D1070407

For Duty and Destiny

THE LIFE AND CIVIL WAR DIARY OF WILLIAM TAYLOR STOTT
HOOSIER SOLDIER AND EDUCATOR

EDITED BY LLOYD A. HUNTER

Indiana Historical Society Press | Indianapolis 2010

Printed in the United States of America

This book is a publication of the
Indiana Historical Society Press
Eugene and Marilyn Glick Indiana History Center
450 West Ohio Street
Indianapolis, Indiana 46202-3269 USA
www.indianahistory.org
Telephone orders 1-800-447-1830
Fax orders 1-317-234-0562
Online orders @ http://shop.indianahistory.org

The paper in this publication meets the minimum requirements of American National Standard for Information Sciences—Permanence of Paper for Printed Library Materials, ANSI Z39. 48–1984

Library of Congress Cataloging-in-Publication Data

Stott, William Taylor, 1836–1918.
For duty and destiny : the life and Civil War diary of William Taylor Stott, Hoosier soldier and educator / edited by Lloyd A. Hunter.
    p. cm.
Includes bibliographical references and index.
ISBN 978-0-87195-290-5 (alk. paper)
1. Stott, William Taylor, 1836–1918—Diaries. 2. Soldiers—Indiana—Diaries. 3. United States. Army. Indiana Infantry Regiment, 18th (1861–1865) 4. Indiana—History—Civil War, 1861–1865—Personal narratives. 5. United States—History—Civil War, 1861–1865—Personal narratives. 6. Indiana—History—Civil War, 1861-1865—Regimental histories. 7. United States—History—Civil War, 1861–1865—Regimental histories. 8. Educators—Indiana—Franklin—Biography. 9. Franklin College (Franklin, Ind.)—Officials and employees—Biography. 10. Franklin (Ind.)—Biography. I. Hunter, Lloyd Arthur, 1940– II. Title.
E506.518th .S76 2010
973.7'472092—dc22
[B]
                                          2010025119

For Jan, my love and
"the wind beneath my wings"
for our family
and for
my students and colleagues
at Franklin College

And in memory of
fellow Hoosier historians
Alan T. Nolan and
Robert M. Taylor Jr.

*For Duty and Destiny: The Life and Civil War Diary
of William Taylor Stott, Hoosier Soldier and Educator*
is made possible through the generous support of
Margot Lacy Eccles and Franklin College.

Contents

Preface

I call him "Will." I am fully aware, of course, that it is not considered kosher for a historian to refer to his subject by first name, much less a nickname. Yet, that is what William Taylor Stott's family, comrades in arms, and colleagues in academe called him, and it seems natural for me to do the same. For, you see, I feel that I have known him for years.

My introduction to the enigmatic "Dr. Stott" came three decades ago, when I arrived on the campus of Franklin College as a novice professor. Being curious about my new setting in life—a handy trait for a historian—I began to examine the school's heritage. At every twist and turn along the way, Stott loomed large. A native Hoosier and an 1861 graduate of the college, he later became the president who took the college from virtual bankruptcy in 1872 to its place as a leading liberal arts institution in Indiana and "the West" by the turn of the century. Indeed, the story of Franklin College, I discovered, was the story of Stott. Nor was his influence confined to the school's parameters. Stott was an inspirational and intellectual force in the Indiana Baptist community, a foremost champion of small denominational colleges and of higher education in general, and a figure of note in local politics and the Grand Army of the Republic. I also learned that he had fought in the Eighteenth Indiana Volunteer Infantry during the Civil War, rising from private to captain by 1863. But that was about all I knew—until 1984.

That year was Franklin College's sesquicentennial, and Professor of Music Sam Hicks and I were asked to write and direct a musical drama of the school's history to celebrate the event. We called it "Jubilee III," and the research for it brought me even closer to Stott, for he would figure prominently in many of its scenes. More about his wartime experiences surfaced, but little that provided a fuller picture of those years. Then, beginning in the late 1990s, I portrayed Stott in Johnson County's living history group, "Telling Our Story," and, through further study in preparation for performances at church and civic events, I caught a glimpse of his daily life and personality.

It was a chance encounter, however, that led to this book. One autumn day in 2001, John Erickson of the college's media relations department stopped me on the first floor of Old Main. He told me that he had a Civil War diary that he thought I might like to see. When I asked him who wrote it, he replied, "Dr. Stott." One can imagine my reaction, since I did not know such a document existed. Now one thing led to another. After perusing the 1940 typescript of the diary that Stott's grandson, Cyril R. Parker, had edited, I realized its potential value for scholars and other students of the Civil War and of Indiana's story. Next came visits with Stott's descendants, particularly great-granddaughters Rosemary "Boo" Laycock of Carmel, Indiana, and Frances Killpatrick of Alexandria, Virginia, and great-grandson Douglas Stott Parker of Austin, Texas. All were eager to have me edit Stott's original diary for publication. The Stott family also donated to the college archives Will's camp chair, sewing kit, shot and powder, and the handwritten diary. This allowed me to use his original words for the editing process. Having a sabbatical leave for the fall of 2003 and funds from a college travel grant and the Roger D. Branigin Chair of History, which I occupied, I proceeded to visit every battleground on which Stott fought and to gather reams of primary research material from repositories in six states. I was able to put my shoes on the ground where Stott and his comrades "saw the elephant," sense the terrain and woods that surrounded him, read the accounts of his fellow officers and soldiers, and gain some perspective on what he encountered in the ranks.

Through it all, Stott has come alive for me in ways he never had before. What the diary reveals is a soldier who was also a scholar in camp and on the march, one who took every available moment to read theology, philosophy, great literary works, the classics of ancient Greece and Rome, and a few novels. He was as familiar with Burns and Byron and Hugo and Pope as he was with ramrods and knapsacks. Theologically, while amazingly ecumenical for that era, he was nonetheless a Baptist through and through. He insisted on baptism only by immersion and displayed a hatred of alcohol and its effects on his cohorts. A scion of Baptist preachers, Stott championed temperance in the army and inherited an antislavery fervor that prompted his belief that, in God's eyes, there were no walls erected between the races. He was a Thoreau in uniform, loved solitude, embraced nature, and contemplated its lessons in periods of reflection and self-cultivation. Many were his meditations on God, humanity, race, and relations between the sexes. Will the thinker, however, also had a playful side, slyly exposing a dry wit and a sense of humor that can sneak up on the reader.

Given these intriguing facets of his nature, the fact that he fought in all three theaters of the war and was a leading figure in Hoosier educational and religious history, I chose to place the diary in the context of his entire life. I do so through biographical accounts of his youth in Jennings County, his years as a student at Franklin, and his leadership of the college from 1872 to 1905.

In fact, it is *context* that shapes this study. By placing Stott's Civil War service in as full and clear a setting as possible, it is hoped that the reader will better appreciate what he encountered while wearing the Union blue. The book is intended for the general reader, not for the scholarly community alone. It therefore seeks to provide enough detailed background to give all readers a sense of precisely what Stott and his comrades faced, and thereby help them understand his reflections on it. For that reason, Stott and those who fought around him are allowed to tell their own stories in their own words. This is especially true of the soldiers in the Eighteenth Indiana and associated regiments from Indiana and other states. The men of the Eighteenth, after all, were Stott's primary community, a fact that makes this study a "first" of sorts, for no other book-length scholarly work has been written on that important Hoosier regiment. Furthermore, seeing Stott "in context" also unveils much about Jennings and Johnson counties, Franklin College and higher education in Indiana, and the role of the Baptists in its religious life.

A brief comment on style is in order. In the diary, the original spelling, punctuation (or lack thereof), capitalization, and grammar have been retained in most instances. *Sic* and bracketed notations are used sparingly and only when needed for clarity. The same is true for the observations of other soldiers. Wherever possible, persons mentioned in the diary are identified in the notes; the unidentifiable remain so. Apparently, Stott transcribed his jottings in the field into the massive ledger-style book that now rests in the Franklin College Archives. The latter volume served as the source for the diary as it appears here, and not the edited version of his grandson, which was replete with missing words and phrases and contained many inaccuracies.

Anyone who writes or edits a book knows that such labor never occurs in isolation. Many folks in many places contributed to the completion of this work. As indicated above, the permission and support of Stott's descendants have been essential and invaluable. My gratitude particularly goes to the Boo Laycock and Frances Killpatrick for providing me with

Will's postwar letters, family remembrances, and photos, along with an even more meaningful gift: genuine friendship. Sadly, Boo's recent death robbed her of the joy of seeing this treasure of her family published, but her dedication to the project alone brought her much satisfaction.

My colleagues at Franklin College assisted in numerous ways. President Jay Moseley and Vice President for Academic Affairs David G. Brailow offered steady encouragement, and both read drafts of the manuscript and made helpful recommendations for improvement. My thanks go to Brailow and the Faculty Steering Committee for granting me a sabbatical and a generous allocation from the Clifford and Paula Dietz Travel Fund. Tom Howald, professor of philosophy and religion, and Mary Alice Medlicott, longtime curator of the college's special collections, saved me from embarrassing errors. Howald guided my attempts at Latin translations, and Medlicott helped in identifying members of the First Baptist Church of Franklin during Stott's era. The staff of the Hamilton Library likewise gave invaluable assistance. Director of the Library Ron Schuetz was always available with wise counsel, and the late Patty Nolting greeted all my requests for inter-library loans with cheerfulness and an uncanny ability to find even the rarest of volumes in the strangest of places. The college archivist, Ruth Dorrel, deserves special kudos. From my home in Florida I called her all too often to check something in the diary or track down other obscure information. The consummate researcher, she always came through and usually in record time. Ruth "saved" me more times than she knows.

At the Indiana Historical Society, the staff of the William Henry Smith Memorial Library made manuscript research a delight with their courteous and genial service. Two of them deserve the highest accolades, and not *just* because they were among the finest students I ever taught at Franklin College. Susan Stanfield Sutton, coordinator of visual reference services, and Suzanne Crowe Hahn, director of reference services, went well beyond the call of duty by searching out details only available in Indiana and thus preventing me from making some major mistakes. They receive As for their assistance! I am likewise indebted to Paula Corpuz, former senior director of the IHS Press, and Kathy Breen, editor, for their copyediting, and to Ray Boomhower, senior editor, for his encouragement. My gratitude is extended as well to the staff of the Indiana

State Library, especially Reference Librarian Darrol Pierson, and Elizabeth Wilkinson and Jill Campbell, manuscript librarians in the Indiana Division.

Other Hoosiers who contributed include Stephen E. Towne, associate archivist at IUPUI, who directed me to small-town newspaper articles on the Eighteenth Indiana, and Calvin Davis, PhD, of Greensburg, professor emeritus of history at Duke University, who shared his knowledge of Moncrief family history. The staffs of Indiana county historical organizations were likewise invaluable aides in finding information on the Stott family, especially those at the Genealogical Room of the Johnson County Museum in Franklin and the Jennings County Historical Society at Vernon.

Like other students of the Civil War, the professional and kindly guidance of National Military Park historians richly enhanced my research. The late Douglas Keller at Pea Ridge—the "Little Big Man," as his friends called him—readily opened the park's archives for my use, and Sherman L. Fleek, program manager of the Shenandoah Battlefields Foundation, gave me helpful directions to hidden spots at Cedar Creek.

Vicksburg Military Park Historian Terry Winschel's warm greetings, gracious assistance in helping me find essential sites beyond the main battlefield, and cordial hospitality while I perused files in his office will never be forgotten. Nor will his willingness to share suggestions and advice in subsequent telephone contacts. Richard Sommers and the staff at the U.S. Army Military History Institute provided useful assistance in locating sources among its voluminous holdings. Thanks as well to Geraldine D. McGloin of the Nueces County Historical Commission in Corpus Christi, Texas, and to the staffs of the Helena (AR) Public Library; the Iberia Parish Library at New Iberia, Louisiana; the Archives of the University of Louisiana at Lafayette; and the Western Historical Manuscript Collection at the University of Missouri, Rolla. Jim Ambuske, director of special projects for university advancement at Miami University of Oxford, Ohio, assisted greatly in my search for the elusive "Miss. L. M." Likewise, Sally Dodgson, PhD, of East Rochester, New York, provided essential information on Rochester Theological Seminary during Stott's student years. These long-distance contributors also receive my gratitude.

Finally, my deepest thanks go to my wife, Jan. Without her love, support, and patience, this book could not have been written.

PROLOGUE

1

Learning Duty and Sensing Destiny

In 1836, the year of William Taylor Stott's birth, Jennings County, Indiana, was still mostly frontier. Though the county seat of Vernon, near which little "Will" was born, had been established twenty years before and was now a hub of almost endless activity, the countryside surrounding it retained earmarks of a wilderness. Small farms and log churches dotted the landscape, primarily along the main water routes that penetrated the county, but getting to them was a laborious and sometimes dangerous task. The principal ways through the dense forests were winding trails freshly blazed with the aspiration of becoming roads, and even these were frequently under water and impassable. Communication was slow, with mail, newspapers, and neighborly messages carried on horseback with unpredictable schedules. And, as one observer recorded, the traveler would be "serenaded on his way by howling wolves, hooting owls, and creaking frogs"—a sort of natural "music lesson." After awhile a fire in a clearing signaled the nearby presence of people, and soon the sojourner, on horseback or on foot, would spot a cabin, approach it cautiously, and shout the customary warning, "Hello the House!" In the countryside, Jennings County folks held to their pioneering ways.[1]

There were those, however, who hoped to push the region to new levels of development, and among them were members of young Will's own family. His ancestors were, in fact, greatly responsible for the founding of the county, the town of Vernon, and Baptist churches throughout southern Indiana. Great-grandfather Jesse Vawter, great-uncle John Vawter, grandfathers William Vawter and William Taylor Stott, and father John Stott all played leading roles in those endeavors.

The patriarch, Jesse Vawter, was the first ordained clergyman in Jennings County. Born into a Virginian Episcopalian family in 1755, he broke with his parental faith at the age of nineteen, having felt a call to the Baptist ranks. After his marriage to Elizabeth Watts in the spring of 1781, the young couple and its rapidly growing family joined the movement westward that was characteristic of that era, arriving in Scott County, Kentucky, in 1790. There they were swept up in the religious fervor of the Great Revival that stirred the spirits of plain folks across the upper South. Under its impetus, the Vawter children, including William and John, were converted, and Jesse himself was ordained. From that time on, his zeal for the Gospel and the launching of churches was unceasing. As historian I. George Blake notes, to Jesse "building a meetinghouse was as important as building a town."[2]

And build them he did. Once the Vawters moved in 1806 across the Ohio River to Mount Glad, north of Madison, Indiana, Jesse's labors at church "constituting" (as the Baptists put it) were tireless. Wherever a fresh settlement emerged, he went to it, preached, and laid the spiritual foundations for a new faith community. His work took him to Switzerland, Ripley, Jefferson, and Clark counties—and, of course, to Jennings. In the latter location, he presided over the founding of Vernon Baptist Church, the first religious organization in the county and a primary influence in his great-grandson Will's growth. A sense of Jesse's achievements can be gleaned from his own words: "I have been at the constitution of twelve churches, have aided in the ordination of eight ministers, and have baptized persons in eighteen churches; the highest number was eighteen, and the greatest in any one church one hundred and twenty-seven."[3] Apparently, Jesse also was persuasive in the pulpit. Charles Lard of Vernon recorded in his diary: "The first sermon I ever recollected anything about was preach'd by Elder Jesse Vawter, the father of my friend and the friend of our family, Elder John Vawter. . . . His text was 'The Master has come and calleth for thee.' From that day untill now I have been a Baptist of the Kentucky Jesse Vawter school." No wonder his great-grandson could write of him in 1908, "His name was a household word in almost every church of the three Associations—Silver Creek, Coffee Creek and Madison," all of which he had founded.[4]

While Jesse planted churches, his son, John Vawter, planted the town of Vernon and oversaw its development. John also was a man of incessant industry, but his interests and pursuits were much broader in scope than Jesse's. Although a Baptist preacher, and often present at the creation of new faith communities, John's primary focus was on civic and entrepreneurial endeavors. Even before he came to Jennings County he served as the first magistrate of Madison, sheriff of both Clark and Jefferson counties, and U.S. Marshal for the Indiana Territory by appointment of President James Madison. Trained as a civil engineer, he accepted many governmental requests to survey large areas of the future state. One such trip sent him to Jennings County in 1813. There he became so enamored of the county's beauty and potential for habitation that he chose a spot on the banks of the Muscatatuck River for a future homestead. Two years later he platted the town of Vernon, erected a cabin, and brought his wife, Polly, and their three young children there. By the autumn of 1815 other families began to arrive, including that of William T. and Mary Ann Stott, Will's paternal grandparents. The newcomers looked to Vawter for leadership, a role he gladly and earnestly assumed.[5]

Virtually every facet of the evolution of Vernon in the early years bore Vawter's imprint. In April 1816 he joined his father, the Stott family, and others in founding the Vernon Baptist Church, becoming its first pastor. An active force in the creation of churches throughout the Vernon area, he also served as colonel of the county militia. Moreover, he was the appointed "agent for the transaction of all such duties as are required . . . for fixing the seats of justice" and host of "all the courts of justice" that, by law, were held at his house.[6] When Vawter and David McClure offered land for the building of the county seat in 1817, they insisted that lots be set aside for churches or schools, a commitment to cultural activities that prompted Vawter to erect the first schoolhouse on the Vernon "Commons," at the very heart of the new town. He also directed that 10 percent of all sales of town lots be used to establish a county library.[7]

Beyond these efforts for education, John and his younger brother, Achilles Vawter, took the lead as entrepreneurs. As early as 1816, John built a saw- and gristmill on the Muscatatuck River, but torrential rains and heavy flooding destroyed it before it could reach full operation. Undaunted, John built a new mill at a higher level on the bank and later engineered, along with Ebenezer Baldwin, the famous four-story Tunnel Mill, considered "one of the most remarkable industrial constructions of pioneer days." The latter met farmers' needs by grinding grain and making flour. Achilles's contribution as a businessman was quite different: he owned Vernon's first tavern, a hotel and restaurant where clientele could procure breakfast and supper for 25 cents each, dinner for 37 ½ cents, lodging for 12 ½ cents, and a half pint of whiskey at the latter rate. Despite these "exorbitant" prices, county residents showed their appreciation of Achilles's trustworthiness by making him the first elected mayor of Vernon, postmaster, and judge of the probate court.[8]

Unquestionably, though, the most influential and far-reaching venture of the Vawters for the future of Jennings County was John's vigorous advocacy of a railroad, connecting Vernon to Indianapolis. A Whig and a firm believer in "internal improvements," Vawter fought for the new line during his five terms in the state legislature, in part because his trips to the capital on horseback, and that city's seemingly "bottomless mud," were so excruciating. Vawter ran potentially fatal political risks at home in championing the railroad, for there was deep-rooted sentiment throughout the county that a railroad would undermine private industry and thus ruin the economy. He prevailed, however, and the first rail line appeared in Vernon shortly after Will Stott's birth. Clearly, more than any other person in Will's lineage, John Vawter was the foremost supporter of moving Jennings County beyond the frontier stage. "He was an intelligent, forward thinking person," one historian says, "who realized the opportunities in the 'Western Region' and relished the challenge."[9]

One of the "opportunities" John took left a lasting mark on the Vawter and Stott families and particularly on young Will as he grew up in the midst of the nation's sectional crisis of the 1840s and 1850s. As a Baptist believer in "soul liberty," John hated slavery. Jennings County was a noted place of refuge for runaway slaves. Vernon itself had a black settlement labeled "Africa," where both free and fugitive blacks resided. Slave traders knew about it, however, and visited it in their search for runaways. Frequent were the instances of blacks, both escapees and free, being wrenched from their homes and families by traders seeking to sell them into slavery. Such events generally caused Vernon's white population to hate the "peculiar institution" even more, and no one acted upon these feelings with greater determination than their beloved "Uncle Johnny." He often interceded to buy the blacks himself and grant them their freedom. In the case of Sam Carr, for example, who had been charged with theft and sentenced to be sold into slavery, Vawter stepped forth, purchased Carr for $500, and then "sold" Carr "to himself for $0."[10]

William Vawter, John's closest brother in age and Will's maternal grandfather, shared his sibling's aversion to slavery, but he was not one to display his political views publicly nor to engage heavily in civic matters. William was most deeply committed to preaching the Gospel. His spiritual journey, however, was not a smooth one. It resembled those of Martin Luther and Jonathan Edwards who, as young men, found it hard to believe they were worthy of God's acceptance. "In the eighteenth year of my age," William wrote, "I was struck under conviction for my sins, and I labored very hard in my own way to bring God under obligation to save me for my works, but, instead of getting nearer heaven, I seemed to get farther off, . . . I could not see any way that God could save such a sinner as I was unless He changed, and I did not wish Him to change to save me." So William went to church, hoping the people there could help him "get religion." There he was astonished when "they received me as a fit subject for baptism."[11]

From then on, William's lifework revolved around farming and the church. In his younger years, near Madison, he tended several farms, including his father's, married his cousin, Frances Vawter, and began a family that eventually numbered ten children. At that time, his preaching was infrequent. But in 1829 he took his family to Jennings County, traded his land near Madison for property north of Vernon overlooking the Muscatatuck, and began his formal ministry. His farm produced wheat, corn, and oats prodigiously, featured an apple orchard, a hay-producing meadow, and a vegetable garden, and it was home to horses, cattle, sheep, and hogs. It was also one of Will's favorite places for play and labor in his youth, and its success meant that Grandfather Vawter could devote all his spare time to preaching and launching churches.[12] Though not yet ordained, he delivered sermons frequently in neighborhood churches, and, in 1835, became the first pastor of Zoar Baptist Church, an offshoot of the Vernon church. Among its members were a young couple named John and Elizabeth Vawter Stott. The daughter and son-in-law of William and Frances Vawter, the Stotts soon became the parents of infant Will. Yet another occasion linked the Vawter and Stott families. In July 1839 William T. Stott, Will's paternal grandfather and pastor of Vernon Baptist Church, ordained William Vawter "by fasting and prayer and the laying on of hands."[13] Apparently, the family ties were as much ministerial as conjugal.

Like Brother Vawter and most of the Baptist leaders of that era, the elder William Taylor Stott was a farmer-preacher—and a revered one. In the words of his grandson and namesake, he "was one of the best known and best loved ministers in the Association and in southern Indiana." The younger Stott made his observation, of course, through loving, familial eyes, and thus his view could be dismissed as understandably prejudicial. Other accounts of the elder Stott's ministry, though, consistently verify its truth.[14]

A native of Woodford County, Kentucky, "Uncle Taylor"—as he would be known in Vernon—was baptized at age thirteen and took his vows with utmost seriousness the rest of his life. Immediately upon his arrival in Vernon in 1815, he and his family became active in the community, joining John Vawter and others in founding the town's Baptist church. Ordained in 1825, he assumed its pastorate and remained in that post for twenty-five years. In 1854 the church recalled him as its leader, and he served until December 1866. During those same years, he simultaneously ministered at Zion Church, near Sullivan's Mills, and shared leadership of Freedom Baptist with Vawter. In order to fund his clerical activities, he first worked land on the North Fork of the Muscatatuck River, then, in 1830, moved his farming operations to property a few miles east of Vernon. Accounts suggest, however, that he was often absent from the farm, holding protracted meetings, taking preaching tours, or assisting in the birth of a new church. Around the time of Will's birth, the Indiana Baptist General Association appointed Stott as a missionary assigned to Jennings and three adjacent counties—this while he was serving the Vernon church![15]

His parishioners and people throughout the county viewed "Uncle Taylor" as a superb biblical scholar and preacher. In a tribute to Stott in 1867, the Madison Association asserted that "Like Timothy, 'from a child he has known the scriptures.'" Many testified to his power in the pulpit, in which "he often rose to great heights of genuine eloquence, and to his authoritative presence and excellent singing voice." Furthermore, while he was "firm and decided on religious principles," he demonstrated an amazing openness toward other denominations in an age when religious bigotry was rampant. Likewise, he was a strong advocate of missions and education, undoubtedly a major component of his influence on his grandson. In 1884 the sixty-six-year-old Stott gave up housekeeping and moved in with his son John Stott and his family, and these traits—especially the love of scripture and singing, of preaching and teaching—no doubt had a daily and profound impact on eighteen-year-old Will. Certainly they took firm root in the life and character of the younger William Taylor Stott.[16]

So also would the nurture and example of his parents, John and Elizabeth Stott. John was born in Kentucky and came to Jennings County in 1815 at four years of age. As a young lad, he engaged in farm labor on his father's spread. In his late teens he went to Vernon, where he learned the tanning trade from his uncle, Richard Stott, onetime justice of the peace and county sheriff. On April 7, 1831, he married Elizabeth Vawter, and, after a brief residency in Vernon, they settled on a farm near North Vernon. There John also opened a tanyard, thus giving him two occupations—farming and tanning—with which to provide for his growing family. But a third, even stronger, calling beckoned, and in 1848 he was ordained to the ministry at Zoar Church. Thus began a lifetime of service analogous to that of his kinsmen: serving many churches as pastor, laboring to strengthen weaker ones, and supporting the denomination's missionary and educational ventures. According to his son, John had a conspicuous ability to lead "many a man and woman . . . to the Savior by means of gentle, earnest, personal appeals."[17] Not surprisingly, the son demonstrated the same traits in his work with students and colleagues decades later.

In all likelihood, Elizabeth had the greater nurturing effect on Will. Given that John was frequently away from home in pursuit of his ministry, the primary responsibilities for child rearing and even for the farm fell to Elizabeth. Like all the other ministers' wives in the family, she learned to bear the burden willingly and viewed it as her duty to God and family. She exhibited a calm, modest nature, but was clear and firm in her religious convictions. As one of her children said of her:

> When mother spoke we always knew she meant what she said and we did what she requested. Father was a preacher and in those days preachers received no remuneration for their services, but gave time and effort freely. . . . The time given to traveling about preaching was just so much time taken away from the work by which the family lived; so the wives of preachers had more to contend with than other women. My mother was often worried in the early years of father's

preaching because of the time spent away from the farm, but later grew reconciled and became the most patient person I ever saw. Everyone was attracted by her sweet, lovable disposition. Her Christian influence on her own family was most marked. She and father labored and prayed for the conversion of their children, and lived to see them all, except Vawter, who died in infancy, members of the Zoar Baptist Church.[18]

The mention of Vawter Stott, who died before his third birthday, testifies to one of the realities that plagued young families in frontier Indiana: high infant mortality. Many stones in early graveyards of the county marked the resting places of children younger than five, in some cases as many as five or six in a single family. The Stotts were more fortunate, however, for they had four children who lived to adulthood: Martha E. (born in 1834), William Taylor (1836), Mary F. (1840), and Jennie M. (1842). The Stott home was an affectionate, nurturing, and supportive one. As Will wrote of his parents in 1908, "Their children honored and loved them for their sterling christian characters, and unswerving fidelity to duty and their never failing parental affection and care."[19]

Will's words—"fidelity to duty"—accurately address the nature of his lineage. When he was born on May 22, 1836, he entered a family of robust, industrious, and intrepid Christians. They were, in short, a people of duty with a sense of destiny. While they have been described as "Hardshell Baptists," conservative and decided in doctrine, they were at the same time pioneering in the forward-thinking sense, forerunners in the pursuit of advancements in both civic and religious matters. Perhaps these relatively progressive traits can be seen best in the quarrel that tore at the fabric of the Indiana Baptist churches over missions and education. The explosiveness of these two issues often divided the churches and even families, as in the case of the Vawters. During the period of the conflict's eruption, from territorial days through the 1830s, it centered on the growing desire of many Baptists to engage in missionary endeavors beyond the local church, such as Isaac McCoy's work among the Indian tribes, and efforts to establish an educated ministry. As belief in such ventures grew, so did antimission and antieducation sentiment. So heated did the rhetoric become that historian John F. Cady concludes that no Baptist controversy in Indiana has ever exceeded "in virulence and in extent of misunderstanding the division over the issue of missions and benevolent enterprises." Blake agrees. "Indeed," he writes, "there was hardly a Baptist church in Indiana, nor an association, that was not ravaged by internal troubles over missions. The Baptist Church was divided against itself. In many instances parents and children, brothers and sisters, were separated in their church relations."[20]

Such was the case with the Vawters. Cady contends that "the Vawter family as a whole were typical of a considerable group of the older leaders who were never sympathetic with the missionary program." Certainly that was true of John. He deeply resented the young, educated missionaries from New England, who, from his perspective, were "telling him and the church what they should do." And yet his brother, William, was an ardent "friend of education," who in his second will bequeathed a portion of his estate to "the Franklin Baptist College in Indiana." Moreover, as a leader of the Sand Creek Baptist Association, William endorsed John Stott's resolution to put the member churches "on record as favorable to missions." Zoar Church, which he pastored, had one of the first Sunday Schools in an association that sent a large number of young men to Franklin College.[21] The Stotts were even more supportive of missions and education. As already indicated, the elder William T. labored as a missionary for the state association and, though he was less enamored of education, favored the General Association's contention in 1837 that "next to the religion of Jesus Christ, education is the most important acquisition of the present world."[22]

The Vawters and the Stotts were also at the forefront of Baptist efforts to address the social issues of the day, from the keeping of the Sabbath and advocacy of temperance to opposition to slavery and support of the Union. All of Will's ancestors were against the use of alcohol, except for medicinal purposes, and they no doubt agreed with the declaration of the General Association that "the seller of liquor was little better than a murderer." So Will came to his strong temperance stand as a soldier quite naturally. Likewise, his outright repugnance toward slavery was a legacy from his family and church. It was, after all, his Grandfather Stott's Vernon church that asserted in 1818 "its disapproval of correspondence with slave-holding Baptists" and its opposition to "oppression in every form." The Vawters, too, were antislavery and active in the Underground Railroad.[23]

Forward-looking, mission-oriented, antislavery, and proeducation, these were people of duty with a sense of destiny. Such was William Taylor Stott's heritage.

———————◆◆◆———————

Little is known of Will's early life. He left no record of his youth, and his college experience can be gleaned only through external sources. The recollections and observations of relatives, friends, teachers, and historians, however, provide informative glimpses into what Will's interests, education, and character might have been. In addition, an examination of life in and around Vernon and North Vernon furnishes at least a sketch of the social and environmental forces that molded his life.

Obviously, the most formative factor in Will's social experience was religion. Not only did his heritage and home revolve around things ministerial but the mores of Jennings County virtually dictated that the church be the center of community life. Every able-bodied person was expected to be there on Sunday and attend a prayer meeting or Bible study in someone's house on a weekday evening. As in the earliest pioneer days, when the church served as a vehicle of comfort and guidance in dealing with the hardships of lonely frontier living, so in Will's youth the meetinghouse was the place to which neighbors came to renew friendships, get a firm handshake, and talk about their farms and families. Presbyterians, Methodists, Baptists—all seemed, in the words of a later article in the *Vernon Journal*, to be "gospel hungry."[24]

One suspects that Will's involvement with the church was even more mandatory, given the expectations of parents and grandparents. His "home church" was Zoar Baptist Church, the community of faith his parents and others founded at a site six miles northeast of Vernon in 1834, and of which his Grandfather Vawter was pastor. Like his sisters, Mary and Jennie, for whose 1854 baptisms documentation exists, Will probably was immersed in the creek that ran through a hollow near his grandfather's farm—and, if it were winter, someone broke the ice in the stream to make the occasion possible. Zoar, at the time of Will's birth, was housed in a tiny log building, but it was quickly attaining prominence and became the birthplace of the Sand Creek Association in 1844.[25]

If there was such a thing as a "cathedral" church in the Baptist tradition, for Jennings County it was the Vernon church, which sat atop the highest peak in the town, overlooking the Muscatatuck valley. Since his grandfather was the pastor, Will likely attended it frequently and knew it well. As a young lad, he may have stood in awe of its sturdy, square brick structure with its four-sided roof, topped with a small belfry that resembled a chicken coop. Hanging from the belfry was the "musical triangle" that Will's great-uncle Achilles, the tavern owner, gave the church to take the place of a bell. As one Vernon resident recalled, "Save the sound of falling waters, such as we hear in Vernon's city of the dead, there was no sound to me so sweetly solemn, as the tolling of the triangle."[26] The building's interior also would have impressed a small boy. Tallow dips in sconces on wood pillars provided the sanctuary with light, and two fireplaces, one on each side of the pulpit, gave warmth in the colder months. Often worshippers switched places during the service to allow those farther from the fire to move forward and "thaw out." The high, boxlike pulpit was the centerpiece of worship, elevated as it was almost five feet from the floor and completely enclosed by wooden sides and a door in the rear to shut in the pastor during the sermon. In one of the congregation's lighter moments, a child, after watching the preacher flail his arms in passionate and seemingly interminable proclamation of the gospel, exclaimed, "Why don't they let him out?" Regardless of the length of the homilies, though, it was to this revered place that country folk came from miles around for spiritual nurture until rural meetinghouses began to appear in the countryside. As for Will, it is quite possible that, of the two churches, Zoar and Vernon, the latter left the greater mark on his ultimate decision to train for the ministry. Not only was its historical and architectural presence stirring, it was also a leading voice in the General Association and the mother church for at least five other faith communities, including Zoar. Furthermore, Will did not join the Zoar church until 1854 at age seventeen, which suggests that he made his commitment to Christ, for whatever reason, even later in his life than did his younger sisters.[27] As will be seen, he was not always the most pious of "preachers' kids."

Given that Baptist church life consumed most weekends—with association meetings on Saturdays, worship on Sundays, and John away from home for both—young Will's weekdays were necessarily spent working with his father on the farmstead and in the tannery. As John's only son, he doubtless learned to do much of the heavier, cumbersome tasks of cultivation and harvesting, along with tending the livestock on a daily basis.

It was labor in the tanyard, though, that seemed to make the greatest impression on him. One of his granddaughters recorded how he liked to talk about "grinding the bark they used in tanning." A description of the Stott tanyard offers a glance at the work involved:

> Large vats were dug in the ground, each vat being about four feet deep. These large vats were filled with alternate layers of hides and oak bark. In six months the hides were removed from the vats, and the hair scraped off, then returned to the vats with layers of pulverized oak barks between them. At the end of six months the hides were removed a second time and dressed. The dressing consisted in stretching each hide on a log and rubbing it with an iron tool made for the purpose. The tanyard was used by the community and when the hides were dressed, the owner of each had boots or shoes made from it. The lightweight leather was used for the uppers and the heavy for the soles.[28]

The tanyard thus supplied the Vernon vicinity with critical leather goods, and, along with the crops and other farm produce the Stotts could sell, exposed Will to some rudimentary merchandising skills. Harrison Burns, Will's cousin and an insightful annalist of early Jennings County, explains that all the families in the neighborhood "took butter and eggs to town and traded for sugar, coffee and other groceries." The Stotts were no exception, and Will was certainly a participant in such transactions. Of course, Will would be expected to take his turn at the daily chores of the household as well. For example, given that none of the houses, whether log cabins or more spacious dwellings, were ever airtight, someone needed to "mind the flies" in the summer and keep the fireplace fully supplied with wood in the winter—a truly man-sized job.[29]

Of course, life was more than work. Family and community gatherings replenished the spirits of isolated, often lonely, farm families. For the Stotts, it meant visiting the homes of relatives for recreation and sumptuous meals. Burns recalled the Vawters and Stotts going to George King's place where "there was always an abundant table." King was Will's uncle by marriage to his aunt, Frances Vawter, and he owned "a buckwheat field and a sugar camp, and when time came for buckwheat cakes there were heaps of them baked on a griddle at the fireplace, and syrup there was in plenty." Will's folks loved to entertain as well. Their farm was near Zoar Church, so when the Sand Creek Association met there for assembly the

Stotts put tables out in their yard and hosted "as many as seventy-five people" for dinner.[30]

One of the favorite spots for the children was Grandfather Vawter's farm. It contained much rolling land right along the Muscatatuck River that could be explored just for play or for more intriguing adventures. Furthermore, with an orchard and sugar camp on the farm, springtime meant plenty of syrup for flapjacks, and summer brought good fruit. Besides, those areas under cultivation could give the older grandchildren a chance to help out behind "a yoke of oxen and a cart and wagon with which all the hauling was done." Then there were those wonderful evenings before the huge fireplace in the five-room dwelling's largest space where grandmother cooked abundant meals for family gatherings. Located about three miles from Vernon, the Vawter farm, Burns wrote, "was about an average one of that day, and . . . his family was considered fairly well to do for his period of life." Burns, who lived with his grandparents for more than two years after the premature death of his mother, saw his grandfather's life as fairly typical of the times. "To describe his situation, the manner of his life and the joys, hardships, or pleasures of the members of his family from 1840 to 1860," Burns observed, "would be to describe the general condition and habits of a large number of the inhabitants of the locality in which he lived."[31]

Among those "habits" were a host of occasions for socializing. Harvesting, for example, was often a community activity, neighbor helping neighbor, especially in times when weather threatened to impede progress. "Cabin raisin's" still brought people together during Will's youth, and these could be elaborate affairs. Men and boys carried axes, chisels, saws, and froes to the site, and women and girls supplied enough food for all. The same was true of barn raisings, wood choppings, hog killings, and log rollings. At one of the latter, in fact, Reverend Stott, dirty and sweaty from labor, received a request to perform a wedding. He accepted the invitation and performed the ceremony for Samuel Campbell and Chloe Prather in his work clothes![32]

Schools and social groups, too, offered a wide variety of events that appealed to everyone. There were spelling bees, debating clubs, literary societies, and—surely Will's favorite—singing schools. Will loved to sing, as his Civil War diary shows, and, besides, that enterprise offered a

chance to escort a young lady to her home. There was one popular amusement, however, formed in Will one of his foremost antipathies: alcohol
consumption. "It was almost a universal custom," Burns recalled, "to
have a jug of liquor at all public gatherings such as log rollings, house and
barn raisings, etc." Jennings County housed many small distilleries that
converted corn—for which there was little market—into whiskey, and
bottles of it were plentiful on social and political occasions. Burns, in fact,
remembered a great uncle "who kept a keg of whiskey" at home and was a
Baptist to boot, though he did not know if he was "of the thirty-six gallon
variety or not." Although the 1830s brought a strong reaction to such
intemperance, and reform groups began to call for war against it, the first
temperance meeting in the county did not occur until 1849. By then Will
was probably fully ensconced in his lifelong hatred of alcohol.[33]

Perhaps the entertainment most eagerly anticipated for those who
lived outside Vernon was the occasional trip—usually on Saturdays—to
the county seat. There, Will and his family could catch up on the news,
see other relatives, and play with friends. By the time he was school age,
Vernon had become "a thriving town" and a leading cultural center. It
began in 1816 as a port for flatboats, a place where the big event was the
arrival of raftsmen to deliver or procure goods. But by the 1840s it was a
hive of business, education, and small industries, to which stagecoaches
and later the railroad brought merchants, traders, and travelers to and
from Indianapolis and Madison. Now, in addition to the gristmills and
sawmills, there were numerous stores, blacksmith shops, shoemakers,
wagon makers, saddleries, offices of attorneys and physicians, and Uncle
Achilles Vawter's tavern, where men sat in chairs tilted against the wall,
telling stories and eyeing all the passersby.[34]

One of Will's favorite haunts had to be the North American House.
Thomas J. Storey, the son-in-law of John Vawter, built this hotel around
1836 as an inn for stagecoach and railroad travelers. Storey's Son, Riley
Clark Storey, was one of Will's close friends, even though Riley was six
years younger. They shared a love of books and were highly curious, so
they may have joined other boys in their fascination with S. W. Storey's
carding machine at his home on Brown Street. The machine turned out
"an endless succession" of "long smooth white rolls" of wool, while the
boys rode on the treadmill powered by an old, tired horse. The girls,
meanwhile, watched eagerly to see if the boys wound up under the hooves

of the horse or got knocked on the head by the upper beams. Nearby was the weaving and fulling operation of Mr. Robb, which children frequented to watch the process, and where the owner exhibited remarkable patience with his youthful visitors. So did Kurtz, the hatter, who entertained the youngsters by making stovepipe hats—a prize possession for a lad.[35]

That Will would have enjoyed most of these amusements is certain, for there was a humorous, playful, perhaps even mischievous side to the boy—and later to the man. This is evident from family accounts and from entries in his Civil War journal and letters. Three incidents might give credence to his carefree, high-spirited nature. On the night of March 8, 1862, only hours after he first "saw the elephant" in full-scale combat at Pea Ridge, Stott wrote in his diary: "On Friday at Leetown a ball struck one of our Band—Billy Martin, but the Picture of the girl in his vest pocket saved his life. The ball did not get through it. If the picture was so valuable what must be expected of the *original*. He may experiment in that direction." Just weeks later, while still in camp in Benton County, Arkansas, Will wrote to Mag and Mattie Stout back in Franklin County, Indiana. He began by expressing his gratitude for the valentine and the copy of the *Ladies' Repository* they had sent him. Then he gave them warning: "If I were there I should propose a visit to Mary's, then I should propose a walk down to the road where is an abundance of <u>mullen</u> [mullein] leaves and lastly, with all the dignity I could summon I certainly should propose—to rub your faces well."[36] Decades later, in April 1881, John and Elizabeth Stott celebrated their golden wedding anniversary. At one point in the festivities, someone asked the couple "which of their children had been most difficult to govern." The answer was that "William had not always been as pious as he might have been." But the point was rapidly made that "Will is all right now and is President of one of the most flourishing colleges in the State of Indiana."[37] This aspect of Stott's personality reveals one of the secrets to what later made him successful as a leader in higher education—a bit of playfulness at times and a healthy sense of humor.

Of course, before Will could become president of anything, he had to have an education, and Jennings County was a good place to start. Education was a major priority of its early settlers. This goal was in keeping with the precedent set by both the Northwest Ordinance of 1787 and the 1816 Indiana Constitution. Article 3 of the Ordinance stated that "Schools and the means of education shall forever be encouraged" in the new territory. The state's first constitution called upon the legislature "to provide, by law, for a general system of education, ascending in regular gradation from township schools to a state university, wherein tuition shall be gratis and open to all." That the people of Jennings County were committed to these aims can be seen in the results of the state election of August 1848. Voters were to register their views on whether the Indiana General Assembly should assess a tax "to support free common schools in every district in the state." Jennings County voters approved this law for free schools with a majority of 79.55 percent, making it one of only twenty-four counties out of the state's ninety-two to favor the measure.[38]

With solid support for education so prevalent in the county, schools became major centers of community life, much like the churches. Indeed, families valued schoolteachers almost as much as they did ministers, considering the "master" critical to the social fabric. Most were young men who "boarded around" in neighborhood homes while being paid small sums "per scholar." In the early years, tuition was low—about a dollar and a half for a twelve-week term—organization was virtually nonexistent, and only one "course" received much attention: spelling. The spelling book was the primary text, and teachers who trained top-notch spellers were the most esteemed. Reading and writing also got considerable stress. Oral reading to the teacher or the class was a requirement each student had to fulfill regularly. The teaching of writing skills focused largely on penmanship, rather than composition or creativity, with students endlessly replicating the "copy set" placed before them by the teacher. The highlight of the year was the "performance at the close of the school." These "exhibitions," as they were called, were usually held at churches at night so that the entire community could attend. In Vernon, the preferred location was the Presbyterian church, where the pillars were best suited to the trimming of the candles needed for illumination as the students read their "spoke pieces." Wherever held, though, the site was lavishly decorated, and "the public square would be filled with wagons which had brought loads of folks in from the country."[39]

Unfortunately, there is little verifiable recorded information on the precise nature of Stott's early education. Biographical sketches offer few specifics, and there are no extant records of any of the schools he attended. That he went to the common school, and thus experienced the stress on spelling, penmanship, and exhibitions, seems certain. One biographer suggests that he did so until he was sixteen, at which time he entered the Sardinia Academy in adjacent Decatur County, where he remained for three years. Another indicates that Stott "was not satisfied with the education afforded him" in the common school, and, upon completing its course, left for the Sardinia program.[40] Some local historians identify Stott as a scholar at the Jennings County Seminary, an attempt at a higher level of learning than that attainable at the common schools. Founded in the 1830s, the seminary occupied a two-story building in Vernon, and, according to Alice Bundy, "was the educational center of the county." The *Vernon Journal* of December 26, 1902, stated that within the seminary, "Education took on a new meaning; it was no longer simply cramming with facts, but learning to think and reason." Students there— including such luminaries as the future founder of Butler University, Ovid Butler, and Robert Sanford Foster, who became a brigadier general in the Union Army—were expected to parse Joseph Butler's *Analogy* and John Milton's *Paradise Lost*.[41] Given Stott's love of Butler's works, the seminary may have given him his first exposure to that renowned theologian.

While a detailed impression of Stott's schooling is elusive, two vignettes can furnish some insight. One comes from the pen of Philemon C. Vawter, Stott's uncle, who attended and taught at the log schools near Vernon before becoming a student at Franklin College in the early 1850s. In 1883 he wrote his nephew, then the president of the college, to reminisce: "Why Mr. President it seems but a little while since you & I were school boys at the log house in the woods—the house with a back wall across one end for a fireplace, & a flue of sticks & mud for a smoke escape; or since at another log house I made my debut as a 'School-Master' with yourself as a 'scholar.'"[42] In such a setting, Stott launched his quest for knowledge. Another of his teachers was Eliza Jane Fink who, at age fifteen, became Stott's first mentor at a country school, located "a short distance from the Stott home." Fink boarded with the Stotts for a while and had a reputation for influencing "a large circle of young people for two generations, perhaps as many as any other teacher, of that time." The supplier of the candlesticks used by the students at the annual exhibitions, she also supervised a Sunday school on the second floor of the seminary where she played a primary role in "the building up [of] characters." Years later, when Stott assumed the reins as president of Franklin College, he visited Fink, who lived in Franklin as Mrs. Eliza Jane Clarke. When she congratulated her former pupil on his new position, he made this playful reply: "Well, Jane, if I make a failure of this, it will be your fault because you did not start me right."[43]

In such an environment, Stott developed a powerful longing— "calling" might be more accurate—for a higher education. As Elba L. Branigin, one of his future students, wrote of Stott in 1913, "he never relinquished this determination, though the necessity of his assistance in the work of the farmstead postponed for a time the attainment of his desire. However, he had one advantage, in that his parents were in hearty accord with him in his plans and gave him all possible encouragement." So, after completing his studies at Sardinia, Stott taught school near Columbus, Indiana, to earn enough money to reach his goal and, at the ripe age of twenty-one, entered Franklin College.[44]

———◆——

Its original name was "Indiana Baptist Manual Labor Institute." Though it bore a cumbrous title, it represented the realized hopes of pioneering, mission-minded Baptists who wanted an educated ministry to further enhance their efforts at spreading the Gospel. But it did not come easily. The men who dreamed of such a school, who championed its cause within the church, and who formed the Indiana Baptist Educational Society as its vehicle of creation, did so under tumultuous conditions. Passionately opposing them were the more numerous and vociferous anti-mission, antieducation forces in the denomination. Perhaps the Reverend W. N. Wyeth best captured the plight and pluck of the founders of the institute through the use of biblical imagery. When he addressed a crowd gathered in 1884 to celebrate the fiftieth anniversary of the school that was by then known as Franklin College, Wyeth reminded his listeners that the founders "worked, like the pious Jews, with the trowel in one hand and the sword in the other." Wyeth explained: "The foundation had to be laid in troublous times when the Philistines were many and large, and constantly opposed them."[45]

The message of the "Friends of Education," as the designers of the new school called themselves, was clear. When they convened at the Baptist meetinghouse in Indianapolis on June 5, 1834—traditionally considered the college's birth date—the fourteen ministers and laymen present set forth the goals of the Education Society. The initial aims, expressed in a series of resolutions, were simple: given "the importance of the Subject of Education as it Relates to our Denomination," the Baptists of the state "need an Institution of learning under their immediate patronage and subject to their direction." It should be "adapted to their present wants" and based on a system of manual labor in which the students did much of the physical work. The Society also agreed to future meetings for site selection and to entertain other proposals, and it voted to ask Jesse Holman, a leading Baptist clergyman and judge of the U.S. District Court in Indiana, to write a constitution for the school.[46] Holman's work came before the Society in January 1835. Its second article stated the purpose of the institution: "To promote the more general knowledge of Science Literature and Biblical Criticism throughout the Baptist connection in Indiana but it shall be open for the benefit of all young men who may wish to avail themselves of the instruction afforded so far as the funds of the Institution will admit." While open to all for admission, preference would be given to Baptist applicants, and the faculty would be confined to "men belonging to Regular Baptist Churches whose qualifications would recommend them to any similar institution." The school would be run under the jurisdiction of the Education Society and located on the east side of Franklin.[47]

Once officially launched in 1836–37, the fledgling school faced rocky times. Finances were grim, with the Baptist constituency unwilling or unable to provide adequate support; attracting students, teachers, and anyone capable of supplying steady administrative leadership proved difficult; and the little frame house that served as the college's only building was far too small. Some bold, forward steps were taken: young women gained admission in August 1842, and a "young ladies' department" appeared in the preparatory program.[48] Yet, even these advances fell short of fruition due in part to lack of adequate instruction and administrative guidance.

Clearly, the most critical need was for a president, not only to oversee the educational enterprise, but also to canvass for essential funds. In August 1843 George C. Chandler, pastor of the First Baptist Church of Indianapolis and head of the Education Society, assumed the presidency, and the college, as Stott knew it, began to emerge. A native of New England, Chandler guided the adoption of a curriculum resembling that of the foremost eastern liberal arts colleges. Steeped in the classics, students were to read Livy, Horace, and Oedipus Tyrannus in Latin, and Herodotus and Homer in Greek, and were required to write in both languages, along with French and Hebrew as possible electives. The other pillars of the curriculum were mathematics and science, with Natural Philosophy and Moral Science during the junior year and a focus on religious courses for seniors. Students could skirt around the classics and obtain a certificate after two years in the Scientific Department, and a preparatory department allowed younger scholars to lay the foundations for entrance into the full collegiate program.[49]

The Chandler years brought many other changes and advancements. The construction of the first brick building, later named Chandler Hall, furnished needed space for classrooms and student housing. Literary societies came into existence, genuinely enhancing student life as well as academics. The faculty grew stronger with the addition of Professor William Brand in mathematics and languages; John W. Dame, the college's first graduate (1847), as tutor; Achilles Vawter, as librarian; and Professor John S. Hougham, the first permanent "fixture" in the teaching corps and instructor in multiple disciplines. Most crucial of all, the financial picture improved, largely because of Chandler's indefatigable efforts—usually on horseback—at soliciting funds from Baptist and other constituencies and making the college "a part of the missionary program."[50] Of course, Chandler had his faults, one of which, according to Stott, was rigidity. Chandler "admired back-bone and had a full share of it," wrote Stott, "but made the mistake that many make in supposing that the best back-bone consisted of only one bone; whereas the Creator has taught us that it is composed of many, and that a degree of flexibility is perfectly compatible with great strength."[51] Then again, maybe Chandler's rigidity was a plus, for after his resignation due to failing health in 1849, the college confronted another financial crisis. So heavy was its debt that some even suggested "a sheriff's sale of the buildings and grounds." Enrollment also fell precipitately in the 1850–51 term. Fortunately, because of Acting President John S. Hougham's energetic leadership and the board's courage in making many difficult decisions, the college avoided exigency and paved the way for a new day under the presidency of Silas Bailey, PhD.[52]

When Stott arrived on the Franklin College campus as a classical preparatory student in 1856, it was Bailey who made the strongest and most lasting impression on him. The new president was a big man in every way—physically, intellectually, spiritually—and his effect on students and faculty was equally huge. A Massachusetts native, he was a graduate of Brown University, where his own role model was its renowned president, Francis Wayland. Bailey thus came to Franklin in 1852 not only with extensive experience in the pastorate and educational administration, but also with a rich background in theology and pedagogy. To his students he seemed demanding and tireless, and yet caring, cheerful, and receptive. "He took a strong personal interest in the welfare of his students," said one of Bailey's scholars, Thomas Jefferson Morgan. "He seemed to have literally a *father's* regard for us." Stott agreed, noting that Bailey's "immediate pupils all loved him and deferred to him in ultimate authority."[53] The president's industry also was legendary. Given the lack of teachers (only four or five during his ten-year presidency), he taught all the theology and philosophy courses, plus English grammar and mathematics. At the same time, he oversaw all discipline of the school, preached at chapel daily

North Edifice, Æd. 1844.   South Edifice, Æd. 1854.

Franklin College in 1856. This would have been Will Stott's first glimpse of the college as he approached from the railroad that fall.

and twice on Sunday, and guided the overall academic program. On top of that, Stott recalled seeing Bailey "planting trees on the campus, repairing fences, or hauling gravel for the walks on Saturday afternoons, putting to shame the lounging students who did not share his spirit of industry."[54] Stott thus found in his mentor another sterling example of duty.

He also was receptive to Bailey's views on destiny. The president was a steadfast Calvinist. In Stott's words, "Loyalty to Christ" was "the reigning motive of his life," and he displayed it in the classroom. The Reverend Henry Day, in his "Memorial Sermon" for Bailey in November 1874, quoted Stott as saying that when his late mentor "would near a grand thought, especially a new view of some of the staunch old doctrines of God's justice, or mercy, or love, his heart would begin to melt and tears would come unbidden to his eyes." Another student, Jeremiah H. Smith, said of Bailey that "the Sense of God and God's prevailing presence and ordaining influence is a thought that he made upper most and gave the deepest impression at the time." Smith added that from Bailey "the Students learned to regard everything however minute as a part of God's plan."[55] In his wartime diary, Stott reflected on insights gleaned from Bailey and his faculty, especially classicist Jeremiah Brumback. Valedictorian of the class of 1856, Brumback immediately attained faculty status, becoming, in Stott's estimation, one of the best teachers in Franklin's history. "He knew," wrote Stott, "how to make his students apply themselves to study with rare success."[56]

Students entering the college in that era needed the sense of duty these instructors embodied. Most of the young men were, like Smith, "one of the greenest of the green boys." They arrived on either the Madison and Indianapolis Railroad or the Louisville and Indianapolis, both of which stopped at the Franklin Depot. They then would walk, baggage in hand, through the streets of what the college catalog described as the "thrifty county seat with a population of twenty-five hundred, and rapidly on the increase," to the eastern edge of town and the small campus. The next step was to find someone to help orient them to their new experience. But that was a difficult task, since the faculty mostly "boarded around" and were not always readily available. Smith, for instance, was told to find Dame who was "off a few squares engaged in house building"—in an effort, probably, to supplement his meager faculty income. William Harrison McCoy, who had made his first commitment to the college at age seven when he gave "a single 'Bit'—12 ½ cents" to the scholarship fund, came as a student in 1854. On his arrival as "a green, beardless boy" of seventeen, he was sent by Bailey to find Dame somewhere in East Franklin where he was "building a fence." Once located, Dame took the anxious young men to the college buildings, of which there were now two, Chandler Hall to the north and a new structure to the south, later to be named Bailey Hall. Riffling through "a great bundle of keys," the tutor opened their rooms for occupancy. Smith discovered that his room was "full of rat holes" and rather dirty, but he worked hard to "right [it] up." McCoy selected his own room, and he, too, got it "fitted up."[57]

Barnett "Barry" Wallace's experience was somewhat different. His father, a member of the school's board of directors, asked him in the summer of 1853 if he wanted to attend college that fall. The answer being affirmative, "Barry" wasted no time in getting to Madison, which he considered "the business metropolis of the state," to purchase a new suit, a tall silk hat, and other items of attire appropriate for a college man. When he got to Franklin with his father, he discovered that he would be residing, not in the college buildings, but with Doctor and Mrs. Bailey in the old Chandler House south of the campus. This pattern of boarding with private families was the one preferred by the trustees. They saw it as "more conducive to health" for the students and a shield "from the temptations to which they are exposed in their absence from home."[58]

Unfortunately, no records exist describing Stott's first days at Franklin, but they surely resembled those of Smith, McCoy, and Wallace, all of whom became Stott's good friends. Even though Stott entered in the preparatory department, it is quite possible that he resided in Bailey Hall, since he was much older and more mature than others in that program, who could have been as young as fifteen.[59] His room would have contained a bed, table, and stove, but all other furnishings, including linens, he would have to provide. For these accommodations, he paid $9.00 for the academic year. Since all charges had to be paid in advance, Stott quickly settled with the officials for his room, his $21.00 tuition, and $3.00 for "incidental expenses"—a total of $33.00 per annum. It is also likely that he made friends rapidly. In his preparatory class was Fielding C. Eddleman, whom Stott probably already knew from his academy days in Eddleman's home town of Sardinia. Eddleman also would be his closest comrade during the Civil War. Among the upperclassmen, Stott became close to George Washington Grubbs and Thomas Jefferson Morgan of Franklin, Casabianca Byfield of Dupont, and Simpson Burton of Mitchell. In fact, on April 28, 1860, Stott, Byfield, Grubbs, and Morgan founded the Indiana Delta Chapter of Phi Delta Theta, the first Greek organization at Franklin College.[60]

This socialization was important in the adjustment to college, but it was the academic and religious life at Franklin that was Stott's main focus. During his preparatory year, he studied English grammar, geography, and algebra. As his diary entries during the war reveal, however, the courses that attracted him most were those in Latin and Greek, for they constituted the essential foundation for the classical curriculum in the collegiate department. Grasping the rules and elements of each language, and reading Sallust, Virgil, and Xenophon's *Anabasis* were prerequisites for the study of Cicero, Horace, Thucydides, and Homer under Brumback. One of Bailey's critical curricular innovations, which was firmly fixed in place by the time Stott matriculated at Franklin, was a broadening of the course of study in the sciences and "the more useful languages of French and German." Stott balanced his examination of the classics with exposure to chemistry, specifically the texts of Benjamin Silliman, and courses in analytical geometry, trigonometry, and calculus. Unquestionably, though, as his wartime reading and reflections testify, the courses in philosophy and theology with Bailey had the most profound and enduring effect on Stott. The careful, steady preparation for daily recitations on William Paley's natural theology or Richard Whately's approach to logic served to reinforce his commitment to duty and strengthen his interest in the life of the mind. Long would he contemplate—and reread—Francis Wayland's *Moral Science*, John Foster's *Essays*, and Butler's *Analogy*.[61] They would, in fact, guide his thoughts and mold his worldview while in camp and on the march during the coming war.

So would the sense of duty he had to develop in order to meet the college's stringent requirements. In 1857, Stott's first year at the collegiate level, a new ruling mandated that all students "submit to examinations in all subjects at the close of each session, in the presence of a Committee appointed by the Trustees for that purpose." It also stated that "the premature departure" of students seeking to avoid that process would not be tolerated, and it elicited parental support for the examination program.

The catalog referred to the curriculum as "liberal and extensive"; the work in metaphysics and moral philosophy, in particular, were "all that the most liberal range of study could demand."[62]

"Demand" seemed to be the operative word, and the college rules for behavior reinforced it. During the academic year preceding Stott's arrival on campus, on Sunday, January 22, 1856, an event occurred that one chronicler described as "perhaps the most serious internal trouble the college has ever experienced"—the infamous "snowball rebellion." According to the faculty report on the incident, a group of students in the Scientific Department, after an apparent night of "whiskey and drunkenness," began a snowball fight outside the campus buildings. The battle continued after some went inside and were still being attacked by those who were outside. Retaliation followed, and the results were considerable damage to property, "noise and riot," and an administrative decision to seek prosecution of the students involved. The event may well have been blown out of proportion, for some students called for Bailey's resignation and even a few faculty members expressed concern over his handling of the affair. Fortunately, cooler heads prevailed, and the rebellion, like the snowballs, melted.[63] From the crisis, however, an inevitable tightening and enforcement of college laws emerged, so that, when Stott and his fellow students enrolled the following fall they heard a loud and clear exhortation to "maintain an honorable and gentlemanly deportment, at all times." This meant:

> Every student shall maintain a sacred respect for the property, as well as the persons of others; shall not enter the room of another, at any time, without permission; shall pay strict attention to cleanliness in his person, in his room, and in relation to every part of the College buildings and grounds; shall avoid all unnecessary noise or disturbance; shall not play at cards, or other games of hazard; shall not keep in his room or use intoxicating liquors of any kind, except when prescribed by a physician; shall not associate with persons of immoral character, nor use profane or obscene language, nor keep in his room fire arms, or other deadly weapons; neither shall any student attend balls or dancing parties of any description.[64]

Along with academics, Stott naturally embraced the religious life on campus. Happily for Bailey, the faculty, and students such as Stott, who sought spiritual growth, the year after the "snowball rebellion" brought a revival of religion at the college. There were two possible reasons for this renewal. One was the success of Bailey's efforts "to make the College of more direct service in the training of ministers." Through a series of Sunday afternoon lectures, specially designed for those considering the ministry, the president maintained support both *for* the students and *from* the school's Baptist constituency.[65] The second, and probably more productive, basis for religious growth was the existence of a congregation on the campus itself. Known as the East Franklin Baptist Church, this body formed on March 26, 1853, when forty-three members of the First Baptist Church of Franklin withdrew to join a "new interest" at the college. Among them were Professors John W. Dame, William Brand, John Hougham, Mark Bailey, and Achilles Vawter, future student George Grubbs, and President Bailey, who became the new church's pastor. The East Franklin church was a powerful attraction for the students and faculty. Stott transferred his membership to it from Zoar on November 7, 1858, and many of his fellow students, including Thomas J. Morgan and F. G. Lukens, were baptized by Bailey "down near the bridge" in Hurricane Creek, just across the railroad tracks from the college. The faculty reported on April 7, 1857, on the "work of grace" that sparked an "increase of religious interest in the College Church & among the students" and pointed to the "tones of prayer" and the labors of evangelism that now characterized student life. State denominational leaders likewise lauded "the influence of the church upon the Students" and described it as "salutary in a high degree."[66] There can be little doubt that Stott's faith strengthened in such a college environment.

Of course, college *was* college, and Stott *was* Stott. His fun-loving nature was evident in some of his escapades both on and off campus. Only a few have been recorded, two of them by his friend Wallace. It seems that farm animals had relative freedom to roam around Franklin. Such was the case with a massive sow on the Wilson-Branham farm near the campus. "Mrs. Sow," as Wallace called her, was not only big, but she was intelligent enough to open the front gate to the campus behind Chandler Hall, giving her access to foraging activities at the college. School officials, seeking to put a stop to her uprooting and thievery, built a stile with a gateway atop it. The clever hog climbed the stile and opened the gate! It was time for drastic measures. Stott and Wallace talked to Hougham about the matter, and the mentor offered to supply drugs to use on the animal "if the students would administer the same." There was talk of using anesthesia, but that seemed too ineffective, so lethal amounts of anodynes were first used, then huge doses of arsenic—all to no avail. Finally Stott and Wallace put "strychnia enough to kill a military company of men" on a biscuit one day and stood at the third-floor window of the laboratory to observe the results. The sow showed up as usual, rooted around awhile, ate the biscuit, and then lay down in the warm sunshine. A twitch of one hind leg left the impression of a "strychnia spasm." The students and professor kept watch, only to see "Mrs. Sow" get up, stretch, and amble on to more rummaging. They learned a science lesson: "hogs are poison proof."[67] During his senior year, Stott learned another lesson. He was rather adept at impersonations, but chose a bad time to perform one. Hougham had spent a study leave at Brown University, where he picked up a habit from Professor Herman Lincoln of ending his lectures with the words, "Even so at the present day, young gentlemen." It was a trait Stott could not resist copying. At that time, Wallace, who had graduated in 1860, was a tutor at the college. He was in his own room talking with Hougham one day about a faculty concern, when Stott, in his characteristic impetuosity, came down the hallway and, without knocking, burst into the room and in a loud voice mimicked Hougham, crying, "Even so at the present day, young gentlemen!" There is no record of Stott's reaction at seeing his mentor standing there.[68]

There were also fun activities with friends in town. On May 6, 1860, Stott wrote to Carrie Morrison about the "Union Pic-nic" the Sabbath schools of the various churches in Franklin were going to host. He explained that there would be music by a class from the Christian church and some brief speeches. Then he joked that it was to be a *Basket Dinner*," so "it would not be best for you to come without your basket" (perhaps a hint for her to bring the food for both of them). He went on to discuss one of his favorite activities: "They have quite a *singing* at Prof. Brumback's this afternoon, if I can judge from the 'fuss.' The singing class is prospering as usual." Stott also thanked Morrison for the valentine he received from her in February. "It was an excellent sentiment I found inside it," he added. "I suspect Miss Crain penned it for you."[69]

Almost exactly one year later, Ginni Crain wrote to Morrison from Memphis, Tennessee, reminiscing about Franklin and "Mr. Stott with his books under his arm." She also peered into the future. "I suppose by the time I visit Franklin," she mused, "he will be among the Faculty of Franklin College and settled in some snugg Cottage with a certain friend of mine the personification of happiness. You see, I have got it all pictured out, but I hope you will give me the privilege of beholding the reality." Crain revealed another reality as well, one that would make Stott's 1861 graduation exercises unique. "I suppose the students are thinking of commencement now," she noted, "although the war question has broken into some of their arrangements."[70]

Commencement Day, Wednesday, June 26, 1861, truly *would* be different than in previous years. For one thing, the class of 1861 had six members—the largest in the school's history to that time. The "Order of Exercises" called for all six to deliver orations, but only four were given. George W. Grubbs, a future judge, talked about "Law in the Distribution of Intellect." William H. McCoy, destined for teaching and work at the college, chose "The Power of Knowledge." John W. Potter, a student for the ministry, told listeners that "Christianity is the Essential Element of Civilization." Stott spoke on "Development Gradual." But there were asterisks before the names of the two remaining graduates, and that was the truly distinct feature of this commencement. The asterisks denoted the fact that Thomas Jefferson Morgan and Benjamin Franklin Adkins were already in the U.S. Army.[71]

After Fort Sumter surrendered on Saturday, April 13, 1861, Indiana responded vigorously and in large numbers to President Abraham Lincoln's initial call for volunteers. So it is no surprise that, even though no major land battles had yet been fought, Franklin College's commencement two months later would feel the war's effects. On the Monday after Sumter's fall, April 15, the residents of Franklin held a meeting outside the Johnson County Courthouse. On the dais stood recent Franklin College graduate Casabianca Byfield, seniors George Grubbs

William Taylor Stott, class of 1861.

FRANKLIN COLLEGE COLLECTION, FRANKLIN COLLEGE ARCHIVES, B. F. HAMILTON LIBRARY, FRANKLIN COLLEGE and Thomas Morgan, and Professor Jeremiah Brumback. Their speeches, along with others, stirred the "large and enthusiastic" crowd. The purpose of the gathering—which turned into a rally—was to make preparations for organizing a company of volunteers. When the call went out for recruits, says one account, "there was a general rush for the secretary's desk" to be enrolled.[72]

Though he was surely there to support his friends, Stott chose not to sign up that day. During the following months, however, destiny called to his sense of duty, and Stott was off to war.

PART ONE

2

A Missouri Odyssey and the Battle of Pea Ridge

Indiana was not prepared for war in April 1861. In the entire state there were only six militia units, all of them recently formed, poorly organized, and containing in total fewer than five hundred men. State officials, including the adjutant general, did not even know where the commonwealth's leftover arms and military equipment from the Mexican War were stored, much less their usability. Uncertainty and confusion reigned on the political scene as well. The new governor, Republican Oliver Perry Morton, had just ascended to that office from his post as the newly elected lieutenant governor because Henry S. Lane—in a previously calculated move—resigned his governorship by appointing himself to a vacant seat in the U.S. Senate. Morton, therefore, as one historian correctly phrases it, "was a young and untried member of a young and untried party." Moreover, he was a former Democrat who left that party in 1854 in anger over Stephen A. Douglas's Kansas-Nebraska Act, so his support from either party was, at best, tenuous and qualified. Finally, there was the economy. In mid-February the state treasury held a meager $10,368, most of it earmarked for specific purposes and unavailable for military use.[1]

The vast majority of Hoosiers, however, did not care about the lack of governmental preparation. Patriotic to the core, they were eager to enter the fray. As in Franklin, "war fever" pervaded virtually every community. When the news of Fort Sumter reached Indianapolis on Sunday, April 14, a massive number of residents assembled in two huge halls, overflowed each, and gathered in the streets. There they heard Morton and orators from both parties call for unity and the will "to repel any treasonous assaults . . . peaceably, if we can, forcibly, if we must."[2] Such scenes occurred in towns and villages across the state. To President Abraham Lincoln's

Colonel Thomas Pattison.

April 15 call for 75,000 volunteer soldiers, Morton responded the same day with a telegraphed offer of 10,000, a figure vastly exceeding the state's quota. Men began enlisting in droves at specified locations throughout the state, and women prepared their sewing supplies for the task of creating regimental, state, and national flags. So overwhelming was the flood of recruits pouring into Indianapolis, in fact, that the governor and the first wartime adjutant general, Colonel Lew Wallace, hastily established a recruitment and training station at Henderson's Grove, the site of the state's fairgrounds. Named Camp Morton, within a matter of days it became the temporary home of the first three-month regiments.[3]

This brisk tempo of recruitment continued throughout 1861. After visiting Indiana in October, U.S. Adjutant General Lorenzo Thomas declared: "We found that the State of Indiana had come nobly up to the work of suppression of the rebellion. She had raised and equipped a larger number of troops in proportion to her population that any other State in the Union. The best spirit prevailed, and it was manifest that more troops could easily be raised." And, indeed, they were. By the end of the year, Hoosiers had three cavalry regiments and twelve artillery batteries in the field, along with infantry regiments numbering "up to the Fifty-ninth."[4]

Among them was the Eighteenth Indiana Volunteer Infantry Regiment, organized on August 16, 1861. It was hastily formed in urgent response to the disastrous Union defeat at Wilson's Creek, Missouri, only six days before, and to the state of alarm that loss created across the Midwest. Initially provided with a severely limited supply of essential equipment—antiquated muskets, just five Enfield rifles per company, and *gray* uniforms—its recruits soon reconciled themselves to the spartan nature of their provisions. Their willingness to settle for such shortages was due in large part to the trust and admiration they had for their commander, Colonel Thomas Pattison of Aurora, a native of Ireland and veteran of the British army.[5]

Like most Hoosier regiments, the ten companies of the Eighteenth represented particular counties or local communities. For example, Company A's personnel drew largely from Dearborn County, while the men of Company K hailed from Shelby County. Company I was the Johnson County unit, led by Captain Jonathan H. Williams, a prominent editor and publisher in Franklin. On the company's original muster roll, compiled by Williams on the day of its organization, appear the names of eighteen-year-old Corporal Riley Storey and two older privates, Fielding C. Eddleman, age twenty-five, and William T. Stott, age twenty-four. Interestingly, the names of Eddleman and Stott are squeezed into the company roster, as if an afterthought, to maintain alphabetical order, causing Williams to adjust the numerical listing accordingly. Although the roll bears the date "16 August 1861," the captain probably made these changes after the Eighteenth had already arrived at its first military destination in Saint Louis, for Eddleman's and Stott's situation was a unique one. They had enrolled early on August 13, and, for some unknown reason, returned to Franklin, thereby missing their regiment's departure from Indianapolis on April 17 and reporting for duty at Saint Louis almost a week later.[6]

<hr>

Upon landing at the famed Mississippi River port, the men of the Eighteenth found the "Mound City" to be a bustling staging area for Union military operations throughout the river valley and the guerrilla-infested state of Missouri. They also learned that fame attended their commander, Major General John C. Frémont, the legendary "Pathfinder" of the American West. Though his tenure as leader of the Western Department proved controversial and contentious, and his lack of military skills quickly became apparent, the troops felt so privileged to serve under him that they named their encampment "Camp Jessie" in honor of Jessie Benton Frémont, the general's wife. Private Walter Stanley of Company G in the Eighteenth described it as "the prettiest camp we ever saw in Missouri," and a Saint Louis woman, visiting her husband at the site, marveled at how "Beautiful Lafayette Park, with its brilliant flower beds and stretches of green swards, looking like emerald velvet, was turned into a great military camp," where "campfires were burning and men were cooking the evening meal."[7]

Not only was their campsite in Saint Louis a pleasant surprise, but so also was their reception by the city's residents. Initially, suspicion abounded on both sides. The Indiana soldiers were under the impression that secession sentiment was rampant in the city and thus they expected hostility, while Saint Louisans feared Hoosiers would bring chaos and disorder to their town. Harry Watts of the Twenty-fourth Indiana reflected, "We expected to be saluted with Brickbats and other missiles from every Housetop." To the contrary, he noted, "we passed through the City without any insult being offered us everything was very quiet." A private from the Eighteenth concurred. In a letter to his father on August 19, Samuel B. Voyles of Company G wrote that the regiment "had ten rounds of ammunition as we came down and had orders to fire if we were interrupted in Saint Louis and we would have done it too," yet, "we had nothing to disturb us as we came through." From the perspective of the citizens, a reporter for the *Saint Louis Democrat* commented on the "excellent order" that characterized the Union camps. "In all regiments," he observed, "we have not heard of a single case of disturbance or disorderly conduct among the soldiers, or improper actions toward civilians." He credited this peaceful state to the "manly disposition" of the troops and "strict military discipline."[8] Stott would differ with the columnist about the "manly disposition," but he testified to the discipline—daily drills, dress parades every afternoon, and even some "skirmish drills." He and his comrades truly were in the army now.

The men of the Eighteenth would look back upon their stay in Saint Louis as a leisurely rest stop compared to the remainder of their odyssey through Missouri, which took them on a severe winter trek over alternately frozen and muddy ground, exposing them to the shock of friendly fire, and sending them on a seemingly endless chase after Confederate forces, both organized and guerrilla. It began on August 28 when orders came to break camp in Lafayette Park and prepare to march by rail to Jefferson City, the state capital. "All was bustle and confusion," Stanley recalled, "tents were finally struck, and we were at last stowed away on the cars in the same manner as any other kind of 'livestock.' After thumping and crashing along the road until 11 o'clock a.m. the next day, we stept off the cars and took a good look at Jefferson City." There was not much to see, however, and no time to see it, for the Eighteenth moved that afternoon to a location about a mile up the Missouri River on the left bank, a place they labeled "Camp Pattison."[9]

Preceding them to Jefferson City was the officer who would be their division commander for the next seven months. Colonel Jefferson Columbus Davis, having been appointed acting brigadier general by Frémont, came to the city's military headquarters on August 28 to relieve its commandant—a brigadier general named Ulysses S. Grant—and to assume command himself. With his customary zeal, Davis began fortifying the city and preparing his troops for combat. The Eighteenth and Davis's own Twenty-second Indiana pulled picket duty for the first time and, according to Gilbert Denny, they drilled for six hours every day, despite "Bad ground to Drill on." Stanley reflected that, under Davis, "We had a pretty lively time of it. Dress Parade and Battalion Drill were the standing orders of the day."[10]

Davis pushed his men hard, for rumors spread that Confederate forces under General Sterling Price, possibly as many as 16,000, were along the Osage River and set to attack Federal fortifications at Lexington, Boonville, and Jefferson City. To prepare for that threat, Davis requested reinforcement by two infantry regiments, two batteries of light artillery, and "some heavy guns"—all from Indiana. He gratefully received a shipment of muskets and rifles from Governor Morton, "total nine hundred sixty (960) equipments in full."[11] While Davis readied his men for battle, Frémont issued a proclamation that stiffened Confederate resolve in Missouri and drew the ire of Lincoln. On August 30 the department commander established martial law throughout the state, asserting that "The property, real and personal, of all persons . . . who shall take up arms against the United States . . . is declared to be confiscated, and their slaves, if any they have, are hereby declared freemen."[12] In the context of this unfortunate proclamation of emancipation, Davis's forces set out to meet the enemy, who was now on the move.

On September 12 Davis notified Frémont that numerous recent dispatches from the West left "no doubt" that Price was at Warrensburg with a large force and was "moving on toward Lexington" in the northwestern part of the state. The next day Davis wired his commander that Confederate Colonel Martin E. Green was pressing on Boonville, only forty-five miles from Jefferson City, and that Hoosier troops would be sent on "force march tomorrow so as to get in Green's rear." As Davis's biographers correctly observe, Missouri was now clearly "in a state of fluidity militarily." During the afternoon of September 14, Lieutenant Colonel Henry D. Washburn, temporarily in command of the Eighteenth, received orders from Davis to take his regiment and a detachment of the Twenty-second and advance by rail to Syracuse en route to Boonville.[13] After a typical period of "hurry up and wait" lasting for hours, the troops climbed aboard Pacific Railroad cars and rode to the little town of Tipton, where they disembarked, had a brief respite, and at night began the twenty-five-mile march to Boonville—their first forced march of the

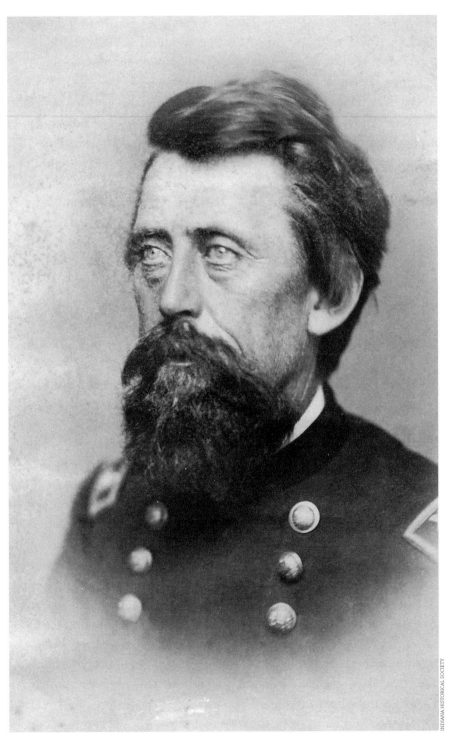

Colonel Jefferson C. Davis.

war. It was a trying one. After treading only a few miles, heavy rain set in and lasted all night, making the road muddy and virtually impassable. At stops along the way, the exhausted troops had no trouble sleeping in pouring rain, and at Boonville they relished the chance to rest and dry out.[14]

Their time at Boonville, however, was brief, for the situation at Lexington had become critical. Price's Confederates were advancing rapidly toward the little Missouri River town where Colonel James A. Mulligan's Irish Brigade and hundreds of Missouri Home Guards had hastily fortified Masonic College Hill against the impending Confederate onslaught. Frémont had inexplicably delayed sending assistance to Lexington until September 20, when he directed Davis to "concentrate a force strong enough, in your judgment . . . and push forward to relieve Mulligan." Frémont's order was too late, since Mulligan surrendered that same day. Anticipating such a directive, however, Davis had already commandeered transport steamers to carry his men up the Missouri River to Lexington.[15]

The Hoosiers started up the swift current of the river on the "beautiful, clear day" of September 19 on four steamers. Most of the Eighteenth squeezed onto the *Iatan*, with the Twenty-second on the *War Eagle* and the Twenty-sixth in advance on the *White Cloud* and the *Des Moines*. As the crowded vessels neared Glasgow, a tiny village on the north bank of the river where the Confederates were rumored to have a battery, officers chose to land the boats, station pickets on guard, and scout the area. The Twenty-sixth, under Colonel William M. Wheatley, began reconnaissance, just as night fell. Soon it heard "the regular tramp" of marching soldiers and saw in the moonlight the glint of arms moving "along a road which ran between the woods and a corn-field." Assuming this was the enemy, sentinels gave the order to fire and, from only sixty yards away, shots were returned. What later generations would call "friendly fire" continued until thirteen men had fallen and Major Gordon Tanner lay mortally wounded. Stanley later recalled the volleys as "simultaneous and murderous" and the loss of both sides as "severe." A horrified fifteen-year-old of the Twenty-second, John Prentiss, wrote his sister about the "fight amongst ourselves" that took place in a "thick papa [paw paw] thicket on both sides." With the men shaken and confused, the expedition toward Lexington came to a halt. Only the Twenty-sixth proceeded in its direction, while Davis sent the other Hoosier units marching toward a Union staging area around Glasgow and Sedalia.[16]

———◆———

The remainder of 1861 found the Eighteenth and its brigade slogging through the torrential rains and deep mud of a disease-ridden autumn and stepping lightly across snow and ice in a bitterly cold Missouri winter. Its destination was Springfield and the Confederate army there, which Frémont now intended to drive from the state. Under increasing criticism for the Lexington debacle, and fearing the loss of both his prestige and position, the Pathfinder mobilized his army for a major offensive. "I am taking the field myself," he informed General Winfield Scott, "and hope to destroy the enemy." Scott replied that the president was pleased and "he expects you to repair the disaster at Lexington without loss of time." The day after Mulligan's surrender, Frémont issued General Order No. 16, reorganizing the Union forces and placing Davis's Indiana troops in the First Brigade of Brigadier General John Pope's Second Division.[17] For the soldiers this meant a long, wet, and cold march through southwestern Missouri.

In late September and early October the army confronted dreadful conditions. Rain fell in torrents daily, transforming roads into quagmires and raising the threat of disease. In a circular letter from Tipton on October 11, Frémont commented, "The state of the roads is such that trains may be uncomfortably delayed," so troops should carry ample provisions and pioneers should be ready "to repair the bridges and roads wherever impassable." Two days later Davis issued a special order at Georgetown, stating that disabled wagons were to be "turned out from the column" until repaired and no one was to ride in the wagons "except by certificate" from a physician. Clearly, the two ordeals of poor roads and spreading illness now overlapped.[18] When Eddelman penned a letter to Maggie Stout back in Franklin County, Indiana, on October 1, he indicated that he and Stott were well and that "the general health of this division of the army is good." But by October 4, Stanley recalled, the Eighteenth was "Badly crippled from sickness . . . and with drooping spirits," and Davis noted a week later "the rapid increase of the sick list," to the point that the courthouse had to be used for "Post Hospital purposes."

Later in the month Pope grumbled to Frémont about the "extraordinary (appalling) sickness" Davis's brigade suffered and the fact that most men were "without overcoats, with only a lone blanket, and their other clothing nearly worn out." Despite these conditions, Stott and his comrades continued their October trek from Georgetown to Otterville, Warsaw, and Humansville, a quaint little village with a unique name whose residents greeted them with waving flags and "Huzzahs" for the Union.[19]

Pope's division left Humansville on the evening of November 1, proceeding toward Springfield, where rumor placed Price's army. It was the first night march of the war for Davis's brigade and it moved slowly, still suffering from the debilitating illnesses of the past month. On Sunday, November 3, it finally encamped on the bank of Wilson's Creek, the site of Union defeat only four months before. The men fully expected to see combat soon, perhaps even on the morrow, but they were not prepared for the startling news that trickled through camp: Frémont had been relieved of command. Although his immediate subordinates expressed pleasure at the move, many officers and men in the ranks threatened to resign or return home, and they greeted the Pathfinder with outbursts of approval when he took his leave several days later. Captain Albert Tracy of a Union Missouri unit considered the dismissal a "crushing insult to one who had labored so long and so earnestly," and a member of the Twenty-second reported that the change of command prompted "universal regret."[20]

Following the dismissal of Frémont, and the realization that Price had left the area, the Union forces retraced their steps in a sad and sullen march over the same road that had taken them to Springfield. George Herr of the Fifty-ninth Illinois said the men "moved like automatons, with no purpose," and John W. Foster, an officer in the Twenty-fifth Indiana, declared the whole Missouri campaign "a very barren affair." "It may suit a fellow who likes long walks and heavy marching," he reflected, "but there has not been much of war in it." There had been deaths that November, however, as the Eighteenth Indiana alone lost fourteen privates and one officer to disease.[21]

December was no better, since winter set in with all its fury. Actually, it made its first appearance in late November, bringing severe cold and high winds. Foster told his family that the men of the Twenty-fifth were "shivering around our campfire . . . stuffing our tents with straw, blankets, and buffalo robes to keep warm. . . . These Missouri winds are such winds as Hoosiers don't know anything about." As the days passed, the weather grew more unbearable. Temperatures were often below zero and snow depths frequently reached four to six inches. These conditions did not prevent officers from keeping troops busy with regular drills and reviews, such as the one Davis held on December 3, the day after a four-inch snowstorm![22] Marching also resumed in mid-December as Pope pressed toward Warrensburg, on the banks of Blackwater Creek. At this location, in response to scouting reports that a large body of Confederates had assembled along the creek, Pope sent Davis, his cavalry, and some artillery to pursue the enemy. December 18 was a day Davis's brigade would never forget, for he not only prevailed over the foe but also captured "1300 prisoners, 1000 stand of arms, 1000 horses, and 65 wagons." Davis received promotion to permanent brigadier general, and some in the Eighteenth, including Stott, proudly escorted the prisoners to Sedalia.[23]

———■◆◆———

Another December event shaped the life of the Eighteenth for the next nine months and set the stage for its first combat experience. On Christmas Day, Major General Henry W. Halleck, now in charge of the Department of Missouri, issued Special Order No. 92, assigning Brigadier General Samuel R. Curtis "to the command of the South Western District." The fifty-six-year-old Curtis, who was regarded as "a fine-looking old man," was an 1831 graduate of West Point, a civil engineer, lawyer, and railroad man who fought in the Mexican War and briefly served in Congress. The day after his appointment Curtis established his headquarters at Rolla and soon sent orders to his three division commanders, Franz Sigel and Alexander Asboth at Rolla, and Davis near Sedalia. He also sent Colonel Eugene A. Carr and his "cavalry expedition" to Springfield in pursuit of the retreating Price "or as far as to feel the enemy, and, if in broken ranks, fall on him and cut him to pieces."[24] Such were Curtis's early actions in creating what he called the Army of the Southwest.

Halleck and Curtis were in a hurry, wanting to expedite the movement westward and quickly bring pressure on the Confederate army in southwest Missouri. But it was winter, the weather was changeable and uncooperative, the young volunteers in Curtis's charge were eager for action but raw and untried, and supplies were few and unevenly distributed. Regarding the latter, when Curtis's new quartermaster,

Brigadier General Samuel R. Curtis, commander of the Army of the Southwest.

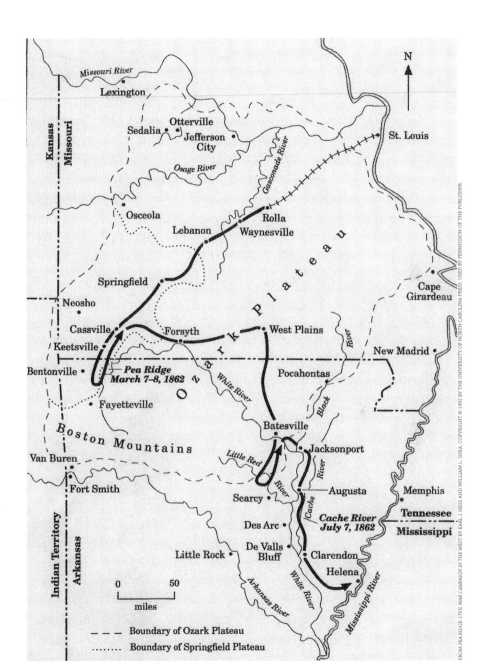

Route of the Army of the Southwest during Stott's first year as a soldier.

youthful Captain Philip H. Sheridan, reached Rolla in late December, he discovered the supply system and the whole "logistical situation" to be "defective"—indeed, in one biographer's description, "an unholy mess." Although Sheridan zealously and successfully "labored day and night" to correct the system, he and his superiors recognized, as historian William L. Shea observed, that "the Army of the Southwest would have to travel light if it was to travel at all."[25] It would also travel slowly. Despite stringent limitations imposed on camp equipment, baggage, and even food and clothing—all of which could have inhibited the pace of the army— the trip into southwestern Missouri occurred in horrendous weather. Storms of snow and freezing rain were followed by rapid thaws, creating "mud without mercy." These were obstacles men, animals, and wagons could barely navigate as they tread across the Ozark Plateau, a region of rolling, rocky hills and narrow valleys. Battling land and elements all the way, the army finally reached its primary objective, Lebanon, Missouri, on February 1. That same day Davis's division, whose travels from Otterville were equally treacherous, camped only a mile and a half away. The Eighteenth now joined the Army of the Southwest, swelling its manpower to 12,095 troops.[26]

Greeting his newly assembled army at Lebanon, Curtis praised the troops for their dedicated marching "during the coldest and most stormy period of a cold winter." You advanced "your trains and equipment through snow, mud, floods, and frost," he marveled, "without . . . a murmur and without loss of property and men." Now they would have to renew and extend their resolve, for "We must strip for a forced march and final conflict."[27] To transform his disparate military units into a compact, functional field army, on February 9 Curtis reorganized his force into four divisions. The First and Second divisions, under the overall command of Sigel, were to be led by Colonels Peter J. Osterhaus and Asboth, respectively. Davis would command the Third Division, made up of the Eighth, Eighteenth, and Twenty-second Indiana, Thirty-seventh and Fifty-ninth Illinois, two batteries (Martin Klauss's First Indiana Light and the Peoria Battery, the Second Illinois Light), and the First Missouri Cavalry. A new Fourth Division of Iowa, Illinois, and Missouri troops had Colonel Eugene Carr as its chief. Once again, Curtis wasted no time. In the early morning of February 10, all divisions began the march south to Springfield with flags aloft and bands striking patriotic airs. The divisions "marched independently but parallel to each other" on separate roads, Carr's biographer records, for the purpose of presenting a strong, formidable front.[28]

Fortunately, the weather had moderated. Two diarists of the Eighteenth noted that it was "clear and cold" as they left Lebanon, but "the roads being froze and in pretty good order, we made good time." Soldiers in other units viewed road conditions differently; the regimental historian of the Fifty-ninth Illinois said "the roads were very bad," and the annalists of the Thirty-sixth Illinois spoke of "quagmires" and a "half fluid condition" that caused "uncertain stoppages." Still, these were minor obstacles, for they were on their way to stop their nemesis—"Old Pap" Price, who had retreated to winter quarters and was relying, one historian has written, on "his powerful allies, Gens. January, February, and March."[29]

The Federals arrived at Pierson's Creek, just eight miles from Springfield, on the evening of February 12. Davis's division, in the advance and following Curtis's instructions, had taken the road past Leslie's store and was pitching camp at Piper's farm when his pickets became the targets of "brisk firing." Hearing the musketry, Curtis ordered artillery and infantry forward to support Davis. Brief skirmishing sent the enemy back toward Springfield. This Confederate "retreat" was in fact a mere cover, allowing Price to vacate the city during the night. Of course, Private Enos E. Johnson of Company B in the Eighteenth did not know that when he confided to his diary that night: "Great excitement in camp. Load our guns. Tremendous splutter and riding to and fro of officers—pale faces of privates. Deep anxiety everywhere manifested. Doubtless the eve of battle."[30] Davis's men arose at two o'clock the next morning and were on the road by four, "still expecting an attack." When they reached the fortifications outside town, however, all that greeted them, according to Stanley, was "a strip of primeval oak, covered with 'frowning batteries' . . . The word passed along the line, 'Price has skeddadled.'"[31]

Curtis entered the town itself at 10 a.m. and immediately wrote Halleck, "The flag of the Union floats over the court-house at Springfield, Mo." He and his warriors saw abundant evidence of the hasty, frantic departure of the enemy. It seemed like everything had been left behind or destroyed. Sigel, who knew the beauty of the "garden city" well, found it now "desolate and bleak" with empty houses, trees reduced to stumps, and ornate fences broken in pieces. Confederate stragglers and hundreds of their sick or injured, storehouses of supplies and food, camp equipage, even military records—all had been abandoned. Johnson saw a full meal sitting on a camp table attended by cooking vessels and found the scene "amusing."[32] Stott grabbed a pair of "secesh" boots, thus joining countless other Union foragers in helping themselves. There was no time to dawdle, though, for Price was on the run and Curtis intended to catch him.

The chase began the next morning, February 14, as the Army of the Southwest proceeded southward in two columns. Sigel's First and Second divisions marched down a westerly route, a poorly kept road covered with ice left by a storm the previous evening. Curtis hoped that Sigel might bypass Price's main body, get south of the enemy, and prevent its further retreat. Curtis himself joined the Third and Fourth divisions on Telegraph Road, also called Wire Road, the primary commercial and mail track to Arkansas, and Price's escape route. With Davis's division in advance, the men in blue reached Wilson's Creek, some expecting Price to fight them there on the grounds of his earlier victory. Instead, the Federals encountered a vision of what might lay ahead. Johnson saw "signs of old battle. Buildings, carts—old cannon balls and shell." Worse, the skeletons of hastily buried soldiers lay uncovered, the work of the elements and scavenging animals over the past months. Shaken but undeterred—and with a distinct "psychological advantage" over their weary, hungry, fugitive prey—the army pressed on in what historian William Shea correctly labels "the most dramatic pursuit of the Civil War."[33]

Of course, many a foot soldier at the time may not have deemed it so. All of the marches, after all, were forced, often at quickstep. They started at the first light of day and ended—save for ten-minute breaks along the way—as dark set in. (It is significant that Stott could find no time to make daily entries in his diary on this march.) For many the march may have seemed a blur, interrupted only by running skirmishes, camping within sight of the enemy, and going to bed hungry because supply wagons lagged behind. An infantryman of the Thirty-seventh Illinois said, "Day after day we followed where the enemy led; day after day we were told that Price would make a stand at some certain place; and day after day we were disappointed." He did add, however, "Sometimes our advance would come up to their rear guard and have a brush."[34]

One such encounter in Missouri occurred on the army's first night out of Springfield, February 14. At Crane Creek, Colonel Calvin A. Ellis of the

First Missouri Cavalry of Davis's division, misunderstanding a directive from Curtis not to bother the enemy, opened artillery fire on Confederate camps in the valley. This misstep led to the capture of some Confederate surgeons and soldiers, but it also prompted Price to speed up his push into Arkansas. Lyman G. Bennett, a civilian employee of the U.S. Army with the Thirty-sixth Illinois, wrote disparagingly of Ellis's effect on the enemy, opining that he had only "spanked them and hurried them off."[35] Now the blueclad warriors moved even faster, passing through the towns of Cassville and Keetsville, where retreating Confederates had informed the residents, said Samuel McKay of the Thirty-seventh Illinois, "that the yanks are coming, destroying everything that came in their way." Consequently, Johnson of the Eighteenth noticed that "Inhabitants nearly all fled on our approach." On February 16 the Federals reached Cross Timber Hollow on the Arkansas border. There the Third Division once again clashed with the enemy, this time on Big Sugar Creek, where Price had halted, hoping for reinforcements from Brigadier General Ben McCulloch's Texans.[36]

On February 17 Curtis led his army onto what he called the "virgin soil" of Arkansas. Traversing the state line was a noisy affair, with hearty cheers accompanied by bands playing uplifting tunes—"Arkansas Traveler" and even "Dixie"—with special exuberance. As he rode along, Curtis lauded his men and, once the telegraph was ready, he paused long enough to wire Halleck: "The flag of our Union again floats in Arkansas." Later that day, though, bearers of the Stars and Stripes engaged in the first Civil War battle on Arkansas turf. Price, now reinforced by McCulloch, took a stand at Little Sugar Creek. "His batteries opened on us," reported Curtis, "and were very soon replied to by mine. After a few rounds of shot and shell, I ordered a cavalry charge, which drove them from the high grounds they occupy, with the loss of many killed, wounded, and scattered. My loss was 13 killed and 15 or 20 wounded." Once again, it was Davis's division in the lead. "By being ordered out ahead," Henry Curtis of the Thirty-seventh Illinois told his beloved Lucy, "we were the *first* Union infantry that ever profaned the Sacred Soil of Arkansas!! Think of that."[37]

The confrontation at Little Sugar Creek forced Price and McCulloch to fall back and establish a cantonment eight miles south at Cross Timber Hollow, which an Iowa cavalryman later described as "one of Nature's fortifications," where they could stage a "strong resistance perhaps a successful one." General Curtis made no immediate pursuit. He knew his army needed rest, and it had outdistanced its supplies. He did dispatch scouting parties "to see if Cross Hollow could be outflanked" from the west and ordered Asboth's Second Division to reconnoiter the area around Bentonville. Then, on February 20, Curtis received word that the Confederate forces had left Cross Timber Hollow for better quarters at Fayetteville, so he promptly began a slow advance to Cross Hollow down a frightfully muddy Telegraph Road. Reaching the former Confederate encampment on February 22, Curtis remained there the rest of the month.[38]

It was clear that the long campaign from Rolla had taken its toll. The men were exhausted, wagons and mules were played out, and the supply situation was grave. Curtis wrote home that "many of the men are no better than barefoot," and Nathan Harwood of the Ninth Iowa remembered soldiers walking on blistered feet because they "had worn holes in their shoes." Clothing of every sort was needed, and food provisions were equally scant. Surgeon George Gordon of the Eighteenth recorded in late February, "We have had no rations for the last week," though "half rations" had arrived the day before. Still, he feared, "it looks like starving if we do not save rations." Fortunately, although the Confederates burned most of the buildings they abandoned at Cross Timber Hollow, along with stores of foodstuffs, General Curtis was able to report on February 22 that "Considerable he did not burn and we are using it. Most of our provisions for the last ten days have been taken from the enemy."[39]

With his long supply line strung dangerously thin, Curtis concentrated on refitting and redeploying his divisions, strengthening his line of communication back to Saint Louis, and developing strategy. He learned that the armies of Price and McCulloch were now under the overall command of Major General Earl Van Dorn of Mississippi, a feisty, daring, and potentially formidable opponent. As March dawned, Curtis took a defensive position. He could have proceeded into the Boston Mountains to challenge the enemy or moved back toward Springfield for supply and communications purposes. He rejected both choices, however, and deployed his troops so as to corner the enemy, should Van Dorn attack. Carr's Fourth Division stayed on the Union left at Cross Timber Hollow, or "Camp Halleck" as the soldiers called it. Osterhaus and Asboth, under Sigel, gathered their divisions at McKissick Creek near Bentonville, thus forming the Federal right. On March 1 Davis's units returned to Little Sugar Creek, where they became a strong central reserve charged with building defensive emplacements. That same day near Fayetteville, Colonel Henry Little of the First Missouri (Confederate) Cavalry Brigade prepared his men for action. On March 3 Asa Payne of that unit recalled, "each man took three days' rations, one blanket and forty rounds of ammunition and began to march to attack General Curtis who had halted at Pea Ridge forty miles distant." The Eighteenth would soon "see the elephant" and find him ugly.[40]

On Tuesday, March 4, Van Dorn's Army of the West left the Boston Mountains and began its march northward in heavily falling snow. In its commander's mind, this was the first step toward victory over Curtis and the eventual recovery of Missouri for the Confederacy. The Confederate force's sheer size hinted at success: 16,000 men compared to Curtis's 12,000 (with even fewer Federals in effective fighting shape) and a four-to-one advantage in artillery. Indeed, as historians William L. Shea and Earl J. Hess contend, "Never did a Confederate army march off to battle with greater superiority." Yet, Van Dorn's eagerness proved hard on his men. He pushed them at a "killing pace" in wintry weather, passing Fayetteville by nightfall and pressing on toward Bentonville the next morning.[41] Around two o'clock on the afternoon of March 5, Curtis heard of Van Dorn's advance from scouts, fugitive Arkansas Unionists, and a Federal spy embedded in the Confederate ranks. Orders went out swiftly to all divisions "to move immediately to Sugar Creek" and concentrate around Telegraph Road. Davis, already there, deployed his Hoosier First Brigade to the right of the road and, under Pattison's direction, had it "falling timber and throwing up some small entrenchments." To the left of the road, Colonel Julius White's Illinoisans likewise wielded picks and shovels, erecting artillery redoubts in bold defiance of a "blinding storm of snow and sleet."[42]

Thus began the Union defense at a place called Pea Ridge, a rough, cragged plateau that ran from east to west at a height of some 160 feet above surrounding farmland. This elevation formed the northern edge of a sort of parallelogram, with Telegraph Road as its eastern boundary, Bentonville Road on the west, and Little Sugar Creek on the south. Within it the impending battle would be fought, with several natural and manmade features playing leading roles in the martial drama. Historic Elkhorn Tavern on Telegraph Road, a large, frame house that had functioned since the 1830s as an inn, stagecoach station, and private dwelling, was surrounded by shot and shell on both days of the battle and served each army as a hospital and surgical ward. The tiny hamlet of Leetown and the nearby thickly timbered Morgan's woods, some two miles southwest of Elkhorn, became the locale of Stott's first major combat experience.[43]

The prelude to the bloody encounter came on March 6. While Sigel was enjoying a leisurely breakfast at the Eagle Hotel in Bentonville that morning, a courier brought news of the rapid approach of Confederate forces. Sigel abruptly ended his meal and hurried to join his men in the field. As the sun arose behind the hills, a heavy artillery exchange ensued, and the German general soon recognized that the intensity of the assault required him to fall back. This launched a day of constant "fighting and re-treating"—repeatedly checking the enemy advance with effective artillery barrages, then falling back—all the way to the Union position on Sugar Creek.[44] Meanwhile, back at the creek, the divisions of Carr and Davis continued to labor, felling trees with which to blockade Telegraph Road and constructing formidable breastworks on the hills overlooking the valley. Curtis, who had been at that site since 2 a.m., also worried about being

Elkhorn Tavern.

"outflanked on the right" at Bentonville Detour. Colonel Grenville M.
Dodge of Carr's First Brigade recommended a blockade of that route similar to the one on Telegraph Road and proceeded, under Curtis's orders, to
erect one.[45] As the day progressed, Gordon wrote, "We begin to hear the
music again of artillery, and now . . . of musketry, up towards Bentonville." The Confederates had "tried to cut Genl. Sigel's command off from
ours," he surmised, but "the Old Dutchman was too much for them on the
retreat." An Illinois infantryman concurred in more colorful and accurate
language. "Sigel had been following his best style of fighting—fighting in
retreat," said McKay, "and it became a saying in our army that 'Sigel can
whip the whole Confederacy if they will only follow him,' and no doubt he
gave the rebs the same opinion that day."[46]

Sigel arrived at the Union defense line at dusk, with Van Dorn on his
tail across Little Sugar Creek. Both armies spent a restless night. Curtis
was at his headquarters at Pratt's store, halfway between Elkhorn Tavern
and the fortified works at Little Sugar Creek. He could see the Confederate campfires, twinkling like earthbound stars, when he peered across
his breastworks, and he felt ready for any attack. "Every one expects a
fight tomorrow," observed Iowan Henry Dysart. "Gen. Curtis was heard
to say this evening, 'I will either fight them tomorrow or they me!'" The
Eighteenth's Stanley recalled, "That night we lay on our arms. Few slept."
And Bennett of the Thirty-sixth Illinois presciently confided to his diary,
"Tomorrow will reveal more than many will wish to know of the movement of the enemy."[47]

As for the Confederate troops, they too slumbered little and anticipated much. Their leaders, however, decided to advance during the night.
In a council of war in Van Dorn's tent that afternoon, officers haggled
over the best course of attack. McCulloch and Brigadier General James M.
McIntosh, over Price's vigorous objections, proposed a nocturnal march
up the Bentonville Detour to the west of the Union emplacement. They
contended that this would avoid what they correctly assumed would be a
strongly defended Telegraph Road and enable the Confederates to circle
around Curtis's right wing and assault him from the rear. The idea appealed to Van Dorn's daring nature, and he "resolved to adopt this route"
and move with all "speed and secrecy." At around 8 p.m. the Army of the
West abandoned camp, leaving its campfires lit to deceive Curtis, and
marched up the chosen path. "Speed" soon dissolved, for the troops suf-

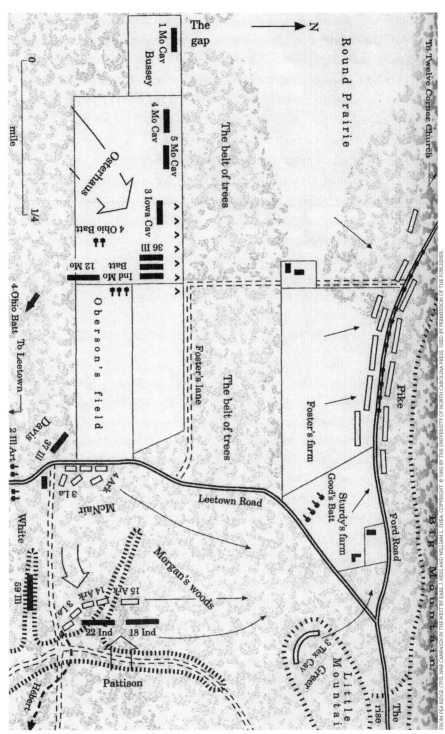

The Eighteenth Indiana at the battle of Leetown (Morgan's woods), March 7, 1862.

fered greatly from exhaustion, illness, and inadequate provisions. It was in this "tired and demoralized" state that they encountered icy streams to ford or bridge, along with Dodge's well-placed obstructions. The result was a delay of almost eight hours. By morning the Confederate army was less fit for a fight than it was the day before.[48]

Friday morning, March 7, dawned bright, clear, and frigid. As Union soldiers tried to unwind after a night on snow-covered ground, steaming tins of coffee in hand and their muskets within reach, Curtis met with his division commanders at Pratt's store. Around eight o'clock, Provost Marshal Major Eli Weston entered to report that within the past two hours Price's forces had driven back Union pickets and skirmishing had broken out at a tanyard less than a mile from Elkhorn Tavern. This meant that Confederates were behind the Union lines. "On Friday the never to be forgotten 7th," Iowa cavalryman William Rogers told his brother, "wee found that the enemy were in our rear and surrounding us." Davis put it more formally in his official report: "It was ascertained that the enemy was making an effort to turn our right flank and attack us in rear." In any language, it meant that the battle at Pea Ridge had begun.[49]

At Pratt's store, some advised retreat. But Dodge and a determined Davis argued, as Dodge wrote later, "we had come to fight; that it would never do for us to refuse, now that we had the opportunity." Curtis agreed and promptly sought to grasp the tactical advantage. To do so meant turning his entire front 180 degrees, the only such movement in the face of the enemy in the entire Civil War. The army accomplished this unorthodox feat in six hours, while simultaneously engaging in stiff combat—an exercise hailed as "a landmark achievement in American military history" by historians Shea and Hess.[50] Curtis immediately sent Carr, with his Fourth Division and a detachment of the Eighth Indiana, to Elkhorn Tavern and the declivity beyond it, in full confidence that Carr "would clean out that hollow in a very short time." He then dispatched Osterhaus to the area around Leetown, Morgan's woods, and Samuel Oberson's farm, now on the army's left. This mission was to be "a cross between a reconnaissance force and a spoiling attack," but the German colonel quickly confronted a storm of fire from McCulloch's and McIntosh's troops and Albert Pike's Cherokee Indian Brigade. After "grimly and steadily" holding his own against vastly superior numbers in bloody fighting at Oberson's cornfield, a contest that left both McCulloch and McIntosh dead on the field, Osterhaus requested reinforcements. In reply, Curtis sent Davis's division to Osterhaus's aid, thus exposing Stott and the Eighteenth to its baptism of fire.[51]

Davis and a large contingent of the Third Division—some 1,400 in all—marched on the double-quick through Leetown and a quarter mile beyond. At about 2 p.m., the reinforcements found Osterhaus at the southern edge of Oberson's field. The two officers conferred, Osterhaus entreating Davis to take his troops to the right into Morgan's woods where the grayclad warriors of Colonel Louis Hébert's infantry were making dangerous inroads. Having dropped their knapsacks and other cumbersome items at Leetown, the Illinois and Indiana soldiers entered the dense woods fixed for speed and freedom of movement. They needed that capability, for the terrain they encountered was a thick snarl of vines, underbrush, and trees, many toppled by recent severe storms. In this jumble, visibility was severely limited, maintenance of regimental formation was virtually impossible, and, since cavalry and artillery were ineffective in such confined quarters, infantry combat was at extremely close range, the smoke from which further restricted the ability to tell friend from foe. Indeed, as Hess observes, the fighting in Morgan's woods was "much closer than in most Civil War battles." While these conditions did allow officers to pull their men back into cover periodically to reform their units, Stott's regiment was apparently an exception. "Of the Federal infantry," Hess notes, "only the 18th Indiana engaged in fighting lasting more than a few minutes at a time."[52]

The Union advance opened with heavy shelling of the forested area by Captain Peter Davidson's Peoria Battery, which Davis had placed at the southeast corner of Oberson's field. From that spot the Thirth-seventh Illinois filed right into the woods in line of battle to "within one hundred and fifty yards of the enemy's front," reported its commander, Colonel White. Their opponents were Hébert's Third Louisiana, in historian Hess's view "the best infantry unit in McCulloch's division." Each line moved steadily toward the other without firing until only "sixty or seventy yards" separated them. Then, White wrote, "the fire opened almost simultaneously from both sides, and was maintained for about three quarters of an hour, with very little intermission at very short range." One reason his regiment held its fire was that the Confederate flags and uniforms closely resembled their own. Thinking they may be Union, McKay recalled, "we advanced without fear or hesitation till we were met by a withering volley that nearly destroyed the 'right wing' of the regiment." Once begun, the fighting grew in intensity. The Fifty-ninth Illinois of White's brigade came up from behind the Thirty-seventh, only to be met by Hébert's Louisian-ans, now reinforced by Arkansas and Cherokee fighters. So heavy was the fire that one Union unit "fought them flat on their bellies on the ground," and an Illinois infantryman said the smoke-laden air was "literally filled with leaden hail. Balls would whiz by our ears, cut off bushes closely, even cut our clothes." In this tempest of fire, White's regiments advanced and fell back three times until a gap between them provided Hébert with a possible wedge for a breakthrough.[53]

At this point, hearing the increased volume of Confederate musketry, and fearing White could no longer maintain his line, Davis ordered Pattison's First Brigade into the maelstrom from its position on the southern edge of Oberson's field. Placing the Eighteenth Indiana to the right of the Twenty-second Indiana, Pattison led them "in double-quick time through the timber to a small hill." There he discovered the Fifty-ninth Illinois retreating in such confusion and disarray that it momen-tarily ran into the advancing Eighteenth, breaking the Hoosiers' line until Washburn could again close it up. With his primary goal being to outflank the enemy, Pattison halted the brigade, ordering it to wheel to its left, a

Morgan's woods today.

maneuver that put his men in position to pour fire into the Confederate left. They did so at the precise moment when Hébert's forces were gaining on the Peoria Battery at the edge of the woods.[54] Sustaining consistent volleys against the Confederates proved difficult because of poor visibility. Judson Tyler of the Eighteenth wrote his cousin that "it would be allmost impossible for a person in the situation that our Regt. was in to tell much how the battle was going," since "the whole country [was] beclouded with smoke." Yet, Tyler's comrade, Johnson, contended, "We peppered them down as fast as we could see them." The dense smoke, though, did not prevent either of the soldiers from seeing that, as Tyler put it, "The Rebels took one of our batteries & turned it on us."[55]

Davidson's guns were in a vulnerable position when Hébert's forces came upon them. According to McKay of the Thirty-seventh Illinois, the artillery company "had lost so many of their horses that two of their pieces had to be abandoned." Those two guns attracted "the full attention of the rebs," McKay wrote. Soon the Southern captors manned the battery and, remembered Stanley, "a murderous enfilading fire was opened on us, which swept the entire line from left to right." But because of Pattison's left wheel earlier in the action, his brigade, and especially the Eighteenth Indiana, was in position to move against the captured artillery. Around this time, Lieutenant Colonel John A. Hendricks of the Twenty-second Indiana fell from two mortal wounds, leaving his men in confusion. Assuming command of the leaderless regiment, Pattison sent the Eighteenth forward. As First Sergeant Louis Knobe of Franklin recorded in his diary, "our Regt was ordered to left half wheel and retake the 22nd ground and charge the battery and retake it at all hazards which we accomplished finly within 21 minutes time and with but Little Loss on our side." Actually, the capture of the guns was not quite that easy. Washburn, who led the assault, reported that his men had to proceed toward the battery under the "canister and shell" it belched forth and did so "through a dense growth of timber and underbrush." Arriving "in the rear of the enemy," who "turned upon [the Eighteenth] and made a vigorous attack," Washburn ordered his men to fire while lying down.[56]

The struggle for the Peoria Battery basically ended the fighting for Stott and the Eighteenth Indiana that day. Capping off their successful combat was the capture of Hébert and more than thirty of his men by Pattison's brigade as the Confederates "skedaddled." The Third Division and its officers had accomplished much in the "battle of Leetown," and they rightfully earned the praise heaped upon them by Curtis and Davis in their official reports. With the fighting over in their sector, the soldiers of the Eighteenth searched through the woods for the wounded and the dead, then finally bivouacked on the battlefield.[57]

Two miles northeast of Leetown, the bloody contest that swirled around Elkhorn Tavern all that day was only half over, subsiding because of the onset of dusk. When Colonel Carr, riding ahead of his Fourth Division, reached Elkhorn Tavern that morning to check out the reported Confederate presence in Cross Timber Hollow, he recognized two critical facts almost immediately. As he later wrote to his father, "the enemy had on our North about fifteen thousand men," compared to his own two thousand. At the same time, though, the terrain was such that Carr occupied a superb position from which to mount a defense against those odds. Down in the hollow, a densely wooded, rocky, and narrow valley, were Van Dorn's forces under his personal command. Price on the left in Williams Hollow, Colonel Little's Missourians at the center near the Tanyard Ravine, and Colonel William Y. Slack's men of the same state on Little's right—all were primed for battle up the rocky ridge. Carr's big guns opened fire on the hollow in late morning, Captain Henry Guibor's artillery answered, and the soldiers in the ravine nervously prepared to climb the ridge in the crossfire. "Here was a place that tried men's souls," Payne of the "Flying Missouri Brigade" recalled. His unit "double-quicked to the top of the rise and the Federal line was in full view and I could hear something going zip, zip all around and could see the dust flying out of the trees and the limbs and twigs seemed to be in a commotion from the concussion of the guns." The Confederate warriors overtook Elkhorn Tavern near dusk, and what had been the Union headquarters and hospital became the same for the Confederates. The Union line wavered and Van Dorn renewed the attack, sending his opponents down into Ruddick's field south of the inn as night fell.[58] But there would be another day.

Utilizing his interior lines, Curtis spent the late hours of March 7 solidifying his disparate regiments into one ready fighting unit. "My only anxiety for the fate of the next day," he wrote, "was the new front which it was necessary to form by my weary troops." His first step was to direct Davis to abandon his spot near Leetown and move to join Carr's division on the southern edge of Ruddick's field. At midnight the Indiana and

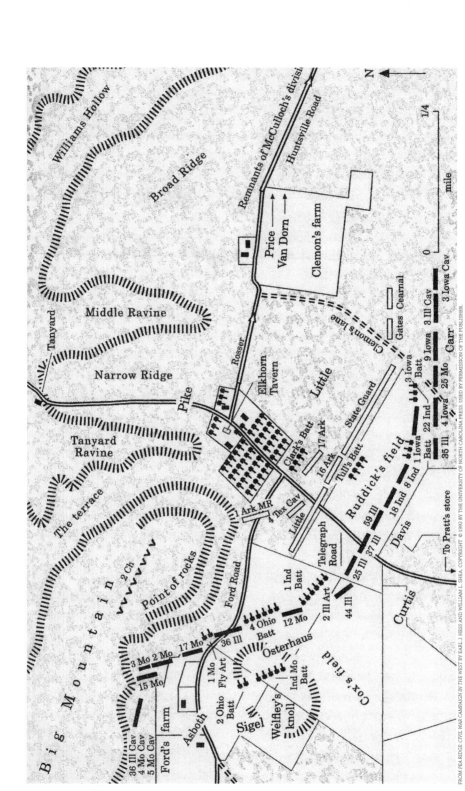

Positions at Elkhorn Tavern, morning of March 8, 1862.

Illinois regiments began the quiet walk that would take them past Pratt's store and up Telegraph Road. The outset of the march was dreary, not just because they were battle weary and the night was cold, but because of what they saw: the dead and dying of both armies on the roads and in the fields. A member of the Fifty-ninth Illinois described the scene. "The road is so bestrewn with rebel dead that a detail of soldiers is necessary to turn them out of our path," George Currie wrote. "Overhead a full moon in a clear sky sheds its beams directly on the upturn[ed] faces of the dead, rendering them still more ghastly and making their gray clothes almost white in the moonlight."[59]

When the Third Division reached Carr's position, Davis placed Pattison's brigade to the right of Telegraph Road, with White's to the left. There it spent a long, cold, fearful night. They "formed a Line of Battle among the heavy timber," Knobe confided to his diary, "and hear we Laid until morning and not being allowed any fire we all most froze." With a bitterly cold north wind sweeping down the ridge, Gordon, Pattison, Washburn, and Major DeWitt C. Thomas shared, with chattering teeth, "a few cold biscuits that had been made with flour and water and nothing else," along with a box of sardines. Then Gordon, Washburn, and Thomas tried to sleep under a single blanket, and, according to Gordon's diary entry, "blessed was the man that got in the middle." But chills and hunger were not all the soldiers felt that night. John D. Crabtree of the Thirteenth Illinois remembered it as one of "deep anxiety," in which "many of us had gloomy forebodings for the coming day."[60]

On March 8, 1862, the sun rose bright and early, and all seemed quiet at first, except for some movement in the Confederate ranks. There were some Confederates walking about in what looked like "white blankets," which were, in fact, the light uniforms of Little's First Missouri Brigade. "Our troops that rested on their arms in the face of the enemy," Curtis noted, "seeing him in motion, could not brook delay, and the center, under Colonel Davis, opened fire." The weakened Peoria Battery threw the first shots around seven o'clock, soon followed by Klauss's First Indiana Light Artillery, and the "white blankets" and other Confederate regalia disappeared for awhile. The Union guns ceased firing and an eerie silence fell upon Ruddick's field. Perhaps the Confederates had taken off, some in the Eighteenth thought. But then the quiet was broken as Confederate batteries unleashed grape and canister in overpowering volleys. Now Knobe knew that "shure enough they ware there" and in such volume "it seemed about 100 pieces." And the Eighth Indiana's Samuel P. Herrington proclaimed, in typical soldiers' lingo, "the ball opened and the dance began."[61]

The first rhythmic steps taken were those of Union soldiers and artillery—backward to avoid the "perfect storm of shell and grape-shot," as Washburn described it. "The fire was so hot," he reported to Pattison, "as to oblige the battery and infantry on our right to retire in some confusion." His Eighteenth Indiana, however, "remained in their position until ordered by you to fall back . . . and we avoided a heavy loss by lying down." For over two hours the firing continued. Soldiers depicted it in many ways: "a wonderful cannonade," during which "the earth trembled and horses shook like aspen leaves"; a time when "all nature seemed convulsed"; "a continual thunder, and a fellow might have believed that the day of judgment had come." From the vantage point of scholarship, historians Shea and Hess call it "the most intense sustained artillery barrage ever to take place on the North American continent up to that time."[62]

Eventually the men of Dixie started to waver. Van Dorn sent his infantry out of the woods below Elkhorn Tavern, but it received raking fire from both Union flanks and fell back behind the tree line. At this point, Curtis took the initiative. Having been among his troops throughout the artillery duel, exposing himself to fire, personally placing batteries, and rallying the soldiers' fighting spirit, he now sensed that the enemy had been "softened up" sufficiently to justify a Union assault. The word went out all along the line. The divisions of Carr and Davis moved forward onto Ruddick's field. With Sigel's help, Davis refused his flanks and aligned them with Sigel's infantry on his left, noting that his "Jeffs"—his old Twenty-second—"had fire in their eyes again." About ten o'clock Curtis gave the "order to charge . . . which was received with cheers, the line advancing steadily with fixed bayonets, increasing to a double-quick." At the head of Davis's division ran the Eighteenth Indiana. Washburn proudly observed "the coolness and courage displayed by the men and officers of my command." To many it was a moment of martial beauty—bayonets sparkling in the sun, banners flying aloft, and Federal voices seeking to exceed the volume of the Rebel yell. Gordon called it "the grandest sight I ever beheld," and the "Yankee Dutchman," Sigel, shouted, "Oh dot was lofely!" The faster the Federals fired and ran, the quicker the Confederates departed. Within an hour, the Third Division reached the woods on Pea Ridge and began driving the enemy another ten miles or so before it turned around and rejoined the rest of its victorious army.[63]

While elation certainly entered the spirit of every exhausted Union soldier, they could not escape the horrors of the battle's aftermath. "Great God, what a scene is presented," Bennett of the Thirty-sixth Illinois penned in his diary. "The mangled trunks of men are thickly scattered around. From each tree or sheltering rock the groans of the wounded arise. Muskets, saddles, horses, blankets, hats and clothes hang on every bush or in gory mass is [sic] strewn upon the ground." Even in the midst of devastation, though, Bennett caught a glimpse of human kindness: "[I]t is good to see the stalwart soldier giving water from his canteen to the wounded and thirsty Southerner, who but now was panting for each other's life. They are enemies no more." The next days were gruesome, as soldiers began the grisly task of burying the dead. March 9 was warmer than usual, and a light rain fell. The sudden heat and the mammoth number of decaying bodies made the job of the burial details, including that of Stott, even more grim and pressing. The dead had to be buried fast. "[J]ust dig a hole and throw them in and cover them up," Herrington described the process. "[A]lways wrap their blankets around them it looks horrid but they don't know anything about it poor fellows." Even after both sides had buried the human remains, dead horses and bloody debris littered the field. Consequently, Curtis ordered a hasty departure to Bentonville.[64]

The next three weeks were quiet for the Army of the Southwest. While the soldiers had a chance to rest and refit, the officers were nonetheless aware that Van Dorn and his army were only as far away as the Boston Mountains. There were no confrontations during these weeks, but Halleck and Curtis thought it best to place some units along the Missouri-Arkansas border as a buffer to Confederate incursion into the Show-Me State. The only real concerns the soldiers had centered on the weather—cloudy, rainy, and muddy in early spring—and a critical lack of supplies. Foraging proved to be difficult in the region, so diaries and letters reflected frustration over provisions. "Commissary drained," Johnson recorded in his diary on March 12, "no prospect of supplies and hunger staring us in the face. Had to live on parched corn or bread made of parched corn meal ground on Coffee mill—with about ¼ rations of beef." The next day's entry read: "Still no bread, no coffee, no salt, little meat." Johnson recorded the arrival of some bacon, coffee, sugar, and flour on March 17, but by the end of the month, supplies were again scanty. "Our provisions have to come 200 miles by wagons so that our supply from Government is <u>slim</u>," Stott informed his friends Mag and Mattie Stout, "but we have learned to steal from the Rebs and by this means 'make up the deficiency.'" On April 4, however, the stagnant and stationary army got some welcome news. Curtis issued Special Order No. 134. "The army in the field," he stated, "will move tomorrow, the 5th instant" toward Cassville, Missouri. Of course, this *was* the army, so it left a day late, April 6, with Stott's Third Division in the rear.[65]

3

Diary: August 1861–April 7, 1862

Friend;

Here are the notes taken during a period of more than three years in the U.S. Army. They were written under a great variety of circumstances. It is singular how many different and even opposite moods one will be in, during no more than a day.

Scholarship is not pretended.

You see here somewhat into the inner life of a soldier during a campaign in Missouri, in Mississippi, in Louisiana, in Texas, and in Virginia, including 15 battles and 10,000 miles marching.[1]

I hope that you will ever appreciate the Government made sacred by the blood of thousands of my comrades.

> Wm. T. Stott, 18th Ind. Vet. Vols.
> Army Diary.
> Transcribed—[2]

August 1861

On Tuesday Aug 13th F. C. Eddelman and I joined Capt. J. H. Williams Company at Indianapolis. We then returned home and remained till Saturday 18th on which day we "started for the wars." On arriving at Indianapolis we found that our Regiment—the 18th Ind Vols—had gone to St. Louis, so we remained until Monday 20th when we started under care of Lt. Davis of Co "D" In the mean time we lodged at Mrs. Cooks'. On Sabbath we attended church at the Masonic Hall—Rev Mr Simmons—In the afternoon I attended 1st Presbyterian Sabbath School and was treated very kindly by the Superintendent. The teacher to whom I listened was quite dogmatical. In the evening we listened to a sermon at the Christian Chapel by a young minister from New York. It was a good sermon and delivered well, and was very patriotic in its nature. The boarders at Mrs. Cooks, in commenting upon it, gave clear evidence that they were not right according to our standard.[3]

On Monday at 11 ½ A.M. we started according to programme, via Lafayette. On the way we had dinner and reached the city about 4 P.M. I soon began hunting the home of Uncle A. J. V. But our company determined to go on so I gave up the search, and we were soon on a train on the Great Western R.R. Our immediate point was Stateline City. On the way Eastman, one of our Brass Band, particularly anxious to make a display—of his talent—did so by acting <u>dog</u>. It seemed quite natural to him, but sensible passengers did not relish it. The ride however was interesting as it was through beautiful prairies. The sight of a large prairie expands the thought and breaks in under the fetters which are wont to hold it. We saw too a Young Niagara with a fall of 30 to 50 feet.[4]

About sundown we reached Stateline City where I met my friend Hardy of Covington. He was just starting to Ohio but found me a place to stay for the night. My friend R. C. Storey was with us. He belongs to Co "I" also.[5] We were taken to the house of an old gentleman—Lowring by name. He was graduated at Brown in 1800. He made the time pass pleasantly by relating incidents and accidents of College life. This was particularly interesting to me as I had just finished a course at Franklin College. He had taught for 30 consecutive winters. When he first came to live in the West, he had to go to Chicago for groceries. Then Indians were far more numerous than white men. Deer were plenty as sheep now.

The old man smiled as he told how he used to wear buckskin pants. Said he if you should let them get wet then pull them off to dry. They will become stiff enough to stand alone. His family implored God's blessings upon us as we started, and I shall long remember them. The only thing to mar my peace while there was a <u>buggy bed</u>, perhaps a little singular from some persons, I would at any time prefer a <u>wagon bed</u>.

We are off at 10 ½ A.M. We found Illinois all alive to the Cause of the Union. The citizens cheered us in every village. Companies were waiting transportation in many places. We passed Springfield the Capital of the State. The scenery is fine. The next important place we reached was Alton on the Mississippi. It was dark before we got there, but by lamplight and pale moon light we could see that it is a romantic place on the side hill. In an hour we reached St. Louis Mo. Took the street car for Camp Jessie. Passing Gen. Fremont's Hd Q we came to Lafayette Park, where the camp is. Got into camp at 10 P.M. We had had no supper and now had to lie down on the ground for a bed. We thought that this perhaps was a good introduction to soldiers life.

————◆————

And here before I get farther in my Diary I shall give the reasons that lead me to join the Army. I cannot better do it than by transcribing to these pages "Soldier's Thoughts,["] written while still at home[:]

Time will bring its changes. The thought that I should ever be a soldier was as foreign to me as that I should be a monarch, till within six months. I had anticipated a long life in teaching and accordingly had gone through a long course of study to prepare myself for the proper discharge of the duties of the Teachers profession. But just as my College course is finished, and my diploma is being tendered me, the cry comes—that Rebels are attempting the destruction of the Union.

After querying whether it is my present duty to serve my country as Teacher or Soldier, at last without a full conviction that I am doing the more advisable thing, I am determined to enlist.

Upon this decision, serious doubts crowd themselves upon me, to some of which I will give utterance. I leave the home of my childhood and youth. Here I first learned to lisp a mothers name, and know a sisters love. Here I lived in careless ease, knowing that a fathers strong hand would provide for all my wants. Here too I have often sinned and been reproved, and hence learned that subjection without which I might today have been a pest to society and a grief to my friends. In the language of another,

> "Here, a child I sinned and strayed
> Here my parents disobeyed
> Here I trust returned to God
> Here found redemption in His blood"

Here often secluded in well known groves I have kneeled and held communion with my Maker. I must too leave true friends, those with whom I have taken sweet counsel. By such a decision, many fond hopes are blasted forever.

But I turn to the Cause which demands such a sacrafice, and the importance of it overrides all obstacles. I go forth to defend the rights and blessings vouchsafed to me by the blood of my ancestors. I cannot deny the same to those who shall come after. Besides there is a just God rules over the destiny of individuals as well as nations. If it be His will I shall be spared in the day of Battle. If not, then existence will not be blotted out forever, but be just begun. With a firm trust in God I go forth to do and if need be die. I think I understand the importance of the issue and will do my best to meet it.[6]

For several days we fared hard on account of the poor management of the Orderly and Cooks, and the hoggishness of the men. They were not more so than others in camp, but I was not used to such way of living. I got sick of soldiering, not on account of physical hardship, but on account of the low grovelling disposition of those with whom I was associated.[7] We remained at Camp Jessie near two weeks during which time I got acquainted with a few with tastes somewhat similar to my own, and this had the effect to make camp life more tolerable. Besides we got a daily paper and sometimes letters.

Letters from home do none more good than soldiers. Things kept the even tenor of their way, mostly while at this camp. We drilled daily, had Dress parade each afternoon and once went out on the prairie for skirmish Drill. Visitors came to Dress parade every day. A large, good-looking gentleman with his three little girls and a small boy came one day, and stood close to me. A drunken soldier began swearing at a great rate. This gentleman stepped up to him and said kindly, Sir I wish you would not swear in the presence of my children. I at once appreciated the great anxiety of the father that his children might not even know of the evil of the world. And I was impressed with the sacredness of the family, and how much that is commendable in the world must emanate from it.

Aug. 28th to Sept. 21st

We were ordered to Jefferson City Mo. We packed up and after a warm and fatiguing march we reached the Depot of the Pacific R. R. We waited two hours and then boarded boxcars. The soldiers were specially gifted with swearing and low talk. After riding all night and half the next day we arrived at our destination, marched up to the court yard rested and took dinner. This is a small City for the Capitol of a State. At 2 P.M. we marched ½ mile south of town and pitched tents, calling the camp Pattison in honor of our Colonel.

On the first night I stood guard, and was quite sleepy, having rode all the night before, but I did not sleep on post. We remained at Camp Pattison more than two weeks, during which time we went through the regular routine of camp duties. There were some incidents and accidents here that deserve mention.

One night about 12 ½ we were aroused with the alarm that the enemy was upon us. This was a fit time for men to show their peculiarities, and they embraced the opportunity. Some were in great fright, and fearing lest they might have forgotten the "Manual of Arms," began going through the whole of it with all the earnestness of a Philosopher. Others were cool. One man, Mr. Comstock, who is certainly a rare specimen of humanity, being denominated by Eddelman and I the "Old Maid," lost his shoes, and while we were all in line awaiting orders to form the regiment he took a candle and went along the whole line hunting his shoes. I could not refrain a smile. He has an impediment in his speech commencing about each sixth word with a "ha." Said he, ["]I "ha," thought someone might "ha" perhaps have taken "ha" my shoes."[8]

Another was of a more serious nature. A young man named Haman Commissary Sergt., stabbed one Davis Sergt. Major. They both came in Capt Holmans company and had quarreled before enlisting. The affair was certainly a disgrace to the Regiment. They were both acquaintances of Col Pattison.[9] He manifested very much regret. We had a great deal of rain at this camp, sometimes so hard as to come right through the tents. The scenery was fine as we were on the banks of the Missouri.

I often went to the river and read and wrote. While here I recd some good letters from Miss Rate and Lizzie.[10]

Eddelman and I sometimes read each others letters—nearly the same as getting a new one. At last one afternoon we were ordered to be ready for marching in ten minutes. In that time we were ready but did not go. But at 11 ½ A.M. of the last named morning we went down to the railroad and boarded the cars not knowing whither we were going. We ran westward passing several small towns many of which seemed almost deserted. We frequently stopped and sent out scouts before we could proceed with safety.

Lt Col Washburn commanded, the Col being absent. Lt Tilson remained at Jefferson City. Half the 22nd Ind Vols was with us on the campaign.[11] After starting out from some station we saw a man approaching on horseback, as if a courier with important dispatches, So mightily did he wave his white hat that the Engineer under orders from the Commander, halted. When the train stopped so that we could hear him, he sang out, "There's a mighty fine train of you, aint there?" We saw then that we were sold and so started on.[12] He was only trying to show his joy at seeing Federals. At Six we reached a small place called Tipton. Here we rested two hours, drew a days rations and started on foot for Booneville, distant 25 miles north. We had marched but a short distance when it began raining and it continued all night. Very hard marching, dark, rainy, muddy, and we carried from 30 to 40 pounds weight each. Many a poor fellow fell over stumps and stones into the mud. Some threw knapsacks away, Some lost one shoe and some got on well. We waded all the streams. At 3 ½ A.M. we halted and went aside into a prairie field to sleep till day. The ground was covered with water, so we made beds of rails, and notwithstanding the rain and hard bed we all slept soundly. The next day the roads were very muddy. The roads were hilly as we neared the river. I slept each time the Regiment halted. The advance guard took a few prisoners and captured some horses and it may be some chickens.

One of Co I went to the house of a secessionist, and told the widow that he belonged to Jeff Davis's Army. (Col Jeff Davis commanded the brigade). So she told him to take a horse, and he did so. At Booneville when the sun was low, we took quarters in the Thespian Hall.

I never was more tired than when we reached Booneville. Eddelman said the same. We did not rest long till we went to the river and washed our feet knowing that this, and the exercise of going and coming would greatly prevent soreness and stiffness. After washing we concluded to take supper at a Hotel, so we did and found great satisfaction in it.

(On the route from Tipton to Booneville the boys showed a great disposition to "Eyeball" peaches. Missouri is celebrated for its fruit.)[13]

On the next afternoon we marched to the fair-grounds and stayed there two days, managing as best we could without tents or cooking utensils. We found there a Regiment from Illinois. On the second afternoon Lt

Johnston, Eddelman, Storey and I got a pass and went to town.[14] We had
not gone far when our ears were saluted with the sound of musketry and
balls came whizzing past us. This was not very agreeable.

Wm Snow had broken guard and the guards were sending balls after
him.[15] He ran directly towards us. He should have been punished for that.
Lt. Johnston delivered him to the guard. We took dinner at the Bakery,
and the Baker would not let us pay for it, so thoroughly Union was he. He
and his wife told us of a lady living near Thespian Hall who was anxious
to give us something. So Storey went over and got six cakes of corn bread.
We shall long remember those ladies and indeed many at Boonville. We
have a negro in the Regiment who shot his master here in a fight not
long since. On the next morning our Regiment was ordered to embark on
the Iätan. When we got on board, we found three other transports there.
The "War Eagle" for the 22[d] Ind and the Des Moines and White Cloud
for the 26th Ind. About 9 AM all four started up the river in the direction
of Lexington Mo. Having gone some 40 or 50 miles all put to shore for
the night and believing that the enemy was not far off, scouts were sent
out from each boat. In the course of two hours there occurred what I am
sorry to record.

Col Wheatly took charge of the scouts of the 26th Ind and Major Tanner
those of the 18th Ind and 22[d] Ind. As it was dark the moon shining faintly,
and as there was not a proper understanding between the two parties of
scouts they soon began firing on each other, thinking it to be the enemy. After a few shots exchanged the mistake was apprehended. Soon I
saw two of our men carried in corpses. I do not know the loss from each
Regiment Report said 15 to 20 altogether. There was a feeling of intense
mortification amongst us all when the fact of the mistake was known
We lay down on our arms, ready for any emergency. In an hour I was
awakened by a volley of musketry. Volley after volley was fired and at
length men were seen running to the boats with all speed, abandoning
guns hats & so on. I was sure Prices men were near.

But alas, notwithstanding the mistake of an hour before, <u>again</u> our men
were firing at each other.

The 26th had got on one side and the 22d the other and were concentrating their fire on the 18th which fell flat on the face, so that but one was
killed. Where the blame of this unsurpassed carelessness will finally and
truly attach I cannot tell. It is said without being confuted that the 22d

and 26th had whiskey on board. We had not.

One or two of Co "I" when the firing was heaviest had to examine the rope coil very carefully and to do so got behind it.

On looking over the Battleground on the next day we found guns bayonets hats etc etc. The <u>Battleground!</u> Posterity—if it wishes to erect a monument here—will find [it] on the left bank of the Missouri 4 miles below Glasgow.

We expected to find a blockade at Glasgow but there was none.

The 22d contrary to orders went back to Boonville. The 18th went 8 miles above Glasgow and brought away the <u>Sunshine</u>.[16] The 26th went still farther up, but meeting with difficulty it came back. We all got back in that day, and went to a grove half mile south of town for a camp. Having purchased a small diary, I shall keep it regularly.

Sep 22d

Pleasant day. Camp life is far superior to traveling on transports as civil life is to camp life. One has so much more room. I shall soon go to Sabbath school.

23d

Last evening Col Pattison came back. The mail brought me a letter from Wallace.[17] This morning we were awakened by the report of gun. One of Co D shot his hand accidentally. Ever since I have been in camp we have had to use River water and it is very muddy. Now we have that which is clear and pure. One peculiarity of this State is the lack of birds in the forest. The news has come that Col Mulligan had to make a complete surrender at Lexington.

24th

We rec'd orders last night to <u>strike</u> tents at 4 this morning. It has proved to be all a hoax. Fifteen men were sent out last night from each company to press teams and wagons——Those of us who have Mr. Goodman for cook have a <u>good man</u> sure enough. The other messes are very quarrelsome and gluttonous. Yesterday I sent a letter home and one to Miss M. Stout. I cannot sleep much on account of a pain in my breast. "Poor old man."

25th

Believe I am fast becoming misanthropic. There are some men here whom I loathe; they are so devoid of all that is manly or cultivated.

Yesterday Storey started back to Jeff City. His arm is nearly useless. Awakened again this morning by the report of a gun. Voorhees had shot his foot.[18] The enemy it seems is not so much to be feared as <u>carelessness</u>.

26th

At 11 A.M. we start on a march to Georgetown distant 35 miles. The roads were good and the weather was cool so it was pleasant marching. After going 11 miles we camped in a field using rails for fires. Eddelman was on guard this night away down in the brush.

A <u>secesh</u> reported to be a captain was taken here.

27th

Quite early we start this morning. The advance guard took several prisoners belonging to the family of fowls. We encamped at 4 P.M. in a grove by the roadside. No sooner were arms stacked than some treed a squirrel. From the hallooing and jumping and clubbing it was plain to see that the Ho[o]sier Boys were little daunted by a days march. Some of the 18th got drunk having found some whiskey on the road, notwithstanding the extreme care of the Col that his men should act in no way inconsistent with real manhood. I had the pleasure of seeing Henry McCanlon and Richard Stott of the 26th Ind. They were encamped near us. Henry spoke of the great profanity in his Regiment.[19]

28th

Company "I" is detailed as train guard. Sometimes we keep up, sometimes not. At 2 P.M. we reached Georgetown. It is a dreary looking place. The citizens are generally gone. All realize that an army is a dreadful thing, and flee from it. Camped two miles north in ploughed ground. As our wagon tongue broke, our tents did not come up till 9 P.M.

29th

Cool day. This morning we washed our shirts and socks thinking tidiness necessary to holiness. A letter from Uncle P.C.V. and The Examiner from Wallace. Interesting matter in both.[20]

30th

I am for guard. Drilling is begun again. This is Camp Thomas. So far as I can learn there are six Indiana regiments here ready to march on Lexington, 8th, 18th, 22d, 23d, 24th and 26th. Lexington is now in the hands of the Rebels. Gen Fremont intends sending force enough to take it.

Oct 1st

Chills are creeping into camp. We should never have camped on this plowed field. The mud is worse than it ever was in the oak flats of Indiana.[21] Persimmons are plenty here, and an abundance of peaches and apples. We have no grove however, which is a great necessity to an agreeable camp.

2d

Several bits of news are a place around the campfires today. In an engagement near Washington the Rebel loss was 40,000, federal loss 18,000. The Federals gained a victory at Paducah Ky with the loss of Col. Wallace. And still another that Gen Pope had destroyed 1,000 rebels while they were attempting to cross the Missouri. To all of these possibility, only, attaches.[22] Drill ground is a mile from camp. I wish I could carry some books. I fear that my intellect will have become shrivelled and inactive. I can do nothing more here in camp than to jump at general conclusions and even to do this takes an effort. I find that Eddelman likes company better than I do. I seek solitude. But such is the difference in our dispositions.

3d

Had a long talk last night with some man in Capt. Jenks company.[23] The general theme was the army. It is said that there are 20,000 troops here about Georgetown. The news of a fight near Washington is confirmed. I learn from the guards that a man by the name of H. R. Stott passed them yesterday. He doubtless belongs to the illustrious family of Stotts to which I belong!!

4th

I am on duty today on the most beautiful part of the "Rounds." Away off in the distance stretches the landscape. The clouds are rich and beautiful. One even in camp may feel poetic. In the evening however I willingly let my mind down to the world of <u>realities</u>. The cold rain poured in torrents, and Aeolus did his best with the winds, and I out all night without shelter or sleep.[24] We have been hunting the Rebels in Missouri for six weeks but alas they are not to be found. "Like the wicked (whom they are) they flew when no man pursueth."[25]

Through sheer carelessness Daniel Kelly shot his hand, so that he is unfit for service.[26]

5th

Passed the day in sleeping and reading Youngs Night Thoughts. Rec'd a good letter from Miss L.M.[27]

6th

I find in Young rich solid thought especially in his estimate of the immortal man, in contrast with the mortal. He says, Many give to Time, Eternity's regard. I have a much nearer approach to the Throne than in civil life. How real and necessary Christianity appears to me now.

7th

Our chaplain had neither sermon nor Sabbath school yesterday. He has done nothing for several weeks. Co "I" goes on <u>Picket</u>. Henry Storey came over last evening. Answered the letter rec'd a day or two ago. Beachly is not liked for Captain.[28]

8th

My post on Picket was on the roadside in the prairie. In the afternoon Eddelman and I went on a scouting tour. We found some grapes and then went to a <u>secesh</u> house and got some apples. We afterwards learned that a wounded Rebel was in the house. I stopped at another house and got some red-pepper. In the morning we went to another <u>Secesh</u> house and got breakfast. The lady said she sposed she could get us something to eat. She hoped that Price would take us prisoners. She respected us but thought that we were in a bad cause. We remarked that we could not be in a better one. She treated us kindly. Her daughter thrummed the piano for us.

Rec'd a letter from my friend Thorp. Sunrise on the prairie is fine. Today rec'd payment in specie from Hon Will Cumback, P.M.[29]

9th

Went to Georgetown to be reviewed by Gen Pope. To one unused to so many men in uniform it would be an imposing sight. I got mad, the company showed so little training and the Captain shows as little himself. He curses if the men go wrong and don't know how to tell them to go right. I could train a company far better. On returning for a second review we did some better. The whole affair seems to me a dream. There are the long dark lines of men. The Aids galloping over the field and the bands playing. Met Robertson of the 26th Ind. He was a College friend.[30]

10th

Read several chapters in Night Thoughts.

11th

Weather is quite changeable in Mo. A detachment went off this morning to take charge of a mill. Capt. Williams went in charge. The report is that we shall soon leave this camp.

12th

Eddelman is sick, and so also some others. There is general depression of spirits, all owing I say to our camping on <u>plowed ground</u>. Had some fun last night with Perkins.[31]
Johnston & Eddelman were talking pretty freely of his <u>laziness</u> not knowing that he was near. After some time he raised himself up slowly and remarked in slow time that "It wasn't altogether <u>laziness</u>," and then lay down again, as before.

13th

Good Sermon. Text—God is our Judge and King and he will save us. 1st A history of the events which led to the utterance of this language. The two principle individuals were Hezekiah and Senacherib. Byrons effusion on the event was aptly quoted. 2nd An application made to our Army. God is in all history. He has been Governor amongst the nations and he will be. 3d. The sinfulness of the vices of camp was shown in a strong light. I frequently recall my Baccalaureate Sermon preached by Dr. Bailey. "Man Shall not live by bread alone." Man's nature requires more much more. Christianity meets most of his wants.[32]
Wallace sent me a Journal.
I find in me a great desire to be spared the ravages of War, that I may yet attain far higher ground in intellect and piety.

14th

Up at 4 A.M. to get ready for a march. All is <u>hum</u> and <u>buzz</u>. I shall have to wait till we get there to tell where we are going.

15th

Our route was eastward parallel with the Pacific R.R. Marched 15 miles and camped in a large prairie. Sunset was grand. It seems as if there is so much room for everything out here on a prairie. Scenery is grand. Many men gave out on the march. Col Davis is in command. The day is consumed in arranging camp. Five Indiana regiments are here and not six.

16th

Rained last night incessantly. The whole camp takes the appearance of a dirt road on the breaking up of winter. I had to take care of Abbott and West, sick. A general complaint against officers prevails. It is said Col Davis refused to let men have straw to lie on. Lt Popp and Capt Davidson were arrested today for aiding some negroes to run away from their masters. I cannot say but that they were right. I am often led to think of the dependency and even <u>slavery</u> of the soldier, And yet concentration of power is necessary to an efficient army. But it ill suits us just [?] Americans.[33]

I certainly would pass time slowly were it not for the Examiner and Journal sent by Wallace and my Diary, which is as necessary to my calculations of time as was Alexander Selkirk's <u>notched stick</u>. To it too I tell all my confidential thoughts.[34]

17th

Out in the rain today attending to the sick and parching the coffee for the cook. Perkins came and crawled into our tent although we had told him that we did not want him. I think he is too lazy to live long. And if he's a Christian, it will be better for him to go right up to Heaven where he will have to keep tidy.

The St. Louis Republican intimates that we are to go to Warsaw, Mo.

18th

Gave all my blankets to the sick last night, depending on a clear conscience and some hay to keep me warm. The <u>spirit</u> of the Brigade is increasing as the weather gets cooler. I am thankful that I am not on the sick list. The sick cannot be properly cared for here.

19th

The Examiner came again today. It says editorially that we must have a conquered peace or none. So say I. Col Davis was over today to see our Col. He looked pleased with the appearance of things. This morning the 8th, 18th and 22d Ind start for Warsaw on the Osage.

20th

I enjoy the Sabbath although on the march. I think of the many thousands in my own State, met and worshiping.

21st

Camp on a prairie wind cold.

22d

All lively and full of fun this day. Part of the time we go on "double-quick." I came near chilling and could scarcely keep up. In the evening had fever.

23d

Chill got after me again today.

24th

I am quite convalescent. Shall be well soon. Tomorrow we are to move across the Osage, on Gen. Fremonts celebrated bridge.[35] There are a great many troops in the vicinity. Some say 80,000. Price it is said is not far off. We are to have overcoats on next Saturday. The Jennings County folks are making up Socks, mits, blankets, &c for the troops which have gone from that county.

25th

Got up at 4. Warsaw the county seat of Benton looks desolate indeed. Roads dusty. See better timber than usual. Camp near Quincy. The mail brought me three letters.

26th

Remain in camp. All this time in the army seems as if it were a dream, I cannot realize that our country is at war.

27th

Moved camp a short distance; for what I certainly cannot tell. All these days we footmen think that if we could only ride we should have no want unsatisfied. Rec'd a letter from home.

28th

I've nothing to say, further than that the sun rose as usual, in fact Natures laws all seem to be in force.

29th

March again today over prairie and then over branches of the Ozark mountains. Camp by a well, somewhat after the custom of the Israelites when marching through the wilderness. A few of us sat up late at night telling jokes. Whether this was practiced by the Israelites I do not think Revelation is very plain on.

30th

Resumed the march. In the afternoon, come upon a small town called Humanville with several human beings in it. Six union flags in triumph did wave. We took possession of two Stores. Went south of town and camped on a low field used but a short time before by Lane with 25,000 Cavalry.[36] Here is the largest and clearest spring that I ever saw or partook of to quench my exceedingly great thirst. I cannot forget this fine spring. It is so much like an oasis in a desert land.

Gen Davis (Gen now) is sick so Col Pattison takes command. Pope's Division now marches together. 1st Brigade, 8th, 18th and 22d Ind. 2nd Brigade, 5th Iowa, 9th Mo and 24th Ind. Gen Sturgis was at this place a few days ago. Gen's Fremont and Sigel have gone to Springfield.[37]

31st

Get another drink from the big spring.

Nov. 1st

Met H. C. Coffey, a former student of F.C. I think we used to call him winders on account of his long legs.

We shall start for Springfield today. I shall be on rear guard. The Brigade moves out at six P.M. We of the guard at 10 ½ P.M. The night was very dark and the road full of boulders. Many the stumble, and many the fall. The officers of the guard basely left us when we got near the camp. I shall never forget them. We had to stand in the road for an hour. We finally built fires and had got somewhat warm when those officers came up and told us that we should have march[ed] on. We slept two hours and [abrupt ending]

2d

Caught up with the Brigade at 3 p.m. on a nice large prairie. Here we were relieved and told that we should have to start on for Springfield in two hours, as the enemy was approaching us. How tired I was! But I would go on with the rest. The teams were left back. We started half an hour before sunset. It was a grand sight to see 6,000 men moving out this time of day on a clean nice prairie, on a winding road, banners flying and bands playing. But we soon came to rough roads and darkness and blinding dust, then the <u>poetry </u>was all gone again. I <u>gave out,</u> told Eddelman I thought I could go no farther. But fortunately we camped there.

3d

Start on again at 7 A.M. March till 1 P.M., when we come out onto a clear nice stream here we halt and rest and some of us bathe. I did and felt much better. In an hour we pursued the march, and at 4 P.M. camped on the left bank of Wilsons Creek, the same stream on which the gallant Lyon fell.[38] I remember climbing a tree here for grapes. At dusk orders came to strike tents and be ready to move on to Springfield, distant six miles. The report was that the enemy would fight us there. Now as there was to be battle I watched countenances. I must give to Christianity her dues. Those who were moral—religious—were cool. Those who had been very immoral either engaged in horse laugh to try to conceal their concern, or else showed some evident signs of quaking.
One of Co "D" noted for profanity as we were starting stepped up to his Lt. and asked half-crying, if he might go back to the doctor and get some medicine. At 8 P.M. we halted in an oak-grove one mile north of town. Here was Fremont's army, such a conglomeration of noises it seemed to me I had never heard. Teamsters hallooing mules bellowing wagons rumbling axes chopping officers commanding and so on.
We slept till day.

4th

The report is that Price has fled to Kentucky, leaving but six thousand at the old Battleground at Wilsons Creek, and that we shall follow them. It is also ascertained that Gen Fremont is superceded by Gen Hunter. At 10 A.M. he passed here accompanied by his Body-Guard and Band on his way to St. Louis. There are many gloomy faces on learning of his removal. We all liked him. But we must be subject to the powers that be.

5th

Wrote a letter home. In the afternoon our tents came. So we probably shall stay here several days.

6th

Recd a letter from Miss L.M.

I am sick again. chills and fever.

We are officially informed of Gen Fremont's supercedure.

7th

Glad that dreams are not realities. So are we all.

8th

It is said that the <u>secesh</u> have captured our provision train between here and Otterville. The cavalry passed back at 2 A.M.

9th

The rumor still prevails that Price has fled. Pope's Division starts back for Otterville tomorrow. It will be a long tedious tiresome dusty march. We all wish we could go back by some new route. Such is the general desire for novelty in man.

I shall consolidate my diary for the march back again. We usually rested two or three times during a day, one of these for eating dinner. We usually arose at 3 in the morning. After halting in the afternoon we got wood by the time the teams came up. Some days we marched 20 miles. We shall never forget how Col Pattisons full voice would ring out "Attention Battalion." Passed the same towns as in coming down the more important of which are Warsaw Bolivar and Coal Camp. When about half way back we met our overcoats and drew them. Each days duties was like the others. When we halted I was always tired and could not sleep well at nights for coughing. Eddelman stood the march far better than I did.

After 8 days continuous march we reached our old camp at Otterville on Sat. afternoon.

What was accomplished by our campaign down to Springfield I am sure I do not see, except the initiation of the troops to campaigning.

17th

Davis Brigade starts for Syracuse. We pass through Otterville where we are joined by some who have been left there. Camped a mile from

Syracuse. We know little of Sabbaths having been marching on five successive ones.

18th

Weather getting cold. I hope we shall soon get to winter quarters where I shall have time to answer my correspondents.

19th

We expect to start for St. Louis on the train tomorrow. Several changes in officers have been made of late. The war seems to be progressing slowly.

20th

Company drill. Recd a letter from home and one from Uncle P.C. Vawter.

21st

No news nor even rumors.

22nd

Read a Republican of the 19th Inst.

23rd

Lt Johnston has the chills. He will go home soon, unless he recovers which is not probable.

24th

Sermon. Christ came to save that which was lost.[39] Got a letter from Rate. I learn that one of my uncles is in sympathy with the Rebellion.

25th

Wash day in camp.

26th

Drew our new uniform. It is blue. Our first was grey. I like the blue much better. And in fact we feel more like gentlemen and say nicer things and think neater thoughts with our new clothes on.

27th

Answered Miss LM"s letter. Lt. Nebeker of Co. "C" died yesterday. He was liked very much.[40]

28th

Here we go again. We are to go back to the Lamine River. I met Hickman King here. He has grown very much since he was in my school.[41]

29th

The day was spent by us mostly in conjecturing where we were likely to go next. We got a daily. The train at night brought up six of our Hospital boys. There is a kind of stone here which when crumbled looks just like sugar. Several boys put it in their coffee.

30th

Chaplain distributed some <u>Tract Journals</u>. Old Dr. White of Wabash is dead. Died of an apoplectic fit.

Dec.1st

Sabbath has come and of course we must go <u>somewhere</u>. March back to Syracuse. Eddelman built a furnace here for our tent. It drew well, but the wrong way.

2d

On waking up we found four inches of snow covering the ground. Winter sure enough. Whether history will laud us as heroes for all this privation and exposure I do not know.

3d

Battalion drill. We are to receive pay in a few days. A letter from Mack and Mat.[42]

4th

Wrote a letter to Rate.

5th

Wrote a letter to Mr. Hart a member of the Phi Delta Theta society.

6th

Recd pay. Col Washburn came back.

7th

The water in our tent got to be four inches deep. We ditched. At 8 A.M <u>go back to the Lamine</u>. To build quarters.[43] At night slept on a big log.

8th

Sermon by the chaplain of the 25th Ind. Vols.

9th

Very agreeable day and we are going to work at the cabins.

The Republican gave me a clearer idea of the difficulty between the President and Sec Cameron on the slave question, than I had before. It is emancipating and arming the slaves or <u>not</u>.[44]

14th

Just as we had cleared off our new campground we were ordered to get ready to march immediately. At night went two miles beyond Smithland and camped.

15th

Marched 18 miles. Eddelman had a chill.

16th

On the road at 4 A.M. March briskly till noon when Col Davis informed us that we should soon have the privilege of meeting the enemy, and that to reach a certain crossroad that he must tax our endurance. We made the point, it being 36 miles from the place of starting that morning. The best marching on record!! Such work as this tries what stuff a man's made of.

17th

Alas, the enemy was gone. We proceed on in the direction of Warrensburg. I suffer egregiously from new small shoes, being obliged to go part of the time barefoot.

18th

Get today to within 2 ½ miles of Warrensburg and halt. The cavalry has brought in 100 prisoners.

19th

Pass on through Warrensburg and direct our course towards Sedalia. Yesterday I met Vandevender, Capt in 8th Ind.[45] Today I feel gloomy as I feel sure the Rebels have sneaked off to their homes to congregate again as soon as we have passed. Our boys got one good dinner prepared for the Rebs, at any rate. But the artillery is rushing past, and the German Artillerists shouting, "Now we ketch 'em." The cavalry has all gone before. There must be something ahead. When the infantry had halted for the night, the cheering news came back that the cavalry had surprised a Rebel camp and taken 1,300 prisoners. Good enough!

Col Davis led the charge in person when they surrendered, arms and all. There were two Colonels, Alexander and McGoffin.[46]

20th

Camped where a secesh was killing hogs so we had fresh Pork.

21st

Camped near Sedalia having passed through Georgetown, where we saw many long faces, as the prisoners passed through. The prisoners are a motley lot. Some have white blankets some red some quilts, and nothing some. Co "I" has to help guard them tonight. Very cold and snowy. The prisoners will get their southern proclivities frozen out tonight, I should think.

22d

Take the prisoners to Sedalia to put them on the cars, for St. Louis. They gave our boys tobacco and seemed well disposed toward us.

23d

The 18th Struck tents and after a hard days march over icy roads, reached the spot of ground cleared off for Winter quarters, on the Lamine. When we got to Otterville the artillery attempted to pass us. Col Pattison ordered Co "A" to file left and fix bayonets. Then said he to the artillerists, "If you know what's best for you, you will fall in the rear.["] They obeyed. At dark we got to the place mentioned above.

Oh how gloomy and cheerless the prospect. Weather very cold. Snow covering everything, no fire, nothing but green wood near, our tents nor cooking utensils likely to get up till midnight, and we all tired and stiff from marching. However we shovelled away the snow and built fires as best we could. Finally our tents came. And we got to bed as best we could. Even the stoutest men could not endure such exposure as this, oft repeated.

24th

Somewhat more agreeable this day.

25th

Christmas. The day is not forgotten although we are far away from home, and those with whom we are accustomed to associate on such occasions.

Our mess has a Christmas dinner—chicken, cornbread, surup and coffee, and withal we are quite jovial. Wrote a letter home. Have been looking for one from Miss L.M.

Am sorry to say that quite a number of our company are drunk.

26th

Busy in fixing campground. Henry McCanlon visited us here.

27th

We are to have Sibley Tents.[47] Eddelman is sick.

28th

Three of us were negotiating with Eastman, Leader of the Band.

29th

Get the Examiner again. On guard.

30th

Have some reason to believe that Mason and Slidell are to be given up to England. Hope not.[48]

31st

Gen Scott thinks they can be given up without sacrificing the dignity of the government. I shall watch the correspondence of Seward and Lyons. Col Pattison has charge of the Brigade. This is the last day of the old year. It has been frought with changes O how great!

1862, Jan 1st

The New Year has come. Who can tell what will be consummated in this year? I am thankful to God that my life and health have been preserved, while the shafts of disease and death have been thick on every hand. And I ask him for the restoration of my comrade who is very sick of fever.[49] Had inspection of Camp today by Inspector General Van Rensalaer. Can this year witness the conquering of the Rebels and the restoration of Peace?

2d

Eddelman is recovering slowly. I feared at one time that he would have to die.

3d

Rec'd a good letter from Rate and a package of Papers. She is in full sympathy with the soldiers and she has a kind heart.

This morning I moved Eddelman to Capt. Williams Tent, he having gone home for a time. Sims and Hoeffer are in it too whom I shall attend to I suppose.

Mr. High came back today. I have not the fullest confidence in his patriotism.[50] I have made a <u>writing desk</u> and it makes me really think of civilization.

4th

The sick are convalescent. I have found that two of them have "bodyguards" so I shall move Eddelman back to our own tent.[51]

5th

We heat our tents by kettles of coals.

6th

Busy as company Clerk, on Descriptive Lists, Special Requisitions &c.

Our donation goods came and were distributed today. I must say that the goods did honor to the good ladies of Johnson Co. The blanket we got was donated by Mrs. Joel Williams.[52]

7th

I shall fill out some blank discharges today. Some of the company are to be discharged. We are getting used to the cold weather. I have no letter from Miss L.M. yet. Strange!

8th to 19th

During this period nothing special has transpired in camp or in the country.

Dick Pattison died last Sabbath from the effects of drunkenness. His father—the Col—is very sad.

He can but grieve that his son should have died under such circumstances. He is himself strictly temperate.[53]

Capt Williams has returned.

There are some changes in the Cabinet Sec. Cameron is to be minister to Russia While Edwin M. Stanton is to be Sec. of War.

The Burnside expedition has started.[54]

20th

I take delight in singing the songs we used to sing at College. Such as Ariel, Pray for the Peace &c, Blessed is the People, Boylston &c, &c. Our class can sing them quite well.

21st

On provost Guard at Otterville. One thing especially annoys me. I frequently meet with a soldier whom I take to be intelligent and of good taste.
I get him into conversation and find to my sorrow that there is nothing to him.

22nd

Rumors of marching again. Destination not stated. On sabbath last sent a letter to Miss L.M. Its characteristic was candor.
There has been a fight near Somerset Ky in which Gen Zollicoffer and 275 Rebels were killed. The federals gained a decided victory. The 10th Ind Vols lost 75.[55]

23d

Today put up and moved into our new wall tent. Eddelman will go to Otterville when we start on our campaign.
Recd another package of papers from Rate. She refers me to an article on School Government, written by Mr. Venable of Vernon. Fannie is reading Maria Antionette, Queen of France.

24th

March to near syracuse. Camp in the snow. We are somewhat better provided as to tents than on the two preceding campaigns. We gathered cornstalks for beds.

25th

As we still go on towards Tipton we hope we shall go on to St. Louis. On we went till we got into the suburbs of the town, all the time leaning toward the left hand road as grandfathers horse used to always bear off towards a meeting house. (Grandfather is a minister). But sure enough the head of the column turned to the south. Then "Springfield" was heard all through the troops. Camped six miles south of Tipton.

26th

Receive two months pay. Then go on passing through Versailles, the seat of Morgan. Camped on a bleak knoll. Capt Woods got mad at somebody and spoke very firm and decided. If <u>ex uno, disce omnes</u> I think he would be an efficient captain.[56]

27th

Very bad roads some of the transportation did not get up at all. I understand this is Jeff C. Davis' own expedition. –independent.
We shall have to remain here several days. Baggage has to be lightened up.[57]

28th

Lt G. W. Kimble is Quartermaster.[58]

29th

Recd a letter from McTilson and one from Miss L. M. The latter is going to Oxford. She is in the Senior Class.

30th

March on only half mile. The wagons and artillery have to be drawn up the hill by hand it is so steep and icy. It was a big job to draw all the train up. We only advanced 1 ½ miles this day with it, when darkness compelled us to stop.
The infantry went on and had to camp without tents or blankets.

31st

I went back to get up a wagon which had been upset with Lt. Popp and Eastman in it. They had set a barrel of Cartridges on fire and had been severely burnt and so had to be drawn. While under the influence of whiskey they had put fire to the barrel.[59] Caught up with the Regiment at Gravois River. Recd a letter from Rate.

Feb. 1st

Rested, after a march of only six miles.

2d

Reached the Osage River at Lynn Creek. For two days we have been coming through romantic country Mountains and Valleys. It is Government land at 50 cts per acre. There are copper and coal mines in these hills.

3d

Col Davis ordered some captured whiskey to be distributed to the troops. How I regret such a thing. Yet I cannot help it. But a man need not drink it. Recd a letter—a good letter from home. Storey and Bogart got some bread and a guinea.[60] We let the citizens know we are around. We are camped in a grove. My tent has a stove. Indeed we are quite comfortable.

4th

Soon after we had gone to bed the order came to be ready to cross the river. We went to the ferry and after waiting till 1 o'clock A.M. got over on the little boat Silver Lake.

5th

We had just got over and our tents pitched and to sleep when the order came again, <u>strike tents</u> and load up. I was vexed, sore vexed. We went but a few rods to get better ground. The news came here that an Iowa and a Nebraska regiment had been drawn into an ambuscade between Rolla and Lebanon, and had been routed. Lynn Creek is a clear small stream reminding me of some in my native State.

6th to 21st

The next place of note that we reached was Lebanon distant from the Osage where we crossed sixty miles. We camped three miles north of the village and remained till Monday. Here Evan Jones of our company died. Capt. Williams treated him shamefully. Here Eastman came with the horns. Since which time we have had brass music the soldiers cheer and delight.

Here I recd a letter from Uncle PCV and three for Eddelman.

The next point was Springfield where we were to meet Old Man Price. By this time our army consisted of Davis's, Asbottes [Asboth's] and Sigels divisions. Sixty pieces field artillery and six regiments Cavalry.

We approached to within four miles and camped for the night.

Co "I" was called out on picket guard. I was on camp guard, and met a student of Franklin—Mason. With a full expectation of a battle the ensuing day, my thoughts while I walked to and fro on my post were turned to it. I could repose all my whole destiny on Him in whom I had believed with a confidence which I had never felt. And I was <u>ready</u> for what was to come. The next morning we started early and proceeded to within sight of what was supposed to be one of the enemy's forts. Our Brigade was drawn up in front of this fort. The skirmishers under command of the Adjutant started in advance. The Cavalry with drawn sabers dashed by on a reconnaissance. The artillery in our rear and above us, our pieces loaded and capped, and all looked like a fight sure enough (only we could not see the enemy) Col Benton commanded "left half wheel" and just then Gen Davis (he is General now) came galloping up with the announcement that Springfield was taken! Then went up a mighty cheer from the whole line of troops. There was then a mighty relaxing of nerves (if this be not a paradox). We advanced quietly into Springfield and learned that Price with his whole force had fled but the night before. His campfires were still burning and his forage still lay on the ground. That night we covered his camp. He left his sick in our hands, at the C.H. [Court House] The graveyard had scores of fresh graves. Along the streets lay broken gunstocks and barrels and occasionally a broken wagon. J.R. Johnston and I had a romantic time wandering through the rebel camps. I found a pair of boots and appropriated them. They look just like secesh boots.[61] For several days we pursued Price closely keeping but one day behind his train. We had four Pieces [?] of "flying artillery" which with the Cavalry went forward in the morning but could not stop the Rebel army till we could come up. We were so close at one time that we had to double quick two miles through mud and creeks, it having been thought that he had halted. But he had not. We passed the gorge where it was supposed that he would give us battle. At last one afternoon the firing of cannon announced to us that there was fighting we did not catch up. It was the Battle of Sugar Creek in which we lost of the enemy 30. Gen Davis was in the fight.

Dead men and horses could be seen for quite a distance round, a sight not to be sought.

Some prisoners were taken who remarked that they could not stop to cook but that we were giving them shells. Here we quit close pursuit and awaited our provision train. We for several days had to press in what we got to eat. In fact for five days we had to live on parched corn.

22d to March 1st

After two days we proceeded passing Cassville and Keatsville, and not long after passed the Arkansas line. Just as we crossed the line the band gave us "Dixie" and the troops gave several lusty huzzas.

We were further south than any other troops in the Southwest.
We all felt glad that we were at least out of Missouri where we had been seven long months. We marched 30 miles into the State and camped on a prairie, Camp Halleck. The water is such that horses at home would not drink it. Storey left us at Springfield. It is rumored that he is captured. I was sick here three days but am now well. Recd a letter from Eddelman. He tells me that High, Hunt, Robbins, Mappin and Hendricks are discharged.[62]

It is now Spring here. Various rumors are afloat as to where we are to go. The latest is that Tennessee is about to declare in favor of the Union; as a consequence, Arkansas will if we will cease to invade, so that we may recross the line. Cap Williams says if reports be true we shall be home in sixty days. I have no hope of it. I call to remembrance the theme of my last oration, "Development is Gradual."

March 1st

I am very much settled in the belief that the people of the South are deceived by their leaders. I am told by prisoners that Price made the citizens believe that the Federals in their course would steal all their property burn their houses and ravish their women. Consequently we found almost every house between here and Springfield deserted. One prisoner stated that he enlisted to catch horse thieves who were infesting his vicinnage and was told afterwards that he was a "regular" soldier.

This is a beautiful day. My thoughts often wander back to home. I have also had great delight in reading the Psalms.

We at last march back to Sugar Creek to the Parched Corn camp. We are told that Lane and Hunter are coming up, when we shall pursue Price. Six miles beyond Camp Halleck there were Secesh Barracks where the Arkansas gentry soldiered. A spring furnished water there for two good flowing wells. There were rooms enough for three thousand men. They were made of pine lumber.

The State had built the Barracks at an outlay of $200,000.00/100.

2nd

This morning we haven't so much spring. It is earnest winter. I have read somewhat in Buck's Exposition of Prophesy.[63]

3d

To our right is a high hill, a nice place for meditating. There are some chestnut oaks, the first I have seen. At the foot of the hill is the largest Dogwood I have seen. It measures 33 inches in diameter. I have passed most of the day in reading. At night a large train came in from Springfield, with it our Sutler, the mail and Storey. I got a letter from home and one from College.[64]

4th

Snowing again. I shall have agreeable days reading. At present we have plenty of books, captured books. I am reading Wm Buck's Philosophy of Religion.[65]

5th

Buck insists that all prophesy is to be interpreted literally. He finds three distinct terms spoke of in Mat. 28th. The destruction of Jerusalem, the prevalence of the Gospel and the Second Coming of Christ.

6th

At 12 last night orders came to draw and cook two days rations. About the same time I heard the light Artillery passing back toward Springfield. This morning I understand that Price is advancing, and that we may expect an attack here in the course of 24 hours. How much truth there is about it I cannot tell. At 8 A.M. we struck tents, ready to march and went two miles north to another camp. Our teams came up. In a few moments we were ordered to take our axes and picks and proceed to the hill spoken of a few days ago. We proceeded to build Rifle pits, the first for us. We slept on our arms here with the expectation that we should be attacked by daylight. I was Vidette Guard. In the afternoon we heard cannonading toward Bentonville. We ascertained that it was Sigel who was skirmishing with the rebels advancing on our left.

7th

We hear brisk cannonading in the same direction as yesterday. We finished the pits, then proceeded to the wagons, but no sooner had we stacked arms than we were double quicked back to the place of starting. We formed in it and awaited attack. Finding that the Rebels were coming up in another direction we marched two miles north where our troops were opposing McCullough.

In passing Leetown most of the boys unslung knapsacks. I did not We passed on beyond the town and filing left followed a road leading West, and parrallel with our Battery. In our front, when we had fronted was a large level field on the opposite side of which was the Rebel line. We passed three men killed by one ball.[66] Finding we were not needed here, Gen Davis sent us to the right half mile. We made a left half wheel and then forwarded in line to flank if possible the enemy who had taken our Battery. An Illinois regiment (59th) fell back through our line in confusion. We had to advance through thick brushwood.

When the enemy saw us they fled in haste, seeing how nearly they were flanked. The enemy then all concentrated on the right where Sigel had been opposing them during the day but without effect.

The 22nd Ind, while we were wheeling gave back, so that some rebels passed between the two. Some Indians were seen. We "faced by the rear rank" and so got a few shots at them. Today Co "I" had but one wounded. We "faced by the front rank" continued our wheel and soon came into the open field where we saw the Battery safe. On the opposite side of the field there were still a few rebels, but under cover of darkness, they too went over to the right.

We drew back into the woods and built small fires.

Here our "grub" came to us. We had Co "B" 9th Iowa, which had been taken prisoners the day before, but had escaped. They had had nothing to eat for two days. So we divided. At 11 P.M. we were ordered to march and to refrain from making any noise. We went back to the main Fayetteville road and proceeded east till we passed all the camps, then filed to the right passed into the skirt of woods in the rear of a fence. We were ordered to lie down without fire and with all equipment on. We could plainly see the enemy pickets as they were only a few hundred yards away.

8th

At daylight all was ready and just after sunup Our Battery opened, but it soon was compelled to retire a fire being concentrated on it. We lay in line for four hours, the shot and shell coming thick and fast. At first the range was high clear above us, but finally the missiles came down disagreeably near. By this time we had pretty well learned what we termed <u>Bushwhack drill</u>. When the shells got to be too scorching we withdrew, a few rods. As we had made no reply the enemy concluded that we were <u>not there</u> so he ceased firing in that direction. By this time Sigel on our left had opened a brisk cannonade and while attention was directed to him we taking advantage of it, moved forward, our Battery proceeding. Then by a rapid movement we passed to the rebel left our brigade charging two Batteries. (When we retired a short time before the enemy shouted <u>tremendously</u> supposing we were driven. But alas for them we were only getting ready for a charge). Davis' division went far up to the right and then forward just in time to see the rebels <u>skedaddle</u>. The day was ours.

In our advance this morning I saw a nice white lamb quietly and innocently feeding on the battlefield, unaware that the missiles of death were flying all around. It was a touching sight. Our Generals Curtis and Davis passed up the lines. Before them a Rebel flag drooping, ours up and floating to the breeze. This scene to inspire the poet. We remained here some time and then went back to our camp of Thursday.

On Friday at Leetown a ball Struck one of our Band—Billy Martin, but the picture of his girl in his vest pocket, saved his life. The ball did not get through it. If the picture was so valuable what must be expected of the <u>original.</u> He may experiment in that direction. Our company was the fullest in the Regt. Capt Williams did well. In some companies, the officers showed <u>coward</u> decidedly.

Our Adjutant was daunted "never a bit" Col Washburn exceeded in coolness and self-possession all our expectations. Col Pattison lost none of his dignity and discretion. Col Hendricks 22nd Ind was killed while intoxicated. Capt Williams says on the strength of that he is almost a tetotaller. I have contended all the time that not a "drap" of whiskey should ever come into an army's lines. On Sat a private of the 36th Ills shot Gen. McCullough.

Co. "I" was as cool as the rest. I saw one man discharge his piece at an angle of 45° as well as I could judge. I shall not comment on my own conduct. The rebel prisoners say that on Sat they were fully expecting to whip us.

But were sure that

> "Being in a just quarrel,
> We were thrice-armed."[67]

A train came in today from Springfield. We sleep soundly tonight having slept none for two nights. The Battle of Pea Ridge will have a place in History.

9th

I and Amos Vaught were detailed to gather up and bury our dead. This was a dismal work. We went on the field near Leetown. We found there three of our Regt., all of Co. "E."[68] We buried one Secesh. We came across one dead Cherokee. He was savage-looking even in death. At the hospital burying ground were bodies torn in every way. One whom I helped to bury had his head torn off by a cannon ball. The only pillow we could get for the corpses was a board.

There those three will perhaps lie as we placed them till Gabriel shall sound his reveille.

I saw scores of horses lying dead and riderless, some with those who rode them lying beside them silent in death. This Sabbath has scenes connected with it which I shall never forget. All detail left but Bishop of Co. "C" and I. We worked nearly all day.[69]

10th

The day spent in washing.

Some rebel cavalrymen came in under a flag of truce to bury their dead. At or near noon some musketry and a few shots of artillery were heard. Our Regt was in line and out in the field in 7 minutes. Some ones had mistaken these cavalrymen. There was a general running to and fro; finally the mistake was understood and we settled back to quiet as hornets do after being stirred up.

Strike tents and pack knapsacks. March 6 miles toward Bentonville and sleep on our arms.

At night I recd the Witness from Rate and a letter from Miss LM. The latter is at Oxford and will graduate next June.[70]

11th

Still in camp expecting to march again. Put up tents, "Grub" is very scarce. We have made graters of our tin plates and by boiling the corn we can keep ourselves in a kind of bread. My own impression is that Prices forces will not propose another fight for some time to come. The Federals are being victorious everywhere. The question at issue will have been decided by 4th of July next I think, or at any rate hope.

I look for Eddelman soon. I have not seen him since Jan. 24th. I should like to have him back.

Mrs. Lincoln has given a Ball, which all condemn.[71]

12th

Nothing strange. We are in great want of "Grub." An old citizen told us that he could show us 800 stand of small arms left by the Rebels in their flight.

13th

Mail goes out today. Some of our boys have come up from Springfield. The papers that come have none but cheering news.

14th

We look for a supply train in from Springfield tonight. That is cheering. There is such a thing as hunger. I have the mumps, though slight. Johnston Bogart and Storey are sick.
Col. White's men found those arms.

15th

Rainy and cool. Saw a proclamation of Gen. Curtis to the citizens of Arkansas, in which he says to them that safety consists in laying down their arms, and peacably returning to their homes.

16th

Wrote to Miss LM. This Sabbath is not so solemn as last. No preaching. Have had no chaplain for several weeks.

17th

Wrote a letter in the afternoon Had a drill a contemptible drill. Sergt Knobe can't drill at all.[72]

18th

Got some bacon today.

19th

Got orders to draw three days rations and get ready to march. We suspected Price might be coming. At 8 A.M. the 18th was ordered back half mile on Picket.
At 4 P.M. we quit our post and started on after the main force. While it was day the roads were excellent, but when night overtook us the roads were <u>terrible</u>. It was so dark that one could not even see his file leader, our only guide was a slight reflection of light from the gun barrels. In the darkest part of the night I lost my Journal and Portfolio. I could not think

of leaving them so I went back along the road and felt for them with my hands—and <u>found</u> them smack in the road. A hundred had walked over but had not stepped on them. This was a tiresome march.

20th

Everybody in an ill humor. Even the captain is so pettish as not to allow anything taken out of the company wagon. Marched on 4 miles towards Keatsville. Then <u>about face</u> and go back 6 miles across the Arkansas line. We don't wish to leave the State, I suppose.

21st

Snowed all day. The pickets say that every house within 4 or even 5 miles of the Battleground is a secesh hospital. The rebs acknowledge that they were terribly whipped.

22nd

Mail today. The question was up today whether the army was a fitting place for study. A mind bent on study, it is said will study anywhere. I need all the helps I can get, such as study, plenty to eat and persons around me from whom I can catch inspiration. If hell be only a concentration of wickedness and degradation of camp I want to get to heaven among people of talk.

23rd

Didn't know it was Sabbath till I took up my Journal at noon. I have been highly entertained today reading a number of the Ladies Repository sent by Miss Mattie and Miss Mag Stout. They filled in quite a number of select pictures. Sweet Home by Lilly Lichen was the best article.[73] Col Washburn has gone home.

24th

I should like to ramble over the hills today but I cannot. There is such a thing as living for today and such a thing as living for the future. There is a <u>higher life</u> which the vulgar crowd knows nothing of. Blacked my shoes today. First time since I have been in the service.

25th

The Paymaster is expected. Bogart and Storey have gone foraging.

26th

Days come and go, and onward drifts the great current of events. Nations are ever busy settling questions with their neighbors or with themselves, sometimes by the ballot box and sometimes by the cartridge box.

How insignificant an <u>individual</u> looks in the great mass, be he high or low. In a short time he will pass away and no longer have an identity. But to the Christian there comes the pleasing thought[:] If he die he shall live again. If he have the great Advocate to plead for him he is secure.

27th

McClellan has charge of the eastern troops, Halleck of the Western and Fremont of the Middle. Fremont, having given a satisfactory account of his stewardship is given a command, which he deserves. Reports are now to be made to the Sec of War directly. The President in his special message wishes the passage of an act declaring the government ready to assist any State that wishes to emancipate its slaves.[74]

28th

Beautiful morning. The birds are singing, the soldiers are busy, and every-thing wears a cheerful face. Sent a letter to Uncle P.C.V. This is a land of scorpions and rattlesnakes. Never since old Mother Eve was so fooled by a snake, do I want anything to do with them. I object even to the <u>snake flag</u>.

29th

Rumors that we shall march shortly. Lt. Tilson has come bringing paper containing an account of Pea Ridge Battle. Mike of Co C was a prisoner. He came near starving at Fort Smith.[75]

30th

I hope we shall have a sermon today not having heard one for months. "I was glad when they said unto me let us go up to the house of the Lord."[76] Answered Mat and Mag.

31st

A Cavalry scout, with the "Bulldogs" went toward Fayetteville. The object, I suppose, is to find where the rebels are, and not to let them get too close up towards our camp.

April 1st

Of all places in camp for thought, on guard at night is best. The surroundings are inspiring especially to the soldier. As I stood on my post last night guarding the thousands in camp from danger I thought of how many ties these are bound to their friends at home by. Then I recalled the object for which we are here. A rebellion of the South caused us to be here. It said slavery shall live and spread. The Government said <u>No</u> and that <u>no</u> is what we are all saying, and will continue to say, till the South hears. Rebellion is no new thing in this world. Its history is but a succession of Rebellions. There were the conspiracies of Rome and Greece, the cruelties and revolts against Papacy, the Revolution of our Fathers, &c, &c. But during all this time the love of liberty has been growing. Like <u>truth</u>, crushed to earth, twill rise again.[77]

2d

As soon as paid some of the boys went to gambling and by night had no money.

I was surprised to hear that Capt Williams was gambling last night. Vice looses its enormity when those whom men look to as examples engage in it. In the language of Byron, Vice is a monster of such frightful mien That to be dreaded needs but be seen. But seen too oft, alas, familiar with his face, We first endure, then pity, then <u>embrace</u>.[78]

Rec'd a letter from Mack and Mat. They are well.

3rd

The scouts say that Price is not in many miles of our camp. Old Uncle Achilles Vawter of Vernon died a short time since of apoplexy. He was one of the first settlers of Vernon.[79] Sixty-one wagons of Ammunition were up as far as Keatsville and were ordered back to Springfield. I judge from this that we are going back. An effort is being made to present Col Pattison with a horse and sword as a memento of regard.

4th

Read a novel through. My theory is that after one has built his mind on substantial reading, he may read fiction.

5th

Curtis's spies report Price going up White River, it is not known whether to the Mississippi or to Rolla. We shall soon know. The 22nd Ind Sutler has brought up Harpers and Leslies each with a drawing of the Pea Ridge Battle.

The Monitor has proved an unparalleled success. Ericson is a Swede and 60 years of age.[80]

6th

The order for the march has come at last. The day is warm and the roads dusty. After traveling a few miles I heard a tremendous hallooing in the advance. An insane negress was standing near the road naked and dancing around as if she thought it entertaining.

7th

March at 6 A.M. in an easterly direction through woods all day. Make 15 miles. After camping I went and passed an hour alone. Such are among the happiest hours. I am grateful that I am yet alive. Many who enlisted with me are dead, or in hospital.

PART TWO

4

To the Mississippi and the Vicksburg Campaign

In early April 1862 the Army of the Southwest was on the move again, this time marching in an eastward direction through southwest Missouri. Its presence back in that state stemmed from decisions made by the high command. General Henry "Old Brains" Halleck, having received word that Earl Van Dorn's Confederate Army of the West had abandoned its stronghold in the Boston Mountains and was heading to new quarters at Pochahontas in northeast Arkansas, directed General Samuel Curtis to return to the Ozark Plateau in order to protect Missouri's exposed southern border. Curtis warned his superior that crossing that rugged territory would be a "long, rough road" and that "matters of supply may retard me," but he resolutely prepared his men for the struggle ahead.[1]

And a struggle it was. The first few days of the trek brought the troops across familiar ground—through Keetsville, Cassville, and along the banks of Flat Creek—areas they had trudged in chasing Sterling Price just a few months before. Then, however, difficulties began to mount. As Curtis had predicted, the lack of supplies reached frightening levels. The first eight or so miles east of Cassville, a soldier in the Fifty-nine Illinois noted, the soil was strikingly arid and covered with a top layer of white flint stone. For lack of water, even the blackjack oaks seemed to fight "for a scanty existence." The land farther east was heavily forested, further reducing the availability of food. Consequently, Curtis chose to denude the countryside in every way necessary for the support of his army. "I will leave nothing for man nor brute in the country passed over by my army," he reported. "I am sure no rebel army will find subsistence in Southern Missouri or Northern Arkansas." Nor was it just food that was in short supply. Toward the end of the month, having arrived at West Plains in the center of southern Missouri, Curtis sent a flood of requests for wagons, teams, and other supplies. "The cry," he wrote, "is for shoes (horse mule and men) and pants."[2]

Equally troubling for the foot soldiers were the rugged terrain and the endlessly wet weather. Will Stott commented on how winding the roads were on the rocky mountain ridges and how "they added greatly to the beauty." Yet they were also treacherous. The historian of the Fifty-ninth Illinois recalled how the slender roads in the "God-forsaken" land dropped "down through a rather narrow defile, with hills two hundred feet high on either side, the base of the hills so close at the foot as barely to admit the passage of a wagon." The valleys were not only threadlike, but they were often flooded. As countless soldiers' diaries attest, pouring rain was almost constant, and crossing the region's numerous creeks became a major undertaking. On April 15, for instance, Stott recorded that the Eighteenth Indiana crossed Bull Creek "27 times" because the meandering road, more like a mere path, was so frequently under its overflowing waters. His comrade, John C. Swift of Company A, said "the teams forded the creek about 32 times," and the soldiers waded the "knee deep and very cold" stream some "14 times."[3] The combination of daunting terrain and rainy conditions even affected the commander of the army. On April 10, from the "dilapidated town" of Forsyth, Curtis explained that "high water detained" his arrival there and that the "country is very rough" and "not cultivated." While he reported some skirmishing with the Confederate cavalry's rear guard and the taking of some prisoners, Curtis's account captured the essence of his army's experience in southern Missouri: more a struggle with nature than with Confederates.[4]

Perhaps this explains why there was a discernible boost in troop morale when, in late April, Curtis directed his army southward and reentered Arkansas. "That simple change of direction," William L. Shea and Earl J. Hess note, "acted as a tonic," for now the thought of chasing Confederates once more rejuvenated the exhausted Union soldiers. Although Van Dorn's army had vacated Arkansas and crossed the Mississippi River, the threat of a resurgent Confederate force in the state was still real. In Little Rock, the capital city and Curtis's ultimate goal, Major General Thomas C. Hindman had assumed command of the South's Trans-Mississippi Department. The Tennessee native was working tirelessly to enforce conscription, impose martial law, fortify Little Rock, and employ the cavalry, under the colorful Missourians Jo Shelby and John Sappington Marmaduke, to harass Union forces and cut off their communication and supply lines. It was to confront this menace that Curtis personally led his cavalry in a surprise raid on the White River port of Batesville on May 2 and proceeded to establish a formidable encampment south of town at the tiny village of Sulphur Rock. The Eighteenth Indiana remained in this vicinity until the end of June.[5]

Around Batesville, life for the Army of the Southwest consisted largely of rest, reorganization, and, of all things, recruitment. The Eighteenth, for instance, served the entire time as the occupation force in Batesville, with its beloved colonel, Thomas Pattison, in command of the post. Private Gilbert H. Denny of Company G wrote his father on May 31: "The 18th is posted here to guard the town & neighborhood untill further Orders we Don't expect to be attacked here Soon the nearest Cesesh force we can hear of is at Little Rock 100 miles Southwest of here."[6] With the war seldom intervening and a large proportion of Union sympathizers in the local population, Batesville provided opportunities for interaction with the community. The stay there also brought command restructuring and unexpected recruitment efforts. On May 6 Halleck, now in field command at Corinth, Mississippi, directed Curtis to send half of his infantry to reinforce Halleck's army. This resulted in an essential reorganization of Curtis's command into three new divisions, with the Eighteenth Indiana now in the First Division, under Brigadier General Frederick T. Steele.[7] Since many local residents were Unionist in sentiment, and there was a growing opposition to Hindman's imposed draft, an impressive number of Arkansans joined the Union ranks. Forty members of the Williams family of Van Buren and Conway counties, for example, were among the volunteers that one of Curtis's staff said were "flocking in from all quarters."[8]

Reorganization and new recruits, however, could not prevent the crises that attended Curtis's army in late May and June. For one thing, supply problems had not gone away. During most of their days around Batesville, the troops supported themselves by extensive foraging, but they soon exhausted the immediate vicinity's resources and faced fierce enemy resistance when seeking food in remoter areas. By mid-June they were down to half rations. The Eighth Indiana, like many of the regiments, had a daily allowance of only a little meat and four ears of corn for each soldier. Scarcity of water led many to drink from "muddy holes that contained water 'the color of chocolate.'"[9] More discouraging was the effect on the Little Rock expedition. Under directions from Hindman, Confederate cavalry and irregulars increased the number and intensity of their attacks on Union supply trains and foraging bands. Despite their assaults, Curtis believed his forces were of sufficient strength to move on Little Rock. On May 31 he began his advance on the capital. It soon became clear, though, that maintaining lines of communication and supplies with their base in Saint Louis, over rough land and through enemy-infested country, would be virtually impossible. Soon Curtis learned from his quartermaster that the overland supply line was collapsing. In the words of Shea and Hess, the army "had reached the end of its tether." Forty miles from Little Rock, Curtis turned his army around and marched it back to Batesville.[10]

With his eyes still on Little Rock, Curtis called on the navy for help. He requested Halleck to open a water route for supplies by sending Union gunboats via the Arkansas and White rivers. In mid-June a fleet of transports and four large ironclads left Memphis in answer to Curtis's call. On the seventeenth, the flotilla fought its way past Confederate defenses at Saint Charles, Arkansas, then turned up the White River, only to be completely stalled by low water at Clarendon. Curtis's only choice was to take his army to the flotilla, since it could not come to him. This meant cutting his army off from all supply routes and relying totally on the countryside for support—the first time in the war that a Union army took such a risk.[11] In late June, the Army of the Southwest began its trek along the east side of the White River toward Clarendon. The Eighteenth Indiana was the last regiment to leave its pleasant base in northern Arkansas, departing on June 30. "We waved adieu to the romantic little town of Batesville," recalled Walter Stanley of Company G, "and 'marched gaily away' to the old familiar strains of the 'Girl I left behind me.'"[12] Stott did not find the departure so cheerful. "I was loth to leave it," he confided to his diary, for he had found new friends in Mrs. Hirsch and her "merry and kind" daughter, Alice.

Nor would the next few months be happy. Though Stott undoubtedly felt gratified at his promotion to corporal on July 1, he shared with his comrades the suffering they confronted on the march to Clarendon. Still existing on sparse rations, the troops tramped along in extreme heat, amid clouds of dust and swarming insects. With a scarcity of potable water, men and animals sought "to quench their thirst from stagnant swamps." Given the necessity of living off the land, the army often went beyond foraging to pillage and destruction. At Augusta on July 3, as Stanley noted, "the Eighteenth adjourned to the river to take a swim and assist in plundering the town." Devastation followed in the wake of the marching ranks, with anything edible consumed and the nonedible destroyed.[13] Furthermore, Hindman was up to his old tricks, rousing natives to torment the Union army in every way possible and erecting blockades of felled trees across the narrow roads in order to provide opportunities for attacks. Perhaps Denny explained best what the men in blue faced. In a letter home on June 14 he wrote, "we have saw the hardest time yet own [sic] this march our roads was blockaded for miles and we have to stop and cut out a new road and the rebels would be killing our pickets while we was at work." Denny assured his family that he was still "rite side up with the forked end down" and then told them about a big battle at the most dreadful of all blockades. "[T]here was 2 regiments of texan rangers attacked our men and our own men killed and wounded 200 of them and I guess the rest of them has no[t] quit running yet." This engagement was the famed July 7 battle at Cache River, a Union victory and the last formidable barrier before the army reached Clarendon.[14]

When the Union forces reached their destination, the worn and weary soldiers confronted a harsh reality: the flotilla they were to meet had left Clarendon the day before and was now floating back down the river. The last hope for supplies was gone. Curtis's private reaction spoke for many. "The disappointment," he uttered, "is overwhelming." The goal of taking Little Rock paled into insignificance, for the redevelopment of a supply route had to come first, and that meant getting to the Mississippi River with dispatch. On July 9, the Army of the Southwest began another long trek, this time to Helena, Arkansas, some forty-five miles away. Already bone tired and hungry, the troops found no solace on the road. C. P Alling, a musician in the Eleventh Wisconsin, recalled making "the longest and hardest day's march of our entire four years" that day. They went "more than thirty miles in a boiling hot sun" with dust up to their shoe tops and "scarce a drop of water." Alling spoke of "considerable loss of life as a consequence" of those conditions, and Samuel Voyles of the Eighteenth Indiana wrote his father of a "few cases of sickness," perhaps the result of marching "3 days on 4 crackers."[15]

The bedraggled army arrived at Helena on July 12, having traveled since Pea Ridge five hundred miles by foot in three months. Some without footwear, wearing ragged uniforms, and ravenously hungry, they learned on entering the town that rations were at least several days away. A number of soldiers spent that time going back, often many miles, to locate sick or worn-out comrades in the roadside, bringing them to their new campsites. Others worked with local slaves at constructing earthworks on the town's perimeters. Though the troops exulted in finally reaching the Father of Waters, which a soldier of the Eighteenth said "inspired us with as great a joy as did its discovery the followers of DeSoto," the primary reaction to Helena was less than joyous. Many called it "Hell-in-Arkansas," and Sylvester Bishop of the Eleventh Indiana proclaimed it "as miserable a place as I ever saw."[16] A living rogues' gallery and magnet for unsavory characters, the town lived by the "code duello" and, as Stanley reported, "*double-distilled quintessence of deep damnation!*" could be bought "at two dollars and a half a bottle." But, worst of all, Helena was a haven for subtropical diseases. Frequent rains transformed streets into mosquito-infested mud holes, stifling heat and humidity, rancid water, crowded encampments on swamplands, and poor diets—all contributed to outbreaks of ague, malaria, cholera, dysentery, and scarlet fever. Muster rolls, diaries, and letters revealed the murderous impact of disease, as one out of every six infected soldiers died in the town in the summer and fall of 1862. Rhonda M. Kohl rightly concludes that the Union army at Helena "spent the majority of its energies fighting disease, not Confederates."[17]

Fortunately for Stott, he escaped the worst of the disease-ridden days at Helena. On August 25 Stott left on the *Polar Star*, having been granted leave to return to Indiana on recruiting service. The Hoosier State's boundless enthusiasm for the war and support of the troops made it a ripe place for the "picking" of fresh soldiers, and the depleted Eighteenth and other regiments desperately needed them. "There is one recruiting officer gon home to recruit for the Regt.," Denny informed his father. "Tell the boys now is the time to come out and fill this company that we want the company filled with boys we no. Tell Frank Early to come out here if he goes attall." For three months Stott canvassed counties in the central part of the state for viable recruits. As his diary reveals, he naturally found time to visit his family, friends, and alma mater. While he performed his military duties at home, his brigade was transferred to the Army of Southeast Missouri, under the command of Brigadier General John Wynn Davidson. Stott rejoined it at Pilot Knob, Missouri, on November 28, 1862.[18]

Colonel Henry D. Washburn.

Historians have largely ignored the service of Union troops in the southeast quarter of Missouri, probably because little of military significance occurred there. Even veterans of the campaign acknowledged that fact. The official chronicler of the Thirty-third Illinois Infantry, writing in 1902, noted that the campaign was seldom "mentioned or even alluded to" in Civil War accounts. He mused that this oversight no doubt reflected the fact that the soldiers in it "did absolutely nothing worth telling." But it was not their fault, he contended, for "this expedition was conceived in stupidity and commanded by a military lunatic." Although it eschewed such caustic remarks, the brief account of the Eighteenth in the Indiana Adjutant General's report stated only that it "remained on duty in southeast Missouri during the winter." Of its companion regiment, the Eighth, the description was similar, noting that it "marched and counter-marched through the south eastern portion of the State, until March 5th, 1863." The *OR* underscores the latter point in the "Record of Events for the Eighteenth Indiana Infantry," for it gives nothing but a list of marches from Pilot Knob to West Plains and back.[19]

Although there were, of course, some memorable moments, none of them shaped the war in any substantial way. Happily, illness no longer threatened the soldiers on a daily basis. On November 27, 1862, the new commander of the Eighteenth Indiana, Colonel Henry D. Washburn, wrote home, "Our regiment is in rather better health than while camped at Helena." Labeling his own health "tolerable," he noted that his men were physically able to engage in "building a bridge across Black River and repairing the roads generally."[20] Though fully convalescent, their battles during the winter months of 1862–63 were still with nature, not Confederates; skirmishes were few, but raging floods and snowstorms were plentiful. Mid-December brought five straight days of heavy rain. In the early hours of Monday morning, December 15, when all but picket guards were asleep in their tents on the Black River, an alarm went out that the river, as Surgeon George Gordon of the Eighteenth put it, was "on one grand spree." Water flooded the camps with lightning speed. Erastus W. Burget of Company I heard the pickets cry that it "would soon sweep us away if we did not get out of there. This I couldn't hardly believe," he wrote, "for I was so Sleepy that I didn't Care much, but I got up & Stuck my head out of the tent & Shurenough the water had surrounded us & was in a few feet of our tent on every side." Mules drowned, tents and rations floated away, and one member of the Thirty-third Illinois lost his life.[21] The rain continued into January, so the river remained dangerously high, supply trains could not get through, and the army was back to half-rations again. Then came the snow, often six or seven inches deep, along with bitter cold. Gordon spoke for many when he recorded in his diary on January 15, 1863: "It has rained or snowed all day and is snowing now. I have not had a tent but 2 nights in the last 15." And, along with other doctors, he was busy daily treating severe cases of frostbite.[22]

One can certainly understand, then, how Private Will R. Lee of Company F felt when he wrote his hometown newspaper on March 3, 1863. "There will be a grand shout when we finally cut loose from south-east Missouri," he declared, and leave behind "our marching and countermarching from village to hamlet and hamlet to village; . . . the rapid streams to cross with the pontoon train limbering along two days in the rear; . . . the imaginary enemy always in front." He longed to "give three cheers for 'Dixie' and the stirring scenes of siege and battle," for he believed "it is not too distant when Vicksburg will be ours; and the Mississippi open to the mouth." Lee, Stott, and their fellow soldiers did not have a long wait. Two weeks later they boarded the *City of Alton* at Saint Genevieve, Missouri, for the fateful trip down the mighty river to Louisiana and the campaign for Vicksburg.[23]

By the time the Eighteenth Indiana reached Milliken's Bend in the Pelican State, Union efforts to capture Vicksburg had been in operation for months. In fact, they had an even longer history. The eyes of Union strategists had focused on the Mississippi River, and the port city Jefferson Davis had labeled "the Gibraltar of America," from the very outset of the war. During a meeting of military and civilian decision makers at the home of Major General George McClellan in November 1861, Abraham Lincoln stressed Vicksburg's importance in no uncertain terms. As naval officer David Dixon Porter remembered the scene, the president pointed at a map and asserted, "See what a lot of land those fellows hold, of which Vicksburg is the key. . . . The war can never be brought to a close until that key is in our pocket."[24] Not only was the city the opening device to the land surrounding it and to the arterial waterways that could carry supplies to the rest of the Confederacy, it was the key to the Mississippi River

Brigadier General Ulysses S. Grant, commander, Union Army of the Tennessee.

itself. To control Vicksburg was to master the Father of Waters, to sever the Confederacy in two, and to remove the Trans-Mississippi from the war. Furthermore, as Brigadier General Ulysses S. Grant noted years later, it would give the northern forces domination of the Southern Railroad of Mississippi, the primary east-west link at Vicksburg between "the parts of the Confederacy divided by the Mississippi."[25]

With these goals in mind, the groundwork was laid for an all-out move on Vicksburg. On October 9, 1862, Lincoln, after weeks of courting and conniving by former Illinois congressman, Major General John A. McClernand, and in need of Democratic support for his policies, authorized McClernand to recruit soldiers from the western states for the purpose of leading a campaign against Vicksburg. Meanwhile, Halleck, now the general in chief of all Union armies, who distrusted and disliked the ambitious and vainglorious McClernand, proceeded to undermine the politician-general's command. On October 16 Halleck created a new department of the Tennessee, appointing Grant as its commander. The new department was extensive, enveloping the entire Mississippi Valley exclusive of the Union-held area around New Orleans. Halleck empowered Grant to pull troops from Curtis's Department of Missouri—hence, the incorporation of the Eighteenth Indiana into Grant's Army of the Tennessee. Realizing that a strong, united operation could not have two commanders, Grant assumed full command of "the expedition against Vicksburg" on January 30, 1863, thus restricting McClernand's command to that of the XIII Corps.[26]

When the Eighteenth Indiana disembarked at Milliken's Bend as part of the XIII Corps, Grant was in the process of making crucial strategic decisions regarding the next stage of the campaign.[27] His attempts to take Vicksburg by way of inland waterways north of the city—at Chickasaw Bayou, Yazoo Pass, and, only days before, at Steele's Bayou—had all met with disaster. Likewise, the incessant efforts of the troops in digging canals on the Louisiana side of the Mississippi for the purpose of creating watercourses for bypassing the Confederate batteries at Vicksburg, or at least allowing Union forces to travel southward by flatboat, had failed. As Michael Ballard succinctly puts it, "Grant had had enough" with canals by the end of March. He also knew he had to get his army on the move and in a campaign mode, not only to relieve them of the unpleasant canal work and prevent boredom, but also to avoid camp fevers and other diseases that tended to break out during lengthy encampments.[28] In the early spring of 1863, therefore, Grant met with his corps commanders, McClernand of the XIII Corps, William Tecumseh Sherman of the XV Corps, and James B. McPherson of the XVII, to discuss strategic options. One was to conduct an amphibious assault across the Mississippi River and then storm the Vicksburg batteries. Another was to revert to Memphis and try an overland course through northwest Mississippi. A third

Major General John A. McClernand, commander, XIII Army Corps.

alternative, however, became the chosen one: search for a land route through Louisiana that would take the army south of Vicksburg, past its fortifications, to a point at which it could make a safe crossing to the east bank of the Mississippi River. This would mean opening a passageway from the Union bases at Young's Point and Milliken's Bend southward to New Carthage, the place chosen by Grant as the staging area for the transfer of troops across the river. While the army operated by land, small vessels could float from Duckport Landing through a succession of bayous to provide supplies, and Porter's gunboats could run past the Vicksburg batteries in order to later escort the troops' invasion of Mississippi soil.[29]

The task of finding a route to New Carthage fell on McClernand's shoulders. On March 29 Grant ordered his senior corps commander to begin an advance southward from Milliken's Bend along the banks and levees of a chain of bayous toward the little village of Richmond, near Roundaway Bayou. McClernand gave the job of directing the expedition to Brigadier General Peter J. Osterhaus of the Ninth Division who, in turn, sent Colonel Thomas W. Bennett's Sixty-ninth Indiana in the lead to probe for open passageways. Bennett's infantry, along with the Second Illinois Cavalry, two mountain howitzers, and a company of engineers, left Milliken's Bend on Tuesday morning, March 31. The army's advance to New Carthage was a distinct challenge. The force trekked over waterlogged ground on the way to Richmond, fought off a small Confederate force stationed there, crossed Roundaway Bayou on small boats while under fire, and arrived at Smith's plantation on April 3 only to discover that the land from there to New Carthage was entirely underwater. Despite these obstacles, and with the aid of flatboats "wrested from the enemy on Bayou Vidal," McClernand's van of one division reached New Carthage, twenty-five miles below Vicksburg, on April 6.[30]

The fact that the army was finally moving lifted its morale appreciably; the spirits were high back at Milliken's Bend as the first troops of the XIII Corps set out for New Carthage. Yet, "hurry up and wait" was again the order of the day. The Eighteenth Indiana did not march toward Richmond until April 11, and the rest of the division and other units began the trek during the next several days. It was slow going again. As Francis Vinton Greene wrote three decades later, "owing to the necessity of making and repairing roads through the soft, black soil, and of constructing a large number of bridges over various minor bayous," it was not until April

25 that the entire corps would catch up to McClernand.[31] Engineering efforts were not the only deterrent. At first, water was the primary enemy, with the land to be traversed basically a "boggy mass." The only dry areas were the natural levees, but even their "narrow tops" could be treacherous. A soldier of the Eleventh Wisconsin described them as "often so wet and slippery as to require an acrobat's skill to keep from skidding into the water, which in fact some did." Historian Bruce Catton correctly said the land was "better suited to the alligator and the catfish than to an army corps." And, with stagnant water everywhere, an Illinois private reported that "the mosqetoes was very bad so that it kept me busy to keep them from taking me prisoner."[32]

But these conditions did not deter the soldiers from observing the countryside and its residents. Many men in blue, for instance, found Richmond and its environs attractive. Colonel James R. Slack of the Forty-seventh Indiana wrote from nine miles south of Richmond that the town "is a very pleasant little country village of 500 or less inhabitants located in the midst of as rich a Country as ever the Sun of Heaven shone upon." Bernard Schermerhorn of the Forty-sixth Indiana concurred. He estimated the town's population at "2 or 3 hundred" and labeled its surroundings "the finest country I ever saw without any exception."[33] Capturing most attention were the plantations. Some were so large as to be self-sustaining towns, while most were of smaller acreage with modest homes. All, however, sported the gay colors of roses, magnolias, and noble oaks. Some, though, were in ruins, like the outbuildings at Perkins plantation, all burned down, according to Gordon of the Eighteenth Indiana, "by the 'Old Reb . . . himself,'" and the mansion of a large spread south of Milliken's Bend that was "fired by the owner before he fled."[34]

Likewise, the Union soldiers sensed the war's impact on residents, white and black. The former often displayed a morose disposition, and they did not hide their "hatred of the soldiers with the blue uniforms." As Sergeant Aquila Standifird of the Twenty-third Iowa remarked, "The citizens is reb from top of head to the toe nails. They think we will never take Vicksburg." The plantation slaves, however, mostly welcomed the blueclad troops. Many followed them as they marched by and brought with them, as Samuel Carter III records, "arms laden with hams and chickens, jugs of molasses, sacks of flour." Most of the slaves left behind by their retreating masters were women, children, and "old Bucks," and many found their customary pattern of life uncomfortably disrupted by Yankee plunder of their plantation homes. Iowan Taylor Peirce wrote his beloved Catharine, "The negroes are all run off and the plantations deserted and are fast being laid waste by the soldiers." But, then again, he asserted, the planters "brought it on themselves by their inhuman conduct and thirst for power and they must reap their reward."[35]

The main attraction for Union soldiers in mid-April, however, was not what they were doing and seeing on land but what naval forces were accomplishing on the Mississippi River. A primary component of Grant's grand strategy for the taking of Vicksburg was for Porter's Mississippi squadron of ironclads, small gunboats called "turtles," and transports to run past the Vicksburg batteries. That mission accomplished, it would be ready to support Union troops south of the fortress city, possibly assault fortifications at Grand Gulf, and provide transportation for the army to the Mississippi shore. At ten o'clock on Thursday night, April 16, the fleet got under way. It was a quiet, moonless night, and the vessels were equally silent and dark, floating with the current with their lights extinguished. With Porter's flagship *Benton* in the lead and Grant watching from a nearby transport, the single-file fleet edged slowly past DeSoto Point on the Louisiana shore. Suddenly, fires flared up on the Louisiana side, the result of buildings set ablaze by Confederates on the Point, and the Vicksburg batteries belched forth shot and shell. Now backlit from the west and fired upon from the east, the Union fleet formed a silhouetted target. The battle went on for several hours, gunboats and transports receiving heavy, continuous fire, with the transport *Henry Clay* completely destroyed. "The sight," said Grant, "was magnificent, but terrible." Yet the fleet made it through, its surviving vessels still functional and its destination attained.[36]

The foot soldiers in Louisiana shared Grant's perspective on the navy's trial and triumph. A Union veteran thought the bombardment of the fleet was "disagreeable music," but the annalist of the Thirty-third Illinois saw it as "one of the grandest spectacles of the war." Members of the Sixty-ninth Indiana, watching the *Benton* "round the bend" from the balcony of the Ione plantation on the morning of April 17, erupted in full-throated cheers. Joshua James, an old Confederate who lived there, shouted "My God! This is the entering wedge!" and proceeded to weep "as if his heart would break." W. M. Littell of the Twenty-third Iowa agreed with James's

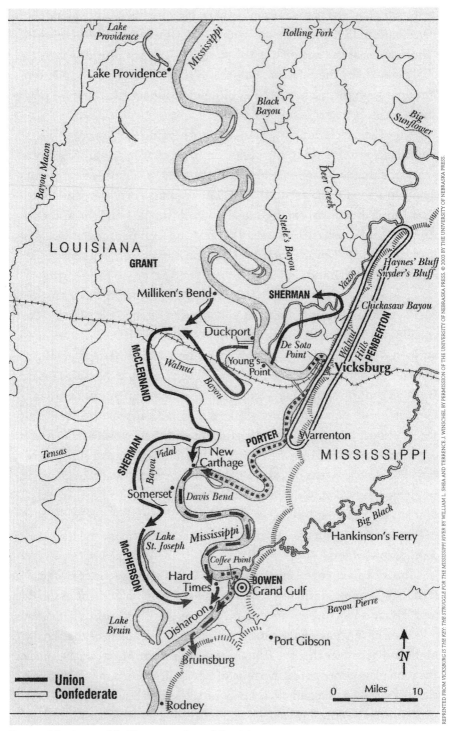

Route of the Army of the Tennessee through Louisiana.

assessment but rejoiced instead. Writing his wife from "Backwoods La.," he concluded that Porter's success meant "Uncle Sam is diong [sic] quite a large business here now in the way of moving the army."[37]

The Army of the Tennessee now moved more rapidly than ever. The naval victory of April 16 and its continued runs past the Vicksburg defenses rejuvenated the Union land forces. Alling of the Eleventh Wisconsin claimed that these developments "incited a spirit of courageous daring that made every man a hero; and the spirit of our invincible leader, Grant, seemed, like Elijah's mantle, to be upon every man." There was some truth in Alling's allegations, for Grant's tireless energy during the rest of April was a model for an army eager to fight. On April 18 Grant met with McClernand and Porter at Pliney Smith's Pointe Clear plantation near New Carthage to consider their next steps. All of the XIII Corps, including the Eighteenth Indiana, was in place there and ready for the move across the river. Grant next returned to Milliken's Bend to expedite the departure of McPherson's XVII Corps for its march to join McClernand.[38]

Two things were evident to the commander: (1) he needed to secure a staging area closer to Grand Gulf, and (2) far more supplies would be required once the whole army assembled at the embarkation point. On April 20 Grant informed McClernand that "Six Steamers I hope will be ready to run the Enemy's batteries tonight." The boats contained, he added, "6.00 thousands rations and a very considerable quantity of forage." The same day Grant's adjutant, John A. Rawlins, issued Special Order No. 110 that detailed the plans "to obtain a foothold on the east bank of the Mississippi River, from which Vicksburg can be approached by practicable roads." Once again, McClernand's corps would take the advance, followed by McPherson's, and then Sherman's. All officers and soldiers were to travel light with few tents, and the XIII Corps was "authorized . . . to collect all of the beef-cattle, corn, and other necessary supplies in the line of march," although "wanton destruction," insults to citizens, and unsanctioned searches of houses were strictly forbidden.[39]

Final orders having been given, on April 21 the Eighteenth Indiana and its division began marching toward Judge John Perkins's Somerset plantation, another potential staging area eight miles southeast of New Carthage. Again, the going was tough. An intense thunderstorm halted progress on the first day, and rafts were needed to cross bayous, "the fields all being covered [in] several feet of water." Then artillery fire interrupted their nightly rest, for six transports ran the gauntlet past the Vicksburg batteries on the night of April 21–22, each ship receiving hits and one, the *Tigress*, being sunk. Augustus Sinks of the Forty-sixth Indiana recorded in his journal: "Although 25 miles distant, the reports of the guns made the doors and Sash rattle in the house in which I was sleeping."[40] The Eighteenth Indiana finally reached Perkins's plantation on April 25, and it immediately caught the fancy of Stott and his cohorts. Once a majestic estate, it still featured lavishly landscaped grounds covered with evergreens, magnolias, a large beech grove, and marble monuments. Its mansion, though, was in ashes, having been burned by Perkins—reportedly a Confederate congressman—to prevent it from falling into Union hands. Camping there was pleasant but brief, Grant having determined that there was no "practicable" way Somerset could serve as an embarkation point. Now it was off to Hard Times, a hamlet located right across the river from Grant's goal: the Confederate fortifications at Grand Gulf.[41]

From his headquarters at Perkins's on April 27, Grant ordered McClernand to "Commence immediately the embarkation of your Corps or so much of it as there is transportation for." He also informed his corps commander that the assault upon Grand Gulf would be up to the navy but, once the guns at that heavily fortified position were silenced, McClernand's corps was to be ready to cross the river. The next day, April 28, according to McClernand's official report, the XIII Corps left Somerset "without wagons, baggage, tents, or officers' horses" and "embarked on steamers and barges" on the Mississippi for Hard Times. Eugene A. Carr's Fourteenth Division, of which Stott's brigade was a part, traveled uncomfortably on multiple vessels, all crowded and some leaky. The Thirty-third Illinois, for instance, was on board the *Forest Queen*, while the Ninty-ninth Illinois and Stott's Eighteenth Indiana floated in "barges lashed to the steamboat's beams," and the Eighth Indiana occupied the *J. W. Cheesman*. Upon landing at their destination, all were united in a common focus.[42]

Grant knew, of course, that the naval assault at Grand Gulf and the subsequent acquisition of a foothold on Mississippi soil could fail. He was aware that, as Warren Grabau cogently states, "the possibility existed that it would prove too tough a nut for the navy to crack." But this was Grant and, as Gordon observed, "Grant goes to win before he quits, that is the way."[43] So, at 7:00 a.m. on Wednesday, April 29, Union gunboats started for Grand Gulf, Porter in the pilothouse of the *Benton* and Grant look-ing on from a small tug. That same morning McClernand received orders "to embark all the troops from his corps that our transports and barges could carry." Some ten thousand men of the XIII Corps climbed aboard the vessels, but not Stott's unit. As McClernand reported, "General Carr's division remained at Hard Times, waiting for the return of troops to bring them on, too. But that never happened." For more than five hours, Porter's eight gunboats and the Confederate batteries at Forts Wade and Coburn blasted at each other, but the Confederate defenses proved the more formidable. "About half-past one the fleet withdrew," wrote Grant, "seeing their efforts were entirely unavailing."[44]

During the bombardment, Stott and hundreds of other blueclad men watched the awesome but disappointing scene unfold. Hoosier Asa E. Sample, aboard the *Empire City*, had "an excellent view of the location of the enemies batteries." "Nature," he opined, "had done much to assist the rebels to fortify this place. The banks being very bluffy enabling the en-emy to dig down and make breastworks almost formidable." Alling stood on the Louisiana shore "and with field glasses could see the frowning muzzles of the great guns . . . directly in our front," and Sergeant Charles Hobbs of the Ninety-ninth Illinois noticed "one old monster, hidden and protected by embankments and cotton," that never went silent. A soldier in Stott's division reflected: "We could stand at our camp and watch the bombardment, and it was a terrible but grand sight." It may have been a spectacular display, but as Iowan Israel Ritter sadly recorded in his diary, "The attempt was not successful."[45]

Even before he launched the effort to take Grand Gulf, the ever-resourceful Grant had an alternative plan in mind. Now he put it into ac-tion. After the firing ceased, the general went aboard the *Benton* to confer with Porter. Standing amid the bloody carnage on deck, the two officers agreed on Grant's scheme to move their combined forces down the river to a new embarkation point. That night, as McClernand's and McPher-son's corps marched unseen across Coffee Point southward to Disharoon plantation, Porter's gunboats provided cover fire for the empty transports to run in the same direction around the Point. At Disharoon the two forces reunited, the army enjoying dry land upon which to camp and the navy able to tie up safely on a sturdy bank.[46] Grant's original design was to land his troops the next day as far south as Rodney, Mississippi, from which a road led to Port Gibson, a feasible starting point for the advance on Vicksburg. Late that night, however, soldiers escorted an "intelligent contraband" to the general's tent. The slave told Grant that a better, more accessible road to Port Gibson could be found at Bruinsburg and that it would intersect with the road from Rodney. Furthermore, Bruinsburg possessed a bank that could accommodate many steamboats and was only about five miles down river from Disharoon. This intelligence dictated Grant's decision: destination Bruinsburg. Meanwhile, his men confronted their own reflections. The next day they might "see the elephant" again, which gave Stott, and no doubt many of his brothers in arms, "sober thoughts" about duty and destiny, about life and death.[47]

<hr />

Sample of the Fifty-fourth Indiana wrote in his diary on April 30 that "the morning came bright and beautiful, and by sunrise we were on board steaming down the river." Actually, the embarkation was not that smooth. Seventeen thousand troops had to be squeezed onto an armada of steamboats, damaged transports, and barges in sweltering heat, the men still silent and apprehensive, the vessels crowded and progressively riding lower in the water. Only sailors and soldiers were on decks, no wagons, tents, or horses, save those needed for artillery; even Grant's steed was left behind. Once on board, the men continued to be anxious, searching the shore for signs of Confederates or their guns, cleaning their own pieces for combat, and wondering what may lie ahead. Then, as paddle wheels churned and the boats chugged through the murky water, a band aboard the *Benton* struck up the tune of "Red, White, and Blue," and cheers emerged from every throat. The Army of the Tennessee—"said to be the finest army that has ever been together," Peirce proudly wrote to his wife—was going to bring the war to Vicksburg. At noontime most of the XIII Corps was on Mississippi soil, its arrival unchallenged, its pickets at the foot of the Bruinsburg bluffs. Grant recalled years later the relief he felt at "being on the same side of the river with the enemy. All the campaigns, labors, hardships, and exposures . . . that had been made and endured were for the accomplishment of this one object."[48]

On the afternoon of April 30, 1863, there was no time to reflect on the meaning of the moment, for there were more pressing matters on the commander's mind. Grant moved with haste among his men, urging them to quicken their pace toward the summits of the bluffs, since securing them was essential both to their safety and to their progress inland. Around noon, as Grant was set to order a rapid march, he received unwelcome news: the XIII Corps was without rations! It was customary, in the absence of wagons, for at least three days' rations to be issued to troops to carry in their haversacks. However, neither McClernand, his division commanders, nor his commissary officers had distributed them. This oversight caused a four-hour delay, and, as a result, the corps did not reach the crests of the bluffs until an hour before sunset.[49]

The XIII Corps began its march toward the high ground at 4:00 p.m. with Carr's Fourteenth Division, including the Eighteenth Indiana, in the lead. The long blue line must have been a bizarre sight. In his urgency to get his forces on the road, Grant had chosen to delay the issuance of rations to individual soldiers. Instead, officers assigned two men to carry each of the large boxes of foodstuffs on the march until suppertime allowed for their distribution. "Weary must these sturdy fellows have been," wrote First Sergeant Hobbs of the Ninety-ninth Illinois, "with the weight of cracker boxes, barrels of meat, provisions." Even after the boxes were opened and their contents dispensed, there were large portions of meat that could not fit in haversacks. So soldiers improvised. "The bayonets were placed on their guns and run through the meat," an Iowa lieutenant explained, "so each man had his extra ration of meat fixed on his bayonet. Then at right shoulder shift, we proceeded on our march." The military train also seemed mighty peculiar. Grant ordered his men to grab everything along the way that could provide transportation, so donkey carts, oxen, farm wagons, even ladies' buggies accompanied the marching ranks. And Carr straddled "a great big ugly poor mule, his sword and belt hanging on the horn of his saddle."[50]

In this manner McClernand's men and artillery slowly climbed to the heights of the bluffs. At the top their eyes feasted on what Vicksburg Military Park historian Terrence J. Winschel depicts as "a panorama beautiful in the extreme." They not only saw large patches of corn and a forest of stately oaks and colorful magnolias, but also directly in front of them stood an imposing, ornate mansion unlike any they had seen in Louisiana. Windsor plantation, the creation of owner Smith Coffee Daniell II, was new, completed by Daniell just two years earlier, and rimmed with more than twenty-five Corinthian columns, reaching forty-five feet to the

Brigadier General William P. Benton, commander, First Brigade.

skies. Here the troops put down their weapons, ate some of their fresh rations, and lay back, for they had seen no Confederates during their entire march. The respite was brief, however, because McClernand decided to plunge on toward Port Gibson in a forced night march. Back on the road, they passed Bethel Church, at the steeple of which some rapscallions in blue could not resist firing their small arms—a sound probably heard by Confederate scouts or their informants.[51]

Just beyond the church, the marching ranks turned left onto the Rodney Road, a dusty path leading eastward. So far their trajectory had been southerly, but now the soldiers' energy quickened for, though weary, they knew they were at least going toward Port Gibson. Out in front as skirmishers was the Eighteenth Indiana, followed by the rest of William P. Benton's First Brigade, the Eighth Indiana and the Thirty-third and Ninety-ninth Illinois. As they tramped along to the sound of clattering artillery wagons, amid clouds of dust, they passed plantations and farms where slaves turned out to watch the peculiar blue line. Samuel P. Herrington of the Eighth Indiana noted that these observers were "from one year up to 100 years old," and the younger children and women wore "dirty colored white dresses" of material "almost like our flour sacking in Indiana." The troops, he said, would "cheer them & that makes them show their ivory they knew their day of Jubile [sic] had come." The Ninety-ninth Illinois's Hobbs told of an "old darkey" who "gives us his blessing, but fears there will be but few of us return."[52]

As darkness began to set in, McClernand replaced the skirmishers with a small patrol led by a black man named Bob, who knew the area intimately. The reconnaissance unit had orders "to advance on the road, and go forward until fired on by the enemy." A bright full moon clearly revealed the complex, nearly surreal, terrain the army was entering. Grant later said that the land in that region "stands on edge," its intricacy making it "easy for an inferior force to delay, if not defeat, a far superior one." Narrow ridges alternated with steep ravines, often as deep as one hundred feet, and both ridges and hollows were covered with tangles of brush, trees, vines, and "canebrakes so dense," writes Grabau, "that a man could not see a companion ten feet away." Rodney Road itself, like many others described by Grabau, seemed to be "at the bottom of a small canyon . . . with vertical sides."[53] And the Eighteenth Indiana moved along it in the dark with moonbeams casting light on strange, eerie objects on all sides.

Even though there had been no traces, thus far, of Confederate presence, could the enemy be on the next ridge? In the deep ravine? That he was not far away would soon become evident.

Brigadier General John S. Bowen, commander of the Confederate forces at Grand Gulf, had assumed that the logical place for a Union beachhead south of Vicksburg would be Rodney Road. Accordingly, on the morning of April 30 he ordered Brigadier General Martin L. Green to take his brigade of Arkansas and Missouri troops to Port Gibson and establish a position west of town. Green did so by late morning, placing infantry and artillery near Magnolia Church on the Rodney Road. That afternoon, Bowen rode to Green's headquarters with the news that Union troops had entered Rodney Road near Bethel Church. The two officers decided to divide their forces between Rodney and Bruinsburg roads, and then wait for the Union forces to arrive.[54] The long wait, deathly silence of the night, and increasing talk of a Union advance made Green antsy. Around 12:30 a.m. he rode west to check on his picket line near the house of Mrs. A. K. Shaifer. There he found the panicked ladies of the household hastily loading their goods in a wagon. Just as Green sought to calm them, a volley of musketry burst forth from his pickets and the Union patrol, some of whose fire struck the Shaifer house and packed wagon. As Littell of the Twenty-third Iowa reported, "we came too close to a rebel battery to be

The Shaifer house, Rodney Road, Port Gibson.

healthy, they threw grape and shell right into our midst, one of the *fruit* of the *vine* striking close enough to me to throw sand in my eyes." Infantry fire increased from the Union side, and soon Standifird, another Iowan, said, "we was ordered to get to the side of the road for the Indiana Battery to pass." Henry C. Leeson of the Eighth Indiana wrote proudly that "Our Duch Boys was ready as soon as the flash of the enemys cannon showed them where to aim, . . . Then Father is when your Boy trembled in his Shoes" because "the Shot and Shell came thick and fast." The exchange of fire began to abate after about an hour, and the guns went silent at 3:00 a.m. The Eighteenth Indiana, only three hundred yards from the Shaifer house, received orders from Carr to abandon the road and get some sleep on their arms.[55]

A few hours later McClernand rode from his headquarters at Windsor and arrived among the troops "about day-dawn." The sun peeping through the haze of early morning slowly brought the soldiers out of their brief and uneasy slumber, some more alert than others. Leeson, for example, was "up at early dawn ready for the May party (It being May Day)." McClernand, on the other hand, cared little about the date. He and his commanders were busily reconnoitering the area, especially Magnolia Church ridge and the plantation road that led north to Bruinsburg Road. From their inspection it was clear that the Confederates held ground that was perfect for a defensive stand—a maze of rims and hollows and virtually impenetrable tangles of vegetation. It was then, the politician-general wrote, that he "learned from a fugitive negro that the two roads diverging at the Shaiffer's led to Port Gibson, one to the right by Magnolia Church, and the other to the left, passing near Bayou Pierre." Acting upon this intelligence, the corps commander deployed his forces, ordering Osterhaus's division up the plantation road to the left and sending Carr's down the Rodney Road toward Green's position at Magnolia Church.[56]

Receiving his orders at 6:15 a.m., Carr acted immediately. He deployed Colonel William M. Stone's Second Brigade to the left of the road, then sent Brigadier General Benton's First Brigade, that of the Eighteenth Indiana, to the right. With his infantry solidly supported by Iowa and Indiana batteries, Carr opened the contest in earnest. While Stone engaged in a holding action, Benton's men plunged forward, their goal being the Magnolia Church ridge. Benton's "way lay through woods, ravines, and a light canebrake," McClernand reported, "yet he pressed on until he found the enemy drawn up behind the crest of a range of hills intersected by a road. Upon one of these hills, in plain view, stood Magnolia Church." Amid the canebrake and ravines, Benton recalled, "the battle raged in great fury," his men forcing the stubborn enemy back "at the point of the bayonet," on the double-quick and "under a galling fire of shell and musketry." The Eighth and Eighteenth Indiana led the way behind Major Thomas V. Brady of the Eighth, with the Ninety-ninth Illinois in ready reserve. The latter unit's Hobbs remembered following the Hoosiers just as "a battery opens on us at easy range of less than 500 yards." With grapeshot "hurtling, whistling, whizzing above us, around us, and through our ranks," he said, "I think we quickened our speed as we heard that music." Stott's company was on the far left of the brigade, the very spot where "the heaviest fire" occurred, according to First Sergeant Louis Knobe. "[O]ur Regt. was placed on a high ridge sloping of[f] in the rear of us down to a deep holer," so its men could fall back into the ravine to load, "then advance to the top of the ridge to fire." Schermerhorn, whose Forty-sixth Indiana soon came forward to support its fellow Hoosiers, watched as they fought over "one continuous succession of hills and ravines & absolutely the roughest country we ever passed over." On such terrain, and with constant firing, Benton's troops attained their goal, and Washburn's Eighteenth rested a few yards from Magnolia Church, "immediately in front of the enemy's battery." "Now came the 'tug of war' in good earnest," Benton wrote.[57]

Green's Confederate line, now reinforced by the Twenty-third Alabama and two guns of the famed Botetourt Artillery, lay only two hundred yards away, across a seemingly bottomless ravine. But, unfortunately, atop the church ridge where the Union forces perched, confusion set in. Benton's right flank had stubbornly fought the rugged ground, clinging to cane and vines for leverage as it climbed to the top of the ravines, and was threatening to envelop Green's left flank. In the process, however, it had drifted away from the rest of its brigade, opening a gap in the center of the Union line. Furthermore, the terrain and the large number of regiments involved were taking a toll on the original battle lines and the soldiers of many units were inextricably mixed together. Given these conditions, and concerned about the unfortunate gap, McClernand sent the fresh troops of Brigadier General Alvin P. Hovey's Twelfth Division into the breach.[58] By the time Hovey's men reached Magnolia Church, the ridge had become a killing field, with the Eighteenth Indiana suffering a heavy portion of the casualties. Sharpshooters on both sides poured forth steady volleys. Two of Hovey's troops found that, while "the 8th and 18th were holding their own," the adjutant of the Eighteenth "implored us to hurry up as his Regt. and the 8th Indiana were being cut to pieces." To Ritter of the Twenty-fourth Iowa, "It appeared that all the forest was crashing to pieces." Around this time, according to historian Winschel, "Sharpshooters of the Eighteenth Indiana crept close to the Confederate line and began firing on the artillerymen with deadly accuracy," killing several battery officers and horses. The Botetourt, however, did not give way easily, and the blueclad line briefly fell back.[59]

Then, shortly after 10:00 a.m., Hovey shouted the command to charge, and McClernand's total force around Magnolia Church pushed forward in direct attack. Men from many regiments—three from Indiana—drove on the Botetourt guns, capturing them and turning them on the fleeing foe. Some two hundred Confederates surrendered, and soldiers of the Eighteenth Indiana seized the regimental flag of the Fifteenth Arkansas. In his General Order of May 6, Carr recorded that "Capt. W. S. Charles, Company H, Eighteenth Indiana, was the first man to jump on the enemy's guns," and Stott wrote in his diary, "I was helping Capt. Charles to turn two pieces which we had captured on the enemy." Benton's report of the battle likewise gives the credit to Charles. The debate over who actually secured the guns continues to this day, and, as Ballard observes, "the answer is elusive." The judgment of Edwin C. Bearss, a dean of Civil War scholars and master of accurate detail, seems most credible. "Even though the regiment that first reached the guns will forever remain a mystery," Bearss writes, "it is possible to award the 18th Indiana the ultimate honor, for they were the men whose deadly marksmanship made the capture possible."[60]

At the time the guns were seized, none of the soldiers cared about who actually was first at the guns. They simply stood alongside the two twelve-pounder howitzers, trophies still hot from extended firing, and cheered, waving their hats lustily as they watched the enemy run away. The jubilation continued when their commanders rode up. "Old Grant heard us fighting and come on the field about 11 o'clock," Iowan Peirce told his wife, "and when the victory was complete you ought to have heard the shout rung out. . . . It was enough to pay us for all the fatigue and dangers." McClernand called to an aide, "A great day for the northwest!" and

Governor Richard Yates of Illinois joined in the celebration. Ever the politicians, they both grasped the climactic moment as prime time for stump speeches, congratulating the men on "a glorious achievement." Grant quietly but impatiently listened, then gestured toward the east where the enemy busily prepared for another defense. There was still fighting to be done.[61]

During the remainder of that fateful May Day, the Eighteenth Indiana's brigade saw less action. Though McClernand "ordered Generals Carr and Hovey to push the enemy with all vigor and celerity," obeying that command was difficult. Again the puzzling terrain impaired the views of McClernand and his troops as they renewed the assault through dense underbrush and canebrakes, and the corps commander feared he might send them into a trap. Though most of Carr's regiments, spent from the morning's combat, were held in reserve, even they felt the confusion and the Confederate presence. "We would move one direction," wrote the sergeant of a reserve unit, "and then ordered to Some other part of the field we was kept moving but was at no time out of reach of the enemy's Shell and often in sight of the enemy." McClernand, never a subtle general, nevertheless smashed his way through, repeating the tactics that worked at Magnolia Church. At one point in the late afternoon, Benton called upon the Eighteenth Indiana and Ninety-ninth Illinois to face Confederate guns again, and, for more than an hour, the Union regiments drove back the intrepid Colonel Francis Cockrell's grayclad Missourians. The Confederate line broke, and the day belonged to the Union.[62]

The Battle of Port Gibson was over, and it was one the Eighteenth Indiana never forgot. Not only did it obtain a bridgehead in Mississippi, force the Confederates to vacate Grand Gulf, and remain in Grant's memory as "one of the most important [triumphs] of the war," but also, as Emma Lou Thornbrough notes, "At Port Gibson the Eighteenth Indiana suffered the heaviest losses of any regiment in the Union army." Washburn reported "19 enlisted men killed, 3 officers and 61 enlisted men wounded—total 83."[63] Stott and his comrades also remembered the feelings and images they shared with others that afternoon. Colonel Slack of the Forty-seventh Indiana told his dear Ann, "the fight at Port Gibson gave me enough. It was terrible indeed." He saw "men upon every side of me fall as dead as though a thunderbolt had stricken them," and "where the contest waged the fiercest," there were Confederates "lying on top of each other. . . . How soon we become accustomed to such scenes," Slack concluded. Hobbs witnessed "a youth of not more than 17 with a bullet through his body. Ghastly white his face, and the pain he was suffering caused his muscles to twitch and the blood to beat in the veins of his forehead. Poor fellow! though a foeman." And everywhere were the signs of hasty retreat: abandoned guns and equipment, dead animals, and discarded muskets and knapsacks. The exhausted Eighteenth Indiana slept that night in the midst of the carnage and debris and without a campfire.[64]

Early the next morning, May 2, once it was light, McClernand's troops started for Port Gibson. The town presented a welcome contrast to the slaughter and death of the day before! Virtually all who reflected on their entrance to the village that morning commented on how pretty it was—and how empty. "A most beautiful place," Ritter wrote, "high and fine buildings, four large churches. . . . Nearly all the citizens are gone, much property taken . . . best place I ever saw South." Hoosier Sample called it "a neat little rural village," and Standifird, Twenty-third Iowa, noted how the streets were "well shaded by large trees" and rimmed by "lawns with their Evergreens and flowers of different colors." Hobbs of the Ninety-ninth Illinois looked beyond the grandeur, however, to consider its implications about southern society. He went to plantation houses "with their fine furniture and elegant grounds. . . . Rare melodeons and pianos, all showing the signs of the rich at the expense of the poor. No wonder that aristocracy is King," he reasoned. "How awfully are the poor white men of the south deceived, when they fight for their own enslavement," Hobbs concluded.[65]

Although perhaps "deceived," the poor whites in General William E. Baldwin's brigade certainly were not quitting. North of Port Gibson, on the primary route to Vicksburg, the Confederates burned the bridge over Little Bayou Pierre, seeking thereby to delay the Union advance. Though disappointed, Grant saw the maneuver as no obstacle, for as Sample penned in his diary, as early as May 2 "The 'miners and sappers' were at work and would have the bridge ready by four in the morning." The pioneers completed a "raft-bridge," using materials taken, Grant said, from "wooden buildings, stables, fences, etc., which sufficed for carrying the whole army over safely." On May 4 Stott recorded, "the 18th Indiana and two pieces 1st Indiana Artillery" crossed the new span and marched another seven or eight miles before halting to construct what they called "Fort Washburn."[66]

———————•◆•———————

The overland campaign in Mississippi was under way. Grant's goal was to reach and cut the Southern Railroad, the Confederacy's vital communication and supply link between Vicksburg and Jackson. To do so, he chose to send his army of 30,000 eastward into the heart of the state, rather than directly north to Vicksburg and the 60,000 Confederates commanded there by Pennsylvania native Brigadier General John C. Pemberton. The move to the east would also allow ample time for Sherman's XV Corps to arrive in Mississippi and swell the Army of the Tennessee to a full strength of about 43,000. Furthermore, it meant campaigning with a radically thin supply line, in defiance of military standards and Halleck's explicit directions. Grant, however, knew how fruitful Mississippi agriculture was and that his army could "live off the land." He wrote Sherman on May 3: "The road to Vicksburg is open. All we want now are men, ammunition, and hard bread. We can subsist our horses on the country and obtain considerable supplies." Besides, Grant intended to move rapidly. He marched his men more than two hundred miles in the seventeen days it took to reach Vicksburg's defenses, fighting five battles along the way.[67]

Obviously, such campaigning required incessant movement, with little opportunity for extended encampments or even much time for meals and rest. The Union army was, after all, in the heart of Confederate country, without a steady base and dependent on the land for sustenance. These factors, among others, created a campaign replete with hardships yet marked with heightened morale, because the soldiers knew they were now on the heels of the enemy. As early as May 5, reflecting on experiences in Louisiana and now in Mississippi, Major Luther H. Cowan of the Forty-fifth Illinois unwittingly offered a preview of what was to come. "We have marched about ninety miles in eight days," he informed his daughter, "through rain, mud, dust, the hottest kind of weather, without tents to lie in and on short rations, foraging and subsisting the men in great measure on the country. But the men have stood it remarkable well."[68]

Cowan's comments underscore a primary reason for difficulties on the eastward march, particularly in its early stages: a scarcity of rations and other supplies. Men in Stott's brigade bewailed the problem. Sitting in a cornfield about twenty miles south of Vicksburg, the Eighth Indiana's Leeson wrote his father, "We have no tents, but few cooking utensils and but scant provision to cook in them there is no wagons allong only Ammunition and what we capture." He complained that "we have been living on corn meal," which, unfortunately, had given "the Boys" the intestinal "quickstep." Similarly, Lieutenant George Smith of the Thirty-third Illinois

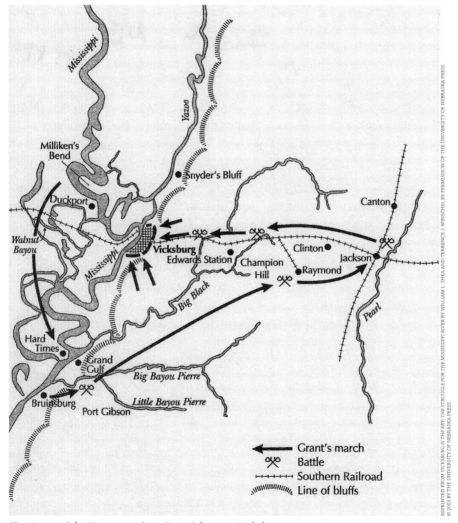

The Army of the Tennessee from Port Gibson to Vicksburg.

remarked that when his unit reached Bruinsburg "we had nothing . . . not even cooking utensils." "Even the officers," he said, "have had a sorry time. Gen. Carr lives on 'hot-cake and sow belly.'" Stott's corps commander, too, felt the pinch. An angry McClernand wrote a series of letters to Grant expressing concern that his corps was being overlooked when it came to allocations of all kinds. "During these thirteen weeks," he later declared in his official report, "my command subsisted on six days' rations and what scanty supply the country in the immediate vicinity of the route afforded." On May 8 McClernand even told Grant that he could not advance "as ordered, because his men did not have rations enough!" That night, however, a train of two hundred wagons arrived with full loads of food and ammunition, and the supply situation began to improve.[69]

Another factor affecting the inland movement, as Winschel observes, was "the availability of water." Unlike the campaign in eastern Louisiana, in which an overabundance of water impeded Grant's progress, the Union forces confronted a perilous lack of water in Mississippi. The number of miles men could march each day, even the direction of their trek, depended on the presence of water. With no rain falling during the first two weeks of May and mostly sultry days, men and animals became easily parched on dusty roads, and small streams ran dry. "Water scarce; weather hot; roads dusty; rations short; houses poor shabby things," a foot soldier succinctly summarized the conditions. On the entire journey from Port Gibson to Jackson to Vicksburg, it only rained appreciably one day, May 14, when Stott said it came "in torrents," creating mud "knee deep" for the next day's march.[70]

Despite these trials and the justifiable laments they elicited, the morale in the Army of the Tennessee was at high levels all the way to Vicksburg. Grant noted that grumbling and straggling were at a minimum. "My force is composed of hardy and disciplined men," Adam Badeau heard Grant say, "who know no defeat and are not willing to learn what it is."[71] The experience of the Eighteenth Indiana and its entire corps demonstrates the accuracy of this assessment. Of the three corps of Grant's army, the XIII was most often in harm's way on the drive east to Jackson, forming the vanguard of the army closest to the Big Black River and thus to Pemberton's forces. As was the case in leading the trek through Louisiana and being in the van across the Mississippi River, McClernand's corps, as Shea and Winschel stress, "was at all times at the point of danger" in its march through Mississippi. Grant's plan, once Sherman's XV Corps arrived, was to have "three parallel columns within supporting distance of each other": McPherson's XVII Corps on the right or southern route, McClernand's on the left or northern, and Sherman's in the center, slightly behind the other two. It was XIII Corps's job to ward off any Confederate attacks on the left flank, a responsibility it fulfilled with exceptional vigilance and courage.[72]

The early stages of the inland campaign were relatively quiet. After its brief stay at Fort Washburn, where it patrolled the northern road leading from Port Gibson to prevent any Confederate encroachment, the Eighteenth and the rest of Benton's brigade moved on to Willow Springs on May 5. There it rejoined the other three divisions of McClernand's corps, and some, including Stott, grabbed a chance to bathe in a small stream. The next day the Eighteenth was on the move again, this time to Rocky Springs, where Grant set up headquarters and continued to plan maneuvers that he hoped would deceive Pemberton. His scheme was to send out detachments and patrols in the direction of Vicksburg, creating the impression that he was headed straight to the fortress city. Meanwhile, he pushed his main forces eastward, to Edwards Station, near Big Black River and along the Southern Railroad, and thus midway between Vicksburg and Jackson. To that end, the pace now quickened, keeping the XIII Corps on the road—to Big Sandy, Cayuga, Five Mile Creek, Old Auburn, and Fourteen Mile Creek, which it reached on May 12 after some stiff resistance from grayclad skirmishers. Union forces were now within seven miles of Edwards Station and a concentrated enemy force. By this point, Sherman had been in Mississippi for several days, the long-awaited supplies had arrived, and, Grant later recorded, "our movements had been made without serious opposition. . . . In all our moves, up to this time, the left had hugged the Big Black closely, and all the ferries had been guarded to prevent the enemy throwing a force in our rear." Bearss calls attention to yet another result of the Union army's northeastward march of May 3–12. By taking that route, Bearss observes, "Grant interposed his corps between the army Pemberton had marshaled for defense of Vicksburg and the rebel forces rumored to be assembled in and around Jackson."[73] This deployment set the stage for a crucial change in Grant's plans.

On May 12, the same day McClernand's corps fought off Confederates at Fourteen Mile Creek, McPherson's XVII Corps soundly defeated Brigadier General John Gregg's Confederates at Raymond in severe and bloody combat. This sent the survivors in gray on a hurried dash for Jackson. At 9:15 that night, Grant sent McClernand word of a new game plan. "I have determined to follow [the fleeing Confederates]," he wrote, "and take first the Capitol of the state." Sherman and McPherson, Grant explained, would go directly to Jackson, and McClernand's orders were to take three of his divisions by way of Dillon's plantation toward Raymond early the next morning to counter any move by Pemberton. McClernand recognized that "the movement ordered was a delicate and hazardous one, but was calculated to deceive the enemy as to our design."[74] While Sherman's and McPherson's men marched to Jackson and battle, the XIII Corps would, in essence, be their reserve force. But, as several historians rightly claim, McClernand's job was the toughest. Not only did he have to split his corps, but his men also had the longest march. In addition, they had to somehow withdraw their vulnerable flank and rear from the proximity of the Confederate stronghold at Edwards Station. Yet, McClernand's sturdy and seasoned western warriors did so, Grant testified, "with much skill and without loss." Leaving Smith's division to maintain position at Fourteen Mile Creek, McClernand sent a portion of Hovey's division toward Edwards Station early on May 13 as a diversion to shield his departure southward. "We marched at 8 o'clock," Ritter of the Fourteenth Iowa wrote, "made an attack on enemy in direction of Edwards Depot. Only a feint attack. Laid in line until noon then left cutting across to within four miles of Raymond." As the feint occurred, the divisions of Carr and Osterhaus left for Raymond, reaching Dillon's plantation near the town around midnight.[75]

That night Grant ordered McClernand to divide his corps again by sending one division northeast to Clinton, another to Mississippi Springs and beyond, and a third to Raymond. McClernand immediately directed his division commanders to advance to the three locations at dawn the following morning, May 14. Osterhaus remained at Raymond to garrison the town. Carr's division, including the Eighteenth Indiana, left for Mississippi Springs with four siege guns and settled at Forest Hill Church, only six miles from Sherman's corps. Hovey proceeded farther north to Clinton to support McPherson only four miles away. This deployment, ranging from Raymond in the south to Bolton in the north, provided an effective shield against any interference from Pemberton and, at the same time, furnished ready reinforcements for the Union forces at Jackson.[76]

Getting the force to its assigned position, however, proved to be the hardest task. A violent, driving rainstorm turned the trek into a mud march. "This was the most fatiguing and exhausting day's march that had been made," McClernand reported. Talk of rain and mud dominated soldiers' diaries and letters. Recounting the trip to Forest Hill Church, Ira Wasson Hunt of the Eleventh Wisconsin told his wife: "We marched at six A.M. Rained all day. The roads were perfectly awful. We were wet to the skin. We marched slowly all day. . . . I could hardly put one foot before another and had to sleep in my wet clothes." His commander, Carr, called it "our hardest march" and noted that not all the division completed the whole twelve miles. Many halts were needed; a member of the Thirty-third Illinois recalled having to stop for three hours at Mississippi Springs before his brigade could continue to Forest Hill Church. But the end of the day brought good news. Grant informed McClernand from Jackson, "Our troops carried this place about three o.clk this p.m. after a brisk fight of about three hours," and the enemy under General Joseph E. Johnston had abandoned the city.[77]

In the same message, Grant indicated that the Confederate forces were seeking to go north of the Union forces and "beat us to Vicksburg." To prevent this, he directed McClernand to "Turn all your focus towards Bolton Station and make all dispatch in getting there." Grant's sense of urgency evidently stemmed from intelligence he had obtained from a Confederate messenger who was, in fact, a Union agent. The courier had delivered to McPherson a copy of a May 13 letter from Johnston to Pemberton, urging the Vicksburg commander to strike at Clinton. Once McClernand got Grant's orders, he wasted no time enforcing them. At daybreak on May 15, the divisions of the XIII Corps were under way. Those of Osterhaus and Hovey moved rapidly toward the railroad village of Bolton, securing it by 9:30 a.m. Carr's troops left Mississippi Springs, marched through Raymond, and then advanced toward Edwards Station. Smith's men followed Major General Frank P. Blair's division of Sherman's corps on a brisk trip to Raymond, where both arrived around 9:00 p.m. Late in the day McClernand reported to Grant that intelligence suggested "the enemy were moving in strong force upon me," especially on the roads from Edwards Station to Bolton and Raymond. His reconnaissance parties ran into "skirmishing at intervals . . . throughout the day, and just before sunset the enemy undertook to feel my positions and force. He was promptly met and repelled."[78]

By dusk May 15, the Army of the Tennessee had seven divisions, 32,000 men, in supporting distance of each other on the three roads leading to Edwards Station: Jackson Road on the north, Raymond Road on the south, and the appropriately named Middle Road in the center. The Eighteenth Indiana camped on the Middle Road, Carr's division quartering just behind that of Osterhaus. The night was quiet, the men felt battle ready, and they would get a full night's rest. As they talked around the campfires, McClernand received further orders. Writing from his Clinton headquarters, Grant instructed the politician-general to move early the next morning, to be on the alert for Pemberton's approach, and, most importantly, to "not bring on an engagement unless he felt certain of success."[79]

At about 5:00 a.m. on May 16 two employees of the Southern Railroad came to see Grant at Clinton. They had come through Pemberton's camp the previous day and learned that the Confederate commander had about 25,000 troops and was planning to attack the Union rear and supply lines. Grant acted on this intelligence promptly, calling on Sherman to move with the greatest possible speed to Bolton and directing McPherson to go rapidly up the Jackson road in support of Hovey. At 5:40 a.m. Grant ordered McClernand to "disencumber yourself of your train, select an eligible position, and feel the enemy" as the rest of the army came up behind him. "The utmost celerity" should be employed, Grant advised, but McClernand was not to "bring on a general engagement till we are entirely prepared." Once again, as McClernand understood it, he was to refrain from attack. Yet his XIII Corps occupied positions on all three roads to Edwards: Hovey on the Jackson road, Osterhaus and Carr on the Middle Road, and Smith with Blair's detachment on the Raymond Road.[80]

Grant's instructions to all his corps commanders were to "move cautiously, with skirmishers to the front to feel for the enemy." This was precisely what McClernand did, having some of his troops on the march even before he got Grant's message. The divisions of Osterhaus and Carr, with the Eighteenth Indiana in the latter unit, moved carefully, but without hindrance, on the Middle Road. All seemed quiet. But a little after 7:00 a.m., firing could be heard off to the left on the Raymond road, Smith and Blair having encountered enemy skirmishers and begun an artillery duel. Hearing the cannonading, Osterhaus pressed forward but still slowly, with Carr held in reserve. Brigadier General Michael K. Lawler of Carr's Second Brigade reported that at midmorning "heavy artillery and skirmish firing was heard in our front," Osterhaus having come upon "the enemy strongly posted on a range of hills bordering Baker's Creek." Lawler's brigade remained "a few hundred yards to the rear" on the left of the road with Benton's on the right. In late morning, Osterhaus's force came to a halt because of difficult terrain, a stubborn Confederate defense line, and consistent orders to move with utmost caution. Meanwhile, on the Jackson Road, Hovey's men and those of Major General John A. Logan of McPherson's corps launched a full-scale assault on the sturdy defense lines of Brigadier Generals Stephen Dill Lee and Alfred Cummings on Champion Hill, just south of the large plantation of Sidney and Matilda Champion. This "hill of death," as it became known, was the highest point on the battlefield and witnessed the heaviest and bloodiest combat of the day.[81]

With the roar of artillery, the crack of musketry, and the shouts of fighting men all around them, the troops on the Middle Road could not understand why they were not being sent into action. As Steven E. Woodworth notes, they were "studies in passivity." Years later, a soldier in Stott's brigade recalled how perplexed his comrades felt. "For four hours we stood there listening, waiting and wondering why we were not put into the fight," wrote the veteran of the Thirty-third Illinois. "Fifteen minutes would have put us into the battle any time that day. It was a matter of speculation at the time, and long afterward." In disbelief, Herrington of the Eighth Indiana, who was even closer to the battle lines, recorded that his men "layed down by a hill near the hardest fighting and was so anxious and ready but was not ordered up till in the afternoon."[82]

Only later would they learn the reasons for their inactivity on the Middle Road. A primary factor was their commander's dogged adherence to Grant's orders "not to bring on a general engagement" until all forces were fully ready. Consequently, the normally aggressive McClernand waited for further orders, concentrating early in the day on the only command he could control—that on the Middle Road—and contenting himself with the exchange of skirmish fire between Osterhaus and Confederate sharpshooters. Sometime before 9:30, Hovey sent word to McClernand that the enemy on Champion Hill was "strongly posted in front" of Hovey's division and asked if he should "bring on an impending battle." McClernand, having learned that Grant was moving toward Hovey's position, referred the issue to his superior officer. He forwarded a letter to Grant regarding Hovey's situation, suggesting McPherson "should move up to the support of Hovey," and then asking, "Should I hold or bring on an engagement?" Because his courier chose not to "cut across country," but to take a round-about course over the Bolton and Jackson roads, and since confusion reigned on the battlefield at Grant's location, McClernand's query did not arrive in Grant's hands until 12:30 p.m. At 12:35 Grant replied, ordering McClernand to "throw forward skirmishers and feel the enemy, and attack him in force if the opportunity occurs." He added, "I am with Hovey and McPherson, and will see that they fully co-operate." Since McClernand was only a few miles away, Grant assumed his senior corps commander would receive his orders quickly. He did not. The message did not reach McClernand until about 2:30 p.m., at which time he ordered Osterhaus and Smith to "attack the enemy vigorously and press for victory" with Carr's and Blair's support.[83]

These orders brought the Eighteenth Indiana directly into the fray. The men of Osterhaus's and Carr's divisions pressed forward until they were several hundred yards from the crossroads where the Middle and the Jackson roads intersected. At that point, sometime between three and four o'clock, Grant rode up to find "the skirmishers of Carr's division just coming in." As Osterhaus arrived from the south, Grant ordered Carr "to pursue vigorously as far as the Big Black, and to cross it if he could; Osterhaus to follow him." This now gave Grant a solid line of assault. A key portion of it was Stott's unit, Benton's brigade. It reached the left flank of General Bowen's division, which, after hours of rough fighting, was drained of energy and ammunition. Getting within artillery range, Benton called forth Captain Martin Klauss's First Indiana Light Battery. The Hoosiers poured heavy fire into the Confederate lines, prompting Bowen to withdraw rapidly toward Big Black River Bridge. Likewise, General Stephen Lee saw Benton's column coming quickly and, "having had enough fighting for one day," sent his Alabamans in the same direction.[84]

The remainder of the battle was a bloody race for Edwards Station. The regiments rushed "forward through as thick woods and underbrush as you ever saw," Hobbs related, "through ponds of water and across deep gullies, over the railroad embankments and cuts, . . . in cornfields and oat fields." And they ran over other objects as well. Herrington, Eighth Indiana, said, "we could have stepped on bodies of the rebels for 50 yards or farther where they had made a desperate stand . . . it does look terrible." A private in the Thirty-third Illinois noticed that death showed no partiality. "One could walk for many rods by stepping alternately upon the dead body of a Union soldier and then upon that of a Confederate," he wrote. Hobbs observed the same mixture as he passed a captured battery: "A moment's halt here has the power to make me sick—the only time I felt this sickness at all. I grew heartsick at the carnage. Yes, carnage is the word."[85]

Leaving the "hill of death," Benton's brigade was the first to arrive at Edwards Station, reaching it around 8:00 p.m. Hobbs heard "the continual report of shells bursting" as the soldiers approached the town, as if "somebody was using artillery in front of us still, and Gen. Carr, Steele and Benton wonder and swear a little." When the Union troops entered the village limits they discovered that the retreating Confederates had set afire a cotton gin and railroad cars filled with ammunition and supplies. The weary bluecoats spent much of the night helping residents extinguish the flames, their last act in the battle of Champion Hill, considered by many chroniclers to be *the* decisive battle of the Vicksburg Campaign, and perhaps of the entire Civil War.[86]

The next day, though, brought yet another critical engagement. Carr's men were up and on the road westward by 3:30 a.m., after sampling the few rations available for breakfast—for some, just cornmeal mush in a tin cup. Their food was sparse but not their enthusiasm, for they were eager to follow up the victory of the day before. Again Benton's troops led the way, slowly and cautiously until daylight dawned. The evidence of the hasty Confederate retreat—cartridge boxes, knapsacks, and even stragglers left behind—prompted more rapid movement. Some four miles out of Edwards Station, Union skirmishers began attracting enemy fire, and soon they saw a milelong and strongly fortified Confederate entrenchment at the railroad bridge across Big Black River. They sent word back to Carr who hastily deployed forces on both sides of the railroad tracks, forming the right of the Union line with Lawler's brigade at the extreme right near the river.[87]

Facing the formidable Confederate breastworks, the Thirty-third Illinois, as skirmishers, and Klauss's Hoosier battery formed "in an old cottonfield," Herrington wrote, with "5 lines of Battle behind us." "As soon as our batteries was in position," he continued, "they commenced the fun we were ordered to lay down and we obeyed orders the balls Shots and shells flew over us fast and thick." Leeson, also of the Eighth Indiana, agreed. "I lay as close to the ground as I could get," he told his father. "One Shot would have hit me if I had been Standing but my nose was in the ground." As this heavy barrage persisted, the six-foot, three hundred-pound Lawler, whose motto was "if you see a head, hit it!" unleashed his brigade from its position inside the tree line on the far right. In a charge McClernand called "eminently brilliant," the coatless Irishman, yelling at the top of his voice and swinging his sword above his head, led his troops, with bayonets fixed and on the double-quick, directly at the Confederate left flank. According to those who followed him, the assault was "through a perfect sheet of lead and hail which left near one half of our men on the field," some from pure exhaustion. The rest stayed behind their burly chief over a cotton field and through a "muddy, shoulder-deep bayou," sweeping the enemy before them. The attack, with the full support of Benton's brigade, took just three minutes—one of the shortest of the war. Grant noted that there was little resistance and the Confederates "fled the west bank of the river, burning the bridge behind them." The charge confirmed an earlier assessment by Grant: "When it comes to just plain hard fighting, I would rather trust old Mike Lawler than any of them."[88]

The triumph at Black River Bridge on May 17 opened the way to Vicksburg. With eighteen Confederate guns and 1,751 prisoners in their possession, Union troops set out at once to build a new bridge across the river, working all night on a temporary span. By daybreak, May 18, troops began to cross it, flags flying, and accompanied by martial airs from a brass band. The XIII Corps initially proceeded up the Jackson Road, then turned left and took Baldwin's Ferry Road to Vicksburg. This brought McClernand's men to a position southeast of the city, while McPherson settled due east and Sherman to the north in closer contact with the navy on the Mississippi River. By nightfall of May 18, the XIII Corps was within two miles of Vicksburg, and Union pickets along its eastern perimeter were exchanging shots with Confederate defenders. The struggle for the Confederate Gibraltar had begun.[89]

As Union troops reached the outskirts of Vicksburg, Grant met with his corps commanders. All believed that the fortress city could be taken by a strong, forceful storming of its defenses. After all, the Southern soldiers had to be worn out and demoralized, especially after Champion Hill and Black River Bridge. Only Grant had reservations about an assault. He knew that Confederates had repeatedly shown an amazing capacity to rebound from defeat, and, as Grabau puts it, "time was on their side." Any delay could result in a recovery of morale for the men in gray. Then, of course, there were those defenses lining the city in a tightly woven semicircle. True, they had stood there unoccupied for months, and the wet winter had broken them down somewhat, but they were still awesome to the eyes of Union soldiers. To call them "formidable" was an understatement. "A long line of high, rugged, irregular bluffs, clearly cut against the sky, crowned with cannon which peered ominously from embrasures to the right and left as far as the eye could see" was how W. E. Strong of McPherson's staff described them. "Lines of rifle-pits, surmounted with head logs, ran along the bluffs, connecting fort with fort, and filled with veteran infantry. . . . The approaches to this position were frightful—enough to appall the stoutest heart." And the defenses ran from the Mississippi River on the south to the Mississippi River on the north, completely surrounding the city. They contained, not only rifle pits and trenches, but also redoubts, lunettes, and redans—fortifications with thick parapets and deep, wide ditches in their fronts, lined with abatis (interlaced timber, brush, and tree tops). Carr's division faced two such positions: the Railroad Redoubt, protecting the Southern Railroad, and the Second Texas Lunette, a smaller fort that guarded the Baldwin's Ferry Road.[90]

Given these facts, Grant decided to go forward with an assault the next day, May 19. He knew the confidence level of his men was high and that of the enemy was depressed. Under those conditions a quick attack could succeed, particularly since, in the words of Ballard, Grant "knew his men wanted to finish the job." On the night of May 18 he alerted his commanders to his plan and the next morning issued Special Field Order

No. 134. It called for all corps to get into position as close as possible to the Confederate works and charge them at 2:00 p.m. Every corps found it difficult to attain a good position on the morning of May 19, for the terrain resembled that of Port Gibson. McClernand rode forward and discovered that he was three thousand yards from the earthworks, with tangled brush on ridges and ravines in between, and his corps would remain at too great a distance to accomplish much. Nonetheless, at precisely 2:00, three artillery volleys signaled the attack. By then McClernand's line had moved only "a half mile and was within 800 yards of the enemy's works." He was proud that his men "bravely continued a wasting conflict," eventually getting "within 500 yards of the enemy's lines." During it all, Stott's regiment remained in reserve along Baldwin's Ferry Road and thus saw no action. It did advance to the hill overlooking the Confederate line, far enough, Stott wrote, for "shot and shell" to come "over and around us thick and fast." The assault failed, however, at every point along the lengthy defense line. A Confederate artilleryman looked out upon fields "blue with Yankee dead and wounded."[91]

Evidently Confederate morale was not as low as Grant assumed, and certainly the strength of Confederate defenses was greater than anticipated. While Union soldiers used the night of May 19 to erect their own works around artillery emplacements, Confederates burned houses fronting their lines to open fields of fire in anticipation of further attacks. Grant met with his senior commanders on Saturday, May 20, for what Sherman called "a mere consultation" during which Grant ordered his officers to make necessary arrangements "for a renewed assault on the twenty-second at 10 A.M." The next two days Union soldiers of every corps readied their positions. "Carr's men dug like badgers all that night [May 20]," Bearss writes, "and when dawn arrived on the 21st, the Texans in the Rebel works were astonished to find a line of rifle-pits extending almost continuously across their front." Stott's Franklin comrade, Knobe, exulted in the progress that brought his brigade "about three forths of a mile from the rebel works" and that the whole army had a "Line of battle from one side of the river to the other 12 miles in Length." Steamboats brought new supplies, foodstuffs arrived at the front, ladders came for use in the assault, and soldiers confiscated buildings to be used as hospitals. And Grant made his decision: with Johnston's Confederates "only fifty miles away" and possibly sending Pemberton reinforcements, it was time to attack. "But the first consideration of all" in Grant's thinking was that "the troops believed they could carry the works in their front, and would not have worked so patiently in the trenches if they had not been allowed to try."[92]

The soldiers of the Army of the Tennessee may have been eager to grab the prize called Vicksburg, but few of them slept well the night of May 21. As mortar shells spewed forth from Union gunboats on the river and fell on Vicksburg, many troops busily arranged for their most precious keepsakes-—letters, rings, watches, pictures of loved ones—to be placed in the hands of someone who could get them to their folks back home in case they should not survive the next day. At dawn on May 22— Stott's twenty-seventh birthday—the guns along the Union line opened on the Confederate emplacements. Where the XIII Corps lay in wait, McClernand recorded, "three 30, six 20, and six 10 pounder Parrotts (in all thirty-nine guns)" belched forth grape and canister in "a well-directed and effective fire . . . breaking the enemy's works at several points." Corps commanders had synchronized their watches so they could simultaneously launch their units forward at precisely 10:00. The colonels of Benton's brigade drew lots to determine which regiment would lead the charge on the Second Texas Lunette. The Ninety-ninth Illinois had the "post of honor," followed by the Thirty-third Illinois, then the Eighth and Eighteenth Indiana. Carr, in tactical command of his division's assault, chose Lawler's brigade to head the attack on the Railroad Redoubt. As for the soldiers, Stott noted that "Some faces of men were pale, but determined." Herrington observed two men of the Eighth Indiana who "went up in the bushes got down on their knees & prayed that they might be spared in this terrible charge." Some had more solemn thoughts. Hobbs, destined to charge with the lead regiment, wrote candidly, "well we know it is the last some of us will have to live," and the Eighth Indiana's Leeson told his father, "everyone I Spoke to Said they knew that we never could take the works and it would be nothing but a slaughter."[93] Sadly, Leeson's words proved to be all too true.

At 10:00 the Union bombardment abruptly ceased, leaving a momentary silence that Confederate General Stephen Lee, at the Railroad Redoubt, found "almost appalling." Then the soldiers of the XIII Corps burst forth from their sheltered positions and, as one body, streamed double-quick toward the enemy fortifications. They appeared to Lee "to spring

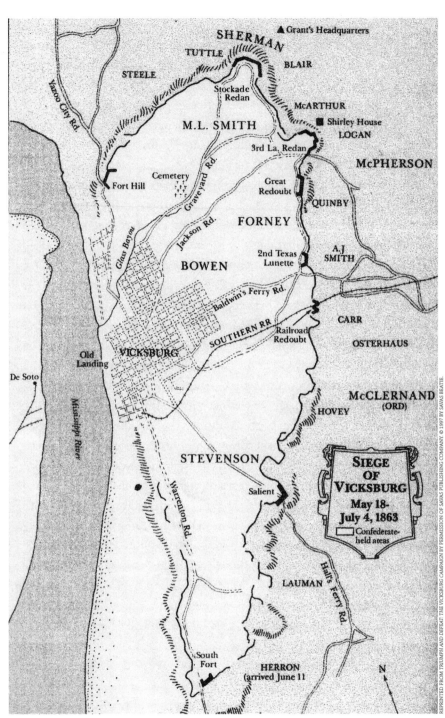

The Siege of Vicksburg.

almost from the bowels of the earth, dense masses of Federal troops, in numerous columns of attack, and with loud cheers and huzzahs, they rushed forward at a run." They formed "a swarm of blue," he said, transforming the color of the landscape and charging "with the determination of a machine gone wild." Lawler's brigade, supported by that of Colonel William J. Landram of Smith's division, made perhaps the fiercest assault of McClernand's corps that morning. Storming the Railroad Redoubt with about forty fifteen- to twenty-foot ladders for scaling the fort's walls, the Union force sought out the redoubt's most vulnerable points. About a dozen Iowans penetrated a spot that had been battered down by artillery, clambered inside the fortification, and engaged in hand-to-hand combat. But increasingly heavy Confederate fire forced them back through the same opening they had entered. The Confederate counterattack gained in ferocity all along the walls of the redoubt, pushing the Union lines into its surrounding ditch and beyond. "We were exposed to a murderous fire from the front and each side," Hunt wrote his wife the next day. "They threw lead at us of all shapes." In the failed assault, Lawler's brigade left 54 dead and 285 wounded on the ground in front of the fortification—the heaviest losses in the corps.[94]

Four hundred yards to the north, Stott's brigade under Benton launched itself at the Second Texas Lunette. Like most lunettes, though shaped somewhat irregularly, it had four faces broken by three salient angles and a deep ditch at its front. Toward the foremost of the looming angles, the Ninety-ninth Illinois led the charge, some screaming "Vicksburg or hell!" The Eighteenth Indiana, according to Captain James Black of Company H, was slated to stay in reserve "because of the excessive loss [it] suffered" at Port Gibson. This assignment, however, did not last long, for the Eighteenth was soon needed. McClernand reported that Benton's brigade, supported by that of Brigadier General Stephen G. Burbridge, "fired by the example" of Lawler's early success at the nearby Railroad Redoubt, "rushed forward and carried the ditch and slope" of the lunette, "and planted their colors upon the latter." This reference was to the heroic action of the color-bearer of the Ninety-ninth Illinois, Thomas Higgins, who carried his regiment's banner all the way to the Confederate trench line while tripping over the bodies of fallen comrades. His valor so stunned the grayclad defenders that they shouted to their fellow compatriots not to "shoot at that brave man again," and to Higgins, "Come on, Yank, come on!" The lad reached the top of the parapet only to be greeted by a row of bayonets aimed at his heart. Though he became a prisoner, his courage earned him a Congressional Medal of Honor.[95]

As this dramatic event unfolded, many of the charging Union line fell like wheat struck down by scythes. Two men of the Ninety-ninth Illinois recorded the impact of Confederate shot and shell. Hobbs noted that the regiment found itself "under the galling fire of infantry behind the breastworks, and the cross fire of three forts so situated as to command each other and deal death to an advancing foe with terrible certainty." Looking around as he ran, he saw "our brave boys dropping around me, and how anyone could escape seems but an interposition of providence." Captain Asa G. Matthews recalled years later that "over a third, and possibly a half of the men of that regiment, who reached the road, were shot down and either killed or wounded." He went on to report that the first three of Benton's rushing regiments "received no support until the 18th Ind. . . . cautiously moved up the hill in our rear."[96]

Once the Eighteenth arrived on the battlefield, it fought with grim resolve. Colonel Frederick W. Moore of the Eighty-third Ohio, which "maintained the same line" with the Eighteenth, saw the Hoosiers in action. "By a vigorous fire they for a time prevented any serious reply from the enemy in front," he reported, but they "were soon exposed to enfilading artillery fire from the forts, both to the right and left, and suffered from it to a considerable extent." Out in front of the Eighteenth was Major John C. Jenks of Newport, a member of Benton's staff and one of the most respected officers in the brigade. Waving his sword above his head and pressing his men forward, he received a mortal shot in his right thigh. Grape and shell came thick and fast as the men of the Eighteenth, "standing crowded along the front of the lunette . . . on the glacis and in the road," assisted the Chicago Mercantile Battery by "drawing up" their gun with rope to a position within thirty feet of the fort. There, reported McClernand, it poured double-shot fire into one of the lunette's embrasures.[97]

Stott's most vivid memory of the day, though, was his experience in the ditch at the foot of the lunette. Bearss indicates that fifty men of the Eighteenth Indiana "succeeded in gaining the ditch fronting the lunette, while the remainder crowded up to its edge, Sergeant Francis M.

Foss planting the colors there." Stott was among those who entered the ditch. At the time, said Black, the regiment was "marching by the flank and moved into a gully that led directly to the last ditch of the redoubt, a considerable number from different companies jumping into the deep and wide ditch, where they were out of sight of those who remained on the glacis." Once in the trench, the men fired incessantly upon the ramparts and gun emplacements above them, harassing the Confederate defenders. Hurt by this offensive, the Confederates placed a bale of cotton into the embrasure of one gun. This prompted the Hoosiers, Black recalled, "to set fire to it by putting on top of their bullets wads of tow taken from artillery cartridges, with which tow the men had provided themselves for the purposes of cleaning their guns."[98]

Trapped in this precarious and dangerous place, the soldiers in the ditch discovered that they could neither get out safely on any side nor, as Stott stated in his diary, "scale the fort." With the enemy "watching us closely," he wrote, the Hoosiers' only recourse was to keep up the fire "on that part of the fort where we saw shots come from." But, being pinned down, his comrades were being killed or wounded at his side. In May 1902, when the Vicksburg National Military Park Association sought to ascertain how the soldiers escaped this death trap, Black encouraged its secretary, William T. Rigby, to write "Rev. W. L. [sic] Stott, D.D., President of Franklin College" for information. In March 1903 Stott wrote Rigby on his college letterhead, relating his experience as his brigade "started up the ravine toward the Confederate works." Colonel George K. Bailey, leading the Ninety-ninth Illinois, was wounded, he said, "Col. (Park) was scared like a hare," and confusion reigned. Stott then proceeded to explain how he and his comrades made it out of the trench:

> After we had been in the ditch a short time we saw clearly that we could not get out, for the Confederates were pouring a hot fire into us. The only commissioned officer with us was First Lieut. G. W. Kimball of Co. F 18 Ind. He came to me, for I had known him well, and I suggested that we must dispatch to the regiment; accordingly, we placed the dispatch and some balls in a silk kerchief which I happened to have, and threw it toward the Regiment; in a short time a dispatch was thrown back saying that the Regiment would keep up a brisk fire and we must crawl out under the fire. This we did, but with the loss of several comrades.
> Shortly after we were out the ditch was filled with Confederate hand-grenades.

In a subsequent letter, Black told Rigby that, once they received adequate cover, the men who were not too badly injured "made holes in the side of the ditch, and climbed out among the men in front of the ditch."[99]

Like the assault of May 19, that of May 22 failed abysmally at every point along the Confederate defense line. Not a single Confederate fortification fell, and Union losses were horrendous. Grant sent 40,000 troops into the fray and lost 502 killed, 2,550 wounded, and 147 missing; total Confederate casualties were about 500. James R. Arnold contends that it was "the fourth costliest Union assault of the war," only Fredericksburg, Cold Harbor, and the Crater at Petersburg being more devastating. Edward Stanfield of the Forty-eighth Indiana called it an "assault made contrary to the dictates of common sence [sic] & the opinion of everyone," and an Iowa soldier, Henry Ankeny, saw it as "a useless expenditure of life." The costly bloodshed of that May Friday did make it clear, though, that Vicksburg could only be taken by siege. Ankeny noted that the failure "satisfied our generals that the enemy works cannot be taken by storm." But, whether by assault or siege, most Union soldiers were still certain that Vicksburg would fall. Laying "under the Vicksburg fortifications," James Leeper of the Forty-ninth Indiana wrote his wife, "Its defenders are obstinate and determined but no more so than our own men who are now sanguine of success. . . . The place must succumb, we are determined." Likewise, Gordon of the Eighteenth Indiana confided in his diary on May 24, "Our loss on the 22nd was awful," yet "we have gained everything but this place and we will get it by time and fighting."[100]

Gordon's assessment of what it would take to capture Vicksburg— "time and fighting"—was strikingly accurate. It would take six long weeks of digging, constructing approaches, launching artillery bombardments, sharpshooting, planting mines, and living in trenches to gain the objective. Some of it began the night of May 22, as Woodworth suggests, even "before the last shots had been fired" in the futile assaults. Soldiers started digging in wherever they ended up at nightfall, whether near the enemy's works or back in the rear in safer places. Along the line occupied by Carr's division, the survivors of the fights at the Railroad Redoubt and Second Texas Lunette were anywhere from within ten to sixty yards of the enemy's ditches. On May 23 Knobe wrote of his Hoosier company, which included his friend, Stott: "our sharpshooters have advanced so near the enemys fort that they have . . . full power of disabling the rebel cannoneers from Loading their guns by keeping up constant firing into their port holes while at the same time our Land batteries are taking advantage of throwing shells into their forts and rifel pits." Six days later Surgeon George F. Chittenden of the Sixteenth Indiana told his wife about "digging every night Since we came." The result was that "each night we approach the Enemy a little with a Strong breastwork that completely protects our Soldiers." The official orders for these activities did not come until May 25, when Grant directed his corps commanders to "commence the work of reducing the enemy by regular approaches," hopefully with few Union casualties.[101]

That same day Pemberton sent a flag of truce and requested a halt in the firing to allow Grant to remove his dead and dying troops who still lay in the scorching sun on fields or in trenches or ditches. Not only was it hard for soldiers of both armies to witness the carnage, but the stench had also become unbearable. As one Southerner put it, "the Yanks are trying to stink us out of Vicksburg." From 6:00 p.m. until about 8:30 p.m., as flags of truce flew and men in blue carried out their grisly task, grayclad troops came on the field and exchanged greetings and taunts with those they had fired at only three days before. To some degree, this fraternization lessened the horror of burying blackened and swollen corpses, many unidentifiable and some "piled up alternately cross-wise." Knobe commented on the "quite friendly chats" the enemies had with each other. Others observed blue and gray exchanging coffee, tobacco, or liquor, and four from the opposing armies even started a card game. In a few cases, relatives, estranged by their national loyalties—fathers, sons, brothers, cousins—had brief reunions. But then, as Knobe recalled, "as soon as time had run out the ball was again open as hard as ever trying to shoot each other's head of[f]."[102]

As the siege developed, Union forces slowly and determinedly tightened the noose around the Confederate stronghold. As one chronicler describes it, "there was a routine of systematic strangulation." It was a matter of digging some thirteen separate approaches all along the Confederate lines. The goal of the operations, writes Ballard, was "to crack the defensive perimeter," and thus draw closer and closer to the enemy's works. When the process began, Grant noted, the Union lines were "six hundred yards from the enemy," but the approach at Carr's position, aimed at the Railroad Redoubt, reduced the distance to within eighty yards by mid-June. To protect the "sappers," those who dug the "saps" (the offensive trenches used to undermine Confederate fortifications) and placed mines at their terminal points, soldiers put bulletproof sandbags atop their parapets "far enough apart to make loop-holes for musketry," and then set logs above the bags. In addition, a shield called a "sap-roller"—a cylindrical object resembling a wicker basket thick enough to ward off bullets— was placed in front of the sappers as they toiled. Understandably, troops found this work tedious and unappealing, so they seldom left accounts of their labors. Some from Benton's brigade, however, were exceptions. Swain Marshall of the Eighth Indiana, for example, told his sister on June 8 that he had "dug rifle pits closer to their works" and was "within fifty yards of their fort," even though "there is bullets whistling over our heads all the time." The Eighteenth Indiana's Denny wrote his parents two days later, "We are tuneling under their Forts and Nearly Done the tunels and there Will Be one of the Biggest Blows up here Some of these Days." And Amos York of the Eighth Indiana recalled the work schedule. "We was on gard one night," he said, "then rested the next night. We were on duty every other night of the Seage."[103]

Along with the efforts to push closer to the Confederate forts and literally undermine them, came the daily thunder of artillery and the endless "banging away" of sharpshooters. Both dominated the consciousness of soldiers and their comments in diaries and letters. Perhaps Oliver H. Hunt's correspondence appearing in the *Ottawa* (IL) *Free Trader* best captured the routine. "From sunrise to sunset," he remarked, "there is one constant and continuous cannonading going on, and this is also accompanied with constant fire of musketry and rifles." Naturally, the artillery barrages came from both sides and reached long distances; troops in the Union rear were in as much danger as the soldiers and citizens in the heart of Vicksburg. Some Union soldiers found the exchange fascinating, while others felt that it "made timid hair on our head stand upright." Daniel Roberts of the Eighth Indiana gave his folks a lengthy and graphic description of the bombardment from the river, depicting the slow climb of a mortar shell as "a glim spark like a meteor half aglow." Then, he said, the sound of "the discharge would come swinging along the air with a sullen boom" as the shell "hangs for a moment as if poised" before "accelerating its velocity" as it plummeted to earth. The sensitive Roberts reminded his family, though, of what such warfare meant for noncombatants. Not only were houses destroyed, and animals and men killed, but also "the women and children are burrowing through the bowels of the city, like the ancient Christians through the catacombs of Rome." Occasionally, officers and soldiers in the trenches also had closer encounters with the fruits of artillery than they wanted. "The Rebels sent me their complements this day in the shape of a 64 pound percussion shell," Gordon of the Eighteenth recorded. It landed only five feet from the doctor but never exploded, so he "picked it hot" and placed it under his cot as a souvenir.[104]

Although cannonading occurred round the clock, save for a silent lull now and then, sharpshooting was largely a daytime phenomenon. It was far more personal, the targets being individual soldiers. Union soldiers became adept at firing through the holes between sandbags and then ducking down instantly, since Confederate sharpshooters were equally talented at using puffs of smoke as targets. Knobe was amazed on May 24 that the Confederates had done little firing, but he reasoned that "it is well they don't for every time one shoes [shows] his head there is not less than fifty shots fired at him." Another soldier said that during the day "not even a hand could be safely raised above the parapets." In mid-June Peirce wrote his beloved Kitty (Catharine) several times, calling war "a strange thing," with a shot being fired "every 5 minutes . . . and the muskets are all the time firing and sound for all the world like a wood-chopping." As their rifle pits got within "40 or 50 yards of the reble breast works," Peirce and his company would lie in the pits "and if a reble shows himself we shoot him." With Union soldiers ordered to fire "a designated number of rounds each day," sharpshooting became commonplace and bruised shoulders a fact of life.[105]

Amid these daily stresses of the siege, troops sought ways to cope. The continuous threat of death or incapacitating injury was accompanied by debilitating heat, a siege much longer than anticipated, invasions of lice and larger mosquitoes than up North, sickness from inadequate diet and polluted water, and an exhausting monotony that caused listlessness. But the men in blue found ways to live with it all. Soldiers on picket duty often conversed across the lines, sharing news stories, jokes, or food with their Confederate counterparts. During the evenings there would be dialogues from trench to trench, often poking fun at each other. When a

Yankee asked how the Confederates felt about their new general, a gray-clad defender queried, "What General?" "Why General Starvation," came the reply. The more such conversations occurred, the more the Union forces learned about their enemy's plight. "The reble soldiers are all tired of the war," and feel "uneasy," Peirce told Kitty. "They are getting hungry . . . and our Pickets gave theirs cracke[r]s and coffee nearly every night as they seem almost starved." Besides fraternization, soldiers wrote and received letters, studied their Bibles, had visits and obtained supplies and provisions from agents of the Sanitary and Christian Commissions (including Stott's uncle, James Vawter), perused readily available newspapers, and played cards or chuck-a-luck. The latter game involved gambling, and one Confederate groused, "I always noticed that chuck won and luck always lost." One particular event undoubtedly caused a distraction and provided grist for conversation in the XIII Corps. On June 20 Stott noted in his diary: "Gen. McClernand is relieved by Maj. Gen. E. O. C. Ord. Gen's Grant and McClernand could not see eye to eye."[106]

Two weeks later, as the siege ended its sixth week, some in the XIII Corps witnessed a moment that changed the course of the war. On Friday morning, July 3, everything was unusually quiet. There was no firing. One could hear the scraping of the sappers as they widened the tunnel leading to the Second Texas Lunette, but just barely, and only if you were a picket close to their location. At ten o'clock Herrington, Eighth Indiana, was on guard in his "corner in the Rifle pits," when suddenly "out came three men horseback with a flag of truce they came out on the North side of the fort the one our men was undermining." The cocking of rifles could be heard up and down the line, all pointed at the riders. Two of the horsemen rode forward, and the officer in charge of the pickets asked what they wanted. The reply was that the two Confederates were sent to meet with Grant about terms of surrender. Ushered behind the lines, the two officers introduced themselves as Major General John S. Bowen and Lieutenant Colonel Louis M. Montgomery. They handed Smith a letter from Pemberton asking for a brief armistice to allow commissioners from each army to negotiate capitulation in order "to save further effusion of blood." Grant received the message but denied the request. "The useless effusion of blood you propose stopping by this course," he informed Pemberton, "can be ended at any time you may choose, by the unconditional surrender of the city and garrison." Naturally, the news of this interchange spread quickly to all parts of the Union line. Officers and soldiers, Grant recalled, felt that all their efforts were coming to a close "and the Union sure to be saved."[107]

At three o'clock that afternoon, Grant and Pemberton, along with their corps commanders and staffs, met about a mile from the place where the flag of truce first appeared five hours earlier. Near what Grant called "a stunted oak-tree," the two commanders approached each other with hesitant steps and clearly different perceptions of what should occur. Their words led to an impasse. Bowen, a former neighbor of Grant's at Saint Louis, suggested that Grant and Pemberton draw aside to converse while the subordinate officers talked about the deadlock. Since there were, as Arnold notes, "too many sticking points, prickly issues of honor and substantive details," all agreed to end discussion and allow Grant to restate his surrender terms by 10:00 that night.[108]

In accordance with orders, Union soldiers greeted the next day, July 4, by firing blank-cartridge salutes to the national holiday. Atop the parapets of Union and Confederate entrenchments soldiers eyed each other in wonder over what their superiors had resolved. Stott walked from battery to battery, checking on their placement and personnel. As he returned to his unit he "heard more than ordinary bustle in the regiment." He then peered out at five miles of small white flags above the Confederate works. It was 10:00 a.m., and Herrington, in shirt sleeves in his corner again, saw the flags go up, some of them "bunches of cotton and anything white." Moments later Confederate troops emerged in front of their forts and began stacking arms, and the Stars and Stripes ascended above a Confederate entrenchment. Soldiers of both armies "mingled freely together," the effect of which, Stanfield exclaimed, "has been wonderful." Diaries and letters told the story succinctly: "July 4th! I am now able to give you the glorious tidings of the *capture of Vicksburg*"; "The Gibraltar of America has fallen"; "Vicksburg is ours"; "Happy is no name for our joy. . . . Hurrah, Hurrah for the Old Flag!" Stott, Herrington, and countless others streamed into the empty, decimated city even before the army made its grand entry at 12:30 p.m. with its marching ranks, martial airs, and unfurled colors. Stott and Herrington saw the "Star Spangled Banner raised" above the courthouse as Grant and Porter shook hands beneath it and "Saluted the Soldiers on shore and the navy on the Boats." They no doubt also winced at the unbelievable devastation throughout the city, as did other men in blue. Daniel Roberts, of Herrington's regiment, wrote that there was not "a place 10 ft. square, but what has been struck with a ball of some kind. . . . I never seen such a cry for something to eat in my life as their [*sic*] is among the prisoners & citizens." And William Winters of the Sixty-seventh Indiana saw homes that mortar shells penetrated "straight down through the roof to the cellar."[109]

Vicksburg was Stott's home for more than a month. On July 5, as the rest of the Eighteenth Indiana followed Sherman back to Jackson to secure that city again, Stott was placed "in charge of the convalescent camp," where eighty-two sick or wounded soldiers required care. During these weeks, Stott saw much of Vicksburg, burial grounds, huge Confederate cannons on the waterfront, and military red tape. He also found time to read and reflect on the issues of the day, including the equality of slave and free in God's eyes. On July 29 he became Captain William T. Stott of Company I, Eighteenth Indiana.[110]

5

Diary: April 8, 1862–August 20, 1863

[April] 8th [1862]

Traverse romantic country. The pine forests are nice, absolutely. We passed most of the road on a mountain range.

The ever-changing view which so winding a road gave added greatly to the beauty. The soldier though it is often thought that he beholds forms of beauty with the "eye of an ox" really appreciates many of the beauties of nature. It can be told by the brightness of his eye, and the cheerfulness of his whole being. At noon camp at Flat-Creek. I think it's time I was having a letter from home and Miss LM. Eddelman will return soon.

9th

March again today.

10th

Camped a mile south of Galena. Crossed the river on a wagon-bridge. Called camp Goodnews. News came of the fall of Island No. 10 the capture of six thousand prisoners and more small arms, and one hundred pieces artillery.[1] Saw here the burial of a citizen. He died of Dyspepsia. His neighbor drew the corps[e] to the burying place on an ox wagon. The train of mourners was meager enough. There was none at all. His neighbor had nothing but a <u>hoe</u> to bury him with.

11th

Camp on Bull Creek (not Bull Run) within 8 miles of Forsythe. A recruit came to Co. "F" through Forsythe. He reports 1,600 Secesh cavalry there.

12th

The sun is actually shining today.

13th

Gambling at <u>Chuckaluck</u> is almost universal. Some who said that they never would gamble have been driven into the vortex.

Principle is neglected, and whatever is popular has made adherents.

I must confess that I am tired of this kind of soldiering. It is more like the life of an ox than of an intelligent human being. But this is not saying that I would falter in my efforts for the suppression of the Rebellion.

14th

Secretary Stanton has publicly acknowledged the valor of the Western Troops. He mentions several of our recent victories. The chaplains throughout the army are to publicly acknowledge our thanks to God for our recent victories.

Maj. Thomas says that we shall be home by middle May next. Hempstead and Daniels have deserted. Wrote to Wallace. Listened to a sermon from the Chaplain 22nd Indiana. The theme was The blessings of Peace. The analysis was not clear. He tried to establish the proposition that Peace is normal. I know that all history is but the record of wars.[2]

15th

Start up Bulls Creek. Cross it this day 27 times. Camp in an old peach orchard, which was planted many years ago. A very nice family of refugees camps with us. "Old Cooper Has Come" Corinth is taken.[3]

16th

As I look upon the blooming trees I enjoy spring although limited by the discipline of Regulations. A mail is to come in today. I must get a letter from home and Mag. Col. Benton will be made Brigadier, but he has not a tithe of the right to it which Col. Pattison has. Real merit is often overlooked.

17th

The rain is pouring and the pond-frogs are croaking. Who wouldn't feel dismal. Read in Harpers an article on The Contest in America by John Hill of England.[4] The English are beginning to see that there is dignity and power to the United States

A Journal here in the army is necessarily tame and insipid. The surroundings are monotonous and often far from inspiring. Unless the Journal keeper has a fund in himself from which to draw, his Journal will scarcely pay perusal.

Parson Brownlow says Secession is a dead dog.[5]

18th

Sister Mat's birthday—28. But yesterday it seemed we were children, enjoying the sports of childhood. F. C. Eddelman has come up at last, very much to my satisfaction. He brought me some pants from home, and a nice Housewife from Rate. I am glad to hear so much from home. Our dog is grown. Charlie (horse) is still alive. Our folks are making maple molasses.

Eddelman brought a paper 10th containing a full account of the battle at Pittsburg Landing. Gen. Johnson (Secesh) was killed. He [Eddelman] brought me Bishop Butler, I am glad of that. It is the masterpiece of English literature.[6]

19th

Two Cavalrymen are to be tried for insulting a woman. They should be severely punished.[7] We march over hills and through ravines as usual. Do not see a house the whole day.

20th

March Northeast. The scenery is romantic. The hills and cliffs are covered with flowers. The clear springs run at the foot of the hills The pines in the distance look clear and green. Our team did not come up. I visited Cap Vandevender, the special object was to get supper, and I got it. We talked of the old College times. He was surprised that I came into the service as a private. I rather wonder at it myself. Lt. McAllister is quite affable. He is somewhat literary.[8]

21st

[no entry]

22d

Co's F, D, I and C do not march this morning, our teams not having come up. 1½ P.M. we are ready and overtake our troops at Beaver Creek.

23d

March 18 miles. I should like to ramble over these hills, though marching is not so nice.

24th

Col Washburn has come up.

We expect a mail soon.

I shall write to Cousin Mattie V tomorrow. Our captain governs very much as would a driver of slaves. He has never treated me amiss, but he does others. I cannot look over it.

Capt. Jenks of Co "C" is my ideal of pleasant and yet firm commander.[9]

25th

For variety we remain in camp. Our Division has already marched 1500 miles.

26th

Caceothis Scribendi non est.[10]

27th

Our new Lieutenant has got a sword. But has not been mustered nor even received his commission. Col Pattison would march us no farther.[11]

28th

Camp at West Plains. Here comes the Provision train. Down on the crackers.

29th

Muster tomorrow. Write to Rate. Storey has "jined" the Brass band.

30th

March at 8 A.M.

May 1st

In a jocular way we talk of our May Day promenade.

2d

Made some fun for the boys.

3d

We marched today to the tune of 28 miles reaching Sulphur Rock, Independence Co, Ark. Pass Evening Shade, and capture some Camp and Garrison Equipage. I saw for the first time a cotton press, cotton Bale, cotton field and cotton growing. O King Cotton thy fibrous majesty will have to come down. Thou canst no longer rule.

The citizens along here are Union. Coleman and McFarland are at Batesville with some Rebel troops. Jackson Port is 18 miles east. It is rumored that New Orleans is taken by Farragut and Butler, and that Corinth is evacuated.[12]

4th

There is a strong element of Unionism here. Coffee has been $1.00 per pound here, iron 22 cents and cotton cords $14 00/100 per pair. We have passed of late a few church houses.

5th

All is good cheer. We are in a shady grove. The birds sing the Bands play and the boys are even scratching the flute and violin out of their knapsacks. I say that music in an army <u>pays</u>.

> Who has not music in his soul,
> Is fit for dark and woful deeds.[13]

I really have enjoyed Barne's introduction to Bishop Butler.
How rich is the world of thought. Let all who can[,] read Butler.

6th

I am appointed to make some <u>peach pies</u>. Soldiers are great admirers of extras. A letter from Oxford is looked for. Whiskey was distributed again last night. O Tempora! O Mores![14] Many soldiers were drunk. Gen Benton made a drunken speech.

7th

Just finished Butler's chapter on a future life. It does not appear so faint and undefined as when I first read it at College. I have also finished Dick's chapter on the wisdom and goodness of God. Prof Brumback calls him Dreamy Dick. I like him, notwithstanding. Col. Washburn says that Memphis is taken.[15]

8th

More good news came last night to the effect that Yorktown was taken with 40,000 Prisoners.[16] Gen Curtis is at Batesville, the second town in Arkansas.

9th

Mr. Grissum and family of Vernon live near here. I shall visit them. Part of Curtis Troops are <u>enroute</u> for Little Rock. I have gained some ideas from

Dick today. He comments on the first and second commandments thus: The first forbids idolatry in all its forms, the second ratifies the first and specially forbids giving to the Diety any <u>material</u> form. In prayer we must think of Him as an immaterial, omnipotent being, forming our conceptions from what we see of his visible works, the earth with all its wonders, and the heavens a study of which will give us some insight into the immensity of His operations.

I find myself frequently assigning to God some form, I am not, however, satisfied with Dick's explanation. Ellis of Franklin started home this morning.

10th

It is said that Yorktown was <u>evacuated</u>. Johnston, Storey and I went to Mr. Grissoms. We got a genuine pass and bounded beyond camp lines as free and glad as if we had been cocks let out of the coop for the first time in nine months.[17] We cut all kinds of antics, physical and <u>witical</u>. Johnston has genuine wit. Was it possible that we were out of sight and hearing of drums and fifes. No roll call to answer, no drill, in fact we are travelling without gun or cartridge box or knapsack (but not without haversack). We kept ahead of all cavalry. We stopped at one house to get some milk and pie. The <u>head</u> of the family was out ploughing with one mule, I suppose they have no Agricultural Associations or publications here in this part of the vineyard.

The family regretted having no more nor better pies. But we sat up to the table, actually took our <u>hats</u> off.

When we had got seated, Johnston, unused to those incumbrances in eating overturned my glass of milk. Sitting to a table, seeing beds and dishes and chairs and the father and mother and the faireyed daughter and dutiful son, besides a whole raft of little ones reminded me vividly that for once I was in civil life again. The lady said 15 cents apiece would do but the father said a dime would be plenty. She readily assented, but she said she thought she did right in charging Major Underwood 15 cents. So did we[18] They live happy. Some day the maiden will leave them, "as it hath been from the beginning."[19]

Afternoon we reached Mr. Grissoms. He was not at home. We got dinner. I found the rudiments of domestic taste exemplified. Wooden frames enclosed wood-cuts. The wall where the 6x8 mirror hung was ornamented with papers posted on it <u>somewhatly</u>. But here was the reign of happiness. We started to Widow Reeves to get some eggs which Storey had engaged. I left Mrs. Grissom by shaking hands, supposing that if I left any peace with her it would also mantle her offspring. The girl, however—what quick things girls are—looked at if she had been passed by. We went to Mrs. Reeves. She had however gone to a log-rolling—a very good place for a widow to go—but her daughter whom I could see had imbibed some of the pertness of the widow mother, received us and conducted us into the <u>sitting room</u> at least a room with <u>chairs</u> in it. The most prominent object in it was the bed. It was a log house, but had a very nice door shutter, it having once belonged on the cabin of a steamboat. The transom extended far above the door, so that it was fulfilled, "we see through a glass darkly."[20]

This girl said she had a risin in her head and so she couldnt hear very well, which latter we ourselves soon discovered. While Storey and the <u>gals</u> caught some chickens, Johnston and I went over the way a quarter to get some eggs. We met a land lady with one "hope of the world" and her sister with another. But they went back and found us six eggs. They wanted us to buy a rooster and some hens, but we only wanted the <u>hen fruit</u>. The rooster in question as if to <u>show off</u> and tempt us to purchase, deliberately walked into the sitting room, exhibiting himself to the best possible advantage. I can scarcely think there was any collusion between the widow and her property. They referred us to another widow, on about a quarter, who they thought could let us have some eggs. We found her hunting some kind of root to cure her boy's poisoned foot. She was Union, though her <u>man</u> had jined and died in the Rebel army. She looked as if she thought it was the <u>best thing he could have done</u>. She called specie Union money, but did not really know whether two <u>dimes</u> were the same as <u>twenty cents</u> or not. She could curse easy.

We came back to the Reeves estate and had some interest in talking to the natives, and in drinking buttermilk. Johnston surrounded 5 glass fulls. Soon we started to camp. Stopped at the <u>pie house</u> but as "he" hadn't got no flour, "she" hadn't made no pies nor nothin'. The daughter, it may be expecting us, had on her new calico dress. She looked quite neat.

The sun was setting as we went to camp. The cows were going to their homes, the farmers were <u>turning out</u> from the plough. I walked on alone, outwalking the others.

Had it been a little later, I could have quoted part of Gray's Elegy

"The curfew tolls the knell of parting day

The herd winds slowly o'er the lea.

The ploughman homeward plods his weary way,

And leaves the world to darkness and to me."[21]

The day's ramble convinces me more of the curse of slavery. Those children had bright eyes, but they were poor, and being in a slave state, they
had no schools. As it is Society drags its slow length along.

Gen Davis with the 22nd and 25th Ind, the 37th and 59th Ills starts for Cape
Giredeau [Girardeau] on a forced march. The 18th guards Batesville. 8th I
don't know.[22]

11th

It is said there is a church in a mile of camp.

12th

Nothing to say.

13th

The "College Miss" frequently has its name taken in vain. McClelland is
advancing to Richmond. President Lincoln has been in the field looking
sound. He dined with Gen'l Wool.[23]

14th

We all feel lazy, as it is so warm. The Aurora, a southern magazine, has
occupied my time today.

15th

The birds sing joyous in the trees.

O'er its pebbly bed the clear brook flows.

While here and there are busy boys

At labor these, amusement those.

We are to go to Batesville today. Col Washburn addresses us on the importance of discipline in the place where we are going. At ten we reach Batesville; all at once it came into view, so well is it hid in the woods. It is full of
blooming roses and flowers. We passed to the west side of the Bayou and
camp in a nice cedar grove. The nicest camp that we have had. We can hear
the church bells, the first that we have heard for six months. When I first
heard them I was alone. It made me think of my College days.

"Those evening bells, those evening bells,
 How many a tale their music tells
Of home and friends and that sweet time
 When first I heard their soothing chime."[24]

I got a cot for Lt Tilson and me. We anticipate that Old Morpheus will be pleased with our offering and will shower his blessings on us in profusion, and that,

"Sleep, tired nature's sweet restorer" will be allotted to us in large doses.[25]

16th

Programme for this camp to be as follows:
Reveille—5 AM
Company Drill—5 to 6 AM
Breakfast—7 AM
Battallion Drill—7 ¼ to 9 AM.
"   " —4 to 6 P.M.
Dress Parade—6 P.M.
Retreat—Sunset
Tattoo—7 ¾ P.M.
Taps—8 P.M.
I do not write all in my Journal that I think or feel. Passion sometimes would make me say hard things.
Physicians say we should not rise in this climate till after sun up. There are such dense fogs.

17th

While at drill this morning Lt Adams verbally detailed me to go over to town as clerk for the Provost Marshal. The Captain peremptorily refused, and swore. There however came a written detail and I went. I reported to Capt Tyler 24th Mo. There are some books in the office. I shall enjoy the place, I am sure.[26]
I shall go to church tomorrow.

18th

It really looks like Sabbath here in town. Found some strange names yesterday, Laughinghouse and Dollarhide. There is a Baptist and Presbyterian and Methodist church in town.

19th

My bed <u>caved</u> in last night. Union loss small, enemy's not known. Answered L. W. Billingsley. I am reading 3d Vol "De Aubigsus Reformation"[27]

20th

Price is at Corinth. He has 200,000 men there—50,000 are sick.[28]

21st

Business brisk. There are many laughable incidents in connection with the examination of Candidates for Allegiance. It is a fine place to study human nature.[29]

22d

I suppose I am 26 <u>aetat</u> [Latin for "of age"].
Twenty-five took the oath today. There is a nice little girl in selling cakes.
Rev. John Cowle, the Methodist Minister took the oath today.
White River is quite large here.

23d

There is quite a history connected with the flag that hangs above the Court House. It was in the Mexican War. When the Rebellion began a Union man secreted it in the belfry and thought so much of the flag as to weep. He is now a Col in the Rebel army. Alas for human weakness, for human resolution.
The flag now floats there proudly.

24th

One fellow asked if Doctors had to take the same kind of an oath of Allegiance as others, and if the taking it would hinder him from neighboring with those who had not.

25th

I had some fun today, stealing Bogarts fish and Lt. Tilsons steak. Analysis of a sermon (Methodist)[:] The importance of retired meditation and devotion. In support of it he said Enter into thy closet and when thou hast shut thy door, pray to the Father, etc.[30] When this is done it promotes purity and sincerity. The Ancients were accustomed to go out by themselves at eventide for meditation.

26th

Settle up in camp and move my boarding place. "I owe no man anything."[31] I find in the Office that almost all men are carried along by the current of popular opinion. Few escape.

27th

Two prisoners were brought in today from the Red River Skirmish. Lt Bell is Brigade Quartermaster and Adjt Marshall Aid to Benton.[32] I wish Eddelman had a place as Clerk.

28th

Capt. Williams has the appointment of Provost Marshal. There are several important cases now before the Committee of Investigation. Capt. Tyler has resigned.

29th

The weather is waxing hot, at least hot enough to melt wax. Our landlady Mrs. Hirsch is going to move into upper town, nearer the office. I shall after this sleep in the office.

30th

The day passed without any strange developments. The telegraph will soon be up, then we shall get the news daily. It is now as far as Pocahontas.

31st

Bowens battalion had another skirmish on White River. We had one killed. The "flat boat" that we had been looking for is aground, and Mr. Thomson the Secesh owner wants to sell it to Uncle Sam. The Provost's office is a fine place for picking up items, learning facts. There is a theo-retical and there is a practical knowledge, I say as I see some illiterate men shrewd business men. The two must be united to have the highest effect.

June 1st

Strove to find church today, but failed.

2d to 8th

Business has been pressing and the weather warm. We are sometimes busy till 9 at night. I like Maj Weston's demeanor very well except his

<u>drinking</u>. He has good business tact. Noble, the Judge advocate, I like. "Fayel" the correspondent is a pleasant man. And I should do injustice to the Union Cause if I should omit to state what a fine family is Mrs. Hirsches. Alice is interesting company. I am not <u>loving</u> her yet I like her. The Boarders are Capt Williams Eddelman Wyand Boggs Lowes and I.[33] I can tell but little of Society here, for all is suppressed while the "feds" are here.

This is almost civil life.

9th

News from the South is good.

10th

Fort Pillow Tenn., is taken.[34]

11th

News grand! Forts Randolph and Harris, and Memphis taken and also Vicksburg, and our boats commanding the whole river. Ten boats chartered to come up White River to us with supplies. On Friday Col Pattison leaves for home. His resignation is regretted by all. No man in the service has more true manhood. He was always temperate, moral. He leaves on account of ill treatment.[35]

12th

This has been a busy day determining the proper ownership of horses, Hearing those who wish to reclaim their slaves, &c, &c, &c., giving letters of Protection and &c, &c, &c. Alice told us of a fellow in the 9th Iowa who wished to attract her notice and love and so made himself some shoulder straps.

I told her no "Hoosier" would do so.

13th

We are looking anxiously for those boats.

14th

A most busy day.

15th

Listened to a sermon by Mr. Lee. It was after the old Methodist sort. Yet it was pretty good for these times. The time flies swiftly. A few months ago this place was quiet and prosperous. Upham recommends meditation.[36] I have little time for study or reading.

16th

Mondays are the busier days in the office. I suppose the citizens meet of Sabbath and come to conclusions, and concoct plans, and so come on Monday to perfect them while the matter is fresh in the memory.

17th

Capt Williams is relieved by Lt. Wm L. Freeman 11th Wisconsin. His removal I take it was on account of his giving a slave owner a pass through the camp to hunt up his slaves. This proceeding is not in tone with the spirit of Gen Curtis' administration. The slaves are to be freed. Positions in the army are as ephemeral as the fancies of childhood.

18th to 22d

Alice is quite a companionable girl, and quite in for fun. She is proud in spirit. Part of Gen Steeles troops leave for Jacksonport, the remainder will leave in a few days[37]

23d to 29th

There are left at this post but the 18th Ind Vols 3[d] Ill Cav Vols and Davidsons Battery. We are erecting breastworks. Yesterevening the pickets were driven in. We were in line and ready. I was ordered out to the cupola of the court house as lookout. One picket was killed. The vidette had ten ball holes in his body. I have found readable in the Southern Fifth Reader. Last night out on secret patrol. I like it. Citizens are watched closely.

30th

At night (last night) orders came for the Post to report to Gen Curtis at Jacksonport. Lt Freeman and I went to overhauling papers, and at 12 M were ready. So still were we all that many of the citizens did not know of the preparation to leave. At 3 AM I went to Mrs. Hirsches to tell her so she might have breakfast in time. She and Alice were frightened at being awakened at that hour, till I told them what the matter was. Then they were more so. They said the Secesh would burn the whole town. I consoled them as best I could. I mounted my pony went to camp to Col. McCrellise's, then back to breakfast. Then I must start from Batesville.

I was loth to leave it. Mrs. Hirsches house was something like home. Alice was merry and kind. After delivering to Mr. Adler his mule and Mr. (Secesh) Cox his keys we marched away. We on horseback got ahead of the command so had "to turn back any more." Here met Lt Freeman and by his order turned over the prisoners to their respective regiments.

July 1st

I went on with John Lowes who told me that Wyand came away without paying his board bill. He is a rascal! Crossed Black River on a Pontoon. Here we report to the Provost Marshal General. Turned over all property, guns, papers, money &c, &c. Maj Weston remarked to the Lt that he might want him again soon. Well, he said, all right, but I must have the same clerk. "Certainly, I have been thinking of detailing him for the General." I shall reflect with pleasure on the short but agreeable association with Lt Freeman. And shall appreciate him for what he has done for me.

2d

March on in the direction of Augusta. Catching up to Steele's division at 1 o'clock. Had poor water, from a pond.

3d

Roads dusty; passed many a good corn and cotton field. Ran the notorious blockade which the Rebels thought so effective. Ran into what I deem unique growth, <u>Cypress</u> <u>Knees</u>.
At first I supposed them to be stumps but soon found that they were alive. These swamps are covered with water a great part of the year and I take it that these knees are the results of roots stretching their heads up above the water to get air. Reached Augusta at six P.M. Two companies went on, on a scout as far as Duvals Bluff.

July 4th

Fourth of July, Hurrah! Glory, and all other expressions of joy at remembrance of the day. Many a heart is sad today which was merry last Fourth. Many soldiers sleep the last long sleep. Our army it is said is destined to Little Rock. Augusta is nearly deserted. I return thanks to God who has been and is my Protection from disease and death moral and physical. At noon we were ordered out on Review. The Artillery roared grandly. It was a dusty hot review. But to relieve the memory of it at 3 P.M. Gen Benton was to make a speech. He did make a marketable speech. He alluded to one of our boys, who had been taken prisoner and killed his captor. He was followed by Col Hovey, 33d Illinois. He spent his breath in telling boys not to steal. Next Col Bussey 3d Iowa Cav. He followed the <u>stealing speech</u>. Next Col Washburn who would divert the attention to the day which we celebrate.[38] He enumerated the past and depicted the future. He is a Western man all out, action action action. In the evening the Col and I had a chat on slavery. Gen. Curtis has come up.

5th

It is rumored that the boats will come up.

6th

Pass nice farms. After having made 4 miles, we were ordered forward double quick, it being told us that the enemy was attacking. We are already hot marching but this double quick a mile and a half, made us hotter by far, when we had reached the place we were nearly overcome but we deployed and advanced two-thirds through the blockade, the cavalry falling back. The cavalry had killed one man, John H. Bell, a planter. Camp here after ascertaining that the Rebels are gone. In the afternoon one of our men was shot. Cap Williams was very much excited by this little flurry. How he swore![39]

7th

Sam Slick is humorous, but not of that high tone of Irving in his Knickerbocker.[40]

8th

Marched to the Battle field of Cotton Plant. Camp beside a pond. No provisions; scarcely worth the naming. Called out by an alarm. If the roads were muddy we could not proceed at all. But fortunately they are dry. The "Yanks" don't care much for blockade.

9th

Made a long days march, reaching Clarendon at 10 at night. The teams got in at one. Bogart and I were horribly tired but as neither of us had ever fallen out of ranks each was ashamed to propose it to the other. At last Bogart said let's rest. But just then the Battalion rested so that both kept our reputation. Mr. Suyg was captured near Cotton Plant. In vain we look for boats, they have gone. We now shall have to march to the Mississippi. It will be a terrible march for we have no provisions yet.

10th

Spent the day in camp. Bathe in White River.

11th

At 10 A.M. start for Helena on the Miss. Our train took one road, we another. Very strange!! Found some molasses and helped ourselves to full rations. A severe rain came in the afternoon We were glad of it Bivouaced at 12 on the wet ground on the strength of no supper.

12th

Still we march. Have not heard of the train. Bivouaced on Big Creek. Several of our boys have "gin out." Start at 3 AM. Pass nice country. Reach Helena at 2 P.M. having marched 65 miles without rations. Camp on the River bank and again sleep without tents, or bread.

13th

[no entry]

14th

Early this morning our train came in. There was nothing along with the train but the sick and the Pioneer squad. It had to bridge two swamps. 100 Rebels could have taken the whole train. Sergt Young is very sick. He has always been robust, but the march was too much. Now he is pale and poor. Boats are in sight.
Spent most of the day in Helena. Gen Curtis has Rebel Gen Hindman's house. It is nice. Lt Freeman is quite sick. Maj Weston still offers me a Clerkship. Trenary has come from St. Louis.[41]

15th

No mail. I write to sister Mollie and Miss LM.[42]

16th

Several boats are below. There are <u>full rations</u> again. I am on a detail to store crackers. It rained famously. We had a gay time getting back to camp and found it submerged, and boys wading around in their tents hunting their breeches and coats. The hard rain had raised the water into the tents two feet high in some places. All was laugh and joke. One fellow said he was diving down after his clothes. Rec'd a letter from home, Rate, Fannie and Morgan.[43] Johnston sent me a paper of the 15th. Sergt Young has started home.

17th

The negro question is <u>the</u> question.

18th

Things take the even tenor of their way.[44]

19th

Inspection and drill. Storey has gone to St. Louis and perhaps home. Wrote answers to letters rec'd. The 8th Ind has gone to town.

20th

There is a breeze from the North. I appreciate it because it is from that direction. I wrote to PC Vawter on the Negro question.

21st

We are to move camp at 2 PM. Some of the knowing ones say we are to go to Richmond. But we move back west onto the hills. It is a good idea. There is a good clear spring. Each company takes a knoll. This is really something similar to retired life. All is quiet and the Beech trees give deep shade.

I have been watching with some interest my <u>moralometer</u>. When I came into the service obscenity and profanity grated upon my sensibilities harshly and I, when I could turned away. Now though I determined not to get used to such things, I confess that a vulgar expression does not grate as shockingly as it did then. I endeavor to keep up the distinction of the holy and the unholy, the pure from the impure. —Write to Wallace.

22d

The long looked for mail came at last. I recd a letter from Rate and Wm King.[45] Rate gives a history of the commencement at Franklin. I am gratified to receive what she is pleased to term an <u>Extra</u>.

23d

Capt. Tyler 24th Mo is Sutler with Avery. Lt Tilson paid $20 00/100 for a trunk. Such at home is worth $10 00/100.

24th

The 11th Ind is camped near.

25th

Lt Knobe cried like a baby as he thought Tilson insulted him. A sterner policy is to be inaugurated.

26th

I have a new mess. H Wells cook. The Regiment parades in its new suit.

27th

Saw the Memphis Bulletin. It reports the adjournment of Congress. The Confiscation Bill was somewhat modified.[46] Many a mother this day prays for her son, as she worships. Many a sister as she enjoys the quiet of Sabbath at home prays for her brother and mayhap he is lying listless with the dead. This is pay day.

28th

Whatever is ennobling or instructing should be sought and practiced in the Army even. With this view I have established a mess that will not be in too much of a hurry to converse at meals. At the other each seemed to specially appreciate that scripture which saith "Whatsoever thy hand findeth to do, do it with thy might."[47]

29th

We eat, we sleep, we wait, we wonder.

30th

Cloudy, productive of sober reflection. I have heartily wished that the war was over. I find nothing congenial in the army. All is quiet. Richmond is the point of interest. Gen Pope is in Virginia. Today the nation lauds a man to the skies, tomorrow it sends him to the regions of Pluto. I say praise to all who have stuck to the ship through good report and evil report. Fremont and Pope will be recorded as no ordinary friends of the Union.

31st

Had a long talk on men and things. At once upon Religion, at another part on the independence to stick out. Thomas Martin sent his regards. "Jim" Lane is going out into the field. Seward does not subscribe the sterner policy of the Administration. He is quite conservative at last.

August 1st

We were sold today by a camp rumor that Richmond was in our possession. I am given the 1ˢᵗ Corporalcy in Co. I. "Mirabile dictu" "Id cum honore et reverentia requoque abundat."[48]

2d

I visited the fleet Two gunboats and several transports. It was amusing to see the tugs hopping around. Well, not hopping exactly but swimming so fast, and turning so quick.

3d

I kept a part of this day holy by sleeping (?) We have been here three weeks today. Josephus is an interesting historian. He gives the number of slain at Jerusalem 1,100,000 or more than the United States has in arms at the present time.[49]

4th

T. J. Morgan and G. W. Grubbs (classmates) are going out, in the 70ᵗʰ Ind. Indiana is alive for once, says Mrs. Tilson.[50] Morgan 1ˢᵗ Lt, Grubbs 1ˢᵗ Sergt. The rebels are crowding us of late west of Helena. A squad went out for them.

5th

After dress parade we marched to town. Our regiment is getting the corners worn off, but still is somewhat uncouth. Our writing desk here under this beech tree is the best we have had. There are no beech trees west of the Miss river except at this point. We shall never forget this desk. The soldier is valued for his physical endurance, and the skill with which he can perform the various movements in drill. He need not think where he is going or what he will do when he gets there. The drum tells him when to eat his meals even; when to go to bed and when to get up. This is the life of ease but the ease of the slave.

6th

The doctrine of continuance is not without power. The child sees the sun rise for several times and so says it will rise again, simply because it has risen for several times and it cannot see anything to prevent its rising again. And so a brother who is accustomed to see his sister in the family adding to its pleasure and comfort cannot believe that the time will come when she will <u>not</u> be there, though her lover be present and wooing her away to his own roof. So the soldier, accustomed to the routine of camp, cannot realize that the time will ever come when he will <u>not</u> be a soldier. I have written 18 letters and recd but <u>4</u>. My <u>House</u> will fail if the <u>credits</u> do not come more nearly up to the <u>debits</u>.

The canal has been abandoned. Many of the slaves were sent back to their masters. I don't like that. Lew Wallace is speechifying in Indiana. I do want more news, but I suppose <u>nec scire omnia fas est</u>.[51]

7th

Warmest day of the season. Gen Curtis has gone east. Indiana has <u>ten</u> of the eleven regiments in the field. This is written by moonshine.

8th

The <u>more</u> sensible article on the War is in Harpers of the 26th ult. It views matters in a common sense light. It is not disposed to loudly laud every General who <u>succeeds</u> nor to <u>trample</u> the one who does not. It shows that measures which are adopted now, could not have been adopted a year ago. Public opinion was not then ready. Lt. Knobe has recd his commission. Ben Schenck it is said, is in the Rebel army.[52]

9th

Last night as I lay on my blanket I thought an enormous musket [mosquito] was singing close to my ear. I began brushing it away. But it wouldent <u>brush</u> for it was the voice of some slaves in the distance singing hymns. As the singing became more distinct I heard the peculiar <u>trill</u> which the negro has. I will say it was touching to hear those old tunes sung which I learned in childhood. The music was good. Between the hymns could be heard the fervent prayer of the slave for himself, his kindred and the Federal Army. And those are slaves, owned <u>body</u> and <u>soul</u> by man. Can it be? No, not long. The Slave shall be free.

10th

One year ago Gen Lyon fell at Wilsons Creek. Tom Woods was up. We are to have a Chaplain before long. Eddelman and I went to a peach orchard. Pope is advancing. Belle Boyd has been captured. She betrayed us at Fort Royal.[53]

11th

Review and inspection by Gen. Benton. We shall have to begin active operations soon. Each company is to have two teams.

12th

Maj. D. C. Thomas is to be Colonel 93rd Ind Vols so that Capt Holman will step up to the Lt Colonelcy. The North had in 1860, 1,900,000 men liable to duty. The South 1,200,000.[54]

13th

The 8th Ind has presented Col Shunk with a sword. He replied, remarking in the course that the question at home was not who should <u>enlist</u>, but who should stay at home.[55] I was told last night that I was to go home on recruiting service. I am indebted to Lt Tilson for this. Maj Thomas says a Majorcy in an old Regiment is preferable to a Colonelcy in a new.

14th

At night Capt Williams was detailed to report on a boat. Mission secret. There is no stir about the recruiting squad.

15th to 23d

Had a severe attack of fever and am quite weak. Gov Phelps has arrived at Helena. Cassius M. Clay is to have a command on the Mississippi. Dr. Bailey promises me a book on the War. He remarks in the meantime that before He or I am three score Slavery will have been abolished, let statesmen manage or mismanage as they will. <u>Providence</u> is doing His work. Wm H. McCoy is teaching at Mitchell.[56]

24th

If I were at home I and Jennie and Mollie would march to church and then come home and spend the evening in reading. But I am here in camp. But one Capt. Williams is going on the Recruiting service. Disappointment is the common lot of man. "The best laid schemes of mice and men aft gang agley."[57]
Two of the 1st Ark were hung near here. My friend James Thorp is dead. He was a Christian man respected by all.

25th

We are now drilling in the McClellan Bayonet Exercise. It is a nice drill. Spent the rest of the day on the Pay Rolls. At 3 P.M. Col Washburn came up and inquired if I was able to go home. So he told me to get ready by 6 P.M. Lt Col Thomas was with us. We could get no transportation except on a contraband boat, so we paid passage to Memphis on the Polar Star. Sergt. Ford and I got a room and went to bed.[58]

26th

Took a walk up the river. Breakfast at 7. We shall start on the Ed Walsh at 10. I am delighted to think of getting to Indiana.

27th

I hunted in Memphis for Miss Crain [Ginni] but did not find her. The Adriatic passed up with negroes on board they were singing a melancholy song and tune. I said the captive is free and this is his song of melancholy joy as he leaves the slave fields to start on a new life.

28th

I got vexed at a cotton speculator. He accused Gen Curtis of all things mean. It was because he had ordered all cotton traders out of his department. He said he paid taxes to support the war and might as well make something out of it. The Rascal! The soldier may give himself up a living sacrifice to his country, but of course he's not right to trade in cotton. I say make such men shoulder a musket at thirteen dollars a month and it will cool down their red-hot patriotism.

29th

Passed Island No. 10. It is apparently about the middle of the river. This is where Gen Pope did so finely. Helena to Memphis 90 miles. Memphis to Cairo 230 miles. The Ed Walsh goes slow. Having passed Bird's Point we came to Cairo at 8 P.M. Ford lost his carpet bag in 10 minutes. Stopped at the St. Charles. Paid 50 cents to sleep on cots amongst the mosquitoes till 3 A.M. Instructed the clerk not to miss having us up.

30th

On the train at 4. Ill Central Road. Place thought he would go it cheap so he would not go to the Hotel. So he got left and had to pay his fair [sic] to Mattoon, not saving much at last, on the other hand losing about 3 dollars. The southern part of Illinois is rough and comparatively poor. Reached Mattoon at 2½ and changed cars for Indianapolis via Terre Haute. Reached Indianapolis at sundown. It was almost like getting home.

Lt Col Thomas recommended us to go to the soldiers home and get board free, so we went and sure enough I was <u>freely bored</u>. It may be as good as circumstances will permit, but I am in Indiana not Arkansas so I shall establish my <u>headquarters</u> at the Spencer House.[59]

31st

As is usual for the soldier I went to work. Wrote most of the day for Col Thomas in the Palmer House. In the afternoon Gen Davis came in and talked some time about the Battle of Pea Ridge. Col Thomas and he were both there. The general does not admire Gen Curtis. Col Thomas is a large souled man. But he drinks strong drink.[60]

Sept 1st

Started on the Jeff [Jeffersonville] train at 6 A.M. Got to Franklin called on Mrs. Grubbs and Wallace. Had a pleasant interview with my friend Sumner who has a room in College.[61] Boarded the Madison train and at 6 was at <u>home</u>. Our folks supposed that I was at least 700 miles away till I crossed the threshold. They could hardly believe their own sight. How shall I describe my own emotions on nearing the parental roof? I was made to recognize that it was God who had protected me and I knelt and silently thanked Him. I am blessed with a great blessing. The gate had the same latch which I had made. The clock still went on measuring time and when it struck the sound was as the voice of a friend. Mollie nor Jennie looked so healthy as I had hoped to see them. Mother was somewhat fleshier, father the same as before. Grandfather [Stott] is as full of life as usual. He is an example of cheerful devoted old age. May my days be as free from sin.

2d

All went over to Macks. Mat and he were glad to see me. I have always prized them.

Jennie can read. Emma is a close observer of things.[62] Came home in the afternoon. Other friends came in so we had a social feast. Many questions were asked and I answered all I could. In the evening some went away whom I never expect to meet again.

3d

Mat and Mack went home. Father and I to Sardinia. Stopped a short time at Mr. Eddelmans, the father of my comrade and friend. Reached my home out there. Aunt Anna was there. We had been there but a short time when a messenger came riding up a full speed announcing that the rebels were threatening Cincinnati and that every man must report at Greensburg. Well, I was interested to watch the excitement. Even some cool men got excited. I thought within myself what will these <u>do</u> when they get their guns. A <u>company</u> of drilled troops could whip a <u>regiment</u> of them. They met at the village and exhibited as much variety of opion [opinion] as of uniform dress.

Finally the fever heat gave way to coolness, and finally to apathy.[63]

4th

Start home at 10 A.M. I did not get to talk long to anyone, not even Fannie Rate Mag or Aunt Anna. Stopped a minute at Uncle Wm. Striblings. Took dinner at Mr. Eddelmans. Phebe is an intelligent and interesting girl. Afternoon prayer meeting at Aunt Frances Kings. Called at Grandfathers coming home. They said they did not expect to see me again. For if I was spared they would in all probability be numbered with the dead.

Lizzie Burns went home with me. I reread my last oration thought I could make improvements.[64]

5th

Take the train at N. Vernon for Franklin. Grim has joined Co. "I." Met many friends Dr. Bailey and Mrs. Bailey Prof Brumback and Mrs. Brumback, &c, &c. Begin my work recruiting. Find many who are almost persuaded to enlist. Met Mrs. Lt Johnson, and Mrs. Rawlings.[65]

6th to 7th

Took dinner with Dr. Bailey he says the war will not end till slavery does. Almost all think so.

8th to 9th

Lt Tilson has a fine wife. So Miss Dungan is a fine lady.

10th

Called on Mrs Mars. Went up to Prof Brumback's study. I enjoy his company. Was in my old room. There hangs my old map. There is my old table. Everything makes me think of "long time ago." When I go up the stairs I involuntarily or rather without thought start for my old room. How strong is habit!! Take the recruits to Indianapolis.

11th

Drew blankets for the recruits.

12th

Go to Hopewell. The hope may be well enough but the recruiting business was dull. Took dinner with Mr Wm McGill. Went to Union Village. It is soaked with the juice of the Butternut. They all with one accord began to make excuse. Was invited to a peach pearing [sic] at Mr Demutts. Had a pleasant evening. The ladies were intelligent.

13th

Got into town at <u>nine</u>. In the evening called on my friend Miss [Carrie] Morrison. She is good company. On coming back found Sumner. We had an argument on <u>morals</u>.

14th

Dr. Bailey preached from "All good works proceed from faith."[66] None suits me so well as my old President. None so clear and solid.

15th to 16th

Went to Edinburg but those intending to enlist were gone. Got a letter from home.

17th

Heard a speech from old Gov Wright.[67]

18th

Dined at Mrs. Forsythes. Evening attended prayer meeting.

19th

Went to Liberty. Took dinner with Mr. Wylie. His house was papered with <u>horse bills</u>. Curious wall paper thought I.
There stood Sir Blackhawk in all his glory.

20th

Evening at the Baptist Church Choir meeting.

21st

Went into Old Webster Hall. I sat at the window an hour calling up old associations.
Heard Dr. Bailey preach, "Reasons why Christians should pray for God's set time to favor Zion, to Come" Afternoon strolled down the creek where

when I was a student I used to walk. Evening heard Mr. Morey preach, "I Thirst" I differ in the meaning of the words. They only refer to the physical man.[68]

22d

Shall go to the Regiment soon.

23d

Went to Indianapolis.

24th

Met my old friends Gideon Moncrief and Thomas Martin. "Postage Stamps" are used for change entirely.

25th

Buell is at Louisville.[69]

26th

To Edinburg again. County Fair.

27th

Went home, had lots of fun.

28th

Communion season at Zoar. I partook but not with all the self-examination I could wish.

29th

At P C Vawter's and O F Feagler's.[70]

30th

I start again from home, having thoughts serious, and full of emotion. Gen Davis shot Gen Nelson. Right! Buell is removed. Good![71]

Oct 1st

Rebellion is still in the land. There will yet be some action campaigns.

2d

Sigel has resigned. Met Milas Hendricks. Attended prayer meeting again.

3d

Met Wylie Burton. He is Lt 67th Ind Vols. Mrs. Clark, my old teacher, lives here in Franklin. I am tired of staying around town.[72]

4th

Went to Mr. Dungan's. Met Miss Anna Tilson. I like her manner. Lt Tilson got home tonight. He looks pale. He says Eddelman was the means of saving him from the grave.[73]

5th

At church again; led the choir. The Dr [Bailey] preached from "They spake often, one to another."

1st—Those with the same tastes hopes and fears naturally associate together. As soon as Peter was lossed [loosed] from the prison he went straight to the prayer meeting.[74]

2d—The object of our speaking together, should not be complaining. Better not speak at all. But it should be for planning for the interests of Zion and our piety.

6th

Got the names of the drafted men of the County.

7th

Mr. Taylor's school will have a rehearsal tomorrow evening.

The students of the College help to fix the stage.—Gen Grant is busy—Eli Thayer has a good plan for settling the South.[75] Visited Prof Hougham. Prof Brumback remarks that the present national contest is between two civilizations, Aristocratic and Democratic, and that the latter is destined, while God sits on the great high throne, to conquer. May it be so.

8th

Miss Crain is at Cor Monroe and Desoto Streets, Memphis. Wrote a criticism for the Young Ladies Exhibition.

9th

Attempt a vindication of myself. Charges serious, but not fearful.

10th

There are lots of things which I do not know. Is it a manly confession. It is evening I am in my cozy room alone, and I shall write some of my thoughts.

As the duties of ladies and gentlemen to each other in their intercourse whether it be for matrimonial or social purposes, has been brought up, by circumstances, it may not be amiss to dwell upon them. It is expected that those of opposite sex associate. It is natural and therefore right. Affection between individuals of the sexes often grow without the intention, at least without the settled determination of either party. Sometimes the affections of the one are engaged, and not those of the other. So that I suppose it to be well for those associating to have a clear understanding as to whether each desires the growth of the affection. This might save many from anguish.

<u>Honesty</u> is demanded here if it is anywhere under the sun. The gentleman is expected to make advances, not the lady.

But let some <u>married</u> one give advice.

11th to 15th

Busy Election Day. Somebody got some of our men drunk thereby expecting to get their votes But I was a little ahead and got their votes in all <u>right</u>.

16th

Spent the day in Indianapolis. Making Muster rolls.

17th

Boarding at Littles Hotel. Doing nothing.[76]

18th

Bigney and I selected the Jubilee to take to camp.[77]

19th

Went to Dr. Day's church.[78] Took Dinner with Claudius Miller an old school fellow. To Sabbath school in the afternoon with Charlie Ball. Evening to Episcopal Church. Fine large organ.

20th

Col Thomas proffers to recommend me for a Lt in a new regiment. Charlie and I go to Franklin.

21st

Got signatures recommending me to a lieutenancy. We shall stay here a week longer. I supposed we would have been at the Regt. by this time.

22d

The Baptist General Association is at Madison. I am reading "13 Months in the Rebel Army" Steeles and Osterhaus's Divisions are at Pilot Knob.[79]

23d

I have been thinking of going into the Regular Service. But I apprehend, that though they are better taken care of, they are not regarded as very absolutely patriotic. Soldiering is their <u>business</u>. They are regarded more in the light of mercenaries. Write two letters. I shall not go to camp till I go to the field. <u>Soldiering</u> at home will not do.

24th

I am living very idly. I shall read Festus today.[80] I shall get my dress coat pressed. A soldier should be very tidy. I sometimes feel that I am losing time. But when I reflect, I know that it is not lost, while in the service.

25th

Col Charles takes the place of Col Thomas. He proposes that we stay till another payday. In fact he says our detail is for six months. An Extra says that Gen Schofield had attacked the enemy 7,000 strong near the old Pea Ridge battleground. Evening go to Columbus.[81]

26th

Got up at 7. No sign was given that breakfast was ready. I somehow heard the dishes rattling and guessed at the thing. While sitting in the barroom I got a good insight into the taste of people there. The conversation was principally about dogs. Some time consumed in talking of other subjects even less inviting that [sic] His Canine Majesty.
I met R. C. Storey and we went to Rev. J. D. Huston's church. Text, "Seek the Kingdom of God."
Afternoon went to Mr. Olcotts, the Teacher, expecting to find Mr. Hart. Sociable family. A soldier there was most desperately in love. I could but pity him. Evening went to Mr. Dickey's church. He read his sermon, but not well. He seems fearful to leave his manuscript as the babe is to let go the leading strings. A Speaker should be so well acquainted with the subject as to be able to leave the manuscript and follow the thought.[82]

27th

Visited the high school. Mr. Olcotts room is under good discipline. Mr. Harts was not conducted well. Miss McClellan has a good infant school. Afternoon went to Uncle George Butlers.

28th

"Marched" up to Joe Wynn's. It's a fine place to go. Afternoon "marched" to Mr. Stouts.

29th

Rate Mag and I went visiting.

30th

Got home at 11 A.M. Aunt Sylvie there. She Jennie and I had a long talk after the rest had gone to bed.[83]

31st

Took train to Indianapolis. Rate sent a present to Lt Martin.—At least I took it.

Nov 1st

Visited the State Library. Several trophies there from Pea Ridge. One cannon ball that had killed three men whom I saw. There was a piece of Gen Ben McCullough's shirt. I have a piece. Afternoon Tutor Wallace came up. Went to the camp of the 68th Ind Vols. Met Capt Patterson, George Hankins. Joab Stout is very sick there. His wife is nursing him. This Regt. (68th) was captured.[84]

2d

Took a long walk up past Camp Morton. Heard Dr. Day again. Theme: The Object of the Mission of Christ. Religion is not an accomplishment, but a change of heart. The 54th Ind is in Camp. Here near Camp Morton. Has barracks.

3d

Rawlings has come here from the regiment. He is going back tonight. I shall send some books to the boys.

4th

Spent the day in the State Library.

5th

Have the promise of more recruits.

6th

I actually start for home again. Arrive at Uncle W. D. Vawters in the afternoon.[85]

7th

Afternoon went to San Jacinto for Jen who teaches there. She has a good school.

8th

Make the acquaintance of Cousin Mary Stott. Afternoon at Cousin Nell's. This last cousin has a nice lovely home.

9th

Had to teach Miss Fink's class at Presbyterian Sabbath school. Sermon by Rev Mr Sims. He is a clear, intelligent expositor.

1st Men are <u>saved</u> as soon as they are converted. 2d The means of salvation is faith. 3d The reason of Salvation: It is Gods will. 4th The time of the determination of this salvation was before the world was.

10th

Went with Cousin Jen to school. She had forgotten her key. So we broke the door open. Saw my old friends, Cox and Randsdale.

McClellan is superced [superseded]. Good![86]

Cousin Mary Stott came home with me.

11th

I went squirrelling but cast on the <u>wrong side</u>.

12th

Took Cousin Mary home.

Went up to Mat's.

13th

Went to Butlerville. Gid is in the store. He does not like the service.[87]

14th

Jennie and I went to Mr. McCallisters. Evening attended a Soldiers Aid Society supper at Vernon, I was not edified. I was too much of a Stranger.

15th

Attended what is called a chopping at Grandfather Vawters.

16th

Went to Sardinia, to church. Capt. Williams writes me that we shall start soon.

17th

At home. Help father pull and put away the turnips.

18th

Go to Indianapolis <u>again</u>.
My Photographs are poor. I hardly know whether to distribute them.
Eddelman sent my letters from the Regt. One from Miss LM. The prospect
is that our Regt will go down the Mississippi. I judge the plan is to have
our troops far into Rebel territory by the 1ˢᵗ Jan 1863, the time at which
the Proclamation goes into effect.[88]

19th

Write a long reply to Miss LM. I consider her a paying correspondent. She
thinks and possesses true womanhood.

20th

Recruiting is now very slow.

21st

One squad went to the Regiment. Visited H. H. Young of the Indiana
School Journal.

22d

Sit all day reading in the state library. Buy Studies from life.

23d

Hear Dr. Day <u>again</u>. Thanksgiving sermon: Resons [sic] for Christians
giving thanks,
He should give thanks that there is a foundation on which he may rest;
and <u>such</u> a foundation.
He should give thanks that <u>he</u> was placed on such a foundation.
For the joys arising therefrom.
For the prospects of the future. He has the promise of eternal life.

24th

I witnessed the workings of the fire engines. We shall go soon.

25th

Getting ready to go to the regt. Two of the Recruits had <u>scattered out</u>.
They were not to be found.

26th

Draw rations for the party. 10½ evening we are off at last. Rode all night. Weary time. We all gape and yawn and stretch several times before morning.

27th

Arrived at St. Louis at 10½ AM. Went to the Everett House. The boys slept in the Hall. It was Thanksgiving Day and the House has an <u>Extra Dinner</u>. Fare $2.00 per Diem.

28th

Start at 6 AM on the Iron Mountain R.R. We first got transportation for Helena, but by accident that our Regt had not yet gone down the River. Reached Pilot Knob [Mo.] at noon. A train was just starting to the front. The mules in the train were novices. So we had a large amount of fun getting the teams along. One wagon tipped and landed two men in the mud, mud beneath above on all sides, it clothed them as a garment.

29th

We start on, jolly as <u>early settlers</u>. Camped at Mr. Williams farm.

30th

At noon arrive at Pattersonville. The 18ᵗʰ Ind is 18 miles to the front. I and some others went to Mr. Fultons. He is emphatically a Union man. He has an intelligent wife and daughter. Charley Purcell our old drillmaster was there with his wife. Hall came there very sick. I sat up and waited on him.[89]

Dec 1st

We shall come up to the Regiment today. I stopped at Mr. Pettitts for dinner. He is rank <u>secesh</u> I know. As I came in sight of the Regt, I was made thankful that my life and health had been spared and I asked for protection for the days to come. The boys met me gladly. I was detailed by Col Shunk as Clerk to the Brigade Quartermaster. John Lowes has my thanks for this. Eddelman is Hospital Steward and is pleased with the place.

2d

Consumed the day in getting acquainted with my duties in the QM department. I think I can soon Master the Forms. I have had several long talks with the Company. They all say that Lt Knobe is a <u>wooden man</u>.

3d

Writing all day. Evening sang at the Hdqrs of the 8th Ind. Asst Surg Brown is the better singer.[90]

4th

It is said that the enemy is 20,000 strong down toward Currant River. Met Col Washburn today. Loaned him the Eclectic.

5th

Nothing beyond the routine of camp.

6th

Congress is talking of raising the wages of the army, and of abolishing West Point and giving it to the States to establish military schools. Lt Lowes is going back to Co "K" and Lt Kimball will become Brigade Quartermaster.

7th

Our choir sang two hours. If I do say it, we make good music. I am again away from churches and Sabbath schools, but I trust that I shall not become forgetful of God. Answered Sister Jennie's letter.

8th

Had a sermon yesterday from Rev. Mr. Skinner, 8th Ind.[91] Gov. Morton has urged the increase of the soldiers' pay to 15 dollars per month.

9th

Had quite a confab with Lt Kimball on the proper object of Masonry. He at first claimed for it something beyond temporal assistance (that is, material assistance) and moral culture, but finally was willing to limit it to these.
I claimed that <u>nothing</u> could take the place of Christianity, and that a man was safe enough against starving if he was a member of the real house of Israel.

10th

Acker, the nominal forage master, went out after forage today. Lt Lowes and I went with the train. Acker was so ignorant of where to go that we took charge of the matter and got the forage. Acker is quite a <u>blow</u> fish.[92]

11th

Mrs. Williams Arta's mother is dead. When I was at home she was full of life and quite patriotic.

12th

Sent in report on transportation.

13th

Report that Burnside has burned Fredericksburg.

Had an argument with Lt Kimball as to the object for which man is placed here. He asserted that it was evidently <u>pleasure</u>. I, that it was <u>God's glory</u>. His theroy [sic] is the popular one, but it cannot be sustained.

14th

I was much interested in the perusal of an article on the Treatment of the Insane. An illustration of the proper treatment is found in Christ's conduct toward the man whom he found among the tombs. Kindness and care are the surer cures. There has been a mistake too in the treatment of culprits, until the reformation of Howard.[93]

15th

Awakened by the hallooing of those who had found the <u>River up into their tents</u>. We just had time to move when the water was all over the ground where we had lain. All was hurry. Some had to abandon tents, some some goods, &c. Some of the 33d Ill's were surrounded by water, and so had to remain on the Island. We moved back to the foot of the hill, feeling assured that the river would not rise much higher. The promise was that the earth should not be again deluged with water. It was time for the exploits of the daring. Gen'l Benton and many other distinguished ones, swam their horses to and from the island. And as they were so exposed to <u>dampness external</u> they thought it proper to dampen the <u>internal</u> so became <u>drunk</u>.

Capt. Vandervender, who was once an earnest seeker after conversion of his soul, was drinking with the rest. I hope he may yet be reclaimed. Col Washburn will start home soon sick.

16th

I subscribed for the Witness. It has not come.

17th

Gen. Benton on Saturday night married a widow lady near here Mrs. Pettitt. He saw her first a month ago. She had 11 slaves. A soldier told me that the General had never gone to see her sober. I say he is a <u>fool</u>-ish man. Worse than all he was married drunk. He may be sane but I think he needs some <u>hellebore</u>.[94]

18th

River still high, too high to be crossed.

19th

Went into the country ten miles to hunt some forage. Engaged oats of Mann and corn of Heckwith, formerly of Indiana. For Dinner at Mr. Manns had cornbread pork and Sassafras tea.

20th

Start with the train for some forage. These citizens love to misrepresent each other. Human nature is found away down here even. Get to camp and find that the command is to move.

21st

Although it is Sabbath and we have been here a long time idle, and there is no prospect of meeting the enemy and the President has said that the armies should observe the sabbath except on extreme cases, yet we go. The roads are very bad. The teams do not get up.

22d

I hunt for oats but fail.
I have not received a letter since I came back. We are again among the pines. Work in making Blank Vouchers.

23d

Had reveille at 3 AM. We shall reach Currant River today. Other troops are to join us here.

24th

Rearranging camp is the order of the day.

25th

Christmas! One year ago today we were on the Lamine. Peach pies for dinner.
There was a big spree tonight in the 8th Ind & 11th Wis.

26th

It is probable that there will be a change in the Cabinet. Seward is too <u>Conservative</u>.

27th

Saw Dr. Smith Campbell, 23d Ioway. He is as gassy as ever. The Rebels have made a raid into Grenada and Holly Springs.[95]

28th

Wrote an essay on Providence. Our nation now has come fully to believe in Providence. Negroes are to be armed and to garrison forts. <u>This is right</u>.

29th

Busy with monthly Reports.

30th

Mail came in. A letter from home. My friend and schoolmate and pupil George McCanlon is dead. He but a few years ago was as robust as I. Now he sleeps with the dead. He was respected by all.
Miss L.M. says that my article was read at the Social at Franklin. Grubbs does not think the service so poetic as he did.

31st

Eddelman is going to see the New Year come in. I shall go to bed and risk its coming. "Times and seasons shall not fail.["][96]

1863

Jan 1st

<u>The important day</u> in five centuries! Today is made the Proclamation of freedom to the Bondmen of America. By so much is the country rising to take its place as Teacher of all nations. I am glad that I have lived to see this day. "The year of Jubilee has come"[97] I told Henry that this day the slaves were freed. Said he, "Thank God for dat." I am surprised that although living amidst the conquest of the great principles of popular government, I am so indifferent to it.

2d

Company "I" started back last night to Pilot Knob with a train.

3d

I must get to reading more.

4th

In the morning went to Dr. Daughters tent to sing.[98] Wrote three letters.

5th

Start the reports for December. I finish our QM Desk. It is handy. All is quiet on the Currant.

6th

The 18th Ind is to move camp. I am reading Newman's Rhetoric. The first and last [illegible word] is in good style, as any article that I have read. A telegram says that Col Holman is at Pilot Knob drunk. Shame for the Lt Col of the 18th Ind. Maj Brady of the 8th Ind has gone to relieve him. He <u>may</u> do better.[99]

7th

The news comes again that Vicksburg is ours, and that Gen Rosencrans has had a decisive victory at Murfreesboro, Tenn, Things assume a brighter appearance.[100]

8th

Some of the 18th are arrested for refusing to do duty.

9th

Vicksburg is <u>not</u> ours. Banks did <u>not</u> come up, and unless Sherman is reinforced, Sherman will have to retreat. It seems that Sherman was <u>fast</u> that time.[101] The rebels reinforced from Jackson Miss. Their force was 65,000.

10th

The work which I am reading [Newman] insists that a man must have the gifts of an orator to be an orator. This is not precisely in accordance with the Latin "<u>Oratores finit; nascunter Poetae.</u>"[102]

11th

It is a most beautiful day. I have read several psalms. Heard Mr. Skinner preach. Got a present from Rate. It is an odd one. She is a good Correspondent. I hope we shall march to Batesville. I would then get to meet my friend Alice.

12th

We never <u>know</u> anything in the Army. We march tomorrow in the direction of Batesville. Henry McCanlon was wounded in the foot at Prairie Grove.[103]

13th

Move across the river. Rains all day.

14th

March again. The wagons can scarcely make a mile an hour. The medicine wagon of the 18th Ind tipped over. Camped on a bridge covered with pines.

15th

Four inches of snow on the ground. Most of the troops had to bivouac. This is hard service even for soldiers.
Recd a letter from Rate.
It is pleasant to live with a high aim. To live for pleasure is to die.

16th

Jeff Davis urges the holding of Vicksburg and Port Hudson. He appears pleased with the prospects of the Confederacy.
The Editor of the Richmond Examiner says that news from the West is always flattering at first but bad enough at the last.[104]

17th

Moved ten miles. Cover one of Davis camps as he came from Sulphur Rock.

18th

Crossed Eleven Points River and camp. Forage has to be brought on horseback for the teams to draw the wagons the roads are so nearly impassable. We are one day behind Gen'l Davidson.[105]

19th

Teams swamp all along the road. It is a dismal dark rainy muddy day. As we neared Alton we met the 18th Ind going back. Carelessly, it was ordered to come on when it was to have remained whence we started. Everybody was fighting mad. I got into camp about nine at night after issuing forage to the Regiments and the Battery.
But we had a good supper, and although I was wet and cold and muddy and hungry and tired, I soon convalesced.

20th

Here at this point (Alton) is a nice court house. Some guerrillas were taken here.

21st

We are having much trouble about forage. We cannot get more than half enough, especially for the Battery. The post is slow. These days I live in a kind of torpid state.

22d

Things take the even tenor of their way.

23d

A. P. Daughters is appointed Surgeon 18th Ind. I like him much better that Dr Gordon. Lt Col Holman is resigning. We march tomorrow. Warrens forces are to join us.[106]

24th

One year ago today we started from the Lamine. Moved 3 miles south of Alton. There are two camps near. Recd a letter from Sister Jennie. Alice Stott is married. We almost always camp in the woods. The pleasures arising from intimate and virtuous friendship are indeed great. Friendship will form a part of the pleasures of Heaven. Friendships in the Army are frequently lasting. He by the side of whom I stood in battle I shall never forget.

25th

Read most of Samuel. I have learned something of Ichabod—"The glory is departed from Israel" David could have slain Saul his enemy but he would not.[107]

26th

We conjecture that Little Rock is taken. We are 65 miles from Batesville. The 18th Ind is said to be the best Regt. in the Army.

27th

March in the direction of Thomasville. Lt. A B Lowes is now Captain. A lady not far from here has always feigned sickness when soldiers were around. Her bed was examined and there were found 7 U.S. blankets. They were taken. She also dressed her negress in men's clothing. But few will know what for.

28th

Marched again. I rode one of Joe's mules. Our horses have gone again.

29th

Lt Wright, 33rd Ills, is a talkative man.[108]

30th

Reached West Plains. I recognize the big spring in town. Wallace tells me that Pres. Bailey has resigned. The Presd't thinks the reason of the dissatisfaction with the college was not its locality but its theology. Many of the Baptists of Indiana strangely deny the doctrine of Predestinarianism.[109]

31st

Non est.

Feb 1st

Read through II Samuel.

2d

Bill, the pony, is found.

3d

Finished our Reports and Returns.

4th

Recd a letter from Mag and Fannie. Hooker has Burnside's place.[110] A flag of truce came in yesterday. I am satisfied that there are but few Quartermasters who do not deal in contraband stock. —7 inches snow.

5th

Nearly half our men are barefoot.

6th

The Order for marching this morning is somewhat Sybilistic. We shall march toward the base of supplies. None knows where that is, in our Dept. Johnston has bought some land in Minnesota, so Ditmars, Ryker and Trautwain. Loafers are quite burdensome.[111]

7th

Our shop goes with the 8th Ind to Eminence on Currant River. I had some fun after we had the tent up. Lt. Kimble appreciates a joke.

8th

I had divers thoughts. Fancy pictured my future habitation. She made a nice one. Camp on Jacks Fork of the Currant river.

9th

I saw some children sitting on the stones used for <u>andirons</u>. Their faces looked as if they were <u>freesoilers</u>. The little boy said that a man came there and took a dodger and two <u>twilts</u>.

10th

We took a prisoner riding on a Jack. He looked somewhat like one himself.

11th

I have been reading Titcomb's Lessons in Life. He says that Religion is made up of a heart full of love to God, and not of forms. Church members do not profess to be perfect hence we may expect to find difficulties amongst them.[112]

12th

March. There was said to be a house along the road with a library in it. I <u>hope</u> I shall get to see it. It would be a refreshing sight.

13th

Camp today at Cave Springs. The bluffs rise perpendicular and the hills are covered with pine. Today a soldier in shooting a rabbit shot a hole in another soldier's ear. Maj Brady has come back from Batesville where he went under a flag of truce.

14th

One of the Iowa cavalry accidentally shot himself while rolling rocks down the hill. Word comes that we soon shall be out of the mud and on boats going down the Mississippi.

15th

Got into Eminence at 8 AM. On the west side is said to be a spring 400 feet deep. There is a little mill. Yesterday two young ladies came to mill, one riding on an ox, the other on a bull. They used men's home made saddles. The boys very ungallantly stole their sacks of corn. They were "willin' to gin up the corn to the soldiers, but they was mighty anxious to keep the sacks for they had had 'em for five years." Wouldn't such a lady as one of these be a glorious <u>helpmate</u>. Our Messenger was shot by a guerrilla. And then the latter was shot by order. A ram has passed the Vicksburg batteries. We start in the morning for the Mississippi.[113]

16th

I went a near route and got 4 miles ahead of the command, so I had
to retrace.

17th

Adjt Dunbar of the 8th is a B.P. of Greencastle. Gen Bentons wife is to meet
him at Pilot Knob.

18th

March 12 miles.

19th

Reach Centerville, a small town.

20th

Camp at Belle View Valley, six miles from Pilot Knob. The valley is rich.
Teams do not come up. We <u>bivouac</u>.

21st

Mail! A letter from Miss LM. She writes good letters.
The Indianola has passed Vicksburg.[114] Col. Shunks verbal order was that
every man was to get drunk. And in quite a measure it was obeyed.

22d

Washingtons birthday. He yet lives in the hearts of his countrymen. I
went to the railroad for forage. All of the teamsters nearly, got drunk. Paul
does not overdraw the picture of man's <u>depravity</u>. I am glad to believe that
heaven will have no mud nor drunken men in it.

23d

Nothing to say.

24th

The mortar boats have begun shelling Vicksburg.

25th

Recd a letter from home. David Glover is dead. So also is George Kendrick.
The Conscription Bill is on the verge of passing. Hope it will.[115]

26th

Gen Carr now commands this division.

27th

I am very tired of living amongst such profane and low minded men as are here.

28th

Rain came again, quite a frequent guest.

March 1st

The fortunate circumstances are all coming together. 1st We are where we can get the Dailies. 2d We get plenty of Rations. 3d We are to have some dishes. 4th About half dozen nice ladies are visiting our Regiment. Col had dress parade for them. A hollow square was formed and they and we sang the Star Spangled Banner and E Pluribus Unum. I was glad to meet Indiana ladies. My toast is, "Woman, long may she wave."

2d

Queen of the West is captured by the rebels.

3d

No fight at Vicksburg yet.

4th

The Indianola is captured by the rebels.

5th

Fort McCallister near Savannah, reduced by our ironclads.[116]

6th

Wrote to Rate and Cousin Mattie.

Highest Peak, Pilot Knob

I had long wished to be up here. Men here, as I passed below, seemed mere birds in size. Now I am upon the highest point; and what a feast for the eyes! Houses below, look more like childrens toys. To the right: the village is busy with all the multiplied departments for supplying the army. But what do I care for that. I am cut loose from all <u>below</u> and shall have this hour to myself. The commons dotted here and there with white spots indicate that an army is around. The strong arm of Power bears rule, government is not left <u>now</u> to the peaceful citizen. He feels his impotence in this hour of trial. And can most effectually enforce the laws of his country by joining the ranks of the armed host.

There stands the church with its finger pointing above. The sick soldier in it would be glad to be here. While scores are suffering there I am here in all the vigor of health. Up the valley, white tombstones remind me that many an one sleeps there, all unconscious of the anxiety and sorrow which his brethren are undergoing. They had not dreamed of war when they sank quietly down to their last long sleep.

All around stretch the hills, the everlasting hills. The farthest seem as clouds in the distance.

Underneath lies an inexhaustible bed of iron. Scarcely touched yet it will supply iron for ages to come. The very peak where I sit will be torn away and its metal wrought into implements of industry, and it may be of war, for the ages to come. These mills will be worked and the world will witness the effect of their working, when all we are as those in yonder graveyard. Again my eyes sweep the horizon. I see the valleys and hills and clouds and sky, and with reverence I am made to say, "What is <u>man</u> that Thou visitest <u>him</u>, or the son of man that Thou art <u>mindful</u> of him."[117] I go down to mingle again with the busy crowd, glad that I could even for a time abstract myself from men and feel the emotions which the view gave.

7th

One year ago today we were in the Battle of Pea Ridge, Ark. I still can recall my emotions there. The day was celebrated by a greeting between all the officers of the Indiana Brigade and Gen Carr.

8th

How many events are crowded in a year. Took dinner with Eddelman.

9th

Sergt Campbell is going home on furlough. Lt Tilson has offered his resignation. The Indianola is doing the rebels no good. "Henry["] is going north to Kimble's.

10th

Start for St. Genevieve on the river. Pass the village of Iron Mountain. Then there is a turnpike from there. How nice it goes to travel on good roads. The pike was built to ship iron and coal on. Today I <u>passed</u> a <u>school</u>. I dismounted and went in. The Elementary Speller was used and Mc-Guffeys Readers, But it seemed as if these worthy gentlemen had not brought on a supply for quite awhile. I asked a girl what the teacher was paid. She said <u>ten dollars</u> a <u>month</u>. I believe he <u>boarded round</u>. I had a curiosity to see the apostle so I waited till he came. I can best express my opinion by saying that he was the "<u>Missouriest</u>" man I have seen. He had standing collar and cotton cravat. The corners of his collar came well up and flanked the face on each side, so that he could turn neither to the right nor to the left but had to keep straight forward in his conduct. If tobbacco should get scarce and high-priced, I really think that it would take his wages to <u>run</u> him.

11th

We passed Farmington. It is a nice southern village. There were pretty ladies.

12th

Reach St. Genevieve at 2 P.M. It is a pretty village. The buildings are neat and substantial. It is settled by Catholic French.
Eddelman is quite sick. Bilious fever.

13th

Our army is to be reorganized here.

14th

The transportation is to be turned over to the Post Quartermaster at Pilot Knob, and we embark tomorrow for "below."

15th

Gen Benton came; and ordered a salute of 11 guns in honor of his arrival! ha! ha! Wrote to Mag. I shall certainly reap a bounteous harvest of letters judging from the amount of seed sown.

16th to 24th

Left St. Genevieve Tuesday. After a tedious waiting got aboard the City of Alton, with the 8th Ind. When we got to Cairo we find that our mail had been sent to St. Louis. Get to Memphis Saturday. Stop off to cook rations. I found Eddelman on the L. M. Kennett. He is convalescent. I attended church in Memphis. The Minister prayed only for the soldiers who were sick. I suppose he took it that well ones might take care of themselves. I could not find Miss Crain. Wrote two more letters.
Got to Helena Sabbath night. The place does not look much as it did. The

river is very high. When we were camped there it was quite low. Gen Benton started with his wife on board but the guards ruthlessly forbade her going on board. So he, poor fellow, had to go alone.

Pass the <u>Yazoo pass</u>.[118]

25th

Lay at Lake Providence. The plantations are getting large and rich.

26th

Just as the troops had got on shore and into camp, the Hamilton came down with Gen Carr who ordered all aboard again. My horse got loose and was loping away to the farthest corner of a large pasture. I exercised my "physical self" somewhat before I got him. Dr. Chittenden of the 16th Ind came on board. We "round to" at Milliken's Bend.

27th

Our Division disembarks and camps on a Plantation near the river. The ground is low and damp and all seems silent and sluggish. Flowers are in bloom.

28th

I have been discussing with myself as to the propriety of getting some new clothes. We are now not far from Vicksburg. We can hear the shelling there. But all our news from there has to come <u>via</u> Cincinnati, and St. Louis. If we get into a fight we probably shall know it before the <u>Gazette</u> or <u>Democrat</u> does. We belong to the 13th Army Corps.

29th

Well indeed last night was a memorable night. About twelve o'clock a storm arose. The lightning flashed, the thunder rolled, the wind blew, the rain poured. Our office tent no longer able to brave the storm fell, and in its fall it overthrew the desk scattering the books and papers and inks and pens, hither and thither into the mud and into the water. It was no delightsome task to get up at such a time of night, under such circumstances and hunt round in the dark for lost papers. Some had blown down into the camps.

I still hope to get some letters before the war is over.

30th

I wandered off to a plantation to get something to sleep on. Found a cot. The planter had been rich. But the evil day had come. "The cries of those

who had reaped his fields had come up to the ears of the Lord of Sab-
baoth."[119] A hundred harrows stood in his sheds but the hand of the slave
would no more come upon them.

31st

Sergt Campbell is back again. He says that there are lots of Copperheads
north. He saw Ira Stout.[120] "Henry" did not get through.

April 1st

Our new organization is—14th Div, 13th Corps, 1st Brigade—8th Ind, 18th
Ind, 33d Ills, 99th Ills, 1st U.S. Infantry and six siege guns. 2d Brigade—
11th Wis, 21st, 22d and 23d Iowa and 1st Ind Battery.

2d to 7th

I have finished the last reports and will soon go back to Co. "I." I met the
Burtons and Merit Read in the 67th Ind. Rec'd a letter from home. Milton
Stribling was instantly killed while helping to raise a log house. Nan will
feel lonely now.[121]
Lt. Tilson has gone home.
Gen. Grant is to Review our troops today. We always take it that we are
to march.

8th

Today the Review was. And by McClernand.

9th

I am in Co "I." Things <u>are</u> as they <u>were</u>. Very muchly.
The <u>Witness</u> reached me but it is not much more a <u>positive</u> than a <u>nega-
tive</u> thing. William Snow came back after an absence of 10 months.[122]

10th

I take great interest in tactics. Tonight we serenade and I must prepare.
The relation of <u>Ideas</u> to <u>realities</u> is a fruitful theme. The evolutions of the
brigade tiresome as they are, are but a <u>realization</u> of <u>Ideas</u>.

11th

March towards Richmond, La and camp on a farm owned by Mitchell,
a brother in law to Jeff Davis.[123] Six gunboats were to pass Vicksburg
tonight.

12th

The right wings of the regiments were ordered out with spades. Could the enemy be so near? But it was only to make roads. Government is confiscating large amounts of cotton through here. The negroes are all at Monroe 90 miles west.

13th

March. Camp in a cotton gin. Our tents are to be left behind. I have learned something of the "quarantine laws."
Our cottages at home are neater than these places.

14th

Get two letters from home and one from R. C. Storey.
Thomas Stribling died in the service.[124]

15th

Resume our march down the Bayou Rondaway. Camp on the Dawson Plantation. This country would be a paradise if it were not for the low ground, hot weather and slavery.

16th

There are 1500 Rebels annoying us on this side of the river. There is a number one Steam Mill and Gin on this plantation
We are making lumber for rafts or boats.

17th

James Feagler is in the 54th Ind. His father is identified with the opposition. Read Dr. Breckenridge's oration at the laying of the cornerstone of Clays monument. It is rich. The old Doctor is far different from his son, J. L. Breckenridge—the Rebel leader. I make the acquaintance of Johnny Ridenour.[125]

18th

A large lot of ammunition is brought around with us in <u>flats</u>.[126] We anticipate going to Port Hudson. The China trees here make nice shade and they are beautiful to look upon. The hedge-rose is beautiful, too.

19th

Col. Washburn has just proposed that we enforce the Regulation in reference to swearing. One fellow said in an undertone, "It will take all my wages to pay for my swearing."

20th

J. R. Johnston proposed to get commissions in Colored regiments. Col. Washburn does not want me to go. He says that he may soon have a place for me in my own regiment.

21st

Orders to march. We <u>march</u> on the levy [levee] and ride on rafts across bayous and where there is no levy.

Quite romantic campaigning. We halt on the levy during a severe rainstorm. Johnston Carson and I shelter ourselves under <u>one</u> oil blanket and take it cool as martyrs.[127] Johnston quotes appropriate stanzas quite profusely. After the rain was over and gone we marched on to a Cotton gin and took quarters. Here on the river we saw the <u>rams</u> and other stock that had come past the Batteries of Vicksburg. One singularity that I find is <u>female rams</u>; for instance, "The ram, <u>Queen</u> of the West." Altogether this is the merriest day that I have seen in the service. Its no use to be moody.

22d

We think we shall help Banks to <u>roll</u> his <u>logs</u>; then he in turn will help us. His are at Port Hudson.[128] David M. Smith is wounded.

23d

In the evening, by moonlight, the fields all being covered several feet in water, The Lowes, Dr. Bigney and I built a raft and floated out into the field, and sang some of our "soul stirring pieces."[129] After we had been in sleep for some time we were aroused by the sound of artillery. More boats were passing Vicksburg. The sound jarred the buildings, and Vicksburg is 30 miles distant.

24th

Six transports started past the batteries, one, the Tigress, was destroyed. The others are, or will soon be serviceable. They are the Anglo Saxon, Cheesman and Moderator besides two others. They brought down a large supply. While I write, the orders are, to get ready to march.

25th

March on down the levy to the Perkins plantation. He, the owner, burned his buildings rather than let them fall into our hands. Mr. Perkins had great notoriety here as a judge. There are two monuments in the garden.

The sentiment on one is, "She lies in the garden she used to adore[.]" The other, "Solid blocks of pure marble, amongst flowers, best represent him." This last one was lost on the Arctic in 1851. Met James Feagler.[130]

26th

Heard an excellent sermon by the Chaplain of the 33d Ills. "For the joy that was set, etc."[131]

    I.   What was the joy before him?

    a.   The establishment of the true religion

    b.   The eradication of false ones

    c.   The conversion of man

    II. The joy set before the soldier of the Union.

I am detailed clerk to the Mustering Officer of the Division, Meinhold.

27th

Our Brigade is the first in this camp. Afternoon a review, which was honored with Gov Yates in attendance. He made a speech. The idea now to which we are all to bend our energies is the taking of Grand Gulf. Rec'd two letters. I have been busy getting acquainted with my new business. In the afternoon we have orders to embark. I was told to stay with the other clerks, but I borrow a gun and join Co. "I." We went down the river several miles and land again on the Lousiana [sic] side. We can see Grand Gulf. I am put on picket guard.

28th

[no entry]

29th

The Ironclads have attacked the batteries. There is a furious cannonade. We expect every moment to be ordered over to charge. Supposing we are so near a battle I have sober thoughts. Life to me today has seemed pleasant. If I am numbered with the slain in the approaching contest, the thought that my sacrifice will help bring peace and continue liberty to thousands who shall come after, takes away the regrets. I trust in that same God who has ever been my Preserver.

30th

The Battle did not come yesterday, but it may soon. This is Fast day, and I observe it punctilliously [sic], for I have nothing to eat.

Eddelman ran the Grand Gulf Batteries on the Moderator. We march down the levy some distance, then embark on transports, gunboats and barges, and steam down to Bruinsburg. Here we disembark and march back up the Mississippi side. Berry hurried to get possion [possession] of the hills.

We camp on a nice farm covered with Magnolias. It belongs to one Smith Donalds.[132] The details had to carry over boxes of crackers up to this place—three miles.

The mansion and furnishing cost $100,000. There is great activity and energy displayed by our troops. I begin to see how the rebellion may be conquered in a few months. The possession of the Mississippi will give us great advantage. It can be used as a base proceeding with the armies eastward from it. I am very hopeful. I know that many prayers are ascending the throne for us. March on at 7 o'clock. Gen Grant gets his information as to roads from a negro. At 2 o'clock at night we came onto the Rebel pickets. Cannonading was kept up for an hour, when all remained quiet until daybreak. We were quite close up to them. Capt. Klauss knew how to direct his pieces. We lay down with all our accoutrements on.

May 1st

True to himself, the sun sent twilight in advance, then sent his direct rays upon us discovering the position of the enemy and what we were to do. This will be a fatal Mayday to many a soldier. We were moved over the brow of the hill and cannonading began. Grape and canister flew about us fast. Maj. Brady 8th Ind took command of our skirmishes and maneuvered them superbly. We followed on and as soon as he found the position of the enemy exactly we went at them. The 8th and 18th rushed through the first strip of woods and in climbing the next hill were met with a withering fire. We returned it, but could advance no further. From our regiment to the enemy was not more than 50 or 60 yards.

We kept up a heavy musketry fire on each side for an hour or more. I moved to the fence twice to see if there was any danger of our being flanked, and I <u>withdrew</u> pretty rapidly when the balls began tipping the fence around me. I had fired my musket so often that it could not be loaded again. Sergt Campbell aided me, but both of us could not force the ball down. McCarty of Co. "C" was wounded near me so I took his rifle.[133] Reinforcements did not reach us readily, we had almost exhausted our ammunition. Victory weaved to and fro. We knew we should not be able to hold the position much longer in that place. Then a general feeling that we must charge, pervaded the ranks, and without orders the whole line started forward with a yell, we fired as we ran. We got within a few feet of the rebel line before it began to give way. Several prisoners were taken. The Rebels ran gloriously. Several of our men had been killed.

While I was helping Capt Charles to turn two pieces which we had captured, on the enemy, someone took my rifle, I got another though. We saw some horses starting off with the caissons. So we shot the horses and thus got the ammunition. As I was taking a prisoner back, he dodged at the firing of our own pieces. I told him not to be afraid. Neagly of Co. "K" captured the flag of the Regiment in our front—the 15th Arkansas.[134] Grim did fine. Some of the boys were scared and didn't do much fighting. We captured quite a lot of ammunition. But the first line only was routed. We reorganized and proceeded on to the second. Col. Bailey 99th Ills was with coat off Musket in his hand and on foot at the head of his regiment. He will fight. Fortunately, in the afternoon we were on reserve. We were close up to the rest. About sundown a charge was made on the left, when the hardest firing had been transferred, and then all was silent. We laid down on the field in line of battle, expecting a still severer fight tomorrow. Gen Benton didn't do well.

2d

The enemy retreated last night beyond Port Gibson, and destroyed the bridge over Bayou Pierre. At 10 AM we reached the beautiful village of Port Gibson. We remain till we build another bridge. Gen Grant and his son ride about constantly, anxious to get the troops forward. He is a cool energetic man.[135] We camp near a school-house. The text books are still there. I suppose it to have been a flourishing school.

3d

Grand Gulf is evacuated. As Gen Grant is with us I suppose this is to be the direction that the main army will take. We shall soon reach Vicksburg. In the afternoon our Division went to the lower bridge to meet any force that might be there. Found breastworks but no enemy. We returned to Port Gibson.

4th

We crossed the bridge and proceeded on 7 miles where we found some cotton at a crossroads. The 18th Ind and two pieces 1st Ind Artillery were ordered to remain there and build a fort of the cotton which we did calling it Fort Washburn. One of these roads leads to Willow Springs, the other to Jackson. It is said that a detachment of the Rebels is in a <u>trap</u> and that we are here to prevent escape.

Contrabands are thick around camp.[136] We found thousands of pounds of Bacon which the citizens had collected for the Rebel army.

I went across to the mansion of the Rebel General Humphreys. Our soldiery had destroyed everything that was left in the rooms.[137]

Judge Baldwin a rank Secesh was here today under guard, claiming two horses which Major Jenks had captured off his farm. He owns six large farms, or plantations.

He is a real Southerner, and looked as if he could see us all slain at a single breath.

5th

Marched up to the remainder of the troops. Some half dozen of us go bathing in a nice clear river.

6th

Wrote a note home and to Fannie, simply stating that I was unhurt.

7th

Start again in the advance. We come near to Black River. It is said that the enemy is fortified on the opposite side. There was some cannonading in the afternoon.

8th

Steele's, Sherman's and other troops are coming up. Sam Clark has come up.[138]

9th

Johnston, Ditmars and I think of collecting a colored company. We go back to Grand Gulf, but the contrabands there are all put to work. I wandered all over the Rebel fortifications there. They had been strong. The siege pieces were down on the beach and marked Captured by Porter. Now I think they were captured a good deal more by us who fought on the 1st day of May. But if Government lets D.D. Porter claim the capture, <u>all</u> <u>*right*</u>.

10th

We go back to the front. We came down with ox teams for ammunition. Sergt. Hoves [?] was Wagon Master. I shall never forget how peculiarly classic one lady looked as she sat, in her mansion door. She was dressed in black. She had the elongated face and vacant stare which told but too plainly the sorrows caused to her poor heart by the invading <u>foe</u>. Won't she commit suicide or not? She laughed when she heard the result at Bull Run, but her gladness has been turned into mourning. If she wants to kill herself, why just let her do it. There now, she rises and goes away to <u>hang</u>—the bird cages!

11th

Cap Williams don't see how it is that we went away without consulting him.

12th

In line of Battle. We march within six miles of Edwards Depot, and having driven in the pickets we withdraw and will direct our course up the river I think.

13th

Marched 8 miles and <u>put up</u> in negro quarters, a heavy rain having overtaken us. The soldier must be proof against wet and cold weather. Sometimes he is perfectly drenched with rain, sometimes almost suffocated with dust and heat.

McPherson has the right wing, Steel the center and McClernand the left. Sherman is still in advance of us.

14th

We were on the road early. At 10 AM we pass Raymond, the rain pouring in torrents. Still all were cheerful. Four miles beyond Raymond we take quarters in Dr. H. J. Holmes Female Infirmary. We are here ten miles from Jackson. I went to a pond, doffed and washed my shirt and drawers, without soap. Just as I had them washed and <u>wrung</u>, the order came to <u>march</u>. I put them on and dried them by means of wearing them. Better that than not to wash at all.

I think if we keep whipping the rebels and wading through this mud as vigorously as we have begun the Rebellion cannot last.

15th

Start again in the rain. The mud is knee deep in some places. We hear that one corps met and drove the enemy from Jackson. We bivouac in the wet woods. While all were discussing busily the probabilities of a fight tomorrow, Col Washburn in a loud tone commanded attention! Said we must go now. But he finished by announcing that Gen Grant's Hdqrs were in the Capitol of Mississippi. One universal shout rang throughout camp. Hooker and Rosencrans have another victory in Tennessee.[139]

16th

We countermarch. As we get into Raymond, Gen Benton comes dashing with the news that "Richmond is ours and the Rebels cut all to H—l." Good if true. I throw up my hat. The enemy is now following up. He expects to fall upon our rear, but fortunately we are all <u>about</u> faced and what was our <u>rear</u> is now our <u>front</u>. This is a strange life. We sleep when we get time, either by day or night. We are marching most of the time. This is the <u>prose</u> of soldiering. The ladies of Raymond proffered their services in our Hospital. After a severe Battle [Champion Hill] in which our loss was quite heavy, the enemy was driven back seven miles. Our Division was in Reserve, till in the afternoon when the enemy began to Retreat. Then we followed them up double-quick, capturing a large amount of supplies and Edward's Depot. The Rebel dead were thick along the road.

17th

Our Division is in advance. We find the Rebels fortified at Black River Bridge. The 18th Ind was ordered to support the 1st Ind battery. The shot and shell came over us thick and fast. Our troops advanced gallantly. Soon the right of our line charged through a swamp or lagoon to the Rebel fort. This charge was so quick and so unexpected, that all in the fort who did not run away surrendered. A sutler of an Iowa Regt volunteered to go in this charge and was killed. <u>Peace to his ashes</u>. The Rebs indicated surrender by sticking their ramrods with cotton on them. One entire Tennessee Regiment was taken this morning.

We took 17 guns and 3,000 prisoners besides small arms.

Company "I" was thrown out as sharpshooters till 10 at night. When we came in and went to bed tired and sleepy.

18th

The Pioneers were to get a bridge thrown up last night so we shall advance again today.

Will it not be glorious for us to get Vicksburg, that stronghold!

Rec'd some mail, a letter from Miss Eddelman. Mrs. Mary Martin is dead. We advance to within six miles of Vicksburg. We are ordered to have no fires that will show, and to make no noise. We are all very much exhausted.

19th

Start again at six A.M. This will be an eventful day. We advance to within gunshot of the breastworks around Vicksburg, in support of our Batteries. Shot and shell came over and around us thick and fast.

20th

This morning at 2 o'clock our batteries and our sharpshooters open again. We could hardly scale the works if we were to charge. We are sure of the place by <u>storm</u> or <u>siege</u>. We communicate with the river above at Haines Bluff, and so will get plenty of supplies. Five days rations have done us 20 days. Our investment is complete. In the afternoon our division advanced, forward and to the right into a hollow. Several were wounded and some killed. Co "I" went out as Sharpshooters again. We had not been firing long till a ball passed through Doan's body cutting the belt on both sides. He threw up his hands, said "Cap I'm shot" and died. He was brave. He knew no fear. But he was wicked. Some of our men were killed and wounded this afternoon by the explosion of shells from our own pieces.[140]

21st

I cannot see that we are accomplishing anything by this sort of process.

22d

This is my birthday. How strange and varied my life has been. There were my childhood and youth. How many pleasant memories are associated with them. Five years in College, come up distinctly. Then my army days. Our boys have been hallooing over to the Rebels. I heard one ask Where's the Capitol of your State? and Where's the Capitol of your Confederacy? (Gen Benton had announced that it was ours) and Where is your Gen

Pemberton? To this last they answered, "He's <u>here</u>!" About 10 o'clock the rumor spreads fast that we are to charge the works. Some faces look terrified the most look cool and ready.

Well, this was a memorable <u>birthday</u>. We made the charge. The 18th was to be in reserve, but soon it was in the advance. Gen Benton got the regiments in the order desired and then gave the order right face forward on to victory. No sooner had the advance started up the ravine leading to the fort than a murderous volley met them. The Col of the 99th Ills was wounded and the Lt Col <u>ran</u>. Men came running back in the greatest confusion. It seemed for a time as if the thing would fail. We advanced slowly. We did not know where to find that part of the Brigade that had gone before, and there was no one to tell us Major Jenks had been wounded. So we went straight up to the fort. 40 of us getting into the outer ditch of the fort. Several were killed and wounded in the attempt. The rest of the regiment did not follow us for some reason, and so there we were. We could not advance for we could not scale the Fort. Lt [John] Lowes was wounded in attempting to reach the ditch. Pucket and Halfacre were killed and others wounded by my side. Wiley was wounded in both legs and hands.[141] The enemy was watching us closely. Our only safety was in keeping a bead drawn on that part of the fort where we saw shots come from; already we had one killed and one wounded by them. Grim again displayed the greatest courage. Not a moment was to be lost. We could not stay there. By means of a kerchief and a dispatch we communicated with the rest of the regiment. We were told that we could come out under cover of the fire from the regiment. This we did safely, and we had no sooner cleared the ditch that [than] the rebels began throwing hand-grenades into it which would have killed or wounded most of us. We had to leave Wiley there. The regiment held its place out side all day. A piece of artillery was drawn up the ravine by hand and with it and our fire the Rebels were kept down well.

About sundown our brigade was relieved by Gen. Burbridge.[142] His troops not as familiar with the operation as we the Rebels got the start of them. We had no more than stacked our arms than they came running back <u>pell mell</u>. I was sad at that. We had as I supposed lost the work of the whole day. Company "I," although it had been on picket two nights was called on again and went without murmur and without a cracker. Cap Williams was slightly wounded. At last we were drawn back to a hill and permitted to sleep on our arms. The great fault of the charge was want of courage in our general (Brigade Commander). I say this because I <u>know it</u>. Cap Charles acted the part of a brave soldier, Cap Woods the part of a <u>coward</u>. Vicksburg is not ours by <u>Assault</u>.[143]

23d

A siege, regular, is to be established. Our men are greatly exhausted. I am detailed Clerk for Regt'l Qmaster. I go back and take a wash and put on clean clothes and take a sleep and feel as if "old things had passed away, and behold all things had become new."[144] I wish the rest could have the same privilege.

24th

I feel still more exhausted. All energy is gone. I am perfectly stupid. I was surprised today to see Uncle James Vawter. He is a Sanitary Agent. He brought our new Regimental flag. Our troops are beginning to throw up fortifications.

25th

Mortars are to be brought round and planted, so that we can shell from two sides. Maj. Jenks is dead. He was admired by all. He while a captain was the model captain of the Regiment. John Lowes is convalescent. Cap Vandervender is dead. Cap ODaniels was killed.[145]

26th

The siege is becoming more systematized, and hence easier. I got a good long letter yesterday from Miss LM. Lt Crane is Quartermaster. He is sick and peevish.[146]

27th

J. R. Johnston is appointed to collect a company of negroes. He will I suppose be commissioned. Sergt Campbell is dead. All speak in praise of Grim. None will doubt that Christianity makes a better soldier in the future.

28th

Busy in the office. Grant's army is the subject of the highest interest and I feel sure that it will realize the highest hopes.

29th

A brisk fire was opened on the enemy. He scarcely replied. One or two magazines were fired yesterday. Rate and Mag are quite unwell. I must write them even if they cannot answer.

30th

Several men are sick owing to the excessive heat and fatigue. Miss Nannie Steele, Johnston's correspondent is a good letter writer.
Johnston [Confederate Gen. Joe Johnston] is said to be coming in the rear, but Gen. Grant provided for that.

31st

Eventful May is closing. On the first day of it we fought the first battle of the campaign, on this last day we are close investing Vicksburg our object. Many brave ones have fallen and sleep with the patriot dead.
Hooker has had a battle East, but was repulsed. Rosencrans in Tennessee is getting ready for offensive movements. Lt. W. G. Burton is dead. He enlisted in the 67th Ind soon after graduating. Simpson his brother came for him. He died at home. He was not a brilliant scholar, but students and faculty respected him. He is the first of our graduates who has died in the service.[147]

June 1st

Our convalescents have gone to the river.

2d

Several citizen surgeons have come here from Indiana. We move quarters to a much pleasanter place.

3d

I assist in issuing the supplies. Some one brought a letter for me, but alas, it was for William Scott, Co. "C." Lee James is dead. He was wounded at Port Gibson. He was a noble fellow.[148] When I reflect on the many worthy young men who have fallen, I ask reverently why do I still live.
As I was coming from the Hospital in the evening I was called to notice the rapid firing of the mortar boats. So I sat down by the roadside and watched the shells as they quickly followed each other. The moon was shining. The scene was thrilling. There were the heavy guns of the boats grumbling out their wrath; along the lines in front was the occasional

shot of the Sharpshooter. In the rear was the sound of the wagons as they went to and fro transporting supplies of ammunition and provisions. At the hospital nearby were the sick and wounded. Here and there a surgeon was sitting by a candle penning lines to those he remembered at home, or recording the experience of the day. In the huts were negroes chanting their hymns of Praise. The mocking bird in the bush was singing his best "peeces" [*sic*].

4th

[no entry]

5th

I am told our forces are undermining a fort, the one where we charged 22d May. Pemberton tells his men that Johnston will soon drive the Yanks away. I was out in the country getting plums. I have a treat in Fields Scrap Book.[149] Wrote three letters. The Black River Hospital has moved up[.] This indicates a looking for Gen. Johnston.

6th

A shell came over this morning "before breakfast" and exploded near but did none any harm. I see plenty of men in the army who <u>simply live</u>. They seem not to think of the past nor of the future. They do not perceive nor understand nor reason much. They sleep a great deal just to get the time to pass along faster.

7th

Eddelman is going to quarter here. The Reg't came back to rest but soon got tired and wanted to go to the pits. Letter from home. John T. Butler, Jacob Holsclaw and John Carroll are dead. Died in the service. John Carroll died quite suddenly. Rate talks of going to the water cure.[150]

8th

Some force made an expedition to Yazoo City and captured the place and the Navy Yard. The Indiana legislature failed to make an appropriation to pay the interest on the State debt. Gov. Morton is running the machine on his own responsibility.[151]
We have been here 20 days, and can stay 60 more if necessary.
Miss Savage I know must be a good woman and <u>true</u>.

9th

More firing than usual. Rec'd a letter from home. Uncle P. C. V. has gone to Lafayette. Jennie is teaching. Gid Moncrief pulled a <u>butternut</u> off a young man's bosom in church. Good for Gid.

10th

Lt. Daniels, Co. "B," relieves Lt. Crane. The latter is going home—sick. Capt Williams is staying here while his leg is lame. Deserters come in every day. The negroes proved themselves good <u>soldiers</u> at Milliken's Bend.[152]

11th

There is to be an election for Lt Col and Major today. Candidates have multiplied of late. There were six for the Lt Col'cy. Lt Laken with his squad has been taken prisoner. He has not been heard from for <u>nine</u> days.[153]

12th

Capt Charles was elected Lt Col and Capt Williams Major. I shall soon be commissioned Captain. I happened into an argument on the relative importance of the different Professions on Society. I claim that it is not material what profession a great man chooses. He will settle to his proper work anyhow. I love to read the writings of great men of the past.

13th

We are being reinforced by General Herron's troops. It is probable that we shall be attacked by Gen Johnston.[154]

14th

[no entry]

15th

Heavy siege guns are planted on our lines. The boys work all of every night at the tunnels and rifle pits. We are now quite close up. The 26th Ind is somewhere on the line.

16th

The Paymaster is here. The news of it "doeth good like a medicine."[155]

We were talking last night of the pleasure of being <u>alive</u>. No studious man can but rejoice that he does exist. Annihilation is of all things the most horrible. Let me live! Let me live! Is the cry of the soul.

17th

There are in Grant's army the following Indiana regiments: 8th, 11th, 12th, 16th, 18th, 24th, 26th, 34th, 46th, 48th, 49th, 54th, 57th, 60th, 67th, 69th, 83d, 93d and 100th. Will McCoy is married to Miss Potter. He is the first of our class to offer himself up a sacrifice upon the Hymeneal altar. Long may they wave! Gen Schofield relieves Gen Curtis. Logan expects soon to have a Rebel fort.[156]

18th

These days are monotonous. None craves something new more than the soldier. Government is organizing an Invalid Corps for Garrison duty. I don't like the idea.[157]

19th

Eddelman and I started for the 26th Ind. Met Capt Stott, Lts Read and Story and Henry McCanlon, John Carroll, George Carroll, Monroe and Sircu Marsh and Charlie King. They all look healthy. One would recognize readily that it was an Indiana Regiment. They have the 1st Missouri artillery. "Dicky" makes a good captain the boys say.[158]

20th

There was very heavy firing today. The pits were to be filled and if any corps Commander saw that he could carry a fort, he was to telegraph to the others, and try it.[159]
Gen McClernand is relieved by Maj Gen E. O. C. Ord. Gen's Grant and McClernand could not see eye to eye.

21st

I have been reading the march of the Israelites. Joshua exhibited more military skill at some times than the best of our Generals, not excepting McClellan. He lost a battle at Ai because some soldier contrary to Gen Order No 1 had stolen a golden wedge. But he took Ai by a sharp trick. He had some ambushed just outside the walls. He attacked in force and fell back. They supposed that they were "driving" him, so they pursued. When they were well out[,] those ambushed went in and set the city on fire and then attacked the Aians in the rear. All of them were slain but the King and he was hanged. Is our age more intelligent than the past ages? We think that we do not need the assistance of God very much, especially since the <u>monitors</u> have been built. If the 70th Ind is here I shall get to see my classmates Grubbs and Morgan. The last Greek we read was <u>Oedipus Tyrannus</u>.[160]

22d

My journal is not <u>Pro Bono Publico</u> but <u>Pro Bono</u> myself and my family. One month ago we made the famous charge. It is said that the Rebels are trying to escape.

23d

This morning the Rebels threw a steel pointed ball into Osterhaus's Hospital yard. It struck where a dog had been lying a moment before. Some of our men say that we shall have Vicksburg in 3 days.

24th

We are getting the Regimental oven nearly done. Lt Adams is going to resign because he was not elected Lt Col.

25th

It is rumored that Port Hudson is taken.[161]

26th

I heard that there was to be a charge yesterday afternoon so I went up. At the blowing of the fort in front of Logan, the whole line was to fire as fast as possible for half an hour. I never before heard <u>such</u> cannonading. The rebels I suppose had their knees smite together.

27th

Our bakery is operating well. Cap Charles has gone home sick. One of the Givans is in the 26th Ind.

28th

Busy all day in the office. Lt Crane has turned all over to Lt Daniels. Continued my history of the Israelites to as far as where Egleon was struck with a stone by a woman, and then commanded his orderly to kill him that it might not be said that he was killed by a <u>woman</u>. Was that chivalrous? Yes.[162]

29th

A butternut shot a Miss Brougher in the leg near to Brewersville, because she was a Union girl. He ought to be executed.[163]
Rate is still indisposed. I hope I shall see her again

30th

The musketoes flies and gnats are monopolizing most of the time. One attacks by day the others under cover of the night. How do musketoes know to sing about ones ear so tormentingly?

July 1st

We have moved our quarters nearer to the front, not more than three hundred yards back. We have excavated a room in the side hill.
The weather is very hot.
Our forces are close up to the rebel line. In some places they are within a few feet. John Potter is now an ordained minister.[164]

2d

The 18th Ind has gone to Black River in expectation of an attack there. Shelling is going on briskly in front.

3d

We were startled by the cessation of firing. I went up to see what was the matter. A flag of truce had passed up to Gen Grants Hdquarters. During the truce Federals and Rebels climbed to the top of their works and sat and stood there silently looking at each other as strangely as if they had all just been created, and were looking at their surroundings. Or they, as they climbed up in quick succession, looked somewhat like fowls flying to the top of the fence after the summer shower is over and the sun shines out again. I took the opportunity to go over all the ground we could. I saw Doans grave. I recognized the ground we charged over on 22d May. When the truce passed back all as if instinctively crawled back to the ditches and began firing as usual. In the afternoon the flag came out again, and after some time passed back.
It seems to be the tacit understanding that the Rebels want to quit. No firing. How glorious, We all say if they should surrender tomorrow. But if they don't we are ready to administer an <u>extra</u> dose of salt peter, for we were always used to shooting on the Fourth of July anyhow!
A general good feeling pervades. Vicksburg will not much longer be in Rebel hands. By means of incessant labor day and night we have superior works to the enemy, and we have more <u>effective guns.</u>

4th

The firing of the National Salute, I not thinking took to be a resumption
of hostilities. But soon it ceased and I started toward the left to see all
I could see. I went three miles, finding Battery after Battery placed and
well manned, only waiting orders. I had hardly got back when I heard
more than ordinary bustle in the regiment. I looked and behold! For five
miles on the enemies lines small flags waved above every fort. They were
intended for white flags, but they were more dirty looking than white.
Then I knew that Vicksburg was ours. At 10 A.M. the Rebels marched
out in front of their works and stacked arms. Most of the pieces were
loaded. Immediately a chain guard was thrown around the entire line,
but fortunately I got inside and directed my steps with no delay to
Vicksburg proper.

I passed the rebel camps. There seemed to be great harmony and good
feeling between Federals and Confederates. The city was desolate and de-
faced by our shells. Many of the cave dwellers were just getting out from
their cave houses. All things had the appearance of war. It is estimated
that we have taken 30,000 prisoners, 40,000 small arms and 300 pieces
artillery including the heavy pieces fronting the river.

The rebels had been eating mule meat.

I reached the Court House, saw the Star Spangled Banner raised over it
and heard the Star Spangled Banner sung while the Marine Brigade at the
landing, together with the gunboats were coming in strong on the chorus
with booming of cannon. Hail Fourth of July! The most eventful since
1776. The Rebellion is sick. May it soon be relieved of its pain by death.

5th

The troops all but enough to garrison the place march towards Jackson
under General Sherman. Gen Joe Johnston may as well look for a place to
retreat to. I am left in charge of the convalescent camp. There are 82 in the
camp. The troops took all the rations away so that I have to get to work to
find some more. The boys had great fun last night sending up rockets.

6th

I got a cart and mule for the boys to move their traps to a new and better
camp. When done with him they very kindly turned him out, for others
better disposed to hunt up.

Lt Scott asked me to clerk for him, but I will not leave Lt Daniels.[165]

7th

Rations being issued I started early to Vicksburg. I first went up the river. The first piece I examined was the <u>Memphis</u> Caliber 10 inches, with a good magazine and plenty of ammunition. The next was the <u>Tennessee</u> Caliber 7 inches. The next was ["]<u>Whistling Dick</u>."[166] I saw several balls made from shells thrown by our mortars. There were still many more pieces of various calibers. And all well mounted. I've no doubt but that the rebels said one to another when they mounted all of them, "No Yankee boat can ever pass here, it will be absolutely impossible.["] Boats can be seen from these upper batteries long before they are round Youngs Point. It is a wonder that any vessel could pass.

Next I went to the burying ground. They dig long deep narrow ditches. As one of the burying party told me that they bury two deep, I estimate the number buried at this yard 1,000. The ridges gave the place the appearance of a potatoe patch.

There were but two tombstones; on one, put there in memory of Grain, 2d Tenn Cav, by his company was these lines:

"Lowly may be the turf that covers
The sacred grave of his last repose
But O, there's a glory round, it hovers
Broad as the Day-break, and bright as its close."

Next to the left of the city. I found here about the same number of pieces and same caliber as those on the right though farther back from the river. I then went to the Arago and got dinner. The wharf is busy. The arms are being brought in. The fort which Gen Logan blew up was very much mutilated. Dirt was thrown 200 feet.[167]

In the hills and in the cuts, for roads were excavations, with front large enough for the ingress of one at a time. Here resorted the aged father, the mother, the fair daughter and the little ones from the wrath of the Yankee army and navy. Mayhap lovers have met in those and amidst the death that reigned without have in gentle whispers vowed <u>eternal love</u>, let come life or death.

8th

James Starr came over. He is better but paralyzed as to his right side.[168] The Regiment is beyond Black River. The railroad is being repaired to there.

9th

I dreamed of being an Army spy.

10th

I have been reading Godey for 1841. It has some affecting <u>affection sto-ries</u>. There was a fight at Helena on the 4th Price was badly whipped. He lost 3,000 prisoners. And Mead[e] is confronting Lee near Harrisonburg. Foster is threatening Richmond. Breckenridge is hovering around Port Hudson as Johnston was around this place.[169]

11th

The squad has increased to 100. "I had rather be a doorkeeper in the house of my God than to dwell in the tents of wickedness."[170]

12th

I was far up to the right of our line viewing the ditches and forts. Several Confederates were buried in the fort blown up by Gen Logan.
The ditches are all silent now. No sound of a musket is heard, the cricket sings his song undisturbed when late was the thunder of war. I met S.[Simpson] Burton again. He tells me that Morgan and Grubbs are well.

13th

Port Hudson is taken! Got a Gazette giving full particulars of the fight in Pennsylvania. Agate, who is <u>really</u> the Gazette's best correspondent and really <u>agate</u> for cutting, gives a description of it. It was at Gettysburg Meade whipped Lee fairly. None could reasonably ask for greater success than we have had this summer.
Marshal Grinstead was wounded at Murfreesboro. His father went for him.[171]

14th

At day break our cook came and awakened me saying "Hugh is <u>dead</u>." He had gone out of his tent at night for water and died getting back. His wife having been asleep did know nothing of it till on waking this morning. He was very old and lame. Harriet said that she was sorry that he died without her knowing it. She has not the refined affection which we would expect in a cultivated woman, but still she had affection. She tells me all her troubles. While the rest make fun of her and her dead husband, I cannot do it. My reflection is that negroes are <u>human beings</u>. Two nice little birds have built a nest here in my desk. Nicer way of having <u>pets</u> than in cages. "I am in league with the fowls of the air."[172]

15th

Went to the Commissary Boat for rations. Here is the <u>red-tape</u> process of getting rations at this post, 1ˢᵗ Get a pass to town, takes an hour. 2d Get the provision Return signed by the Provost Marshal, takes two hours, 3d Get it signed by the commander of the Post, takes two hours, 4ᵗʰ Get the order for the provisions at the office of the Commissary, takes two hours, and 5ᵗʰ Takes two hours to get waited on at the <u>issuing</u> department. And lastly it takes from <u>two</u> to <u>four</u> hours to get a pass of the Provost Marshal to get back to camp. This is no exaggeration. It took me all of a long summer day to <u>grind through</u>. There were several ladies at the Commissary Boat. Some of the young ladies were pretty I suppose. I can hardly risk my judgment in such a momentous matter. They wore long flowing garments as angels do.

16th

Florer and I discussed farming till 12 at night. So far as I am able to judge, we discussed it <u>ably</u> and <u>at length</u> especially the latter.[173] I drew today a barrel of sugar instead of a barrel of flour. The boys shall have it for sirup.

17th

We have Bob the barber for cook. He is lazy. I am reading "Practical Thought," published by the Tract society.[174] Several start for the Regiment today. Wrote a note to Miss C.G. of Granville.

18th

Our cook is not very cleanly in the kitchen arrangements. I deplore it. I hope my wife will be neat in her dress and fastidiously cleanly in her management of the kitchen. If she is not I shall feel somewhat the mortification of Mr. Woodbridge in Godey.

As I stood at the door of the Provost Marshals office, awaiting my turn to get in, I hear an old sober-looking negro murmuring to another that when he got to Heaven he supposed he should not be <u>pushed back</u>. (He had been pushed from his place all morning.)

Was there not great reason for his consolation? Black and white will not be known there.

19th

We shall have to move our camp inside the works. I don't like it—but "anything to crush the Rebellion."

20th

Gen. Grant has taken about 42,000 prisoners since May 1st 1863.

21st

In town to the Express Office. Saw a <u>Steamer</u> (sail-rigger) from New Orleans. Port Hudson was taken on the 8th. 9,000 prisoners. Morgan was in Indiana, on a raid. If <u>six</u> <u>thousand</u> after Morgan at home can't stop nor catch Morgan, let all complaint about <u>mismanagement</u> of our <u>armies</u> be restrained.[175]

22d

Here comes another <u>22nd</u> but there's no use charging Vicksburg now. The stars and stripes wave unquestioned.
There has been a fleet attack at Charleston. Our troops will be in tomorrow. Johnston evacuated Jackson.[176]
Sure enough, Morgan passed near Vernon. He demanded a surrender; but the place did not see fit to let him have the place so he didn't <u>want</u> it; and went on. Good for the pluck of my native town.

23d

Our Division will be in this afternoon.

24th

Rate and Mrs. Beck Wynn are at Columbus. Water cure.[177] Recd a letter from Mat and Miss T. The rumor is that we shall go to New Orleans.

25th

G. N. Hawley of Franklin College was to see me today. He was in my S. S. class. He is now a member of the church. He is in the 76th Ills. Saw Merit Read[178]

26th

Charleston was attacked vigorously.

27th

We camp on the back of the River in the sand.

28th

The victories at Vicksburg, Gettysburg Helena and Port Hudson occupy the Journals.

29th

My Commission came. I get mustered. I hope to be able to show myself a worthy Captain. I think I can make soldiering as pleasant for my men, as is possible.

30th

Receipted for the Company property.

31st

The weather is exceedingly warm.

August 1st

Expressed to John L. Vawter for the Company $560.00.

2nd

The discipline of Co. "I" was very poor.

3rd

Lt. Knobe starts home. I send a walking stick to Barney Wallace. Dr. Bigney is sick.

4th

Morgan is captured. He and his staff are in prison.

5th

We have Ordnance Inspection today.

6th

Nineteen more Ironclads are about ready. I was entertained (?) till 12 last night by a certain loquacious Surgeon. I listened because I did not know how to avoid it.

7th

Expected to be inspected but passed without being subjected, which thing we might have suspected.

8th

We had a gale.

9th

Is it possible that a soldier is so careless as to his soul? It is shocking. When he looks back on this life from the light of eternity; they will explain themselves.

10th

Began Battalion Drill again. And had Dress Parade—the first for <u>four months</u>.

11th

Co. "I" reports <u>seven</u> sick; the weather is intensely warm. I have reported a man I found furnishing whiskey to the Regiment.

12th

A large mail. A letter from home and Miss Carrie G. and Lt. Morgan. Kelly Sims Buckner and Hall are going north.[179]

13th

Rev. J. S. Donaldson has been elected Chaplain 18th Ind.[180] We shall soon go down the river.

14th

Battalion Drill is interesting.

15th

It is said that a man should always be on good terms with himself. To be so one must do what he himself approves, and do so at all times.

16th

Heard a Methodist minister preach. His illustrations were all from the <u>farm</u> when they should have been from the <u>camp</u>, the <u>march</u>, or the Battlefield.
Took dinner with Merit Read of 67th Ind.
Co. "I" had a nice Inspection this morning.

17th

Lt. Pelser has a severe attack of cramps.[181]

18th

The opening of the Mississippi brings an urgent demand for <u>trade</u>. But the opening of trade now will not be best.

19th

We were served up with three papers, 12th 13th and 14th, all having the same news.

20th

A sad accident occurred today. The City of Madison, just loaded with ammunition, blew up. About fifty lives were lost mostly colored men. The explosion was caused by the explosion of a shell.

PART THREE

6

In Cajun Country and "On to Texas"

While William Taylor Stott spent the long, hot days of late summer
1863 ministering to sick and wounded soldiers in Vicksburg, Union officials devoted much of their time to considering the question of what to do
about Texas. Unknown to Stott, it was the Abraham Lincoln administration's desire to establish a firm foothold in that state that shaped the next
chapter of his own Civil War story.

Following the Union successes at Vicksburg and Port Hudson, Major
General Nathaniel P. Banks set his eyes on Mobile, Alabama, a primary
conduit for Confederate supplies from abroad, which he believed could be
captured easily. He proposed such a movement to the War Department,
only to learn that Washington had a different target in mind. On July 24,
1863, General-in-Chief Henry Halleck informed Banks that "every preparation should be made for an expedition into Texas." In three subsequent
messages—dated July 31, August 6, and August 10—"Old Brains" urged
Banks to begin operations into the Lone Star State with dispatch. As
Banks himself reported, Halleck "fully appreciated" the Massachusetts
general's plan for operations against Mobile, but they would have to wait,
for "there were reasons other than military why those directed in Texas
should be undertaken first." In fact, as Banks understood the matter,
"there was no choice."[1] Besides, Halleck was not alone in his sense of urgency. Lincoln, on July 26, requested Secretary of War Edwin M. Stanton
"to organize a force to go to Western Texas" and stressed his personal
belief that "no local object is more desirable." A week later Banks received
a letter from Lincoln insisting that "recent events in Mexico" made quick
action in Texas "more important than ever." Within a few days Lincoln

Captain William Taylor Stott, Company I.

also urged upon General Ulysses S. Grant "the importance of re-establish-
ing the national authority in Western Texas as soon as possible."[2]

There were several "other than military" reasons why Northern leaders deemed Union presence in Texas to be vital. One was economic, and
it swirled around a commodity coveted by both nations—cotton. Long
before the disunited states went to war in 1861, northeastern textile
manufacturers hoped to populate Texas with Yankees who would intro-
duce free-labor agriculture there, raise cotton for northern mills, and thus
"save Texas for freedom." The coming of war made that prospect more attractive, and in 1861 the influential Massachusetts textile tycoon Edward
Atkinson lobbied in Washington for "a free-labor invasion of Texas." His
proposal gained support among many of the North's most persuasive
political figures, including senators, generals, and three members of the
president's cabinet, Postmaster General Montgomery Blair, Secretary of
State William Seward, and Treasury Secretary Salmon Chase. The "Conquer Texas" lobby, as one historian labeled the group, was obviously heard
in the highest places. A second economic factor was one of the "recent
events" to which Lincoln referred in his correspondence with Banks. Now
that Vicksburg and Port Hudson had fallen, the only truly open path to
foreign markets for the western Confederacy lay through Texas in the
Trans-Mississippi Department. That state bordered the neutral nation of
Mexico, and trade across the Rio Grande, though difficult, was indispens-
able for the Confederacy's sale of cotton and acquisition of foreign goods.[3]
Planting the Union flag in Texas could cripple Confederate efforts.

Mexico itself constituted another potent motive for movement into
Texas—a political and diplomatic one. Foremost of the "recent events"
troubling Lincoln were those that occurred in Mexico on June 7, 1863,
when the French forces of Emperor Louis-Napoléon entered Mexico
City, toppled the republican government of Benito Juárez, and erected a
puppet regime to be run by Louis-Napoléon's relative, Archduke Maximil-
ian of Austria. The fear in Washington, and particularly of Lincoln and
Seward, was that Louis-Napoléon's incursion in Mexico would foster a
potential French-Confederate alliance against the United States. Further
rumors abounded that the French monarch had imperialistic designs on
Texas, Louisiana, and other former Mexican holdings, even possible an-
nexation. From Seward's perspective, France's occupation of Mexico was a
bold violation of the Monroe Doctrine. The secretary of state therefore de-

manded that "the flag be restored to *some one point in Texas*" as a reminder that it was still U.S. property. Hence, as Halleck told Banks, military operations in Texas were necessary "as a matter of political or State policy, connected with our foreign relations."[4]

In his directives to Banks, Halleck stated his personal preference for an invasion route, namely a "combined naval and military movement upon the Red River" to northern Texas. Neither he nor the president, however, dictated the strategy to be employed, leaving it up to Banks to formulate the most suitable plan. Banks, however, had a personnel problem. The forces in his Department of the Gulf had been greatly reduced by the removal of twenty-one regiments whose terms of service had expired, leaving Banks with less than 13,000 men with which to face Major General Richard Taylor's grayclad troops in the Louisiana bayou country. Fortunately, beginning in mid-August Grant filled the vacuum by sending the battle-tried XIII Corps, a total of 14,712 troops fresh from their triumph in Mississippi, to bolster Banks's army.[5]

So it was that Stott and the Eighteenth Indiana stepped aboard the steamboat *North America* on the night of August 20, 1863, for a two-day excursion to Carrollton, Louisiana, six miles north of New Orleans. While on the river, Stott became ill with fever and remained so throughout his stay at Carrollton, his friend F. C. Eddelman, now a hospital steward, providing him with medical care. Understandably, Stott left little record of those days in his diary.[6]

His comrades, however, shared with diaries or folks at home some of their impressions of the trip and their new locale. Also aboard the *North America* was Daniel Roberts of the Eighth Indiana, who found the sights on the Mississippi shores overwhelming. Natchez especially caught his eye. He could barely see it, since it was "up on the hills," but judging by "the looks of the dwellings & the country around it," it appeared to be "a splendid place." Equally impressive were "the great estates lining the banks where the planters houses are very large & costly . . . built on the ancient style with heavy columns & porches all around[,] one to each story." Even the slaves' quarters seemed stately, arranged in "nice rows" and surrounded by "the nicest shrubbery I ever saw." The corps's new campsite in and around Carrollton likewise met with the soldiers' approval. Located on the east bank of the river and close to Lake Pontchartrain, it was, in Roberts's opinion, "a great bathing place." Lieutenant George S. Marks of the Ninety-ninth Illinois declared it a "fine and Pleasant Place for a camp," and the Sixty-seventh Indiana's William Winters considered it "the nicest campground that we have ever had."[7] Though the weather was hot and sultry during the day, the nights were cool, and the close proximity to New Orleans made up for any climatic discomfort. As Colonel James S. Slack of the Third Division explained to his wife, Carrollton was "really a part of New Orleans," and trains ran from it to the city "every hour during the day & charge 10 cts for the trip." Every day without a grand review by Banks or Grant, or some other pressing obligation, could be a field day in the big city. Roberts and Marks recorded their excitement at going "to Jackson Square, seeing the Henry Clay Monument at Lafayette Square, and spending time at the 'Ship Landing,'" where these midwestern landlubbers enjoyed a rare sight—"15 or 20 men of war." To Roberts, New Orleans "beat Cincinatti all to pieces." Besides, Private Gilbert Denny of Company G in the Eighteenth noted, there were "plenty of women here," and the Vieux Carré provided opportunities to meet them over custard pie, flowing wine, and other delicacies.[8]

Stott's chance to see New Orleans, however, would have to wait. In early September, before Stott had fully recovered, the XIII Corps, now under the command of Major General Cadwallader C. Washburn, crossed the Mississippi to Algiers, Louisiana, a place Captain John William DeForest of the Twelfth Connecticut called "a dirty, rascally suburb of New Orleans." At Algiers the men of the Eighteenth, joined by the regiments that had fought beside them in the Vicksburg campaign—the Eighth Indiana, Thirty-third Illinois, and Ninety-ninth Illinois—boarded the New Orleans, Opelousas and Great Western Railroad for Brashear City on Berwick Bay. The train ride made it clear that this expedition would differ from that of Vicksburg. The crammed cars sped across "verry poor country," according to Private David S. Scott of the Eighth Indiana. It careened through cyprus swamps and low, marshy, wet prairie populated, said Roberts, "by Moccasin snakes, Alligators & Musquitoes," the latter "sitting on the top of trees whetting their bills, ready to pounce down upon us as quick as they found out where we were going to camp."[9]

Thus began what the chronicler of the Thirty-third Illinois called a "fool expedition" akin to the "uselessness and stupidity" of the campaign in eastern Missouri of the previous winter. Many agreed because once again the soldiers did much marching back and forth and had little contact with the enemy, only this time in the southern Louisiana bayou country. Another disappointing development emerged as well, for now the midwesterners of the XIII Corps were to serve alongside the New England troops of Banks's XIX Corps. The easterners viewed the newcomers from the West as "strangers in this army" who exhibited "peculiar habits and singular style of doing duty." One New Yorker had heard that they were "evidently, excellent fighting men" but "they had a wonderful disregard for personal appearance" and a penchant for rowdiness and destruction. The new Army of the Gulf was a strange mixture, at times resembling oil and water. Yet, as historian Richard Lowe points out, it was a "formidable military machine"—one molded at little Brashear City.[10]

Brashear was not much better than Algiers. "We have escaped Algiers by getting sent back to Brashear City," mused DeForest, "which is something like being delivered out of purgatory into hades." Besides the extreme heat and humidity, he complained, "the largest part of the native population, if not the worthiest" were "mosquitoes and other insects, including alligators." As a result, DeForest added, it was "one of the sickliest spots in Louisiana," with unhealthy, briny water that bred critters attracted to army tents, what another soldier described as "moccasin snakes of domestic tendencies." The city hardly deserved that lofty title. Gouverneur Morris of the Sixth New York called it an "abortive sort of place," and a Louisiana black contraband, one of many who flocked into the Union camps, said Brashear had been "borned and had'nt growed." It sat at the head of Berwick Bay, had around five hundred human inhabitants, and owed its existence to the railroad. A turntable, lodgings for train crews and station agents, cattle pens, small shops and stores, a hotel, and a bar lined the tracks, but the rubble of burned dwellings and unsightly earthworks beyond were reminders of the ravages of war. In short, wrote Dan Camp of the Twenty-fourth Iowa, Brashear was "a miserable little town" and "anything but a pleasant place to be encamped."[11]

The Eighteenth Indiana and its companion regiments avoided Brashear by camping on Bayou Boeuf, seven miles from the village, but conditions there were about the same. The deep, navigable, and slow-flowing waters of the bayou were unfit for use, so the troops dug wells. The water they uncovered, however, was "little better." It was also at Bayou

Boeuf, as Isaac Elliott of the Eighth Indiana recalled, that the soldiers of
the First Brigade "first made acquaintance with alligators," and some of
the "young saurians were pets in the regiment." A Bedford, Indiana,
corporal said that their bellowing, "like a herd of lost bulls," could be
heard for miles.[12]

Brashear City and its environs may have been a nasty place to camp,
but it provided the locale for the creation of a new army. The arrival of the
Union troops increased the local population fourfold. Trains brought Yankee brigades and regiments, artillery and caissons, and ambulances and
wagons. Soldiers scattered throughout the countryside, creating tent cit-
ies, excavating latrines, erecting supply depots, and virtually taking over
the entire area. Here were fifty-one infantry regiments, fourteen units of
cavalry, and sixteen artillery batteries, an army one biographer contends
was "possibly the largest to ever take the field in Louisiana." And here,
around tiny Brashear, Banks fashioned a fighting force out of a peculiar
blend of "westerners" and "easterners," all experienced combat veterans
but none too sure of each other. He chose General William B. Franklin, an
officer with a checkered career, to be the field commander of his roughly
30,000 men, so that Banks himself could concentrate on fulfilling his
charge to plant the Union flag in Texas.[13]

In his eagerness to do so, the Massachusetts politician-general had
already sent a sizable portion of the XIX Corps under Franklin's direction
seaborne from New Orleans along the Texas Gulf Coast toward Houston.
Franklin's orders were to advance to the mouth of the Sabine River and
employ the navy to secure a landing so that his army could move quickly
inland to Houston and Galveston. The attack on September 8, however,
was a "comic-opera affair" in which poor planning and multiple blunders
led to failure, leaving Franklin no choice but to return to New Orleans.
The Sabine Pass debacle caused some in the ranks to wonder if their
commander would live up to his nickname of "Nothing Positive" Banks.
Bernard Schermerhorn of the Forty-sixth Indiana wrote his wife: "There
does not appear to be the same amount of brains & skills exhibited in the
conduct of affairs in this department as there was in the Dept. of Tenn."[14]

The skills may not have been there, but Banks's anxiety to invade
Texas persisted. This time he opted to move his army up the Bayou Teche,
north to Vermilionville, and then west across the southern Louisiana
grasslands. On September 13 he informed Halleck that "preparations for

an overland movement" were under way. His hope was to convince Washington that specific steps toward Texas were being taken as he "bought time for another naval invasion of that state via the Gulf of Mexico." Banks decided to put the army in motion again. At six o'clock on the morning of September 25, two divisions of the XIII Corps crossed over the bay to Berwick City, another "city in name only." In fact, Augustus Sinks of the Forty-sixth "looked in vain for the City unless the half dozen houses Scattered on the plain could be called a City." The troops no sooner set up camp than torrential rains set in. What Stott termed an "Equinoctial Storm" lasted for days, causing the men to hunker down in the "Small and Delapadated Town," until the Bayou Teche Campaign, also called the Texas Overland Expedition, began on October 3, 1863.[15]

The First and Third divisions of the XIII Corps received their orders for the new operation on Friday, October 2. They were to carry two days rations in their knapsacks, and the First Division—Stott's unit—was to be in column by 6:00 a.m. the next morning. Dawn on the day of departure could not have been more beautiful. The endless rains were over, and the grateful soldiers stepped off for the north, gladly leaving their soggy campsites behind. Greeted by a brilliant sun and a cool, crisp wind coming from the north, their spirits brightened at the thought of seeing fresh territory. Although Franklin's XIX Corps preceded them in the van and cleared obstructions left in earlier battles along the Teche, it was not long before the western troops saw clear signs of war. First they saw the bare hulk of the Confederate gunboat *J. A. Cotton*, destroyed in a bloody engagement the previous January in which Union losses were severe. Just beyond the *Cotton* were the remains of the Confederate fortress at Bisland, leveled in combat that April, and near it the skeletons of horses left where they had died and attended by large flocks of carrion crows. Elsewhere could be seen charred chimneys and shells of destroyed dwellings.[16]

Yet the trek along the Teche would be remembered by most of the western troops for its "pleasant marching and plenty of food." Soldiers treading along the banks of the bayou, which resembled a snake winding through the land (the stream derived its name from an Indian word, meaning snake) almost universally used the words "beautiful country" in their diaries and letters. Stott wrote, "We are passing the nicest country

I ever saw, level, rich, well-cultivated"—though he insisted that "Yankee farmers" could make it more productive. Illinoisan Marks concurred, saying "the Country through Bayou Teche is the finest I ever seen in my life," and C. P. Alling of the Eleventh Wisconsin praised its "grand climate and extreme fertility, producing cotton, Cuban cane, corn, all varieties of vegetables, oranges, figs, bannanas, etc." Perhaps nothing turned the heads of these westerners more often, though, than the vast plantations that fronted the Teche, with their stately mansions, abundant land featuring lush gardens, and large warehouses full of sugar and rice. As Roberts told his family, "You had better believe we live well on this trip, for their is plenty of hogs, cattle & poultry, & sugar, & molasses all through here, and sweet potatoes."[17]

Of course, there were other sides to the story. Those who took a closer look at the area saw that some of the finest estates were now desolate, having been touched, and even torched, by war. *New York Herald* reporter Henry Thompson considered the region the "paradise of the south" but noted that many mansions were "silent and deserted" and their slave cottages "tenantless and fast falling into ruin." Nor did the remaining residents take kindly to the foraging bluecoats. In the same letter in which he exulted about "living well," Roberts commented: "The citizens make right smart of fuss about us taking things" and flash "their protection papers as a plea that we ought to let their stock alone." These protesters were Creoles or Cajuns, descendants of the Acadians who had been driven from Nova Scotia years before, and they now constituted the majority of whites in the sugar country. They were of French-Catholic extraction, still spoke French (as did their slaves of all ages), and claimed either French or British protection, brandishing documentation to prove it. Along with holding these papers, which irritated Union troops, hundreds of Cajuns had taken the oath of allegiance to the Union. They had suffered enough already at the hands of Texas Rebels and hoped now to protect themselves from further harassment by either side.[18]

Another unpleasant development on the "idyllic" march through the Teche country was the growing tension between the western troops of the XIII Corps and their eastern counterparts in the XIX Corps. Both were cocky and certain of their superiority, and the more they marched together, the stronger became their bitterness toward each other. The New Englanders regarded all the men from the West to be gambling, bragging

"Hoosiers," while the western troops saw the eastern men as stuffed-shirt, starched-collar, white-gloved "Pilgrims." One soldier concluded, "I think either side would rather shoot at each other than at the Johnnies." No wonder the generals of both corps eventually separated them "on the march and in camp."[19]

Aside from these distressing aspects of the early stages of the campaign, the XIII Corps proceeded up the Teche in relative ease and with little sign of the enemy. As the long blue line wound through small towns along the bayou, they found their cleanliness and beauty inviting. Citizens of Centerville and Franklin lined the streets to view the Union troops parade through town. Harry Watts of the Twenty-fourth Indiana said the residents of Centerville "looked surprised to see us and were very inquisitive to know where we were going," but, of course, the soldiers revealed nothing. In Franklin, in the early morning of October 5, the marchers went past a crowd of onlookers standing in front of padlocked stores and buildings displaying flags—the Stars and Stripes intermingled with French, Prussian, and Spanish banners. A member of the Sixty-ninth Indiana saw "French and negroes of every hue and complexion" in the throng but thought the town itself bore "the appearance of a deserted village."[20]

That same day the blue line continued on to New Iberia, the very heart of Cajun country. The skies were cloudless and the sun blazing, so by midmorning the heat transformed the roads, still rutted from wagons during the recent rains, into clouds of dust that "choked and blinded the men" and gave their clothes and bodies a brownish tint. They had started that morning in high spirits—drums rolling, bands playing, and all singing along. But now the prominent sounds were curses and moans as they suffered from blistering feet, unquenchable thirst, and weariness that made them stumble. On top of that, the Confederates, camped west of New Iberia and toward Vermilionville, were watching the army's movements. Taylor informed the Trans-Mississippi headquarters on October 6 that "the enemy is advancing in very large force." Since he could not predict the enemy's exact destination or plans, the Confederate leader determined to play a "cat and mouse game" in response to his every move.[21]

Unlike the XIX Corps, which, still in the advance, had a two-day rest in New Iberia while Banks and Franklin deliberated over which route to take next, the weary men of the XIII Corps passed rapidly through the town—"March *suddenly*," Stott wrote—on their way to Vermilion Bayou.

The Eighteenth Indiana reached the latter place on Friday, October 9, on the heels of a battle in which the army, led by the Union First Texas Cavalry, succeeded in chasing Confederate forces "in a brisk fashion" toward the village of Vermilionville. The Eighteenth saw no action, but two units in its division, the First Indiana Artillery and Colonel Lionel Sheldon's Third Brigade, participated in the assault that led to "bloodless victory for the Union." The overblown skirmish, in which only five Union soldiers received minor wounds, did not even earn mention in Stott's diary. Nor did much else that happened during his regiment's stay along the Vermilion, primarily because little of significance occurred. DeForest confided in a letter on October 10: "I cannot imagine what we are here for unless it is to make believe to carry on war, and so furnish an excuse to keep General Banks in charge of the department." All the army really accomplished, he wrote, was to follow some Confederate "mounted infantry" who did little more than "burn bridges and then scamper away."[22]

DeForest did mention one major concern, illegal foraging. "We forage like the locusts of Revelation," the captain declared, and the westerners "plunder more than our fellows." Each brigade had an "official foraging party" to bring in dairy products, crops, and livestock, with the responsibility of giving owners receipts for confiscated goods. Yet, unauthorized raids on local farms, ranches, and other homesteads—and even some sanctioned ones—got so frequent and so out of hand that General Edward O. C. Ord, now back in corps command after an extended sick leave, angrily ordered all pillaging and violence to stop. Furthermore, he empowered residents of Vermilionville to organize patrols to protect "Themselves, their families, and personal property against marauders and thieves, white and black." Many soldiers, and even general officers, felt that Ord's policy was an overreaction and rather ludicrous; some simply looked the other way when hungry soldiers sought prey. Stott, for instance, joked that, while passing Vermilionville, "A hen flew into one of my boys hands. Will Gen. Ord care for that?!" And the historian of the Thirty-third Illinois recalled that foraging continued unabated, for "There was not a 'neutral' stomach in the first brigade."[23]

On Tuesday, October 20, after almost two weeks of brigade drills, roll calls, and little else, the Eighteenth Indiana made a "rapid march of twenty-five miles" past Vermilionville northward toward Opelousas. The next day the Eighteenth was within about eight miles of its destination when it learned that some skirmishing with Confederate guerrillas had occurred the day before. Franklin's XIX Corps, along with the Third and Fourth Divisions of the XIII Corps had been in the advance for several days, pestered by strikes from General Thomas Green's grayclad cavalry. Franklin had, in fact, so scattered his brigades that their small units actually invited enemy attacks. Both sides, blue *and* gray, were perplexed: Confederate leaders found the indecisiveness of the Union officers, and their avoidance of any engagement, confusing; on the Union side, the soldiers believed they were "On to Texas," but their commanders seemed to have little idea how to get there. As historian William Arceneaux puts it, "the Great Texas Overland Expedition seemed stalled."[24]

Bewilderment and apathy began to penetrate the ranks as well. Schermerhorn of the Forty-sixth Indiana told his wife on October 18 that "Every officer nearly from Gen. Franklin down seems to be disappointed in the manner in which this campaign has been conducted," and he pointed to insufficient planning for supplies as one sign of mismanagement. Yet another Hoosier rejoiced that "for once in all our campaigning, the old 13th corps is in the rear. And you may be assured we are not grieving over the matter, and are perfectly willing that somebody else shall go and do the fighting for us . . . <u>we have been there</u>." Under such circumstances, General Franklin no doubt was relieved to hear, on October 20, that a supply train with hundreds of wagons, along with Colonel Henry D. Washburn's brigade and Lieutenant Lawrence Jacoby's First Indiana Battery, were on the way.[25]

Even with this good news, Franklin still faced complications. After repeated requests for orders from Banks, who was in New Orleans preparing for a naval operation against the Texas coast, Franklin received no instruction from his superior. Unsettled about how to proceed and, according to scholar Richard Lowe, "unwilling to take the initiative himself," Franklin opted on October 21 to quarter both his corps at Barre's Landing on Bayou Courtableau, near Opelousas. He saw this as a choice location for a supply base, given that the bayou connected with waterways to Brashear City. Unfortunately, the army's arrival at Barre's Landing coincided with a cold front, torrential rains, and a lengthy delay in the arrival of the expected supplies. Because the vicinity of Barre's Landing had been depleted of crops and livestock during previous military operations, it was a wretched place for foraging. Moreover, the weather made the men, many of whom had no tents, into "so many drowned rats," virtually paralyzed as an efficient military force.[26]

Faced with these conditions, on October 26 Franklin proposed to headquarters that his army should begin to move south where foraging would be possible and supplies more available. To his amazement, he soon got word that Banks, off on another naval foray to Texas, "had left orders for Franklin to send a few of his regiments back down the Teche for ultimate transfer" to the Texas coast. Banks also directed his lieutenant to travel in such a way as to convince the enemy that his force was still the "real one" in the campaign to invade Texas, thereby concealing Banks's naval expedition. Thus began the retreat to Berwick for the purpose of joining Banks's efforts to plant the Union flag in Texas. With Stott's division, under General Michael Lawler's command, leading the way, the Army of the Gulf retraced its earlier route back to New Iberia. It was a difficult march, for the eager Lawler set a brutal pace in a late-October driving rain. The men following him, many with blistered feet or barefoot, "lugged at a quick step their heavy load," trying to keep up. Upon reaching New Iberia, all seemed calm until Friday, November 6, when word spread "that the enemy was close upon us." The Indiana regiments went into line of battle west of town, with the two Illinois units in reserve. They stayed on alert that night, only to discover that "there was no enemy in the vicinity." The official record of the division's return to New Iberia stated: "No events of special importance have transpired thus far in the campaign."[27]

Nor would there be during the rest of the trek to Berwick, a fact that deepened the sense of disappointment and dejection the veterans of the XIII Corps were already feeling. The whole campaign up and down the Teche now seemed like a waste. For men who had fought behind Curtis and Grant, and had never met defeat, the dearth of action and accomplishment on this operation was embarrassing. Then, when word arrived at New Iberia of the rout of Franklin's forces at Bayou Bourbeau on November 2–3—despite the valiant efforts of the tenacious Third and Fourth divisions of the XIII Corps at containing the Confederate attack— the feeling of humiliation and anger toward their eastern leaders mushroomed. Many no doubt agreed with Hoosier Watts, who fought at Bayou Bourbeau and later grumbled, "This was the first time the 13th Corps ever turned its back." It was obvious, he wrote, "that the bubble burst and the Great Texas Overland Campaign was a failure all owing to too much strategy by Gen. Banks."[28] Perhaps it was in an effort to push these emotions aside that Stott said nothing in his diary about the events of the few days remaining on the trip to Berwick and, instead, devoted those entries to reflections on Robert Burns. It was more rewarding than mulling over a barren and moribund campaign.

———•—•———

As the bulk of the Army of the Gulf retraced its way to Berwick, Banks scouted the Texas coast near the mouth of the Rio Grande. On November 2 his small array of 7,000 troops landed at Brazos Santiago, its goal being the capture of Brownsville. Despite some fumbled efforts at coordinating naval and land forces, Banks's men met no Confederate resistance and the garrison at the town fell to them on November 6. Within a matter of days, Banks decided to bring more troops from Louisiana in order to seize the islands and ports from the Rio Grande to the Sabine River.[29]

Among the first brigades to be mobilized for the new operation was that of the Eighteenth Indiana. At 3:00 on the afternoon of November 12, Stott and his compatriots stepped on the decks of the steamship *St. Mary* at Berwick, presumably "On to Texas." Their orders gave no clue as to their actual destination, so all surgeon George Gordon could tell his diary was that they were heading to "some point in Texas, I guess." That day, wrote Roberts of the Eighth Indiana, they "went about 25 miles" and dropped anchor. The next day was a slow one as well, for the ship "struck the sand bars at the mouth of Berwick Bay" around midmorning and "had to lay by untill the tide raised so that we could get out." A row of sandbars blocked the vessel "as far as sight can reach," and timbers were strewn in front of the ship. At 3:00 p.m., though, the tide came up, permitting the inexperienced seafarers to cross the sandbar and head into the night. For these westerners, few of whom had ever seen the sea, the experience of looking at nothing but water was, as Stott exclaimed, a "grand sight." But on November 14 the sea lost its grandeur. The wind rose, the billows became rougher, and the *St. Mary* tossed about on the roiling waters. "A great many of the men and officers," Roberts wrote, "got very sick," and Stott had a moment when he made "such gyrations as did the whale in releasing Jonah." That afternoon, said Roberts, the soldiers could not sit "still, without holding to something." As the storm hit full force that night, few slept. With waves splashing as high as the second deck, Roberts explained, "we couldn't lay still, half the time our feet were higher than our heads." Gratefully, on the morning of Sunday, November 15, the sea was calm again, bringing the troops in sight of land—Point Isabel, near Brazos Santiago.[30]

The Hoosier regiments did not disembark that day. They remained on deck, marveling at the sight of a blockading fleet, with two men-of-war "formed in line of battle." From their vantage point, they could see a French fleet at the mouth of the Rio Grande and catch a glimpse of the Mexican coastline. They expected to land at Corpus Christi, but later in the day the steamer started northward, running slowly along the banks of the coastal islands. On the morning of November 16, they were "still agoing," as Roberts put it, on a smooth sea but "out of sight of land again." At about 3:00 p.m. the ships "hove up to the mouth of the Bay" to reconnoiter the land from afar but "could not tell . . . whether the rebels had it fortified or not." As night fell the vessels neared the shore and the order went out for the Eighteenth Indiana to "Jump out." It did so "in shifts," wading waist-deep to shore amid powerful breakers. Once on the beach, the men gathered driftwood, ignited fires, hovered around them in attempts to dry their clothes, and then settled down on the sand to sleep. This was Mustang Island, a seemingly barren place with white-sand beaches and, beyond them, varieties of scraggly grasses interspersed with stunted scrub bushes.[31]

At dawn the next morning, the men of the Eighteenth began a north-ward trek on the beach, a strange and difficult walk for Hoosiers. Salt spray, swirling sand, and uncertain footing made it "hard work" for Stott and his company, but its uniqueness took their minds off their "pains and aches." They marched twenty-two miles, each man carrying all of his gear, including cooking utensils, and became increasingly thirsty from the salt spray. The weary soldiers arrived at Aransas Pass at the head of the island in time to witness the aftermath of a successful Union assault on a Confederate fortification placed there to protect blockade runners. With shells booming forth from a man-of-war off shore, Brigadier General Thomas E. G. Ransom's force had attacked the works and taken one hundred prisoners and three siege guns without firing a shot.[32] Now the Eighth and Eighteenth Indiana regiments assisted in the occupation of the fort. The next four days on Mustang were bitter ones in which little could be done. A Texas "Norther" came up with piercingly cold winds and stinging rains. Since much of the camp equipage was still on the ships, the regiments lacked adequate shelter and the wind prevented the making of comfortable, lasting fires. Besides that, the Forty-ninth Indiana's James Leeper wrote, "the sand drifting in heaps like snow filled our eyes till we could scarcely see. What we eat is half sand, we sleep in sand, and cover our tents with sand to keep them from blowing away, our very existence is in Sand half knee deep." Things got so bad that, on November 19, smaller boats anchored off shore were tossed about, even landing on sandbars. On one of them, Chaplain Henry C. Skinner, Eighth Indiana, "offered up a Prair that they might all be spaired." That night the wind settled down and the waves quit roiling.[33]

Nevertheless, the gales and heavy rains continued through November 20, causing Stott to believe that more prayers were being lifted up, even by those "not accustomed to it." Such petitions, however, may have been refocused because of developments on the twenty-first. That day, after troop inspection, the Hoosier regiments joined Major General Washburn, the Thirty-third Illinois, and a portion of the Eighteenth Indiana on the steamer *Clinton* when it arrived on a sandbar off the head of Mustang Island. On Sunday, November 22, Washburn received orders to lead "an expedition up the coast, for the purpose of capturing" Fort Esperanza, a formidable Confederate defensive facility at the northeastern tip of Matagorda Island. Acting swiftly, Washburn crossed to St. Joseph Island on the *Clinton* with the brigades of the XIII Corps he had with him. He sent troops under Ransom in advance, with instructions to reach "the pass between St. Joseph and Matagorda Islands," also known as Cedar Bayou. While Ransom moved on ahead, Washburn's own force, including the Eighteenth Indiana, had to contend with yet another "norther" that delayed troop movements for two days, during which only Buffalo chips could provide effective fuel for warmth. When Washburn's men finally reached Cedar Bayou on November 24, it was obvious that bridging the three hundred-yard bayou, with its strong current agitated by the "terrible winds" that still prevailed, was impossible. Fortunately, Washburn's train of wagons contained four yawl boats that soldiers linked together on November 25 to provide a passageway for his "troops, wagons, and artillery," while his "horses and mules were swum across." "We are progressing fairly in crossing," he told Banks. "The process is slow and tedious, but I will have ferried over during the coming night. I will advance my headquarters to-morrow at least 15 miles, and will invest the fort the day after."[34]

Washburn's estimate was largely on target. All the troops crossed Cedar Bayou by midnight, marched some eight hours, and caught up with Ransom's advance brigades. According to Colonel Washburn, the commander of Stott's First Brigade, the men rested a few hours, then made "a very hard march through the sand of 23 miles," after which they cheerfully camped for a full night. The next morning, Friday, November 27, the brigade proceeded to a lighthouse that stood as a beacon for ships passing from the Gulf of Mexico into Matagorda Bay. Elliott of the Thirty-third Illinois remembered reaching that place around noon, pressing north, and finding "Fort Esperanza in plain sight and in easy artillery range." The view invoked fear and respect, as Roberts suggested. "It is the largest and best Fort I ever seen," he wrote, "it goes far ahead of anything they had at Vicksburg." With several lines of outworks manned by Confederate sharpshooters, the fortress housed five hundred troops, seven 24-pounder smoothbore cannon, one 128-pounder Columbiad pivot gun, and two smoothbore field pieces. Built to defend against naval attacks, its parapets stood ten feet high with a thickness of fifteen feet and were skirted by water.[35]

Leaving the majority of his command near the lighthouse, Washburn moved "cautiously up the beach" toward the fortifications with one company from each of his regiments, supported by the Thirty-third Illinois. His goal was to discover "the strength and position of the enemy." Driving in the Confederate pickets, the small reconnaissance force found a safe haven among "a range of sand hills, within 300 yards of the outer works of the enemy." Now within rifle shot, it soon was the target of shells from the fort. As one soldier of the Eighteenth Indiana expressed it, they "had the fun, if fun it might be called, of dodging a few 128-pounders." Feeling certain of the placement and strength of the Confederates, and with night falling, the colonel and his task force rejoined its brigade in order to be out of the range of fire.[36] Regrettably, they were *not* out of the range of "the worst 'Norther' that ever blew over Texas." A combination of rain, sleet, and snow hit that night, causing the Union soldiers to dig in for limited shelter in which they "slept plenty cold" as the wind blew right

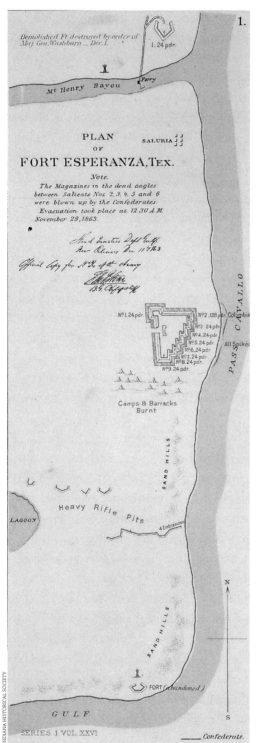

Confederate Fort Esperanza,
Matagorda Island.

through their blankets. The storm maintained its severity the next day, impeding all operations save the digging of rifle pits and advancing of artillery. As the Thirty-third Illinois's Elliott recalled, "the only fight we had was to keep from freezing."[37]

On Sunday morning, November 29, as the gales continued their icy blasts, Union batteries opened fire on Fort Esperanza. At "early dawn" the Eighth Indiana moved out of its rifle pit, followed by the Thirty-third Illinois, and "took possession of the outer works about 400 yards from the fort." There was little resistance from the grayclad infantry, which quickly retreated to the main Confederate defense line. Meanwhile, the Union artillery and gunboats found their targets, thereby prohibiting the Confederates from effectively using the guns in their fort. Moreover, Confederate rifle fire proved wild, giving the blueclad chargers confidence to expose themselves "in the open prairie," sometimes recklessly. Finding his troops "more successful that [he] had dared to hope," Washburn ordered the Thirty-third Illinois "to advance as fast as prudence would allow" in an attempt to find a position where artillery could be made even more operative. That task being accomplished, Washburn ordered his adjutant, William W. Zener of the Eighteenth Indiana, to move two pieces of the Seventh Michigan Battery up to a position from which it could lob shells into "the enemy stronghold, . . . driving them from their guns." Washburn also sent the Eighteenth Indiana rapidly to the support of the Eighth Indiana and Thirty-third Illinois. In doing so, the Hoosiers ran under heavy fire from the fort, but the Confederates "threw nothing but solid shot," small enough to be avoided. As a result, only one Indianan was killed. All day the Union forces accomplished these feats in bitter cold and strong winds. Advancing across resistant sand "with balls & shells flying all around us," Sergeant Samuel P. Herrington recorded, "we had to run facing the wind & sand as the air was full of sand & it was very slow running."[38]

As night approached, the men of the First Brigade occupied positions among the sand hills near the fort, the Eighth Indiana closest to their objective and the other three regiments not far behind. Their colonel proudly reported: "The men, although the night was raw and cold, remained upon the field and in their position." A detachment from reserve regiments moved four guns of the Seventh Michigan closer to the works held by the advance troops, and a regiment of the Eighteenth Indiana, under Stott's friend Abraham Lowes, reinforced a critical spot to the army's right. As Washburn made plans for a general assault by the whole brigade to be made the next morning, Confederate Colonel William S. Bradfute and his officers met as a council of war inside the fort, deciding to abandon the fortress during the night and leave nothing behind that could be of use to the Union army.[39]

At around 2:00 a.m., Swain Marshall slept soundly alongside his comrades of the Eighth Indiana. Suddenly, he "was waked up by the explosion of one of the rebs magazenes." That first blast signaled that "the enemy [was] on the move." Herrington said the blast occurred at one o'clock and was accompanied by "nice fires outside the Fort burning up some of their [Confederates'] traps." Washburn instantly ordered an advance on the fort, during which another magazine exploded, throwing Herrington "back agane the wall of the entrance" and sending timber in all directions, covering him with "dust & splinters." When Washburn entered the fort, he "found that the enemy had fled, leaving behind him stores and ammunition and the personal baggage of the officers." Around the stocks of ammunition lay large piles of cotton with gunpowder spread across them. Altogether as many as seven explosions erupted, one of which, Herrington observed, sent debris higher than "a flock of gees [sic]" that flew overhead. With Fort Esperanza in Union possession, the Thirty-third Illinois raised its flag over the ruins—the first banner to mark the victory.[40]

The XIII Corps remained on Matagorda Island until December 23. That day the First Brigade, now under the command of Brigadier General Fitz-Henry Warren, sailed to Indianola on the Texas mainland, reaching the town in late afternoon. Situated on Lavacca Bay, Indianola ranked second among the busiest ports in the state. But when the Federal soldiers arrived, it was mostly vacant. Confederate General John B. Magruder had recently declared that he would burn the town, a threat that prompted hundreds of residents to flee. Their departure left empty houses that now provided lodging for the men in blue.[41]

The Eighteenth Indiana's long sojourn in the Indianola vicinity may best be described as cold, hungry, and militarily uneventful. The turn into the New Year of 1864, for example, was especially harsh because of bitter weather and lack of rations. References to chilly rains, fogs, and occasional "northers" punctuate Stott's diary, and New Year's Eve morning was the coldest he had known in the South. On January 7, Leeper of the Forty-ninth Indiana, stationed at DeCrow's Point just across the bay from Indianola, told his wife about yet "another Cold Spell" that started the previous Sunday as a "slow misty rain" that poured all day and then "blew off cold and freezing" that night. The whole week was "cloudy dark gloomy looking" and featured "a severely cold north wind" that still blew that Thursday. In the same letter, Leeper mentioned a second factor that made life rough for the soldiers: "Hunger and severe cold weather, with the Slim conveniences we have to keep ourselves comfortable, render our conditions anything but desirable." Hunger! Stott spoke of it, too. For four straight days in early January his diary entries began with the plaintive plea: "No rations." And, from nearby Pass Cavallo, William Winters wrote his beloved Hattie that things were the same for the Sixty-seventh Indiana. Though it was warmer on the day he penned his letter, he reflected facetiously on earlier days when "our rations got most confounded short, and a good many of the Reg had no bread for a week, and between that and the cold north wind, we had a butiful time of it." Leeper laid the blame for the shortage of food squarely on "the thieving conduct and glaring rascality of these Eastern villainous officials," namely the quartermasters back in New Orleans who made money off the sutlers before allowing them to "bring stores here" rather than "provision and forage." "So now we have nothing to eat," he carped, "while these Quart'rs are Strutting about Orleans spending with a lavish hand their ill gotten gain." Apparently, the clash between the XIII and XIX Corps had not ceased.[42]

Conflicts with Rebels, however, seemed to have ended. Except for occasional bloodless encounters with enemy pickets, the military labors of the troops at Indianola centered on three activities: (1) the holding of courts martial; (2) the arrival of the black Corps d'Afrique, whose assignment was confined to "work in intrenchment" ("their proper sphere," as XIII Corps commander Napoleon J. T. Dana contended); and (3) the erection of fortifications "as strong as possible against attacks, both by land and water"—assaults that never came.[43]

As the weather became more mild in late January and February, other matters emerged at Indianola that elicited the soldiers' attention, particularly that of Captain Stott. Marshall wrote his father on February 18 about the desire of many in his Eighth Indiana to reenlist as "veterans" soon, thereby extending their terms of service. But he ended his letter rather abruptly, saying he would have to quit in time to attend that evening's temperance meeting. He explained that such gatherings were held "three times a week" and that "eight hundred from our brigade and the third have signed the pledge . . . not to drink any intoxicating drink while in the United States Service." Swain assured his father that he "need not be afraid of me braking it." Here was a cause that naturally touched Stott's very soul. His lifelong advocacy of temperance led him to take an active role in the new venture. Launched through the "untiring efforts" of Chaplains Henry C. Skinner of the Eighth Indiana and John S. Donaldson of the Eighteenth Indiana, the temperance society grew rapidly and, in the estimate of the historian of the Eighth, reached one thousand members. Its growth paralleled that of a religious society founded by Donaldson. The influence of both groups, to Stott's delight, spread throughout the whole corps.[44]

Marshall's letter touched on the other major event in the life of the XIII Corps: veteranizing. As early as June 1863, the War Department recognized that the reenlistment of men already serving would greatly strengthen the army. On the twenty-fifth of that month, the Adjutant General's Office released General Order No. 191, "For Recruiting Veteran Volunteers." The document detailed the regulations through which "armies now in the field" could enlist as "Veteran Volunteers" for another "three years or during the war." These veterans would receive a month's pay in advance, plus a premium of $402, and at the completion of their present terms of service be granted a thirty-day furlough in their home state. Later orders authorized the furloughs for the month *before* the soldiers' terms expired and called for regiments to "be furloughed in a body." The question of veteranizing was before the whole army during December 1863, and talk in the ranks often revolved around it. Three of the four regiments in the First Brigade chose to become Veteran Volunteers, only the Ninety-ninth Illinois opting out of the program. On January 1, 1864, twenty-eight-year-old, gray-eyed, light-haired, "5 ft 11 in" Capt. William Taylor Stott, who declared his occupation as "student," officially mustered into the veteran service at his current rank. The Thirty-third Illinois had already left on furlough, but Stott's unit had to wait.[45]

On March 14, 1864, the Eighteenth Indiana left Indianola and returned to Matagorda Island. With the corps once again under its old commander, Major General John A. McClernand—a move that William T. Sherman concluded meant that McClernand had been "ingeniously disposed of"—the troops had as their mission the rehabilitation of Fort Esperanza to enable its use against Rebel assaults. Apparently, for Federal officials the anticipated attack, as scholar Lester N. Fitzhugh observes, was "a threat generated in their minds by four months of inactivity surrounded by hostile pickets." Taylor Peirce of the Twenty-second Iowa, however, could not understand this concern. Commenting to his wife on the "extensive scale" of the rebuilding project, he confessed: "What we have moved back for is more than I can tell for we have seen no signs of rebles for some time and we constantly hear of their leaving for the north and attempting to cross the miss [Mississippi] to reinforce the Rebles east of that stream." All he could fathom from "the best informed" was that they were to stay there "so that if the texians will not come in we will have a place to commence from." It would be a long time before commencement, though, and the days would be filled with hard work.[46] Official reports on the progress at the fort indicated that around 1,700 officers and men worked almost daily, constructing revetments, shoring up redoubts and lunettes, and sodding the interior of the fortress as well as its exterior slopes. The Eighteenth Indiana, including Stott's Company, invested much of its time in laying sod. Their progress met frequent delays due to a lack of lumber, an inadequate number of work animals, and fiercely high winds. When not at work, there was little to do. Officers kept soldiers busy through regular inspections and a grand review, and Stott found time to practice his writing skills and enjoy the camaraderie of singing with his friends. While on the island, the Eighteenth Indiana also received authorization "to have inscribed on their colors the names of the several battles" in which they fought.[47]

It was with great pleasure, then, that the Eighteenth Indiana learned on April 16 that it would be off to New Orleans the next day. "Hail Columby" was Stott's exaltation. The Hoosiers had a glorious sendoff on the morning of the seventeenth. Accompanied by a brass band, they passed through rows of cheering Iowa troops. They boarded the *Clinton* once again and headed out to sea. It was a rough trip at first, many of the men getting ill from the rolling of the vessel—getting to "New York," as Stott put it. A Confederate ship sought to intercept them, but its "shots fell short," and it gave up the chase. Arriving at New Orleans, the men of the Eighteenth donned their fresh uniforms, waited for pay, and learned that they were to go to Baton Rouge. On the day they left for their new post, Major General J. J. Reynolds, in charge of New Orleans's defenses, reported that among the new regiments heading north was the "Eighteenth Indiana Volunteers (the latter under orders for furlough which has been long delayed)."[48]

The delay lasted for nearly another two months, during which the regiment did post duty at Baton Rouge. Only once was that tedious job interrupted by combat. Confederates in the region, hearing that Banks's Red River Expedition was suffering setbacks, sought to move against Baton Rouge. This threat mobilized the Federal forces stationed there and, with the Eighteenth Indiana in the van, they confronted the enemy on Tuesday, May 3, at Olive Branch Bayou near the Comite River. The fray has been described as a "hot engagement of five hours duration" (Stott said six hours). The result was a complete rout of the Rebels, for which the Eighteenth Indiana received praise for its "coolness and bravery." As he awaited furlough at Baton Rouge, Stott continued his temperance work, read voraciously, and even joined a choir at the Presbyterian Church.[49]

Finally, the day came! On Thursday, May 28, the regiment started northward on the Mississippi River aboard the *Pauline Carroll*, which took them to Cairo, Illinois. Traveling by rail the remainder of the way, the regiment arrived at Indianapolis as the sun was going down on Saturday, June 4. Two days later the men of the Eighteenth marched again, this time down Washington Street in the capital city. Throngs lined the way, and a local newspaper noted that "the regiment moved with even tread as one man, erect and proud." At the Statehouse, Governor Oliver P. Morton delivered a moving tribute to the soldiers, and Colonel Washburn gave "a speech of fiery eloquence," lauding his men for their courage. Looking back on their reception, however, the men might have remembered the words of Mayor John Caven, who urged them "to endure a little while longer." For two weeks later, on June 20, the Eighteenth Indiana became part of the XIX Corps. There was still fighting to be done—in Virginia.[50]

7

Diary: August 21, 1863–July 12, 1864

[Aug.] 21st to Sept. 6th [1863]

Embarked on Steamer North America. Was aboard two or three days, during which time I became sick. Arrived at Carrollton near New Orleans, where we went into camp. I was sick here all our stay ten days, scarcely able to leave my tent. Fever was the ailment. Eddelman medicated me. Lt Carson was sick at the same time. Capt. [Richard] Stott and Lt. [Joseph] Storey came to see me. Had $150 stolen from my Pants pocket. Sergt. Young had charge of the Company, and did well.

We move again. Cross to Algiers. Then take cars to within seven miles of Brashear City, La., on Berwick Bay. I went on to the city and remained two days and nights, by which time I was able to go to camp again. The regiment is camped on Bayou Boef (Beef). My impression is that we are to go to Texas by land, if wet weather does not prevent. I don't remember to whom I have written or from whom I have rec'd letters so I shall have to guess at it.

The country here is very <u>low</u>. Lakes and Bayous and Lagoons are on every side. Oysters <u>are made</u> not far from this place. Oranges are plenty.

7th

Have a sweeping gale. 69th Ind 54th Ind are here.

8th

Spent some time building a shed to our tent, Built of leaves and brush-wood. The water here is all salty.

We have a fine Brass band camped near.

9th

The railroad bridge is filled with fishermen.

10th

Battallion Drill is instituted already.

11th

As Brigade O.D. I was ordered to relieve the guard at 9 P.M. as we would march at 7 today.[1] We reached Brashear City by 10 o'clock. Lt. Knobe came in the evening. The 19th Corps failed in their expedition to Sabine Pass. The tide going out, the gunboats could not operate.
It is probable that the 19th will let the 13th try it. And we will <u>succeed</u> too, if we do. We have never failed <u>yet</u>.

12th

There is no news from the East. I presume that we shall have to go to <u>making</u> news. "Sam Huston" is up with goods.[2]

13th

Went up to town and got Jordan out of the <u>Calaboose</u>. Found Lt. Wood, 11th Ind.[3]

14th

The New Orleans Era contains a letter from Pres. Lincoln to the Louisiana Convention. It is a logical and laconic letter.

15th

I am still learning new lessons in human nature. If one should ask me what motive governs the actions of most men I should reply <u>Selfishness</u>. I could not even give it the dignity of <u>self-love</u>. Another thing which I am very much confirmed in is this, that "the man makes the place" and <u>not</u> "the place makes the man." A man of strong points will show himself wherever he be.

16th

Made an extra Muster Roll. Co I has had 113 men in toto.

17th

Lt. John who had a bookstore in Franklin, called on me. There are 23 Army Corps in the U. S. Service. Gen Grant is Maj Gen of Regulars. Met my old friend Sam Foster. He belongs to 87th Ills.[4]

18th

Troops are crossing over to Berwick City.

19th

Rosencrans' Army is crossing the Cumberland mountains.[5] Drew a plat of the fort near.

20th

Our troops are improving fast in military appearance. Rec'd a letter from my new correspondent.

21st

Rosencrans occupies Chattanooga. Gillmore is now in possession of Morris Island.[6] Sentiment is rapidly changing in some of the southern states.

22nd

Little Rock is ours. Tennessee is clear of Rebel rule. Fort Smith is ours. The news is good everywhere.[7]

23rd

I am glad we have a chaplain. We have long done without one.[8] Col. Washburn sends up another recommendation for himself. It was made by the soldiers and officers of this Brigade.

24th

Not an item to ruffle the smooth transit of this day.

25th

Cross over the Bay. Have a nice camp. In the evening the chaplain initiated himself. He spoke familiarly and yet earnestly. It is well that we are reminded again that there is a God, and of our relations and obligations to Him. I shall strive to have my company benefitted as much as possible.

26th

I am very much dissatisfied this morning with Col. Washburns administration in reference to some men of my company. But militarily I must acquiesce.

27th

Inspection then church. Whatsoever thy hand findeth to do, do it with thy might.[9] Wrote to Miss CM.

28th

Read the story of a "Volunteer" in "Greenwood Leaves." It is well written and gives Margaret a most lovely disposition.[10]

29th

We have the Equinoctial Storm. It is later by a few days owing to the disturbed state of the country (?).

30th

Rained very hard. Henry had to arise and take up his bed.

October 1st

There has been a great Battle in Tennessee. It was fought on the 19th and 20th ult. Victory poised but finally balanced in our favor. Rosencrans took 15,000 prisoners. Col. Tripp was wounded. The Southern Chivalry don't whip us <u>one</u> to <u>five</u> quite so much in reality as <u>on paper</u>.[11]

2nd

No further news from Rosencrans.

3rd

So we are off for Texas. The roads are in a bad way. Camp 12 miles from the place of starting, and on the same Bayou, or rather an arm of it.

4th

4 A.M. The country grows nicer. Pass Centerville. Camp in a nice green lot. In the evening have a service. Moses chose rather to suffer with the children of God, than to be called the son of Pharaoh's daughter.[12]

5th

Pass Franklin. It is a neat southern village. Co "I" is rear guard.

6th

We are passing the nicest country that I ever saw, level, rich, well cultivated. What vast wealth is in this soil yet undeveloped. The cultivation though good, does not bring out one fourth what it might under Yankee farmers. British Protection flags are very <u>flourishing</u>. Boats come up the Teche river as fast as we proceed by land.

7th

We are permitted to remain in camp.

8th

March <u>suddenly</u>. Pass through New Iberia and turn off the road to the right. Camp at 10 P.M.

9th

March to Vermillion Bayou. Come onto the rear of the 19th Army Corps. Cross the Bayou and camp in nice woods.

10th

It is supposed that John W. Frampton is captured.[13]

11th

Two sermons today. The soldiers attend well.

12th

It is reported that the 26th Ind is captured.[14] Strict orders are issued against foraging chickens potatoes &c. <u>Gen. Ord is with us</u>.

13th

Col. Shunk is relieved from duty, on account of allowing foraging.

14th

Wrote to Miss C. G. Our transportation is cut down to two teams to the regt. <u>Mirabile dictu</u>.[15]

15th

Col. Charles does not drill well. How I wish this cruel war was over!

16th

Strange, but I dreamed of being an engineer. I have obtained the names of all the line officers asking for Eddelman an Assistant Surgency.

17th

The Regiment is out on Picket line. Have the fever again. Providence is dealing out victory now in small quantities that we may not become haughty.

18th

Two sermons today. Also a Bible class meeting.

19th

Reading Robert Burns' life and Poems. His verses are good. His "Cotters Saturday Night" is unique. Some of his poems are immoral in their tendency. He was licentious. Before marriage, he was father to a child.
On the occasion of seeing a louse and lady's bonnet at church he wrote: "O for the gift to see ourselves as others see us."[16]

20th

Pass Vermillionville at sunrise. A hen flew into one of my boys hands. Will Gen. Ord care for that!
Thomas Hall was captured today.[17]

21st

March to within reach of Gen. Franklin's Camps.

22nd

Catch up to our Brigade at Barry's [Barre's] Landing. All business on these farms is suspended. The Rebels have retreated from Opelousas to Washington.

23rd

Hall has been paroled. No, he was recaptured. Tom McCracken and two others started to Brashear City this morning in a skiff to report our whereabouts.[18]

24th

Had a good solid chat this morning with Capt. [Abraham] Lowes. He is expecting to study for the ministry.

25th

Sabbath in the woods! The groves were God's first Temples.[19]

26th

Burns' "Nanie's Away" is fine and his Mousie.[20]

27th

March by a new route on retreat but cover the camp which we did just one week ago.

28th

The dirge reminds us that one of our number is lain with the dead. The 33d Ills buried him, and we march on.

Soldier rest, they warfare's done,

Sleep the sleep that knows no waking.

The mounted men went on a scout. Boggs captured a man. We are always cheerful marching if it be good weather.[21]

29th

Reach St. Martinsville. Cross the Bayou on a Drawbridge. The dwellers are still <u>black</u> and <u>dark</u>. It began raining and how <u>terribly muddy</u>. We had to leave the road altogether.

30th

We shall be paid in a few days. The 54th Indiana is at New Iberia. We shall go there today. The 54th is going home.

31st

After pay the camp was as busy as Wall Street. Some collecting, some paying and striking bargains some. Received a letter from Fannie S. George Hankins is supposed to be killed.[22]

Nov 1st

Sermons morning and evening. There is no clear analysis so that I cannot recall the points readily.

2nd

Move camp. Busy making out Muster Rolls.

3rd

Brigade Drill. No time for writing.

4th

There is a report the substance of which is: the enemy attacked McGinnis's Division, 60 wounded and killed. Some of the Louisiana Cavalry deserted to the enemy and gave him the situation of the camp.[23]

5th

A large mail came in. I got a good share of those welcome visitors.

6th

At 3 AM marched back past New Iberia and drew up in line to await the enemy, but none came. Hardly a week passes but that we are ordered out to <u>be ready</u>. It has a tendency at any rate to wear away any <u>scariness</u> which any might have.

7th

Robert Burns in speaking of the value of a private Journal says: "Nor am
I sure, notwithstanding all the flights of Novel writers, and the sage
philosophy of Novelists, whether we are capable of so intimate and
cordial a coalition of friendship, as that one may pour out his heart, his
very inmost soul, with unreserved confidence to another without hazard
of losing that respect, which man deserves from man; or from the unavoidable imperfections attending human nature, of one day repenting
his confidence."

8th

One should keep his own secrets. He [Burns] makes one exception which
I cordially grant. That the closest intimacy may exist between those of
opposite sex whose hearts are knit together in love, and that the intimacy
decreases not but augments the happiness. My wife shall know all that
I do, worth knowing, if she wishes the knowledge. There are very few to
whom it is wise to unbosom oneself.

9th

I really think that a perusal of Burns has been profitable. I shall be the
more able to shun the vices which he fell into. We are going back
to Berwick.

10th

Marched to Franklin and boarded the Starlight. Reached our destination
at dark. I did not on leaving this camp expect the pleasure of seeing
it again.

11th

Northern papers say that Hooker has had a fight with some of Braggs
men and repulsed them.

12th

The order is for the four companies on the right to be ready to board the
steamer lying at the wharf, to take us to Brownsville, Texas. (The <u>order</u>
did not say where we will go.) We are to have 5 days provisions and one
hundred and forty rounds ammunition. We anticipate a prosy time.
At 3 PM we go aboard the ocean steamer St. Marys and go down the
Atchafalaya about 20 miles and anchor for the night.

13th

Start over the bar but soon run aground. We shall have to wait for the tide. In the mean time a pilot from the lighthouse comes to us. He gets us over by four in the afternoon and takes his skiff and rows to his <u>solitary home</u>—what a palace he has for thought! All night he hears naught but the lashing of the waves. Has any pilot living in a lighthouse written a poem?

Now we are in the Gulf, the land can't be seen in any direction. It is a <u>grand sight</u>.

14th

In the morning on waking up and getting up, half the officers and men are sick, <u>sea-sick</u>. The vessell rocks from side to side. There is a great deal of sport at the sick ones expense. Col Washburn goes to bed, ashamed to be caught <u>sea-sick</u>. I am Officer of the day, and by the time I get through with my work it is too late to get sick. Well I did once make some such gyrations as did the whale in releasing Jonah. In the afternoon the captain says we will have storm so we get ready for it.

15th

The sea is calm today. We are propelled at the rate of 13 miles per hour. We expect to reach our destination by 4 or 5 P.M.

At 4, come to Point Isabel. Find several steamers and find Gen Banks. We see off at the mouth of the Rio Grande a French fleet. Some of our troops are off here at Brasos Island. Some of them embark again. And they and we are ordered to some other point. After one of our steamers chases a blockade runner an hour or two, we all start north direct. It is said that we are bound for Corpus Christi. We advance in line of Battle. The boys have learned a great many nautical phrases. In the afternoon we had divine service. Chaplain Skinner preached. Ours was quite too sick.

16th

We have to run slow to keep in line. I cannot conjecture why we did not land at Brasos Island. It may appear at some time. I should like the sea well. I have read some grand passages in the Bible while on the voyage. Some of the officers on board spend the time in drinking gambling and swearing. Are such real patriots? I fear that some are "hirelings whose own the sheep are not."

We are <u>nine month men</u>.

The Captain Barstow is a shrewd Yankee. There are three ladies aboard. It is supposed that we shall have to do some fighting to effect a landing. It is the point where Gen'l Taylor landed in 1846—Corpus Christi.[24]

At night the 18th disembarks onto Mustang Island. No one can imagine our surprise when yet quite a distance from the shore, the steersman of the yawl gave the words, jump out. The breakers were running high. I supposed for the instant that the yawl was about to be capsized and that we had to swim to shore the best we could. Our anxiety however was relieved when we knew that we had only to <u>wade</u> to shore. But wo[e] to him whom the breakers caught out there. He was almost sure of an <u>immersion</u>. The boys called the breakers <u>big wrinkles</u>. We are glad to get on shore even on sand. We sleep as best we can.

A few rations are put ashore.

At least we didn't have a "dry time."

17th

Early we start down the beach. We were able to find no water all day. The spray—salt spray—made us quite thirsty. Marched 22 miles, but it was hard work. The marching along the beach was novel and so tended to make us forget our pains and aches.

Although marching alongside the Gulf of Mexico we could get no <u>water</u>. Got to camp at 5 P.M. A three gun battery had been taken and the Rebs had been captured.

18th

Such a gale has come up that it impedes the further progress of our expedition.

19th

We can scarcely get provisions enough to subsist on. There are some cattle on the island. There is nothing to do but get ones back toward the blowing sand and take things <u>cool</u>. One vessel is wrecked.

20th

The schooners with our blankets and coffee pots and so on, were towed in. And they were a motley mess. Blankets and trunks and provisions were never so eagerly <u>grabbed for</u>. Those in the schooners outweathered a severe gale. I've no doubt it had the effect to make some pray, who were not accustomed to it. And so it was a blessing.

21st

Inspection. We now go aboard the Cliffton with the remainder of the 18th Ind. Dupree a deserter came up. A mail met us here. Morgan is Maj. 3rd U.S. Colored Infantry.[25] Fannie has been to Brookville. Marshal Grinstead is at home.

22nd

On a bar nearly all day. Got off late in the day. Camp on St. Joseph's Island. Left Bogart and Warren in charge of the baggage.[26] Here I am no tent no bed no supper. Are <u>volunteers</u> sinners above all men? Then why not give us some transportation.

23rd

After fitting out we get started at 12M and March 16 miles up St. Joseph's Island. At midnight we were suddenly roused by a "Norther." How sudden and disagreeable they are one cannot well imagine. All we could do was stand up and face the way the wind did not blow. There is no wood on these Islands.

24th

I do nothing but eat and <u>scrounge</u> around the scanty fire. The boys bring in 12 or 15 deer. I wonder that they live on this Island. Snow says he saw a hundred in one flock.[27]

25th

Inspection. The other Brigade is crossing to Matagorda Island. If Patmos was any such island as this I can see that it would be a fitting place for the Revelations.[28] With perhaps not another individual on the island, he could give his whole soul to the matter. He would be capable of the profoundest thoughts.

26th

Marched till two o'clock at night on Matagorda Island. Then got tired out, and out of humor. It was too severe marching. I could scarcely stem the current myself. Camp at 2 and sleep till daylight. I was too tired to sleep much.

27th

Marched 27 miles. At night it rained again. We have severe times these days. Got near the Rebel fort. Our skirmishers drove the Rebel skirmishers in. The fort is surrounded by water.

28th

Not much is being done today as it is so severely cold. Lt. Fifer was wounded while with the skirmishers.[29] The sea is so rough that the navy can do nothing.

29th

At two PM we were summoned to get into line, for the purpose of moving forward. About sundown we started to "run the gauntlet" We had to advance about one fourth of a mile in plain view and in good range of the Fort. While we were passing there were I think nine solid shot from a 128-pd Cannon hurled at us. But we <u>went</u>. Fortunately but one was wounded. This was serious <u>ball-play</u>.

At night occupy the Rebel advance Rifle pit. The artillery keeps a brisk fire till dusk. About 2 at night an explosion of a magazine in the fort indicated that the Rebels had evacuated it. We advanced and were there soon after the enemy had gone. A few prisoners were taken.

30th

The prisoners told us that 5 more magazines would explode. So we kept <u>from under</u>. And they did explode, throwing timber several hundred feet. Several men were killed by them. One came into my gunstack and broke a gun. Our capture was six prisoners 8 heavy pieces and a few tents. This was the best fort on the coast. It is called Fort Esperanza.

Dec 1st

One boat came up the Bay and went in pursuit of some rebel vessels. The 23rd Iowa is to garrison the Fort. I saw for the first time the Texas horned frog. It does not hop, but walks. It's horns slope backward as a goat's. It is smaller than our Yankee frogs.

2nd

We get an avalanche of mail. I seven letters. John Carson gets his Commission. Butler takes Hunters command in North Carolina.[30]

3rd

Amongst other letters was a <u>good</u> one from Miss L M. I am blessed with good correspondents. We shall stay here several days.

4th

Ben Fisher has gone back to New Orleans for our transportation.[31]

5th

Employ the day in answering Correspondents. If it is possible for one to get lonesome amidst thousands of men, I get lonesome.

6th

Will the <u>real</u> ever come up to the <u>ideal</u> When the mortal shall put on immortality, when the soul free from the "cumbrous clay" shall <u>grasp</u> what it now can't conceive of, will the real be up to the ideal? or will the ideal still advance, and keep man continually <u>striving</u> to <u>realize</u> the <u>ideal</u> It is well for us here to be aiming at something beyond what we are or what we possess at the present. The language of the professions is worth studying. The language of the legal profession for instance aims at exactness, regardless of circumlocution or tautology. That of the Military profession aims at <u>perspicuity</u> and <u>brevity</u>. A very good example is <u>Veni, Vidi, Vici</u>.[32]

7th

Had a short sermon today.

8th

I am so fortunate as to get my tent trunk and mess chest. So that I shall have a <u>home</u> separated from the rest of the world by the thickness of heavy canvass at least.

9th

A salute of 34 guns was fired this morning in honor of <u>something</u>. Report says a victory over Bragg by Grant. I shall not huzza till I <u>know</u> something about it. It is not pleasant to know that one has rejoiced over <u>falsehoods</u>.[33]

10th

Reading Wayland's Moral Philosophy. His style is plain and straightforward. His conclusions are generally undesirable.

Moral Philosophy is but a development of the relations and consequent duties of man as found in the Bible. Bishop Whately is dead. He was a native of Ireland.[34]

11th

We have not had a "Norther" since we took this fort. Before, every fourth day. The news from Grant is confirmed.

12th

Time passes swiftly on. There was a high tide today caused by the conjunction of sun and moon. I have heard soldiers accounting for high tides by high winds. The regularity of these tides would confute such an idea if there were nothing else.

Wayland comes to some serious conclusions: "Man is accountable for all the moral sensibility, and the actions correspondent, which he would have possessed had he lived as holy and immaculate a life from the first as did the Lamb of God himself." How much then one needs a Savior. How vigorously one should accept the one sent.

13th

Gen Benton and Col Shunk come over on the St. Marys. A mail came.

14th

The ladies Fair at Chicago was a success. Sam'l Huston, Esq. has brought a schooner and is shipping for himself.

15th

The Paymaster favors us. Co. "I" sends home $700. Gen. FitzHenry Warren now commands the 1st Brigade, Col Harris the 2d, and Gen Lawler the 3d. Gen. Benton the Division.

16th

The boys say only 8 months more! I am full of hope buoyant hope, as to the future. Lt. Daniels is appointed to enlist the Veterans.

17th

It is cold for us thinblooded folk this morning. Some of Co. "I" have reenlisted for three years. It will pay better than the past three years. The pay will be more, the hardship less.

18th

Had a speech from Col. Washburn encouraging enlistment in the Veteran Army. The bounty is $400.

19th

A Temperance meeting. Lecture by the Chaplain 23rd Iowa. He was followed by the Chaplain 18th Ind.[35]

20th

Mail again. Miss C. M. don't know whether I am a captain or a colonel. I suppose I must inform her. Rev. Mr. McKee is at Franklin again.

21st

Detailed on court martail [*sic*]. Capt Bell and Lt. Crane and Eddelman are messing with me.

22nd

We shall march tomorrow morning at 7 A.M. Gen. Warren enjoins order and discipline on the march.

23rd

Co's "I," "G" and "B" have the honor of escorting Gen. Warren on the flagship "Granite State." About 4 P.M. we reach Indianola. No resistance offered by the enemy. There are empty houses for 3,000 troops. I captured two houses [or horses?] while establishing the picket line.

24th

Employ the forenoon while fixing up our quarters. Afternoon we drill. Evening eat our Christmas Eve chicken.

25th

Hail Christmas! Had a sermon by the Chaplain. "Peace on Earth and good will to men." He told of the great joy at Christ's birth and how we should celebrate the day as often as it occurs.[36]

26th

At 7 A.M. we start for Lavacca. Routed a rebel picket on the way. When we got near the place the Rebels tried to burn a bridge over which we had to cross. But we were too fast. Dr. Hughs, who was once in the Rebel service, came to us there and intends staying with us. I found a map of Texas in the village. Some of our regiment got a rebel flag.

27th

Start back to Indianola, which we reach at 2 P.M. Sermon at night by the Chaplain. "Behold the Lamb of God.["][37]

28th

Our Company box came up at last. I got but four of the guns left at New Orleans. Sam'l Huston Esq has come with his schooner laden with goods. He ran into a Rebel Post on his way over, passed himself off for "Confederate" got the Captain and Mate of a Gunboat on his craft as if he would <u>treat</u> them, then took them prisoners; finally the bargain was made that he should let them go if they would not disturb him but let him run out to sea.

29th

Eddelman has come up.

30th

Had an alarm. We were on the road to meet the attack in a short time. As no enemy came on we lent our attention to <u>street drill</u>. The ladies were very much scared. The "Veterans" were very cool.

31st

This is the coldest morning that I have witnessed in the South. The "Matamoras" lies out on the sand, having been blown there by the wind. Sermon—"Give account of thy stewardship for thou mayest be steward no longer."[38] This is a direct appeal to the sinner. We hoped that the end of this year would find the end of the war.

1864

Jan 1st

I hope that the wicked will lose their authority, and that righteous Government may pervade the whole land this year, for "When the righteous beareth rule the people rejoice, but when the wicked are in authority the people mourn."[39]

2nd

Rainy and cold. Been on picket.

3rd

Moved over into a separate room. I anticipate a good deal of time to read. There have been meetings every night for three weeks.

4th

The "Matamoras" is off at last.

5th

Officers school in the evening.

6th

No Rations.

7th

No Rations.

8th

No Rations. I am put under arrest for letting my men get wood at an old Boatyard.

9th

No Rations. no wood. And still 38 men of Company "I" re-enlist for 3 years more. When was ever such endurance and patriotism exhibited? Rebellion may reel when those who have seen a score of battles coming at it by the thousands.
Let history record it.

10th

Sam'l Esq's schooner is safe and some papers. A Bill is introduced increasing soldiers' pay. The 18th Ind. is Veteran.

11th

Had a speech from Col Washburn and "Gen'l" Sam'l Huston, Esq.
    The latter promises us a nice banner. And he still wants to Sutler us. The veteran fever ran high. A few did not catch it.

12th

Temperance meeting. Dr. Hughs says that there were ten physicians here. Seven drank whiskey, three did not. The seven are all dead, the three still live.

13th

The 3rd Brigade came up.

14th

Still cool and foggy. Co. "I" did not elect me captain, and again it did. I used no persuasions. My resignation was already at Regimental Hdqrs when the committee announced that I had been elected.

15th

Nothing novel.

16th

Considerably ditto.

17th

The Brigade church numbers over two hundred. The Chaplain is a working man.

18th

Brigade drill regularly under Gen. Warren.

19th

An Ohio Battery has come up.

20th

Plenty of green apples in the "city" at 8 ⅓ apiece.

21st

I am having leisure to read The Spectator.

22nd

There was a most beautiful <u>mirage</u> this morning. Lavacca was seen as if banked upon a beautiful hill. Lavacca is about 15 miles distant.

23rd

Nice warm weather.

24th

We use the Methodist Church for worship.

25th

Detailed on General Court Martial. The first case is Col. Park's 99th Illinois.[40]

26th

Adjourn as the Judge Advocate cannot be here.

27th

Making papers for muster into the Veteran Service. It only requires 17 different Rolls.

28th

The 33rd Illinois has gone home on furlough. We are ready before the 8th Ind. and Gen. Warren says we shall go. To prevent it Gen Benton (my special favorite!) puts Gen Warren under arrest, and places Col. Shunk of the 8th Ind. in command of the Brigade. It's trickery.

29th

Our court proceeds slowly. I got a good letter, as I always do, from Miss LM.

30th

In Lowell's Satires we find the following:

> "We kinda thought Christ went agin war and pillage
> And that 'Eppylettes' war'ent the best mark of a saint,
>> But John P.
>> Robinson, he
> Says this kind o' thing's an exploded idee."[41]

31st

Byfield is married; so Burton and Miss Graves. Elgin is Chaplain. Billingsley 2nd Lt.[42]

February 1st

Not mustered yet. Gen. Warren is released.

2nd

Grass is growing fast. The place is being fortified. I have begun the second volume of Poland.

3rd

We have to make and entirely new set of "Veteran" papers.

4th

Our papers keep me busy all day.

5th

We are mustered this morning for three more years. There seems to be the best of good feeling towards me by all my company except two or three.

6th

A full mail. Rec'd a letter from cousin Lib Collins. And one from sister Jennie. Lucian Gray and James W. Feagler are in the cavalry service. Capt.

Patterson is home wounded. George Hankins has not been heard from.[43] We hope to start home soon. I shall be glad that those who have not been home for three years get to go. It is right.

7th to 14th

Still at Indianola. Transferred 23 men to the 49th Ind. Co. "I" has 46 veterans. Court martial still in progress. I like the business. John [Hunt] Morgan has escaped. Rec'd a letter from home.

Enjoyed a feast at the temperance meeting. More than a thousand of the bluecoat tribe are in attendance. The village school furnishes us some good declamations, some peculiarly antic. I was touched as the neat little boys one after another mounted the little stand and one after another delivered their pieces so gracefully, so cool and so distinct. But as the little girl came out with a coronet on her head and said in a feeble but dis-tinct voice: "x x x x x x I hope you veteran soldiers will not forget us little children of Indianola when you get to your homes at the far north,["] not many soldiers eyes but were moistened with a tear.

15th

Have read Wayland's Nature of Virtue. 10 P.M. the hum of camp has nearly died away. "Now I lay me down to sleep."

16th

Capt. McCallister has joined the Temperance Club.[44]

17th

I must make out a lot more of rolls.

18th

Very cold. I offered a strong resolution in the Temperance Club all were afraid of it.

19th

Dr. Brashear leads a singing class of Dr. Brown Dr. Bigney Eddelman and me. He is number one, an amateur.[45]

20th

I visit Mr. Heely's school.

21st

I am very lazy. The day is warm.

22nd

Washington's birthday. Convention at Indianapolis.

23rd

We are at work on fortifications.

24th

Temperance Club meets tonight.

25th

The grapevine in the arbor is budding.

26th

Deserters come in frequently.

27th

Sent out a flag of truce.

28th

The truce had a long talk with the Rebs. Exchanged papers and so on.

29th

This is Muster-day. Cold again.

March 1st

We are under marching orders from Indianola to Fort Esperanza. The citizens pray us to stay here.

2nd

Rec'd a letter from Mrs. C. B. and wrote to "Substitute."[46]

3rd

I am on another court martial. The 99th Ill's. Sutler had goods stolen by a guard.

4th

Wrote to mother.

5th

Some of my boys are preparing to take home a horned frog.

6th

Sermon by Reb. [Rev.] Mr. McCrea, he is terse and solid.

7th

Our singing club meets.

8th

Gen McClernand will be here soon.

9th

He is here. Also Gen Hamilton, Military Governor of Texas.[47]

10th

We are preparing to move our baggage.

11th

A most disagreeable day.

12th

We tear down buildings so as to ship the lumber to Fort Esperanza.

13th

March and camp at 4 P.M. at the first Bayou.

14th

Get across at 9 A.M. 30 men were drowned yesterday by the sinking of the pontoon. Fearful carelessness!

15th

Find our camp 5 miles south of Fort Esperanza. In passing Gen. McClernands Hdquarters we gave him three cheers. We are to draw Shelter tents.[48]

16th

Tim Hays, Co. K, was killed on a boat last night while drunk. Heed the lesson!

17th

Lewis Williams got for me an old wall tent.[49]

18th

Several refugees are with us, having come from Indianola. Dr. Hughs, Capt. Sheppard and Mr. Woodman are camping with us.

19th

Went to the beach but found but one shell. The best arranged camp on the Island is that of the 114th Ohio Infty Vols We are building immense fortifications.

20th

An exciting inspection. Sergt Butler had the cleanest gun.[50] Quite a rage for clean guns. Gen Warren at night sends a very puerile order around. All noise is to be <u>dried up</u>. He did not think it proper for us to be whooping, he said, like the Comanches. I like to hear the halloo and laugh. It denotes cheerfulness.

21st

Draw a supply of clothing.

22nd

At work on the fortifications. In the afternoon some steamers come in. Mail comes. The two James Vawters are married. One an uncle; one a cousin. Prof. Brumback and Tutor Wallace only, remain at Franklin college. Wallace says he will support me for Tutor if the Faculty is filled. Several of the sabbath scholars have joined the church, Eliza and Harry Hougham Julia Johnston Mary Meixwell, &c. Alice and Dora Forsythe are both dead. How disconsolate their mother must be. David McCaslin is dead.[51]

23rd

Sand flies like frost. Capt. Bell is a citizen.[52] Indiana has nominated Gov Morton for Governor and Pres. Lincoln for President. 38 Indiana Regiments have veteranized.

24th

Our tent blew down and we got wet as <u>rats</u>. But we had been <u>out in the wet</u> before.

25th

Read an article on sheep-growing in Minnesota. Visited Rev. Mr. Mc-Crea.[53] A portion of the 13th A.C. [Army Corps] is up Red River.

26th

Evening. "David went out to the fields at eventide to meditate." And it shows the Christian scholar. None can have as grand and pious thoughts in the throng as alone. Read an article in the Atlantic on "Northern Invasions Promote Civilization."[54]

27th

Correspondence is one of the great sources of pleasure to the soldier.

28th

Still at work on the defences. It is stated that Grant is now Lt General. I should be glad to be so situated that I should have to write write write. My style is crude and not perspicuous.

29th

Brigade Officer Day. Gen Warren has a most sensitive temperament. He could not sleep well unless the chain guards were on a perfect line. Our chaplain wet the foreheads of five candidates today. It was no baptism. It was hardly an apology for it. The chaplain says he will baptize any way. How generous! Does Christ warrant such generosity and conservatism Another question comes up. What are these men joining? It is not a church. There is no church here. I am considered very indifferent but I cannot give my influence to what I think to be wrong.

30th

I mingle with men of all tastes and aspirations. One of the lessons that I learn is, Most men are unlearned and not even consistently thoughtful. I analyze my own nature and actions and I find myself guilty as the rest. Strong proof everywhere of Total Depravity.

31st

Had a grand Review, Sand blew horribly. The Rhode Island colored troops are under arrest for mutiny. They refuse to receive seven dollars per month, saying that they were to have thirteen. They are right.[55]

April 1st

We have had our own "April fun." Several soldiers came up to my tent and looking quite serious said, "Did you wish to see me, Captain?" The other had sent them to sell them. Lt Crane is a citizen.[56]

2nd

Skirmish drill at 10 A.M. The blowing has given rise to a new song in camp:

"Never mind the weather
So the wind don't blow, &c"

3rd

Today Lt Crane, our companionable friend and witty mess-mate starts home. He is too nervous for almost any business.
Gen Warren commands the Division. Col Washburn the Brigade. Several citizens came down for something to eat.

5th

We ardently hope to see a steamer come in.

6th

The 8th Ind. is at New Orleans still.

7th

Mr. Clendenning is dead. So Mrs. Storey.[57] We shall start home very soon. It will be nice weather by the time we get home. I am anxious to go.

8th

James Bridges is quite low.[58]

9th

The officers of the Regiment have asked Col Washburn that he recommend a man from Indiana and *not* from Texas for Surgeon. He is very wrathy but I guess won't hurt anybody.

10th

After a sermon, I went down the Island by myself alone and had profitable cogitations. They were principally on the "Importance of heeding the Mountains of Conscience." A Mr. Small called on me today. I know his uncle a very pious and intelligent man.

11th

We met for singing.

12th

Worked all day sodding the fortifications.

13th

Visited the Hospital.

14th

Transferred some ordnance.

15th

Our going home is slow.

16th

We are to leave tomorrow for New Orleans. "Hail Columby" Our Non-Veterans are retransferred and then transferred again. They are to be left here.

17th

Start at 8 AM. Escorted by the Brass band and 21st 22nd and 23rd Iowa. We were heartily cheered as we passed through the opened ranks of these regiments. Get aboard the Steamer Clinton, Capt. Baxter. He had not much ballast and the vessel rolled very greatly. It did not take long for most of those on board to get to "New York."
A vessel tried to hail us but we could not think of stopping. Her shots fell short.
Finally she gave it up and <u>stood</u> the other way.

18th

Run steady and fast, will reach the Balize by midnight.

19th

Passed over the bar at one AM. The boys are getting well. Nice plantations along the river. Banks has met a reverse up the Red River. I get to learn that our troops had fallen back to Grand Ecore. Gen. Ransom was wounded.[59] We camp in the Union Cotton Press.

20th

Peddler women "are thick and fast." We have adopted the Veteran uniform.

21st

We have to make some more Rolls yet before we are paid. We are to go to Baton Rouge. I purchased here Victor Hugo's Les Miserables, and have read his account of the Battle of Waterloo.

22nd

Get aboard the Belvidere. I finish Waterloo. Victor writes as if he knew something of war.[60]

23rd

Reach Baton Rouge. Get into camp at 12 M. Just got our tents up when we were blessed with a fine April shower. The fortifications here are very poor.

24th

A lovely Sabbath morning. The ground is carpetted with green, the trees afford a deep shade. To add to all this, the village bells toll for worship. "I was glad when they said unto me let us go up to the house of the Lord." Sermon by Chaplain Brakeman.[61]

25th

Went to French Market.

26th

The Companies are to have a prize drill when we get to Indianapolis. So we go to work in earnest. I shall certainly get some letters soon.

27th

Took a stroll around town.

28th

The 33rd Ills. Veteran has come back to the field but is dissatisfied with Col Lippincott. I do not wonder at it. He is a <u>sot</u>.[62]

29th

Strolled into the graveyard by the Fort. Scores of Union soldiers lie there sleeping silently, quietly. On one monument of a citizen, David Martin who was born in New Jersey in 1815 and died in 1856 this singular inscription is found, "His last words were, 'I die a Christian and a Democrat.'"
The generations to come will wonder what he meant by Democrat, and may wonder too whether he was more a Christian or a Democrat. He must have been a monomaniac.
Went to Freedman's night school. Taught a class.

30th

I receive a good mail. The members of the Webster Society at Franklin College did a horribly mean thing. I say it to their shame. G. E. Moncrief is at Sardinia. Ol and Marshall are at Franklin College. A Miss Emma Stott was married here a day or two ago.

Gen Philip St George Cook, commanding here, is author of Cavalry Tactics. He has a son in the Rebel army. I don't think the Gen'l is doing his duty here. The condition of things testifies to it.

Citizens are permitted to take out of the lines almost anything they wish. Some take supplies for the Rebs I think.[63]

May 1st

Hail gladsome May Thou dost cover the earth with flowers. In thy warm breath the lambkins skip.

I have read a good Thanksgiving sermon by Chancellor Ferris of New York. "Render unto Ceasar [sic] the things &c &c"[64] Dr. Bigney has an old Plantation hat. Bridges should have a furlough. I fear he will not recover unless he has the bracing atmosphere of the North. This May Day I am full of gladness and praise.

2nd

Temperance meeting at the M. E. [Methodist Episcopal] Church. Several colonels made speeches. Some confessed that they yielded to intoxication but would do so no more. There are more sober colonels in this detachment than in any I have been in before. Heavy dews as we have will I think produce chills. At 5 P.M. we on the march for Clinton or some other point. Col Sheldon 42nd Ohio commanding expedition. March till 12 o'clock at night.[65]

3rd

Up at two and on the road. 18th Indiana in the advance. Routed the Rebel Pickets at daylight. After marching four miles further Col Sheldon began to prepare for a fight. The 18th Ind formed in line on left of the road, Co's A and K to the right of the road as skirmishers. The 24th Ind filed right and formed on the right of the road. The battery kept in the road. The cavalry pitched in wherever they could to best advantage.

After a sharp little fight we drove the enemy's cavalry from Olive Church by charging. The order of battle was now changed and the other regiments went in front. Co. "I" was stationed out to the right flank to watch the enemys movements. Our forces advanced to the bridge across Comite River where the Rebels were intrenched so we withdrew. The Col 4th Wis Cav was killed. We had six or eight men killed or wounded. We came back 12 or 15 miles and camped, tired and sleepy.

4th

Resumed the march at six[,] reach camp at Baton Rouge at 11 AM all with sore feet.

This was a remarkable scout for infantry. From 5 PM Monday to 11 AM Wednesday we marched 50 miles and was in the engagement 6 hours. If it was simply to find the position of the enemy, it was a success.

5th

The Western States have offered a lot of hundred days men.

It is said that Gen'l Warren will command here. The genius of Gen Grant's administration is concentration.

6th

A large escort followed the remains of Col Boardman, 4th Wis Cav to the boat L. M. Kennett. The coffin was drawn on a cannon wagon by 8 large black horses.[66]

In the Judgment the Col. will have to stand with the private. The high and the low; the rich and the poor, the learned and the ignorant, the small and the great will meet together. The favor of God is all that can shield one then.

7th

I am gloomy. I feel chagrin and disappointment and sorrow and anger because of the drunkenness of some of my men. Here are half-dozen of them drunk fools. I have by example and precept tried to induce them to habits of soberness. Cursed is he who sells the intoxicating stuff, and the son of a curse, he that permits it to be sold.

I suppose that amongst drunken men we see the distinct beginnings of that state where the worm dieth not and the fire is not quenched.[67] Father Above grant me a pure heart and fit me for the mansions of the pure holy and good.

We have received pay on the Muster Out and Muster In rolls.

8th

Rec'd a letter from Fannie. Rate is still at Greensburg. Henry McCanlon and George Carroll are at home.

9th

It is said that if we wait a week or two longer we shall be paid again.

10th

I adopt a sterner discipline.

The 26th Ind. will be down today.

11th

Read Maud Melvin, Grant's Spy.[68]

12th

Get our new uniforms costing $31 25/100.

13th

Grant is at work in earnest.

14th

Write to Miss M. M. We are all ready to start home, so far as we know. I however shall attempt to be content and make my boys so till we <u>do</u> go.

15th

Grant and Lee have come together. It is said that Lee will have to fall back to Richmond.

Heard Rev. Brakeman in the forenoon and Rev. Chaplain in afternoon. He made a distinction between courage and bravery.

Had a Dress parade. Gen. Birge was present. Mrs. Foley a very just widow says she shall write to some of the northern papers about what a fine appearance we made. The General said that we should have orders to start home soon.[69]

16th

Part of our Brigade has gone. We are glad of it for we get a supply of lumber, bricks bunks, &c.

Capt. R. H. Stott and David Burns passed down but I did not get to see them. Answered Miss L M and M M.

Grant crossed the Rapidan at three fords. Butler has advanced from the South and divided Beauregards forces.[70]

17th

Had a long and tedious drill.

18th

Again on duty. Grant has reached the south side of South Anna River. Longstreet was wounded.[71]

19th

The weather, if I <u>must</u> remark upon it, is considerably as it used to be in olden times. The 18th Ind is to furnish Provost guard. Capt Kimble, Lt Daniels and 60 men. Eggs 80 cts per a dozen.

20th

Lee has gradually fallen back. Sheridan's cavalry has got in Lee's rear. Sherman has advanced to Dalton [Georgia]. Ingalls dispatches—"We've got 'em this far." Discipline that stern but sensible old man has command in camp again. Long live his honor!

21st

Have a rigid Inspection after Regulation style. Rec'd a letter from home.

22nd

One year ago today we made the charge at Vicksburg. Thoughts, emotions recollections come thick and fast. Many re-lived their whole lives. Though the trial of courage was great, I could see written in the countenances, "I will do my best." I remember how my nerves began to steel how the excitement of the battle roused me. I have remarked to several that we were so intent on taking the fort that we could have built a bridge of dead bodies and walked over it, to accomplish our purpose. But once the nerves were relaxed, we could not even <u>look</u> at those bodies without emotion. For three weeks after the Battle I felt exhausted and dull. I indulge the hope that May 1865 will find our country at peace.
Heard a fine sermon from Chaplain Bates, 14th Maine. "I have overcome the world." It was written.[72]

23rd

An officer was arrested in bed with a woman of the town. Both were taken to jail. He I suspect wishes he had not been caught.

24th

Grant is resting and putting fresh troops in advance.

25th

Sherman has advanced to Kingston. Sigel has been defeated.[73]

26th

At 5 P.M. four of us and four ladies met at the Presbyterian Church for rehearsal. It is for the purpose of getting up a choir. Gens Warren and Benton are in town.

27th

The Paymaster is here. The getting the Ironclads down Red River again is due to the sagacity of Col Bailey 4th Wis. Uncle P. C. V. thinks the days of Franklin College are numbered. Unpleasant reflection.[74]

28th

At 10 AM we were ordered to the wharf to <u>start home</u>!!! There was the Pauline Carroll a nice large boat. Before we had proceeded far one of Co. H in attempting to shoot another, shot a sergt. of Co. "E." The guilty one was put ashore to be put in irons at Baton Rouge. Ed Dupree is drunk.

29th

"All's Well." No guerrillas trouble us yet. Prof Hibbens of Bloomington preached for us. I don't like the looks of the man. I am decidedly of the opinion that trade on the Mississippi should be stopped. It is a great means of furnishing the rebels with supplies. At Grand Gulf today the boat discharged several thousand dollars worth of goods, for three or four ladies. I say stop the trade. Don't let's feed and fight the rebel army too.

30th

Co."I" is on Picket on deck. As we pass the vessels of Porters fleet, the commanders tell us to keep well off the Columbia side. The Rebs have a Battery there.

31st

I had scarcely come on duty when we heard firing from the Western shore. The citizens scampered and hid like hunted rats. The guard had fired fifty shots before I could make it hear "cease firing"
Coming up I have read "Peculiar." A friend Mr. Frinck had it. Most of the cabin passengers spend the time playing cards and chess and in drinking and dancing.[75]

June 1st

We shall soon reach Memphis. I shall if possible find Miss Crain. Her friends at home will be glad to hear from her.

2nd

Sat up from 1 AM with a sick gentleman from Chicago. He had been practicing law in Vicksburg. I was surprised to find several officers of the 18th slipping to bed having gambled nearly all night.

3rd

Started on the train from Cairo at daylight. Col Washburn and Capt. Lowes had gone on to Terre Haute. The boys got to shooting at dogs geese &c from the cars. I made as if I was Officer of the Day and had it <u>dried up</u>.

4th

Reached Terre Haute at 8 A.M. The citizens had prepared for us a good breakfast. We felt as if we were getting amongst <u>friends</u>. After breakfast we marched out to the grove of the Female Institute to have a reception by the ladies who had presented to us a banner. After a good speech by Col Thompson and Col Washburn, we had a <u>dress parade</u> and drill which were highly complimented.[76] We were then taken to another grove and partook of a nice dinner, the ladies serving us. I made the acquaintance of a tall handsome young lady who I really admired. She was so amiable and intelligent.
Reached Indianapolis at sunset with about one third of my men drunk. Took quarters at the Soldiers Home.

5th

After getting my drunk men straight, I went to Dr. Days church. The new house is finished. Met Smock, Wallace and my good friend Miss Riesa Adams.[77]

6th

The papers announce our public Reception today. At 10 AM escorted by Col Blake we paraded Washington street preceded by the City Band. At 12 ½ the ladies had dinner for us at the soldiers home. When all was ready and all was right, Col Blake commanded: "Attention! Ready—Aim—Fire!" And we <u>fired</u>. After dinner three cheers for the ladies and then to the State House. Speeches by Gov Morton, Mayor Caven and Col Washburn. At 4 P.M. went to University Square and have a Dress parade and Drill. I shall say they were splendid. The <u>Indianapolis Journal</u> says so too.[78]

[Long undated clipping from the *Journal* inserted here]

7th

Removed my Hdqrs to the Spencer House.[79]

8th

Visited Miss Adams at the Institute. She had executed a very fine paint-ing[,] design original. Next called on Mrs. Dr. Brown and Miss Jordan. At 4 PM came down to Franklin. Met many warm friends. Sat till 12 ½ with Wallace.

9th

Vistied Mrs. Forsythe and Prof. Brumback's family. There were Miss Brumback and Miss Ella Graves. Afternoon visited Miss Morrison. Evening at Prayer meeting.[80]

10th

We are all down with Fremont now, however much we admired him be-fore. He has accepted the nomination for the presidency on a Butternut Platform. I think very strange of it, indeed. There is talk of establishing a military Professorship at Franklin. A professorship endowed by the old students, of the army. At 6 P.M. met Father Mollie Jennie and all Uncle WD Vawter family at Vernon. At 9 P.M. met mother at home.[81]

11th

Some visitors come in. I am tired.

12th

Met Miss Leon DeHoff at Sabbath school.

13th to 20th

Have visited and met almost all my former associates and friends of the neighborhood. Read "The Joneses." [82] Cousin Mary Stott is out to see us. I like her very much. Jennie and I go to Sardinia. Met my good friends at Uncle Abners. It is a <u>whole souled</u> family. I regard the place almost as home. I have been there a great deal in the past ten years.

21st

Eddelman and I start for Cincinnati. Arrive at the Gibson House at 12. John Fink and Mr Hutchings are with us.

22nd

After dispatching several trades, we seek conveyance for Brookville. Find a "Bus" at the Brighton House. It was crowded amazingly. But there was "room for one more." After the rain was over I got up with the "Engineer." The gentleman just mentioned had a great deal to say about <u>dogs</u>. I should think that he had observed dogs <u>principally</u>. I was really surprised to see the number of <u>Enquirers</u> thrown off the route. The greater number of papers thrown off were <u>Enquirers</u>. I could scarcely think that I was in Ohio. The country is hilly but cultivated. There is a Tavern each 6 to 10 miles. Each has a large yard attached for wagons and stock. And when I saw out here on the pike, not 20 miles from the Queen City such orthography as "Waggon Yard" I said it speaks ill for the education of the people. I fear the <u>schoolmaster</u> has not been at work. Reached Harrison at 6 PM. It is a quiet neat place. We had a good supper for 30 cts. We had not paid less than 50 for three years. I gave up my seat <u>above</u> as night came on and made myself content to sit with those <u>below</u>. A nice married lady with a well trained child was aboard. I appreciated her more that she wanted to share her basket supper with us. Said I mentally, "You have a woman's <u>soul</u>." How different from the fashionable ladies who expect attention from every one, and bestow it upon <u>no</u> one.

At 11 PM we reached the Valley House, Brookville.[83]

23rd

Wake up to find myself in Brookville. It was not as large a place as I anticipated, nor was there as much taste displayed, and to add to my disappointment, here came the newsboy sticking up to me the <u>Brookville Democrat</u>, the most traitorous sheet in comparison with its ability, in the North! And I, standing there with a Federal uniform on, I say a majority must patronize the sheet or it would be <u>rooted out</u>. After breakfast took a stroll over town. Like the looks of the place a <u>little</u> better. Found our Host a gentleman and loyal. At 10 started out to Uncle Ira Stouts. (I say <u>uncle</u> for that I have heard him always named so.) Arrived at 12M. I was able to reconnoiter while Eddelman held the horse, I went at it by asking for a drink of water. While drinking I saw Mattie coming from the milk house. She did not know me. I looked through the door into the room to see if Fannie was there. She was. At first, she did not recognize me. Mattie has an intelligent husband. Uncle Ira is a cheerful Christian man. In the afternoon some of us went down to Mrs. Shirks. Met there Mrs Shirk Cousin Beck, Lizzie and Lida McNutt and Mollie—and Elbert Shirk. Pleasures cup was filled to the brim. We retired at <u>Baptist</u> bedtime.[84]

24th

Enjoyed the forenoon in reading talking walking, &c. Lizzie and Lida baked bread and pies. In the afternoon took Fannie up home to get a dress for Sabbath. Then we came back. At noon attended a burying at Big Cedar Church. Lizzie showed me the graves of her mother brother grandfather and others. Lida, Eddelman, Lizzie and I took the buggies and drove to Mr. Owens. Miss Rate Owens his daughter received us cordially, James his son is a graduate of Oxford.[85] In coming back we lost the road and so did not get home as soon as we might otherwise. I was a stranger to the roads and Lizzie had not been home for two years, hence having forgotten them. Cousin Beck is still full of <u>fun</u>. Mrs. Shirk told me that she must soon pass to that land, whence none return, and that she hesitated not to go.

26th

Went to Sabbath school. It is a poor school. Few are good teachers, fewer still can conduct a Sabbath school efficiently. At five bade our friends good afternoon and started for Brookville. Met there Capt. Kimble. Attended M.E [Methodist Episcopal] church, heard Rev. Mr. Kiely preach. The sermon was clear and forcible. The church was neat the behaviour good and the singing fine.

27th

Start at 2 AM on stage. Reach Cincinnati at 10 AM Bought some Photograph albums. Reach Moores Hill at 8 P.M. Prof. McCoy comes home with me.

28th

Spent most of the day at home. Evening Mollie Jennie Miss Lou and I went to Grandfathers. He has sold his farm.

29th

Visited friends. Evening at home. How I enjoy the quiet of home and the affection of parents and sisters. None has a pleasanter home than I have. There is a regard for me which I fear I do not deserve.

30th

Some of us attend the exhibition of Mr. Wells high school. Aunt Leah took us up and got for us the best seat. Thanks for her <u>strategy</u>.

July 1st

Met Uncle P.C.V. at Wm. Holsclaws.[86]

2d

We are in the photograph business. I must go see Mat again or she will think me a negligent brother.

3d

At Sabbath school I made some criticism on the singing and for it (I suppose) was made singing clerk. Miss Lou came home with us.

4th

Fourth of July! Celebration at North Vernon. There was a speech by Rev. Mr. Dolph and Terrill. Daugters was there. Late got to Mat's. Mack not at home.

5th

Got to Vernon at 12 M. Visited cousin May and Lib.[87]

6th

I shall soon be off to the wars again. I leave with less emotion that at the first. [S]till I realize that I may never see my home nor parents nor sisters again. I go prepared for any fate. My trust is in God.

7th

It is somewhat sad to part from those we love when the probabilities are that we shall not see them again.
10 AM at Franklin. Take dinner at Mrs. Dr. Paynes after which Wallace and I took a walk out to the grave of his Arta.[88] We conversed freely on death[,] on affection, on the pleasures of a home. Accompanied Miss Ella Graves to prayer meeting.

8th

11 AM At Indianapolis. Found a few of the 18th Ind.

9th

We go into camp. A rebel raid into Maryland is announced. Franklin captured.[89]

10th

Attended Dr. Day's church. Mrs. Dr. Brown and Miss Jordan there.

11th

Most of the Regiment is in.

12th

Democratic Convention today. McDonald nominated for Governor and Turpin Lt. All went off quiet.[90] I want to get to the field as soon as possible.

PART FOUR

8

With Sheridan in the Valley

When Captain Will Stott declared himself ready "to get to the field as soon as possible," he assumed that the Eighteenth Indiana would head south again. In fact, on July 14 he and his comrades earmarked the baggage they took to the depot in Indianapolis for delivery to Cairo, Illinois, a primary entry point to Dixie for western troops. That same day, however, as Stott put it, "the order for going south was countermanded," and the Eighteenth received directions "to report at Washington," the nation's capital. The trip by rail took at least three days, but the soldiers looked forward to it with elevated spirits. Few had ever been to the District of Columbia—a place that held for them a mythic, almost sacred, aura—and stories of the fighting all around it had already reached legendary proportions. Furthermore, the excursion eastward would take them through gorgeous country and lift their emotions during some highly inspiring moments.

The men of the Eighteenth got on board the Pittsburgh and Fort Wayne Railroad at Indianapolis around noon on Saturday, July 16, 1864, and began rolling east at one o'clock. Stott spent a sleepless night, staring at the moon deep in thought and reflecting on the past. Others, no doubt were also anxious about the future, especially the new recruits such as eighteen-year-old Eugene Houghton of Daviess County who had just enrolled in Company E earlier that day. The train rumbled shakily through Indiana and Ohio, stopping at a number of small towns, and then it sped into Pennsylvania, where it crossed the Allegheny River and pulled into Pittsburgh at eight o'clock on the evening of July 17. There the Hoosier boys received a royal reception. According to James J. Osborn of Company F, the regiment "marched to the City Hall where we partook of a sumptuous supper prepared by the patriotic ladies of that city." After the dinner, Stott recorded, the troops "promenaded and sang" a rousing rendition of "Rally 'Round the Flag" with "the whole regiment coming in on the cho-rus" and lifting cheers of gratitude to the women of Pittsburgh. Climbing aboard the Pennsylvania Railroad at about 12:45 p.m., the soldiers spent all of July 18 absorbing the scenery of the beautiful Alleghenies on their way to Baltimore, arriving there in the dead of night.[1]

But it was the next day, July 19, which made the deepest impression on Stott. Wakening from a short night's sleep, he led his company to the city's Soldiers' Rest for breakfast and then marched to the Washington Depot for their four-hour ride to the capital. With only a little time to freshen up on their afternoon arrival in Washington, D.C., orders came for the Eighteenth Indiana to march through the city to a steamboat land-ing along the Potomac River. Parading down Pennsylvania Avenue evoked feelings that renewed Stott's deep-seated sense of duty and destiny. "How one's soul swells with emotion as from this perspective he views the na-tion struggling to crush a gigantic Rebellion," Stott wrote. "And when one reflects what this nation is yet to be, he says, come what may[,] hardship or disease or death even, the country is worth the sacrifice of all the ease and enjoyment of life and life itself. I have never felt more like doing my whole duty than now." Stott's later visits to Washington reinforced this resolve to fight again for his country.[2]

When the Eighteenth Indiana left Washington at nine o'clock that night aboard the steamship *Idaho*, it began a month of relatively unevent-ful campaigning. (It did so, however, during the early stages of Brigadier General Ulysses S. Grant's lengthy siege of the strategic railroad hub of Petersburg, Virginia, and the Eighteenth's travels took it to some of the significant locations of that operation—City Point, Bermuda Hundred, Deep Bottom.) The steamer took the regiment down the Potomac River, past Point Lookout, and into the Chesapeake Bay. As the ship approached the mouth of the James River, the famed Fort Monroe (also known as Fortress Monroe), a stone bastion of coastal defense since the 1820s, came into view. Its huge guns kept watch over the waters of Hampton Roads, where the ironclads *Monitor* and *Virginia* (formerly USS *Merrimack*) dueled without mercy in March 1862. The trip up the James River toward City Point, Grant's headquarters and primary supply base, brought to mind the unsuccessful campaign George B. McClellan had led on the Pen-

insula not long after the ironclads clashed. Arriving at City Point around
11:00 a.m. on July 21, and reporting to Grant, the Eighteenth received
orders to advance immediately to Bermuda Hundred, three hours farther
up the James. There the regiment would bivouac temporarily with Major
General Benjamin Butler's Army of the James.[3]

Although Stott believed that his unit had been sent to Butler "by mistake," he was pleased to be back "in <u>camp</u> again." The brigade's tent city
on the west bank of the James River was a bit "too near" the river for
Stott's comfort—only about fifty yards from the water. Yet, Houghton
proclaimed it "a good place to swim," and Taylor Peirce of the Twenty-
second Iowa praised the location as "a nice old Virginia farm." Stott and
the other veterans of the hot Louisiana campaign also appreciated its
"bracing" air. Compared to the "deadning [*sic*] influence of the extreme
south," Peirce wrote, "the atmosphere here seems to diffuse an elasticity
to the frame that gives a corresponding action to the mind which is truly
invigorating."[4] Stott therefore made the most of the Eighteenth's week-
long stay. He walked to the Appomattox River, returned to City Point,
where he witnessed the busyness of a major landing, and attended an
African American worship service with its heartfelt prayers and lively
songs. Only the occasional sounds of cannonading or heavy musketry
and some harsh thunderstorms, interrupted his largely pleasant time
at the Hundred.

On Wednesday, July 27, orders came to cross the James River and
report to Brigadier General Robert Sanford Foster's garrison on the
bridgehead called Deep Bottom, nine miles southeast of Richmond. Both
Foster and Stott were natives of Vernon, and the Hoosier boys of the
brigade valued their few days under Foster's command. Placed in the
front rifle pits, the Eighteenth also saw some action in line of battle. With
Confederate videttes clearly visible, skirmishing and picket duty "under
the sound of the enemy's guns" prompted Stott to confide in his diary:
"We are now where it is as necessary to <u>watch</u> as it is to <u>pray</u>." On July
29 the Eighteenth advanced on some Confederate works, shelling them
freely and laying in wait of possible assault. Noontime on Sunday, July 31,
however, brought new orders, and in just twenty minutes the Eighteenth
was off to Washington again, in swirling dust on one of its hottest and
driest marches of the war. By sundown its men were packed tightly on the
decks of the *Patapsco*, set to retrace the route they had taken less than two

weeks before. On this excursion, one moment brought a sense of awe to the soldiers. As the vessel steamed up the Potomac River, the men stood silently as they saw Mount Vernon, the home and burial place of George Washington, and, at the next turn of the winding river, got a full view of the dome of the Capitol—a juxtaposition of scenes that once again evoked the troops' patriotism.[5]

Upon reaching Washington, the Eighteenth Indiana received orders to report to Brigadier General Cuvier Grover, a top-ranking West Point graduate of 1844 who had fought in McClellan's Peninsular Campaign, at Second Bull Run, and in Major General Nathaniel P. Banks's operations in Louisiana. He was now commander of the Second Division of the XIX Army Corps stationed at Tennallytown near Georgetown, about four miles north of Washington. Setting up camp at that site on August 3, the Eighteenth became part of a provisional brigade with the Twenty-fourth and Twenty-eighth Iowa. Upon the arrival of the Eighth Indiana nine days later, the four regiments constituted the Fourth Brigade of Grover's division, Colonel David Shunk in command. Being so near Washington Stott took every opportunity, when he could break free from his paper work, to go to the city "on business." There he worshipped at Fourth Presbyterian Church with his friend, Captain Abraham Lowes, bought a new camp chair, and stood in the Capitol rotunda admiring the paintings and statuary. But such leisure could not last. Thursday, August 11, found the men of the Eighteenth, with Stott partially in charge, cutting under-brush and bushes around Fort Bunker Hill and other installations some ten miles from Washington. This activity was essential, as Will R. Lee of Company F explained, "so that if the Rebs advance on them again the men in the Fort could see them before they get close upon them." After two days of labor, the "slashers" received orders to return to camp and make preparations to march. They were to go to the Shenandoah Valley where they would join a former colleague from the Pea Ridge Campaign, Philip Henry Sheridan, now the commanding general of the newly constituted Army of the Shenandoah.[6]

Before the summer of 1864 the region through which the Shenandoah River flows, known simply as "the Valley," was a miserable place for Union forces. It was the major avenue Confederate armies had used in putting pressure on Washington and in launching invasions into Maryland and Pennsylvania. It served also as the foremost granary and garden of the Confederacy, its products capably offsetting the effects of Union blockades on overseas trade early in the war and now providing the last source of food for Robert E. Lee's beleaguered Army of Northern Virginia at Petersburg. The 165-mile corridor also handsomely provided manpower for the Southern ranks. Furthermore, Union military efforts in the Shenandoah Valley had been uniformly unsuccessful. Thomas "Stonewall" Jackson's famous campaign there in the spring of 1862, in which he pummeled three Union armies and diverted Washington's attention during McClellan's poor performance on the Peninsula, still stung the Union high command. Nor were the initial clashes of 1864 in the Shenandoah Valley any consolation. Franz Sigel's movement southward in May met with disaster at New Market. David Hunter's parade of destruction the following month led to his realization that, faced with the combined forces of Jubal Early and John C. Breckinridge at Lynchburg, he could not prevail against that valuable railroad link to Lee's army. Hunter was left with no option but to withdraw into the Allegheny Mountains. Now Lee had let Early loose to storm down the Shenandoah Valley toward Washington. During his rampage, Early defeated Lew Wallace at Monocacy, Maryland, and raided the environs of Washington on the very days the Eighteenth Indiana's slashers were seeking to improve Union vision. Early then beat a Union force at Kernstown, Virginia, and proceeded to plunge into Pennsylvania where, on July 30, his troops burned the town of Chambersburg in retaliation for its citizens' refusal to pay Early a monetary tribute.[7]

By the end of July, it was obvious to Grant that, if he were to be successful in taking Petersburg and defeating Lee, something had to be done to subdue the Confederates in the Shenandoah Valley. First, there was Washington to consider. Northern newspapers were screaming over the easy access Confederate forces had to the capital. A *New York Times* editorial said the situation looked like "the old story again. The back door, by way of the Shenandoah Valley, has been left invitingly opened." Besides, it was a crucial election year, and, as historian Jeffry Wert cogently observes, "If President [Abraham] Lincoln expected to win reelection, the 'back door' needed to be shut." Moreover, a stronger, more mobile Union army in the Shenandoah Valley, under solid leadership, could press Early's forces and possibly destroy the rail links supplying Lee's troops.

This would allow Grant to retain George Meade's Army of the Potomac and Butler's Army of the James for the Petersburg operations, while freeing the XIX and VI corps for service along the Shenandoah. So it was that Grant chose to yoke his Petersburg offensive to combative action in the Shenandoah Valley.[8]

Grant began by conferring with Lincoln at Fort Monroe on Sunday, July 31, the day after Chambersburg went up in flames. While the primary concern for both men was the security of Washington, they agreed that "a unified command under an aggressive Union commander" was essential to wipe out Early's Army of the Valley, destroy the vital Virginia Central Railroad, and thus cut off Lee's source of supplies from the Shenandoah. Grant and Lincoln then discussed possible candidates for the new command: Generals William B. Franklin, Meade, even McClellan. When Grant proposed Sheridan as overall commander with the retention of Hunter as chief of the "geographical department," Lincoln concurred. The next day, Grant wrote Chief-of-Staff Henry Halleck: "I want Sheridan put in command of all the troops in the field, with instructions to put himself south of the enemy and follow him to the death. Wherever the enemy goes let our troops go also."[9] In two sentences, Grant named the man and defined the strategy.

Some officials, Secretary of War Edwin M. Stanton and Halleck in particular, had some doubts about the *man*. Sheridan was, after all, only thirty-three years old, rather young for such a high-level appointment. Even Lincoln momentarily worried about the age factor. Nor was "Little Phil," as his men called him, an imposing figure. Five foot three inches tall, weighing about 120 pounds, with broad shoulders and a barrel chest atop short legs, he was, as one historian puts it, "an odd-looking runt." Civil War artist James Taylor, however, after only a few minutes in his presence, described Sheridan as a "little mountain of combative force." And Grant's closest lieutenant, William T. Sherman, congratulated his chief on his selection. "I am glad you have given Sheridan the command of the forces to defend Washington," Sherman wrote. "He will worry Early to death."[10] Indeed he would, as his men could tell you. As the fiery cavalry commander of the Army of the Potomac, Sheridan had an electric effect upon his troops. "He was the only commander I ever met," said one of his subordinates, "whose personal appearance in the field was an immediate and positive stimulus to battle." A cavalry surgeon noted that Sheridan's "appearance in front of the line of battle, without saying a word, charged the character of every man in a moment." Later, Grant himself would praise Sheridan's "magnetic quality of swaying men which I wish I had—a rare quality in a general." In the end, Sheridan proved to be more than a match for Early.[11]

As for the *strategy* Grant proposed, the youthful appointee embraced it in a heartbeat. The plan called for an energetic offensive, not just against Early's butternuts but against the land as well. At a meeting on August 6 at Monocacy Junction, Grant handed Sheridan detailed orders to that effect. He was to drive Early up the Shenandoah Valley in such a manner that "nothing should be left to invite the enemy to return." While buildings should be spared and the people personally unmolested, the valley itself should be so devastated that "even a crow flying over it would be compelled to carry his own provender so as not to perish." Drive the enemy south, Grant later directed, giving him "no rest, and if it is possible to follow the Virginia Central Railroad, follow that far. Do all the damage to railroads and crops you can. Carry off stock of all discreptions [*sic*] and negroes, so as to prevent further planting." In short, the general-in-chief wanted the Shenandoah Valley to become "a barren waste," totally useless as a resource for the Confederacy. Yet, Grant warned, Sheridan should not engage the enemy unless forced to, for defeat could further threaten Washington, possibly cost Lincoln his re-election, and thus prolong the war. As Sheridan recalled in his memoirs, "I deemed it necessary to be very cautious; and the fact that the Presidential election was impending made me doubly so."[12]

Before strategy could be implemented, however, an army had to be created. There had never been a unified command in the Shenandoah Valley, where Union forces had met only defeat. Now Grant and Sheridan intended to rectify that situation. The first step toward doing so occurred when, in Sheridan's words, Hunter made the "unselfish request" to be relieved of his departmental post. Consenting to Hunter's entreaty, which he saw as a sign of "patriotism that was none too common in the army," Grant proceeded by presidential order to merge four geographical districts into a new Middle Military Division temporarily under Sheridan's command. In essence, this laid the foundation for what Sheridan called the Army of the Shenandoah. Initially, it brought together Major General Horatio G. Wright's VI Corps, out of the Petersburg lines; a portion of

Major General Philip Sheridan, commander, Army of the Shenandoah.

Major General William H. Emory's XIX Corps, recently transferred from Louisiana; Major General George Crook's Army of West Virginia, now designated the VIII Corps; and sizable divisions of infantry and cavalry from the Army of the Potomac.[13]

It has been described as "an amalgam, a hybrid army," and "hardly more than a loose aggregation." Yet, it became, according to historian Charles C. Osborne, "the largest Union force ever to serve in the Valley," three times the size of Early's army and molded by Sheridan into a formidable fighting machine. And, in mid-August, it gained further strength through the arrival of Grover's huge Second Division of the XIX Corps, including the Eighteenth Indiana—specifically at Sheridan's request. On August 12, the new commander wrote Halleck from his encampment at Cedar Creek, expressing his "regret that Grover's division was not permitted to come to Harpers Ferry, as I intended to use it as a strong guard for the subsistence trains." Considering the threat of Confederate reinforcements, he added, "Grover should have been permitted to come out." The next day the Eighteenth received its orders to march to the Shenandoah Valley.[14]

The Eighteenth Indiana began its trek to join Sheridan in the early morning of Sunday, August 14. The sun and humidity were blistering that day and, as one member of Company D reported to his hometown newspaper, "it was very hard marching" on rough, dusty roads. The next day brought more of the same and "a great many men were sunstruck," two dying of heat stroke. On the sixteenth the long blue line marched up the Leesburg Pike toward the Blue Ridge Mountains, and it entered the heart of the Shenandoah Valley through Snicker's Gap on August 17.[15]

Meantime, to the northeast, Sheridan was shifting his already extensive army farther down the lower valley. For some days he and Early had been countering each other's movements in what one historian has portrayed as an "elaborate martial gavotte"—one stepping forward and the other stepping back in a repetitious pattern. On August 15 Sheridan abandoned his position at Cedar Creek, which he told Grant was "a very bad one," since he could not "cover the numerous rivers that lead in on both of my flanks to the rear." Besides, the Confederates had established an observation post and signal station on Three Top Mountain in the

Massanutten range overlooking Cedar Creek and the Union encampment. Through Halleck, Grant urged Sheridan "to be cautious, and act now on the defensive" in anticipation of Early's reinforcements. Consequently, Sheridan pulled the major portion of his army back down the Valley beyond Winchester into position on a fourteen-mile line along the Shenandoah River from Berryville in the south to Charles Town in the north. This placed him at a site from which he could "pressure" the Rebels around Winchester. "This retrograde movement," he noted in his memoirs, "would also enable me to strengthen my command by Grover's division of the Nineteenth Corps and [Brigadier General James] Wilson's cavalry." On the night of August 17, after hastening through Snicker's Gap and wading the waist-deep Shenandoah River at midnight, Grover's men reached Sheridan's forces at Berryville near morning. There they "cast themselves, hungry and tired upon the ground and slept." They had made the rigorous march from Washington, a total of sixty-nine miles, in three days.[16]

During the next month, units of the Army of the Shenandoah were on the move almost constantly. The infantry traversed back and forth in the lower valley from Berryville in the south to Harpers Ferry in the north, while cavalry held a defensive line along Opequon Creek near Winchester. At times hounded by Early's graycoats, at other moments dogging them in return, and regularly within the sounds of musketry and cannon, the Union army faced all kinds of weather and saw places that had been touched by history. They also came to know their new leader, who may have been short of stature but looked majestic atop his black charger, Rienzi. On their first day in his command, August 18, the men of the Eighteenth Indiana arose from their short nap at daylight and marched through Berryville "in a drenching rain" and onto the Charlestown Road. While enjoying a brief respite on the side of the road that day, they got their first glimpse of Sheridan. Stott, in fact, had a chat with him, during which the general pumped Stott with questions about his brigade and company and wanted to know when it had arrived. As others watched, Sheridan's modest, approachable demeanor, a trait praised by an officer of the VI Corps, may have struck them. "One thing pleased us at the start," Surgeon George T. Stevens recalled. "Our new general was visible to the soldiers of his command; wherever we went he was with the column, inhaling the dust, leaving the road for the teams, never a day or two behind the rest of the Army, but always riding by the side of the men." Perhaps it was the assurance provided by this commander's presence—

that of "one born for the din of battle"—that made Stott declare a few days later, in the face of a seemingly imminent fight: "I am ready for duty and destiny."[17]

Stott penned these words on Sunday, August 21. That same day Swain Marshall of his brigade told "Friends at Home" that, since the butternuts were "advancing on us, we commenced fortifying and by dark had very good works thrown up." But, he explained, "the enemy left the road we were on, and moved around our right, attacking the VI Corps driving them back toward Charlestown [sic]." The next day the brigade passed through Charles Town, where John Brown, the abolitionist raider of Harpers Ferry, had been tried and hanged. The town was mostly deserted, chimneys standing lonely, its famous courthouse now in ruins, and the jail "a shell of tottering walls." Soldiers and bands, however, could not resist filling the air with the strains of "John Brown's body lies a mouldering in the grave, His soul is marching on."[18]

For weeks after that, as summer heat gave way to fall chills, diaries, letters, and official reports echoed the observations of Marshall's letter. In late August a soldier of the Eighteenth Indiana informed the Vevay newspaper that one day "the Johnnies are still skirmishing with us," then the next "All [is] quiet along the line." Pennsylvanian Henry Keiser penned these entries in his diary: "received orders this morning to march at a moment's notice"; "the pickets kept up a fire all day, also an occasional cannon shot"; "pretty heavy musketry on our left where the VII and XIX corps are in line." During the same period, Peirce, Twenty-second Iowa, told his wife, "This is the most fatiguing campaign that we have had since the Siege of Vicksburg." And Captain John W. DeForest of General Emory's staff, describing himself as "dirty from head to foot," complained of the "uncommon amount of severe guard duty, night alarums, sudden orders to fall in, and unexpected movements." Their commander noted the incessant action, too. Sheridan reported to Halleck on August 24: "This morning General Crook made a reconnaissance, driving in the enemy's advanced line, . . . capturing twenty men belonging to Early's corps. General Emory . . . encountered a strong force in his front. I will commence operations with the cavalry to-morrow."[19]

There were, of course, more pleasant moments. The charm of the Shenandoah Valley prompted Peirce to exclaim to his sister: "I thought that I never seen so beautiful a country." Its farms displayed "a style of luxury and comfort I have seen no where in the south," he noted, and every village had "a church spire rising above the surrounding trees" that enhanced the land's beauty. In all, he resolved, "this was a nation and a country worth risking his life for." Furthermore, word of the fall of Atlanta sparked celebrations in the camps, as did the news that McClellan's run for the presidency was "fast playing out." As one soldier wrote a friend, the Democratic candidate's "popularity in the army is rapidly declining. In our Brig. which is composed of the 8th and 18th Ind, 24th and 28th Iowa McClellan would not get 50 votes."[20]

Such was the situation on the eve of the new army's first test in combat, a battle that would be known as Third Winchester. On September 9 Grant encouraged Sheridan to continue the course he had been pursuing thus far, that of "pressing closely upon the enemy and when he moves follow him up being ready at all times to pounce upon him if he detaches any conciderable [sic] force." Within a week, Grant came to the conclusion that the opportune moment to push the Confederates from the Shenandoah Valley was at hand. He rode to Charles Town on September 16 to consult with Sheridan about conditions in the valley. Sheridan expressed confidence that he could defeat Early's forces, prompting Grant to ask if it could be done in the next four days. With Sheridan's assurance, Grant said quietly, "Go in." Sheridan immediately laid plans for a westward move on Winchester. Ironically, he received assistance from Early, who, for some inexplicable reason, divided his army. While maintaining young Stephen Dodson Ramseur's crack division in a defensive position along the Berryville-Winchester Road, the Confederate commander sent the equally formidable divisions of John C. Breckinridge, Robert Rodes, and John Brown Gordon north of Winchester to Stephenson's Depot and Bunker Hill. Seizing upon what he called "the disjointed state of the enemy," Sheridan chose to strike the Confederates with the VI and XIX corps down the Berryville Pike, retaining Crook's VIII Corps in reserve "to be used as a turning column when the crisis of the battle occurred." On the night of September 18, the Army of the Shenandoah got orders, as Stott recorded them, "to be up and ready to march at 2 A.M."[21]

Upon arising with the sound of the first call at 1:00 a.m. on September 19, the men of the Eighteenth Indiana worked the stiffness out of their limbs by striking tents and loading baggage on wagons, while the aroma of fresh-brewed coffee awakened their senses. They joined Grover's other regiments "at precisely 2 a.m.," reported corps commander Emory, and set off on the Berryville road for Winchester. Sheridan's plan relied heavily on rapid movement in order to startle the enemy beyond Opequon Creek. But after only two miles of swift marching, both elements—speed and surprise—were lost, for Grover's division, placed in the van of the XIX Corps by Emory, found itself halted by a massive traffic jam. The turn-pike was a long, narrow, wooded ravine, a virtual canyon, and VI Corps commander Wright, contrary to orders, had taken his entire train of baggage, supply and ammunition wagons, ambulances, and rolling stock onto the slender road. The result was a snarled bottleneck that blocked the columns of the XIX Corps. Emory, affectionately called "Old Brick Top" by his troops because of his sandy hair, was understandably furious. After sending a series of staff officers to request that the road be cleared and receiving no reply, he resolutely galloped forward to confront Wright. The VI Corps commander, however, stubbornly refused to move his train. Even though cannons were erupting up ahead, Emory and his men could do no more than watch the wagons roll by. It took an angry Sheridan, who rode to the scene to investigate the delay, to order the teamsters to "Get those damned wagons into the ditch" before Emory could direct Grover's men to proceed around the congestion—in the woods to the right, if need be. By then hours of precious daylight had been wasted, and it was around 11:00 a.m. when the XIX Corps finally broke out of the gorge and got into line of battle on the right of the VI Corps.[22]

Grover formed his four brigades into two lines, with the Hoosiers and Iowans of Shunk's brigade in the second line, directly behind Brigadier General Henry W. Birge's First Brigade of New Englanders. Once in place, they peered across more than a thousand yards of broken, wavelike pastures, rows of corn ready for harvest, and a densely wooded area on the left. Beyond the uneven ground stood their grayclad opponents, stronger than a few hours before. Taking advantage of Union delays, Early had buttressed his defensive line by erecting sturdier earthworks and recalling the troops of Rodes and Gordon, who had come on the double-quick from Stephenson's Depot. It was now clear to Sheridan, as he later wrote, that his "chances of striking [Early] in detail were growing less every moment." Just down the row from Stott, native Hoosier Israel Ritter of the Twenty-fourth Iowa took a minute to reflect as well. "We will probably move soon as firing is increasing," he scribbled in his diary. "I am perfectly composed. Bless my dear ones at home. The nearer death comes the happier the Christian. 'Hope thou in God, Oh, my soul.' I read the 13th Psalm for my lesson as I have had no opportunity before today. 'Tho he slay me yet will I trust in him.'" It was Ritter's last entry. In less than an hour, he would fall with a mortal wound.[23]

At 11:45 bugles blared and the signal cannon thundered, and the Union troops rose up as one body and charged onto the open field. Lee of the Eighteenth Indiana saw the many lines move "forward in splendid style, drums beating and colors flying." The surgeon of the Seventy-seventh New York likewise marveled at the scene. "Stretching three miles across the fields," the blue host, he said, was "as composed as though on parade, the line straight and compact, the various division, brigade, and regimental flags floating gaily in the sunlight." But, Lee noted, "The first line had not advanced more than two hundred yards when they became warmly engaged." The New York doctor recorded that "at every step, men were dropping, dropping; some dead, some mortally hurt, and some with slight wounds."[24]

Grover's division defied the deadly shelling, cleared the hills before them, and carried the woods beyond "with a rush." The Eighteenth Indiana, said Captain James B. Black of Company H, "looked every man a veteran" as they threw their cooking utensils and other unnecessary burdens aside, and "with a loud yell, swept forward at double-quick into the woods." Grover's troops charged the butternut left with devastating effect, even breaking up a division of Gordon's Confederates. Unfortunately, this movement opened a broad gap between the First and Third brigades of Grover's division. Sheridan recalled that this "increased an interval that had already been made" and consequently "destroyed the continuity" of the Union line. Its timing also proved costly. Feeling overconfident because of their success thus far, Grover's advanced troops impetuously hurried toward a second wooded area where rocks concealed Confederate soldiers. At that moment "a terrific front and enfilading fire" poured into the charging Union force, sending it "flying in fragments to the rear" through the ranks of the Eighteenth Indiana. Stott's regiment allowed the fugitives to pass, but stood its ground, rallied three times, and held back the grayclad pursuers for two hours before themselves falling back toward their retreating comrades, leaving scores of fallen men in the woods. Fearing "the day was lost," Stott said he had "scarcely ever felt so sad."[25]

The Confederate counterattack from which the Eighteenth Indiana fled began when Gordon noted that the unrestrained actions of Sheridan's lines had caused them "to halt, bend, and finally to break at different points," forming a gap between the Union XIX and VI corps. The Georgian immediately conferred with Rodes and both saw that "the only chance to save our commands was to make an impetuous and simultaneous charge with both divisions." The decision was no sooner made than Rodes fell from his horse, mortally wounded by a shell fragment behind his ear. His loss deprived Early of one of his most skillful and intrepid lieutenants. Saddened but undeterred, Gordon led his division and Rodes's (now under Ramseur's command) directly into the soft spots of the Union line, driving them back in confusion and with heavy losses.[26]

Around noon the firing began to fade away. As far as the men in gray were concerned, the battle was over, and it was time to rest and enjoy victory. Union leaders, however, had other plans. By 1:00 p.m., Emory began refashioning his depleted lines at the edge of the woods where they had fought that morning. And Grover's shaken remnants reorganized "in good order behind the lines of [Brigadier General William] Dwight." Sheridan rode among his men, and one witness said he "treated the infantry men to a taste of the sweetest swearing they had ever heard." He took after Grover's fugitives in such a furious way as to scare them back to work. And yet the soldiers cheered him as he rallied them, as he told them what they had to do to the Confederates—"give 'em hell." Of course Sheridan knew he still had the numerical edge and, with Crooks's VIII Corps in reserve— his trump card— he could assume the initiative. "I directed Crook to take post on the right of the Nineteenth Corps," Sheridan recalled, "and, when the action was renewed, to push his command forward as a turning-column in conjunction with Emory." As Crook brought his corps up to Red Bud Run across from the Confederate left, Sheridan ordered Wright to "advance in concert with Crook, by swinging Emory and the right of the VI Corps to the left together in a half-wheel." Then, while Crook pushed his men across Red Bud Run and into Gordon's left flank, Sheridan rode up to Brigadier General George Getty, also of the VI Corps, and shouted, "Press them, General, I know they'll run." Stevens, who heard these words, said a cheer from the men then "drowned all the noise of battle." Emory reported that "Nothing could have been more opportune than the attack of General Crook's force, as it was just at the moment that the enemy had been repulsed from his assaults on my line." Crook, Emory, and Wright pressed the Confederates, and run they did. Gordon's left wing collapsed in disorder, Ramseur folded back as Emory and Wright bore down upon him, and Sheridan yelled, "We've got 'em bagged, by God!"[27]

The Battle of Third Winchester was history, and the Eighteenth Indiana had witnessed another decisive victory. When officers called the roll that night, though, the price paid for victory struck home. "Dead," "Missing," "Killed" came the responses from tired men who had eaten nothing since morning and were out of water. The XIX Corps lost more than two thousand killed and wounded during the barrage of Confederate musketry and artillery prior to the final Union assault. Grover's division bore the largest share of the casualties, with 1,527 falling in combat, about 30 percent of the total losses of Sheridan's army. In Stott's company alone, ten men went down in twenty minutes. Yet, behind solid leadership, the soldiers in blue transformed a potential rout into a brilliant triumph. "A great victory," Grant called it when he wrote Sheridan to tell him of the "salute of 100 guns" that would be fired "in honor of it" the next morning.[28]

———·◆·———

By the time Grant fired his promised salute, the Army of the Shenandoah was already at Strasburg, just two miles from Early's encampment at Fisher's Hill. On the night of September 19, Sheridan issued orders for "following Early up the valley next morning—the pursuit to begin at daybreak." After celebrating the night before, the army left the outskirts of Winchester at 5:00 a.m. on Tuesday, September 20, and proceeded up the Valley Pike, the main thoroughfare through the valley. With the cavalry in the van, the infantry columns marched abreast on either side of the pike, the XIX Corps on the right. Spirits were soaring. One Massachusetts soldier wrote that "everybody is in high glee." Not only had they notched a cardinal victory, but also their faith in their young commander and his lieutenants was greater than ever. Besides, they had Early on the run and were hard on his heels. In fact, when they reached little Strasburg that afternoon after a twenty-mile hike, Union pickets were close enough to exchange shots with enemy videttes hidden behind the town's buildings and in the surrounding countryside.[29]

At Fisher's Hill, the main body of Early's Army of the Valley was in a defensive position that DeForest said, "was not a nut to be cracked easily." Indeed, New Yorker Stevens recalled that "the citizens of the valley assured us" the Confederate post "could be held by Early's army against one hundred thousand men." This was certainly an exaggeration, but one of Emory's engineers, having perused the site, predicted, "If they have prolonged their left, they are inattackable." One reason Fisher's Hill was so commanding was that it formed a lofty, natural fortress squeezed between the Massanutten range on the east and North Mountain on the west—the narrowest section of the entire Shenandoah Valley where its width was only four miles. Nestled snugly in this position, the hill seemed to a Vermont veteran to be "a huge, high-fronted billow of earth and rocks, which had some time been rolling down the valley and became strangled between these two mountains and held still."[30]

On this steep bluff overhanging the tiny rivulet called Tumbling Run, Early waited. In the wake of the Winchester disaster and the quiet, dreary retreat up the Shenandoah Valley, Early was satisfied that Fisher's Hill was "the only position in the whole Valley where a defensive line could be taken against an enemy moving up the Valley." He admitted "it had several weak points"—a thin left flank, for example—but having placed his divisions along the ridge behind strong earthworks, Early felt secure enough to remove his ammunition boxes from their caissons and put them behind the breastworks. His troops must have shared his certitude, for they christened the site "Gibraltar."[31]

Upon reaching Strasburg on the afternoon of September 20, Sheridan promptly rode forward to study "Gibraltar." It was clear at first glimpse that the steep and rocky eastern edge on the right of the Confederate stronghold was, according to DeForest, "a spot for Rocky Mountain goats to fight in," not men. Likewise, Sheridan immediately noticed that a frontal assault was potentially suicidal. He also knew that maneuvers could not take place in daylight because his position was clearly visible from the Confederate signal station on the northern peak of the Massanutten. In a council of war that evening, Sheridan and his corps commanders agreed that the Confederatre right was unassailable and a head-on assault absurd. Crook suggested a plan similar to the successful one at Winchester, namely a turning movement at Little North Mountain directed at Early's weak left flank. Emory and Wright were not supportive of Crook's proposal, but Sheridan embraced it and assigned Crook's VIII Corps to accomplish the task. The secret to the strategy's success, Sheridan later wrote, was "to move Crook, unperceived if possible, over to the eastern face of Little North Mountain, whence he could strike the left and rear of the Confederate line, and as he broke it up, I could support him by a left half-wheel of my whole line of battle." Wasting no time, Crook took his men that night to a heavily timbered area on the north bank of Cedar Creek, where they remained hidden the next day.[32]

When the sun rose on the misty, foggy morning of September 21, the men of the Army of the Shenandoah rose with it. The day started routinely enough—brew the coffee, make breakfast, quietly and slowly so as to savor a moment of peace. Most of the morning was leisurely, but as the fog began to lift, those closely observing the Confederate defense line—Sheridan among them—noticed that Early's men had been busy during the night. Their stone-and-earth breastworks had been strengthened, and an officer of the VI Corps noted that "the lines of troublesome abattis" were longer and more formidable than before. Riding with Wright at his side, Sheridan reconnoitered the Confederate works throughout the day and ordered periodic changes in his troop deployments that brought them steadily closer to the enemy's line. Confederate skirmishing and artillery fire punctuated these maneuvers, interrupting their flow but not detaining them. Only once, when Sheridan ordered Wright's VI Corps to capture the high ground north of Tumbling Run, did any significant fighting occur. Wright prevailed due to what cavalry chief Wesley Merritt called "a brilliant charge." Wright now occupied a perfect position for Union guns and, wrote Sheridan, "an unobstructed view of the enemy's works." The XIX Corps then took the ground the VI Corps had vacated between the Manassas Gap Railroad and the North Fork of the Shenandoah River, just southwest of Strasburg. Shunk's brigade, that of the Eighteenth Indiana, "was ordered to the right of the pike" and advanced even farther right in the succeeding hours, erecting fortifications along the way. Francis A. Dawes of the Twenty-fourth Iowa described this operation: "[A]bout noon our camps moved to the front and right gradually advancing as the 6th Corps were getting their place on our right they drove back the enemy's skirmishers about sunrise and continued fireing until after dark."[33]

By dusk the Union front spread for nearly two miles below Fisher's Hill. Along this extensive line, the troops got little sleep, for realignments continued all night. Emory, for example, "received orders to move [his] corps at the break of day to occupy the position occupied the night before by the Sixth Corps" and to remain close to Wright's men as they moved farther right. This kept the Eighteenth Indiana and its companion regiments busy, since Emory's batteries were posted with Grover's brigades, and they had to be dragged to new placements. Although these movements, according to Stevens, "were . . . keeping up a show of determination to attack in front" of Fisher's Hill, Early concluded that Sheridan "was satisfied with the advantage he had gained and would not probably press it further."[34] What the Confederate leader did not know was that Crook's hidden corps was using the darkness of night to cross Cedar Creek and proceed through ravines shaded by heavily wooded ridges to the base of Little North Mountain. Joining Crook near the base was James B. Ricketts's Third Division of the VI Corps. All night and well into the morning of September 22, the artillerymen of the two commands silently pulled their guns up the precipitous mountainside while the foot soldiers marched in columns "with utmost secrecy."[35]

Thanks to Crook's advance, the warm morning of September 22, unlike the previous day, left the Union forces no time for leisure. "[U]p again at 4," scrawled Dawes, "and at 5 we commenced to move to the right and front winding round the hills and thru the cornfields until we formed on the left of the 6th corps Our Brigade in the 2nd line and fortified and moved up as the line in front advanced canonading and musketry going on in front." So it was all along the Union front. "[S]trong skirmish lines were thrown out, the whole army being put in motion," reported Lieutenant Colonel Ed Wright, Twenty-fourth Iowa. Sheridan, concerned that Confederate signalmen might see Crook's maneuvers, and determined to make Early believe there would be a frontal assault, rode up and down his lines, urging his troops to intensify their efforts. Around 11:30 he ordered Emory to "press the enemy" in order to "mask an attack on their left," so Emory promptly sent two pieces of artillery forward with instructions to "shell them vigorously for twenty minutes" and ordered his infantry to charge on the Confederate rifle pits. DeForest received a directive to "keep up a tip-top racket. Blaze away as though you meant to follow up with a charge." The Eighteenth Indiana joined in the show, noisily rushing toward the Confederate leftcenter. So relentlessly did the Union army bang away at Early's works that the Confederate leader actually composed "orders for a nighttime retreat."[36]

Unfortunately for Early, "night" came early. At about 4:00, as the sun started to dip below the mountains, a loud yell arose from the side of Little North Mountain, and Crook's men struck like a thunderbolt at the Confederate left flank and rear. The Union line bearing down on Early's front echoed the sounds and movement of Crook's charge. Grover's assault on Gabriel Wharton's Virginians resembled a tidal wave, engulfing the Confederates' guns and sending the men in full flight. The surprise was complete. In Early's words, "[M]y whole force retired in considerable confusion," though his officers fought gallantly "to the very last." As Southerners shouted, "We're flanked," Sheridan exulted, "By God, Crook's driving them!" Not content with that conclusion, he rode among his warriors, answering every question with "Forward everything! Don't stop! Go on!" And, indeed, they did, turning Early's planned retreat into a "regular skeddadle" and chasing them into the night.[37]

Grover's division led the southerly pursuit, with the Eighteenth Indiana and other regiments often on the double-quick and tenaciously hounding the steps of the fleeing Confederates. Sheridan, it seemed, would tolerate no slowness. In reporting to Grant on his "most signal victory" at Fisher's Hill, Sheridan told his superior, "I am tonight pushing on down the valley." "Pushing" may have been an understatement. Historian A. Wilson Greene contends that "Sheridan drove his foot soldiers mercilessly." Greene cites a New York soldier's assessment of the diminutive commander's zeal. "Neither man-flesh or horseflesh," he exclaimed, "had any consideration from him when garnering the fruits of such a victory." There was not a moment's halting, according to Emory, even though "Night had now come on and it was intensely dark."[38]

The Confederates sought to stop or detain the Union rush at times, but their resistance was haphazard. Five miles into the chase, Emory reported, the enemy stood on a high bank across a creek and "opened on us with artillery and infantry." Though this "produced some confusion," and Union forces in the rear began firing on their own skirmishers ahead of them, order resumed and the Confederates pulled back. At another point, the butternuts erected a road block with two artillery pieces, but it too was easily swept aside. Given the momentum, speed, and inevitable overlapping of regiments in the nighttime pursuit, some soldiers of each army fell to the side, either giving up, seeking sleep, or simply searching for their own units. Large numbers of Southerners were overtaken by Union troops, some simply opting to surrender out of weariness or hopelessness. Bluecoats spotted one demoralized Confererate sitting by a small fire and singing a plaintive tune, the last line of which was, "And Old Jube Early's about played out." Frequent also were reports of a Northern boy finding a spot for rest and awakening to find a Reb at his side who chose to surrender. When Grover's men arrived at the village of Woodstock around 3:30 a.m. to set up camp, the general reported the capture of about two hundred Confederates, thus ending what DeForest labeled "the whole wearisome night" of pursuit.[39]

There was little time to rest, however, for Early was still out there. At Woodstock the Eighteenth Indiana, as Lee told his hometown newspaper, "halted and waited for a few hours for the supply train, as our rations had given out the day previous. The train soon came up. We drew rations and were again after Early." Though trailing behind the Eighteenth, the VI Corps likewise had a short night. At 7:00 on the morning of September 13, Henry Keiser of the Ninety-sixth Pennsylvania recorded, "[W]e started after the teams which left last night. The Rebels are in full skeddadle, with our boys close on their heels." That same morning Early pulled back to Mount Jackson where he "halted to enable the sick and wounded, and the hospital stores at that place to be carried off." Pressed again by Union cavalry, he withdrew to Rude's Hill where, on the morning of Saturday, September 24, Union horsemen threatened his right flank and their infantry advanced on Early's left. Iowan Dawes related the movement of Shunk's brigade that morning. Marching in line of battle, its men heard cannonading in front and saw a "large Depot or warehouse at the Village being burned Bridge also burned we finaly marched by right of Regt to the front waded the north fork of the Shenandoah struck the road in sight of the enemy's rear guard it is a splendid sight our batteries are shelling them." Early watched this advance of Hoosiers and Iowans unfold. "I could see the whole movement of the enemy," he recalled, so "I commenced retiring in line of battle."[40]

On the subsequent march up the valley toward New Market that day, Stott marveled at a sight of martial beauty. "I have today witnessed a military scene," he wrote, "which I can never describe for its grandeur."

Sheridan had put two of his columns on the right and two on the left, leaving those in the center in line of battle following the Union skirmishers. Up ahead was the long gray line of Early's retreating army, its skirmishers drawing back as they fired on the bluecoats. From its place in the right flank, Captain Black remembered, the Eighteenth Indiana had "a view of the whole valley." There was "the undulating valley, shut in by towering mountains on the east, and a line of hills on the west," all dotted with fertile farms and ancient mansions, the sparkling Shenandoah winding through it all. Down the center was the lengthy ribbon of competing armies, each in faultless line of battle, bayonets gleaming in the sun, colors flying, ambulances and wagons "in double line." Early exulted about "the most admirable" deportment of his men as "they preserved perfect order and their line intact." On the Union side, a New York officer called the scene "a grand excursion" and "a spectacle of rare beauty" that caused the Union soldiers to march with "light hearts."[41] September 24, 1864—the romance of war, the pageantry of it.

Another side of war, however, dominated the days ahead—the cruel side, the devastation of land and crops and barns and stock. These would be the days of the "Burning," when Grant's call to leave nothing "to invite the enemy to return" would be enacted in full fury. Arriving at Harrisonburg on September 25, the Union army found the Confederates nowhere in sight, for on the previous night they had receded rapidly toward Port Republic, ten miles to the southeast. The Union infantry remained at Harrisonburg for a number of days, but the cavalry began what Gordon called a "season of burning, instead of battling." With Grant's original directions in mind, Sheridan believed "it was time to bring the war home to the people engaged in raising crops from a prolific soil to feed the country's enemies." For almost two weeks, from September 26 to October 8, Sheridan's orders to his troopers to torch all "forage, mills, and such other property as might be serviceable to the Rebel army" in the upper Shenandoah Valley were carried out daily. To cavalry commander Merritt, such action "was necessary as a measure of war," and Stevens agreed, saying the "destruction, cruel as it seemed, was fully justified" from a military perspective.[42] Infantry joined the cavalry in ravaging the land. DeForest of Emory's staff indicated that "between Mt. Crawford and Woodstock over seventy miles and two thousand barns crammed with flour, wheat, corn, and hay were destroyed" by both branches of the army. Foraging by foot soldiers was also rampant. "The inhabitants," DeForest claimed, "were left so stripped of food I cannot imagine how they escaped starvation." Letters and diaries of Union soldiers cited "all the wheat, corn, oats, and hay in the adjoining country" destroyed, along with "all the grain rebel goverment stores at Stanton [Staunton], &c, &c." But the men in gray painted the most vivid pictures. From mountain tops they "could see Yankees out in the valley driving off the horses, cattle, sheep, and killing the hogs and burning all the barns and shocks of corn and wheat in the fields." Confederate staff officer Henry Kyd Douglas observed "mothers and maidens tearing their hair and shrieking to Heaven in their fright and despair." Another Confederate saw a board on which the bluecoats had written, "Remember Chambersburg."[43]

On the night of October 7, Sheridan wrote Grant that "the whole country from the Blue Ridge to the North Mountains has been made untenable for the rebel army." He listed the amount of crops, mills, stock, and sheep that had been annihilated, informing Grant that "the people here are getting sick of the war." In a prior communication, Sheridan had suggested that "the burning . . . be the end of this campaign, and let some of the army go somewhere else." Grant wired Sheridan to proceed with his plan as long as he left "nothing for the subsistence" of the enemy forces.[44] The "somewhere else" Sheridan had in mind was down the valley, back to the Strasburg-Cedar Creek area. The Army of the Shenandoah passed Fisher's Hill on October 10, and the two corps of Emory and Wright camped north of Cedar Creek that night. Prior to crossing the creek, DeForest noticed that Emory appeared "impatient and worried," doubtlessly afraid that he might have to fight in that precarious position. When his XIX Corps finally "got a chance to move," DeForest said, "it went like an avalanche," the men dashing through the creek and up its steep northern bank. This brought Emory some peace of mind, but his fears were well-grounded, for Early's army, now reinforced by convalescents and Major General Joseph Kershaw's division, was only a mile and a half from Cedar Creek by the night of October 13. Although many Union soldiers inferred that the campaign was probably over, actually the stage was being set for a third act of combat in the drama of the Shenandoah Valley.[45]

In mid-August Sheridan informed Grant that his position along
Cedar Creek was "a very bad one." Two months later it was not much
better, still offering little promise for defense. Brigadier General Lewis
A. Grant termed it "almost defenseless," and another brigadier, Merritt,
later explained why. According to Merritt, the enemy's approach routes
from Fisher's Hill went "through wooded ravines in which the growth and
undulations concealed the movement of troops," which meant that Union
pickets could not be sent "sufficiently far to the front to give ample warning of the advance of the enemy." For these reasons, the October occupation of the land along Cedar Creek "was not intended to be permanent."[46]

Whether the position was fixed or not, Emory, whose two divisions
of the XIX Corps were in the center of the crescent-shaped Union line,
was determined that his encampment would be strong. It was located on
a ridge about 150 feet above the creek and in front of Belle Grove plantation, which served as headquarters for Sheridan and Crook. Emory placed
nearly all his artillery on the crest and had his veterans dig trenches at its
peak edged by timber breastworks and abatis. He planted Grover's division on the extreme left of his line, with the Eighteenth Indiana in ready
reserve there. The emplacement was formidable. "Emory's command," historian Wert notes, "could shatter any frontal attack which had to cross the
creek and scale the 'precipitous' slope." General Wright's VI Corps extended from Emory's right toward a rivulet called Meadow Brook. On Emory's
left, east of the Valley Pike, resided Crook's VIII Corps, behind which rested the reserve artillery, supply wagons, and ammunition dumps. Crook's
force was the weakest numerically, and an unfortunate hole existed in its
alignment that further worried Emory. Another concern stemmed from
the fact that ravines and ridges cut through the terrain, in effect separat-
ing infantry commands from each other.[47]

These matters, though, were far from the soldiers' minds on Tuesday,
October 18, an absolutely gorgeous day. The morning, recalled an Ohio
cavalryman, was "crisp and bright," noontime warm and sunny, and sunset "glorious and still." "It was such a beautiful autumn day," stated historian Wert, "that a man wanted to reach out, grab, and hold it." And that
was precisely what the secure Union army did. There were drills and dress
parades, of course, but any thought of fighting was fleeting at most. There
had been some brief skirmishing on the thirteenth, but that seemed long
ago.[48] So the bluecoats took advantage of the splendid weather to stroll

through neighboring groves and along the creek, visit the many caves in the vicinity, and receive their favorite treat—mail from home. The evening featured gatherings around campfires, pipe smoking, the sounds of flutes and fiddles and lots of singing, and just chatting about the day's letters. In short, as veteran James Franklin Fitts remembered it, "that night was one of dreamful tranquility."[49]

Confederates used October 18 differently. On the preceding day, knowing that a frontal assault on Sheridan's lines would be futile, Early sent Gordon, the meticulous mapmaker Jedediah Hotchkiss, Brigadier General Clement Evans, and Gordon's chief of staff, Robert Hunter, to the signal station on Three Top Mountain. Given that it was a remarkably clear day, they were to examine in detail the Union position. Early also sent Brigadier General John Pegram toward Cedar Creek to investigate the strength of the Union right and center. From their perch atop the mountain, Gordon and company found that "the entire landscape was plainly visible." Through strong field glasses, Gordon spotted all of Sheridan's breastworks "and every piece of artillery, every wagon and tent and supporting line of troops." One factor stood out above all: the Union left was weak, poorly protected by cavalry, and thus much exposed to any force that could reach it secretly. Returning to Early's headquarters after dark, Hotchkiss gave his commander a full report of the team's findings and a detailed map of the enemy's position and camps. After confirmation of the report by Gordon the next morning, Early called a council of war for 2:00 that afternoon.[50]

At the meeting, Gordon presented a comprehensive plan, abandoning any "serious attack" where Sheridan was strong and sending only a cavalry "demonstration" against the Union right flank. Gordon argued, he later wrote, that "the heavy and decisive blow should be given upon the Union left, where no preparation was made to resist us." He and Hotchkiss pointed out a route available for a furtive nighttime march along the base of the Massanutten that forded the North Fork of the Shenandoah River. Early assigned the task around Massanutten to Gordon, with the divisions of Ramseur, Pegram, and Evans under his command. Early supervised advances by Kershaw and Wharton toward the Valley Pike for assaults to occur simultaneously with Gordon's at five o'clock the next morning. All were to proceed in total silence—no words were to be spoken and everything that could rattle would be left behind.[51]

On the Union side of Cedar Creek that night, while soldiers looked forward to a good night's sleep, two corps commanders contemplated plans for the next morning. Wright was apprehensive about weaknesses on the right flank of the VI Corps, which stood rather open along the creek, while Emory continued to worry about the Union left. Just the day before, as Wright, Crook, and Emory inspected the entire front, Emory questioned the security of Crook's position. DeForest heard the general maintain that it did not adequately "command the valley in front of it." Pointing to a gap between two of Crooks's divisions, Emory contended that Confederates "could march thirty thousand men through that defile, and we not know it till they were on our flank." Perhaps with Emory's warning in mind, and despite having already received an intelligence report that all was well in Crook's sector, Wright—acting as commander while Sheridan was in Washington—ordered Emory to conduct another inspection early on the morning of October 19. Emory selected Grover's division for this duty, with "directions to move at early dawn." Shunk's Fourth Brigade, including the Eighteenth Indiana, was to be "under arms" in "the works of the First and Third Brigades" at 5:00 a.m., when the latter units were to go on reconnoiter. The Twenty-fourth Iowa of Shunk's brigade, its colonel reported, "all retired to our 'virtuous couches' on the evening of the 18th" when the order came to man the vacated breastworks at the crack of dawn.[52]

At the very moment Grover's men received these directives, Gordon's grayclad troops were silently, stealthily making their way single file around the narrow base of the Massanutten. Approximately an hour before the appointed time of attack, they reached Bowman's Ford on the Shenandoah River and noiselessly waited in the darkness. The moon had set and a dense fog rolled in. Still, they could hear and see Union videttes stationed on horseback in the middle of the river, "wholly unconscious of the presence of the gray-jacketed foe," Gordon wrote, while his own men, "like crouching lions from the jungle, were ready to spring upon them. The whole situation was unspeakably impressive." The Confederates rested in the grass and brush, their hearts beating in anticipation, their ears hearing rustling leaves, the ripples of the flowing river, or an officer's struck match as he checked the time on his watch. At five o'clock, as 30,000 Union troops slept, the 17,000 men of the combined Confederate force moved forward. Gordon's warriors "rushed into the cold current of the

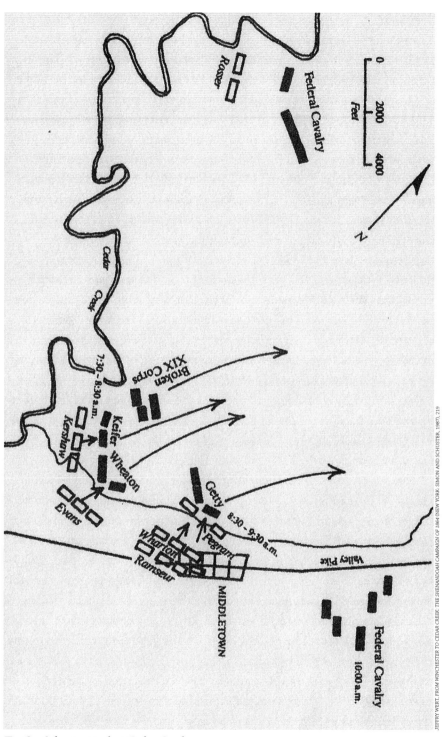

The Confederate attack at Cedar Creek.

Shenandoah" under the dense fog that allowed but a few feet of visibility. Capturing the Union cavalry pickets, they then climbed the river's western bank and, with a ferocious Rebel yell, slammed into Crook's sleeping ranks on the double-quick, Evans's and Ramseur's divisions in the lead.[53]

Crook's command shattered in less than a half hour. Simultaneous assaults by Gordon's divisions from the east and Kershaw's from the south left little time for Union resistance. The attackers poured past the fieldworks and were amid the tents before some bluecoats were fully awake—many, in fact, staggered about partially clothed and unarmed. The few able to make it to the breastworks were subjected to such fierce fire that they quickly retired. Confusion and terror ruled in the face of the onslaught, and even those who could resist found it impossible to "concentrate their firepower" effectively. Whole units disintegrated. Colonel Rutherford B. Hayes's division crumbled at first contact with the enemy, the future president himself narrowly avoiding capture when his horse collapsed under him. One member of Crook's staff described the chaos: "Army wagons, ambulances, artillery, soldiers without commanders, commanders without soldiers, every fellow for himself, moving backwards in sullen discouragement in the faces of yelling victors." With minié balls whizzing through tents, comrades fighting hand to hand using muskets as clubs, too many of them being shot or bayoneted, most of the VIII Corps chose "moving backwards" and fled across Valley Pike toward the XIX Corps.[54]

A hungry DeForest was enjoying breakfast at Grover's quarters that morning. The captain had been up for quite awhile. "I was in the saddle before there was light enough to see my white horse two rods away," DeForset recalled, because it was his job "to see that the reconnaissance" by Grover's men "started on time." As the two officers ate, they suddenly heard "a shrill prolonged wail of musketry" about a mile away on the left front, "followed by scream on scream of the rebel yell." Glancing at each other in "surprise and comprehension," both men jumped to their duty. The general quietly voiced orders to get "the brigade commanders to move their men into the trenches," and the captain mounted his horse and sped to Emory's headquarters." He found Emory "coatless and hatless and uncombed," but saddling his steed. It was clear to the young captain that the old man knew precisely what was happening. As DeForest rode off to find Wright at Emory's request, he heard his chief growl, "I said so; I knew

Colonel David Shunk, commander, Fourth Brigade.

that if we were attacked, it would be there." Due to the density of the fog, Emory found it "impossible to see the position of the enemy or the direction of his advance," so he allowed himself to be "guided by the firing," knowing full well that the poor visibility favored the Confederates. Soon joined by Wright and Crook, Emory accepted directions from Wright to send brigades across the Valley Pike near Belle Grove.[55]

Knowing the XIX Corps's position was basically unfavorable for defense, since its "earthworks ran at right angles to the pike" from where the attack was coming, Emory ordered Grover's division to abandon its works, move to the east beyond the pike, and seek there to hold back further Confederate encroachment. As it hurried to its new position, the Eighteenth Indiana met a stampede of men from the VIII Corps going the opposite direction in considerable disorder. While Stott led his company on the double-quick, he saw the fugitives "running pell-mell." A New York officer observed "stragglers of the Eighth Corps . . . rushing wildly through our camp," and Iowan Peirce said that Crook's panicked men threw his own brigade "into some confusion."[56]

Running through this "incessant stream of fugitives," Shunk's brigade reached the Valley Pike in surprisingly good order. The colonel promptly formed his brigade into a line "extending diagonally across the pike, the right regiment (Eighth Indiana) supporting battery D, First Rhode Island Artillery." At the center stood the Twenty-fourth and Twenty-eighth Iowa, and the Eighteenth Indiana held the far left in support of another battery. Through the thick fog, Colonel Wright of the Twenty-fourth Iowa reported, "it was impossible to tell what was in front of us." Were the soldiers advancing on their line retreating friends or charging foes? "There is, at such times, a dead weight of suspense at a soldier's heart, which is perhaps harder to bear than the fury of battle itself," New Yorker Fitts insightfully noted. "The men who were now beneath my eye were veterans, tried in half-a-dozen engagements; but I noticed that their hands clutched their muskets nervously, and their teeth were all set hard together, as they tried to peer through the impenetrable curtain of fog."[57]

Such was the case for the Eighteenth Indiana when the fury hit. Out of the southeast emerged the three grayclad brigades of Kershaw's division, while those of Evans swooped down from the east. Still, for fear of shooting their fleeing comrades, Marshall said his Eighth Indiana held its fire "for a minute or So," and Shunk reported that even under "heavy

Major Jonathan H. Williams.

fire . . . we did not reply until they charged directly on the battery." The Eighteenth Indiana, hit the hardest on the extreme left and without breastworks for protection, began to give way, but Grover's regiments rallied to check the enemy for a time in the face of "slicing crossfire." This set a pattern for the XIX Corps, Stevens observed. "[A]lthough thrown into confusion," he recalled, "it was not in the panic with which the Eighth Corps yielded the ground." However, the combined Confederate divisions rushed the pike with such force and numbers, and Shunk's men were exposed to "such a murderous fire," that the colonel led his troops back some five hundred yards and aligned them parallel to the road. There they held again, until the Confederate avalanche spread across the pike and threatened to cut the Fourth Brigade off from its division. Again, Shunk's regiments fell back, this time beyond Belle Grove, fighting all the way. As one of Sheridan's biographers has written, "Grover's division, in particular, performed well under the extreme pressure, firing and falling back and taking heavy losses with each temporary stand."[58]

Through it all, Stott fought alongside his Company I. Like the other officers, he "could not distinguish the rebels from our own men" and at first curbed his company's firing. But then the men around him began to "fall fast." Confederates could be seen "on three sides" of Stott's position, so he shouted "Fire!" His "boys stood and fought well," and Stott himself stared at an enemy infantryman taking aim directly at him through the haze of fog and smoke. What happened next is unknown, except that the order came to "fall back." Stott's heart sank, for he was unspeakably "disappointed and chagrined" at the idea of retreat. His concern went beyond any dishonor to himself and his men. "At once the thought came to me," he confided to his diary, "the election is lost[,] the day is lost, the cause is lost." He was further disheartened as he fell back for he found himself amid units in disorder, riderless horses, frightened teamsters rushing their wagons to the rear, whistling bullets, overturned gun carriages, blood-covered men and ambulances, news of fellow officers falling dead or wounded, and lifeless bodies in blue and gray. It was enough to make a Baptist preacher's son utter in disbelief, "O Pshaw!"[59]

As he and his men drifted to the rear, Stott learned that Major Jonathan H. Williams, who had led Company I until his promotion made Stott captain, had been hit and was "too badly wounded" to be taken from the field. Now command of the regiment fell to Stott. After placing Williams in a ravine in hopes that he would be safe there, Stott turned to see his comrades picking up the pace of their withdrawal. William Elliott of Company G told his cousin: "The Rebs got within fifteen paces of me, and you can bet high I got up and dusted at the rate of about 2:40." Some paid swift visits to their old camp, risking their lives or capture to retrieve haversacks or blankets, while "leaving behind the helpless wounded and the dead who needed no succor." Marshall "went back & passed our tent and Saved my knapsack which was more than many of the Brigade Saved."[60]

Though overwhelmed by sheer numbers, the XIX Corps "had done good fighting," one of its officers told his comrades years later. It "retained its organization, and obeyed its officers, although it had been through a fearful ordeal" at the hands of "an enemy who appeared to be everywhere." The Eighteenth Indiana had, in fact, fought and held its ground "so long and stubbornly," one of its captains reported, that it had "thirty-two men taken prisoners" rather than run. As DeForest later observed, the XIX Corps fought against Confederstes "on its flank and at its back" for several hours before its withdrawal ended "between eight and nine o'clock in the morning." No doubt Stott would have agreed with DeForest's summation: "It was time for us to back out of our hole, and we marched rearward sadly diminished in numbers, though not a regiment had entirely disbanded."[61]

With Kershaw and Evans still advancing on its rear, what was left of Emory's corps waded "thigh deep" through Meadow Brook and thus brought the battle to Wright's VI Corps. The latter's three divisions remained intact as a unit and, allotted time by the XIX Corps's lengthy struggle at the pike and in its camps, they were able to establish a defensive position beside the hills a mile to the west. Although Emory's retreating troops created some disorder in Wright's lines as they sped through them, Fitts of the XIX Corps recalled that "the Sixth served as a rallying point for its discomfited neighbors, and we began to hope that our disaster might be retrieved here." Wright had Emory align his men to the right of his own. Emory, now on foot since his horse fell dead under him, and Grover, looking less gallant astride an old mule, quickly arranged their depleted forces into a reasonably firm line of battle, with the Eighteenth Indiana on the extreme left alongside the VI Corps. "But it was all useless," Fitts explained, "except to prolong the time when we must finally quit the field." Fighting continued for another hour, but it became clear that the "wasted lines" of bluecoats had to be reunited. So, Fitts said, "fighting and retreating, we reached the shelter of the woods." Confederate lines faced Union ones, fighting continued but gradually faded, and around noon the Confederate offensive ceased.[62]

To Early, the battle was won. As Gordon and Early rode up to each other in late morning, Early exclaimed, "Well, Gordon, this is glory enough for one day. This is the 19th. Precisely one month ago to-day we were going in the opposite direction." Gordon agreed that the battle had gone "very well so far," but he reminded his superior that the rugged VI Corps was still there, so "we have one more blow to strike." Early responded, "No use in that; they will all go directly." Gordon later remarked that, upon hearing these words, "My heart went into my boots. Visions of the fatal halt on the first day at Gettysburg . . . rose before me." In his own memoirs, Early contended that "it would not do to press my troops further. They had been up all night and were much jaded." Furthermore, his own ranks had become disordered, with troops scattered about, many "engaged in plundering the enemy's camps." It was best, the general believed, "to try and hold what had been gained." Although controversy still rages among historians regarding the encounter between the two Confederate commanders and Early's so-called fatal halt, there is little question that the momentum of the Confederate assault was waning by that time. The grayclad troops *were* weary, hungry, and wearing ragged clothes. The abandoned Union camps, with well-supplied larders, warm clothes, blankets, and ample coffee, understandably led to "every imaginable kind of plunder."[63]

Conveniently, the Confederate "halt" allowed the Union forces to reorganize. Elliott, Eighteenth Indiana, put it simply: "[R]ebs, thinking they had us completely whipped, halted for a while, giving us time to again form our line of battle." Not only were the Confederates now fighting "with less spirit," as one of Sheridan's staff noticed, but Union cavalry had become a nuisance to the Confederate left. Impatient Union infantrymen and their officers were also becoming increasingly determined, said an Ohio colonel, "to prevent disaster from becoming disgrace." Emory, for one, had had enough of going backwards. Captain Benjamin W. Crowninshield of Sheridan's staff came upon Emory lecturing his troops at the top of a hill. He was "telling them emphatically," Crowninshield recalled, "that he would not retreat any further, that there he would stand

and fight," and all around him his men were erecting "breastworks of rails, and even digging a little." Emory's fighting blood was up, and it was transfusing into his men. As reorganization progressed in every corps, DeForest sensed that the troops were beginning to "recover their usual confidence." He reflected on Leo Tolstoy's contention "that it is largely 'the spirit of the army' which wins victories."[64] Then something happened that lifted the spirits of the Army of the Shenandoah to even greater heights: *Sheridan arrived.*

———•◆•———

Upon his return from Washington, Sheridan decided to spend the night of October 18 in Winchester. Arriving there, he dispatched a courier to bring him "a report on the condition of affairs" along Cedar Creek. The message was "that everything was all right." The enemy, he was told, "was quiet at Fisher's Hill," and Grover's division was to conduct a reconnaissance on the next morning. Reassured, Sheridan retired for the night, planning on sleeping late on the nineteenth. At about 6:00 a.m. an anxious officer on picket duty came to Sheridan's room to report "artillery firing from the direction of Cedar Creek." The general assured the young man that it was probably Grover "merely feeling the enemy." Soon the officer returned to report continued firing, though it did not sound like a battle. Unable to sleep anymore, Sheridan requested a hasty breakfast and ordered "horses to be saddled and in readiness." Near nine o'clock, joined by his staff officers, including Major George "Sandy" Forsyth, Sheridan left for the ten-mile ride to Cedar Creek astride his horse, Rienzi.[65]

Sheridan's party rode at a "regular pace" until they reached a slope just beyond a small stream called Mill Creek. At its peak, Sheridan confronted the "appalling spectacle of a panic-stricken army—hundreds of slightly wounded men, throngs of others unhurt but utterly demoralized, and baggage-wagons by the score, all pressing to the rear in hopeless confusion, telling only too plainly that a disaster had occurred at the front." Sheridan proceeded to question the soldiers, and their responses were consistent: the army is in disarray, it has pulled back, and "all was lost." When one frazzled colonel shouted on the run, "The army's whipped!" the little general on the big black horse roared back, "You are, but the army isn't!" Hearing further intelligence that all "was gone" at Cedar Creek, and his headquarters taken, Sheridan's first thought was to stop the rearward flow, "form a new line, and fight there." But, knowing his troops had confidence in him, he decided to "try now to restore their broken ranks, or, failing in that, to share their fate because of what they had done hitherto." Barking orders to his staff to stop the flood of fugitives, turn them around, and send them back to the front, Little Phil shouted, "Come back boys! Give 'em hell, God damn 'em! We'll make coffee out of Cedar Creek tonight!" The general and his entourage then rode hard to the lines of his three corps, galloping across fields adjoining the road wherever it was blocked by wagons and wounded soldiers. As he passed by, uninjured men waved their kepis, put their muskets to their shoulders, and "turned to follow with enthusiasm and cheers." At around 10:30, Sheridan rode up to his field commanders.[66]

His reception among them was both exuberant and awkward. Brigadier General Alfred Torbert exclaimed, "My God! I'm glad you have come!" When Brigadier General George A. Custer saw Sheridan, he hugged and kissed him, causing the embarrassed Irishman to back away, murmuring that there was "no time to lose." Oddly, Emory—he who vowed not to retreat another inch—told Sheridan that his troops were now organized and "could cover the retreat to Winchester." Sheridan burst out, "Retreat—Hell! We'll be back in our camps tonight." After receiving a summary of the morning's calamity and the current situation from Wright, Sheridan ordered the XIX Corps and part of Wright's "brought to the front, as they could be formed on [Brigadier General George] Getty's division" in order to create an extended line of battle. For Sheridan had already determined "to attack the enemy from that line as soon as I could get matters in shape to take the offensive." Once the line was completed, Grover's division, with the Eighteenth Indiana, would be at its western edge.[67]

These decisions having been reached, and the line strengthened, Forsyth suggested that the general might ride along it, thereby letting the troops know that he had returned. It was a brilliant idea. This culmination of "Sheridan's Ride," as historian Wert asserts, had "no equal in the annals of the Civil War." Sheridan rode Rienzi along the two-mile line, waving his hat, voicing encouragement, exuding an irresistible charisma, and sparking cheers and promises to "go back." One soldier said, "Now we all burned to attack the enemy, to drive him back, to retrieve our honor" because

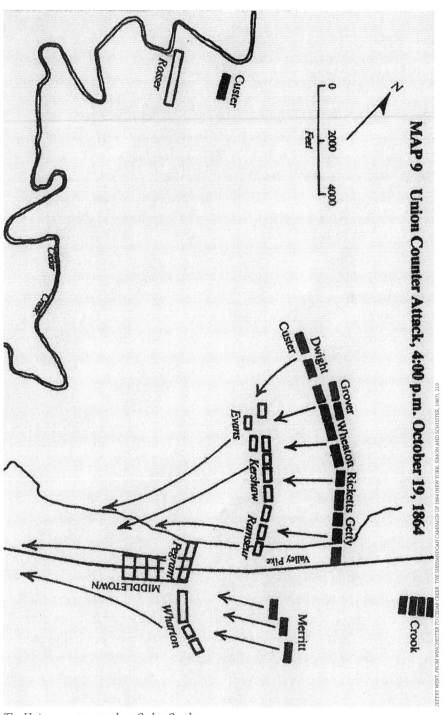

MAP 9   Union Counter Attack, 4:00 p.m. October 19, 1864

The Union counterattack at Cedar Creek.

"every man knew that Sheridan would do it." Stott summed up Sheridan's impact in three words: "we about faced."[68]

Meantime, the nerves of Confederate officers were becoming taut. The sound across the fields suggested that Sheridan had returned, and Gordon was getting "ominous reports" of enemy cavalry and infantry amassing on his front and flank. He sent couriers to Early about the situation, but Early, convinced that Union horsemen were "seriously threatening" his right and also were "very strong" on his left, was in no mood to send Gordon into the Yankee lines. "A repulse at this time would have been disastrous," Early concluded. He did, however, write Gordon that he could test the enemy's position but not launch an assault if it proved too strong. This was all Gordon had to hear. At 1:00 p.m., the Georgian directed Kershaw, Evans, and Ramseur forward toward the section of the Union line held by the XIX Corps. Sheridan alerted Emory to the move, and Emory prepared for defense. "Within an hour they charged my line," Emory reported, "but were promptly driven back, this time, as I believe, the first permanent repulse which they received during the day."[69] As Emory's words imply, it would not be the last time that day the Confederates would be pushed back.

<hr />

Emory's successful defense against Gordon's advance made Sheridan "feel pretty safe" from more Confederate operations. While waiting for a further strengthening of his force by soldiers still returning from the rear, he "decided to suspend the fighting" for a while. But, as a Massachusetts soldier said, Sheridan "never waited for the rebs to get ready. When he was ready he would fight." By mid-afternoon that moment came. Sheridan was prepared to go all out against the foe, sending his entire line on the attack simultaneously. Wright, with his left toward the Valley Pike, was to advance once the bugles sounded, as would Emory on the right. If an opening occurred, the XIX Corps was to swing its regiments on the right flank—the Eighteenth Indiana among them—on a left half wheel, squeezing the enemy toward the pike. Crook's forces would be in reserve east of the pike, and cavalry would occupy both flanks, Custer on the right and Merritt on the left. The hours after Gordon's aborted demonstration were eerily quiet. "The suspense was terrible," one horseman said. In the meantime, Sheridan waited leisurely at his headquarters for stragglers to appear and answered any inquiries about an attack with a terse, "Not yet." At about 3:00 Stott's Fourth Brigade got orders to call in skirmishers, take its place in line, and prepare to advance. Around 3:30, Shunk reported, the Eighteenth Indiana and his other regiments "assumed the offensive and advanced upon the enemy." By 4:00 the entire Army of the Shenandoah emerged from its densely wooded cover and rushed the Confederate lines on the double-quick as two hundred bugles sounded the charge. "From that moment to the end," the chronicler of the XIX Corps recalled, "the men hardly stopped an instant for anything."[70]

Things would be different this time, Fitts said later. "We were in action again," he wrote, "not as in the morning, masked by fog, and flanked by an unseen enemy, but now muzzle to muzzle and breast to breast." Unfortunately for the grayclad troops, one historian noted, Early's "dread of being flanked by the cavalry caused him to so extend his lines as to make them unduly thin." Still, Emory's advance was heavily contested, partly because Custer became entangled in a side conflict with Confederate cavalry, leaving the right flank of the Union infantry "overlapped by Gordon's opposing division." The Eighteenth Indiana was running "into the jaws of a vice," trapped in a deadly enfilade of firepower that for a moment pinned them down. It rallied enough to press butternut skirmishers from the stone walls, only to face another "killing fire." Grover fell with a severe wound but refused Sheridan's pleas to leave the field, insisting on staying with his men "until success was certain." At that minute, though, there was little assurance of success. The Eighteenth Indiana, toiling "blindly in jungle like thickets of trees and vines," faced vicious Confederate volleys in what one Union soldier termed "a square musketry fight." Like the rest of Grover's decimated division, however, the Eighteenth plunged forward, seeking to achieve the coveted left wheel, despite threats from Evans's Confederate brigades on their right. "For half an hour," Fitts stated, "the obstinate currents of the fight wavered" until the sounds of "a thundering gallop" signaled the advent of Custer's horsemen and convinced the Thirty-first Georgia, directly in Custer's path, to take off for Cedar Creek.[71]

The Confederate left began to buckle, prompting more Union divisions to increase the pressure on the decaying gray lines. "An impulse was given to advance," noted Fitts. "Where it came from, no one could tell, a sweeping cry of 'Charge-charge!' ran from lip to lip." When soldiers of the XIX Corps located the weaknesses in Gordon's defense, they soon—in the Confederate general's own words—began "rolling it up like a scroll." Evans's Georgians broke first, followed by Kershaw's and Ramseur's men. As he tried to rally his Virginians and North Carolinians, twenty-seven-year-old Ramseur, who had just learned he had become a father, fell with a mortal wound. Those who had been pursued in the morning now became the pursuers and, a XIX Corps veteran observed, the conflict became "a race and a chase, not a battle." Iowan Dawes of Stott's brigade, taken prisoner during the Union charge and destined for Libby Prison at Richmond, jotted in his diary: "We could see the rebs skedaddling in every direction when we left." An Ohio cavalryman said the Confederates "scattered like sheep to the hills." Peter B. Boarts, a sergeant in the Twenty-second Iowa, portrayed the day as "the hardest battle I ever Saw fought the rebels drove us about 5 miles then We drove them back about 20 miles." Compared to all the other battles he had been in, he remarked, "this beats them all."[72]

Shortly after dark, the Eighteenth Indiana stepped onto the camp they had been forced to vacate in the morning. Many of them sought rest by lying down amid the dead and wounded in blue and gray uniforms. The anguished moans and cries of the injured did not keep the weary and hungry from their sleep. Stott found Major Williams, still alive, one leg ripped off and the other mutilated and stripped of his money, sword, Masonic emblems, and much of his clothing. Near him was the lifeless body of Stott's friend, Edward Bishop of Company C. Elsewhere on the battlefield laid the mortally wounded Lieutenant Colonel William S. Charles, alongside whom Stott fought in Arkansas and Mississippi. At 8:00 the Fourth Brigade broke camp again and marched south to Strasburg. Along the way, Marshall told his brother, they took "a good many prisoners and any amount of plunder [the Confederates] had thrown away in their hasty retreat . . . the road was jam full of artillery, caissons and baggage . . . we recaptured all the artillery lost in the morning and thirty nine pieces besides." Two days later, the Eighteenth Indiana went back to its old camp at Cedar Creek, but it was a sad experience. Many comrades were no longer among them, and those who were could not help but wonder how much longer the "cruel war" would last.[73]

At ten o'clock on the night of the battle, Sheridan described the valiant performance of his men to Grant. "Affairs at times looked badly," he admitted, "but by the gallantry of our brave officers and men disaster has been converted into a splendid victory." From another perspective, Early portrayed the battle as "a glorious victory given up by my own troops after they had won it." At an "unguarded moment," he put it more succinctly: "The Yankees got whipped and we got scared." In a sense, these views of the final battle of Sheridan's campaign expressed by the opposing commanders are emblematic of the experiences of the Union and Confederate forces in the Shenandoah Valley. For Northerners, it had been a scene of nothing but failure prior to the autumn of 1864, but now they had conquered not only Confederate forces there but the land itself. The Southern story was victory after victory beginning with "Stonewall" Jackson's 1862 raid. But by the end of 1864 it was one of bitter and irreversible defeat and devastation, not so much because Southerners "got scared," but because the South was losing the will to fight. As historian Wert correctly contends, Cedar Creek—indeed, the whole of Sheridan's Valley Campaign—"broke Southern morale" and lifted that of the North. Furthermore, along with Atlanta, Cedar Creek ensured Lincoln's re-election, which Stott, in the throes of the battle, feared was lost. No record appears that Stott ever discussed that day at Cedar Creek publicly. He surely had to be grateful, however, that Providence, to whom he attributed "the success of our arms," had spared him to fight in a campaign that Wert claims "forged a tide of Union success that could not be stayed by a beleaguered Confederacy."[74]

Cedar Creek marked the twilight of Stott's military career. He saw no further combat, but he spent the next two months doing his duty as always, visiting familiar sites again—Winchester, Opequon Creek, Harpers Ferry—maintaining the daily records of Company I, conducting train guard operations, overseeing the slashers, and sharing drills and dress parades with his troops. He went through another harsh winter, read and reflected as often as possible, followed the daily events of the war and politics, kept in touch with the folks at home, and worshiped on every Sabbath. On December 10, 1864, while at Camp Russell, Virginia, Stott wrote to his division headquarters: "I most respectfully ask to be honorably mustered out of the United States Service, as an officer of the Army, in accordance with Circular 75, War Department, current series."[75] The next day Stott confided to his diary that he felt "strange in thinking of being a <u>citizen</u>."

But it was time. He had fought in every theater and seen "the elephant" in three campaigns deemed by historians as critical turning points in what Lincoln called "a great civil war"—Pea Ridge, Vicksburg, and Sheridan's campaign in the Valley. During his journey back to Indiana, he spent another exciting week in Washington and stopped to see his friend Lowes, with whom he had talked about the ministry during evenings in camp. Lowes was a student at the Western Theological Seminary, and Stott attended some of his classes, thereby getting a glimpse of theological studies and perhaps of his destiny. He reached his hometown of Vernon on Friday, December 23.

Will Stott was "home safe from the wars"—just in time for Christmas.

9

July 13, 1864–December 23, 1864

[July] 13th [1864]

Spent the evening in the city. Attended prayer meeting.

14th

We had sent all our Baggage down to the Depot for Cairo, when the order for going South was countermanded and we are ordered to report at Washington.

Every man I meet seems to me to be just in the act of saying "May I go home"?

Some have gone home for the night. It will take us three days to reach Washington with a fortunate trip.

15th

[no entry]

16th

At noon Board the train on the Bellefontaine road. I left six men behind. Met Wallace on the street. Took supper at Muncie town. During this night I did not sleep but like some poetic one sat watching the moon and thinking of the past. Even on a smoky dusty shaky car one can think.

17th

Arrived at Pittsburg at 8 PM. We were escorted to the City Hall where we had supper prepared by Pittsburg. After supper we promenaded and sang Rally round the flag, the whole regiment coming on the chorus. Gave [cheers] for the ladies and then off to the Depot of the Baltimore road.

18th

I like Pennsylvania. The farms and the villages look so thrifty.
In the afternoon got on the Susquehana river. The Pennsylvania Barns are
all that they were represented, neat large, substantial.
In winding through the Alleghanies we passed some rich mountain
scenery. Pass a great many iron works. Reach Baltimore at 2 at night.

19th

Sleep till morning. Then go to the Soldiers Rest for breakfast. March
through a portion of the city. At 10 AM start for Washington. Got to the
city at 2 P.M. Had time to wash our faces when the order came for us to
march to the wharf on the Potomac. We paraded Pennsylvania Avenue at
<u>open order cross arms</u> and made a good impression generally.
Well this is the capitol of the nation. How ones soul swells with emotion
as from this standpoint he views the nation struggling to crush a gigantic
Rebellion. And when one reflects what this nation is yet to be, he says,
come what may hardship or disease or death even, the country is worth
the sacrifice of all the ease and enjoyment of life and life itself. I have
never felt more like doing my whole duty than now.

20th

On board the Steamer <u>Idaho</u> bound for City Point Va. Our vessel runs
smooth. I have a good sleep. We go to the James Buoyant and lightsome.
We may return emaciated and sad.

21st

11 AM at City Point. From the Potomac into Chesapeake Bay, from that
into the James. Passed Fort Monroe and what is called the <u>Rip-Raps</u>.[1]
Ordered to disembark at Bermuda Hundred. In <u>camp</u> again. Glad of it. We
hear occasionally the sound of cannonading. We belong to no Division nor
Brigade. We are independent. Sent here by mistake.
Tonight a Sergt of Co. "K" shot his leg accidentally. It had to be
amputated.

22nd

I shiver with cold. We camp too near the river. At last we are on the
"sacred soil"
Uncle Sam seems to be doing a big business here on the James. Within

the scope of 20 miles are gathered thousands of men whose profession is <u>death</u>. We had a dress parade and drew out the praise of the "Red Petticoats" even.[2]

Sherman will soon compel the evacuation of Atlanta

Just at dusk my attention was called to a new machine for killing rebels. It is mounted on a gun carriage on an iron board as base arranged 30 barrels size of Enfield barrels. The cartridges are arranged in cases and are all inserted at once into the breech of the barrels. A single cap explodes all at once. The barrels may be diverged at pleasure also elevated or depressed. It can be discharged 15 times per minute. How Invention has aided us in this contest!

Science constructs instruments for the most delicate music, musick [*sic*] wooing and soft; and instruments with thunder tones whose object is death and destruction.

23rd

Sherman has Decatur and hence the road leading from Atlanta to Richmond. Sergt. Johnston has gone to the front to see his brother.[3]

24th

The atmosphere here is much more bracing than at New Orleans. The soil in clayey. The farms seem to be badly worn. After dinner I took a walk down to the Appomattox. But a short distance up it is the identical spot where Pocahontas saved the life of John Smith. Attended negro worship. One in prayer used such language as this: "Heavenly Fader, hope us for we have a hard <u>bone</u> to <u>chaw</u> and a hard <u>pill</u> to <u>swallow</u>." I also saw them in singing do what is called "patting juber." After services the young <u>Gents</u> took the <u>ladies</u> home in style.[4]

Had some plain talk as to the culpability of associating or corresponding with a young lady without a perfect understanding as to the object of it.

25th

Had a terrible rain and windstorm. My tent lost its hold upon the ground and went flapping round. Everything got wet. Soon the water came running through the bed. This was the cap of the climax. During these inspiring moments I occasionally lifted my melodious voice in singing such appropriate couplets as I could recall.

26th

Capt Lowes and Lt Hickman are messing with us. Two N.Y. Regiments and the 22nd Iowa came in from New Orleans. Heavy musketry firing this morning. I procured a pass and taking passage on the tiny Gazelle went to City Point to spend a couple hours. Found there a busy city. One month ago it was a mere landing. Now there is a RR leading out in the direction of Petersburg. There are fatigue parties of negroes constantly unlading the vessels and lading the cars. There is no confusion no hallooing no cursing. All is system.

Tugs constantly come and go bearing messengers and dispatches. The Q.M. Dept is busy. The C.S. Dept is busy. The Ordnance Dept is busy. The Post Office Dept is busy. And the Sanitary and Christian Commissions are far from idle. How much we of the Army owe to these Commissions for the comfort of the hospital and camp. The best horses and wagons that I saw were those belonging to the Commissions. The best system-atized business was theirs. About 4 PM the John Brooks came in from Washington. As soon as possible I got a position on deck whence I could see all that was being done. First here comes the squad for the mail. There it goes—one—two—five—twenty—fifty—sixty five sacks! One days mail. Next come the boxes and barrels. I supposed that some sutler anxious to accommodate all was having a large supply brought on, but soon the marks "U.S.C.C" and "U.S.S.C." convinced me that they were sup-plies being forwarded by the Commissions. How careful our country is of its soldiers![5]

27th

All packed up ready to march. We are to go where the firing is severest. Gen McPherson is fallen! The country mourns. Hood supercedes Johnston.[6]

The mail has not found us yet. Marched at one P.M. Crossed the James and reported to Gen Foster of Vernon.

28th

We are nearer Richmond than any other troops. We are frequently "under the sound of the enemy's guns." I should like to hear Cousin Mary play it again.

I am extremely interested in old John Fosters Essays. One on Memoirs of

Oneself. He dwells on the fact that men in the main think more of objects around them, of objects of sense, than they do of their own mind and its varied and multiplied workings. He loves to examine that delicate existence the soul. Most men with whom I am acquainted turn no thought inward upon the "Ego"

He says of a soldiers writing (and I remember that he lived in a day of <u>mercenary</u> soldiering, else I would say he is mistaken) "if an adventurer or a soldier writes memoirs of himself for the information or amusement of the public, he may do well to keep his narrative alive by a constant crowded course of facts; for the greater part of his readers will excuse him the trouble of investigation, and he might occasionally feel it is a convenience to be excused from disclosing, if he had investigation, the history and merits of his internal principles. Nor can this ingeniousness be any part of his duty any more than it is that of any exhibition of a public show, as long as he tells us that he professes to tell where he has been and what he has seen, and the more reputable portion of what he has done." I say let the intelligent soldier describe the operations of his <u>inner</u> life under the various and extraordinary circumstances in which he, in a campaign, is thrown, and the recital will be as interesting as the thoughts, reasonings and conclusions of the sedentary scholar. Mr. John Foster, sir, you underrate the inner life of a soldier![7]

We are ordered into line. The gunboats have begun shelling. We are now where it is as necessary to <u>watch</u> as to <u>pray</u>.

29th

At 5 P.M. after advancing toward the rebel works in line and shelling the enemy's camp we were ordered on advance picket. I have charge of Co's. "I" and "C." I anticipated having a fine day with John Foster, but my hopes were blasted. It is too warm to read and I am required to be along Picket line frequently. We see Scesh [sic] pickets plainly. The 2d Corps will withdraw from the right tonight and report to Petersburg. We expect our garrison attacked tonight or tomorrow morning. Frequent exposure to danger takes away in a measure the excitability.

30th

In line awaiting attack. We live much as did the rebuilders of the walls of Jerusalem.[8]

Capt Kimble has gone home. He was a worthy soldier. It is no mean thing for a soldier to have deported himself well for three years. I now know something of what the Peninsula is. On one side is the James river; on the other side the York.

John Foster says, ["]one reason why persons of taste reject Christianity is because so many persons of weak minds embrace it and in the practice of it do many things, which persons without cultivation do, and have a general manner that others, those of refinement, abhor."

He shows that such an objection is entirely without foundation. They do not reason so with reference to anything else.

31st

Capt Lowes and I bathed our noble limbs in the James. In the course of our thoughts we suggested that the ministry, the working, effective ministry after the war is over must come from those who have been in the army. Illustrations from the soldier's life will always draw his attention. Stood in line for three hours awaiting an attack. At noon rec'd orders to report to Washington, D.C. In twenty minutes we were on the road.

The weather was so hot and the roads so dusty that we had many a man to give out before we had gone three miles. Got on board the Patapsco and under way at sundown.

We were horribly <u>crowded</u>. Anchored off City Point. We were well pleased with our place under General Foster.

Aug. 1st

Steam away all day. Pass Fort Monroe.

2d

We shall disembark sometime today. Read an excellent Poem in the Atlantic, "The Heart of the War."[9]

On coming up the Potomac I felt quite an interest in seeing Mt. Vernon. So I climbed to the topmast. I could barely see George Washington's residence, so thickly surrounded by foliage. The roofing was painted red. As I looked at that spot I had thoughts worth very much to me. Soon we passed Fort Washington.

3d

Today we are busy arranging our camp at Tennallytown. The 28th Iowa and we form a Provisional Brigade. Got three good letters. Had green corn for supper.

4th

Day of humiliation and Prayer. Capt Lowes and I went to Washington City. Heard a sermon at the 4th Presbyterian church. The great point was to show the difference between the <u>cause</u> and <u>occasion</u> of the war. We got into the QM Gen'ls Dept. I counted 6,600 boxes of Returns, in one room. I got a camp chair. I left one at home which I got in Texas. The <u>one</u> of these is for my wife, the <u>other</u> for me.

5th

My clerk has finished up my Reports. I go to the city on business and while there I visited the Capitol. As I entered the rotunda from the West, there was on the right <u>first</u>, "The surrender of Burgoyne at Saratoga N.Y. Oct. 1777."
<u>Second</u> "Declaration of Independence July 1776."
<u>Third</u>, "Baptism of Pocahontas at Jamestown Va. 1613."
<u>Fourth</u>, "Discovery of the Mississippi River by Desoto May 1541."
<u>Fifth</u> "The Landing of Columbus, 1492."
<u>Sixth</u>, "Embarkation of the Pilgrims in Holland, July 1620."
<u>Seventh</u>, "Gen'l Washingtons Resignation at Annapolis Md 1783."
<u>Eighth</u>, "Surrender of Lord Cornwallis Yorktown Va. Oct 1781[.]"
In the right wing was a statue of the dying Tecumseh and the bust of the sculptor Crawford. There was also a painting—"Westward the course of Empire takes its way" which was really fine.
There was in this wing also, Gen. Scott lifesize on horseback.
In the left wing are the busts of old John Hancock Thomas Benton and Robert Taney. In the ground rooms are the gas works, and engines for filling the rooms with cool or heated air.[10]
The Navy Yard is a busy place. Ordnance rooms, Plating rooms, Foundry rooms, &c, &c. I saw a gun there taken from the Merrimac. There are hundreds of pieces of various sizes.
On arriving at camp, found a letter from home.

6th

Our baggage is to be reduced, mine to be one small valise. Took a walk with Capt Lowes up to Fort Reno.

7th

The Christian Commission had an agent here—Sure enough, at last, I've got that letter.

8th

Miss L. M. would have me tell my conclusions after my conversation with Wallace. In fact I promised to do so. At last I send in all of my Returns of C. C. and G. E.Trautwine is a good clerk and a worthy young man.[11]

9th

Farragut has got inside Mobile Bay. He has captured the Rebel Ram Tennessee.[12] Sheridan relieves Hunter.

10th

Our new camp is much better than the old—more room, more system. Time passes slow and dull. I today made the acquaintance of the word solidarity—a fellow feeling for those in like circumstances with ourselves. It was used to denote the sameness of mind that existed in the North in regard to Slavery.

11th

Up at 2 ½ AM. ready to go to Bunker Hill to slash underbrush. Passed Forts Meade Totten Slocum &c all connected by well concealed roads, and plenty of finger boards to tell troops where such a fort on the line was. I am a little jealous of those fellows who are garrisoning these forts. They have too easy a time.

They all appear with very acceptable dress and "beards new reaped" and many of them I fear would chill at the sights of the Battlefield. It grinds me to think we have come ten miles to do the work that these men should do. O Charity I need thine aid!

12th

I command the slashers in the forenoon, Lt Carson in the afternoon. Fort Gaines surrendered six hundred men.[13] I should be thought puerile, should I express the annoyance I find from getting the points of the compass wrong. The sun seems to rise in the west. In consequence of the inconvenience I took the wrong end of the street railroad the other day, and so instead of finding myself at Georgetown, I found myself at the Navy Yard.

We shall remain here another day, by order of Gen Grover.

Col [Henry] Washburn is nominated for Congress.

13th

After we had been slashing a while, orders came to have us report to camp preparatory to a march. The men in marching back suffer severely with heat.

We find the right wing of the 8th Ind at camp, so Col Shunk will command the Brigade. Popp is Brigade Q.M. A lightning stroke killed a soldier on post, and knocked down the Chaplain, he is quite numb as to his head.[14]

14th

We march at 3 A.M. There was a great lack of system. Men were soon overcome with heat. Some were sunstruck.

The Eastern Troops can't march with us.

15th

Passed some nicer country than usual. Camp at Broadrim. Today I watched with some interest the sameness of mood that pervades every member of a regiment. At on[e] part of the day all are mirthful and talkative[;] at another, as if by common consent all are taciturn and thoughtful. I think this phenomenon shows at least that all are influenced to a great extent by external circumstances.

This would indicate the propriety of having nice yards and gardens to dwellings and nice scenery near a school building or church.

16th

This day three years ago we were first mustered in the US Service. Many have been the incidents and accidents[,] successes and failures, hopes and fears, in this period.

Reach Leesburg, an old town in Loudoun Co, Va. We passed a stone mill dated 1763. William and Marys College is I believe at Staunton. Dr. Jenkins was once president of it. He is the father in law of "Stonewall" Jackson, but he would not leave the old flag. So he came north. He was once president of Miama [sic] University.

We get plenty of green corn.

There are some of my boys who seek opportunities to have a long talk with me. I enjoy making it interesting for them. Here I bought a gold pen which I hope to keep many years (this book is written with it)[15]

17th

Pass Hamilton We are not far off Snickers Gap. We have been one month from Indianapolis and have had a large experience. Pass a nice stone church. Most buildings are old but substantial. After camping we were suddenly ordered to get ready to march on. We crossed through Snickers Gap, the Shenandoah River and marched on to Berryville, it taking till almost day. How tired we all were I cannot tell. I felt it however. Many could not keep up.

18th

Start off towards Harpers Ferry without any breakfast. A tremendous rain came up. We have to wait on other troops. While lying along the roadside, Gen Sheridan passed us. He asked me several questions—what troops we were, where from, when we came in, &c. I suppose we are retreating. At noon stopped to make coffee. We are now 2nd Div 19th Corps. Corps commanded by Gen Emory, who arrested me for discharging my pieces. When I informed him that it was by order, he released me and hauled up the Col.

19th

In a beautiful grove.
We are near Charlestown.

20th

On Picket, had a wet dark mean time of it. Get a mail which makes all amends. Some one sent me a Harpers.
Wallace is studying medicine with Dr. Payne.

21st

Try our new cook. We have just rec'd an Order requiring men and officers to wear Corps Badges. We are expecting a fight today. I am ready for duty and destiny.

22nd

Pass Charlestown where John Brown was tried. Our Brigade is in line on a ridge and has gone to fortifying.

23rd

Brisk skirmishing we finish our line of works. We all need rest and clean clothing

Grant has cut the Weldon railroad.[16]

Country here hilly. The Rebels have followed us up. They may fight us yet.

24th

Some skirmishing last night on our front. My impression is that the main [part] of the enemy is gone. Vanhoutten is to be Capt Co "D."[17]

25th

Another mail. Skirmishing again. None is able to tell what an hour may bring forth. I exhaust the day in answering letters. In afternoon went to Harpers Ferry. It is indeed in a romantic place. There are high rugged cliffs on every side of it. It is at the intersection of the Potomac and Shenandoah Rivers. It is the garnerdest up place that I ever saw. The landing at Natchez on the Mississippi will not compare. Transportation cut down to one valise to the company.

26th

[no entry]

27th

I do not wish to make "any remarks" today.

28th

I have been charmed, reading the Psalms. The language, how well chosen, the thought how elevated and pure.

29th

Well <u>now</u> we are after the rebels. We march out in four columns. Many a one as we march along would feign lift the veil of the future to see his fate, but fortunately he cannot. I felt like having a chill (may have been scared) In the evening we took position in line of Battle.

30th

We have now lain in line of battle three weeks. Fort Morgan is taken.[18]

31st

Muster Day. The Chicago Convention has not made a nomination yet but will nominate McClellan. Rec'd a letter from friend Lou. Visited a graveyard at Charlestown. Saw the monument to Fontaine Beckham Mayor of Harpers Ferry who was in the John Brown raid Oct 17th 1859. I went into and through the building where Brown had his trial. Saw the jail where he was imprisoned.

Sep. 1st

"The Autumn days have come, the saddest of the year."
McClellan is nominated. Joke on the non-coercionists; the non-arbitrary arrest men &c &c.
Col Washburn goes home to canvas his District. Dan Voorhees his opponent.[19]

2d

The Paymasters are a people whom we like to have visit us. They have not been around for a long while.

3d

March at 4 AM Just before starting the Adj't announced that Atlanta was taken ten days ago.
At night we were suddenly attacked there was rushing to and fro of Aids and orderlies. We capped, finally reclining with our traps on, fully antici-pating that the morrow would witness a severe battle.[20] The Brigade in advance of us worked all night at breastworks.

4th

I was out where I could see the pickets fighting. I always feel safer where I can see.

5th

Draft Day. Though I cannot "resign" I shall feel "resigned."

6th

Rained with a vengeance. I have no place to lay my devoted head. My sergeants invited me in as a guest with them. I shall accept. Jeff C. Davis is making his mark in Georgia.

7th

"Bill Mitchell" came to see me today. He is Bugler 4th U.S. Artillery. In college none had a better mind. Tom Woods has become reckless. Rec'd a letter from Mat and Mack.[21]

8th

Some colored men coming in with forage yesterday stampeded our pickets and won the occasion of calling us all into line. Good Joke!

9th

The great victory at Atlanta will almost insure the reelection of Lincoln. Whiskey is issued again by <u>order</u>. I am glad to know that most of my men <u>burned</u> theirs.

10th

I feel very hopeful of a speedy termination of the war. Everett says that Sherman has broken the big end of the "egg shell" at Atlanta, and that Mead will soon break in the little end at Richmond.[22]

11th

McClellan accepts the nomination but makes his own platform.
Read today the "Maid of the Cabin." Listened to a sermon from the Chaplain of the 28th Iowa who had his pants stuffed in his boots, so Capt Lowes said that we need not expect much of a sermon.[23] It is a lamentable fact that we have a poor set of ministers in the Army. It is a field which needs the <u>best</u>. The powerful doctrines of the Bible preached here would have an effect. But generally those whom I have heard here cannot produce <u>beaten oil</u> It comes in a very <u>crude</u> state. Scarcely extracted from the grain.

12th

Weather growing colder constantly. Sorry to find Lt Woods now a <u>disbeliever</u> in Christianity. I can but recall how fervently and loudly he used to pray when he roomed next to me in College. I pray that he may yet be reclaimed.[24]

13th

Anomalously I get <u>five letters</u>. I feel very well pleased about it.

14th

I am mad, absolutely mad, and I cant tell when I shall get over it. I wish Col Charles was at home enjoying the comforts of civil life.
The 8th South Carolina was captured today. Our Cavalry here is <u>ne plus ultra</u>.[25]

15th

Rev. Mr. Collins of Franklin is dead. Mary Thomas is attending school with Rosa [Riesa?] Adams.
Lincoln is to be re-elected very sure.

16th

A student's worth to mankind is not to be measured so much by what he <u>is</u> as by what he <u>does</u>. The most brilliant scholars are not doing the best service.

17th

Fine day and we all feel well. The citizens can compensate for good weather by rooms and stoves and grates and lights. The soldier feels just as the weather is.

I am reading the "Citizens Manual." In it I find much valuable information as to the form of our Government. The first compromise the North made to the South was <u>slave</u> <u>representation</u>. The second was granting all states Equal representation in the Senate. From the first, the North has conciliated the South even when it felt that was a concession. The history of Congress confirms this.[26]

18th

Sermon in the forenoon. At noon orders come to be ready to march at a moment's notice. We strike tents and load up our baggage and put them in the wagon, which goes back to Harpers Ferry. Night comes and the order is to be up and ready to march at 2 AM

19th

Up and on the Winchester pike at 2. We move in two columns, one on the left the other on the right of the pike the artillery and train on it. Advanced on to the intersection of another road and waited there for the 6th Corps. We finally waited farther on the road till the train of the 6th Corps passed. Artillery firing was heard on our front. At about 10 AM we crossed the Opegnau [Opequon], and moved on rapidly to the Battlefield which the rebels had chosen in front of Winchester. We passed up a ravine, the 19th Corps moved to the right of the pike. We rested a short time and then all things being ready, I having recommended to my boys to unsling knapsacks, Lt Carson having taken charge of Co B, Capts Bowden and Wadsworth having been appointed to act as field officers, we went forth double quick to the charge.[27] Forward went Col Charles with his brother (citizen) by his side across fields and fences.

We were nearly exhausted when we came up just behind the 1st Brigade. It was very near the Rebel line as we came up the Rebels opened such a deadly fire that the 1st Brig gave way falling back through our lines. Then we weaved and wavered to and fro (for the first time in our history) Finally we got orders to fall back and we did pell-mell, no line was preserved Everyone was for himself. I have scarcely ever felt so sad. I thought the day was lost. But when I had ascertained what a position we were in I said no troops could stand there. The enemy was full force in our front, in short range, and on both flanks he had artillery delivering a most murderous fire. I give as an instance that one solid shot passed through the Captain and knocked down or killed the whole front rank of one company. In twenty minutes there I lost ten men killed and wounded. Smith Crawford a noble boy was killed instantly.[28] As we were falling back a Captain of some N.Y. Regiment upbraided me in the most abusive manner for falling back, but judging that I knew as much about <u>war</u> as he did I took my squad back to where the regiment was re-forming. We were in a most deplorable fix. Our Col could not utter a word except in a whisper, Capt Wadsworth was killed and Capt Bowden did not know much about commanding the regiment. Hoso [howsoever] a few of us were ready for anything. But we lacked a commander. The rest of the Brigade was <u>gone</u>, where I do not know. We got back on the line and acted <u>Sharpshooters</u> till we were ordered back to the rear to join the Brigade. None could accurately describe the scene for a few moments after the charge. Dead and wounded were on all sides. Guns knapsacks and tents were scattered everywhere. The Rebels did not follow us up. They were too sharp.

One of Gen Emory's Aides said that the general simply wished us to hold this line until the 8th Corps could come in on the right. We remained till near the time for him to come when our Adjt General ordered us to fall back to where the rest of the brigade was.[29] By the time the Brigade was reformed, quite a number of the scared ones and lost ones came up. Then on we went, 8th Corps 19th Corps and 6th Corps, all straight for Winchester. And the Cavalry as soon as the rebels began to retreat, did some magnificent charging. We could see them. Their praise is on every tongue. Enemy's loss 8,000; ours <u>large</u>. My thanks rise to Providence for this decisive victory. But I am sad for the loss of so many of my company. Camp and sleep without blankets, thankful that we are alive. We could realize in part what a thrill of joy we by this day's work, sent through the whole North.

20th

March at 4 AM. The Rebels had abandoned and burned several wagons Pass Newtown and come on to the enemy at Fishers Hill. Our position is on the extreme left.

We see Round Mountain plainly. It is the lookout of the enemy.[30]

21st

We pass to the extreme right. And work hard all day at fortifications using what hatchets we happen to have. At night our Cavalry succeeded with some infantry in getting on the right flank and rear of the enemy, so that he thought it safe to retreat again.[31]

We started for his position double-quick, and had not left our work more than five minutes before the enemy began shelling it.

Here he lost 21 guns and several hundred prisoners. It is concluded to pursue him tonight. So our Brigade is put on the pike three columns deep. We get along well in the dark for three miles, when suddenly the enemy's rear guard opened on us with musketry and artillery. It caused great confusion in our ranks for a few moments. The horses stampeded and rushed over and through the men at a fearful rate. Lt's Vanhoutten and Bailey were wounded by a ball or the horses. Lt Relser [Pelser] lost his hat and sword. Capt Bowden lost his sword. Two of my men were badly bruised. There were several wounded. Lem Ross lost his bass drum.[32]

I hallooed myself considerably away trying to rally the right wing. Finally found that the Regiment was forming on the other side of the pike. Marched on all night. Reached Woodstock at day. Several Confederates waked up to find themselves in our hands.

22d

After a little sleep and the issue of rations we went on. Took several hundred prisoners.

23rd

Pass Edinburg. Enemys rear in sight.

24th

The country is really fine. I have today witnessed a military scene which I can never describe for its grandeur. Gen Sheridan concluding that it would not pay to stop the army for every skirmish placed two columns on the right flank, two on the left. The center marched in line of battle preceded by its skirmishers.

I saw all. Thousands of troops marching along in perfect order, colors waving bayonets and gunbarrels gleaming.

We were on the right flank and on the side hill overlooking the valley. We saw the enemy slowly receding their skirmishers contesting the advance of ours. Ours advancing fearlessly.

25th

The enemy is entirely gone, when we reach Harrisonburg. We find here 500 wounded men.

26th

Remain in camp.

27th

Gen Sheridan issues an order stating that the 19th Corps did <u>not</u> fail to come up to time at the Battle of Winchester, as stated by a correspondent of the Baltimore American.

28th

Sent a note to Rate and Miss LM. Wm Young has come up. We left him in Texas. Our wounded have gone to Bolivar Heights. Stanton [Staunton] is within 25 or 30 miles. Read some good stories in the "Doctors Book" October and November will to a great measure the fate of the Confederacy. The Presidential election is Nov 8th. Green and Hall the deserters are still at home. Bogart was a true man to the last.[33]

29th

March at 5 AM. through nice country. At 11 we reach Mt Crawford halt, and camp. We are support to Cavalry at Staunton. We take hogs chickens apples butter and <u>applebutter</u>.

30th

<u>Camping in the woods</u>.

This is much nicer than camping in the fields. There is more protection and it seems more like a home. Groups gather under trees and have many a familiar talk of the olden time We like to be under and around trees I remember well some trees in our pasture at home. I could almost greet them as friends. There is the oak near the gate. I never shall forget it. Under its ample deep shade I have had many a talk and play. I have have [*sic*] heard the winds whistle through its brown leaves many a winter night, while I was in my cozy trundle bed upstairs. It had leaves all the year, the old crop giving way only when pressed by the new. I wish we could always camp in the woods.

Oct. 1st

Back in our camp at Harrisonburg. I got out of humor on the march back One of my boys was even boasting of having been drunk. Our provision train has failed to come up. The men are really hungry. I have 26 present—16 absent.

2d

Still no train. For breakfast took a cup of coffee and am satisfied. I miss Capt Lowes. I have no particular associate now amongst the officers of the Regt. Rec'd two letters which were welcome indeed. Col Washburn is making a good canvass. J. K. Howard is assistant at Mitchell Seminary.[34] I have no books no stationery—nothing.

3d

Cousin Lib Collins is at Franklin teaching. I shall watch with the intensest interest the development of these two months. We are to have a peace or a war President. The former would ruin all our hopes. The latter would finally bring order and submission and that honorable peace which we want.

The Baptist church in Vernon has a melodeon. Good for Vernon. A few years ago such a thing would have been considered sacrilege or worse. Of the Books which I wish to read there is no end. I am messing in the Company but protest against it. It is not best. I shall quit soon. Many an officer has <u>sponged</u> his whole living from the rations of his men.

4th

J. G. Whittier the poet is a Quaker and is now 60 or 70 <u>aetat</u>. Miss L M spoke of having read Keats' Endymion. Keats died at Rome aged 26, and requested that his Epitaph be:

"Here lies one whose name was writ in water."

What did he mean? Who'll answer? Here's room_____ [35]

[Stott provided blank space in the original diary for answers to his query.]

In the afternoon I took a stroll to the woods where the 6th Corps is camped. Had a fine view of all the camps. Visited the graveyard. I asked[:] are not many of these inscriptions lies? I fear that "Farewell night, welcome morning" is written over the grave of many a practical infidel. Judgment morning will astonish us all. Many whom we had in our judgment placed on the <u>left</u> will be found on the <u>right</u> and <u>vice versa</u>.[36] How important the subject of Christianity is to mortals. We shall soon all sleep as these. And there is no repentance nor conversion in the grave whither we go. As the tree falls it shall lie.

5th

I have read a good story called "The Lieutenant's Trick." We burn all barns and forage as we fall back.

6th

March at 5 AM. Camp at New Market. The Cavalry detail keeps a big smoke in the distance.

7th

"I" was detailed to go forward to guard a bridge. I stood on the bridge and saw all of Sheridans army pass. Was really interested in reading the <u>faces</u> and <u>figures</u> of men. One cow fell off the bridge. Camp at Mount Jackson.

8th

By nine AM reach Fishers Hill. Fighting in the rear. Cross the Creek and camp just opposite Fishers Hill.

9th

Issue rations at 1 AM. Sheridans operations increase in the importance of their results. Some skirmishing today. Indiana's Gubernatorial Election will be day after tomorrow.

10th

Severe frost at nights. I lay on my bed at night looking up at the stars in the clear blue sky. "How Manifold are Thy works.[37]

11th

The sun rises majestically over Blue Ridge. No man with a <u>soul</u> could have stood with me last evening and have seen what I did without the emotion of sublimity. Here stretch the camp fires far up the valley. The sound of the flute is heard in different parts of the camp. The sound of singing too is heard. "Rally Round the Flag Boys" starts up over yonder. Nearer is the buzz of talking and laughing. Now the distant bugles sound the "Tatoo" Who is there that does not feel gentler and more amiable under the sound of that <u>lullaby.</u>

But here the "Brass Banders" who do not sleep as other men have begun their nightly labor. Time after time sounding in the distance woo us to rest and quiet. "Hurrah—hurrah—hurrah" from the throats of ten thousand brave men rise on the air like a mighty volume of joy. It is caught up by the camps successively, going like a wave till it has reached all.

But what is all this for[?] why Gen. Sheridan announces that "we have taken 300 more prisoners 11 pieces artillery and 40 wagons" Early perhaps will come to think that it wont pay to follow the <u>Yanks</u>.

Above glided the moon and stars in their prescribed paths, glad to do the will of Him who made all things—and I laid me down to sleep—

The prisoners taken state that Longstreet is coming with 50,000 men. Gen Dwight of the 1st Div would make it appear that the 1st did all the fighting at Winchester holding the ground that the 2nd (Gen Grovers—ours) gave up. But he cannot make it appear.[38]

12th

"Things take the even tenor of their way." Lt Carson is appointed Q.M. Sent a letter to Substitute.

Heard around campfire against bedtime <u>ninety seven oaths</u>! Can God bless such a soldiering?

13th

Had a case of discipline.

14th

We expect another severe Battle today. I am prepared entirely.

15th

There was no Battle.

I rejoice that there is an inner as well as outer world. A reconnoitering party went out today. The enemy was gone. Gen. Burbridge was defeated in a raid to some salt works in Va. He had only 2500 men.[39]

16th

On Picket. The "Johnnies" came up in sight. At midnight our forces went to fortifying. We heard the chopping plainly. At this writing (11 AM) all over the North, fathers, mothers, sisters brothers Husband wife and lover are gathered in the sanctuaries for <u>prayer</u> and <u>praise</u> and to listen to the words of wisdom as they are given out by him who stands in the pulpit. Would I could join the mighty throng. <u>Here</u> I receive <u>admonitions</u> from Rebel <u>guns</u> and have to <u>watch</u> more than pray.

17th

We have quite a decent line of works in our front. We have to <u>stand at</u> arms, an hour before day every morning.

A five days supply of rations has come up. The rumor is that Gov Morton got 30,000 majority. I have been reading Havens philosophy. I disagree with Haven in some points—for instance, freedom of the Will. At once he says it is perfectly free, and comes to the <u>conclusion</u> that it is not. He acknowledges the cogency of Edwards logic.[40]

18th

[no entry]

19th

Eventful day! We were up at 5 A.M. and <u>standing at arms</u> as the 1st 2nd and 3rd Brigades of our Division were to go across Cedar Creek on a reconnoitering expedition. After we had stood twenty minutes firing was heard over on the left in front of the 8th Corps. Instead of our making a reconnaissance the rebels thought it time to make one. Soon a strong volley of musketry was heard then a yell. We supposed as we stood there that the Rebels had made a charge and had been repulsed, for the firing had well nigh ceased.

It was not long however till we were ordered to the left <u>double quick</u> leaving everything in camp but our guns and accouterments. Some thought we were getting into a fight. Some thought not. As soon as we had crossed the ravine and had got nearly up to the pike the bullets balls and shells told us that there was enemy near[.]

The 8th Corps had been completely surprised and was now running <u>pell-mell</u>. Soon the Rebel line was in full view after them (Now it was just day) It was with some difficulty that we could distinguish the rebels from our own men, hence firing was restrained for some time. But at last there could be no mistake. [O]ur men fell fast. Our Brigade was there to check the advance, but in a few moments they were on three sides of us. As soon as I saw them come up within plain view and <u>aim</u> I commanded fire. Most of my boys stood and fought well.

I shall never forget how a rebel stood up at full length and took (as it looked to me) aim at me. We had but a moment to decide. We had stood as long as it was possible to stand. Our Field officers had been shot, we could not resist such a force. So the word was <u>fall</u> <u>back</u>. How disappointed and chagrined I was when I knew we had to fall back I never can tell. At once the thought came to me, the election is lost the day is lost, the cause is lost.

Henry Goodman who stood by my side said that as I started back, I exclaimed: "O Pshaw" I know that is the expression of my feelings.[41] As we turned round we saw that the most had "<u>got up and dusted</u>." Henry and I tried to carry Maj. Williams off the field but we could not he was too badly wounded. He told us to leave him. We put him in the ravine where he would be safe, and started on.

Six of my boys had been taken prisoner.

We could hear "<u>Halt</u>" plainly but we did not think it best to halt.

Our color bearer had been killed, another had taken up the colors and had been wounded, so I told a sergt of Co. "K" to take them and on we went. We ran back over the field in all sorts of directions. Ball flipped into the ground all around us. I expected I should be wounded, but on I went about a mile. A recruit of Co. H (a noble fellow) had our banner. We caught up with a portion of our troops. Col Shunk was trying to collect them. All the colors of the Brigade happened to get together perhaps there were a dozen men with each. Col Shunk told me to form the Brigade and that he would go farther back and inform the rest where the line was being formed. Where his <u>aids</u> and <u>orderlies</u> were he did not <u>know</u>.

We got the line formed and soon a number came into ranks. By this time the rebels had nearly caught up to us again.

Although most of our men came up promptly when they knew where to come, there were some <u>cowardly skulkers</u>.

Gen. Grover came up, his hat torn with a shell, and told us where to take position we took it but fell back gradually as the afternoon came on. There were but three of our officers left so I was in command of the Regiment. Lt Hickman and Lt Pelser were the others. When we had fallen back about a mile where it seemed that our army was to take a stand Capt Robinson came up so I took command of my company again.[42] We still fell back and rested a short time, when Gen Sheridan coming on the field we about faced. We passed some two hours in rearranging the lines. Capt Robinson complained of feeling sick so he went to the rear and I took command again. We built temporary breastworks of rails, the enemy shelling us vigorously the while. The 1st Brigade was in our front. It fired a heavy volley, and was about to break again, when Gen Grover and Gen Birge rode right up and made them stand; our line gave them a cheer which had a good moral effect. I said Gen Grover and Gen Birge will do to count on, they were right with us all the time.

Soon the orders came to advance. Some men went to the charge as if they were going to the slaughter sure enough. But we advanced. Whenever I saw any indications of shrinking I urged that part of the line right on. Gen Sheridan rode along after we had got out into a field and swearing told us that we had started the rebels, on we went, some got killed some wounded, but on we went. Near sundown we found that the enemy had made a precipitate retreat. O how the soul was filled with thanks and gladness to know that we had gained the victory after all! The Cavalry knowing well its business was hard on the enemy's retreat. We advanced in line to our old camp passed Maj. Williams. He was still alive. The rebels had taken his watch ring money Mason Badge and sword. The rebel women had taunted him. Bishop was lying near, dead. I admired him for his manliness.

We camped on our old camp till 8 P.M. when our Brigade was ordered to cross Cedar Creek and go to the hights [sic] near strasbing [Strasburg], we went and laid down in line of battle without tents or blankets or anything to eat. The night was cold. I walked till 11 PM, up and down the line. Then Lt Daniels, who had been captured and had escaped came in with a supply of blankets and I slept.

I never was so deceived as to time as today. When I supposed it was ten AM I looked and it was two P.M.

The horses got to sweating and even foaming early in the morning, when as yet they scarcely had been used. It must have been the excitement.

Of my company Henry Wells was killed, Jno F. Abbott, G. C. Eyker and C. Sims wounded, and Sergt Butler, Charles Grim, Wm Glover Thos Flinn Henry Utterback and Wm Young prisoners. I had my hat rim shot early in the morning.[43]

20th

We remain here all day.

I sent two men from each Company to get some beef. We had nothing else. Several prisoners were taken by our men today. Sergt Hover took six.[44] There is an everlasting telling of incidents and accidents today. None seems to tire of telling or hearing some new thing.

Send a detail back to bury the dead At night move to the left of the pike and camp in the woods. Capt Black and Capt Robinson came up.

21st

Move back to our old camp again. There are but 17 of Co. "I" left with us. We all feel melancholy but not cast down. Such is the fate of war. None knows what will be his fate.

22nd

I put up a good board at Wells' grave. The boys burned the letters in it. How we appreciate rest.

The philosophy of the surprise on the 19th is this[:] Gordon's Division (Rebel) came down Massanuten mountain one at a time without making any noise. It took all night. But the surprise was so complete that some of our guns were captured in the stack as soon as the firing began, The enemy across Cedar Creek began and so we were under a cross fire.

The morning was sad for us, the evening sadder for the enemy. We captured 50 pieces artillery.

Sent a note to Father and Miss L M.

23rd

The rebels left ambulances, wounded, dying and dead in our hands.

I like to refer the success of our arms to Providence. He it is that preserved our nation thus far, and will.

I came near losing my Journal on the 19th.

24th

The Republicans in Indiana had a great victory _____ Mrs. Shirk is very low with cancer in the breast.

25th

In talking of the battle some of my boys said that they could do very well while standing or advancing, but that when we went to falling back they got demoralized.

A congratulatory order from the President came for Gen Sheridan and his gallant army.[45]

Our baggage has not been with us since we left Berryville in September.

The mountains look beautiful clad in green red and brown.

A banker in Germany has offered the United States $1,000,000,000. He can trust us.

26th

On Picket. I contested my election but finally concluded to go.

I have Iowa boys. They do fine.

Major Williams is dead.

He was a vigilant soldier but a wicked man.

How sweet is friendship to the soldier! Separated from those he was accustomed to mingle with, he is very glad to keep alive and augment that friendship with correspondence.

Paid at night by Maj Sallada.

27th

We march to Winchester as <u>train guard</u>.

28th

March 22 miles on the Pike.

Reach Martinsburg, a nice railroad town on the B & O RR.

Stone fences all around. None others left.

29th

I help Tom Woods and his wife to the train. Col Washburn met us. Price has been defeated in Mo I go shopping. Buy some clothing.[46]

30th

Write to a friend, then visit the Martinsburg cemetery. Rebels and Federals buried in the same lot.

Aunt Lizzie Vawter is dead. Sallie is a good letter writer.

31st

Shall endeavor to write some today.

Nov. 1st

Shall we have another Battle on the 19th this month? March to Winchester in half a day. It was hard on us all.

2d

March to the front It is raining and cold.

3d

Back again to Winchester. The boys are getting sharp enough to carry rails. I am messing with Dr. Brown Eddelman &c.

4th

Reach Martinsburg at 4 P.M. Get mail. Rec'd a letter from Rate.

5th

Rained today. Harvey Crane is here He has come for Bishop's body.

6th

We scarcely know that this is Sabbath.

7th

The merchants of New York have shown themselves Union <u>men</u>. Rec'd a letter from home. None could wish a better, They had found that I was numbered with the slain. Let others speak lightly of home. I cannot. It is the best place I know.

8th

Day of days! The doings of today will decide the fate of the Union—the fate of Republics.[47]

9th

March to Winchester.

10th

Find the army falling back to within four miles of Winchester. We are relieved as train <u>guard</u>. We are glad of that.
I reduced a Corporal for <u>playing out</u> and staying out of camp. Work till 12 at night building works.

11th

Finish our works. In afternoon I am put to superintending the slashing of timber in our front.
It is expected that Early will attack tomorrow morning.

12th

At 4 A.M. We slashers are out again. It dont feel as if Early's coming. He may be. I have been thinking a great deal of the value of an untarnished character. It is worth more than learning or wealth or honor.

Webster's Dictionary is out again 10,000 words added.

13th

The Johnnies it is found are <u>non extant</u>. Two spies were caught today.

14th

Sherman is all right.

He has swung off from the rest, and with 5 Corps has started through the South, leaving Thomas to take care of Hood.

This is bold design but Sherman can do it. He <u>knows his men</u> and they <u>know him</u>.[48]

Lincoln is Re-elected! Allelujah!!

"Praise God from whom all blessings flow."

Today we take some more prisoners and artillery. What can Early think.

15th

Went to Winchester hoping to see Tilson. But did not find him. He had gone with Maj Williams body. We now connect by telegraph with Harpers Ferry.

16th

McClellan resigned on the 8th Nov.[49]

17th

We are now building <u>winter quarters</u>, the first we ever built.

Ryker, Trautwine and Goodman will room with me. I am on Picket <u>again</u>.

18th

The night was severe and long. The "Spleeny" Col finds great fault with the picket. Well just let him!

I see through him. He is down on the <u>Western Brigade</u>, but it don't care much. I was complimented by the Division Officer of the Day.

19th

Early does not come somehow!!

20th

Chaplain Donaldson preached a short sermon.

21st

Ferrer Robinson and Duncan are mustered out. I am on Picket <u>again</u>!!

22nd

We have a fine warm house. Fire in it.

23rd

Winter has come. We get the Baltimore American Daily. Sherman meets no opposition. The Union League Societies &c of New York &c send Sheridans Army 30,000 lbs Turkey! Ours was spoiled but we take the <u>will</u> for the <u>deed</u>.[50]

24th

Thanksgiving Day! We soldiers have reason to give thanks 1st for the general Health. No Epidemic has visited us. 2nd For the victory that has everywhere crowned our arms. 3rd That Lincoln has been reelected.

25th

Sherman is still going on, 15 miles a day.

26th

There is forcible talk of our Regiment being consolidated. Trautwine is recommended for Sergt Major.

27th

A sermon by Mr. Crawford a citizen. Rev Mr Talmage of Philadelphia has written a most glowing Thanksgiving sermon. Prof Silliman is dead.[51]

28th

Had Brigade Drill. after <u>so long</u>.

29th

Wrote several letters.
We expect the order for consolidation soon.

30th

Sergt Ditmars has come up. Recd a letter from Miss LM. Mrs. Shirk is gradually declining. Will not live long. Miss LM. is teaching. Watches with her grandma half of each night.

Dec. 1st

Chaplain Leozier makes one of the speakers at the burial of Democracy say "Countrymen lend me your ears" and then remarks that is the greatest loan he could have asked them to make.

2d

Part of the 6th Corps has gone.
Rec'd a letter from Mrs Dr Bailey and Mrs J H Williams.[52]

3d

Spent the day in setting up a Drug store.

4th

Sermon by the Chaplain. He dwelt principally on swearing. It was a most appropriate theme. There has been an unusual amount of swearing of late.

5th

Ticknor and Fields have charge of the North American Review.[53]

6th

I looked for the President's Message today.[54] Answered Rate and Miss LM.

7th

Had a fine inspection. Co. "I" had its quarters ornamented with Pine trees. The Inspector gave us the meed of praise.

8th

I am detailed to take a detachment to Stevensons Depot. Cold day. Get back at night. There was some playing out.[55] I reported all such. Read the President's Message. It has the true ring.

9th

Read Sec. Wells Navy report. The oversight of the Navy is a herculean task. My wife's chair is broken but it mended promptly. S. P. Chase is made Chief Justice of the Supreme Court of the United States.[56]

10th

What a snow! The first that I have seen for two years. The ground is in good state to receive it—dry and frozen. We all think of the olden time when the snowbirds hopped about outdoors at home and how we frolicsome lads and lasses went coasting down the hills at noons and recesses of school. And we think of the path shoveled out from the home to the school, and how we rolled together great snow balls, which so scared the travellers horses, when all the other snow was gone, that the <u>Master</u> made us chop them away. Some of us country lads remember how we went hunting rabbits and quails &c, and some of us may remember how <u>manlily</u> and yet how tenderly we caught the girls and washed their faces and how they would make it appear that they did not want us to do so, but did all the time. And we recall the familiar stamp of snowy shoes at the steps as some friend was getting his "understanding" in a condition to be brought into our fathers house. In the snowy times we always take great care to make one warm who comes in out of the storm. I shall soon be home to see some of this.

11th

This is the last Sabbath that I shall spend in the army. I feel strange in thinking of being a <u>citizen</u>. Savannah to be the objective point for Sherman.
The 6th Corps is at Petersburg.

12th

Busy in getting ready to transfer my property. I find that I shall regret somewhat to part from my comrades.

13th

Weather pleasanter today.

14th

Have transferred my property Paid all my debts and am now on my way to Washington City.
Get to Harpers Ferry at 2 P.M. to the Relay House at 9 P.M. to Washington at 12. We Lt Baily and I lodge at the Metropolitan Hotel.[57] We have a pleasant room I expect to have an agreeable sojourn here of 3 or 4 days.

15th

Finish out Lt Bailys and my Reports.
Meet Judge Holman.[58]
The news comes that Sherman has communicated with the coast.

16th

Sherman has <u>reached</u> the coast!

Thomas has whipped Hood, taking 17 pieces artillery and 15,000 prisoners. A salute is fired from the Navy Yard. I go to the QM Generals Dept. The hundred clerks are ever busy. Then we go to the Ordnance Dept. The latter has the more system. Visit the Patent Office. We pay $5.00 per day fare at our Hotel.

I can say but little of the Patent Office for we had a short time to see a great deal in.

There are 300 cases 20 feet long, 15 feet high and 5 feet wide, filled with models. A great many are stowed on the tops of the cases. The cases have four shelves each. There stands Powers' Washington sent from Baton Rouge. It is the best in the United States. It will pay a man of taste to come here to see <u>that</u>.[59]

Saw Washington's sword, Coat, vest, pants, writing case, tent, mess-chest, chair table bureau and dishes. Saw the press which Ben Franklin worked on in England. Also a lot of silk robes presented to our government by Japan. And so on <u>ad infinitum</u>. I [saw] some persons there who had come there to <u>court </u>(if I understand this term) as it is such a nice quiet place.

17th

Went to the Smithsonian Institute. Young ladies and gentlemen were there on the same errand of love and mercy as described above. They certainly appreciate such a place. There we saw all kinds of stuffed beasts and birds and creeping things. Busts portraits skeletons, minerals relics from all countries. Library, &c &c Portrait of Guizot Webster Burr and [S]leeping Innocence.

Then to Stanley's Museum, adjoining. Here we saw the Sarcophagus which contained the remains of some Roman, was intended for Gen. Jackson but he would not be put into it. And the Bastile, and ancient Indian pieces. Next to the lecture room. I wish I could spend a year in this Institution.

Have finished Longfellow's Evangeline.[60]

18th

Gen'l Warren is in town today.

I got Davy Crockett.

I shall go to Dr. Gurleys church in hope of seeing President Lincoln and family.[61]

19th

Read "Human Destiny" nearly through.[62]

First visited the Capitol. On the grounds east of the building is a statue of Washington in a sitting Posture. On one side of the granite on which it rests was "First in War" on another side "First in Peace" and on still another "First in the hearts of his countrymen."

A guide showed me through the building. I overlooked the Senate for an hour. I cant say whether it is "improving" any or not. The Senator from Wisconsin was making a warm speech in favor of fortifying our northern border.

Next to the House. Speaker Colfax presided with ability and grace. The House was not doing much.[63]

Dewey's object in The Problem of Human Destiny is to show the object of mans creation, and he makes it to be <u>cultivation</u>. It falls in with Bishop Butler's ideas in the main.

20th

I shall be unable to settle with Government here. Every Department is slow except the Ordnance Department.

21st

I start on home arrive at Pittsburg, where I meet my friend Capt Lowes. He is a student in the Theological Institute. I stay with him.

22nd

Listen to several recitations in the Institute. I like the Faculty. Dr. Jacobus and Dr. Hodges are authors in Theology.[64] Start on home.

23rd

Reach Cincinnatti [sic] in the forenoon. Met Lt Baily. Afternoon take train for North Vernon. Get home at 10 at night. "<u>I am home safe from the wars</u>[.]"

EPILOGUE

10

The Grand Old Man of Franklin

When William Taylor Stott arrived at his home in the final days of 1864, he no doubt delighted in the warm reception given him by his family and friends. But the agonizing pain he felt in his knees may have dampened his joy. Apparently, the wartime illnesses he suffered in Missouri and Louisiana, along with the wear and tear of endless marching and the rigors of battle, were already beginning to take a toll—a condition that gradually worsened during the rest of his life. Stott would testify in his 1888 "Declaration for Invalid Army Pension" that "at or near a place called Springfield, State of Missouri, on or about the 15th day of September, 1861, . . . [I] contracted malarial poisoning (rheumatism) and chronic diarrhea and disease of respiratory organs under following circumstances: from exposure, sleeping on damp ground, malaria, and drinking impure water." Six years later, in November 1894, he wrote his wife, Arabella, from Jerusalem about the long days he had spent on horseback while he visited biblical sites. He described a "tumble" he had taken when, on "a cold and very rainy day, between Nazareth and En Ganim in the valley of Esdraelon," his horse stumbled into a hole, flinging Stott to the ground amid "many a hearty laugh" from his companions. The impact of his days in—and out!—of the saddle, he said, "made my knees more rheumatic. It was a good deal as I felt when the Civil War was over and I 'came marching home.'"[1]

Of course, the twenty-eight-year-old Stott was not about to let pain deter him from pursuing what he perceived to be his calling: to enter the Baptist ministry. It was a natural step for this scion of preachers and graduate of Franklin College who had spent much time in the camps of the Eighteenth Indiana reading philosophy and theology, discussing the ministry with his friend Abraham Lowes, and counseling soldiers on spiritual matters. So in late summer 1865, Stott left home again, this time for New York where he enrolled at Rochester Theological Seminary, a divinity school of his denomination, studying at the feet of some of the leading theologians and educators of his tradition. Among them was Ezekiel Gilman Robinson, who taught biblical and pastoral theology and became the seminary's president in 1868 before proceeding to the same post at Brown University. Teaching church history and evidences of Christianity was George Washington Northrup, who left Rochester before Stott's senior year to preside over the Baptist Union Theological Seminary at Chicago. Asahel Clark Kendrick, author of several commentaries on New Testament books, taught biblical exegesis, and August Rauschenbusch, the most renowned member of the faculty, pontificated over courses in German as well as biblical literature and theology. A native of southern Westphalia and a convert from Lutheranism, Rauschenbusch held a revered status among German Baptists in America.[2]

Under such mentors Stott received solid pastoral training. Already having a firm background in Greek from his college days, he now added depth in Hebrew to his study of biblical languages. His grasp of the Holy Scriptures grew as he plunged deeper into biblical criticism and basic principles of interpretation, particularly in the Old Testament and the four Gospels. The history of the church and its doctrines supplemented a thorough grounding in systematic theology, and courses in homiletics and "pastoral duties" prepared Stott for service in the local church. When he completed his studies in 1868, he joined two other graduates of Franklin College as recipients of divinity degrees: Thomas Jefferson Morgan, his 1861 classmate, and William Elgin, class of 1862.[3]

Stott's three years in Rochester provided him with far more than a theological education. It was in that city that he met Arabella Ruth Tracy, a student of French and art at the Tracy Seminary for Young Ladies. Bright, attractive, adept at the piano, and known to "cook like a dream," Arabella—or "Bel," as she was called—was about a decade younger than Stott. She was a native of Royalton, Vermont, and the daughter of Isaac Storrs and Mary Pierce Tracy, a descendant of President Franklin Pierce. Isaac, a businessman, had accumulated considerable wealth and property but, through a series of "business reverses," lost most of his holdings. This may have been the reason that the Tracy family moved to Rochester while

Bel was quite young. Shortly before Stott entered her life, she had suffered a devastating loss. She had fallen deeply in love with a young man
named Charles Rossiter, and the two were engaged to be married when he
suddenly fell ill and died, a tragic blow from which Arabella never recovered. For years after Professor Kendrick wed Will Stott and Bel Tracy on
May 21, 1868, the memories of Rossiter invaded the couple's life together.
Their granddaughter, Eleanor Parker Van Cleave, who adored Arabella, recalled that "we all knew as much about Charles Rossiter as we knew about
Gramp." And another relative noted that Bel gave her second daughter
the middle name "Rossiter." Yet, despite being haunted by a specter from
the past, the Stotts were married for more than fifty years. Their union
produced five children: Wilfred Tracy (born 1869), Grace Ellen (1870),
Edith Rossiter (1875), Cyril Hackett (1877) who died of "brain fever" at
age seven, and Roscoe Gilmore (1880).[4]

Shortly after their wedding day the young couple moved to Columbus,
Indiana, where Stott began his pastoral ministry at First Baptist Church
on Franklin Street, one of the town's busiest thoroughfares. On September 24, 1868, clergy from the surrounding counties and the members of
First Baptist gathered in its stately brick edifice to ordain Stott into the
Christian ministry. The new pastor was already familiar with his charge,
for his Grandfather William T. Stott had moderated the meeting at which
the church was founded in 1852, and Will had visited it while he was a college student and on his recruitment trips during the war. Something had
occurred, however, that may have created a distinct challenge for his pastorate. After early struggles to simply exist during the 1850s, the church
enjoyed a remarkable revival of strength under the leadership of Reverend
William Haw. But then, during the war, dissension erupted that, according to a local historian, "weakened the church considerably, and for a time
threatened its destruction." Little is known about the precise nature of
the discord, but it may have stemmed from the charge of a former pastor
that the church's "revivalist effort" was a "Butternut raid and the work
of the devil." In 1863, in fact, the church chose to remove from membership those "who sympathized with the Southern rebels." It is certainly
possible, then, that the newly frocked veteran of the Eighteenth Indiana
may have had to assist his congregation in finding peace in the wake of
conflict. If so, working to heal the parish's wounds—while simultaneously visiting the sick, counseling the afflicted, conducting weddings and

funerals, preparing at least two sermons a week, maintaining time for study and prayer, and leading worship—unquestionably placed exacting demands upon the fledgling pastor.[5]

Amid these duties, his alma mater beckoned. In the early spring of 1869, Stott began serving as an agent for Franklin College in its efforts to procure financial support and new students for the revived institution. In February he joined his friend Barnett Wallace on a "committee to solicit persons to act as agent[s] for the Endowment of the Indiana Professorship" at the school, and in April he received an advance of twenty-five dollars for his own expenses in that work. Then, on May 25, 1869, the college's board of directors elected Stott as professor of natural sciences and acting president at an annual salary of $900.[6] For a second consecutive summer, the Stotts answered a new call. With three-month-old Wilfred, they traveled north to a fresh venture in what, for Stott, was an old, familiar place.

The story of Franklin College while Stott was a soldier and seminarian was one of virtual death and hopeful resurrection. On a Monday in March 1863, student O. M. Merrick wrote in his diary that the prayer meeting he had just attended on campus was "the last one pobably [sic] that I shall ever enjoy here. For if there is a draft it will break down the college." By September he would be a member of the Persimmon Brigade of the 118th Indiana, and more students would follow in his steps. There were, of course, other reasons for the school's decline during the war. President Silas Bailey's ill health led to his resignation and, coupled with the usual financial strains, put the college in a leaderless state of shock. Competing educational facilities, some of Baptist origin, provided alternatives for students from around the state, and the rise of public high schools threatened college preparatory programs. Furthermore, the war spirit sapped the energies of Indiana Baptists, causing, in the words of historian John F. Cady, "a tragic collapse all along the line" in the church's support of education. Yet, it was the war that cut deepest, calling patriotic students to set aside their books and shoulder arms for their nation. By the spring of 1864 there were but two students enrolled, Oliver H. Stout of Greensburg and Marshall Grinstead of North Vernon, and both were lame—clearly not army material. Consequently, on June 1, the board of directors appointed a committee to investigate "the propriety of suspending the exercises of the college at the end of the present Collegiate year." The group's report of June 29 called for the college to be closed until "such time as in the judgement of the board it may be proper to resume operations." The school appeared to be dead, and many Indiana Baptists of means were openly hostile to any revival of the enterprise.[7]

There were, however, loyal graduates and local supporters who were not content to let the college fade away. Among them was Stott's friend Wallace, who was residing in the college buildings when it closed. The year was a sad one for Wallace. On January 15 his wife died, and six months later he witnessed the "death" of his "dear mother," his alma mater. Twenty years later, when the resurrected college celebrated its fiftieth anniversary, Wallace wrote to Stott about the hope he held for its rebirth even as he grieved for it back in 1864. The school, he said, "closed her eyes and stopped breathing and all the family went away. But, somehow, even during those four long weary years, from 1864 to 1868, when there was scarcely a sign of any life about the houses, when even the rats stormed out and left, and your humble servant was the only living thing that slept inside the old walls, it seemed to me it was not death but a bad case of suspended animation."[8] Other alumni, especially those who became ministers or teachers, clung to the same hope and looked for inspiration to the sacrifices many had made to make the institution "the center of Baptist educational endeavor in the state." Some noted that the war's close brought an "alarming dearth of suitable ministers," and they reminded the churches of the need for ministerial education. In 1866 the campus began hosting an annual Ministers' Institute that received the endorsement of some Baptist associations. Since the old board of directors had not dissolved and still held title to the college property, it also leased the buildings to former professor Francis M. Furgason, who conducted a private school in them in 1866–67.[9]

The real breakthrough to rebirth, though, came in 1867 when the board contracted with Professors William Hill and Jeremiah H. Smith, both graduates of the college, for the removal of their Ladoga Female Seminary to the Franklin College location. Agreeing to place the school on a coeducational foundation under the name "Franklin College," Hill and Smith set out to revive it with a complete program of college-level instruction, while maintaining the preparatory department and adding offerings in art and commercial fields. Although the board "undertook no obligation for the support of the school," its members quickly took note of its almost immediate success and launched two fund-raising efforts—the Johnson County Professorship with a goal of $15,000 and the Indiana Professorship set at $18,000. They then resolved in May 1869 to resume "full control" of the college in the coming September. These measures led directly to Stott's call to be his alma mater's president at just thirty-three years of age.[10]

The attainments of the 1869–70 academic year under Stott's leadership were impressive. The college enrolled more than two hundred students, the vast majority in the Preparatory Department, and the endowment reached $30,000. Indeed, as Stott wrote four decades later, the accomplishments of the year were "so prosperous . . . that the board was encouraged to go forward to the election of a president." Joining Stott on the faculty were Professors F. W. Brown in languages and J. E. Walter in mathematics, with Wallace and Doctor Philander W. Payne as lecturers in anatomy and physiology. Although the study of the classics and mathematics remained the core of the first two years in the collegiate curriculum, there was a notable increase in the amount of science offerings and other requirements for juniors and seniors. As the catalogue explained, the college offered a wide range of study intended to provide "thoroughness of scholarship and breadth of knowledge." The faculty received praise for its efficiency, and Stott's personal investment in reaching out to the Baptist constituency brought forth "many warm friends in different parts of the State who were, a year ago, at best, lukewarm." A pledge of free tuition for ministerial students, and the board's commitment to admitting women "to all the departments of study . . . upon the same terms" as males, undoubtedly drew increased support from the churches.[11]

But not all the news was good. Financial troubles arose that first year. The nation broke out in a speculative fever in the early postwar period, and reckless spending and a desire for rapid economic growth prevailed. Unfortunately, the college board caught the fever and, in its ardor to secure the school's future, began what historian Cady labels a three-year "period of inflated expenditure." As early as June 1869 college leaders began investigating the feasibility of installing gas lighting fixtures. By fall they were in place, and the board proceeded to launch other projects— the installation of lightning rods, a new roof for the north building, and renovations in both buildings, all to the tune of $7,000. To meet these expenses the board voted to take out a loan and to execute a mortgage on the college property. Then came more laboratory equipment and additional advertising. By February 1870 the board's treasurer, Wallace, reported "an excess of liabilities over assets of $5,995.06." Such was the school's economic state when the board elected Doctor Heman Lincoln Wayland as president of the faculty on July 20, 1870.[12]

The new executive, the son of acclaimed philosopher and educator Francis Wayland, arrived on campus in September, and his presidency, wrote Stott, "began auspiciously." His solid reputation turned the attention of leading Baptists to the college and, in a paper called *The Campfire*, Wayland placed the labors and needs of the college before the churches in what Stott deemed "an attractive way." A former chaplain in the Union army and professor at Kalamazoo College, Wayland championed an educational focus that stressed the sciences and current social issues, rather than the traditional study of the classics. A self-proclaimed Christian socialist, he brought startlingly new ideas to Franklin. A hint of his thought appeared at the first commencement at which he presided on June 20, 1871. The speaker of the day, invited at Wayland's request, was Congressman William Steele Holman, a former student at the college, son of one of its foremost founders, and an outspoken advocate for labor. His address, entitled "Capital and Labor," was a sharp departure from previous commencement speeches. Holman reminded his listeners of the college's origin as a Manual Labor Institute and asserted that "the noblest temporal purpose of education is to elevate labor and vindicate its rights." He traced the contributions the working class had made to history and attacked the manner in which "unbounded opulence" and "overgrown landed estates" had created "licentiousness and luxury which have overwhelmed virtue and corrupted the very fountains of public justice," with the laborer the chief victim. Unfortunately, such rhetoric did not sit well with Baptist men of means, and it was seen as too radical a break with the school's cultural and theological heritage. As historian I. George Blake put it, among Indiana Baptists "frontier tradition was still stronger than sympathy for the working class."[13]

Inexplicably, in this context Wayland determined that it was the right time to initiate a campaign to acquire a $100,000 endowment, a proposal the board of directors had ratified in February 1871. As Stott recalled,

Wayland contended "that if Indiana Baptists were in earnest about their college they would at once rally to its support when all the facts were presented, and that it was useless to think of securing less than $100,000 additional funds." But the college was still operating on borrowed money and seeking more loans to pay the current expenses. Indeed, as Stott described it, "increased expenses were not balanced by an increased income." Even before Holman's hapless speech in June, the endowment drive was in trouble, for, as Cady correctly observes, the wealthier Baptists "refused to rally to Wayland's support." The grand total derived from the interest on the endowment notes was just a little above $5,000, and the principal was never paid. On November 15, the board resolved that "unless the Endowment can be raised to $75,000 in reliable funds by June 15, 1872 . . . the college at that time will have to be closed."[14]

But the school did not last that long. At the board meeting of January 31, 1872, Wayland submitted his resignation, and the board resolved "that the college so far as teaching is concerned be suspended." Wayland's own report of that moment captures the emotions expressed at the meeting. His words appeared in the Chicago-based *Baptist Standard* of February 15:

> I need not speak of the feelings with which this result was reached. To some who were present the college had been the object of life-long affection, having stood to them first in the place of a parent, and later having received the care and regard and protection due to a child. Tears stood in the eyes of those brethren as they voted. None could fail to sympathize most deeply with Bro. Stott, Dr. Wallace, and Mr. Byfield, and the other dear brethren in the termination of their protracted labors.
>
> Amid the sorrows of the event, the members of the board accepted Wayland's resignation with expressions of their affectionate regard for his "most enthusiastic devotedness" to the college. The fact remained, however, that, if the buildings and grounds should be sold (as the board projected they would be), the college was bankrupt with little hope for revival.[15]

Stott labeled the spring and early summer of 1872 "days of Egyptian darkness for the friends of Franklin College." There was renewed talk of relocating the school to a more favorable place, and its teachers and students scattered to other institutions or new fields of work. Stott, for instance, went to Kalamazoo College as a professor of natural science. During these same months a frank, sometimes bitter, editorial debate between Wayland and college spokesmen flooded the pages of the *Baptist Standard*. At its height, Wayland gave vent to an outburst of presidential exasperation:

> My dear young brother, now burning the midnight oil in the semi-nary, and "dreaming of the hour" when you may be at the head of a college; a word in your ear. Don't. *Don't!* If you want a light, pleasant, gainful calling, with sure pay and learned leisure, enlist as a private in a regiment that is going out to fight the Apaches; ship before the mast for a three-years' cruise to the Northwest; but don't be a President, . . . Fighting rebels is nothing to it: I have tried both.
>
> But there is this compensation. No doubt, in the hereafter, there will be a region of peculiar serenity, a heavenly singular repose, re-served for canal horses, ministers' wives, and College Presidents; to the one, boundless hay and rest; to the second, a back, a contented domestic, and no agents to stay over Sunday; to the last, something that is not in a chronic state of bankruptcy.

Despite Wayland's wailings, there was one member of the Franklin College faculty who, after being at the helm of the college himself for two years, and facing similar financial constraints, expressed genuine appreciation for Wayland. In July 1874 Stott praised Wayland as "a most earnest and able instructor" whose "noble generosity inspired all the students." He commended Wayland's "broad and progressive" ideas and explained that his lack of success stemmed only from his uneasiness with "the slow development of the State."[16]

Happily, the darkness of which Stott wrote soon gave way to glimmers of light. While he was conducting classes at Kalamazoo, friends of the col-lege in Johnson County were busily organizing a group to save Franklin. In fact, at the fateful January meeting at which the college was suspend-ed, these friends—among them Wallace and Casabianca Byfield—calling themselves the "Franklin College Association," proposed "to take charge of the college and property belonging to the same . . . for a term of five years." They pledged to assume its indebtedness, pay all its expenses, se-cure a faculty, and maintain the school "under the auspices of the Baptist Church of Indiana." At first the board accepted this offer, but then the association withdrew it and chose instead to form a joint-stock company that could obtain the institution through direct purchase. Almost immediately, as Stott later reported, "Real friends did rally." Supporters in the city of Franklin and Johnson County, half of them Baptists, realizing that the college's demise would be "an irreparable loss to the community" subscribed to its capital stock at a total of $36,000. In mid-June the Baptist organ *Journal and Messenger* announced: "Franklin College is saved. The subscriptions to the stock have reached $50,000." A month later, on July 25, the old board agreed to "sell to Franklin College Association all the real estate and personal property of Franklin College for $12,731.57," payable either "in cash or taking up our notes." The "Egyptian darkness" was over. "Let Franklin live," penned a *Journal and Messenger* correspondent. "It can do good service for Christ's cause. Put an able, vigorous man at the head of it, and he will soon rally friends and gather means of its support."[17]

———————————

The man selected to accomplish this daunting task was Stott. From the start the members of the new board focused on Stott alone as their choice, for, as one well-wisher put it, he had been "only loaned to Michigan." Another admirer remarked, "No other available man as admirably equipped for the position could have been chosen." Officials at Kalamazoo College evidently agreed, for they graciously released him from his post there and bestowed upon him the honorary degree of Doctor of Divinity. Although relatively inexperienced as an administrator, Dr. Stott had already demonstrated superlative skills in the classroom and he commanded the respect of all at the college and of Baptists throughout the state—the latter being the key to the institution's financial future. These factors alone enabled the school to experience under Stott's leadership what historian Clifton J. Phillips calls "a virtual rebirth."[18]

The thirty-six-year-old Stott threw himself into his new work with youthful exuberance and unflagging energy. Fortunately, he was a man of patience and self-possession, for the early period of his presidency was one of loneliness and frequent discouragement. Upon arrival he discovered that "the interior of the buildings was in such bad repair and the funds of the Institution so scant that I . . . with my own hands tore the ragged paper from the walls & put on a double coat of calamine." The number of people on the campus was no more encouraging. Initially, there "were not more than fifty students present at any one time," Stott noted, and the entire enrollment that first year was only seventy-five. There were only three full-time faculty members, including the president. He set natural science aside to teach moral and intellectual philosophy, a sign of the versatility he exhibited in the classroom throughout his career. Rebecca Thompson assumed the natural science and history responsibilities, and J. E. Walter taught mathematics. The part-time instructor in the "Ornamental Department" was Bel R. Stott, the president's wife. Stott "was obliged to teach whatever he could not conscientiously ask the other two to take." He recalled that all worked exceedingly hard, but "there was manifest a feeling akin to loneliness the whole year through. A college yell would have startled us, but probably done us good." Even in chapel services and prayer meetings, "a feeling of lonesomeness" prevailed. In addition, Stott said, "We had no library worth the name, we had no geological cabinet; we had only fair physical apparatus." Still, everyone evinced "a steady and determined purpose to make the most of the opportunities, and on the part of the leaders a most hopeful spirit."[19]

While the academic program got off to a healthy start and the excitement of resurrecting the college evoked an optimistic spirit, the new president faced two administrative challenges that called for prompt action. First, he was well aware that the foremost worry of the board of directors was the still bleak financial picture. Perhaps emblematic of that concern was the fact that, at the first meeting of the board in September 1872, Stott's starting salary was set at $1,400 (Wayland's was $2,000), given "with the understanding that he donates $100 of said salary to the College." Equally troubling was the imbalance of income and expenditures. With the endowment at the end of the first year (1872–73) at only $47,700, the combined salaries of the full-time teachers was $5,700, but the total income was just $4,000. Furthermore, as Stott recalled years later, "ten of the [twenty] subscribers to the stock had combined to refuse payment." All of these factors created, he said, "an element of uncertainty very trying to both board and faculty."[20]

The second pressing need, inextricably linked to the first, was to strengthen the college's relations with its Baptist constituency, the greatest resource of funds and students. For this task Stott was admirably and uniquely prepared. He was known and liked by both ministers and churches in the Indiana Baptist Convention, and, even among those opposed to education and to Franklin College in particular, he commanded respect.

As Cady correctly observes, "Perhaps the most successful phase of Stott's program was the improvement of relations between the College and its constituency." Since the school's wherewithal hinged in large measure on the generosity of the Baptists, Stott's familiarity with the Convention and its leaders, and his untiring labors among them, were critical keys to the college's economic development.[21]

During the early years of his presidency, Stott and the board vigorously tackled the financial situation, first attempting what Stott called "various measures of reconciliation" with delinquent subscribers to the capital stock. In November 1872 board members received lists of "those who have not paid their assessments" and were enlisted to meet with those parties to encourage payment "as speedily as possible." At the same meeting, the board ordered the finance committee to "bring Suit" against all who refused to pay their subscriptions—an unpleasant but essential step toward procurement of needed funds. The board assigned its president, R. W. Pearson, and Stott to the task of requesting financial assistance from each Baptist Association "to defray the current expenses of the college." It also issued a flyer for distribution to all churches stating forthrightly the needs of the school: an increase of endowment to $100,000, additions to the library, more students and faculty. The brochure also indicated the ways aid could be given, such as through prayer, donations to the college, subscriptions to the endowment, bequests, and the sending of students. Moreover, the board periodically approached the faithful subscribers for a gift of at least 20 percent of their assessments and allowed them to settle their accounts "by notes with personal security" on a ten-year loan. Finally, in order to make fund-raising and recruiting more systematic, Stott encouraged the board to divide the state into five sections, with a committee in each to procure gifts and students. He, as chief executive, would serve as general agent to supervise the work of all committees. Each of these measures brought positive results, some understandably more profitable than others. In every case, though, their productivity benefited from Stott's personal involvement in denominational circles, including the Convention's Executive Committee for Education, to which he secured appointment in 1872 and on which he played a major leadership role. As for the lawsuits to obtain overdue payments, both the circuit and state supreme courts ruled in the college's favor, the latter in May 1876. The news of this judgment provided an occasion, Stott wrote, "to plan larger things."[22]

Although the panic of 1873 affected some of these plans, Stott and the board continued to make resolute strides toward a more solid financial base despite the hard times. Numerous approaches were taken, among them solicitations for bequests, the purchase and sale of real estate, and energetic fund-raising campaigns. In March 1874, for instance, Stott told the board that he had obtained a $5,000 will from Jonathan Allen, explaining that he thought the donor would provide the money at once should the board agree to pay him "8 per cent upon the principal during his life." Another substantial gift came a year later when Rosa Bailey, the widow of former president Silas Bailey, gave one-half of his estate, including his vast library, to the school. Reflecting on this gift, Wallace recalled how Silas used to preach about the "eternity of Franklin College," and now he had shown "a still larger exhibition of faith, when, as he lay dying, he left all his worldly estate to her, whose flame was then only a faint flicker."[23]

Along with bequests, the college gained from investments and sales involving real estate. These transactions ranged from such simple purchases as that of a Johnson County sawmill in 1876 that brought $800 when sold two years later, to the acquisition of hundreds of acres of land—some in places as far away as Missouri and Texas—and their subsequent sale when the school needed an economic boost. A prime example was board member James Forsythe's proposal in 1878 to "transfer eighty acres of land south of Franklin to the college in full payment of his obligations" to the school. Forsythe, a personal friend of Stott, had suffered financial losses and other setbacks but wanted to faithfully fulfill his pledge to the college. In tribute to his conscientiousness, fellow board member Reverend W. N. Wyeth, an editor of the *Journal and Messenger*, commended Forsythe for "putting his property where thieves will not break through and steal—in the heart and minds of other people's children." In 1881 the college realized $2,800 from the sale of the Forsythe farm.[24] Periodically, when college needs dictated, real estate in the form of land, houses, and other buildings, were placed on market "at fair price." In December 1879 the board chose to sell "all the real estate belonging to the College except the College grounds." This released the school from paying taxes on properties in Pike, Gibson, Pulaski, and Jasper counties. Occasionally, the proceeds from real estate simply fell into the institution's hands. A classic case was an 1883 resolution of the Freedom Association that called for the sale of the property of the defunct Ladoga Female Seminary with all proceeds "turned over to Franklin College."[25]

The most ambitious efforts to improve the college's economic foundation, however, were its many capital campaigns. The first attempt during Stott's tenure was a modest one. To fund the construction of a women's dormitory to be called Centennial Hall, the college asked every Baptist in Indiana to donate one dollar and each pupil in the churches' Sabbath schools twenty-five cents to a "Centennial Fund." Unfortunately, this was in 1874–75 when the country was still reeling from the effects of the 1873 panic, crops were failing everywhere, and the times were tough, so the drive had to be aborted. Subsequent efforts, though, met with more favorable results. In the 1880s, Stott personally pressed for funds to establish a Women's Professorship with an initial goal of $20,000. Mrs. B. H. Stuart and Emma Jordan assumed the responsibility of canvassing for the project in 1882, and the president wrote Baptist women across the state, urging them to speak on its behalf. It was successfully completed in 1886. In addition, Reverend Norman Carr of Kokomo became the board's financial secretary and general agent in 1882 and, together with Stott, brought the college's assets from $111,333 to $425,000 over the next twenty years. During the same period, the endowment grew from $62,000 to $225,000. Much of this progress was the result of fruitful campaigns in those decades. Not to be outdone by their female counterparts, a Business Men's Campaign started in 1897. As the drive's title suggests, it reached beyond Baptist circles to appeal to merchants and corporate leaders of all faiths in reaching its goal of $75,000 for the endowment.[26] The capstone of all the campaigns during Stott's presidency, however, came toward its end. Again, it was the outcome of the combined labors of Stott and Carr. At the board meeting of March 19, 1889, Stott presented a letter from Frederick T. Gates of the American Baptist Education Society, setting forth the procedures the board could take to procure a portion of a $100,000 gift from Baptist philanthropist John D. Rockefeller. Over the next thirteen years, Stott and Carr prepared the necessary papers, attended sessions at the Society's headquarters in Boston, and solicited essential matching funds. Their endeavors proved fruitful when the college received

$25,000 of Rockefeller money in 1902. This campaign, and all the others, netted the college, at Stott's retirement in 1905, assets totaling about $500,000, half of it in fertile endowment. And all its bills were paid.[27]

As mentioned earlier, much of this success stemmed from Stott's steady influence among Baptists in Indiana and beyond. As Cady states, "President Stott assumed an unrivaled place of leadership in Baptist educational affairs." In the summer of 1883, Stott received a letter from his uncle, Philemon C. Vawter, a fellow college alumnus. Reflecting on the school's encounter with near bankruptcy in 1872 and its "renewed life & vigorous growth," Vawter offered an intriguing metaphor. "As comes a storm upon the trunk and branches of a great tree," he wrote, "swaying it to & fro, breaking the laterals, & threatening utter destruction, so came that crisis, but instead of utter destruction the result was to stir up the tap-root, causing it to reach down deeper into the subsoil" for support. Stott knew that, and he was determined to be a principal force in stirring up the taproots among Baptists nationwide, not only for Franklin College but also for an educated ministry. As chairman of the Indiana Baptist Committee for Education, he fought for aid to ministerial students wherever they received their education. The program he projected included Rochester, Shurtleff, Kalamazoo, and even Presbyterian Wabash (though half of those training for ministry attended Franklin). It was Stott's conviction, Cady notes, that "it was futile to pray for a better trained ministry unless the churches were ready to aid those already in preparation." He protested against the licensing of unqualified pastors and the unsavory practices of churches that enticed ministerial students away from the classroom before they finished their studies. Besides promoting Franklin before its constituency, Stott also improved the school's relations with the churches by supporting their future pastors and insisting on the highest level of preparation for them.[28]

Sometimes Stott's work as a college executive and denominational leader thrust him into the midst of wider issues in higher education. In the 1880s he was called upon to address two matters that posed potential threats to small church-related colleges. The first arose because of the revival of the University of Chicago as a Baptist institution, due in large part to the labors of prominent denominational educator, Gates, and major funding from Rockefeller. Gates conducted a study of "the state of Baptist education in the West" and presented his findings to Chicago ministers in

October 1888. Among his conclusions was that the resources and enroll-ments of the denomination's colleges in Indiana, Illinois, Michigan, and other states were exceedingly, even dangerously, slim. Most of them had endowments averaging only $78,000 and the normal salary for a profes-sor was just a little over one thousand dollars. Moreover, the schools were not "well-located," being in "small towns, surrounded by an impecunious population, far removed from the centers of western life and means." What was needed, Gates contended, was a grand university in Chicago with an endowment in the millions, large libraries, and other buildings as a magnet for "feeder academies" in nearby states.[29]

The reference to "feeder academies" and the possible dominance of the Baptist institution in Chicago gave rise to anxiety among the smaller denominational schools. At the board meeting of December 16, 1890, Stott delivered his customary report on developments at the college and called for a stronger effort to raise the endowment. He cited the fact that Franklin was "possibly paying the smallest salaries of any college in the state" and desperately needed a full-time librarian and a professor of English. "But there is another reason," he stressed, "why this institution should be wide awake in increasing its endowment. Within 200 miles of us . . . there is shortly to be a Baptist University with money enough to do whatever it decides ought to be done." The president explained that the Chicago school already had 2.5 million dollars in "real estate or reli-able obligations" and the capability of doubling that amount "in the next few years." Franklin simply could not ignore "the fact that this new and large and noble enterprise is going to create new conditions for us and all the Northwest." If the college did not demonstrate an equal fervor toward doubling its own assets, Stott warned, "eyes that are looking this way will look in another direction." Franklin should display "an attitude of independence and vigor and enthusiasm," and nothing would express that spirit more clearly than growing the endowment. He then suggested meeting with representatives of the new university to discuss matters of mutual interest, stressing that the communications should be of a "fra-ternal and liberal kind." Over the next two years, Stott worked with his counterparts at other denominational schools to clarify the University of Chicago's relationship with the smaller institutions. In the spring of 1891 the university clearly indicated that it would not seek to draw students away from Franklin, except for graduate work. During Stott's meeting with the university's president, Doctor William Rainey Harper, at the national gathering that summer, Harper reinforced the university's promise and assured Stott that, in his judgment, Franklin was doing "college work" in preparing students for successful graduate education. Stott's labors thus resulted in productive collaboration with the West's burgeoning research institution.[30]

Another potential threat to small liberal arts colleges arose out of legislation passed by the Indiana General Assembly in 1897. This controversy elevated Stott to yet another leadership post. The issues emerged from the diversion of large amounts of public funds to state institutions of higher education and a decision by the State Board of Education—upon which sat the presidents of the state universities—to favor students from those schools in the granting of teaching licenses. Stott first brought his displeasure over these developments to the college board in December 1896. Its members directed him and Edward A. Remy to "watch state legislation" and correspond with schools of all denominations in an effort to "prevent any kind of legislation looking toward preferment of privileges to students of state schools." They were also to seek modification of the current law. The college likewise urged church associations to discuss the inequalities of the state's actions. A movement among church and private colleges arose to contest further "State school aggression" and to persuade the Indiana Board of Education to expand its membership to include representatives of nonstate schools. Their actions reached fruition when Stott and Earlham president Joseph J. Mills gained appointments to the state body. Although the fears of the small colleges continued, at least they now had a voice.[31]

———————•◦•———————

As crucial as they were, Stott's labors in the realms of finance and church relations never once tore his heart and mind away from what he believed was his most important duty: creating an academic program of the highest quality. Whether he was teaching in the classroom, assembling a first-rate faculty, or molding an atmosphere in which students could not only learn but also grow in moral stature, Stott's example, as his students recalled, was one of "complete devotion . . . that withheld nothing of himself . . . from the service of the college." The school and its educational enterprise constituted "the master passion of his soul." It was with this passion, said the student newspaper at the time of his death, that "he guided the destiny of the institution."[32] Once again, a sense of duty and destiny shaped his endeavors.

Above all, Stott was a teacher, and a good one. Three of his students of the 1870s and 1880s testified to that fact:

> Many distinctions crowned the head of our honored president, as soldier, as patriot, as educator, administrator and divine, but to us, who once frequented his classroom and sat at his feet, he towers pre-eminently as the great teacher. His large and noble conceptions of the teacher's mission and his fine exaction of effort on the part of his students were joined with an intuitive understanding of the student's difficulties and a wonderful patience and simplicity in making things plain. And he loved his students with a deep and abiding affection . . . . Also, his belief in his students was such as inspired in them the effort to realize their highest possibilities.[33]

Martha Noble Carter, class of 1897, had this same perception of Stott. "[H]e loved his students. He made them feel it," she recalled. Then she spoke of his mannerisms. "He would listen with patience while one of us stumbled through some abstruse problems in mental philosophy," she mused. "Soon he would begin to nibble at the ends of his beard . . . then flicking a bit of dust from his coat sleeve, and a twinkle creeping into his eyes, with a quick, keen question the thing that had been so obscure would become luminous." This caused the class to laugh. Stott laughed with them, and the student who had blundered a little "would sit down feeling he had made a fine recitation" after all. And Harriott Palmer told the Indiana State Teachers Association in 1919 of Stott's "strong and kindly face, his cheerful personality and his steadfast character" that inspired all the students. "But his greatest power as a teacher lay through his skillful questioning, in his ability to reveal the student to himself," she claimed. Perhaps Reverend Edgar Fay Daugherty, class of 1898, was one of those students. He reflected thirty years later that "if there is any sanity or integrity in my view of life and the world, it is more due to W. T. Stott than any of the many teachers who had patience with me."[34]

Descriptions of Stott's courses, including his own assessment, appear to substantiate the students' recollections. In the Department of Philosophy, he taught psychology, ethics, mental philosophy, aesthetics, political economy, and a course entitled "Evidences of Christianity." His teaching load was three classes each day of the week. In 1898 the yearbook, *The*

President William Taylor Stott.

Blue and Gold, indicated that the department had two goals: "clear think-ing" and "a strong conviction of the feebleness of mere reason," along with "a higher application of the truths of revelation." Stott discussed his own philosophy of teaching in the *Catalogue* of his last year at the college. In addition to the student becoming "acquainted with the works treating the subject," he wrote, it was his aim "to provoke independent thinking, and this is constantly sought." It was his belief that "to quicken the powers of the student is worth far more . . . than to fill his mind with mere informa-tion, however important." Therefore, class time was "not limited to mere recitation," but questions were "encouraged and sometimes the discussion of the topics being studied takes up a large part of the hour." To Stott, teaching was more than simply imparting knowledge.[35]

For such independent thinking to occur, Stott knew, the students had to have ready access to scholarly resources. For that reason, one of his foremost goals was to strengthen the school's library. When he re-turned to Franklin as president in 1872 the only accessions to the library were the result of voluntary donations, there being no budget for the purchase of books. Thus, the holdings were small and limited primarily to historical and theological literature. The library's first genuine boost came in 1874 with the addition of Bailey's volumes as part of the bequest of his estate. Otherwise, the chief source of funds for book acquisitions derived from annual students' fees, from which the library gleaned one dollar per student by 1901. After 1877 the board also designated gradu-ation fees to the library. Despite the scarcity of funds, Stott persistently kept the library's needs and progress before college officials and donors; his report at virtually every gathering of the board included the number of volumes acquired since the previous session, such as the eighty-eight books received before the December 1888 meeting. Among his other concerns for the library was its staffing, cleanliness, and availability to the students. In 1875 Rebecca Thompson began presiding over the library, now located on the ground floor of the North building, and a "Students' Reading Room Association" maintained an adjacent space to which stu-dents had access one hour each day. Nine years later Wallace wrote Stott regarding his pleasure at how the library was advancing. "In those elder days," Wallace noted, "the library[,] consisting of some old books occupy-ing your present study, would have been amazed at the proportions to which it has now grown."[36]

By the 1890s the library became a focal point of college life. The Dewey system of cataloguing brought it into line with the latest advancements in library science, the facilities were opened to Franklin citizens as long as their use did not "work a hardship to the students," and assistant librarians were employed, including the president's son and daughter, Wilfred and Grace. "The Library and reading table never offered such attractions as they do now," Stott informed the board in June 1894. "And as the facilities increase the demand for more library hours is made." At century's turn, Stott's greatest wish reached fulfillment: plans began for a "new Fire Proof Building" to house the rapidly expanding library. On December 16, 1902, the president reminded the board of the "great need of a Library Building," and the search for architects and contractors started. Completed in 1904, the Jeffersonian-style, domed structure—named Shirk Hall in honor of its donors, the Shirk family of Peru, Indiana— stood just south of the classroom buildings, providing easy accessibility for both town and gown.[37]

While the library was growing to the point of requiring its own building, the classrooms, chapel, and dormitory spaces in the college's main structures were becoming overcrowded, a reality that led to an even more crucial and much larger construction venture. Once again, the pivotal factor dictating the erection of what would become Stott Hall was the desire to strengthen the academic program by providing a larger chapel, additional classrooms, and more spacious laboratories. When Millard Fillmore Kennedy entered the college as a freshman in 1883, the school "consisted of two three-and-a-half story buildings—both of them part dormitory and part recitation halls," and there was "a meager half dozen on the faculty." Three years later, as Elba L. Branigin matriculated for his first year, he noted that "The buildings were antiquated and much in need of repair and fresh paint." Furthermore, it was dingy and chilly in the "poorly lighted and heated" classrooms. Every floor of each structure was crowded. The north building contained recitation rooms and offices for Stott, Thompson, and Columbus C. Hall, meeting halls for three literary societies, the chapel, and men's dormitory rooms, with the attic housing the "frat" men. The south building was almost as tight, having teaching areas for four faculty, along with Webster Hall and the janitor's quarters. The *Catalogue* of 1883–84 reported that, if enrollment continued to rise at the "present rate, . . . the chapel and recitation rooms will soon prove to be too small." In 1884 the board appointed a committee to "consider the propriety of creating a new college building," and the group's report at the next session called for "immediate steps" toward that goal. But progress was hardly "immediate," and for four years Stott brought regular pleas to board meetings from professors whose larger classes required "more room" or "more commodious appointments."[38]

The snail's pace at which the new edifice was built (it was eleven years from the hiring of an architect to completion of construction) was not because of any lack of will on the part of the college officials. Part of the problem was, as Wallace related in July 1884, "Most every *feller* has a plan of his own about that Bldg," and the board committee wanted to "give everybody a chance to say his say before they fully make up their minds." This well-meaning attempt at democracy sparked controversy, most of which swirled around the location of the new structure. Wallace told the chosen architect, Indianapolis-based R. P. Daggett, that the committee was "unanimously and strongly in favor of combining the new Building

Franklin College in 1904. "Old Main" now contains Chandler Hall on the left, Stott Hall in the center, and Bailey Hall on the right. The Jeffersonian-style domed building at the far right is the library, Shirk Hall.

with the old ones," as Daggett had proposed. But, Wallace explained, there was "a very respectable and strong opposition to our plan" from people who preferred "an entirely separate" location. The final decision was to join the new hall to both of the older structures, making it the center wing of a single three-part building. Other factors caused delays as well. Cracks developed in the original buildings because of structural stresses placed upon them by the construction of the new one. There were lengthy debates over the placement of laboratories, the chapel, specific offices, and classrooms. There was the question of how to fund the project while still being "aggressive to increase salaries and employ more professors" and move forward on the promised home for the library. Even the nature and timing of the leaded-glass cathedral windows for the Athenian Hall prompted time-consuming discussions. Despite these and other impediments, Stott and the board pressed forward, and the building reached full completion in the summer of 1895. Later, in 1903–04, all the structures were again totally remodeled and each received a new name. The north wing became Chandler Hall, the south Bailey Hall, and the board honored Stott by placing his name on the center addition.[39]

⸺◆⸺

Of course, scholarly resources and buildings are but the *context* for a successful academic program. It takes *people* to make it flourish. That is why Stott sought to assemble the most capable and dedicated faculty possible, one whose primary focus was on teaching. Given his own skills in the classroom, he naturally led the faculty by example, and a significant aspect of his guidance centered on adherence to the college motto: "Christianity and Culture." Hall, explaining the meaning of the motto in 1897, remarked that Franklin College "puts Christianity first" and considers it the foundation of culture. Christianity, he concluded, furnishes both the "standard" and the "process" of culture—its model and its practice. Understandably, then, in addition to scholarly proficiency and pedagogical skills, the faculty, Stott said in 1898, should consist of "men and women of evangelical convictions and a high standard of religious life, as well as enthusiasm and mastery in their several departments." As Wallace assured the Indiana Baptist Convention in 1901, the ultimate questions in choosing a faculty member were: "Is he or she a Christian gentleman or gentlewoman? Is he a character builder?"[40]

A glance at several of the prominent teachers during Stott's tenure provides a sense of their caliber as instructors and their devotion to the institution and its principles. Hall was in the middle of his senior year at Franklin College when the school closed in 1872. After completing degrees at Chicago University and its neighboring Baptist theological seminary, he returned to Franklin in 1875 as an instructor in Greek, Latin, and science. Hall taught at the college for thirty-seven years and was known to the students as "Our gray-haired, curly-haired Professor of Greek." They lauded him for his amiability and the encouragement he gave to "diligent" students, but they admitted that his "eyes burn like fire and his tongue like sulphuric acid" toward the "indolent and insincere" ones. With a "poetic instinct," Hall exhibited the gift of calling his students "to nobler purposes in life" as well as a genuine love for everything Greek, even the intricacies of the language. Though short in stature—"tall like Zachaeus," wrote one student—he was towering in the estimation of college officials who elevated him to vice president in 1885. Another language professor, Brown, had taught at Franklin in the difficult years of 1869–72. The college recalled him for a one-year appointment in 1887, but because of his superlative teaching he "quickly [won] the love of his students" and remained on the faculty for twenty more years. Teaching modern languages was Jeanette Zeppenfeld, an 1880 graduate of Franklin, who used her paid leaves from the college to enhance her mastery of the field through study in Paris and Heidelberg. She also fought successfully to institute a requirement of one year of modern language for all students.[41]

Among the more versatile faculty members was mathematician and historian Thompson, who combined teaching with responsibilities as director of the library. She also guided the installation and use of an astronomical observatory on the fourth floor of Stott Hall. Under the command of John Wildman Moncrief and Charles Elmer Goodell, instruction in history was exceptional. A graduate of Denison University with advanced study at the University of Leipzig, Moncrief was a tutor in the preparatory department at Franklin in the early 1870s. He returned in 1881 as professor of history and became an outstanding member of the faculty. At the time of his departure in 1894 to become a professor of church history at the University of Chicago, his colleagues told the board that Moncrief had "brought the Department of History from essentially nothing up to a high plain, as compared with the best institutions in the

Country." They also praised him as "a recognized leader" in the state's denominational endeavors. Moncrief's successor, Goodell, a Franklin graduate, took the department to even greater acclaim and encouraged Latin as a prerequisite for the study of history. Goodell's superlative teaching and administrative gifts brought him back to his alma mater in 1917 as its president. The sciences were equally blessed with capable leadership. Until his health broke in 1897, Franklin alumnus David A. Owen literally created ex nihilo the college's offerings in biology, geology, and chemistry. He instituted and managed its cabinet of geological and other scientific specimens, laid the groundwork for an expansion of the laboratories, and taught that "God's invisible hand is felt in each experiment and reaction." Later, Melvin E. Crowell added physics to the curriculum and receive credit for "revolutionizing" the science department "in its appearance and the quality of work done." So pleased was Stott with his teaching corps, which grew from three full-time professors in 1872 to more than ten in the year of his retirement, that he invited board members to "visit the college and hear the recitations as often as possible."[42]

Stott expected his faculty to function in areas far beyond the classroom. He entreated them to hone their pedagogical skills through active membership in "organizations for the promotion of teaching," and such participation sparked periodic discussions on campus regarding the desirability of a yet higher standard of academic performance. Professors also attended a variety of teaching institutes during the summer for exposure to fresh pedagogical methods. Furthermore, in direct service to the college, the faculty joined Stott in student recruitment efforts—again in the summer. In May 1879, the board asked them "to spend at least one month this summer in canvassing for students." This plea may have been in response to Moncrief's report on his recruitment experience of the previous year. The history professor had enjoyed kind and warm receptions across the state and found "a healthy interest growing up . . . on behalf of the college and every indication that it will continue." But, he explained, he had to work hard "to get a hearing" sometimes, due to the ineffectiveness of an "unscrupulous agent" of the college, one P. H. Sumner. Although Moncrief felt he had succeeded in securing new students, he warned of two formidable obstacles. Other colleges in the state either gave free tuition or were less expensive, and Franklin's residents did not seem to display the "same interest in the college and students" that people in other college towns did. From then on, faculty became permanent fixtures in recruitment ventures, and Stott personally set aside a month in the summer to lead the "troops."[43]

On campus, the faculty also played the major role in governing academic life. Besides teaching full schedules of classes five days each week, attending all chapel services, and making curricular decisions, it had to establish and enforce rules and regulations for the students. Most decisions regarding discipline ultimately fell to the president, but the faculty had to address the ongoing matter of class attendance. Sometimes "cutting" recitations—or "bucking" them, to use the student lingo of those days—got out of hand. As one student bard expressed it:

> To buck or not to buck, that is the question.
> Whether 'tis better to the class to go
> And there recite what I don't know,
> When down the line it comes to me,
> And flunk or bluff it's got to be,
> Or homeward wend my lazy way,
> Cut out the farce for one more day,
> Cut out the absences and see
> That just one more will finish me.[44]

Students who frequently missed classes had to come before the faculty and make "satisfactory concessions respecting former conduct." In October 1887 the faculty required a student to meet with them for "leaving class in Book-keeping without permission," and another for failing "to appear at his examinations." Apparently, they were two of many, for the following month the faculty ruled that three unexcused absences would result in the suspension of a student from the class.[45]

Franklin College faculty, 1899.

Perhaps the most important faculty task, however, was the development of the curriculum. When Stott took the helm in 1872, the course of study was much as it was in his student days: focused on the classics and mathematics. But by the 1880s, like most institutions of higher education, Franklin began to incorporate new areas of study. Modern languages and new offerings in the sciences, history, political economy, constitutional law, philosophy, theology, American literature, and the arts became valued additions to the curriculum. Understandably, teaching methods modified to meet the new types of courses. The old lecture-recitation system, for example, began to give way to seminars and the encouragement of original research by the students. The faculty introduced a new grading scale in the late 1880s as well, dropping the old scheme of grading in figures from 1 to 10 and adopting the use of letters: G (85 percent and up), M (70–85), and B (below 70). Consequently, the *Catalogue* for Stott's final year as president, 1904–5, bore little resemblance to those of earlier years, revealing a much more diverse, systematic, and rigorous course of study with a greater focus on current issues.[46]

Student life at Franklin College also underwent remarkable changes between 1872 and 1905. For one thing, enrollment mushroomed. At the outset of Stott's administration, the total enrollment was seventy-five, but in 1887 the president could proudly announce that the figure for the year was "215—the largest in the history of the college." He added that the June graduation class was twice the size of the previous year and that the number in "regular college classes" had increased appreciably. By the 1890s enrollments of more than 250 were customary, with the largest being 273 in 1891. These statistics, of course, include those matriculating in the preparatory department as well as the collegiate ranks. To get a sense of the growth in the degree-granting programs, a review of the alumni roster posted in the *Catalogue* of 1904–05 indicates that during Stott's student years fourteen young men were graduated, but during his presidency 367 men and women received degrees. Furthermore, over the thirty-three-year period, the collegiate ranks swelled as the preparatory waned, a pattern boosted in 1887 through the creation of an "extensive scholarship program."[47]

Another increase occurred in college costs, though the expenses seem ludicrous by twenty-first century standards. Annual tuition, for instance, rose from twenty-one dollars in 1874 to forty-two dollars in 1904. Cady estimates that the total cost at the collegiate level in the eighties, including tuition, room and board, and washing, ranged from $138 to $216. Since Franklin was still a "preacher factory" in those days, tuition for ministerial students and those preparing for missionary service was free, and ministers' wives and children could attend at reduced rates. The school also became more coeducational during these years. Stott presented figures to the board in 1898, showing that the percentage of women in the student body had gone from twenty-nine in 1875 to forty-one in 1898.[48]

As in most colleges of that era, student life outside the classroom at Franklin revolved around the literary societies, which Stott actively nourished. A member of the Webster Literary Society as a student, he knew the value of the organizations in providing social interaction, literary opportunities, and training in public speaking and parliamentary procedure. The Periclesian, Athenian, and Webster societies had their own halls, entered into competitive debates, and held regular Friday evening meetings at which papers were read and critiqued. To Stott the literary societies were the perfect complement to the students' academic work, giving them outlets for the practice and application of what they learned in the classroom.[49] Alongside the literary groups, and also nurtured by Stott, were the Greek organizations. Phi Delta Theta, which Stott helped found

Stott surrounded by the 1898 Webster Literary Society.

in 1860, still existed, and in the 1880s and 1890s the Sigma Alpha Epsilon fraternity and the Pi Beta Phi and Alpha Gamma Alpha (later Delta Delta Delta) sororities were launched. The campus witnessed a contentious rivalry between the Greeks and the "barbarians," as the nonfraternity students were called. Yet, according to S. P. Smith, an 1878 transfer student from Wabash College, Franklin displayed a commendable "freedom from caste and special class distinctions" and the competition between Greeks and non-Greeks was an "honorable rivalry."[50]

It was the literary organizations that helped create what historian Cady called Franklin College's "final essence, . . . a group of students thinking." The fruits of the literary societies can be seen in the emergence of student declamations, orations, and theses. In its June 1881 issue, the student publication, the *Collegiate*, featured the "real oratorical revival" that was occurring on campus. "The literary societies have earnestly encouraged the cultivation of a good delivery," the editors pointed out, "while Dr. Stott has seconded their efforts by giving the rhetorical work of the entire year to the study of oratory. . . . The result is decided and gratifying." Over time, student orations given at chapel exercises, debates, or prize competitions varied in subject, and they distinctly evolved from religious and inspirational topics to a focus on history or politics to objective analysis of social and cultural issues. They also became more liberal, displaying a growing independence of thought. As Cady notes, the students jumped ahead of their professors in their viewpoints. Whereas the conservative Stott preferred to stress "personal morality and good citizenship," the undergraduates sought to address the need for change in society. The Social Gospel had come to Franklin. Other outgrowths of the literary societies were the extensive student journalistic productions that blossomed during Stott's administration. Four successive student newspapers emerged—*Collegiate*, *Clarion*, *Kodak*, and *Franklin*—each of which from time to time espoused progressive ideas.[51]

Whether he agreed with the conclusions students arrived at in their thinking, their growth and well-being remained Stott's foremost concern. As already seen, he commanded respect as a teacher and role model, in large part because he treated them as adults. When George Zoda, the janitor at the school, told Edgar Daugherty that "when a man has completed the college course he knows something," the lad decided to visit the campus. In early September 1892, he went to Stott's office and expressed his interest in becoming a student. The president asked, "What would you like to study, Mr. Daugherty?" The teenager was impressed. "It was the first time anybody had ever addressed me as 'Mister Daugherty'—and 'twas quite a lift toward the maturity of which a boy dreams." Daugherty was not alone. Even when his duty required Stott to enforce discipline, he did so in a manner that evoked respect. Branigin said that Stott "could inflict punishment in fewer words at the chapel exercises or in a heart-to-heart talk than any instructor" he had ever known. Further, the president's personality was "so strong . . . and so kindly his reproof that the delinquent student, though not always repentant, loved him as a man and respected his authority."[52]

Naturally Stott preferred moments when he could tell the board, "The grades for the year have been good and the cases for discipline have been few," or "We have been unusually free from aimless students and those of low tastes." There were, nonetheless, pranks played, alcohol consumed, and rules violated—all of which required him to be the disciplinarian. There were instances of movable property being displaced, the college bell ringing in the middle of the night, buckets of water being set above doors, or students playing tricks on professors. Often Stott ignored such incidents, thus minimizing them. When someone burned "Petersburg," the men's privy, the torching sparked a noisy rally and debate over what to name the outhouse's replacement, which ended only when the town marshal appeared. "Dr. Stott made some humorous comments on the affair in chapel," noted Kennedy, "deftly ribbing the participants for their boyishness, and that was all." Yet, no further episodes occurred.[53] More difficult to manage were individual cases of misconduct in which Stott had to be, in Branigin's words, "chief executioner." In 1883 a Mr. Todd received indefinite suspension for at least a year for "a generally demoralizing influence in the institution," particularly charges of obscenity and profanity. Several students that same year faced the same punishment for visiting saloons and cutting classes or examinations without excuses. In 1884 one student was suspended for "self abuse and pederasty" and another for visiting the ladies rooms "contrary to rules." But the worst case for Stott personally came in 1891 when someone reported that the Hercules Tennis Club was dancing and playing cards at the Overstreet House near the campus. Among the offenders was the president's son, Wilfred. The verdict for *all* involved: placement on probation with the understanding that any repetition of the offense would result in immediate expulsion.[54]

Ironically, Stott discovered that pranks and general misconduct reduced dramatically when the college developed a program about which he initially had grave reservations: athletics. Sports emerged later at Franklin than at other Hoosier colleges, in part because of resistance from college officials, including the president. Yet, as early as 1881, a call for the introduction of "physical culture" on campus appeared in the *Collegiate*. A writer identified only as "W. C. T." asserted that three elements were necessary for the full development of a student: training in morals, intellect, and "bodily strength." Although Franklin had "made creditable attainments with respect to moral and intellectual culture," physical training had been neglected. Except for some who may saw wood, walk to the post office downtown daily, or swing "Indian clubs" when the weather was nice, there was no systematic, regular exercise built into the students' lives. W. C. T. then made a striking point: "[I]f some of the time which is now spent dawdling over lessons were given to regular exercise, students would spend the remaining time in intense study, which would soon tell upon their recitations."[55]

Although games and sports did not develop in direct response to this editorial plea, the 1880s witnessed concerted efforts to make athletics a part of the college scene. In 1886 a student "Athletic Club" petitioned the Board "for the right to level the south end of the campus" for sports activities, namely "Field Days." The board refused to grant any funds for that purpose, but the field was leveled and such events became a regular aspect of campus life in the next few years. Soon after the 1886 founding of the Indianapolis Athletic Club, Franklin joined the football league and played games against Butler, Wabash, Hanover, and Indiana University, though always at home. The faculty had outlawed away games for fear of "trouble" on the road.[56]

With the coming of the 1890s, more clubs and teams arose, such as the tennis squad and the Rialto Cycle Club. When Stott Hall was being built, students clamored for the inclusion of a gymnasium in the new structure. They got their wish. Its musty basement featured workout areas with rudimentary apparatus for both sexes, along with attached dressing rooms, the use of all the facilities to be supervised by the faculty. Still,

there was some opposition from authorities. When Wallace, a true champion of physical culture, met with Stott in December 1898 about making
gymnasium training a requirement for students, he left disappointed.
Wallace wrote to Will Everson, the instructor in the program, saying he
had "failed to get the Dr. convinced of the feasibility of making the work
compulsory at present," though the president was "in favor of the students taking it" and would encourage them to do so. And, when the *Blue
and Gold* wanted to place a picture of the gym in that year's publication, it
instead left the page blank except for the words, "Photograph of Gentlemen's Gymnasium Suppressed by the Authorities."[57]

Athletics prevailed, however. By Stott's retirement in 1905, Franklin
had a full complement of sporting events, including basketball—begun
that year, thus making the school a truly *Hoosier* institution. The final
thrust toward a complete athletics program came in 1897 when the board
approved the formation of the Franklin College Athletic Park Association,
with the understanding that "ultimate and final power to control, regu-
late, and govern athletics rests with the Board of Directors." On campus,
though, a standing committee of faculty and students oversaw all activities. Stott's only input was to insist that the athletic field should be fenced
and that all sports should be "free from bad language." The field would
be named in honor of Goodell, the leading faculty advocate for athletics.
Around the same time, Wallace proceeded to establish a lecture series by
eminent experts on "our physical well-being." The shouts of "Franklin!
Franklin! Rah! Rah! Rah!" now resounded across campus, and Blue and
Gold became the college's official colors, thanks to athletics. At one point,
the board voted to put a ribbon of each hue in the case displaying Stott's
Civil War sword. Something of Stott's was now graced with the symbols of
Franklin College athletics.[58]

Given Stott's adherence to duty, it is no surprise that he would readily
accept opportunities to serve in church and community affairs well beyond his responsibilities as college president. Besides his dedicated service
to the Indiana Baptist Convention as its president, its leading advocate
for education, and the associate editor of the *Baptist Outlook,* he was also
the person who, above all others, the Convention sought for "wisdom and
counsel." One of the founders of the National Baptist Education Society

at Washington, D.C., in 1888, he was likewise prominent in the church at the national level. He was, moreover, the historian of the Indiana Baptist community. In 1908, while in retirement, he wrote *Indiana Baptist History*, the first authoritative study of the Baptist experience in the state. A reviewer hailed Stott as "pre-eminently the man to have written" the book and lauded the balance of the account. Stott had revealed, largely from "first-hand information," the "sturdiness, zeal, and heroism" of the early Baptists, on the one hand, and their "narrowness and intolerance of opinion" on the other—a rare accomplishment for an author whose own involvement in the church's story was so personal. Stott's commitment to his local church was equally impressive. He wrote an insightful and remarkably candid history of the first fifty years of Franklin's First Baptist Church for the *Franklin Jeffersonian* in August 1882. At the same time, he served with his friend Wallace on a committee to direct the building of the church's new edifice at the corner of Jefferson and Home streets. On Thursday, June 16, 1887, the first service held in the structure was the college's commencement, and Stott delivered "the first words from the new pulpit."[59]

Active in the Republican Party, Stott was a city councilman from 1892 to 1896, representing Franklin's First Ward. Though little is known of his work in that post, he was elected to it by the largest majority on record, and his devotion to his party was unquestioned, as an incident during the presidential campaign of 1896 demonstrates. A principal issue in that contest was the Republican support of the gold standard against the Democrats' plea for free silver. GOP candidate William McKinley's front-porch campaign hailed gold, but Democrat William Jennings Bryan passionately called upon Americans not to "crucify mankind upon a cross of gold." That October junior student Chloe Wood brought Stott a gift from her mother's orchard on Monroe Street, just west of the campus. Stott sent a note thanking Mrs. Wood for the "public pears," but cautioned her to not say much about the transaction till *after election*," for fear it might lose votes for the GOP. Yet, he went on, "One thing that pleases me about the pears you sent—they have a *gold* tinge."[60] Another sign of Stott's allegiance to his party, along with his pronounced patriotism, was his membership in the Grand Army of the Republic, the foremost organization of Union veterans and a bulwark of the Republican Party. He belonged to Wadsworth Post Number 127 in Franklin after its founding in 1882 and served at the state level as Department Commander of the GAR. Stott's stature among his fellow veterans led to his selection to deliver the invocation and benediction at the dedication of the Indiana monuments and markers at the Vicksburg National Military Park on December 29, 1908. In the invocation, Stott struck a conciliatory tone. "As we gather today to dedicate these monuments to the memory of our comrades who gave their lives that the Republic might live," he implored God, "do Thou bless us, and help us to resolve upon a deeper devotion to the welfare of our common country, so that these dead may not have died in vain." His hope was that the whole country may "join to make this nation one whose God is Jehovah and whose task is to carry the light and truth to all the nations of the earth."[61]

While it is clear that Stott, in today's terminology, was a "workaholic," driven by his sense of duty to college, church, and community, his love and devotion to his family never wavered. Despite his heavy work schedule, he dedicated a portion of every day to homeschooling his children in his office at the college and, according to family sources, he did so by himself. Also, during his presidency a number of his closest kin came to the Franklin area. His parents, "Uncle John and Aunt Lizzie," left North Vernon in 1885 for the Hopewell region near Franklin. His sister and brother-in-law, Martha and Maxa Moncrief, moved to Franklin in 1879, and another sister, Mary, lived with them beginning in 1885. Jenny, Stott's youngest sibling, taught a private school in the town and died there in 1894. Grace and Clarke Parker, the Stotts's daughter and son-in-law, returned to Johnson County, where Clarke served as principal of Franklin High School. Evidently, the last major family event to take place in the Vernon vicinity was "Aunt Lizzie's" seventy-second birthday on September 16, 1883. She and "Uncle John" had gone to the Sabbath service at Butlerville the day before, stayed there that night, and returned home the next day to a "house chuck full of friends," including some who had raced from Butlerville to get to the Stott home before the Stotts did. After a "sumptuous dinner," Stott's mother was so moved she could not speak, a guest wrote for the *Indiana Baptist*, "but the tears that filled her eyes spoke more of love and appreciation than words could have done." The reporter then added, "We feel that with such ancestry President Stott could not, without violating every principle of nature, be otherwise than what he is—a good man, and a blessing to the race."[62]

Yet, not all seemed blessed in the marriage of Will and Arabella. Maybe the shadow of Rossiter still hovered over it from time to time, or perhaps Will's illnesses were progressing and making him highly sensitive, for he confessed to feeling unappreciated by his wife. His emotions flowed freely in his letters home while on his 1894 trip to Europe and the Holy Land—the only such communications still available from his pen. While most centered on the sites he saw, in one missive from London in September he "opened out" to Bel about their relationship. He insisted, in the first place, that his college duties never "weaned me from home. I haven't been so busy that I could not spend an hour or so after meals (especially during dinner and supper)." And yet,

> Many a time . . . I have gone to my room and found something to do for I felt that there was no other place for me. Almost all our married life, as it now seems to me, your attitude toward me has been one of antagonism. You have set up your judgement against mine, almost as a matter of course. It seemed impossible for anything I did to be right. You have quickly and constantly let the children know that of course I was wrong in my tastes and in my judgements and in my whole make up. . . . And so it has seemed to me you are determined to keep the attitude I speak of.

As for the rest of the family, Will wrote, "I have loved my children as much as any father ever did. I know you don't think so. But I know that I love them with all my heart." Will spoke of the tension that sometimes arose between him and Bel, such as his wish for more affection and for family worship, the latter of which Bel rejected. But the fact remained, he professed, "I can truly say that I have never ceased to love you." True, he pulled himself away when she antagonized him, but "A few strokes of your hand over my face would have turned 'darkness into joy'—and it would do so now."[63]

That Will's love for Bel and the children was genuine is clear from other letters of that time. He admitted to Bel that "Wilfred has almost broken my heart—and yet I do love him." Should his oldest son, whose frequent rejection of right for wrong had hurt his father, "truly repented," Will declared, "I should love him as I did when he was an affectionate and truthful little boy—and I have told him so." One can only imagine the joyful feelings Will must have had when Wilfred wrote him seventeen years later to announce his marriage to Margaret Kellogg, and added, "If I ever do get squared away in the right direction I shall have you to thank for it almost alone. . . . But I thank you for all you have done and thought. I love you very much my father." In his letters of 1894 to his daughters Grace and Edith, Stott encouraged them both in their college work, asked "Ede" if she had joined the Webster Society yet, and chided Grace about being "a big librarian." In writing both girls and "Little Roy" (Roscoe), he reminded them to "help Mama all you can." In one poignant plea, possibly anticipating that his health would deteriorate, he told Grace and Ede: "When I get home help me all you can for my work will be done in the next ten years and I ought to be very useful till then."[64]

When one considers the state of Stott's health during his entire presidency, his achievements seem even more remarkable. Twice the college board granted him paid leaves of absence so that he could recuperate sufficiently to resume his duties with full energy. In March 1885, the board gave him a leave "on account of ill health," and in June allotted him the time and expenses to go "to the woods of Michigan and other secluded place of rest and quiet in the North." In thanking its members, Stott promised to resume work in September and "put into it all the earnestness and devotion at my command." Just before Christmas, 1897, Stott's condition declined to the point that the board resolved that he "should remain away as long as is needed in the Judgment of himself and his Physician for the complete restoration of his health."[65]

A perusal of Stott's voluminous pension file offers some indication of the nature of his illnesses. According to the Federal Pension statute of 1862 and the Pension Arrears Act of 1879, when applying for an Invalid Army Pension, a Union veteran had to prove sickness or disability directly resulting from his military service—especially a condition that made him incapable of performing manual labor. It was under the latter legislation that Stott first requested an increase in pension in July 1888. His pension files are replete with affidavits and other testimonies to his physical condition from physicians, soldiers who served with him, colleagues at the college, and his brother-in-law, Moncrief. These witnesses testified that he suffered chronic diarrhea and disease of the rectum; debility of the stomach, liver, spleen, and nerves, due to malarial poisoning; and rheumatism and disease of the respiratory organs—all stemming from his illnesses in Missouri and Louisiana in wartime. They further stated that he was unable to do physical work. Though rejected by the Pension Bureau twice for "inadequate evidence," Stott's claim was finally accepted in February 1903 and his increase in pension granted by Congress on June 6, 1906.[66]

The steady impairment of his physical abilities, and his own independent judgment that it was time to make way for a younger and more vigorous leader, prompted Stott to submit his resignation as president on June 15, 1904. He stayed one more academic year to allow ample time for the board to search for his successor. Even that extension, however, seemed in doubt by December. Stott reported by letter on the twenty-first that he had "been sick most of the term," and the board expressed "the regret of his illness and high hopes . . . that he will soon be able to be out again." The next month, Professor Elmer B. Bryan of Indiana University's Department of Education accepted the call to be the college's new executive, and on June 14, 1905, the retiring president delivered his final report. He thanked the board for its "confidence and cooperation through all the years" and expressed his belief "that what has thus far been done for Christian education here will prove but the foretaste of the greater and better things that are to be wrought in the future." On the same day, the college bestowed upon him the honorary degree of Doctor of Laws, and Stott remained on the faculty as president emeritus for life.[67]

The early years of Stott's retirement were restful and productive. He enjoyed his home at 847 East Jefferson Street, began work on his history of Indiana Baptists, and spent summertime with Bel, their children, and grandchildren at their getaway cottage at Pine Lake in La Porte, Indiana. Will's health improved enough that he could participate in church and community affairs, and Bel spent many hours at her art studio above their son Roscoe's insurance office in downtown Franklin, within walking distance from their home. Bel, one relative recalled, "was quite a girl," still painting daily. And a granddaughter, who "loved every move" Bel made, remembered her cooking. "She could make the best meringues and bow-knot doughnuts I ever ate," Eleanor Parker Van Cleave said. "She made potato chips before you could buy them. I was happier with Gram than with anybody else in the world." Van Cleave also recalled her moments with her "Gramp" at Pine Lake, the Baptist retreat site that he had helped select years before and upon which he had the Stott cottage built as a surprise for Bel. It was a "double-decker . . . with a porch on two sides, both up and down." There, along the lake and among the woods and hills, Van Cleave and her Gramp walked together. He pointed to things with his cane as he limped along, and then they would return to the cottage where Van Cleave sat on his lap, combing and braiding his bushy white beard. "He was very particular about it," she remembered, and he liked her to brush it "after he had washed it." At Pine Lake Will enjoyed his family, the beauty around him, and the rocker under him.[68]

In late 1907, though, duty called again. Stott's GAR comrades enlisted him to become the new superintendent of the Indiana Soldiers' and Sailors' Children's Home at Knightstown. Founded in the summer of 1865 as the State Soldier's Home in Indianapolis, it moved to a fifty-four acre plot of land at Knightstown Springs in 1866 and began caring for orphans in 1867, while still tending to sick and disabled veterans and their widows. In 1887 the GAR became the major force in renovating the home and providing its trustees and superintendents. Seventy-one-year-old Stott arrived with Bel at the home on January 21, 1908. Together they coordinated the educational department and, interestingly, launched "a more formal recreational program" (athletics, again). Bel served as matron, and they lived, Van Cleave recalled, in "a series of rooms in the

Stott poses with teachers at the Indiana Soldiers' and Sailors' Children's Home at Knightstown.

main building"—"big old Victorian rooms with massive furniture." Their schedule was filled with "Alumni meetings, school operettas, ice cream festivals, lawn entertainment and band trips to GAR state and national conventions." It was a busy retirement for Will, but both he and Bel loved it. The "Centennial Souvenir" of the home features a photograph of Stott surrounded by a group of teachers. He stands with his arms folded across his gray suit, one leg before the other, looking quite dapper and self-confident, and there is a mischievous look on his face and a twinkle in his eye—a throwback to his rascally boyhood days in Jennings County. Stott was still enjoying himself.[69]

In May 1911, the Stotts left Knightstown and moved back into their house on Jefferson Street in Franklin. While no records of this period are extant, and thus little is known of Stott's activities, there is little doubt that, living just a block from the college campus, he spent many days, while still in decent health, visiting colleagues, students, and other friends of the school. In May 1918, Will and Bel celebrated their Golden Wedding Anniversary. At the modest festivities, their son Roscoe—the poet laureate of the family and the college, who wrote the lyrics to its song, "Hail to Franklin!"—described his father as "of the Daniel Boone breed." "He rose from among his people," Roscoe said, "to be a real tower of strength to his denomination . . . . He was born a fighter. Whatever he believed in he fought for."[70]

But there was little fight left in Stott anymore, as his debilitated appearance reflected that day. His health worsened rapidly in the next few months, and in the last three weeks of October, as he lay confined to his bed, all hopes for his recovery were abandoned. On November 1, 1918, the *Franklin Evening Star* announced on its front page: "Dr. W. T. Stott died this morning at 9:30 o'clock at his home on Jefferson Street." The article, headlined "Death of Johnson County's 'Grand Old Man,'" reported that his family surrounded him as "the end came peacefully." It came, however, at an inopportune time for a public memorial service. Franklin, along with much of the nation, was in the throes of a deadly influenza epidemic, and public gatherings had been banned. Though no public funeral could be held, the *Franklin Democrat* reported that "a constant stream of citizens visited the home" on the days prior to the private service held at the house on Monday, November 4. Reverend Robert Homer Kent, pastor of First Baptist Church and member of the college faculty, presided at the "simple, but impressive" event, and a number of speakers paid tribute to Stott, whom the *Baptist Observer* called the "Grand Old Baptist of Indiana." Doctor Elijah A. Hanley, former president of Franklin College reminded the mourners that Stott was "a humble servant of God" and "above all else a teacher . . . whose glory shone in the classroom" and whose legacy was one of "spiritual and intellectual father" for hundreds of students. Following the service, the Student Army Training Corps stationed on the college campus escorted the body in a long procession to Greenlawn Cemetery. "The soldierly bearing of the young soldiers was especially remarked," the *Evening Star* noted. Joining the uniformed students were Stott's wartime comrades and members of the GAR as honorary casket bearers, along with representatives of the college. A large crowd assembled at the cemetery and, fittingly, the Franklin College bell tolled at the conclusion of the graveside ceremony. William Taylor Stott now rested beside his parents.[71]

Tributes poured in from across the state and nation. From November through January, the *Baptist Observer* ran columns of letters, poems, and other expressions of admiration from students, colleagues, and friends. The twentieth edition of the *Franklin Almanack*, however, would probably have meant the most to Stott. Dedicated to his memory, the yearbook

contained a tribute from his close colleague and friend, Hall. Labeling Stott "A Hoosier of the Hoosiers," for whom "the college was the embodiment of his life," Hall added: "His monument is imperishable, the college and the men and women who, in their youth, partook of his abundant life." And the students themselves spoke of "The Grand Old Man of Franklin" who, doing his duty, "for thirty-three years . . . guided the destiny of the institution." How appropriate it was, then, that among Stott's last words were, "Tell all the old students good-bye."[72]

The Grand Old Man of Franklin College.

THE FRANKLIN ALMANACK–TWENTY (FRANKLIN, IN: FRANKLIN COLLEGE, 1920)

Abbreviations

ACWRD	American Civil War Research Database, Historical Data Systems, Duxbury, Massachusetts www.civilwardata.com
AGI	W. H. H. Terrell, *Report of the Adjutant General of the State of Indiana*, 8 vols. (Indianapolis: W. R. Holloway, State Printer, 1865–69)
DAB	Allen Johnson and Dumas Malone, eds. *Dictionary of American Biography*, 10 vols. (New York: Scribner's Sons, 1927–36)
FC Minutes	Franklin College Board of Directors Minutes, 3 Books, Business Office, Franklin College
IHS	Indiana Historical Society, Indianapolis
ISL	Indiana State Library, Indianapolis
Jubilee	*First Half Century of Franklin College, Jubilee Exercises* (Cincinnati: Journal and Messenger, 1884)
MOLLUS	*Papers of the Military Order of the Loyal Legion of the United States*
NARA	National Archives and Records Administration, Washington D.C.
NUC, Pre-1956	*National Union Catalog, Pre-1956 Imprints*
OR	U.S. War Department, *The War of the Rebellion: A Compilation of the Official Records of the Union and Confederate Armies,* 128 vols. (Washington, D.C.: Government Printing Office, 1880–1901). All citations are from Series 1.
PRNMP	Pea Ridge National Military Park, Pea Ridge, AR
SCFC	Special Collections, Franklin College, Franklin, IN
ULL	University of Louisiana, Lafayette, Dupree Library Archives
USAMHI	U.S. Army Military History Institute, Carlisle Barracks, PA
USF	University of South Florida, Tampa, Library
VNMP	Vicksburg National Military Park, Archives, Vicksburg, MS
WHMC, Rolla	Western Historical Manuscripts Collection, University of Missouri, Rolla

Notes

CHAPTER 1

1. Alice Ann Bundy, *A Glimpse of Pioneer Life in Jennings County* (Vernon, IN: Jennings County Preservation Association, 1992), 87; *Minutes of the 39th Anniversary of the Madison Baptist Association* (Madison, IN: Courier Steam Printing, 1867), 8, in Moncrief Family Papers in possession of Calvin D. Davis, PhD, Greensburg, IN; Phyllis Hurley and Mischell Ferguson, *The Way They Were: Jennings County, Indiana* (n.p., 1995), 26; R. Carlyle Buley, *The Old Northwest: Pioneer Period, 1815–1840*, 2 vols. (Bloomington: Indiana University Press, 1950), 1:336. For brief discussions of the origin and early settlement of Jennings County, see Malcolm Deputy, *"The Land of Winding Waters"* (Montezuma, IN: Wabash Valley Press, 1963), 1–3; Bundy, *Glimpse of Pioneer Life in Jennings County*, 5–8; *History of Jennings County* (1956; reprint, Evansville, IN: Unigraphic, 1979), 89–90 (hereafter cited as *History of Jennings County* [1956]).

2. *Hoosier Journal of Ancestry: Jennings County* (Little York, IN: n.p., n.d.), 149; I. George Blake, *Finding a Way through the Wilderness: The Indiana Baptist Convention, 1833–1985* (Indianapolis: Central Publishing, 1983), 162.

3. Grace Vawter Bicknell, *The Vawter Family in America* (Indianapolis: Hollenbeck Press, 1905; reprint, Atlanta: Thorpe and Associates, 1969), 72; *Hoosier Journal of Ancestry*, 149; Bundy, *Glimpse of Pioneer Life in Jennings County*, 33; William T. Stott, *Indiana Baptist History, 1798–1908* (W. T. Stott, 1908), 80.

4. The Lard quote appears in Deputy, *"Land of Winding Waters,"* 8. See also Stott, *Indiana Baptist History*, 80.

5. Blake, *Finding a Way through the Wilderness*, 16; Deputy, *"Land of Winding Waters,"* 3; *Hoosier Journal of Ancestry*, 149–50.

6. Bundy, *Glimpse of Pioneer Life in Jennings County*, 33; *Minutes of the 39th Anniversary of the Madison Baptist Association*, 6; Lois S. Ammerman, April Nicole Compton, and Meredith Ertel, *Reminiscences of Vernon: Stories of the Early Days of Vernon, Indiana* (Vernon, IN: Jennings County Historical Society, 2002), 33; *History of Jennings County: Jennings County, Indiana, 1816–1999* (Vernon, IN: Jennings County Historical Society, 1999), 20 (hereafter cited as *History of Jennings County* [1999]).

7. *History of Jennings County* (1956), 90, 116; *History of Jennings County* (1999), 20; Ammerman et al., *Reminiscences of Vernon*, 38. The school's first teacher was Joel Butler, the grandfather of Ovid Butler, the founder of Butler University. See *History of Jennings County* (1999), 111; Barbara Butler Davis, ed., *Affectionately Yours: The Civil War Home-Front Letters of the Ovid Butler Family* (Indianapolis: Indiana Historical Society Press, 2004), 152–53.

8. Deputy, *"Land of Winding Waters,"* 9, 11; *History of Jennings County* (1999), 105–6, 320; Bicknell, *Vawter Family in America*, 243.

9. Ammerman et al., *Reminiscences of Vernon*, 30–31; *History of Jennings County* (1999), 105.

10. Deputy, *"Land of Winding Waters,"* 18; Ammerman et al., *Reminiscences of Vernon*, 37; *History of Jennings County* (1999), 20, 105.

11. Bicknell, *Vawter Family in America*, 75–76.

12. Ibid., 76–77; *History of Jennings County* (1999), 320.

13. *History of Jennings County* (1956), 6; *History of Jennings County* (1999), 116; Bicknell, *Vawter Family in America*, 83, 104. For a detailed account of Zoar Church, which later became North Vernon Baptist Church, see Blake, *Finding a Way through the Wilderness*, 178–80. It is noteworthy that William Vawter was also an early supporter of Franklin College. Two of his sons, Achilles J. and Philemon C., became students there, with Achilles briefly holding a faculty position. William Vawter wrote three wills, in the second of which he bequeathed funds to the college. See Stott, *Indiana Baptist History*, 236, and Bicknell, *Vawter Family in America*, 85.

14. Stott, *Indiana Baptist History*, 165. See also *Minutes, 39th Anniversary, Madison Baptist Association*, 7; *Hoosier Journal of Ancestry*, 147; handwritten biography of W. T. Stott, Grinstead Papers, W. T. Stott Presidential Papers, 1874–1965, SCFC (hereafter cited as Stott biography). The latter source incorrectly identifies William Taylor Stott as Will's father rather than his grandfather. Its information on Stott is otherwise accurate. Some confusion abounds among historians, who assume the two men were "Senior" and "Junior."

15. *Hoosier Journal of Ancestry*, 139, 147; *History of Jennings County* (1999); *History of Jennings County* (1956), 5; Stott, *Indiana Baptist History*, 165.

16. *Minutes of the 39th Anniversary of the Madison Baptist Association*, 7; Stott, *Indiana Baptist History*, 166; Stott biography; *History of Jennings County* (1999), 43; 1860 U.S. census—Indiana, microfilm, Roll 271, p. 146, ISL.

17. Bicknell, *Vawter Family in America*, 105; Hurley and Ferguson, *Way They Were*, 26; Stott, *Indiana Baptist History*, 238.

18. Bicknell, *Vawter Family in America*, 104–15.

19. Deputy, *"Land of Winding Waters,"* 9; Bicknell, *Vawter Family in America*, 106–8; Stott, *Indiana Baptist History*, 238–39. It should be noted that the censuses of 1850 and 1860 both list the fourth Stott child as "Mariah T." See 1850 U.S. Census—Indiana (no page number) and 1860 U.S. Census—Indiana, 146. This creates a great mystery: Who is Jennie M. Stott? Bicknell, *Vawter Family in America*, indicates on page 105 that John and Elizabeth's last child was "Maria Jane," but in her biographical accounts of the children on 106–8, Bicknell gives a brief account of "Jennie M." and omits "Maria Jane." This editor's conclusion is that "Jennie" was the family name for "Mariah T." or "Maria Jane," since the birth dates and ages of the latter two in the census records are the same as that of "Jennie M." in Bicknell's account. The "M." could refer to "Mariah" or "Maria," and Stott, in his wartime diary and later writings, only refers to a sister named "Jennie."

20. The "Hardshell Baptist" quote is in a brief anonymous and undated biography of William Taylor Stott, the younger, by one of his grandchildren in Stott Family Papers in possession of the editor, courtesy of Rosemary Laycock and Frances Killpatrick. See also John F. Cady, *The Baptist Church in Indiana* (Franklin, IN: Franklin College, 1942), 31; Blake, *Finding a Way through the Wilderness*, 27. For a thorough treatment of the antimission and antieducation dispute see Cady, *Baptist Church in Indiana*, 31–63. See also Stott, *Indiana Baptist History*, 1–60, and Blake, *Finding a Way through the Wilderness*, 19–30.

21. Cady, *Baptist Church in Indiana*, 45; Stott, *Indiana Baptist History*, 235–36; Bicknell, *Vawter Family in America*, 85.

22. John F. Cady, *The Centennial History of Franklin College* (Franklin, IN: Franklin College, 1934), 22; Blake, *Finding a Way through the Wilderness*, 59.

23. Cady, *Baptist Church in Indiana*, 181, 184–92, 195; Stott, *Indiana Baptist History*, 159–60. The Vernon church, in fact, declared against slavery at its founding in 1816. See *History of Jennings County* (1956), 2.

24. Harrison Burns, *Personal Recollections of Harrison Burns* (Indianapolis: Indiana Historical Society, 1975), 26; Bundy, *Glimpse of Pioneer Life in Jennings County*, 33; Ammerman et al., *Reminiscences of Vernon*, 26.

25. *History of Jennings County* (1999), 116; *History of Jennings County* (1956), 6; Bicknell, *Vawter Family in America*, 108; Cady, *Baptist Church in Indiana*, 137. An excellent brief account of Zoar's history may be found in Blake, *Finding a Way through the Wilderness*, 178–80.

26. *History of Jennings County* (1956), 2; *History of Jennings County* (1999), 129; Blake, *Finding a Way through the Wilderness*, 165; Ammerman et al., *Reminiscences of Vernon*, 4, 26.

27. Ammerman et al., *Reminiscences of Vernon*, 26; *History of Jennings County* (1956), 2; Blake, *Finding a Way through the Wilderness*, 165–66; Bicknell, *Vawter Family in America*, 106.

28. David Demaree Banta, *History of Johnson County, Indiana* (Chicago: Brant and Fuller, 1888), 26; *History of Jennings County* (1956), 2; brief undated biography of W. T. Stott by one of his granddaughters in Stott Family Papers, in possession of the editor (hereafter cited as undated Stott biography). The description of the Stott tannery appears in Bundy, *Glimpse of Pioneer Life in Jennings County*, 23.

29. The Burns observation is in Bicknell, *Vawter Family in America*, 79. See also Buley, *Old Northwest*, 1:232–33.

30. The Burns quote is in Bicknell, *Vawter Family in America*, 79.

31. Burns, *Personal Recollections*, 15-18, 24. Harrison's mother was Maria Vawter, the oldest child of William and Frances and sister of Elizabeth Vawter Stott. She married Maxa M. Burns in December 1826, at age seventeen, had nine children, and died in 1846 at thirty-seven years of age. See Bicknell, *Vawter Family in America*, 90, 96.

32. *History of Jennings County* (1999), 110; Burns, *Personal Recollections*, 25; Bundy, *Glimpse of Pioneer Life in Jennings County*, 37.

33. Burns, *Personal Recollections*, 28; Ammerman et al., *Reminiscences of Vernon*, 28; Buley, *Old Northwest*, 1:371.

34. *History of Jennings County* (1999), 108, 110; *History of Jennings County* (1956), 118; Bundy, *Glimpse of Pioneer Life in Jennings County*, 83, 87–88.

35. *History of Jennings County* (1999), 4, 15; Bicknell, *Vawter Family in America*, 63; Ammerman et al., *Reminiscences of Vernon*, 3, 35.

36. W. T. Stott to Mag and Mattie Stout, March 29, 1862, Martha Stout Papers of the Stout-Jacques Families, 1834–1936, IHS. Mullein is an herb related to snapdragons with a fuzzy, woolly texture.

37. Hurley and Ferguson, *Way They Were*, 43–44.

38. *History of Jennings County* (1999), 18–19, 111; Robert M. Taylor, ed., *The Northwest Ordinance, 1787: A Bicentennial Handbook* (Indianapolis: Indiana Historical Society, 1987), 61–65; Buley, *Old Northwest*, 2:326–27; Bundy, *Glimpse of Pioneer Life in Jennings County*, 54–55.

39. Bundy, *Glimpse of Pioneer Life in Jennings County*, 49–50, 53; Ammerman et al., *Reminiscences of Vernon*, 13. For a complete, detailed account of education in the county during these years, see Bundy, *Glimpse of Pioneer Life in Jennings County*, 48–63.

40. Banta, *History of Johnson County*, 659; Elba L. Branigin, *History of Johnson County, Indiana* (Indianapolis: B. F. Bowen and Company, 1913), 597.

41. Bundy, *Glimpse of Pioneer Life in Jennings County*, 56; *Vernon Journal* cited in Ammerman et al., *Reminiscences of Vernon*, 40–41.

42. P. C. Vawter to W. T. Stott, July 4, 1883, in *Alumni Letter Book, 1883–1884*, Franklin College Collection, SCFC. See also Bicknell, *Vawter Family in America*, 40–41.

43. *Vernon Journal*, July 25, 1902, cited in Ammerman, et al., *Reminiscences of Vernon*, 41; Barnett Wallace, "A History of Franklin, Indiana, Especially Jefferson Street," typescript, 1923, ISL, 51.

44. Branigin, *History of Johnson County*, 597; William T. Stott to Carrie Morrison, May 6, 1860, Carrie Morrison Correspondence, SCFC.

45. W. N. Wyeth, "Founders of Franklin College," in *Jubilee*, 23.

46. Minutes of the June 5, 1834, meeting of the Indiana Baptist Education Society, Franklin College History Collection, Box 4, SCFC. For more on the founding of Franklin College and its early years, see Cady, *Franklin College*, 9–44; *Jubilee*, 7–27; Barnett Wallace, "Sketches Concerning the Early History of Franklin College (to 1904)," SCFC.

47. "Constitution for a Baptist Literary Institution for the State of Indiana," handwritten copy, Franklin College History Collection, Box 4, SCFC. See also minutes and publications of the Indiana Baptist Education Society, and Minutes of the Indiana Baptist General Association, 1833–1862, ibid.

48. Cady, *Franklin College*, 30–44; *Jubilee*, 35, 67.

49. *Franklin College*, 48; *Catalogue of the Officers and Students of Franklin College, 1856 and 1857* (Indianapolis: Indianapolis Journal, 1857), 13–16.

50. Blake, *Finding a Way through the Wilderness*, 51; *Jubilee*, 37; Cady, *Franklin College*, 50–53. Interestingly, Chandler Hall stands on the very ground where the founders of the town of Franklin camped in the spring of 1823 when they chose the land as the location for their new settlement. See Banta, *History of Johnson County*, 310; Branigin, *History of Johnson County*, 175–76.

51. W. T. Stott, "History of Fifty Years of the First Baptist Church of Franklin, Indiana," *Franklin Jeffersonian*, August 31, 1882, p. 16, typescript reprint, Historical Room, Johnson County Public Library, Franklin, IN.

52. Blake, *Finding a Way through the Wilderness*, 51–52, 61–62. Just how drastically enrollment fell in the interim years of 1849–52 is uncertain. Hougham reported to the college board that the attendance was at seventy in the second session of the 1850–51 academic year. On May 10, 1851, student Merryman George told a friend that he thought there were "not more than about 40 or 50 at the outside. Yet there is enough of us to keep things pretty lively." See "Report of the Acting President," Franklin College History Collection, Box 1, SCFC; Merryman George to J. R. Holston, May 10, 1851, ibid.

53. Cady, *Franklin College*, 66–67; quotations are in Henry Day, "Memorial Sermon," in *Memorial Volume of Dr. Silas Bailey, D.D., LL.D.* (Lafayette, IN: Spring and Robertson, 1876), 37; Wallace, "Sketches Concerning the Early History of Franklin College," 24–27.

54. Day, "Memorial Sermon," 28; Cady, *Franklin College*, 67. See also W. N. Wyeth, "Memorial Tribute: Impression of a Student," in *Memorial Volume of Dr. Silas Bailey*, 47–53.

55. Cady, *Franklin College*, 74–75; W. T. Stott, "Memorial Tribute," in *Memorial Volume of Dr. Silas Bailey*, 44; Day, "Memorial Sermon," 29; J. H. Smith to W. T. Stott, January 11, 1884, *Alumni Letter Book*, SCFC. Apparently Bailey shared one characteristic with Chan-

dler. Stott observed that he once overheard Bailey's self-evaluation, in which he stated that "when he had carefully studied a proposition and reached a conclusion, Gabriel himself could not make him change his mind." See Day, "Memorial Sermon," 33.

56. W. T. Stott, *History of Franklin College: A Brief Sketch* (Indianapolis: Journal and Messenger, 1874), 9–10. This publication, in pamphlet form, contained the substance of a paper read at an educational meeting at Franklin College, July 29, 1874.

57. J. H. Smith to W. T. Stott, January 11, 1884, *Alumni Letter Book*; W. H. McCoy to W. T. Stott, February 6, 1884, ibid.

58. Barnett Wallace, "Autobiography," *Franklin Democrat*, March 16, 1923, p. 1, in Barnett Wallace, Writings, and Papers, 1897–1927, SCFC; *Catalogue . . . 1856–1857*, pp. 17, 21. The practice of boarding students in private homes was standard throughout the Midwest. See Buley, *Old Northwest*, 2:412.

59. The College *Catalogue* for 1856–1857 states that no student could attend "who has not completed his fourteenth year." To depart from this rule required special permission. See *Catalogue . . . 1856–1857*, p. 19. According to reminiscences of his associates, all evidence points to Stott having lived in Bailey Hall throughout his college career. See in particular, Wallace, "Sketches Concerning the Early History of Franklin College," 30–31.

60. *Catalogue . . . 1856–1857*, pp. 7–10, 17; Walter Havighurst, *From Six at First* (Menasha, WI: Banta Company, 1975), n.p.

61. *Catalogue . . . 1856–1857*, pp. 13–15; Cady, *Franklin College*, 68. The rigorous nature of the academic work can be seen in a report of Brumback to Bailey in 1859. "The Freshmen have read and reviewed one hundred and eleven chapters of the first book of Herodotus, and nearly two books of the *Aeneid*," Brumback wrote. "The Sophomores have read and reviewed some forty chapters of Thucydides, and two books and a half of Cicero. . . . The Juniors have read about two thirds of Demosthenes . . . and practiced daily in rendering English into Greek." See Brumback to Bailey, June 22, 1859, Franklin College History Collection, Box 2, SCFC.

62. Cady, *Franklin College*, 78; *Catalogue . . . 1856–1857*, pp. 19–20.

63. W. C. Thompson, "The Board of Directors," *Jubilee*, 39–40; "Report of Faculty," no date, Franklin College History Collection, Box 2, SCFC; Cady, *Franklin College*, 76–77.

64. *Catalogue . . . 1856–1857*, pp. 22–23.

65. Cady, *Franklin College*, 70–72.

66. Ibid., 72–74; Mary A. Medlicott, *First Baptist Church, Franklin, Indiana, History, 1837–1982* (Franklin, IN: Schumacher Printing, 1983), 6–7; Branigin, *History of Johnson County*, 342; Stott, "History of Fifty Years of the Baptist Church of Franklin," 18–19, 21; T. J. Morgan to W. T. Stott, February 18, 1884, and F. G. Lukens to W. T. Stott, no date, 1884, *Alumni Letter Book*; Faculty Report, April 1857, Franklin College History Collection, Box 2 SCFC; Report of the Committee on Education, 11, *Minutes of the Indiana Baptist General Association, 1833–1862*, SCFC. The two churches reunited in 1859 out of "a sense of duty to the cause of Christ in the community." See Stott, "History of Fifty Years of the Baptist Church of Franklin," 19.

67. Wallace, "Sketches Concerning the Early History of Franklin College," 30.

68. Ibid., 30–31.

69. William T. Stott to Carrie Morrison, May 6, 1860, Carrie Morrison Correspondence, SCFC. Miss Crain is Ginni Crain, a friend of Carrie and Will, who moved to Memphis during the next year. Several of Will's Civil War diary entries refer to his unsuccessful at-

tempts to find "Miss Crain" in Memphis while he was on furlough.

70. Ginni to Carrie, May 28, 1861, Carrie Morrison Correspondence.

71. "Program of the 23rd Commencement of Franklin College, Franklin College Miscellaneous Publications, SCFC.

72. Banta, *History of Johnson County*, 729–30.

CHAPTER 2

1. Joseph A. Parsons Jr., "Indiana and the Call for Volunteers, April, 1861," *Indiana Magazine of History* 54 (March 1958): 1–3. See also W. H. H. Terrell, *Indiana in the War of the Rebellion: Report of the Adjutant General* (Indianapolis: Indiana Historical Society, 1960, 1–4.

2. Emma Lou Thornbrough, *Indiana in the Civil War Era, 1850–1880* (Indianapolis: Indiana Historical Bureau and Indiana Historical Society, 1965), 103–4.

3. Ibid., 103. Terrell, *Indiana in the War of the Rebellion*, 5–7, 19–20; Hattie Lou Winslow and Joseph R. H. Moore, *Camp Morton, 1861–1865: Indianapolis Prisoner Camp* (Indianapolis: Indiana Historical Society, 1940), 239–40; Parsons, "Call for Volunteers," 13–14, 21.

4. The Thomas quote appears in Catharine Merrill, *The Soldier of Indiana in the War for the Union*, 2 vols. (Indianapolis: Merrill and Company, 1866), 1:142. See also Terrell, *Indiana in the War of the Rebellion*, 20. In her masterful history of Indiana during the Civil War, Emma Lou Thornbrough elaborates on the overwhelming support for the Union demonstrated by Hoosiers. She asserts that the "people of Indiana furnished manpower for the Union armies on a scale scarcely matched by any other state" and that "Indiana ranked second among all the states" in its proportion of men serving in the federal army. Thornbrough, *Indiana in the Civil War Era*, 124–26. All told, Indiana contributed 157 infantry regiments, including one unit of U.S. Colored Troops, twenty-six batteries, and thirteen cavalry regiments. See Terrell, *Indiana in the War of the Rebellion*, 151–56.

5. Merrill, *Soldier of Indiana in the War for the Union*, 135, 158; Nathaniel Cheairs Hughes Jr. and Gordon D. Whitney, *Jefferson Davis in Blue: The Life of Sherman's Relentless Warrior* (Baton Rouge: Louisiana State University Press, 2002), 49.

6. *AGI*, 2:372–89; John W. Miller, *Indianapolis Newspaper Bibliography* (Indianapolis: Indiana Historical Society, 1982), 205; Muster Roll of Capt. Jonathan H. Williams, August 16, 1861, William T. Stott Civil War Papers, 1863–1864, SCFC (hereafter cited as Stott Civil War Papers). Though the muster roll shows Stott's age as twenty-four, he had turned twenty-five the previous May.

7. Merrill, *Soldier of Indiana in the War for the Union*, 1:158; *Indianapolis State Sentinel*, September 17, 1862; Louis S. Gerteis, *Civil War St. Louis* (Lawrence: University of Kansas Press, 2001), 141–42. On the controversies surrounding Frémont's performance as the military commander in Missouri, inability to work with the state's officials and lack of responsiveness to the crisis created by the Union defeat at Wilson's Creek, see Edwin C. McReynolds, *Missouri: A History of the Crossroads State* (Norman: University of Oklahoma Press, 1962), 221–22; William E. Parrish, *A History of Missouri*, vol. 3, *1860 to 1875* (Columbia: University of Missouri Press, 1973), 27–29; William E. Parrish, *Turbulent Partnership: Missouri and the Union, 1861–1865* (Columbia: University of Missouri Press, 1963), 48–52; William Garrett Piston and Richard W. Hatcher III, *Wilson's Creek: The Second Battle of the Civil War and the Men Who Fought It* (Chapel Hill and London: University of North Carolina Press, 2000), 188, 307.

8. Harry Watts, Civil War Reminiscence, "Review of the 24th Ind. Vols.," p. 7, By a Corporal, Pro Tem., S1372, Manuscript Section, ISL; S. B. Voyles to Father, August 19, 1861, IHS; Merrill, *Soldier of Indiana in the War for the Union*, 1:162–63.

9. *Indianapolis State Sentinel*, September 17, 1862; Gilbert Denny to Father, September 10, 1861, Letters of Gilbert Denny, Eighteenth Regiment, 1861–1863, IHS (hereafter cited as Denny Letters).

10. Hughes and Whitney, *Jefferson Davis in Blue*, 51–52; James P. Jones, "Jefferson Davis in Blue: The Military Career, 1846–1866, of General Jefferson D. Davis, U.S.A." (MA thesis, University of Florida, 1954), 43–44; Gilbert Denny to Father, September 10, 1861, Denny Letters; *Indianapolis Daily State Sentinel*, September 17, 1862.

11. Hughes and Whitney, *Jefferson Davis in Blue*, 53; *OR*, 3:484 (all *OR* references are series 1); Missouri and Western Telegraph, J. B. Shanks to Col. Jeff. C. Davis, August 31, 1861, Jefferson Columbus Davis Papers, 1849–1875, L41, Manuscript Section, ISL (hereafter cited as Davis Papers).

12. *OR*, 3:466–68. The whole story of the controversy sparked by Frémont's proclamation is beyond the scope of this book. The tussle between the general and the president, along with Frémont's failure to reinforce Lexington, the displeasure of Missouri officials and other men of influence in his performance, criticism from his subordinates, and his general unfitness for command led to his dismissal in early November 1861. For fuller accounts see *OR*, 3:469–70, 477–78, 485–86, 540–49, 553–59; Allen Nevins, *Frémont: Pathfinder of the West*, vol. 2, *Frémont in the Civil War* (New York: Frederick Ungar, 1961), 529–34; Andrew Rolle, *John Charles Frémont: Character as Destiny* (Norman and London: University of Oklahoma Press, 1991), 201–10; Peter Cozzens, *General John Pope: A Life for the Nation* (Urbana and Chicago: University of Illinois Press, 2000), 46–49; Gerteis, *Civil War St. Louis*, 157–59; Parrish, *1860 to 1875*, pp. 34–41; Parrish, *Turbulent Partnership*, 66–75. A sympathetic view of Frémont appears in Robert L. Turkoly-Joczik, "Frémont and the Western Department," *Missouri Historical Review* 82 (July 1988): 363–85.

13. Jefferson C. Davis to John C. Frémont, September 12, 13, 1861, Davis to Henry D. Washburn, September 14, 1861, Davis Papers. See also Hughes and Whitney, *Jefferson Davis in Blue*, 55–56.

14. Merrill, *Soldier of Indiana in the War for the Union*, 1:165.

15. *OR*, 3:180; Davis to Frémont, September 17, 1861, Davis Papers. On the battle of Lexington and the impact of its loss on Frémont's role in Missouri, see McReynolds, *Missouri*, 233–36; Cozzens, *General John Pope*, 43–44.

16. Hughes and Whitney, *Jefferson Davis in Blue*, 57–58; Merrill, *Soldier of Indiana in the War for the Union*, 1:172; R. V. Marshall, *A Historical Sketch of the Twenty-second Regiment Indiana Volunteers* (Madison, IN: Courier Company, 1884), 8–10; David Stevenson, *Indiana's Roll of Honor*, 2 vols. (Indianapolis: by author, 1864), 1:471–72; Jones, "Jefferson Davis in Blue," 46; *Indianapolis Daily State Sentinel*, September 17, 1862; John W. Prentiss to Sister, September 22, 1861, Civil War Papers of John William Prentiss, 1843–June 1862, IHS. See also Davis's report to Frémont on the friendly fire incident, *OR*, 3:182.

17. Nevins, *Frémont in the Civil War*, 529; Rolle, *John Charles Frémont*, 201; Jones, "Jefferson Davis in Blue," 46; *OR*, 3:508. See also Peter Cozzens and Robert L. Girardi, eds., *The Military Memoirs of General John Pope* (Chapel Hill and London: University of North Carolina Press, 1998), 31; Marshall, *Historical Sketch of the Twenty-second Regiment*, 11.

18. *OR*, 3:530–31; Jeff. C. Davis, Special Order No. 16, October 13, 1861, Davis Papers.

In Civil War usage, the word "train" referred not only to the railroad, but also to a convoy of wagons. The word "pioneers" designated a corps of engineers assigned to building and maintaining roads, bridges, and trenches, as well as the handling of repairs. See Webb Garrison, *The Encyclopedia of Civil War Usage* (Nashville, TN: Cumberland House, 2001), 192, 250.

19. F. C. Eddelman to Miss Maggie Stout, October 1, 1861, Martha Stout Papers of the Stout-Jacques Families, 1834–1936, IHS (hereafter cited as Stout Papers); *Indianapolis Daily State Sentinel*, September 17, 1862; Jeff. C. Davis Special Orders, October 11, 1861, Davis Papers; Hughes and Whitney, *Jefferson Davis in Blue*, 63; David Lathrop, *The History of the Fifty-ninth Regiment Illinois Volunteers* (Indianapolis: Hall and Hutchinson, 1865), 27. See also John Foster, *War Stories for My Grandchildren* (Cambridge: Riverside Press, 1918), 18–19; Marvin R. Cain and John F. Bradbury Jr., "Union Troops and the Civil War in Southwestern Missouri and Northwestern Arkansas," *Missouri Historical Review* 88 (October 1993): 41, 45; Muster Roll of Capt. Jonathan H. Williams from 1 September to 31 October 1861. Notice that the spelling of F. C. Eddelman's name is different here. This stems from confusion regarding its spelling in various sources. For example, the adjutant general's report of the State of Indiana, Company I's Muster Rolls, and the Military Records at the Indiana State Archives all spell the name "Eddleman." Franklin College records, Stott, and Eddelman himself spell it "Eddelman." The editor has chosen to spell the name in accordance with the source being used. See *AGI*, 2:386; Military Records, Civil War Muster Cards (microfilm), State Archives of Indiana, Indianapolis; *Jubilee*, 137.

20. Cozzens, *General John Pope*, 48–49; Turkoly-Joczik, "Frémont and the Western Department," 381; Nevins, *Frémont in the Civil War*, 538–40; Ray W. Irwin, ed., "Missouri in Crisis: The Journal of Captain Albert Tracy, 1861," part 3, *Missouri Historical Review* 51 (April 1957): 281; James K. Bigelow, *Abridged History of the Eighth Indiana Volunteer Infantry from Its Organization, April 21st, 1861, to the Date of Re-enlistment as Veterans, January 1, 1864* (Indianapolis: Ellis Barnes, 1864), 10. For the events surrounding Frémont's removal, see *OR*, 3:557–60; Nevins, *Frémont in the Civil War*, 530–34; Rolle, *John Charles Frémont*, 208–10. General David Hunter briefly replaced Frémont only to be superseded by Major General Henry W. Halleck, who commanded from his post in Saint Louis. See Stephen E. Ambrose, *Halleck: Lincoln's Chief of Staff* (Baton Rouge: Louisiana State University Press, 1962), 11–12.

21. Lathrop, *History of the Fifty-ninth Regiment Illinois Volunteers*, 46; George W. Herr, *Episodes of the Civil War: Nine Campaigns in Nine States* (San Francisco: Bancroft Company, 1890), 42; Foster, *War Stories for My Grandchildren*, 22; Report of Col. Thomas Pattison to Jeff C. Davis, December 2, 1861, Davis Papers.

22. Foster, *War Stories for My Grandchildren*, 25–26; Merrill, *Soldier of Indiana in the War for the Union*, 1:190, 195; Special Order No. 25, December 3, 1861, Davis Papers.

23. [Attila Harding?] to Brother, December 22, 1861, Stephen S. Harding Papers, 1848–1959, IHS (hereafter cited as Harding Papers); Marshall, *Historical Sketch of the Twenty-second Regiment*, 12. For full accounts of the Blackwater expedition, see Cozzens, *General John Pope*, 50–51; Cozzens and Girardi, eds., *Memoirs of General John Pope*, 38; Hughes and Whitney, *Jefferson Davis in Blue*, 65–66; Jones, "Jefferson Davis in Blue," 47–49.

24. *OR*, 8:462, 473–74; William L. Shea and Earl J. Hess, *Pea Ridge: Civil War Campaign in the West* (Chapel Hill and London: University of North Carolina Press, 1992), 3–7, 9; Edwin C. Bearss, "From Rolla to Fayetteville with General Curtis," *Arkansas Historical*

Quarterly 19 (Autumn 1960): 225–27.

25. Philip H. Sheridan, *Personal Memoirs of P. H. Sheridan*, 2 vols. (New York: Charles L. Webster and Company, 1888), 1:127–28; Richard O'Connor, *Sheridan, the Inevitable* (Indianapolis: Bobbs-Merrill, 1953), 58; William L. Shea, "The Road to Pea Ridge," *Arkansas Historical Quarterly* 52 (Autumn 1993): 207; Shea and Hess, *Pea Ridge*, 11. For an intriguing insight into Sheridan's predicament, see the memoir of his tentmate at that time in Grenville M. Dodge Papers, 1, PRNMP (hereafter cited as Dodge Papers).

26. Shea, "Road to Pea Ridge," 207–8; Shea and Hess, *Pea Ridge*, 10–11, 13–14; Merrill, *Soldier of Indiana in the War for the Union*, 1:197; Dodge Papers, 1; Diary entry, February 7, 1862, George W. Gordon Papers, 1861–1864, USAMHI (hereafter cited as Gordon Diary); Samuel P. Herrington Diary, February 7, 1862, Rudolph Haerle Collection, USAMHI (hereafter cited as Herrington Diary). On conditions faced by Curtis's army, see Sheridan, *Personal Memoirs*, 1:129; *OR* 8: 196, 540–47. On the march of Davis's division from Otterville to Lebanon, see Bearss, "From Rolla to Fayetteville with General Curtis," 239–40; Hughes and Whitney, *Jefferson Davis in Blue*, 72–73; Muster Roll of Capt. Jonathan H. Williams, January 1, 1862 to February 28, 1862.

27. *OR*, 8:549.

28. Shea and Hess, *Pea Ridge*, 14; Frank J. Welcher, *The Union Army, 1862–1865: Organization and Operations*, 2 vols. (Bloomington: Indiana University Press, 1989), 2:318; E. A. Carr to Father, February 23, 1862, Eugene A. Carr Papers, 1830–1930, USAMHI; James T. King, *War Eagle: A Life of Eugene A. Carr* (Lincoln: University of Nebraska Press, 1963), 43–44; *OR*, 8:550–51; Bearss, "From Rolla to Fayetteville with General Curtis," 244.

29. John C. Swift Diaries, 1861–1863, 2 vols. (February 10, 1862), 2:2, IHS (hereafter cited as Swift Diaries); E. E. Johnson, "Notes by the Way," diary entry of February 10, 1862, Florida Historical Records Survey, USF; Lathrop, *History of the Fifty-ninth Regiment Illinois Volunteers*, 63; L. G. Bennett and William M. Haigh, *History of the Thirty-sixth Regiment Illinois Volunteers, during the Civil War* (Aurora, IL: Knickerbocker and Hodder, 1876), 110; John McElroy, *The Struggle for Missouri* (Washington, D.C.: National Tribune Company, 1909), 293–94.

30. *OR*, 8:554; Hughes and Whitney, *Jefferson Davis in Blue*, 73; Jones, "Jefferson Davis in Blue," 104; Johnson, "Notes on the Way," February 12, 13, 1862. An intriguing account of the skirmish appears in the report of Col. C. A. Ellis, 1st Missouri Cavalry, to Davis, February 23, 1862, Davis Papers.

31. Samuel P. Herrington Diary, 21, USAMHI; *Indianapolis Daily State Sentinel*, September 19, 1862.

32. *OR*, 8:59; Franz Sigel, "The Pea Ridge Campaign," in Robert U. Johnson and Clarence Clough Buel, eds., *Battles and Leaders of the Civil War*, 4 vols. (New York: Century Company, 1887), 1:316; Shea and Hess, *Pea Ridge*, 28–29; Bearss, "From Rolla to Fayetteville with General Curtis," 247; Johnson, "Notes on the Way," February 13, 1862.

33. Shea and Hess, *Pea Ridge*, 30, 32, 34–35; Bearss, "From Rolla to Fayetteville with General Curtis," 247–48; Bennett and Haigh, *History of the Thirty-sixth Regiment Illinois Volunteers*, 116; Hughes and Whitney, *Jefferson Davis in Blue*, 73–74; E. A. Carr to Father, February 23, 1862, Eugene A. Carr Papers, USAMHI; Johnson, "Notes on the Way," February 14, 1862; Shea, "Road to Pea Ridge," 211. On the historic importance of Telegraph Road, see Shea and Hess, *Pea Ridge*, 11–12.

34. Nathan S. Harwood, "The Pea Ridge Campaign," (Nebraska) *MOLLUS*, 25:114; Shea

and Hess, *Pea Ridge*, 35; Norman Clarke, ed., *Warfare along the Mississippi: The Letters of Lieutenant Colonel George E. Currie* (Mount Pleasant: Central Michigan University, 1961), 17; Samuel A. MacKay [pseudonym "Jim Hardtack"], "War Reminiscences," PRNMP.

    35. *OR*, 8:59–60; C. A. Ellis to Jeff C. Davis, February 23, 1862, Davis Papers; Shea and Hess, *Pea Ridge*, 32–34; Bennett Diary, Lyman G. Bennett Collection, 1857, WHMC, Rolla (hereafter cited as Bennett Diary).

    36. McKay, "War Reminiscences," 14; Johnson, "Notes on the Way," February 17, 1862; Lathrop, *History of the Fifty-ninth Regiment of Illinois Volunteers*, 78–79; Stephen D. Engle, *Yankee Dutchman: A Life of Franz Sigel* (Fayetteville: University of Arkansas Press, 1993), 105; Shea and Hess, *Pea Ridge*, 37. Swain Marshall of the Eighth Indiana also reported that Price's soldiers told civilians that "the northern dutch were coming a killing women and children and burning all the houses, and most of the families left everything they had and went with him." Swain Marshall to Father and Mother, March 6, 1862, Thomas Marshall Papers, 1821–1920, IHS.

    37. Shea and Hess, *Pea Ridge*, 39–43; William L. Shea, "1862: A Continual Thunder," in Mark K. Christ, ed., *Rugged and Sublime: The Civil War in Arkansas* (Fayetteville: University of Arkansas Press, 1994), 22–23; Bearss, "From Rolla to Fayetteville with General Curtis," 252; *OR*, 8:61; Ellis to Davis, February 23, 1862, Davis Papers; Henry Curtis Jr. to Lucy, February 18, 1862, Henry C. Curtis Jr. Papers, 1861–1931, *Civil War Times Illustrated* Collection, USAMHI. The Battle of Little Sugar Creek, or Dunagin's Farm, was also the first time the new Confederate battle flag appeared in the Trans-Mississippi theater.

    38. Henry W. Dysart Diary, March 3, 1862, PRNMP; Shea and Hess, *Pea Ridge*, 45.

    39. Shea and Hess, *Pea Ridge*, 50–51; Shea, "Continual Thunder," 27; Lathrop, *History of the Fifty-ninth Regiment Illinois Volunteers*, 80; Henry Curtis to Lucy, February 25, 1862, Curtis Papers; Harwood, "Pea Ridge Campaign," 115; late February 1862, Gordon Diary; *OR*, 8:562.

    40. Shea and Hess, *Pea Ridge*, 52–55, 59–60; Welcher, *Union Army*, 2:712; Arthur B. Carter, *The Tarnished General: Major General Earl Van Dorn, C. S. A.* (Knoxville: University of Tennessee Press, 1999), 46–47; Asa Payne, "Story of the Battle of Pea Ridge," memoirs of Asa Payne, 2, PRNMP. According to historian Jay Monaghan, Curtis knew of Van Dorn's arrival on March 3 from hearing "forty precisely timed discharges" of cannon to the south—"the salute for a major general." See Jay Monaghan, *Civil War on the Western Border, 1854–1865* (Boston and Toronto: Little, Brown, 1955), 233. "See the elephant" was a phrase used by Civil War soldiers to describe combat and its terror. See John D. Wright, *The Language of the Civil War* (Westport, CT: Oryx Press, 2001), 265.

    41. Shea and Hess, *Pea Ridge*, 59, 63; Engle, *Yankee Dutchman*, 107; Walter L. Brown, "Pea Ridge: Gettysburg of the West," *Arkansas Historical Quarterly* 15 (Spring 1956): 8.

    42. Robert G. Hartje, *Van Dorn: The Life and Times of a Confederate General* (Nashville: Vanderbilt University Press, 1967), 126; Carter, *Tarnished General*, 53; Shea, "Road to Pea Ridge," 218; *OR*, 8:197, 245–46; Hughes and Whitney, *Jefferson Davis in Blue*, 75; John D. Crabtree, "Recollections of the Pea Ridge Campaign and the Army of the Southwest," (Illinois) *MOLLUS*, 12:216.

    43. Edwin C. Bearss, "The Battle of Pea Ridge," *Arkansas Historical Quarterly* 20 (Spring 1961): 86; Shea and Hess, *Pea Ridge*, 43–44; Welcher, *Union Army*, 2:715. For more complete descriptions of the Pea Ridge terrain, see Bennett and Haigh, *History of the Thirty-sixth Regiment Illinois Volunteers*, 141–42; Hartje, *Van Dorn*, 137–39. On Elkhorn Tavern,

see John W. Bond, "The History of Elkhorn Tavern," *Arkansas Historical Quarterly* 21 (Spring 1962): 3–15.

44. Engle, *Yankee Dutchman*, 108–9; Stephen D. Engle, "Franz Sigel at Pea Ridge," *Arkansas Historical Quarterly* 50 (Autumn 1991): 259–60; William Baxter, *Pea Ridge and Prairie Grove; or, Scenes and Incidents of the War in Arkansas* (Fayetteville: University of Arkansas Press, 2000), 30; Lyman G. Bennett Diary Collection, 91–93, WHMC, Rolla; Henry Voelkner to Parents, March 18, 1862, Henry Voelkner Papers, PRNMP (hereafter cited as Voelkner Papers; Louis W. Knobe Diary, 1861–1863, pp, 24–25, S1438, Manuscript Section, ISL (hereafter cited as Knobe Diary).

45. *OR*, 8:191, 197–98, 249; Bearss, "Battle of Pea Ridge," 85–88; Shea and Hess, *Pea Ridge*, 67–68; March 7, 1862, Swift Diaries, 2:11; March 6, 1862, Herrington Diary.

46. March 6, 1862, Gordon Diary; McKay, "War Reminiscences," 17.

47. Monaghan, *Civil War on the Western Border*, 237; King, *War Eagle*, 45; Welcher, *Union Army*, 2:715; Hartje, *Van Dorn*, 131; March 6, 1862, Henry W. Dysart Diary; *Indianapolis Daily State Sentinel*, September 19, 1862; Bennett Diary, 93.

48. Shea and Hess, *Pea Ridge*, 80–82; Edwin C. Bearss, "The First Day at Pea Ridge, March 7, 1862," *Arkansas Historical Quarterly* 18 (Summer 1958): 132; Hartje, *Van Dorn*, 130–35; Thomas W. Cutrer, *Ben McCulloch and the Frontier Military Tradition* (Chapel Hill and London: University of North Carolina Press, 1993), 294; Carter, *Tarnished General*, 55–56; Albert Castel, *General Sterling Price and the Civil War in the West* (Baton Rouge: Louisiana State University Press, 1968), 71–73; Robert Shalhope, *Sterling Price: Portrait of a Southerner* (Columbia: University of Missouri Press, 1971), 201–2.

49. Shea and Hess, *Pea Ridge*, 80-82; Carter, *Tarnished General*, 57; Sigel, "Pea Ridge Campaign," 321; Bennett and Haigh, *History of the Thirty-sixth Regiment Illinois Volunteers*, 144–45; Engle, *Yankee Dutchman*, 111; William H. H. Rogers to James S. Rogers, March 16, 1862, Rogers Papers; *OR*, 8:246.

50. Dodge Papers, 3; *OR*, 8:191; Shea and Hess, *Pea Ridge*, 120.

51. King, *War Eagle*, 46–47; Shea and Hess, *Pea Ridge*, 90; *OR*, 8:192, 198–99. For more complete accounts of Osterhaus's handling of the fight at Leetown, see Earl J. Hess, "Osterhaus in Missouri: A Study in German-American Loyalty," *Missouri Historical Review* 78 (January 1984): 162–63; Cutrer, *Ben McCulloch and the Frontier Military Tradition*, 297–302.

52. Shea and Hess, *Pea Ridge*, 118–21; Earl J. Hess, "Battle in the Brush: Davis' Division at Pea Ridge, 7 March 1862," *Indiana Military History Journal* 8 (May 1983): 13, 17–18. See also Bearss, "First Day at Pea Ridge," 150–51; Lathrop, *History of the Fifty-ninth Regiment Illinois Volunteers*, 92; Clarke, *Warfare Along the Mississippi*, 25.

53. Shea and Hess, *Pea Ridge*, 121–27; Report of Col. Julius White to Jeff. C. Davis, March 11, 1862, Davis Papers; McKay, "War Reminiscences," 17; Shea, "Continual Thunder," 33; Hess, "Battle in the Brush," 13.

54. *OR*, 8:246, 249–50; Shea and Hess, *Pea Ridge*, 128–29; Hughes and Whitney, *Jefferson Davis in Blue*, 79–80; Hess, "Battle in the Brush," 13.

55. Judson to Cousin, April 4, 1862, Harding Papers; Johnson, "Notes by the Way," March 7, 1862.

56. McKay, "War Reminiscences," 19; *Indianapolis Daily State Sentinel*, September 19, 1862; Louis W. Knobe Diary, 1861–1863, pp. 25–26, ISL (hereafter cited as Knobe Diary); Washburn to Pattison, March 11, 1862, in Frank Moore, ed., *The Rebellion Record: A Diary*

of American Events, 10 vols. (New York: Putnam, 1862), 4:248–49. See also *OR*, 8:250. Earl Hess contends that "it is entirely unclear" which regiment retook the Peoria Battery, asserting that "the 22nd Indiana or the 37th Illinois were probably the captors." Yet, in his report to Davis of March 11, 1862, Colonel Julius White of the Thirty-seventh gave full credit to Pattison's First Brigade and, specifically, the Eighteenth Indiana. See White to Davis, March 11, 1862, Davis Papers, and the same report in *OR*, 8:247. See also Merrill, *Soldier of Indiana in the War for the Union*, 1:3. Furthermore, the Twenty-second Indiana was in disorder at the time. For more detailed accounts of the fighting in Morgan's woods, see Hess, "Battle in the Brush," Shea and Hess, *Pea Ridge*, chapters 6 and 7; and Hughes and Whitney, *Jefferson Davis in Blue*, chapter 5.

57. Hughes and Whitney, *Jefferson Davis in Blue*, 83–84; *OR*, 8:195–205, 245–49.

58. Carr to Father, March 15, 1862, Eugene A. Carr Papers; Shea, "Continual Thunder," 34–35; Shea and Hess, *Pea Ridge*, 152–54; Payne, "Story of the Battle of Pea Ridge," 1, 4; Bond, "History of Elkhorn Tavern," 9–11; Hartje, *Van Dorn*, 141–44.

59. *OR*, 8:201; Shea and Hess, *Pea Ridge*, 221; Hartje, *Van Dorn*, 151–52; Clarke, *Warfare along the Mississippi*, 30.

60. Hughes and Whitney, *Jefferson Davis in Blue*, 85; Sigel, "Pea Ridge Campaign," 326–27; Harwood, "Pea Ridge Campaign," 118; March 10, 1862, Gordon Diary; Crabtree, "Recollections of the Pea Ridge Campaign," 121.

61. *OR*, 8:201-2, 247; Herr, *Episodes of the Civil War*, 74; Shea and Hess, *Pea Ridge*, 225–26; Knobe Diary, 26; March 8, 1862, Herrington Diary.

62. Report of Washburn to Pattison, March 8, 1862, in Moore, ed., *Rebellion Record*, 4:249; Henry Voelkner to Parents, March 18, 1862, Voelkner Papers; Marshall, *Historical Sketch of the Twenty-second Regiment*, 19; Shea, "Continual Thunder," 36; Shea and Hess, *Pea Ridge*, 236.

63. Shea and Hess, *Pea Ridge* 226–28, 235–36, 252; Sigel, "Pea Ridge Campaign," 328; Hughes and Whitney, *Jefferson Davis in Blue*, 88; Shea, "Continual Thunder," 36; *OR*, 8:250–51; Report of Washburn to Pattison, March 8, 1862, in Moore, ed., *Rebellion Record*, 4:249; March 10, 1862, Gordon Diary; Engle, "Franz Sigel at Pea Ridge," 266.

64. Monaghan, *Civil War on the Western Border*, 249; Bennett Diary, 101–2; Shea and Hess, 271–72, 275; March 9, 1862, Herrington Diary; *OR*, 8:193–95. The *OR* reference is to a series of letters between Curtis and Van Dorn in which they agree to burial arrangements for their respective troops.

65. Hughes and Whitney, *Jefferson Davis in Blue*, 91; Merrill, *Soldier of Indiana in the War for the Union*, 1:207; Johnson, "Notes on the Way," March 12, 13, 17, 1862; W. T. Stott to Mag and Mattie, March 29, 1862, Stout Papers; *OR*, 8:659.

CHAPTER 3

1. It is intriguing that Stott does not include Arkansas in this listing, especially since that was where he first saw major combat at Pea Ridge. The omission is inexplicable.

2. All evidence points to the fact that Stott transcribed his original diary notes into a new handwritten copy in a ledger-style book sometime after his return home from the war in December 1864. This transcription is now in the archives of Franklin College, and it is the copy used in the preparation of the current volume. As mentioned in the preface and acknowledgments, the editor has preserved the original spelling, punctuation (or lack thereof), and paragraphing throughout, using a [sic] or bracketed note only when needed

for clarity. Stott's grandson, Cyril R. Parker of La Porte, Indiana, made a typescript copy in 1940, but he edited it to meet the stylistic and spelling standards of his day. The editor had to "re-edit" Parker's edition to be true to the original.

3. Lieutenant Davis is Second Lieutenant William F. Davis of Patriot, Indiana. See *AGI*, 2:162. Mrs. Julia Cook ran a boardinghouse at 44 North Pennsylvania Avenue in Indianapolis. Reverend James B. Simmons was the pastor of the First Baptist Church of Indianapolis, which was then meeting at the Masonic Hall. The First Presbyterian Church was on the northeast corner of the Circle and Market Street, and the Christian Church was located at the corner of Ohio and Delaware. See *Indianapolis Directory and Business Mirror* (Bowen, Stewart and Company, 1861), 16, 118, 231, 274.

4. Uncle A. J. V. was Achilles J. Vawter of Vernon who was graduated from Franklin College in 1850. Stateline City in Warren County, Indiana, built in 1859 as a railroad town, literally intersected the state line between Indiana and Illinois. Lycurgus W. Eastman was a principal musician in the Eighteenth Indiana. See *AGI*, 4:372.

5. The *Jubilee* volume of Franklin College lists W. R. Hardy of Covington as having graduated in 1861, but he was probably in the preparatory program, since he did not receive a degree with Stott that year. See *Jubilee*, 143. R. C. Storey is Stott's boyhood friend from Vernon.

6. Stott's reasons for going to war reflect clearly the "ideological motifs" that James M. McPherson cites as the primary motivation for entering the war expressed by Civil War soldiers, North and South. In his study, *What They Fought For, 1861–1865*, McPherson arrives at this conclusion after having examined thousands of soldiers' diaries and letters. One New Jersey officer, for example, echoes Stott's thoughts in saying, "the man who doesn't give hearty support to our bleeding country in this day of our country's trial is not worthy to be a descendant of our forefathers." Countless are the Northern soldiers' reflections, indicated McPherson, on the importance of laying down one's life for the country if necessary, and doing so against the "threat of 'dissolution, anarchy, and ruin.'" See James M. McPherson, *What They Fought For, 1861–1865* (Baton Rouge and London: Louisiana State University Press, 1994), 27–28, 32, 34. Note the strong faith context of Stott's motivations.

7. Stott's friend, Eddelman, echoed these same sentiments in a letter to Mattie Stout of October 1, 1861. "You ask why does camp life confirm me in my Calvinistic views?" he queried. "It is simply because men here in camp have thrown all restraint off and I no longer am required to behold them through a glass darkly. . . . By observation," Eddelman went on, "I find them as represented in the Scriptures. 'They cast up mire & dirt continually.' They utter continually the vilest oaths possible without any provocation. . . . Many do, and say, what they do and say, in the vulgarest and lowest way that they possibly can." Stott, as will be seen, repeatedly comments on such behavior in his diary. See Eddelman to Mattie, October 1, 1861, Martha Stout Papers of the Stout-Jacques Families, 1834–1936, IHS (hereafter cited as Stout Papers).

8. The Manual of Arms described the proper manner of loading a weapon or carrying out other operations. See Webb Garrison, *The Encyclopedia of Civil War Usage* (Nashville, TN: Cumberland House, 2001), 148, 154. Amos Comstock of Johnson County was a private in Company I. See *AGI*, 4:386.

9. The men involved in the altercation were Luther T. Hayman and William P. Davis, both of Company A, of which Jesse L. Holman of Aurora, Indiana, was captain. According

to Gilbert Denny, of Washington County, a private in Company G, the incident occurred on September 9. Davis was killed, and Hayman was "Court Marshalled and I guess will be shot." Private John C. Swift of Company A also indicated in his diary that Hayman killed Davis but gives the date as September 10. See Gilbert Denny to Father, September 10, 1861, Letters of Gilbert Denny, 18th Regiment, 1861–1863, IHS (hereafter cited as Denny Letters); September 10, 1861, John C. Swift Diaries, 1861–1863, 2 vols., 1:2, IHS (hereafter cited as Swift Diaries). There is no evidence in the *AGI*, however, that either man died in service.

10. Identifying civilians to whom Stott refers is a difficult job. In many cases there simply is not enough information to make an accurate identification. Such is the case with Lizzie. According to Stott's descendants, Rate's full name was Rate Stout, but Stott's relationship with her is unknown. The U.S. Census for Indiana in 1860, however, reveals that a Margrate Stout lived adjacent to Martha Stout, the Mattie with whom both Eddelman and Stott corresponded. Margrate apparently was married to John Stout, Mattie's brother, and it is quite possible that she is the "Mag" referred to by both soldiers, and thus the sister-in-law of Mattie, and that "Rate" was another nickname for Margrate. The Stout family lived in Franklin County. See 1860 U.S. Census—Indiana, microfilm, Roll 259, ISL.

11. John Tilson of Franklin was a first lieutenant in Company I. See *AGI*, 2:165.

12. In the language of the Civil War soldier, "sold" meant "to be deceived." See Garrison, *Encyclopedia of Civil War Usage*, 232.

13. Many of the comments of soldiers are about the fruit-bearing nature of Missouri, especially in peaches. The chronicler of the Fifty-ninth Illinois described Boonville as "a pretty town, of perhaps one thousand inhabitants," sitting in the midst of "a most splendid fruit country." And Gilbert Denny wrote his father: "They is plenty of fruit in this Country Such as peaches Apples plums grapes pawpaws &c and peaches sell here for 30 cts per Buhel [Bushel]." See David Lathrop, *The History of the Fifty-ninth Regiment Illinois Volunteers* (Indianapolis: Hall and Hutchinson Printers, 1865), 11; Gilbert Denny to Father, September 10, 1861, Denny Letters.

14. First Lieutenant Charles F. Johnston of Company I was a Franklinite, age thirty-six at the time of his enrollment. See Military Records, Civil War Muster Rolls, microfilm, Indiana State Archives, Indianapolis. Interestingly, the Adjutant General's Report gives his name as "Johnson." See *AGI*, 2:165.

15. William S. Snow was a private in Company I. See *AGI*, 4:386.

16. Private Walter Stanley indicated that the *Sunshine* was a rebel steamer captured at Cambridge, but Private John C. Swift's Diary reveals that the capture of the "Steamboat called Sunshine" occurred at the town of Big Arrow Rock. See *Indianapolis Daily State Sentinel*, September 17, 1862; September 21, 1861, Swift Diaries, 1:5.

17. Will Stott's college friend, Barnett (Barry) Wallace.

18. There was no Voorhees in the Eighteenth Indiana. This is probably a reference to either Private John H. Voris or Private Joseph E. Voris. See *AGI*, 4:387.

19. "Henry" is Private Miles H. McCanlon of Vernon who was in Company H of the Twenty-sixth. Richard H. Stott, also from Vernon, was the company's first sergeant. See *AGI*, 4:604–5.

20. Uncle P. C. V. is Philemon C. Vawter, Stott's uncle and teacher, who was graduated from Franklin College in 1855.

21. Walter Stanley described this campground as "the most unlucky spot we were

ever in. Scarcely one-fifth of the regiment was fit for duty in two weeks time. Many died from the effects of measles and improper medical attendance." In 1888 Stott declared for Invalid Army Pension, claiming that, during this period of the campaign in Missouri, "He contracted malarial poisoning (rheumatism) and chronic diarrhea and disease of respiratory organs under following circumstances: from exposure, sleeping on damp ground, malaria, and drinking impure water." It may have been at this spot that his health problems began. See *Indianapolis Daily State Sentinel*, September 17, 1862; "Declaration of Invalid Army Pension," July 3, 1888, Full Pension File, William Taylor Stott, U.S. NARA. Ironically, this day (October 1) was the same day Eddelman wrote to Mattie Stott, saying that he and Stott were well and the "general health" of the division was "good." See F. C. Eddelman to Martha Stout, October 1, 1861, Stout Papers.

22. Paducah fell to Ulysses S. Grant's army on September 6, 1861, but it is unclear to which Colonel Wallace Stott refers. If he was thinking of Lew Wallace and his Eleventh Indiana, they did not arrive at Paducah until September 11. See E. B. Long, *The Civil War Day by Day: An Almanac, 1861–1865* (New York: DaCapo Press, 1971), 115; Ann Turner, *Guide to Indiana Civil War Manuscripts* (Indianapolis: Indiana Civil War Centennial Commission, 1965), 22.

23. John C. Jenks of Newport, Indiana, was captain of Company C. See *AGI*, 2:161.

24. Aeolus was the Greek god of the winds.

25. Proverbs 28:1 (KJV) reads: "The wicked flee when no man pursueth."

26. There was no Daniel Kelly in the Eighteenth Indiana. Company I did contain Samuel Kelly and Allen Kelly, either of whom could have been the victim of this self-imposed accident.

27. Edward Young (1683–1765) was an influential poet, theologian, and sometime chaplain to the King of England. His lengthy poem *Night Thoughts on Life, Death, and Immortality*, published in June 1742, emerged from Young's catastrophic personal loss. In 1741 his wife and two stepchildren, who were the lights of his life, all died within a very brief period. At a time when "He long had buried what gives life to live, / Firmness of nerve, and energy of thought," Young found consolation in the future world, "an eternal state of being, revealed to him in the Holy Scriptures." According to biographer and literary critic James Robert Boyd, who edited the 1852 edition of *Night Thoughts*, Young's spirit was one of "sublime piety and strict morality." So it seems natural that Stott would find Young helpful as he confronted the trials of war. See Edward Young, *Night Thoughts on Life, Death, and Immortality* (New York: A. S. Barnes and Company, 1852). Quotes come from Boyd's "Memoirs and Critical Review" in that volume, 59–60. See also *Dictionary of National Biography*, 22 vols. (New York and London: Macmillan, 1908–9), 21:1283–88. The mysterious "Miss L. M." will be the subject of a subsequent note.

28. George W. Ames, of Greencastle, Indiana, was the chaplain of the Eighteenth at that time. He would serve until April 1862. See *AGI*, 2:159.

29. Since Stott had friends in western Ohio, the Thorp reference is possibly to Private James B. Thorp of the Fourteenth Ohio Light Artillery, who died in Saint Louis on May 28, 1862. Stott refers to his death in his diary entry of August 24, 1862. On Thorp see ACWRD. William Cumback was an attorney and the postmaster of Greensburg, Indiana. See U.S. Census—Indiana, microfilm, Roll, 253, p. 765, ISL.

30. Joseph M. Robertson was a Franklin College student in 1861 and was sergeant of Company B in the Twenty-sixth Indiana Infantry. See *Jubilee*, 164; ACWRD.

31. Private Daniel Perkins of Company I, Eighteenth. See *AGI*, 4:386.

32. The biblical texts for the sermon were from either 2 Kings 18–19, 2 Chronicles 32, or Isaiah 36-37 (KJV). Lord Byron's "effusion" on the events surrounding Hezekiah and Sennacherib are in his poem, "The Destruction of Sennacherib," Stanzas 1–6. See Lord Byron, *The Complete Poetical Works*, edited by Jerome J. McGann, 7 vols. (Oxford: Oxford University Press, 1980–93), 3:309–10. "Man shall not live by bread alone" is found in Matthew 4:4 and Luke 4:4 (KJV).

33. Lieutenant John H. Popp "was commissioned into Field and Staff" in the Eighteenth. See ACWRD. All searches for Captain Davidson were nonproductive.

34. Mariner Alexander Selkirk was the castaway who was traditionally considered to be the model upon which Daniel Defoe based his famous tale *Robinson Crusoe*. See Michael Seidel, *Robinson Crusoe: Island Myths and the Novel* (Boston: Twayne, 1991), 39–40. The "Journal" Stott received from his friend Barnett Wallace was the *Indiana State Journal*, a Republican paper edited by Berry Sulgrove and published in Indianapolis. See John W. Miller, *Indiana Newspaper Bibliography* (Indianapolis: Indiana Historical Society, 1982), 274.

35. In mid-October, as John Charles Frémont's army moved toward Warsaw on the Osage River, it discovered that General Sterling Price had burned the bridge spanning the river. Frémont got a trained engineer to supervise the building of an eight hundred-foot-long pontoon bridge to enable his army to cross the Osage. The bridge became quite an item of conversation among the common soldiers, Walter Stanley labeling it the "celebrated bridge" and describing it as "built of logs laid crosswise on heavy stringers." See Allen Nevins, *Frémont: Pathfinder of the West*, vol. 2, *Frémont in the Civil War* (New York: Frederick Ungar, 1961), 532–33; *Indianapolis Daily State Sentinel*, September 17, 1862.

36. The reference here is to James Lane, a Hoosier who had been Indiana's lieutenant governor and congressman as a "pro-slavery Democrat," but who went to Kansas in 1855, becoming a leader of abolitionist forces during the Kansas border wars. A fanatical opportunist, Lane led a Kansas Brigade into Missouri in pursuit of Price in the autumn of 1861, telling his troops that "everything disloyal, from a Shanghai rooster to a Durham cow, must be cleaned out." See Richard S. Brownlee, *Gray Ghosts of the Confederacy: Guerrilla Warfare in the West, 1861–1865* (Baton Rouge: Louisiana University Press, 1958), 37–38.

37. The Ninth Missouri will become the Fifty-ninth Illinois. Brigadier General Samuel Davis Sturgis was Brigadier General David Hunter's chief of staff. See Patricia L. Faust, ed., *Historical Times Illustrated Encyclopedia of the Civil War* (New York: Harper and Row, 1986), 729–30.

38. Brigadier General Nathaniel Lyon was the commander of Union forces at the Battle of Wilson's Creek on August 10, 1861. Always aggressive and impetuous, he was killed leading a charge at Bloody Hill during this Confederate victory. See William Garrett Piston and Richard W. Hatcher III, *Wilson's Creek: The Second Battle of the Civil War and the Men Who Fought It* (Chapel Hill and London: University of North Carolina Press, 2000), 28–30, 268.

39. The sermon was based on either Matthew 18:11 or Luke 19:10 (KJV).

40. Second Lieutenant Jasper Nebeker was from Newport, Indiana. The cause of his death is unknown.

41. Hickman King, a private in Company C of the Twenty-second Indiana was possibly one of Stott's students when Stott taught in the Columbus, Indiana, schools. See ACWRD.

42. Mack and Mat are Stott's sister Martha (Mat) and her husband Maxa Moncrief (Mack). They were married near Vernon on November 3, 1853, when Martha was nineteen. See Grace Vawter Bicknell, *The Vawter Family in America* (Indianapolis: Hollenbeck Press, 1905; reprint, Atlanta, GA: Thorpe and Associates, 1969), 106.

43. An officer of the Twenty-fifth Indiana described this move as going "into winter quarters." "We will have a large city of log huts, probably 15,000 or 20,000 troops," he wrote on December 7. "We were commencing operations to-day by clearing off our camp, preparatory to building our log huts." See John Foster, *War Stories for My Grandchildren* (Cambridge: Riverside Press, 1918), 27.

44. For some time, President Abraham Lincoln, for a variety of reasons, had been dissatisfied with Secretary Simon Cameron's running of the War Department. In a report to Congress on his department's operations that was to accompany the president's State of the Union address, Cameron, recalling the pleasure with which abolitionists welcomed Frémont's emancipation declaration in Missouri, included a recommendation "to arm slaves . . . and employ their service against the rebels." Lincoln, determined not to allow anyone other than himself to establish "government policy on slavery," notified Cameron of his desire to appoint the secretary as minister to Russia. Cameron resigned his cabinet position on January 11, 1862. See David Herbert Donald, *Lincoln* (New York: Simon and Schuster, 1995), 326.

45. Hiram T. Vandevender, of Anderson, an 1857 graduate of Franklin College, was captain of Company K in the Eighth Indiana. He died of wounds at Vicksburg, Mississippi, May 23, 1863. See *AGI*, 2:55.

46. The reference here is to Davis's victory over the Confederates at Blackwater Creek. The identification of Rebel Colonel Alexander is unknown, but Colonel Ebenezer Magoffin was the son of Kentucky Governor Beriah Magoffin. See Nathaniel Cheairs Hughes Jr. and Gordon D. Whitney, *Jefferson Davis in Blue: The Life of Sherman's Relentness Warrior* (Baton Rouge: Louisiana University Press, 2002), 67.

47. A Sibley Tent, named after its creator Henry R. Sibley, a graduate of West Point who was a brigadier general in the Confederate army, was shaped like a tepee, twelve feet high and eighteen feet in diameter. Made of canvas, it had a door flap and was supported by a strong center pole. Though cumbersome, it had the advantage in the winter of being heated by a cone-shaped Sibley stove. See John D. Wright, *The Language of the Civil War* (Westport, CT: Oryx Press, 2001), 271.

48. James M. Mason and John Slidell were Confederate emissaries to Great Britain and France who were traveling on board the British steamer *Trent* when it came under fire from Captain Charles Wilkes's Union warship *San Jacinto*. They were apprehended and placed on board the American vessel. The incident created a major diplomatic crisis with England for the Lincoln administration, until it was agreed that the men would be released. Major figures in the deliberations over the "*Trent* Affair" were General Winfield Scott, Secretary of State William H. Seward, and England's minister to the U.S., Lord Richard Lyons, all of whom are mentioned in Stott's next diary entry. See Donald, *Lincoln*, 320–23.

49. A variety of illnesses spread through the division during the early days of January, including the fever that gripped Stott's friend, Eddelman. Surgeon George Gordon reported on a large number who were ill in the Eighteenth with "pneumonia, diarrhea, and severe colds" and attributed the sicknesses not only to the weather but also to "dregs

of measles" that many suffered before his arrival in camp. Private Samuel B. Voyles of Company G in the Eighteenth wrote his father that mumps were "prevailing among the Boys," and John William Prentiss of the Twenty-second Indiana told his sister that "the smallpox is pretty bad in the hospital at Otterville." See Diary, December 31, 1861, George W. Gordon Papers, 1861–1864, USAMHI (hereafter cited as Gordon Papers); S. B. Voyles to Father, December 31, 1861, Samuel B. Voyles Civil War Correspondence, 1861–1862, IHS; Prentiss to sister, January 3, 1862, John William Prentiss Civil War Papers, 1843–1862, IHS.

50. Charles A. Sims and Samuel P. Hoeffer were both privates in Company I. John High was the company's wagoner. See *AGI*, 4:386.

51. Soldiers used the word "bodyguards" as a humorous term for lice. See Wright, *Language of the Civil War*, 36.

52. Mrs. Joel (Frances) Williams lived in Franklin Township. See U.S. Census—Indiana, roll 271, p. 91.

53. In his diary entry of January 8, 1861, Private John C. Swift of Company A wrote: "R. R. Pattison as tight as a brick." Later, he records that "Richmond R. Pattison died in camp on Lamine river about 2 oclock in the morning of the 15th of January 1862," and that Swift participated in escorting Pattison's remains to the Depot in Otterville the next day. See January 8, 16, 1862, Swift Diaries, 1:24–25. The Adjutant General's Report listed Pattison as Robert R. Pattison, a sergeant in Company A. See *AGI*, 4:372.

54. On January 11, 1862, a fleet of around one hundred vessels with troops under the command of Brigadier General Ambrose E. Burnside left Hampton Roads, Virginia, for Hatteras Inlet, North Carolina, where they arrived two days later, the delay due to the low draft of the vessels and lack of adequate landing craft. Burnside then assumed command of the department of North Carolina. See Long, *Civil War Day by Day*, 159–60.

55. The battle in which Confederate Brigadier General Felix Zollicoffer was killed occurred on January 19, 1862, and is known by a number of names—Mill Springs, Somerset, and Logan's Cross Roads, among others. See ibid., 162.

56. Peter C. Woods, of Metamora, was captain of Company F. See *AGI*, 2:163. *Ex uno, disce omnes* may be translated, "Out of one, all march away" (or, "all depart").

57. The next few days found travel virtually impossible. George W. Herr of the Fifty-ninth Illinois described "storm after storm" that left roads "beaten by the rains into mudpuddles and quagmires," making it "impossible for the heavily laden baggage trains to keep up." See George W. Herr, *Episodes of the Civil War: Nine Campaigns in Nine States* (San Francisco: Bancroft Company, 1890), 46. See also E. E. Johnson, "Notes by the Way," Diary of E. E. Johnson, Company B, Eighteenth Regiment Indiana Volunteers, January 26–30, Florida Historical Records Survey, USF.

58. Kimble, from Metamora, was first lieutenant of Company F. As quartermaster it would be his responsibility to oversee the living arrangements and transportation for the troops, arrange for the movement of equipment and supplies, and prepare for the burial of the dead. See *AGI*, 2:163; Wright, *Language of the Civil War*, 242.

59. Surgeon Gordon, who treated both Quartermaster Popp and musician Eastman, left a more complete account of how they set the fire and the extent of their injuries. Gordon, who described them as "the worst burned men" he had ever seen, covered "their faces, ears, necks, and hands with Symple carrote and bandaged them barely leaving them a place to breathe." Later, the wagon carting them to the hospital turned over on an icy road

and fell ten feet, but both escaped further injury. See Diary, February 3, 1862, Gordon Papers.

60. "Bogart" is Corporal Henry Bogard of Company I. See *AGI*, 4:386. Surgeon Gordon also recorded the whiskey incident in his diary, indicating that "18 kegs and barrels of rot gut whiskey" had been captured, "one barrel and three kegs" going to the Eighteenth. He said, however, that the colonel (supposedly Davis) "would hold them responsible if any man got drunk." Only members of the Brass Band got inebriated. See Diary, February 3, 1862, Gordon Papers.

61. William Plummer Benton was the colonel of the Eighth Indiana Infantry and later was a brigadier general in the Vicksburg campaign. See Ezra J. Warner, *Generals in Blue: Lives of the Union Commanders* (Baton Rouge: Louisiana University Press, 1964), 30–31. James R. Johnson was a sergeant in Stott's own Company I. See *AGI*, 4:385.

62. Robert R. Hunt, William Robbins, Joseph Mappin, and Miles Hendricks were all privates in Company I. See *AGI*, 4:386.

63. Stott refers here to the work of William C. Buck, an eminent theologian and pastor of the Baptist church of Columbus, Mississippi. A thorough search for his *Exposition of Prophesy* proved fruitless, but Buck contended in his other works that theology should be approached as a science. See note 65 below.

64. Sutlers were civilian merchants licensed by the government to sell their wares at military camps. From them soldiers could purchase newspapers, tobacco, toiletries, cookies, and other foodstuffs. See Wright, *Language of the Civil War*, 289–90.

65. Buck's *Theology* was the Baptist theologian's major work. In it, he insisted that "Theology *as a science*, is too little the subject of earnest and prayerful study" and that such study should focus on the philological rather than the philosophical approach to the scriptures. He thus employed a literal interpretation of the Bible in examining such theological concepts as justification, the person of Christ, the new birth, prophesy, and faith. See William C. Buck, *Theology: The Philosophy of Religion* (Nashville: Southwestern Publishing House, 1857), iii–iv, 5, 8–9.

66. Corporal Randolph V. Marshall of the Twenty-second Indiana described this brutal scene: "A ten pound shell from the enemy's battery took off the head of Corporal Alfrey in the front rank, passed through the neck and shoulder of his cousin, a private in the rear rank, and, without exploding, buried itself in the breast of Lt. Watts, killing all of them instantly." See R. V. Marshall, *An Historical Sketch of the Twenty-second Indiana Volunteers* (Madison, IN: Courier Company, 1884), 16.

67. Stott here quotes William Shakespeare's *King Henry VI*, part 2, act 3, scene 2, line 233. See Yule Shakespeare edition, *The Second Part of King Henry the Sixth*, Tyler Brook, ed. (New Haven, CT: Yale University Press, 1923), 67.

68. The three soldiers of Company E found dead were Sergeant James W. Murry, Corporal Thomas Wilson, and Private George S. McMahan, all of Martin County. See *AGI*, 4:379–80.

69. Private Edward C. Bishop of Vermillion County, who was killed in the Battle of Cedar Creek, November 19, 1864. See *AGI*, 4:376.

70. In this last sentence Stott may have revealed the secret to the identity of the mysterious Miss L. M., one of his primary correspondents. Countless were the hours spent in searching through genealogical materials, census records, Jennings County historical repositories, and other collections, as well as telephoning persons in Indiana, Michigan,

and Ohio, in attempts to determine who this enigmatic lady might be. All the editor had to go on were the initials "L.M." One of Stott's friends from Jennings County, Caleb Moncrief, married a Lydia Moris (or Morris). Could she be the mystery woman? As noted in the preface and acknowledgments, descendants of the Moncrief family assisted me in that search. Finally, the "Oxford" connection proved more fruitful. Through conversations with Jim Ambuske, director of special projects for University Advancement at Miami University, Oxford, Ohio, I learned of an Oxford College for Women, a Presbyterian school from which Lillie Lydia Morris was graduated in June 1863 and at which she briefly taught. She was the daughter of the president of the college, Reverend Desha Morris, and she married a later president of the college, Doctor La Fayette Walker. Although Lillie Lydia Morris seems to be a perfect match with Stott's correspondent, I unfortunately have been unable to substantiate the origin or nature of their friendship. See *Miami University Bulletin: Alumni Directory, Oxford College, 1833–1928* (Oxford, OH: Miami University, 1941), 287; Olive Flower, *The History of Oxford College for Women, 1830–1928* (Oxford, OH: Miami University Alumni Association, 1949), 133–35. The *Witness* was an Indiana Baptist newspaper, first published in 1857 by M. G. Clarke and F. W. Clarke of Indianapolis. See John F. Cady, *The Baptist Church in Indiana* (Franklin, IN: Franklin College, 1942), 173.

71. Mary Todd Lincoln's ball was held on February 5, 1862, and, according to historian Jennifer Fleischer, was intended to be "a grand finale of a year of renovations" to the White House and "her own personal redemption after a season of criticism." Many were troubled by the pomposity of such an occasion at an especially trying time during the war. Senator and Mrs. Benjamin Wade's response to the event was typical: "Are the President and Mrs. Lincoln aware that there is a civil war? If they are not, Mr. And Mrs. Wade are, and for that reason decline to participate in dancing and feasting." See Jennifer Fleischer, *Mrs. Lincoln and Mrs. Keckley* (New York: Broadway Books, 2003), 229.

72. Louis W. Knobe, a merchant in Franklin before and after the war, enlisted as first sergeant of Company I. His name is recorded as Lewis W. Knobe in *AGI*, 4:385.

73. "Sweet Home" was a highly sentimental poem, typical of the mid-nineteenth century. It expressed a longing for home, which no doubt resonated with Stott's spirit at a time of little activity far away from his own community. The poem describes missing one's "gold-haired baby-sister," how "my father will sit in his wonted chair" and "silent and thoughtful my mother will sit." It ends with a prayer: "'Be kept, O Father in Heaven,' by thee, Till I meet them all at home, sweet home." See Lily Lichen [Mary A. A. Phinney], "Sweet Home," *The Ladies' Repository: A Monthly Periodical, Devoted to Literature, Arts, and Religion* 21 (May 1861): 304. The *Repository* was published in Cincinnati by the Methodist Episcopal Church.

74. Stott here refers to Lincoln's proposal for compensated emancipation of the slaves, which the president had been suggesting since the previous November. See Long, *Civil War Day by Day*, 143, 185.

75. Private Michael Whelan of Vermillion County, the only "Mike" in Company C. See *AGI*, 4:377.

76. Psalm 122:1 (KJV).

77. This sentence is an almost verbatim quote from William Cullen Bryant's poem, "The Battlefield." See William Cullen Bryant, *Poems*, 2 vols. (New York: D. Appleton, 1871), 2:164.

78. Stott's memory fails him a bit here. The quoted poem is not from Byron, but from

Alexander Pope's *An Essay on Man*. Nor is it verbatim, but so close as to impress the reader with Stott's exceptional memory. See *Poems of Alexander Pope*, Maynard Mack, ed., vol. 3, *An Essay on Man* (New Haven: Yale University Press, 1951), 81–82.

79. This Achilles Vawter was Will's great-uncle, the tavern keeper and postmaster of Vernon. He died on March 18, 1862. See Bicknell, *Vawter Family in America*, 243.

80. *Harper's Weekly* and *Frank Leslie's Illustrated Newspaper* were the leading illustrated newspapers of the day. The USS *Monitor*, the most famous of Union ironclads, was built and designed by Swedish inventor John Ericsson. On March 9, 1862, it won a tactical victory over the Confederate ironclad *Merrimack*, officially called the *Virginia*, at Hampton Roads, Virginia. See Faust, *Historical Times Illustrated Encyclopedia of the Civil War*, 504.

CHAPTER 4

1. William L. Shea and Earl J. Hess, *Pea Ridge: Civil War Campaign in the West* (Chapel Hill and London: University of North Carolina Press, 1992), 291; William L. Shea, "1862: A Continual Thunder," in Mark K. Christ, ed., *Rugged and Sublime: The Civil War in Arkansas* (Fayetteville: University of Arkansas Press, 1994), 41; John Gould Fletcher, *Arkansas* (Chapel Hill: University of North Carolina Press, 1947), 154–56.

2. David Lathrop, *The History of the Fifty-ninth Regiment Illinois Volunteers* (Indianapolis: Hall and Hutchinson, 1865), 110; Shea and Hess, *Pea Ridge*, 291–92; James T. King, *War Eagle: A Life of General Eugene A. Carr* (Lincoln: University of Nebraska Press, 1963), 50.

3. Lathrop, *History of the Fifty-ninth Regiment Illinois Volunteers*, 110–13; John C. Swift Diaries, 1861–1863, 2 vols., entry of April 15, 1862, 2:29-30, IHS. Enos E. Johnson of Company B of the Eighteenth carefully logged the soggy conditions and their "disagreeable effect on marching in southern Missouri." See E. E. Johnson, "Notes by the Way," Diary of E. E. Johnson, Company B, Eighteenth Regiment Indiana Volunteers April 15, 17, 18, and 20, 1862, Florida Historical Records Survey, USF.

4. *OR*, 8:679.

5. Shea and Hess, *Pea Ridge*, 292; Fletcher, *Arkansas*, 158–59; Catharine Merrill, *The Soldier of Indiana in the War for the Union*, 2 vols. (Indianapolis: Merrill and Company, 1866), 1:208.

6. Merrill, *Soldier of Indiana in the War for the Union*, 1:209; *Indianapolis Daily State Sentinel*, September 20, 1862; Gilbert H. Denny to Father, May 31, 1862, Letters of Gilbert H. Denny, 18th Regiment, 1861–1863, IHS (hereafter cited as Denny Letters).

7. Nathaniel Cheairs Hughes Jr. and Gordon D. Whitney, *Jefferson Davis in Blue: The Life of Sherman's Relentless Warrior* (Baton Rouge: Louisiana State University, 2002), 92; Shea and Hess, *Pea Ridge*, 295; Frank J. Welcher, *The Union Army, 1861–1865: Organization and Operations*, 2 vols. (Bloomington: Indiana University Press, 1989), 2:219.

8. Kenneth C. Barnes, "The Williams Clan: Mountain Farmers and Union Fighters in North Central Arkansas," *Arkansas Historical Quarterly* 52 (Autumn 1993): 293–94. See also Shea, "Continual Thunder," 41.

9. James K. Bigelow, *Abridged History of the Eighth Indiana Volunteer Infantry from Its Organization, April 21st 1861, to the Date of Re-enlistment as Veterans, January 1, 1864* (Indianapolis: Ellis Barnes Book and Job Printer, 1864), 13–14; Merrill, *Soldier of Indiana in the War for the Union*, 1:208-9; Rhonda M. Kohl, "'This Godforsaken Town': Death and Disease at Helena, Arkansas, 1862–1863," *Civil War History* 50 (June 2004): 114.

10. William L. Shea, "The Confederate Defeat at Cache River," *Arkansas Historical Quar-*

terly 52 (Summer 1993): 129–30; Shea, "Continual Thunder," 41–42; Shea and Hess, *Pea Ridge*, 299–300.

11. Fletcher, *Arkansas*, 160–61; Shea, "Continual Thunder," 42.

12. Bigelow, *History of the Eighth Indiana Volunteer Infantry*, 14; Merrill, *Soldier of Indiana in the War for the Union*, 2:245; *Indianapolis Daily State Sentinel*, September 22, 1862.

13. Merrill, *Soldier of Indiana in the War for the Union*, 2:245; Shea and Hess, *Pea Ridge*, 301–2; Kohl, "'This Godforsaken Town,'" 114–15; July 4 and 6, Swift Diaries, 2:79–82; *Indianapolis Daily State Sentinel*, September 22, 1862.

14. Denny to Morris Denny, July 14, 1862, Denny Letters; Shea, "Confederate Defeat at Cache River," 132. The Shea article is the finest and most complete study of the crucial encounter, which Shea, in another article, calls "the most one-sided Federal victory in Arkansas." See Shea, "Continual Thunder," 44. The Eighteenth Indiana did not participate in the battle, having arrived after it had subsided. See S. B. Voyles to Father, July 14, 1862, Samuel B. Voyles Civil War Correspondence, 1861–1862, IHS.

15. Shea and Hess, *Pea Ridge*, 303; C. P. Alling, "Four Years with the Western Army," 2–3, Regimental Files (11th Wisconsin), VNMP; S. B. Voyles to Father, July 14, 1862, Voyles Correspondence.

16. Shea and Hess, *Pea Ridge*, 303; Kohl, "'This Godforsaken Town,'" 115. Shea, "Continual Thunder," 44; Merrill, *Soldier of Indiana in the War for the Union*, 2:248; Sylvester Bishop to Mother, July 14, 1862, in "Indiana Troops at Helena: Part III," *Phillips County Historical Quarterly* 17 (March 1979): 11.

17. Barnes, "Williams Clan," 297; *Indianapolis Daily State Sentinel*, September 22, 1862; Thomas A. DeBlack, "1863: We Must Stand or Fall Alone," in Christ, ed., *Rugged and Sublime*, 75; Kohl, "'This Godforsaken Town,'" 109, 116–18, 123, 137, 142. References in soldiers' accounts of the extent of disease may be found in "Indiana Troops at Helena: Part I, Civil War Diary of James H. Hougland, 1st Indiana Cavalry, for the Year 1862," *Phillips County Historical Quarterly* 16 (March 1978): 21–23, 26; Gilbert Denny to Father and Mother, September 18, 26, 1862, in "Indiana Troops at Helena: Part II, Gilbert H. Denny Letters," ibid. 16 (September 1978): 6–7; Sylvester Bishop to Mother, August 29, October 2, 1862, in "Indiana Troops at Helena: Part III," ibid. 17 (March 1979): 15, 18–19. In the last entry, Bishop reports that the death of his close friend, Kelly, "was almost like losing a brother." See also Muster Roll of the Eighteenth Indiana, 18 August 1862, at Helena, Arkansas, in William T. Stott Civil War Papers, 1863–1864, SCFC.

18. William T. Stott Military Service File, dated May 7, 1895, Individual Service Record and Company Muster Roll for September and October, 1862, NARA; Gilbert Denny to Father, August 29, 1862, "Indiana Troops at Helena: Part II," 5; Merrill, *Soldier of Indiana in the War for the Union*, 2:251.

19. Isaac H. Elliott, *History of the Thirty-third Illinois Veteran Volunteer Infantry in the Civil War* (Gibson City, IL: Regiment Association, 1902), 33; *AGI*, 2:56, 167; *Supplement to the Official Records of the Union and Confederate Armies*, part 2, vol. 16 (Wilmington, NC: Broadfoot Publishing Company, 1995), 383–84.

20. Extracts from November 17, 1862, letter of H. D. Washburn, in the *Rockville Parke County Republican*, December 10, 1862.

21. Diary, December 15, 1862, George W. Gordon Papers, 1861–1864, USAMHI (hereafter cited as Gordon Diary); December 15, 1862, vol. 2, Erastus G. Burget Diaries, 1862, IHS (hereafter cited as Burget Diary). See also entry of December 14, 1862, vol. 3, Swift

Diaries; Elliott, *History of the Thirty-third Illinois Veteran Volunteer Infantry in the Civil War*, 32.

22. Gordon Diary, January 15, 31, 1863. On weather and supply problems, see also Elliott, *History of the Thirty-third Illinois Veteran Volunteer Infantry in the Civil War*, 32–33; Taylor Peirce to Catharine, February 5, 16, 1863, in *Dear Catharine, Dear Taylor: The Civil War Letters of a Union Soldier and His Wife*, Richard L. Kiper, ed. (Lawrence: University of Kansas Press, 2002), 77, 80.

23. *Brookville Franklin Democrat*, March 27, 1863; Bigelow, *Abridged History of the Eighth Indiana Volunteer Infantry*, 16.

24. Earl Schenck Miers, *The Web of Victory: Grant at Vicksburg* (New York: Alfred A. Knopf, 1955), 23; Michael B. Ballard, *Vicksburg: The Campaign that Opened the Mississippi* (Chapel Hill and London: University of North Carolina, 2004), 24–25. See also Terrence J. Winschel, *Triumph and Defeat: The Vicksburg Campaign*, 2 vols. (Mason City, IA: Savas Publishing, 1999), 1:1–3.

25. Stephen E. Ambrose, *Halleck: Lincoln's Chief of Staff* (Baton Rouge: Louisiana University Press, 1962), 108; Ulysses S. Grant, *Personal Memoirs of Ulysses S. Grant*, 2 vols. (New York: Charles L. Webster and Company, 1885), 1:422.

26. Ambrose, *Halleck*, 110–12, 117; William L. Shea and Terrence J. Winschel, *Vicksburg Is the Key: The Struggle for the Mississippi River* (Lincoln and London: University of Nebraska Press, 2003), 35; Ballard, *Vicksburg*, 157; Winschel, *Triumph and Defeat*, 2:57. Grant's subordination of McClernand, who actually outranked Grant, added fuel to the already tense relationship between the two men, a complete account of which is beyond the parameters of this study. Brief insights into their conflicts, however, will be given in subsequent endnotes.

27. The Eighteenth Indiana was assigned to the Fourteenth Division, led by Brigadier General Eugene A. Carr. The regiment was in the First Brigade under the command of Brigadier General William P. Benton. See Welcher, *Union Army*, 2:259–62.

28. Ballard, *Vicksburg*, 172–74; Warren E. Grabau, *Ninety-eight Days: A Geographer's View of the Vicksburg Campaign* (Knoxville: University of Tennessee Press, 2000), 55. On the failure of the canal system and its effects on Grant's thinking, see Brooks D. Simpson, *Ulysses S. Grant: Triumph over Adversity, 1822–1865* (Boston and New York: Houghton Mifflin, 2000), 173; Bruce Catton, *Grant Moves South* (Boston and Toronto: Little, Brown and Company, 1960), 406, 409. Unhealthy conditions during the winter of 1862–63 had already led to numerous illnesses. See James R. Arnold, *Grant Wins the War: Decision at Vicksburg* (New York: John Wiley and Sons, 1997), 62; Steven E. Woodworth, *Nothing but Victory: The Army of the Tennessee, 1861–1865* (New York: Alfred A. Knopf, 2005), 313.

29. Grabau, *Ninety-eight Days*, 16, 51–52; Winschel, *Triumph and Defeat*, 1:6, 18; Francis V. Greene, *The Mississippi* (New York: Charles Scribner's Sons, 1892), 109–10; Samuel Carter III, *The Final Fortress: Campaign for Vicksburg, 1862–1863* (New York: St. Martin's Press, 1980), 152–53.

30. Grant, *Personal Memoirs*, 1:465; Richard L. Kiper, *Major General John Alexander McClernand: Politician in Uniform* (Kent, OH and London: Kent State University Press, 1999), 204; John D. Winters, *The Civil War in Louisiana* (Baton Rouge: Louisiana State University Press, 1963), 188; *OR*, 24(1):139–40; Shea and Winschel, *Vicksburg Is the Key*, 91; Winschel, *Triumph and Defeat,*, 1:18–21. For details on the Bennett expedition from a participant, see Oran Perry, "The Entering Wedge," (Indiana) *MOLLUS*, 362–65.

31. Carter, *Final Fortress*, 153; Terrence J. Winschel, "Fighting Politician: John A. McClernand," in *Grant's Lieutenants: From Cairo to Vicksburg*, Steven E. Woodworth, ed. (Lawrence: University of Kansas Press, 2001), 137; Greene, *Mississippi*, 110; Winters, *Civil War in Louisiana*, 191. Endless mud and the need to ferry around some levees also slowed progress. See Woodworth, *Nothing but Victory*, 319.

32. Grabau, *Ninety-eight Days*, 62; Woodworth, *Nothing but Victory*, 315–16; Alling, "Four Years with the Western Army," 7; Arnold, *Grant Wins the War*, 66–68.

33. James R. Bernard Slack to Ann, April 17, 1863, James R. Slack Papers, 1837–1865, L145, Manuscript Section, ISL (hereafter cited as Slack Papers); Schermerhorn to wife, April 19, 1863, Bernard F. Schermerhorn Papers, 1862–1864, IHS (hereafter cited as Schermerhorn Papers).

34. Grabau, *Ninety-eight Days*, 19; Charles A. Dana, *Recollections of the Civil War* (New York: D. Appleton and Company, 1899), 28; Gordon Diary, April 13, 1863.

35. Ballard, *Vicksburg*, 194–95, 197; April 15, 1863, Aquilla Standifird Civil War Diary, 1862–1865, WHMC, Rolla (hereafter cited as Standifird Diary); Carter, *Final Fortress*, 158; Taylor to Catharine, March 28, 1863, Kiper, ed., *Dear Catharine*, 89.

36. Grant, *Personal Memoirs*, 463–64; Winschel, *Triumph and Defeat*, 1:8–9; Shea and Winschel, *Vicksburg Is the Key*, 98–99; Woodworth, *Nothing but Victory*, 322–25; Arnold, *Grant Wins the War*, 75.

37. Timothy B. Smith, *Champion Hill: Decisive Battle for Vicksburg* (New York: Savas Beattie, 2004), 14; Elliott, *History of the Thirty-third Illinois Veteran Volunteer Infantry in the Civil War*, 37; Perry, "Entering Wedge," 375; Woodworth, *Nothing but Victory*, 323–24; W. M. Littell to wife, April 18, 1863, Regimental Files (23rd Iowa Infantry), VNMP.

38. Alling, "Four Years in the Western Army," 7; Grant, *Personal Memoirs*, 1:466; Winschel, *Triumph and Defeat*, 1:25; Shea and Winschel, *Vicksburg Is the Key*, 101; Kiper, ed., *Dear Catharine*, 100n2.

39. Grabau, *Ninety-eight Days*, 83; Arnold, *Grant Wins the War*, 79, 87–88; Grant to McClernand, April 20, 1863, John Y. Simon, ed., *The Papers of Ulysses S. Grant*, 26 vols. (Carbondale: Southern Illinois University Press, 1969–), 8:96; Special Orders No. 110, ibid., 8:98; Edwin Cole Bearss, *The Vicksburg Campaign*, 3 vols. (Dayton, OH: Morningside Press, 1985–86), 2:297–98.

40. Augustus G. Sinks, "'Four Years in Dixie,' Journal of the Campaign of the 46th Indiana Regiment," 32, S1193, Manuscript Section, ISL. For a full account of the transports' combative trip past Vicksburg, see Woodworth, *Nothing but Victory*, 326–31.

41. Elliott, *History of Thirty-third Illinois Veteran Volunteer Infantry in the Civil War*, 37; Standifird Diary, April 24, 1863; Grant, *Personal Memoirs*, 1:473; Welcher, *Union Army*, 2:864.

42. Grant to McClernand, April 27, 1863, Simon, ed., *Papers of Ulysses S. Grant*, 8:126–27; *OR*, 24(1):142–43, 6:15; Bearss, *Vicksburg Campaign*, 2:295.

43. Grabau, *Ninety-eight Days*, 136; Gordon Diary, April 24, 1863.

44. Grant, *Personal Memoirs*, 1:473, 475–76; Woodworth, *Nothing but Victory*, 335; *OR*, 24(1):142. For an excellent account of the strength of the Confederate defense at Grand Gulf, see Edwin C. Bearss, "Grand Gulf's Role in the Civil War," *Civil War History* 5 (March 1959): 5–29.

45. Asa E. Sample Civil War Diary of Co. E, 54th Regt., 97–98, S1136, Manuscript Section, ISL (hereafter cited as Sample Diary); Alling, "Four Years in the Western Army," 7;

Diary and Letters of Charles A. Hobbs, 1, Regimental Files (99th Illinois), VNMP (hereafter cited as Hobbs Diary); W. M. Littell to wife, May 4, 1863, Regimental Files (23rd Iowa), VNMP; Israel M. Ritter Diary, April 29, 1863, USAMHI (hereafter cited as Ritter Diary).

46. Dana, *Recollections of the Civil War*, 43; Woodworth, *Nothing but Victory*, 335–36; Grant, *Personal Memoirs*, 475; Grabau, *Ninety-eight Days*, 143–44.

47. Grant, *Personal Memoirs*, 1:475; Grabau, *Ninety-eight Days*, 144–45.

48. Sample Diary, 102; Grabau, *Ninety-eight Days*, 145–46; Taylor to Catharine, May 4, 1863, Kiper, ed., *Dear Catharine*, 105; Shea and Winschel, *Vicksburg Is the Key*, 106; Winschel, *Triumph and Defeat*, 1:30; Bearss, *Vicksburg Campaign*, 2:317; Woodworth, *Nothing but Victory*, 337; Grant, *Personal Memoirs*, 1:480–81.

49. Grabau, *Ninety-eight Days*, 146; Bearss, *Vicksburg Campaign*, 2:318–19; Grant, *Personal Memoirs*, 1:481–82. Grant had, in fact, specifically ordered the chief commissary of the XIII Corps to "issue to the troops of this command . . . for their subsistence during the next *five* days *three* rations." See Adam Badeau, *Military History of Ulysses S. Grant*, 3 vols. (New York: D. Appleton and Company, 1881), 1:204. Biographer Richard L. Kiper concludes that "McClernand alone must bear responsibility for that oversight." See Kiper, *Major General John Alexander McClernand*, 221.

50. Woodworth, *Nothing but Victory*, 338; Hobbs Diary, 2; Shea and Winschel, *Vicksburg Is the Key*, 108; Grabau, *Ninety-eight Days*, 147, 149; Bearss, *Vicksburg Campaign*, 2:318–19.

51. Winschel, *Triumph and Defeat*, 1:58–59; Ballard, *Vicksburg*, 222–23; Bearss, *Vicksburg Campaign*, 2:319–20; Shea and Winschel, *Vicksburg Is the Key*, 108–9. A devastating fire destroyed Windsor mansion in 1890, but some of the pillars still stand, vivid reminders of the opulence some enjoyed in the antebellum South. Bethel Church also remains.

52. Grabau, *Ninety-eight Days*, 147; George W. K. Bailey to C. A. Hobbs, May 19, 1885, Regimental Files (99th Illinois), VNMP; Samuel P. Herrington Diary, July 4, 1863, Rudolph Hearle Collection, USAMHI (hereafter cited as Herrington Diary); Hobbs Diary, 2.

53. Bearss, *Vicksburg Campaign*, 2:320, 345, 357, 373; Ulysses S. Grant, "The Vicksburg Campaign," in *Battles and Leaders of the Civil War*, 4 vols., Robert U. Johnson and Clarence C. Clough Buel, eds. (New York: Century Company, 1887), 3:497; Grant, *Personal Memoirs*, 1:483; Grabau, *Ninety-eight Days*, 23, 148, 155.

54. Grabau, *Ninety-eight Days*, 150–52.

55. Ibid., 154, 162; Winschel, *Triumph and Defeat*, 1:62-64; Bearss, *Vicksburg Campaign*, 2:355–56; Ballard, *Vicksburg*, 227–28; Arnold, *Grant Wins the War*, 102; W. M. Littell to wife, May 4, 1863, Regimental Files (23rd Iowa Infantry), VNMP; Standifird Diary, May 1, 1863; H. C. Leeson to Father, May 10, 1863, Mrs. F. A. Thomas Civil War Diaries and Letters, 1813 & 1863, S1301, Manuscript Section, ISL (hereafter cited as Thomas Diaries and Letters). See also *OR*, 24(1):615. The Indiana Battery involved was Martin Klauss's First Light Artillery, a largely German outfit, hence "Our Duch Boys."

56. *OR*, 24(1):143; Leeson to Father, May 10, 1863, Thomas Diaries and Letters; Kenneth P. Williams, *Lincoln Finds a General*, 5 vols. (New York: Macmillan, 1956), 4:347; Shea and Winschel, *Vicksburg Is the Key*, 110; Kiper, *McClernand*, 222, 225.

57. *OR*, 24(1):144, 615-16, 625; Bearss, *Vicksburg Campaign*, 2:373–74; Hobbs Diary, 4; May 1, 1863, Louis W. Knobe Diary, S1238, Manuscript Section, ISL (hereafter cited as Knobe Diary); Schermerhorn to wife, May 2, 1863, Schermerhorn Papers.

58. Ballard, *Vicksburg*, 230, 234; Bearss, *Vicksburg Campaign*, 2:375–76; Woodworth, *Nothing but Victory*, 342–43; Grabau, *Ninety-eight Days*, 157; Smith, *Champion Hill*, 50.

59. Harry Watts, Civil War Reminiscence, "Review of the 24th Ind. Vols." by a Corporal Pro. Tem., 68, S1372, Manuscript Collection, ISL; Sinks, "Four Years in Dixie," 34; Ritter Diary, May 1, 1863; Winschel, *Triumph and Defeat*, 1:71.

60. Winschel, *Triumph and Defeat*, 1:72; Woodworth, *Nothing but Victory*, 343; Arnold, *Grant Wins the War*, 107–8; Grabau, *Ninety-eight Days*, 157; Ballard, *Vicksburg*, 235; *OR*, 24(1):621–22, 626; Bearss, *Vicksburg*, 2:378–81. The debate over which unit was first at the battery began during the war itself and continued among the veterans until their demise, which is one reason it is hard for historians to tell the story with precise accuracy. The regimental files at the Vicksburg National Military Park are replete with conflicting claims. On those of the Eighteenth Indiana, see E. A. Carr to C. A. Hobbs, January 13, 1885, the Eugene A. Carr Papers, 1830–1920, Box 2, USAMHI; *OR*, 24(1):633–34; Knobe Diary, May 1, 1863; Herrington Diary, May 1, 1863.

61. Taylor to Catharine, May 4, 1863, Kiper, ed., *Dear Catharine*, 108; Hobbs Diary, 9; Arnold, *Grant Wins the War*, 109; Kiper, *McClernand*, 225; Simpson, *Ulysses S. Grant*, 191–92.

62. *OR*, 24(1):145; Arnold, *Grant Wins the War*, 112; Smith, *Champion Hill*, 54–55; Standifird Diary, May 1, 1863; Winschel, *Triumph and Defeat*, 1:79–80, 83; Bearss, *Vicksburg Campaign*, 2:387, 392.

63. Winschel, *Triumph and Defeat*, 1:31, 2:1–2; General Order No. 32, May 7, 1863, Simon, ed., *Papers of Ulysses S. Grant*, 8:170; Emma Lou Thornbrough, *Indiana in the Civil War Era, 1850–1880* (Indianapolis: Indiana Historical Bureau and Indiana Historical Society, 1965), 154; Report of Henry D. Washburn, undated, Regimental Files (18th Indiana), VNMP.

64. James R. Slack to Ann, May 11, 1863, Slack Papers; Hobbs Diary, 7; Arnold, *Grant Wins the War*, 118; Winschel, *Triumph and Defeat*, 2:2.

65. Grant, "Vicksburg Campaign," 3:498; Badeau, *Military History of Ulysses S. Grant*, 1:12; Ritter Diary, May 2, 1863; Sample Diary, May 2, 1863; Hobbs Diary, 7.

66. Bearss, *Vicksburg Campaign*, 2:411; Grant, "Vicksburg Campaign," 3:498-99; Sample Diary, May 2, 1863.

67. Grant, "Vicksburg Campaign," 3:501–2; Catton, *Grant Moves South*, 430 (Grant to Sherman quote); Carter, *Final Fortress*, 185, 187; Winschel, *Triumph and Defeat*, 1:9. The reasons Grant chose to go east rather than directly toward Vicksburg are most succinctly and clearly stated in Shea and Winschel, *Vicksburg Is the Key*, 117–18.

68. Catton, *Grant Moves South*, 430, 432; Arnold, *Grant Wins the War*, 127; Woodworth, *Nothing but Victory*, 352 (Cowan quote).

69. H. C. Leeson to Moses Leeson, May 10, 1863, Thomas Civil War Diaries and Letters; Bearss, *Vicksburg Campaign*, 2:461; *OR*, 24(1):146; Grabau, *Ninety-eight Days*, 211.

70. Winschel, *Triumph and Defeat*, 2:15; Shea and Winschel, *Vicksburg Is the Key*, 119–20.

71. Shea and Winschel, *Vicksburg Is the Key*, 120; Badeau, *Military History of Ulysses S. Grant*, 1:215.

72. Shea and Winschel, *Vicksburg Is the Key*, 120; Winschel, "Fighting Politician," 138; Grabau, *Ninety-eight Days*, 199–200 ("parallel columns" quote); Woodworth, *Nothing but Victory*, 350.

73. Winschel, *Triumph and Defeat*, 2:14, 20, 24; Greene, *Mississippi*, 134, 140–41; Bearss, *Vicksburg Campaign*, 2:428, 446, 465, 470–72, 480 (quote); Dana, *Recollections*, 50; Ballard, *Vicksburg*, 259–60; Grabau, *Ninety-eight Days*, 174, 197, 210–14; Grant, "Vicksburg Cam-

paign," 3:502–3; Grant, *Personal Memoirs*, 1:496–97. On the work of McClernand's men in guarding the ferries and the skirmish at Fourteen Mile Creek, see McClernand to Grant, May 7, 12, 1863, Simon, ed., *Papers of Ulysses S. Grant*, 8:173, 204.

74. Grant to McClernand, May 12, 13, 1863, Simon, ed., *Papers of Ulysses S. Grant*, 8:204, 208; Grant, *Personal Memoirs*, 1:499–500; *OR*, 24(1):147.

75. Grabau, *Ninety-eight Days*, 241–42; Winschel, *Triumph and Defeat*, 2:31–32; Grant, *Personal Memoirs*, 1:501–2; Ballard, *Vicksburg*, 271–72; Arnold, *Grant Wins the War*, 138; *OR*, 24(1):147; Ritter Diary, May 13, 1863; Kiper, *McClernand*, 238–39.

76. Grant, *Personal Memoirs*, 1:501–3; *OR*, 24(1):147.

77. *OR*, 24(1): 147, 616; Wasson (Ira W. Hunt) to wife, May 23, 1863, Regimental Files (11th Wisconsin), VNMP; Grant to McClernand, May 14, 1863, Simon, ed., *Papers of Ulysses S. Grant*, 8:215.

78. Grant to McClernand, May 14, 1863, and McClernand to Grant, May 15, 1863, Simon, ed., *Papers of Ulysses S. Grant*, 8:215–16; Michael B. Ballard, *Pemberton: A Biography* (Jackson and London: University Press of Mississippi, 1991), 159; Smith, *Champion Hill*, 110–11; Arnold, *Grant Wins the War*, 144.

79. Smith, *Champion Hill*, 115; Greene, *Mississippi*, 152–54; Ballard, *Vicksburg*, 286–87; Grabau, *Ninety-eight Days*, 259–60; Grant, *Personal Memoirs*, 3:509-10; *OR*, 24(1): 148.

80. Ballard, *Vicksburg*, 289; Greene, *Mississippi*, 152–54; Grant to McClernand, May 16, 1863, Simon, ed., *Papers of Ulysses S. Grant*, 8:224; Arnold, *Grant Wins the War*, 151–52; Shea and Winschel, *Vicksburg Is the Key*, 131. Hovey's division was detached to McPherson's XVII Corps that day. See Woodworth, *Nothing but Victory*, 369–70.

81. Grant, "Vicksburg Campaign," 3:509-10; Bearss, *Vicksburg Campaign*, 2:579, 585, 591; Badeau, *Military History of Ulysses S. Grant*, 1:259; *OR*, 24(2):134; Smith, *Champion Hill*, 155–59; Arnold, *Grant Wins the War*, 148, 153–54.

82. Woodworth, *Nothing but Victory*, 371; Elliott, *History of the 33rd Illinois Veteran Volunteer Infantry in the Civil War*, 39; Herrington Diary, May 16, 1863.

83. Smith, *Champion Hill*, 163, 190, 187–90; *OR*, 24(3):149, 316–18; Simpson, *Ulysses S. Grant*, 199; Ballard, *Vicksburg*, 295; Grabau, *Ninety-eight Days*, 279, 300. Grant laid much blame on McClernand because of his inertness during the decisive battle at Champion Hill. He wrote in his memoirs: "Had McClernand come up with reasonable promptness or had I known the ground as I did afterwards, I cannot see how Pemberton could have escaped with any organized force." Adam Badeau, one of Grant's private secretaries, accused the Illinois politician-general of "an excess of caution" and keeping 15,000 men lingering under his command. McClernand's biographer, Richard Kiper, also criticizes the general's handling of his corps that day. Edwin C. Bearss, on the other hand, asserts that McClernand "was not as derelict as Grant implies." Likewise, Terrence Winschel masterfully defends McClernand's performance under the conditions on the day of the battle. See Grant, *Personal Memoirs*, 1:518–19; Badeau, *Military History of Ulysses S. Grant*, 1:269; Kiper, *McClernand*, 247; Bearss, *Vicksburg Campaign*, 2:639; Winschel, *Triumph and Defeat*, 2:49–72, especially 59–60.

84. Grant, *Personal Memoirs*, 1:517; Shea and Winschel, *Vicksburg Is the Key*, 136; Arnold, *Grant Wins the War*, 193; Smith, *Champion Hill*, 357; Ballard, *Vicksburg*, 307; Bearss, *Vicksburg Campaign*, 2:28–31.

85. Hobbs Diary, 27–28; Herrington Diary, May 17, 1863; Smith, *Champion Hill*, 313.

86. Bearss, *Vicksburg Campaign*, 2:632; Hobbs Diary, 29; Arnold, *Grant Wins the War*,

195. Edwin Bearss, among other historians, contends that Champion Hill "was the most important single engagement of the Civil War," and Michael Ballard asserts that it definitely "sealed the fate of Vicksburg." See Bearss, *Vicksburg Campaign*, 2:637; Ballard, *Vicksburg*, 164. For similar assessments, see Winschel, *Triumph and Defeat*, 1:90–91; James M. McPherson, *Battle Cry of Freedom: The Civil War Era* (New York: Oxford University Press, 1988), 630.

87. Bearss, *Vicksburg Campaign*, 2:659, 663; Woodworth, *Nothing but Victory*, 190–91; Ballard, *Vicksburg*, 313–14; Grant, *Personal Memoirs*, 1:523.

88. Herrington Diary, May 17, 1863; H. C. Leeson to Father, May 27, 1863, Thomas Civil War Diaries and Letters; OR, 24(1):152, 2:135–38; Arnold, *Grant Wins the War*, 227–29; Ballard, *Vicksburg*, 315–17; Bearss, *Vicksburg Campaign*, 2:670, 674; Grant, "Vicksburg Campaign," 3:515; Catton, *Grant Moves South*, 446 (Grant quote); W. M. Littell to William T. Rigby, November 17, 1903, Regimental Files (23rd Iowa), VNMP; Standifird Diary, May 17, 1863.

89. Grant, *Personal Memoirs*, 1:526, 528; Swain Marshall to "Friend at Home," May 29, 1863, Thomas Marshall Papers, 1821–1920, IHS; Osborne H. Oldroyd, *A Soldier's Story of the Siege of Vicksburg* (Springfield, IL: n.p., 1885), 34–35; OR, 24(1):153; Arnold, *Grant Wins the War*, 240; Ballard, *Vicksburg*, 324.

90. Grabau, *Ninety-eight Days*, 46–47, 355, 375; Ballard, *Vicksburg*, 320; Kiper, *McClernand*, 251. The quotation from W. E. Strong appears in Herman Hattaway, *General Stephen D. Lee* (Jackson: University Press of Mississippi, 1976), 93, 245.

91. Ballard, *Vicksburg*, 324–25; Grabau, *Ninety-eight Days*, 355–57; Special Field Orders No. 134, Simon, ed., *Papers of Ulysses S. Grant*, 8:237; OR, 24(1):154; Simpson, *Ulysses S. Grant*, 202–3; Arnold, *Grant Wins the War*, 245.

92. Ballard, *Vicksburg*, 335, 337; Hattaway, *General Stephen D. Lee*, 91; Miers, *Web of Victory*, 204–5; Bearss, *Vicksburg Campaign*, 2:801; Knobe Diary, May 21, 1863; Badeau, *Military History of Ulysses S. Grant*, 1:305–6; Grant, "Vicksburg Campaign," 3:518. For Grant's orders, see Simon, ed., *Papers of Ulysses S. Grant*, 8:245.

93. Oldroyd, *Soldier's Story of the Siege of Vicksburg*, 39; OR, 24(1): 154; Simpson, *Ulysses S. Grant*, 203; Elliott, *History of the 33rd Illinois Veteran Volunteer Infantry in the Civil War*, 44; Grabau, *Ninety-eight Days*, 376–77; Herrington Diary, May 22, 1863; Hobbs Diary, 20; Leeson to Father, May 27, 1863. According to James R. Arnold, this was the first occasion in military history when commanders "synchronized their timepieces" for an assault. See Arnold, *Grant Wins the War*, 247.

94. Hattaway, *General Stephen D. Lee*, 93–94; Kiper, *McClernand*, 259; Wasson to wife, May 23, 1863. The finest recent accounts of the fighting at the Railroad Redoubt are Ballard, *Vicksburg*, 34–42, and Woodworth, *Nothing but Victory*, 417–19. See also the letters of First Sergeant Austin E. Cook of the Twenty-first Iowa to William T. Rigby, April 12, 15, 1903, and Cook's "Recollections," in Regimental Files (21st Iowa), VNMP.

95. Ballard, *Vicksburg*, 323; James B. Black to William T. Rigby, May 15, 1902, Regimental Files (8th Indiana), VNMP; Shea and Winschel, *Vicksburg Is the Key*, 150; Richard Brady Williams, *Chicago's Battery Boys: The Chicago Mercantile Battery in the Civil War's Western Theater* (New York: Savas Beattie, 2005), 113; OR, 24(1): 155; Arnold, *Grant Wins the War*, 252; Woodworth, *Nothing but Victory*, 146; Kiper, *McClernand*, 259.

96. Williams, *Chicago's Battery Boys*, 113; Hobbs Diary, 21; A. G. Matthews to William T. Rigby, December 27, 1904, Regimental Files (99th Illinois), VNMP. Matthews also remem-

bered that the brunt of the fighting "was made by the 99th Illinois and the 18th Ind."

97. *OR*, 24(1):155, (2):37–38; Indiana-Vicksburg Military Park Commission, *Indiana at Vicksburg* (Indianapolis: William B. Burford, 1911), 55; James B. Black to William T. Rigby, May 15, 1902, and November 27, 1903, Regimental Files (18th Indiana), VNMP; Matthews to Rigby, April 13, 1903, Regimental Files (99th Illinois), VNMP; Merrill, *Soldier of Indiana in the War for the Union*, 2:319; Badeau, *Military History of Ulysses S. Grant*, 1:319.

98. Bearss, *Vicksburg Campaign*, 3:828, 830–31; Black to Rigby, May 15, 1902; James A. Abbott to Rigby, November 17, 1904, Regimental Files (8th Indiana), VNMP; Merrill, *Soldier of Indiana in the War for the Union*, 2:317–18.

99. Black to Rigby, May 15, 1902, November 27, 1903; Stott to Rigby, March 9, 1903, Regimental Files (18th Indiana), VNMP. See also *Indiana at Vicksburg*, 188–89.

100. Ballard, *Vicksburg*, 348; Arnold, *Grant Wins the War*, 257; Woodworth, *Nothing but Victory*, 427; Leeper to Mary, May 23, 1863, James Leeper Papers, 1855–1865, IHS; Gordon Diary, May 24, 1863. There was, of course, plenty of blame to go around for the failure of the May 22 assault, but tracing the claims of eyewitnesses and historians who have accessed it is beyond the parameters of this book. Suffice it to say that both Grant and McClernand received the brunt of most criticism. McClernand had urged Grant to reinforce his XIII Corps in its assaults on the Southern defenses, or at least use some of McPherson's men as a "diversion" while the politician-general secured what he saw as potential success at the Railroad Redoubt and Second Texas Lunette. Grant provided such relief but "did not see the success [McClernand] reported" and always felt "misled . . . as to the real state of the facts." He insisted that McClernand's actions caused an even greater loss of life. Grant's other corps commanders joined him in this belief, as did eyewitnesses Sylvanus Cadwallader and Charles A. Dana. McClernand's biographer, Richard Kiper, tends to agree with this assessment, but James R. Arnold faults "Grant's stubborn refusal to acknowledge defeat" as the trait that led to increased bloodshed and suffering. To trace the exchanges between Grant and McClernand, see Simon, ed., *Papers of Ulysses S. Grant*, 8:252–54; Bearss, *Vicksburg Campaign*, 3:835–37; Simpson, *Ulysses S. Grant*, 204; Winschel, "Fighting Politician," 140. See also Kiper, *McClernand*, 259–60, 263–65; Sylvanus Cadwallader, *Three Years with Grant*, Benjamin Thomas, ed. (New York: Alfred A. Knopf, 1955), 89–92; Dana, *Recollections*, 56–58.

101. Woodworth, *Nothing but Victory*, 425; Badeau, *Military History of Ulysses S. Grant*, 1:350; Knobe Diary, May 23, 1863; Chittenden to wife, May 29, 1863, George F. Chittenden Papers, 1831–1913, L31, Manuscript Section, ISL; Bearss, *Vicksburg Campaign*, 3:885.

102. Winschel, *Triumph and Defeat*, 1:13, 129; Ballard, *Vicksburg*, 349–50; Knobe Diary, May 25, 1863; J. C. Nottingham to William T. Rigby, December 12, 1901, Regimental Files (8th Indiana), VNMP.

103. Jim Huffstodt, *Hard Dying Men: The Story of General W. H. L. Wallace, General T. E. G. Ransom, and Their "Old Eleventh" Illinois Infantry in the Civil War (1861–1865)* (Bowie, MD: Heritage Books, 1991), 149; Ballard, *Vicksburg Campaign*, 361; Grant, "Vicksburg Campaign," 3:521–22; Bearss, *Vicksburg Campaign*, 3:935–36; Arnold, *Grant Wins the War*, 260–61; Shea and Winschel, *Vicksburg Is the Key*, 155; Swain Marshall to Sister, June 8, 1863, Marshall Papers; G. H. Denny to Father and Mother, June 10, 1863, Letters of Gilbert H. Denny, IHS; Amos York to W. T. Rigby, January 12, 1903, Regimental Files (8th Indiana), VNMP. McClernand's regular reports on progress in his sector may be found in Simon, ed., *Papers of Ulysses S. Grant*, 8:370. Michael Ballard provides an excellent account

of the work of the XIII Corps in these operations (*Vicksburg*, 370–73).

104. Woodworth, *Nothing but Victory*, 429–30; Oldroyd, *Soldier's Story of the Siege of Vicksburg*, 54; Huffstodt, *Hard Dying Men*, 151–52; Ballard, *Vicksburg*, 376; Roberts to Mother and Sisters, Daniel Roberts Letters, 1861–1864, S1123, Manuscript Section, ISL; Gordon Diary, June 6, 1863.

105. Ballard, *Vicksburg*, 374; Knobe Diary, May 24, 1863; Miers, *Web of Victory*, 223; Taylor to Catharine, June 7, 13, 1863, Kiper, ed., *Dear Catharine*, 113–15; Arnold, *Grant Wins the War*, 268–69.

106. Dana, *Recollections*, 93; Ballard, *Vicksburg*, 373–75; Oldroyd, *Soldier's Story of the Siege of Vicksburg*, 50–53; William Winters to Hattie, June 9, 1863, in *The Musick of the Mocking Birds, the Roar of the Cannon: The Civil War Diary and Letters of William Winters*, Steven E. Woodworth, ed. (Lincoln and London: University of Nebraska Press, 1998), 56; Huffstodt, *Hard Dying Men*, 153–54; Taylor to Catharine, June 13, 1863 (addendum), Kiper, ed., *Dear Catharine*, 116; Arnold, *Grant Wins the War*, 271; John D. Wright, *Language of the Civil War* (Westport, CT: Oryx Press, 2001), 63. The removal of McClernand from command occurred on June 18. Stott's insight gives a minute glimpse into the reasons for his dismissal, the complexities of which are beyond the scope of this book. To say, as Stott does, that Grant and McClernand did not "see eye to eye" is a profound understatement (though Stott would not have known that). The two generals had major personal and professional antagonisms as long as they knew each other. The precipitating action that triggered McClernand's loss of command was his so-called congratulatory order to his troops—General Order No. 72—of May 30, 1863, which was published in newspapers in Memphis, Chicago, and Missouri. His fellow corps commanders, and even his subordinates, vehemently attacked McClernand's apparent assumption of credit for all the successes of the campaign, his aspersions regarding their service, his consistent inaccuracies, and, as Sherman put it, his "effusion of vainglory and hypocrisy." Grant had already considered McClernand less than competent on several occasions and apparently planned to remove him from command after Vicksburg fell. The "congratulatory order" expedited the process and, together with their long-term dislike of each other, led to his dismissal. For a complete picture of the immediate events leading to McClernand's removal, see *OR*, 24(1):137–69; Simon, ed., *Papers of Ulysses S. Grant*, 8:384–85. For secondary accounts dealing with the tensions between the two men, see Bearss, *Vicksburg Campaign*, 3:875–81; Woodworth, *Nothing but Victory*, 430–34; Kiper, *McClernand*, 215–17, 248–50, 267, 304. Terrence Winschel has cogently presented a sympathetic defense of McClernand's leadership of the XIII Corps. He points to the fact that McClernand was Grant's choice to lead the march through Louisiana, which Winschel states was "arguably the most important assignment of the campaign." He was also Grant's selection to handle the left flank of the Army of the Tennessee on the march through Mississippi "at the point of danger being closest to the enemy." In short, Winschel concludes that Grant "entrusted him with a high level of responsibility" because of his aggressive fighting style. See Winschel, *Triumph and Defeat*, 2:16, 49–72.

107. Herrington Diary, July 3, 1863; Woodworth, *Nothing but Victory*, 447–49; Arnold, *Grant Wins the War*, 294. Eyewitnesses and historians differ regarding the number of Confederate messengers appearing that morning, some say two and others three. If there was a third, as Herrington records and historian James R. Arnold affirms, that person may have been the flag bearer.

108. Grant, *Personal Memoirs*, 1:558; Arnold, *Grant Wins the War*, 294–95.

109. Arnold, *Grant Wins the War*, 295–97; Herrington Diary, July 4, 1863; E. P. Stanfield to How[ard], July 10, 1863, Civil War Files of Edward P. Stanfield, IHS; George F. Chittenden to wife, July 3–4, 1863, Chittenden Papers; Taylor to Catharine, July 4, 1863, Kiper, ed., *Dear Catharine*, 124; Denny to family, July 4, 1863, Denny Letters; Gordon Diary, July 4, 1863; Roberts to sisters, July 6, 1863, Daniel Roberts Letters, 1861–1864, S1123, Manuscript Section, ISL; Winters to Hattie, July 6, 1863, Woodworth, ed., *Musick of the Mocking Birds*, 63.

110. Individual Muster Roll, Military Service File, W. T. Stott, NARA.

CHAPTER 5

1. The battle for Island No. 10 in the Mississippi River near New Madrid, Missouri, took place on April 7, 1862. Union forces under General John Pope captured the island, after an unsuccessful naval assault, by sending troops on steamers to the eastern shore of the island. This was a strategic victory, creating a major break in the Confederate defenses and opening the river down to Memphis. See Patricia L. Faust, ed., *The Historical Times Illustrated Encyclopedia of the Civil War* (New York: Harper and Row, 1986), 387; E. B. Long, *The Civil War Day by Day: An Almanac, 1861–1865* (New York: DaCapo, 1971), 196.

2. Major Thomas was Dewitt Clinton Thomas of Salem, who would later be promoted to lieutenant colonel. Privates Henry Hempstead and William Daniel (no "s") were both in Company I and hailed from Johnson County. The chaplain of the Twenty-second Indiana at that time was Episcopal priest Eli P. F. Wells. See *AGI*, 2:158, 210, 4:386. On Wells's denomination, see John W. Brinsfield et al., *Faith in the Fight: Civil War Chaplains* (Mechanicsburg, PA; Stackpole Books, 2003), 205.

3. Though Union forces began to move against Corinth, Mississippi, in mid-April, it was not taken until May 30. See Long, *Civil War Day by Day*, 198, 218.

4. The article to which Stott refers appeared in the April 1862 issue of *Harper's*. Its author was not John Hill but the renowned philosopher and ethicist John Stuart Mill. He declared the American war to be one fought over slavery: "The day when slavery can no longer extend itself is the day of its doom. The slave-owners know this, and it is the cause of their fury." Mill predicted that Congress would soon "declare all slaves free who belong to persons in arms against the Union." See Mill, "The Contest in America," *Harper's New Monthly Magazine* 24 (April 1862): 677–84.

5. William G. Brownlow was a fearless, outspoken, and highly controversial Methodist minister, editor, and politician in Tennessee. Though not an opponent of slavery, he vowed to support the U.S. government and maintained his influential *Knoxville Whig* as the last Union paper in the South until the Confederate government threatened his arrest and destroyed his press and types in November 1861. He later served as the postwar governor of Tennessee. See *DAB*, 2:177–78.

6. Sister Mat was Stott's oldest sibling, Martha Stott Moncrief. A "housewife" was a tiny sewing kit with needles, thread, buttons, and a thimble. See John D. Wright, *The Language of the Civil War* (Westport, CT: Oryx Press, 2001), 151. The battle at Pittsburg Landing was the Battle of Shiloh, fought on April 6–7, 1862, and the bloodiest battle of the war to that date. Confederate Major General Albert Sidney Johnston was killed in the afternoon of the first day. What Eddelman brought was Bishop Joseph Butler's (1692–1872) *Analogy*, which Stott had studied in college and which was particularly influential in his own theological

development. Interestingly, the edition used by this editor was the one that belonged to Doctor Silas Bailey, under whose tutelage Stott first studied Butler. See Joseph Butler, *The Analogy of Religion, Natural and Revealed, to the Constitution and Course of Nature* (Cambridge, MA: Hilliard and Brown, 1827).

7. This incident also was mentioned by the historian of the Fifty-ninth Illinois Infantry who indicated that the men were charged by three women with "creating a disturbance at their house the night before, and sleeping with two young ladies '*nolens volens*.'" Three men were arrested and court-martialed, two of whom were "drummed out of service with shaved heads." See David Lathrop, *The History of the Fifty-ninth Regiment Illinois Volunteers* (Indianapolis: Hall and Hutchinson, 1865), 119.

8. Lorenzo D. McCallister, from Anderson, was the first lieutenant of Company K of the Eighth Indiana. See *AGI*, 2:55.

9. Cousin Mattie V is Mattie Vawter, the daughter of Williamson and Charlotte Vawter of Vernon. See 1860 U.S. Census—Indiana, microfilm, Roll 271, p. 216, ISL. John C. Jenks of Newport, Indiana, was promoted to major in October 1862 and was killed at Vicksburg on May 22, 1863. See *AGI*, 2:161.

10. Translation: "I have no itch for scribbling" or "I have no desire to write."

11. The new lieutenant was John Tilson of Franklin. See *AGI*, 2:165.

12. Commodore David G. Farragut steamed past the forts at New Orleans and entered the city on April 24–25, and General Benjamin Franklin Butler took charge of it as military governor of Louisiana on May 1. See Long, *Civil War Day by Day*, 202–4, 206. As mentioned in note 3 above, Corinth was not evacuated by the Confederates until May 30.

13. Here Stott paraphrases Shakespeare's *Merchant of Venice*, Act 5, scene 1, lines 83–85, which read "The man who hath no music in himself, Nor is not moved with concord of sweet sounds, Is fit for treasons, stratagems, and spoils." See E. B. Harrison, ed., *Shakespeare: Major Plays and Sonnets* (New York: Harcourt, Brace and Company, 1945), 330.

14. Stott quotes Cicero's "First Speech Against Catiline" with these words, which are translated "What an age we live in." See Cicero, *In Catilinam*, I–V, *Cicero in Twenty-eight Volumes* (Cambridge, MA: Harvard University Press, 1977), 33.

15. Stott refers here to Scottish theologian John Dick (1764–1833), whose *Essay on the Inspiration of the Holy Scriptures* brought him much acclaim. He was known for his advocacy of the doctrine of "plenary inspiration," which held that the biblical writers were all directly moved by the Holy Spirit. The chapters Stott read were in Dick's *Lectures on Theology*, in which he contends that divine wisdom and God's goodness are best seen in the "visible creation," that is, earth, its creatures, and their bodies. See Dick, *An Essay on the Inspiration of the Holy Scriptures, of the Old and New Testaments* (Philadelphia: James C. Howe, 1818) and *Lectures on Theology* (Philadelphia: W. G. Wardle, 1844), 1:219, 240. Memphis was not taken until June 6, 1862. See Long, *Civil War Day by Day*, 222–23.

16. The Army of the Potomac entered Yorktown, Virginia, on May 4 after a monthlong siege, Confederate General Joseph E. Johnston having evacuated the town the day before. See Long, *Civil War Day by Day*, 207.

17. Union soldiers could be given passes to move through military lines. These were written authorizations that required the users to be loyal to the government while traveling. See Webb Garrison, *The Encyclopedia of Civil War Usage* (Nashville, TN: Cumberland House, 2001), 187. Stott's companions on this venture were his longtime friend Riley Sto-

rey and Sergeant James R. Johnson. First Lieutenant Charles F. Johnson of Franklin was also in the regiment, but he was mustered out on April 14, 1862. There were no Johnstons in the Eighteenth Indiana. See *AGI*, 2:165, 4:385–86.

18. Major Underwood is a mystery. There was no such person in the Eighteenth Indiana, though there was a first lieutenant and quartermaster on the field and staff of the Twenty-second Indiana by that name. See ACWRD.

19. Quoted from 1 John 1:1 (KJV).

20. 1 Corinthians 13:12 (KJV).

21. The quote, almost verbatim, is from Thomas Gray's famed "An Elegy Wrote in a Country Church Yard." See Edmund Gosse, ed., *The Works of Thomas Gray, in Prose and Verse*, 4 vols. (London and New York: Macmillan, 1902–6), 1:219.

22. The departure of Jefferson C. Davis and the Indiana and Illinois troops was the result of General Henry Halleck's request of May 6, 1862, for Samuel R. Curtis to reorganize his army and send some of his units to the support of Halleck's movement on Corinth, Mississippi. See Nathaniel Cheairs Hughes Jr. and Gordon D. Whitney, *Jefferson Davis in Blue: The Life of Sherman's Relentless Warrior* (Baton Rouge: Louisiana State University, 2002), 92.

23. Stott refers here to Major General George B. McClellan's Peninsular campaign, in which he unsuccessfully sought to reach Richmond. Brigadier General John Ellis Wool was the army's senior brigadier and, in May 1862, was commanding operations to occupy Norfolk, Virginia. This was the occasion during which President Abraham Lincoln dined at Wool's headquarters. See Faust, ed., *Historical Times Illustrated Encyclopedia of the Civil War*, 842; David Herbert Donald, *Lincoln* (New York: Simon and Schuster, 1995), 351.

24. As Stott reminisces, the words of Thomas Moore's "Those Evening Bells" come to his mind. Only the third line is not verbatim. The original reads: "Of youth and home," rather than "Of home and friends." See *The Poetical Works of Thomas Moore* (Boston: Phillips, Sampson, and Company, 1855), 267.

25. Old Morpheus appears in Ovid's *Metamorphoses* as the son of Sleep, supposedly "the most artful imitator of the human form," whom Sleep sends to carry out the orders Isis brought him. See Michael Simpson, *The Metamorphoses of Ovid* (Amherst: University of Massachusetts Press, 2001), 195–96. "Tired nature's sweet restorer, balmy *Sleep!*" is the first line of Edward Young's *Night Thoughts on Life, Death, and Immortality* (New York: A. J. Barnes and company, 1852), 37.

26. David E. Adams of Metamora was second lieutenant of Company F of the Eighteenth Indiana, and Captain Jonathan Williams refused his request. See *AGI*, 2:163. Stott reported to Captain Isaac B. Tyler, the provost marshal. See ACWRD.

27. Lorenzo W. Billingsley graduated from the classical program of Franklin College in 1862, after which he enlisted in the Fourth Indiana Cavalry. He later served as second lieutenant in the Fourteenth Infantry (Colored Troops). See *Jubilee*, 111, 127; ACWRD. Despite a thorough and lengthy search, the editor has not been able to identify the book Stott was reading.

28. Stott's information regarding Sterling Price and his troops is accurate, though his estimate of the number of soldiers and extent of their illnesses may be exaggerated. The Confederate general arrived in Corinth on April 24, 1862, and because of the low, swampy terrain, the hot, humid weather, and impure water, sickness became pervasive among the troops of Price, Earl Van Dorn, and P. G. T. Beauregard. See Albert Castel, *General Sterling*

Price and the Civil War in the West (Baton Rouge: Louisiana State University Press, 1968), 84–86; Robert Shalhope, *Sterling Price: Portrait of a Southerner* (Columbia: University of Missouri Press, 1971), 210.

29. One of the tasks of the provost marshal's office, in addition to policing the army and overseeing conscription, was to supervise the taking of loyalty oaths by citizens in Union-occupied sections of the Confederacy. Union commanders occupying Southern territory frequently sought to control the local population by "requiring them to pledge loyalty to the Federal government." See Faust, ed., *Historical Times Illustrated Encyclopedia of the Civil War*, 453; Wright, *Language of the Civil War*, 239–40.

30. Matthew 6:6 (KJV).

31. Paraphrase of Romans 13:8 (KJV)

32. The new quartermaster was First Lieutenant James A. Bell of Company C. See *AGI*, 2:161.

33. William Fayel was a journalist with the *Saint Louis Republican* and was with the army through the Pea Ridge Campaign and beyond. He was under fire during the battle at Elkhorn Tavern, "gaining the distinction of being among the very few Civil War journalists to come under sustained enemy fire." See Shea and Hess, *Pea Ridge: Civil War Campaign in the West* (Chapel Hill and London: University of North Carolina Press, 1992), 171–72. The boarders at Mrs. Hirsch's that have thus far not been identified are: Corporal James O. Boggs from Vermillion County of Company C, and either First Lieutenant John L. Lowes from Metamora of Company F or First Lieutenant Abraham B. Lowes of Company K. The probability is that it was Abraham Lowes, since he and Stott were close friends. A thorough search has failed to uncover any soldier named Wyand in the units stationed at Batesville at the time. See *AGI*, 2:163, 166, 4:376.

34. Union troops found Fort Pillow deserted on June 5, 1862, the Confederates having evacuated it the day before. See Long, *Civil War Day by Day*, 222.

35. Some of the news Stott exults over was erroneous. Though Union forces did capture Memphis on June 6, the expedition toward Fort Randolph in Tennessee did not begin until September 28. See Long, *Civil War Day by Day*, 222, 272. Vicksburg, of course, was not yet taken. The loss of Colonel Thomas Pattison apparently devastated many in his command. Sam Voyles of Company G was livid. He wrote his father on June 7 that Pattison had resigned because "he has been insulted & mistreated. . . . After commanding the Ind. Brigade at the battle of Pea Ridge and showing his very ableness as a commander," Voyles remarked, Pattison "was then deprived of the command by a mere drunkard, Col. Benton who had the most secret wire workers at Washington." John C. Swift of Company A called the farewell to Pattison "a solemn thing and will long be remember[ed]." See Voyles to Father, June 7, 1862, Samuel B. Voyles Civil War Correspondence, 1861–1862, IHS; Diary, 2:64–65, John C. Swift Diaries, 1861–1863, IHS.

36. Thomas Cogswell Upham (1799–1872) was a distinguished professor of mental and moral philosophy at Bowdoin College from 1824 to 1867. He was the author of more than sixty works, including *A Philosophical and Practical Treatise on the Will* (1834), which is considered a major contribution to modern psychology, and *Principles of the Interior or Hidden Life* (1843), which may be the work to which Stott refers. See *DAB*, 10(1):123–24.

37. General Frederick Steele commanded a division in the Army of the Southwest and later succeed General Samuel Curtis as commander at Helena, Arkansas. See Ezra J. Warner, *Generals in Blue: Lives of the Union Commanders* (Baton Rouge: Louisiana University

Press, 1964), 474-75.

38. Colonel Charles Edward Hovey was promoted to brigadier general in September 1862. Colonel Cyrus Bussey saw action at Pea Ridge on the staff of General Eugene A. Carr and became a brigadier general in April 1864. For both, see ACWRD.

39. The "little flurry" described here was the battle of Cache River, for which the Eighteenth arrived too late to participate.

40. Sam Slick was a comic figure created by a writer who used the pseudonym of "Judge Halliburton." The humor in Sam's "Sayin's and Doin's" was of a backwoods, homespun style, somewhat similar to the early-twentieth-century Hoosier cartoon character Abe Martin, the creation of Frank McKinney "Kin" Hubbard. See *Sam Slick: The Clockmaker* (Philadelphia: T. B. Peterson, n.d.). Stott compares Slick's humor with that of Washington Irving in his Knickerbocker Tales, such as *Rip Van Winkle.*

41. Richard Young of Johnson County was sergeant in Stott's Company I. See *AGI,* 4:386. The Major Weston mentioned here was probably Eli Weston of the field and staff of the Twenty-fourth Missouri Infantry, since that unit was stationed with the Eighteenth Indiana at that time. See ACWRD. Corporal Thomas Trenary returned to the Eighteenth after having been wounded at Pea Ridge. See *AGI,* 4:386.

42. "Mollie" was often a nickname for Mary, so the sister to whom Stott refers is probably his younger sister Mary.

43. "Fannie" is quite possibly Stott's aunt, Frances Vawter King, his mother's younger sister. The "Morgan" from whom he received a letter is undoubtedly his Franklin College classmate, Thomas Jefferson Morgan, who had joined the army before his graduation in 1861. At this time he was directing public education in Illinois, but in August he enlisted as a lieutenant in the Seventieth Indiana Volunteer Infantry. See Grace Vawter Bicknell, *The Vawter Family in America* (Indianapolis: Hollenbeck Press, 1905; reprint, Atlanta, GA: Thorpe and Associates, 1969), 137–38; *DAB,* 13:187–88.

44. A paraphrase of a line in Thomas Gray's "Elegy Wrote in a Country Church Yard." See Gosse, ed., *Works of Thomas Gray,* 1:221.

45. William King is probably Stott's thirteen-year-old nephew, the son of George and Frances Vawter King. See Bicknell, *Vawter Family in America,* 140.

46. The Second Confiscation Act became law when President Lincoln signed it on July 17, 1862. It stated that slaves of all persons supporting or aiding the "rebellion" would become free once they came under "Union control." See Long, *Civil War Day by Day,* 241; Faust, ed., *Historical Times Illustrated Encyclopedia of the Civil War,* 157.

47. Paraphrase of Colossians 3:23 (KJV): "And whatsoever ye do, do it heartily."

48. Translation: "Marvelous in the saying. It abounds with honor and necessary respect."

49. Flavius-Josephus was a Jewish general and historian of the first century CE whose major work was *The Antiquities of the Jews.* See *The Complete Works of Flavius-Josephus: The Celebrated Jewish Historian,* William Whiston, trans. (Chicago: Thompson and Thomas, n.d.).

50. Mrs. Tilson is probably Elizabeth A. Tilson, wife of Johnson County farmer Robert B. Tilson and mother of Ann S. Tilson, quite possibly the "Miss Anna" in the diary entry of October 4, 1862. See 1860 U.S. Census—Indiana, microfilm, roll 271, p. 716, ISL.

51. Stott quotes this Latin phrase from the Roman poet Horace's "Drusus and the Claudian House," in his *Carminum Liber IV,* Ode 4, line 22, which has been translated "nor

is it vouchsafed to know all things." See *Horace: The Odes and Epodes*, C. E. Bennett, trans. (Cambridge, MA: Harvard University Press, 1960), 296-97.

52. The article to which Stott refers appeared in the "Editor's Table" section of the famed monthly magazine. Titled "Victory," it reflected on a number of the moral questions raised by the North's fighting of the war and its expected triumph. See *Harper's New Monthly Magazine* 25 (July 1862):265–70.

53. Belle Boyd was the most notorious of the Confederate spies, who specialized in passing intelligence to Generals Thomas Jonathan "Stonewall" Jackson and J. E. B. Stuart. The betrayal of which Stott speaks occurred at Port Royal, not Fort Royal. See Faust, ed., *Historical Times Illustrated Encyclopedia of the Civil War*, 74.

54. Dewitt C. Thomas of Salem succeeded Henry D. Washburn as lieutenant colonel of the Eighteenth Indiana. He was replaced by Jesse L. Holman, a member of the famous Baptist family of Judge Jesse Holman of Aurora. See *AGI*, 2:158.

55. Colonel David Shunk of Marion was William P. Benton's successor as colonel of the Eighth Indiana. See *AGI*, 2:48.

56. John Smith Phelps was the military governor of Missouri. Cassius Marcellus Clay, a renowned Kentucky antislavery advocate and a founder of Berea College, never served on active military duty of any consequence, even though he was commissioned in 1862 as a major general of volunteers. See Faust, ed., *Historical Times Illustrated Encyclopedia of the Civil War*, 143–44, 580. William H. McCoy was Stott's friend and fellow member of the Franklin class of 1861.

57. Quote from Robert Burns's poem "To a Mouse." The next line in the poem is: "An' lea'e nought but grief an' pain, For promis'd joy!" See Robert Burns, *Poems and Songs, Complete*, 4 vols. (Edinburgh: James Thin, 1896), 1:125. It is clear that Stott is not pleased that Williams is joining him on the recruitment trip.

58. William H. Ford of Patriot was a sergeant in Company D of the Eighteenth. See *AGI*, 4:377.

59. Private Daniel S. Place of Salem was in Company G of the Eighteenth Indiana. See *AGI*, 4:383. The Indiana Sanitary Commission had established the Soldiers' Home earlier that month as a place for military men of all units and states to rest, be fed, and be provided with a "taste of home." It became a welcome refuge for the troops, but, for Stott, it had obviously not yet reached that point. See Emma Lou Thornbrough, *Indiana in the Civil War Era, 1850–1880* (Indianapolis: Indiana Historical Bureau and Indiana Historical Society, 1965), 176; Barbara Butler Davis, ed., *Affectionately Yours: The Civil War Home-Front Letters of the Ovid Butler Family* (Indianapolis: Indiana Historical Society, 2004), 12. The Spencer House was located at the corner of South Illinois and Louisiana streets in Indianapolis. See *Indianapolis City Directory and Business Mirror* (Indianapolis: Dodd, Talbot and Parsons, 1862), 211.

60. The Palmer House was on the corner of Washington and Illinois streets. See *Indianapolis City Directory and Business Mirror*, 184. The General Davis identified here is, of course, Jefferson C. Davis, Stott's commander in the Pea Ridge campaign.

61. Mrs. Grubbs was the mother of George W. Grubbs, Stott's Franklin College classmate. P. H. Sumner graduated from the college in 1862. See *Jubilee*, 171.

62. Stott is visiting his older sister Martha (Mat) and her husband Maxa (Mack) Moncrief, along with their two daughters, Jennie and Emma, ages seven and almost two. See Bicknell, *Vawter Family in America*, 106.

63. The call for troops was in response to a report of September 2 that Confederate forces were near Cincinnati. That city's businesses shut down, and citizens in neighboring counties and states began drilling. See Long, *Civil War Day by Day*, 261.

64. Samuel Eddelman's daughter, Phoebe, was eighteen years old at this time. See 1860 U.S. Census—Indiana, microfilm, roll 271. "Grandfather" is the Reverend William Vawter. Lizzie Burns is probably Stott's cousin, Elizabeth Burns, the daughter of Maxa and Maria Vawter Burns, and the sister of the author Harrison Burns. See Bicknell, *Vawter Family in America*, 91.

65. Charles Grim was graduated from Franklin College in 1862 and enlisted in Company I on September 25. See *AGI*, 4:387. Elizabeth Johnson was the wife of Lieutenant Charles F. Johnson and was a resident of Franklin; Mrs. Rawlings may have been the mother or wife of Private Moses E. Rawlings of Company I. See 1860 U.S. Census—Indiana, microfilm, roll 271, p. 670; *AGI*, 4:386.

66. Bailey probably preached from James 2:17–26.

67. Joseph Albert Wright was Indiana's tenth governor (1849–57). A Democrat, he became the state's U.S. senator during the war, having been appointed by Governor Oliver P. Morton to that post following Jesse Bright's expulsion. See John T. Hubbell and James W. Geary, eds., *Biographical Dictionary of the Union: Northern Leaders of the Civil War* (Westport, CT: Greenwood Press, 1995), 542.

68. Stott has revisited the college. Webster Hall was the meeting place of the Webster Literary Society, one of Franklin College's extracurricular academic groups. The creek he mentions was probably Hurricane Creek in present-day Province Park in Franklin. The scripture passage Morey (the name is not clear in the handwritten diary) preached upon was John 19:28.

69. Major General Don Carlos Buell was in a tight race with Confederate commander Braxton Bragg for possession of Louisville. He beat Bragg to that city on September 25. See Long, *Civil War Day by Day*, 270–71.

70. P. C. Vawter was Stott's Uncle Philemon. Ormand Feagler was another uncle, the husband of his Aunt Mary Vawter. See Bicknell, *Vawter Family in America*, 96.

71. Brigadier General Jefferson C. Davis shot and mortally wounded Brigadier General William "Bull" Nelson at the Galt House in Louisville on September 29, the result of an argument in which Davis felt mistreated. See Hughes and Whitney, *Jefferson Davis in Blue*, 100–26.

72. Second Lieutenant Wylie G. Burton of Mitchell died in the service on May 16, 1863. See *AGI*, 2:618. Mrs. Clark was the former Eliza Jane Fink, Stott's teacher in Vernon.

73. The Elisha Dungan and Robert Tilson families lived on farms near each other in Johnson County. As mentioned in note 50 above, the Tilsons had a seventeen-year-old daughter, Ann, who could well be "Miss Anna." See 1860 U.S. Census—Indiana, microfilm, roll, 271, p. 716. By this point in the war Fielding Eddelman was a hospital steward/assistant surgeon with the Eighteenth. See *AGI*, 2:159.

74. The sermon was based on Acts 12.

75. Eli Thayer (1819–1899) was the founder of the Emigrant Aid Society that supported making Kansas a free state in the 1850s through a process of organized emigration of free-soil advocates to that territory. While a congressman from 1857 to 1861, Thayer proposed further colonization into new lands in western territories and in the border states. See *DAB*, 9:402–4.

76. Little's Hotel was at the southeast corner of Washington and New Jersey streets in Indianapolis. It advertised as "One of the finest hotels in the state," with large rooms, new beds, and sumptuous tables. See *Indianapolis Directory and Business Mirror* (Indianapolis: Bowen, Stewart and Company, 1861), 148.

77. Peter M. Bigney was a principal musician in the Eighteenth Indiana. In January 1863 he was promoted to assistant surgeon. See *AGI*, 2:159, 4:372.

78. The Reverend Doctor Henry Day was the pastor of First Baptist Church, Indianapolis. See *Indianapolis City Directory and Business Mirror*, 81.

79. William G. Stevenson's *Thirteen Months in the Rebel Army* was a highly controversial indictment by a Confederate soldier of the Southern nation and the "backdrop of indifference" in both North and South. Published anonymously, the writer hoped to "stir the North to a profounder sense of the desperate and deadly struggle in which they are engaged than they have ever yet felt." See Stevenson, *Thirteen Months in the Rebel Army* (New York: A. S. Barnes and Company, 1959; originally published by Barnes in 1862), 5, 6, 9–10.

80. Festus was the Roman proconsul of Asia in the fourth century CE. Stott may have been reading his *Breviarium*, a brief history of Rome. See J. W. Eadie, *The Breviarium of Festus: A Critical Edition with Historical Commentary* (London: University of London Athlone Press, 1967), 4–9.

81. At the time of his new appointment, William Stanley Charles of Bloomington was captain of Company H in the Eighteenth. See *AGI*, 2:158, 164. Brigadier General John M. Schofield was commander of the Army of the Frontier and the District of Southwest Missouri at the time. See Faust, ed., *Historical Times Illustrated Encyclopedia of the Civil War*, 661.

82. J. D. Huston was pastor of the Columbus First Baptist Church, and he preached that Sunday on either Matthew 6:13 or Luke 12:31. Ironically, Stott's Grandfather W. T. Stott was moderator of the meeting in 1852 at which the church was organized, and Will himself would later be its pastor. See *History of Bartholomew County, Indiana—1888* (Columbus: Bartholomew County Historical Society, 1976), 103. Reverend N. S. Dickey lived in Columbus, but it is not clear which church he served. See 1860 U.S. Census— Indiana, microfilm, roll 244, p. 346.

83. Aunt Sylvie was Sylvia Hunter Vawter, the wife of Philemon Vawter. See Bicknell, *Vawter Family in America*, 96.

84. Reuben F. Patterson was captain of Company I of the Sixty-eighth. George Hankins was sergeant in the same company and was killed at Chickamauga in September 1863. Sergeant Joab Stout was also in Company I. The Sixty-eighth surrendered to the forces of Braxton Bragg at Munfordsville, Kentucky, on September 17, 1862. See Ann Turner, *Guide to Indiana Civil War Manuscripts* (Indianapolis: Indiana Civil War Centennial Commission, 1965), 208; ACWRD.

85. This uncle is Williamson D. Vawter of Vernon. See Bicknell, *Vawter Family in America*, 92.

86. Randsdale is possibly twenty-eight-year-old Benjamin Ransdale, a farmer residing in Vernon. See 1860 U.S. Census—Indiana, microfilm, roll 271, p. 312. Lincoln removed Major General George B. McClellan from command of the Army of the Potomac on November 7, 1862. See Long, *Civil War Day by Day*, 285.

87. "Gid" probably is Gideon E. Moncrief of Butlerville, the brother of Maxa Moncrief, Stott's brother-in-law. Gideon attended Franklin College in 1853. See Calvin DeArmond

Davis, *A History of the Albert Carter Moncrief Family* (copyright by author), 1997), 41.

88. The proclamation to which Stott refers is, of course, the Emancipation Proclamation, the preliminary draft of which Lincoln presented to his cabinet on September 22, 1862.

89. Richard M. Hall was one of Stott's recruits. He enlisted on October 31. See *AGI*, 387.

90. S. Clay Brown was assistant surgeon in the Eighth Indiana at this time. In July 1864 he was promoted surgeon of the Eighteenth Indiana. See *AGI*, 2:48, 159.

91. Henry C. Skinner of Wabash was a Baptist chaplain who had first served with the Twenty-first Ohio Infantry. He transferred to the Eighth Indiana in November 1862. See *AGI*, 2:49.

92. The exact meaning of "blow fish" is uncertain, but the context suggests that it may be a synonym for a person Civil War soldiers called a "blower" or "blowhard," slang for braggart or boaster. See Wright, *Language of the Civil War*, 33.

93. The biblical story to which Stott refers appears in Matthew 8:28–33 and Mark 5:1–16. Known as the story of the Gerasene Demoniac, it tells of Jesus's exorcism of demons from a possessed man. John Howard (1726–1790) was a British prison reformer who, out of deeply religious convictions, fought to abolish jailers' fees, improve the sanitary conditions in England's gaols, and end a host of abuses in the prisons. See *Dictionary of National Biography*, Leslie Stephen and Sidney Lee, eds., 22 vols. (New York: Macmillan, 1908–9), 10:44–48.

94. Hellebore was a powder extracted from a poisonous herb of the genus *Helleborus* and used by the ancients in treating mental and other disorders. The historian of the Thirty-third Illinois seemed to share Stott's feeling about Benton. He wrote that "Gen. Benton found a widow, a Mrs. Pettit, somewhere in the woods and married her offhand after some ten days' courtship—the most courageous thing we ever knew him to do." See Isaac H. Elliott, *History of the Thirty-third Illinois Veteran Infantry in the Civil War* (Gibson City, IL: The Regiment Association, 1902), 32.

95. Smith Campbell of Adel, Iowa, was assistant surgeon in the Twenty-third. General Earl Van Dorn's army, in a quick move from Grenada, Mississippi, raided Ulysses S. Grant's critical supply depot at Holly Springs on December 20, 1862, capturing 1,500 Union troops and destroying more than a million dollars worth of supplies. See Long, *Civil War Day by Day*, 298–99.

96. A paraphrase of a biblical passage—either Ecclesiastes 3:1 or 1 Thessalonians 5:1.

97. In Hebrew law, as revealed in Leviticus 25:10–54, every fiftieth year was to be the Jubilee Year when all property was to be returned to its original owner or family, all oppression was to cease, and all Jewish slaves were to be freed.

98. Andrew P. Daughters of Moores Hill was the surgeon of the Eighteenth. See *AGI*, 2:159.

99. Samuel Phillips Newman, another leading light of the faculty at Bowdoin College from 1824 to 1835, stressed style, diction, and taste in his works on rhetoric. He insisted that the proper foundations of writing are a thorough knowledge of the subject and "the power of methodically arranging his thoughts." Stott probably read Newman's *A Practical System of Rhetoric; or, The Principles and Rules of Style* (Andover, ME: Gould and Newman, 1835), see especially 16, 20–22, 41, 50. Major Thomas Jefferson Brady of Muncie had a distinguished military career. After leading the Eighth Indiana through the Vicksburg campaign, he was a colonel in the 117th and 140th Indiana and became a brigadier general by brevet in March 1863. See *AGI*, 48; ACWRD.

100. Union Brigadier General William Rosecrans commanded the Army of the Cumberland in its victory in the battle of Stones River, or Murfreesboro, on December 31, 1862, and January 2, 1863. See Long, *Civil War Day by Day*, 302–3, 307.

101. Stott refers to Sherman's failed efforts at Chickasaw Bayou, Mississippi, on December 29–30. See ibid., 301–2.

102. Possible translation: "Speakers end (or have limits); poets grow (or spring forth)."

103. A resident of Vernon, Indiana, Private Miles H. McCanlon was in Company H of the Twenty-sixth Indiana at the battle of Prairie Grove, Arkansas, on December 7, 1862. That company contained many Vernon boys, including First Sergeant (later Captain) Richard H. Stott, a relative of Will's, and Private Joseph Storey. See *AGI*, 4:604–5.

104. The wartime editor of the *Richmond Examiner* was Edward A. Pollard, an outspoken critic of President Jefferson Davis, his administration, and his handling of the war. See Faust, ed., *Historical Times Illustrated Encyclopedia of the Civil War*, 591, 633.

105. Brigadier General John Wynn Davidson was named commander of the District of Saint Louis after serving in McClellan's Peninsular campaign. At this time he was commander of the Army of Southeast Missouri. See Warner, *Generals in Blue*, 112.

106. Brigadier General Fitz-Henry Warren assumed command of the Second Brigade, Second Division of the Army of Southeast Missouri. See Faust, ed., *Historical Times Illustrated Encyclopedia of the Civil War*, 802–3.

107. The reference is to 1 Samuel 4:16–22.

108. First Lieutenant Simeon Wright was also the quartermaster of the Thirty-third. See ACWRD.

109. In his *Centennial History of Franklin College*, John F. Cady indicates that Bailey resigned due to a "physical breakdown," an observation that squares with all other information about his departure. The college at this time was left with only two faculty members, Brumback and Wallace, was in serious financial straits, and was having difficulty competing with other Baptist institutions in the state and contending with some "downright hostility" among its Baptist constituency. See Cady, *The Centennial History of Franklin College* (Franklin, IN: Franklin College), 1934, 84–91, 96–98.

110. Major General Joseph Hooker assumed command of the Army of the Potomac on Monday, January 26, after that army's debilitating defeat at Fredericksburg, Virginia. See Long, *Civil War Day by Day*, 315.

111. Edward Ditmars and John H. Troutwine were both privates in Company I. There were two privates named Ryker, John W. and Teborius C. See *AGI*, 386–87.

112. Author and educator Josiah Gilbert Holland (1819–1881) wrote under the name of Timothy Titcomb. Holland published articles in the *Knickerbocker* magazine, was superintendent of schools in Vicksburg, Mississippi, and later editor of *Scribner's Monthly*. His *Lessons in Life*, first published in 1861, contains twenty-four essays, or "Lessons," on such subjects as "Truth and Truthfulness," "The Rights of Woman," and "Faith in Humanity." The final essay, "Half-Finished Work" is the one on which Stott comments in the diary. See J. G. Holland [Timothy Titcomb, pseud.], *Lessons in Life: A Series of Familiar Essays* (New York: Charles Scribner's Sons, 1881), 315–21; *Appleton's Cyclopedia of American Biography*, James G. Wilson and John Fiske, eds. (New York: Appleton and Company, 1888), 3:234–35.

113. Both Isaac Elliott, historian of the Thirty-third Illinois, and Taylor Peirce of the Twenty-second Iowa record the story of the guerrilla's actions and death, but they add that

his furious, grieving wife came for his body and swore vengeance. See Elliott, *History of the Thirty-third Illinois Veteran Volunteer Infantry in the Civil War*, 33; Taylor to Catharine, February 16, 1863, *Dear Catharine, Dear Taylor: The Civil War Letters of a Union Soldier and His Wife*, Richard L. Kiper, ed. (Lawrence: University Press of Kansas, 2002), 79–80. The Union ram may have been the *Queen of the West*, which ran the batteries on February 2, 1863. See Long, *Civil War Day by Day*, 318.

114. The gunboat USS *Indianola* ran the batteries at Vicksburg along with two barges on the night of Friday, February 13, 1863. See Long, *Civil War Day by Day*, 320.

115. Henry D. Glover of Vernon was a private in the Twenty-second Indiana; he died in Cincinnati in August 1862. George W. Kendrick of North Vernon was captain of Company E, Eighty-second Indiana, when he died of disease in January 1863. See ACWRD. The Union Conscription Act passed the very day of this diary entry, February 25, 1863. See Long, *Civil War Day by Day*, 323.

116. The recent events regarding the *Queen of the West* and the *Indianola* were quite ironic. On Saturday, February 14, the *Queen of the West*, having captured a Confederate vessel, ran aground and fell into Confederate hands. Ten days later, on February 24, the repaired *Queen*, now a Confederate ram, participated in the capture of the *Indianola*. See Long, *Civil War Day by Day*, 320, 322–23. The report about Fort McCallister was incorrect; Union ironclads failed in their attacks on the fort.

117. Psalm 8:4 (KJV).

118. Yazoo Pass was the scene of another failed expedition (March 11–16, 1863) to get to Vicksburg from north of the city. See Long, *Civil War Day by Day*, 328–29.

119. Paraphrase of James 5:4.

120. "Sergt" Campbell is evidently Corporal David Campbell of Company F from Franklin County. The Ira Stout he saw while on leave is the father of Martha (Mattie) Stout, Stott's correspondent. There is no record of Campbell's promotion to sergeant. See *AGI*, 380; 1860 U.S. Census—Indiana, microfilm, roll 259, p. 116.

121. The Burtons were probably Second Lieutenant Wiley G. Burton of the Sixty-seventh Indiana and his civilian brother, Simpson Burton. Both hailed from Mitchell, Indiana, and were graduates of Franklin College during Stott's years as a student there. Wiley died in the service in May 1863. Merritt A. Read, a native of Vernon and former student at Franklin College was a private in the Sixty-seventh. For Wiley Burton and Read, see ACWRD. Milton Stribling of Vernon was the son of Thomas and Sarah Vawter Stribling and husband of Nancy Moncrief. See Bicknell, *Vawter Family in America*, 219, 233; Davis, *Moncrief Family*, 54.

122. William S. Snow was a private in Company I, Eighteenth Indiana. See *AGI*, 386.

123. Jefferson Davis did not have a brother-in-law named Mitchell. His niece, Mary Davis, the youngest daughter of his older brother, Joseph, however, married Doctor Charles Jouett Mitchell in 1838. A Vicksburg physician, Mitchell owned a plantation near Milliken's Bend, just north of Tallulah in Madison Parish, Louisiana, only twenty miles from Vicksburg. He was briefly held captive by Union troops in August 1862. The estate upon which the Eighteenth Indiana camped was that of Doctor Mitchell, Davis's nephew-in-law. See Haskell M. Monroe Jr. and James T. McIntosh et al., eds., *The Papers of Jefferson Davis*, 11 vols. (Baton Rouge: Louisiana State University Press, 1971–2003), 2:7–9, 7:134–36, 8:231–33, 351–53.

124. Stribling, a resident of Sardinia, Indiana, and a private in the Eighty-second

Indiana, died of disease on March 17, 1863, and was buried in the Stones River National Cemetery at Murfreesboro, Tennessee. See ACWRD.

125. Stott is mistaken in his identification of the father of former U.S. vice president and Confederate Major General John Cabell Breckinridge. The general's father, Joseph Cabell Breckinridge, died at age thirty-four, not long after John Cabell was born. The Doctor Breckinridge to which Stott refers is probably Doctor Robert Jefferson Breckinridge, the prominent Presbyterian clergyman and antislavery advocate, who was the general's uncle. See William C. Davis, *Breckinridge: Statesman, Soldier, Symbol* (Baton Rouge: Louisiana State University, 1974), 3, 8–10; *DAB*, 2:6–10. Corporal John W. Ridenour, a resident of College Corner, Ohio, was a corporal in Company H, Eighteenth Indiana. See *AGI*, 4:384.

126. "Flats" was a short term for flatboats or small river barges. See Wright, *Language of the Civil War*, 114–15.

127. John Carson of Franklin was a second lieutenant in Company I. See *AGI*, 2:165.

128. During the time the Eighteenth Indiana campaigned in eastern Louisiana, Major General Nathaniel P. Banks attempted to capture the critical Confederate position at Port Hudson, Louisiana. There was talk among the soldiers of McClernand's XIII Corps that they would be sent to Port Hudson to assist Banks's efforts, after which Banks would, in turn, join Grant in assaulting Vicksburg. See Faust, ed., *Historical Times Illustrated Encyclopedia of the Civil War*, 596–97.

129. As the war progressed, Stott became quite close to Second Lieutenant John L. Lowes of Company F and Captain Abraham Lowes of Company K. Peter M. Bigney was assistant surgeon of the Eighteenth Indiana. See *AGI*, 2:159, 161, 163. Singing was one of their favorite pastimes.

130. Private James W. Feagler of North Vernon was in the Fifty-fourth Indiana Infantry in General Osterhaus's Ninth Division of the XIII Corps. See ACWRD.

131. The scriptural passage was Hebrews 12:2. The chaplain may have been Baptist clergyman Herman J. Eddy. See Brinsfield et al., eds., *Faith in the Fight*, 150.

132. The reference here is to the Windsor plantation, built and owned by Smith Coffee Daniell II, which is discussed in the introduction to this section of the diary.

133. The wounded soldier was Private Bartholomew McCarty of Vermillion County, and his wound was classified "severe." See *AGI*, 4:376.

134. General William Benton reported that the flag of the Fifteenth Arkansas was captured by Private Amos Nagle of Company K, Eighteenth Indiana. There is no Nagle or Neagly listed in the Indiana Adjutant General's report, but there is a Thomas Nogle listed among the privates in Company K. The Indiana–Vicksburg Military Park Commission, however, reinforced Benton's observation, crediting an Amos Nagle with killing the Fifteenth Arkansas color-bearer and capturing the flag. See Report of William P. Benton in *OR*, 24(2):626; *AGI*, 4:388; Indiana–Vicksburg Military Park Commission, *Indiana at Vicksburg* (Indianapolis: Wm. B. Burford, 1911), 177.

135. Frederick Grant, General Grant's son, was with his father throughout the Vicksburg campaign and witnessed the end of the Port Gibson battle. He joined a couple of detachments that gathered the dead and wounded. "Here the scenes were so terrible," he wrote, "that I became faint and ill, and making my way to a tree, sat down, the most woebegone twelve-year-old lad in America." See Terrence J. Winschel, *Triumph and Defeat: The Vicksburg Campaign* (Mason City, IA: Savas Publishing, 1999), 1:87–88.

136. Contrabands were former slaves who were either held by the Union army or sought

safety behind Union lines. The term "contrabands of war" was first applied to ex-slaves as property that could be seized during wartime by General Benjamin F. Butler in 1861. See Wright, *Language of the Civil War*, 70.

137. Brigadier General Benjamin Grubb Humphreys was at that time in Robert E. Lee's Army of Northern Virginia. A native of Claiborne County, Mississippi, he was the state's first postwar governor, serving from 1865 to 1868. See Ezra J. Warner, *Generals in Gray: Lives of Confederate Commanders* (Baton Rouge: Louisiana State University Press, 1959), 145–46.

138. Private Samuel Clark of Johnson County was in Stott's Company I. See *AGI*, 386.

139. This information was incorrect and probably based on the rumors that frequently spread in army camps. Hooker had been defeated at Chancellorsville, Virginia, May 1–4, and had retreated across the Rappahannock River; Rosecrans had seen no action since the victory at Stones River in early January.

140. Nicodemus Doan was a private in Stott's own Company I. See *AGI*, 4:386.

141. Ephraim Puckett and James J. Wyley, both of Johnson County, were privates in Stott's company. Wyley was captured in the ditch by the Confederates. Private Daniel Half-aker of Franklin County was in Company F. See *AGI*, 4:381, 386–87.

142. Brigadier General Stephen Gano Burbridge commanded the First Brigade of General A. J. Smith's Tenth Division in the XIII Corps. See Faust, ed., *Historical Times Illustrated Encyclopedia of the Civil War*, 95.

143. Peter C. Woods of Metamora was captain of Company F. Interestingly, he resigned a month later (June 14, 1863). See *AGI*, 2:163.

144. Paraphrase of 2 Corinthians 5:17.

145. Andrew O'Daniel of Muncie was captain of Company A of the Eighth Indiana. Hiram T. Vandevender of Anderson was captain of Company K in the Eighth and also an 1857 graduate of Franklin College. Both received mortal wounds in the May 22 assault. See *AGI*, 2:49, 55; *Jubilee*, 173.

146. First Lieutenant Harvey D. Crane of Newport was in Company C of the Eighteenth. See *AGI*, 2:161.

147. The mention of General Hooker is no doubt in reference to his defeat at Chancellorsville in early May. Rosecrans was indeed reorganizing his forces for the offensive after Stones River. Wiley G. Burton of Mitchell, who died on May 16, 1863, was an 1862 graduate of Franklin College and Will's close friend. His brother, Simpson Burton, also Stott's friend, graduated from Franklin in 1860. See *Jubilee*, 110–11.

148. Probably Private Jason L. James of Company C. He was the only soldier with the surname James in the Eighteenth. See *AGI*, 4:376.

149. In 1861 William Fields published the second edition of his *Scrap-book* (the first edition appeared in 1851). Described as "a book of eloquent extracts," it was a volume of writings meant to inspire patriotism and love of country. Among the articles included were: "Is There a God?" "Liberty and Revolution," and "Christ on Calvary," as well as other materials such as Washington's Inaugural Address and speeches on the Union by Sam Houston, Daniel Webster, R. M. T. Hunter, and Henry Clay. See William Fields, *The Scrap-book: Tales and Anecdotes, Biographical, Historical, Moral, Religious, and Sentimental Pieces in Prose and Poetry* (Philadelphia: J. B. Lippincott, 1861), 3.

150. John T. Butler, a resident of Columbus, was in the Twelfth Indiana and died at Fort Loomis, Tennessee, on May 10, 1863. Jacob H. Holsclaw of Jennings County was

discharged for disability from the Sixth Indiana; the date of his death is unknown. John Carroll of Vernon was in the Twenty-sixth Indiana and died at Port Hudson, Louisiana, but not until August 8. All were privates. See ACWRD.

151. For the political conflicts between Governor Oliver P. Morton and the state legislature, and the financial machinations of the governor, see Thornbrough, *Indiana in the Civil War Era*, 183-96.

152. Napoleon H. Daniels of Bedford was first lieutenant and now assumed the role of quartermaster. See *AGI*, 2:160. When Confederate forces assaulted the Union garrison at Milliken's Bend on Sunday, June 7, it was successfully defended by Union gunboats and troops that included the African Brigade. See Long, *Civil War Day by Day*, 363.

153. Francis Laiken or Lakin was second lieutenant of Company D in the Eighteenth. No record of his capture has been found, but his commission as first lieutenant was revoked on June 6, 1863. The Indiana Adjutant General's report has two spellings of his surname. See *AGI*, 2:162, 4:377; ACWRD.

154. Major General Francis Jay Herron had served brilliantly in Arkansas, especially in the battle at Prairie Grove. His force joined the XIII Corps at Vicksburg on June 11. See Warner, *Generals in Blue*, 228–29. The expected attack by General Joseph E. Johnston never occurred.

155. Stott quotes a portion of Proverbs 17:22: "A merry heart doeth good like a medicine; but a broken spirit drieth the bones."

156. Major General John M. Schofield took command of Curtis's Department of Missouri on May 24, 1863. See Long, *Civil War Day by Day*, 358. Major General John A. "Black Jack" Logan, former congressman from Illinois, was commander of the Third Division of McPherson's XVII Corps. See Faust, ed., *Historical Times Illustrated Encyclopedia of the Civil War*, 443.

157. The U.S. Government created the Invalid Corps, later known as the Veteran Reserve Corps, in 1863. Made up of convalescent and disabled troops, or others no longer capable of combat duty, its purpose was to serve in support roles—as recruiters, cooks, guards, and nurses—in order to free other soldiers to concentrate on combat-related activities. See Wright, *Language of the Civil War*, 315.

158. All of these soldiers were in Company H of the Twenty-sixth. Richard H. Stott, a merchant in Vernon in civilian life, was more than likely Stott's cousin. Like Stott, Lieutenants Elijah T. Read and Joseph M. Story, Privates George and John W. Carroll, and Sergeant Miles H. McCanlon were all from Vernon. Privates Monroe and John S. Marsh hailed from nearby Brewersville, and Private Charles King, a former sawmill operator, came from Oakdale. Read and Story were both preparatory students at Franklin College. See *AGI*, 4:604–5; ACWRD; 1860 U.S. Census—Indiana, microfilm, roll 271, p. 220; *Jubilee*, 163, 169.

159. Osborne Oldroyd of the Twentieth Ohio Infantry, Logan's Division, described the scene that day in similar terms, but in more detail: "This morning our whole line of artillery—seven miles long—opened on the doomed city and fortifications at six o'clock, and kept up the firing for four hours, during which time the smoke was so thick we could see nothing but the flash of guns." Osborne H. Oldroyd, *A Soldier's Story of the Siege of Vicksburg* (Springfield, IL: n.p., 1885), 69.

160. The story related by Stott is in Joshua 7-8. *Oedipus Tyrannus*, also known as *Oedipus Rex*, was one of Sophocles's most well-known plays. Since he has been reading the

Joshua account and hoping to see his classmates, Stott apparently was reminded of his school days and reading the Greek tragedy. See Sophocles, *Oedipus the King* (San Francisco: Chandler Publishing Company, 1961).

161. This was a false rumor. Port Hudson did not fall into Union hands until July 8, 1863. See Long, *Civil War Day by Day*, 381.

162. There is some confusion in Stott's relating of this biblical story. The man who had his skull broken by a millstone thrown by a woman was not Egleon, but Abimelech, one of the sons of Gideon, who fought his own people to gain power. Indeed, there is no Egleon in the Bible. The assault on Abimelech and his request of his armor bearer to kill him rather than have it be said he was killed by a woman—a disgrace in the eyes of this macho warrior—is recorded in Judges 9:53–56. It is startling that Stott, such a careful student of the Bible, was mistaken on this point.

163. Emaline Brougher would have been twenty-one at the time. See 1860 U.S. Census—Indiana, microfilm, roll 271.

164. John Williamson Potter graduated with Stott from Franklin College in 1861. See *Jubilee*, 111.

165. The word "traps" was the soldiers' term for gear and belongings. See Wright, *Language of the Civil War*, 302. Jesse E. Scott of Richmond, Indiana, was first sergeant of Company C, Eighth Indiana, and assistant quartermaster. See *AGI*, 51.

166. "Whistling Dick" was the nickname given a rifled, banded eighteen-pounder cannon on the Vicksburg heights. Originally cast by the Tredegar Iron Works in Richmond as a smoothbore, it was later rifled by southerners. The spirals created in the process of rifling caused its wobbling shells to emit a peculiar whistling sound. It is considered "the most famous gun in the war," but whether Stott saw the actual gun is questionable, since it supposedly disappeared before Vicksburg surrendered. Some suggest that Confederates buried it in the river to prevent it from falling into Union hands. See Wright, *Language of the Civil War*, 323; Faust, ed., *Historical Times Illustrated Encyclopedia of the Civil War*, 820.

167. The explosion destroyed the Third Louisiana Redan on June 25. See Michael Ballard, *Vicksburg: The Campaign That Opened the Mississippi* (Chapel Hill and London: University of North Carolina Press, 2004), 365–69.

168. James Starr was a corporal in Company B, Eighteenth Indiana. See *AGI*, 374.

169. *Godey's* was a leading magazine of the nineteenth century. As will be seen in his diary entry of July 18, 1863, Stott evidently read the melodramatic story about the newlywed couple, Charlotte Augusta and Harvey Woodbridge. It depicts Charlotte as a shrew, wanting to be a socialite and have all the finest of furnishings, but at the same time, taking two weeks to rest after setting up housekeeping. Harvey tries to stand up for himself, but like his "Pa," eventually gives in to Charlotte, who becomes lazy and slovenly. See E. Leslie, "Mr. and Mrs. Woodbridge," *Godey's Lady's Book and American Ladies' Magazine* 22 (Jan.–June 1841): 2-6, 74–78, 109–13, 168–74. Union forces successfully held off a Confederate attack on Helena, Arkansas, on July 4. Brigadier General George Gordon Meade was following on Robert E. Lee's heels after Gettysburg, and Brigadier General Robert Sanford Foster, a native of Vernon, Indiana, had been opposing James Longstreet's troops in Virginia that spring. See Long, *Civil War Day by Day*, 163; Warner, *Generals in Blue*, 158–59.

170. Psalm 84:10.

171. The *Cincinnati Gazette* employed Radical Republican journalist Whitelaw Reid to cover Ohio troops then serving in western Virginia. He did so under the pseudonym "Ag-

ate," possibly because of his fondness for quartz stones. His work reached a wide reader-ship, especially his coverage of the Gettysburg battle. See Duncan Bingham, *Whitelaw Reid: Journalist, Politician, Diplomat* (Athens: University of Georgia Press, 1975), chapter 2; Gary W. Gallagher, ed., *Two Witnesses at Gettysburg* (St. James, N.Y.: Brandywine Press, 1994), ix–xii. Marshall Grimstead (not Grinstead) of Jennings County was a private in the Sixth Indiana Infantry. He was discharged for disability on October 14, 1863. See ACWRD.

172. Possible paraphrase of Job 5:23.

173. Shepard Florer of Vermillion County was a private in Company C of the Eigh-teenth. See *AGI*, 376.

174. William Nevins wrote this book of inspirational articles in the last months of his life (1834–35) when he had lost his voice and could only interpret life with his pen. His purpose was "to rouse Christians to greater attainments in personal holiness, and through their efforts and progress to bless the world." It included pieces on prayer, teaching Sab-bath School, and heaven. See William Nevins, *Practical Thoughts* (New York: American Tract Society, 1836), 5.

175. In early July 1863 the legendary and colorful Confederate cavalry commander John Hunt Morgan plunged into southern Indiana with some 2,000 mounted troops. His raid through Indiana and Ohio lasted twenty-four days and created panic in both states. Response to Morton's call for defense was overwhelming, and Morgan's hope to arouse Southern sympathizers in the state went unfulfilled. As Stott reveals in his next entry, Morgan met with solid resistance when he reached the outskirts of Vernon. The raid ended with Morgan's capture in Ohio on July 26. See W. H. H. Terrell, *Indiana in the War of the Rebellion: Report of the Adjutant General* (Indianapolis: Indiana Historical Society, 1960), 209–48; Thornbrough, *Indiana in the Civil War Era*, 203–4. For more on the Vernon experi-ence, see Malcolm Deputy, *"The Land of Winding Waters"* (Montezuma, IN: Wabash Valley Press, 1963), 21–24; *The History of Jennings County: Jennings County, Indiana, 1816–1999* (Vernon, IN: Jennings County Historical Society, 1999), 21–25.

176. Following two bloody and unsuccessful assaults on Fort Wagner at Morris Island near Charleston, South Carolina, on July 11 and 18, Union land and sea forces laid siege to the city. Confederate General Joseph E. Johnston withdrew from Jackson on July 16. See Long, *Civil War Day by Day*, 382, 286–88.

177. Joseph and Rebecca Wynn lived in Burnsville, Bartholomew County. See 1860 U.S. Census—Indiana, microfilm, roll 244, p. 155. The nature of Rate's illness is unknown.

178. George N. Hawley was a second lieutenant in the Seventy-sixth. He was in the first class of the College Preparatory program at Franklin College and the Sunday School class of the college church at the time of Stott's graduation. See ACWRD; *Catalogue of the Officers and Students of Franklin College, 1860–61* (Indianapolis: Indiana Journal Company, 1861), 8; *AGI*, 6:75.

179. Lieutenant Morgan is undoubtedly Stott's classmate, Thomas Jefferson Morgan of the Seventieth Indiana. The soldiers mentioned were all privates in Company I of the Eighteenth: Allen or Samuel Kelly, Charles A. Sims, George W. Buckner, and Richard M. Hall, one of Stott's recruits of October 1862. See *AGI*, 386–87.

180. John S. Donaldson was a Methodist minister and was with the Eighteenth for the rest of the war. See *AGI*, 2:159; Brinsfield et al., eds., *Faith in the Fight*, 149.

181. Peter D. Pelser of Metamora was first lieutenant of Company F of the Eighteenth. See *AGI*, 2:163.

CHAPTER 6

1. *OR*, 26(1):18. See also Robert L. Kerby, *Kirby Smith's Confederacy: The Trans-Mississippi South, 1863–1865* (Tuscaloosa and London: University of Alabama Press, 1972), 187; John D. Winters, *The Civil War in Louisiana* (Baton Rouge: Louisiana State University Press, 1963), 294; David C. Edmonds, *Yankee Autumn in Acadiana: A Narrative of the Great Texas Overland Expedition through Southern Louisiana, October–December 1863* (Lafayette, LA: Acadiana Press, 1979), 5.

2. Kerby, *Kirby Smith's Confederacy*, 187–88; Stephen E. Ambrose, *Halleck: Lincoln's Chief of Staff* (Baton Rouge: Louisiana State University Press, 1962), 146; Roy P. Basler et al, eds., *The Collected Works of Abraham Lincoln*, 8 vols. (New Brunswick, NJ: Rutgers University Press, 1953–55), 6:364–65.

3. Richard Lowe, *The Texas Overland Expedition of 1863* (Fort Worth and Boulder: Ryan Place Publishers, 1996), 14–16; Edmonds, *Yankee Autumn in Acadiana*, 5; Edwin Adam Davis, *Heroic Years: Louisiana in the War for Southern Independence* (Baton Rouge: Louisiana University Press, 1964), 52; Kerby, *Kirby Smith's Confederacy*, 165.

4. James G. Hollandsworth Jr., *Pretense of Glory: The Life of General Nathaniel P. Banks* (Baton Rouge: Louisiana State University Press, 1998), 134–35; Kerby, *Kirby Smith's Confederacy*, 187; Ambrose, *Halleck*, 146–47; Lowe, *Texas Overland Expedition of 1863*, p. 19; Davis, *Heroic Years*, 52–53; Richard Kiper, *Major General John Alexander McClernand: Politician in Uniform* (Kent and London: Kent State University Press, 1999), 279.

5. *OR*, 26(1)18; Kerby, *Kirby Smith's Confederacy*, 187–88, 293; Frank J. Welcher, *The Union Army, 1861–1865: Organization and Operations*, 2 vols. (Bloomington: Indiana University Press, 1989), 2:263; Winters, *Civil War in Louisiana*, 293. Taylor's army actually was more meager than that of Banks, and the Confederate general was obliged to spread his less than 14,000 troops thinly over western Louisiana. He also noted that earlier that year major Confederate fortifications "had been abandoned, the garrisons withdrawn, works dismantled, and guns thrown into the water." See Richard Taylor, *Destruction and Reconstruction: Personal Experiences of the Late War* (New York: D. Appleton, 1879), 102; Winters, *Civil War in Louisiana*, 319; Richard B. Irwin, *History of the Nineteenth Army Corps* (New York and London: G. P. Putnam and Sons, 1892), 266.

6. General Affidavit of William Taylor Stott, March 13, 1889, Full Pension File, William Taylor Stott, NARA.

7. Daniel Roberts to mother, sister, and friends in general, August 27, 1863, Daniel Roberts Letters, 1861–1864, S1123, Manuscript Section, ISL; August 25, 1863, Diary, Lt. George S. Marks Papers, Civil War Miscellaneous Collection, USAMHI (hereafter cited as Marks Diary); William Winters to Hattie, September 12, 1863, in Steven E. Woodworth, ed., *The Musick of the Mocking Birds, the Roar of the Cannon: The Civil War Diary and Letters of William Winters* (Lincoln and London: University of Nebraska Press, 1998), 75–76.

8. James S. Slack to Ann, August 16, 1863, James R. Slack Papers, 1837–1865, L145, Manuscript Section, ISL; Roberts to Mother et al., August 27, 1863, Roberts Letters; August 27, 29, September 4, 1863, Marks Diary; Gilbert Denny to Morris T. Denny, August 31, 1863, Letters of Gilbert H. Denny, Eighteenth Regiment, 1861–1863, IHS. See also Edmonds, *Yankee Autumn in Acadiana*, 6.

9. Welcher, *Union Army*, 2:264; John William DeForest, *A Volunteer's Adventures: A Union Captain's Record of the Civil War*, James H. Croushore, ed. (New Haven, CT: Yale University Press, 1946), 154; David Scott to Kate Missimer, September 10, 1863, David S. Scott

Papers, 1862–1865, IHS; Augustus Sinks, "Four Years in Dixie," Journal of the Campaign of the Forty-sixth Indiana Regiment, S1193, Manuscript Section, ISL; Winters to Hattie, November 22, 1863, Woodworth, ed., *Musick of the Mocking Birds*, 85. See also Lowe, *Texas Overland Expedition of 1863*, pp. 34–35.

10. Isaac H. Elliott, *History of the Thirty-third Illinois Veteran Volunteer Infantry in the Civil War* (Gibson City, IL: Regiment Association, 1902), 48; Hollandsworth, *Pretense of Glory*, 136; Lowe, *Texas Overland Expedition of 1863*, p. 34.

11. DeForest, *Volunteer's Adventures*, 148, 154; Morris Raphael, *The Battle in the Bayou Country* (Detroit: Harlo Press, 1974), 48–49; Sinks, "Four Years in Dixie," 51; Lowe, *Texas Overland Expedition of 1863*, p. 35; Edmonds, *Yankee Autumn in Acadiana*, 10, 14–15; D. W. Camp to father, September 16, 1853, "The Civil War Letters of Dan Camp, 24th Iowa Volunteers," 12, edited by Andrew J. Morris, Iberia Parish Library, New Iberia, LA. Brashear City is the present-day Morgan City.

12. Roberts to mother and sister, September 9, 1863, Roberts Letters; Elliott, *History of the Thirty-third Illinois Volunteer Infantry in the Civil War*, 48; Edmonds, *Yankee Autumn in Acadiana*, 18.

13. Lowe, *Texas Overland Expedition of 1863*, p. 35; Kerby, *Kirby Smith's Confederacy*, 243; William Arceneaux, *Acadian General: Alfred Mouton and the Civil War* (Lafayette: University of Southwestern Louisiana, 1981), 105.

14. OR, 26 (1): 18–19; Lowe, *Texas Overland Expedition of 1863*, pp. 21–22; Arceneaux, *Acadian General*, 102–3; Irwin, *History of the Nineteenth Army Corps*, 268; Hollandsworth, *Pretense of Glory*, 138; Bernard Schermerhorn to wife, September 14, 1863, Bernard F. Schermerhorn Papers, 1862–1864, IHS.

15. OR, 26(1):19; Arceneaux, *Acadian General*, 103–4; Edmonds, *Yankee Autumn in Acadiana*, 15; Sinks, "Four Years in Dixie," 51; September 25, 1863, Marks Diary.

16. Edmonds, *Yankee Autumn in Acadiana*, 23–26; Lowe, *Texas Overland Expedition of 1863*, p. 36; Arceneaux, *Acadian General*, 106.

17. Catharine Merrill, *The Soldier of Indiana in the War for the Union*, 2 vols. (Indianapolis: Merrill and Company, 1866), 2:511–12; Edmonds, *Yankee Autumn in Acadiana*, 77; October 14, 1863, Marks Diary; C. P. Alling, "Four Years with the Western Army," 12, Regimental Files (Eleventh Wisconsin), VNMP; Lowe, *Texas Overland Expedition of 1863*, p. 39; "From the Sixty-ninth!" October 22, 1863, unidentified newspaper clipping (possibly *Richmond (IN) Quaker City Telegram*), in Walter Burke Papers, ULL; Roberts to Mother & Sisters, October 7, 1863, Roberts Letters. Confederate General Richard Taylor had similar feelings about the Teche and its surroundings. He labeled the bayou "the loveliest of southern streams" and of the countryside he said, "I cannot recall so fair, so beautiful, and so happy a land." Taylor, *Destruction and Reconstruction*, 104–5.

18. Lowe, *Texas Overland Expedition of 1863*, p. 40; Roberts to Mother and Sisters, October 7, 1863, Roberts Letters; Edmonds, *Yankee Autumn in Acadiana*, 34; Kerby, *Kirby Smith's Confederacy*, 6. On Confederate treatment of the Acadians, see Arceneaux, *Acadian General*, 107–8. This was Evangeline country, popularized in the epic poem of that title by Henry Wadsworth Longfellow. Stott read that work while on duty in Virginia in 1864. See Edmonds, *Yankee Autumn in Acadiana*, 77; George B. Marshall, "A Reminiscence of the Civil War, 1861 to 1865," S2192, Manuscript Section, ISL.

19. Lowe, *Texas Overland Expedition of 1863*, pp. 30–31, 36–38; Elliott, *History of the Thirty-third Illinois Volunteer Infantry in the Civil War*, 47–48; Taylor to Catharine, Novem-

ber 7, 1863, in *Dear Catharine, Dear Taylor: The Civil War Letters of a Union Soldier to His Wife*, Richard Kiper, ed. (Lawrence: University Press of Kansas, 2002), 153.

20. Edmonds, *Yankee Autumn in Acadiana*, 34 (Watts quote), 38; "From the Sixty-ninth."

21. Edmonds, *Yankee Autumn in Acadiana*, 45–46; Lowe, *Texas Overland Expedition of 1863*, p. 44; Davis, *Heroic Years*, 50; "Glimpses of Iberia in the Civil War," 11, Weeks Family Historical Papers, Iberia Parish Library.

22. Edmonds, *Yankee Autumn in Acadiana*, 82–88, 135; DeForest, *Volunteer's Adventures*, 156.

23. DeForest, *Volunteer's Adventures*, 156; Sinks, "Four Years in Dixie," 52–53; Taylor to Catharine, November 1, 1863, Kiper, ed., *Dear Catharine, Dear Taylor*, 147; Carl A. Brasseaux, *Acadian to Cajun: Transformation of a People, 1803–1877* (Jackson and London: University Press of Mississippi, 1992), 67–68; Edmonds, *Yankee Autumn in Acadiana*, 130–42; Elliott, *History of the Thirty-third Illinois Volunteer Infantry in the Civil War*, 49. Historian David Edmonds lays most of the blame for the worst foraging squarely on the western troops, stating that "If a prize had been awarded the state whose soldiers plundered the most, Iowa and Indiana would surely have taken top honors." See his *Yankee Autumn in Acadiana*, 136. One of General Edward O. C. Ord's more notable steps to curb foraging was his arrest of Stott's brigade commander, Colonel David Shunk, "for failing to perform his duty and prevent marauding in his command." The Eighteenth's former chief, Colonel Henry Washburn, succeeded Shunk. See *OR*, 26(2): 763. Vermilionville is the present-day Lafayette, Louisiana.

24. Elliott, *History of the Thirty-third Illinois Volunteer Infantry in the Civil War*, 49; Lowe, *Texas Overland Expedition of 1863*, pp. 48–49; Kerby, *Kirby Smith's Confederacy*, 243–45; Arceneaux, *Acadian General*, 109.

25. Schermerhorn to Wife, October 18, 1863, Schermerhorn Papers; "From the Sixty-ninth"; Edmonds, *Yankee Autumn in Acadiana*, 198, 214.

26. Arceneaux, *Acadian General*, 111; Lowe, *Texas Overland Expedition of 1863*, pp. 60-61; Edmonds, *Yankee Autumn in Acadiana*, 214, 224–29.

27. Lowe, *Texas Overland Expedition of 1863*, pp. 61–62; Arceneaux, *Acadian General*, 112; *OR*, 26(1): 19–20, 336–37, 357; Edmonds, *Yankee Autumn in Acadiana*, 252; Elliott, *History of the Thirty-third Illinois Volunteer Infantry in the Civil War*, 50; Taylor to Catharine, November 7, 1963, Kiper, ed., *Dear Catharine, Dear Taylor*, 153. Interestingly, William Arceneaux questions whether Banks "seriously intended the Great Texas Overland Expedition to be anything more than an exercise for political consumption in Washington and a mask for his more facile and less perilous designs on Texas." See *Acadian General*, 112.

28. Lowe, *Texas Overland Expedition of 1863*, pp. 105–6; Harry Watts, "Civil War Reminiscence," 107, S1372, Manuscript Section, ISL. The Battle of Bayou Bourbeau lies beyond the purview of this book. Excellent accounts may be found in *OR*, 26(1):355–56; Lowe, *Texas Overland Expedition of 1863*, chapter 6; David Edmonds, "Surrender on the Borbeaux: Honorable Defeat or Incompetence Under Fire," in Arthur W. Bergeron Jr., *The Civil War in Louisiana, Part A: Military Activity* (Lafayette: University of Louisiana at Lafayette, 2002), 408–26; Schermerhorn to wife, November 9, 1863, Schermerhorn Papers; Taylor to Catharine, November 11, 1863, Kiper, ed., *Dear Catharine, Dear Taylor*, 156–57; Taylor, *Destruction and Reconstruction*, 150–51.

29. Hollandsworth, *Pretense of Glory*, 141–43; Ralph A. Wooster, *Civil War Texas: A History and a Guide* (Austin: Texas State Historical Association, 1999), 27–28.

30. Entry of November 12, Diary, George W. Gordon Papers, 1861–1864, USAMHI; Roberts to mother and sisters, December 1, 1863, Roberts Letters. See also entry of November 12–13, 1863, Samuel P. Herrington Diary, August 1, 1861, to September 14, 1864, Rudolph Haerle Collection, USAMHI.

31. November 15, 1863, Herrington Diary; Roberts to mother and sisters, December 1, 1863, Roberts Letters; *OR*, 26(1):20; Merrill, *Soldier of Indiana in the War for the Union*, 2:516.

32. *OR*, 26(1):20, 426; Jim Huffstodt, *Hard Men Dying: The Story of General W. H. L. Wallace, General T. E. G. Ransom, and Their "Old Eleventh" Illinois Infantry in the Civil War* (Bowie, MD: Heritage Books, 1991), 169; Swain Marshall to friends at home, December 6, 1863, Thomas Marshall Papers, 1821–1920, IHS; November 1, 1863, Herrington Diary; undated entry, Diary, 37, Gordon Papers; Lester N. Fitzhugh, "Saluria, Fort Esperanza, and Military Operations on the Texas Coast, 1821–1864," *Southwestern Historical Quarterly* 61 (July 1957): 95; Merrill, *Soldier of Indiana in the War for the Union*, 2:516.

33. Merrill, *Soldier of Indiana in the War for the Union*, 2:516; Leeper to Mary, December 18, 1863, James Leeper Papers, 1855–1912, IHS; November 19, 1863, Herrington Diary.

34. *OR*, 26(1):416, 418, 427; November 25, 26, 1863, Herrington Diary; Elliott, *History of the Thirty-third Illinois Volunteer Infantry in the Civil War*, 53.

35. Roberts to mother and sisters, December 1, 1863, Roberts Letters; *OR*, 26(1):419–20, 427; Bill Windsor, *Texas in the Confederacy: Military Installations, Economy, and People* (Hillsboro, TX: Hill Junior College Press, 1978), 7, 40; Alwyn Barr, "Texas Coastal Defenses, 1861–1865," *Southwestern Historical Quarterly* 45 (July 1961): 1–31. Colonel Henry D. Washburn, who had led the Eighteenth Indiana and its brigade from the time of enlistment, was not related to General C. C. Washburn. Not all descriptions of the armaments at Fort Esperanza are in agreement regarding numbers and sizes. The best accounts of Fort Esperanza and Texas military installations appear in Windsor, *Texas in the Confederacy*; Barr, "Texas Coastal Defenses"; Fitzhugh, "Saluria, Fort Esperanza, and Military Operations on the Texas Coast."

36. *OR*, 26(1):420–21; Elliott, *History of the Thirty-third Illinois Volunteer Infantry in the Civil War*, 53; *Rockville Parke County Republican*, February 14, 1864.

37. Elliott, *History of the Thirty-third Illinois Volunteer Infantry in the Civil War*, 53; November 28, 1863, Herrington Diary; Barr, "Texas Coastal Defenses," 28; *OR*, 26 (1):419, 421.

38. *OR*, 26(1):421–22; Elliott, *History of the Thirty-third Illinois Volunteer Infantry in the Civil War*, 53; November 29, 1863, Herrington Diary.

39. *OR*, 26(1):422; Fitzhugh, "Saluria, Fort Esperanza, and Military Operations on the Texas Coast," 97.

40. Swain Marshall to "Friends at Home," December 6, 1863, Marshall Papers; *OR*, 26(1):416–19, 422; November 29–30, Herrington Diary; Elliott, *History of the Thirty-third Illinois Volunteer Infantry in the Civil War*, 53.

41. Merrill, *Soldier of Indiana in the War for the Union*, 2:517; December 23, 1863, Marks Diary; Taylor to Catharine, January 8, 1864, Kiper, ed., *Dear Catharine, Dear Taylor*, 169–70.

42. Leeper to Mary, January 7, 1864, Leeper Papers; Winters to Hattie, January 14, 1864, Woodworth, ed., *Musick of the Mocking Bird*, 95–97.

43. *OR*, 34(2):147–48.

44. Swain to father, February 18, 1864, Marshall Papers; James K. Bigelow, *Abridged History of the Eighth Indiana Volunteer Infantry from Its Organization, April 21st, 1861, to the Date of Re-enlistment as Veterans, January 1, 1864* (Indianapolis: Ellis Barnes, 1864), 25–26, 39; *Rockville Parke County Republican*, February 24, 1864.

45. W. H. H. Terrell, *Indiana in the War of the Rebellion: Report of the Adjutant General* (Indianapolis: Indiana Historical Society, 1960), 32–39; Kiper, ed., *Dear Catharine, Dear Taylor*, 189n2; *Rockville Parke County Republican*, February 24, 1864; "Detachment Muster-out Roll" and "Muster-in and Descriptive Roll of Veteran Volunteers," Military Service File, William Taylor Stott, NARA. As a captain, most of Stott's time in December and early January centered on paperwork dealing with veteranizing. The Eighteenth Indiana did not receive actual veteran status until February 5, 1864.

46. Kiper, *Major John Alexander McClernand*, 279–80; Taylor to Catharine, March 17, 1864, Kiper, ed., *Dear Catharine, Dear Taylor*, 188.

47. *OR*, 34(2):392, 702–3, 771–72.

48. Ibid., 34(3):253.

49. Merrill, *Soldier of Indiana in the War for the Union*, 2:534; *OR*, 34(1):906–7.

50. Undated *Indianapolis Journal* clipping pasted into Stott's diary following the entry of June 6, 1864; *OR*, 34(3):464–65. On the receptions typically held in Indianapolis to greet furloughed veteran troops, see Terrell, *Indiana in the War of the Rebellion*, 40–43.

CHAPTER 7

1. "O.D." signifies Officer of the Day.

2. "Sam Huston" was a sutler, a commercial merchant permitted to sell his products at military camps and specially licensed to do so. Sutlers peddled cigars, newspapers, candies, books, razors, and other personal items. Many were corrupt, selling "shoddy products at inflated prices," though, as Stott suggests, Huston seemed to be honest and informative. His actual identity is unknown. See John D. Wright, *The Language of the Civil War* (Westport, CT and London: Oryx Press, 2001), 289–90.

3. The reason Private Munsford Jordan of Johnson County and Company I, Eighteenth Indiana, had been jailed is unknown. Thomas B. Woods of Crawfordsville was a first lieutenant in Company F of the Eleventh Indiana. See *AGI*, 4:386.

4. Captain Samuel J. Foster was in Company G of the Eighty-seventh. See ACWRD.

5. Stott's information is a little out-dated here. General William S. Rosecrans crossed the Cumberland Mountains in late August, advancing to Chattanooga. On this date, September 19, 1863, his Army of the Cumberland was engaging Braxton Bragg's Confederate Army of Tennessee during the first day of battle at Chickamauga. See E. B. Long, *The Civil War Day by Day: An Almanac, 1861–65* (New York: DaCapo, 1971), 411.

6. After his defeat at Chickamauga, Rosecrans pulled his army back to Chattanooga and formed a strong defensive line around it by September 22. Major General Quincy Adams Gillmore and troops in the Union Department of the South forced Confederates to evacuate Battery Wagner and Charleston's Morris Island on September 7 after a long bombardment by siege guns, monitors, and ironclads. The operation there "constituted a new era in the science of engineering and gunnery," according to some analysts. See Long, *Civil War Day by Day*, 405, 412; Ezra J. Warner, *Generals in Blue: Lives of the Union Commanders* (Baton Rouge: Louisiana University Press, 1964), 176–77.

7. Fort Smith, Arkansas, fell to Union forces on September 1, and Sterling Price's troops

evacuated Little Rock on September 10. See Long, *Civil War Day by Day*, 403, 407–8.

8. The new chaplain of the Eighteenth Indiana was Methodist John S. Donaldson, who began his service with the regiment on August 28, 1863. See *AGI*, 2:159; John W. Brinsfield et al., *Faith in the Fight: Civil War Chaplains* (Mechanicsburg, PA: Stackpole Books, 2003), 149.

9. Ecclesiastes 9:10.

10. Mrs. Jane Clarke Lippincott, under the pseudonym Grace Greenwood, published *Greenwood Leaves: Collection of Sketches and Letters* in 1852. "The Volunteer" is an antiwar story set during the Mexican War. Herbert and Margaret, an engaged couple, quarrel over Herbert's decision to join the army, a move Margaret deems beneath her high position in life. Even though both are against the war, Herbert chooses to enlist, despite Margaret's protestations, and asks Margaret to care for his mother while he is gone. Margaret agrees to do so, but chastises Herbert for acting "not from love . . . but from your *pride*—your hard, unlovely pride." Herbert suffers a number of wounds and returns home "forgotten, abandoned, utterly friendless!" Margaret nurses him back to health and repledges her love to him because of his "worthiness" and "victory over self." See Grace Greenwood, *Greenwood Leaves* (Boston: Ticknor and Fields, 1852), 100–121.

11. Obviously, Stott had received some erroneous information. The battle to which he refers was that of Chickamauga in which the Confederates whipped Rosecrans in tactical victory, although the latter's forces held tenaciously under General George Thomas, the "Rock of Chickamauga."

12. A reference to the story of Moses's call by Yahweh at the burning bush in Exodus 3.

13. Private Frampton of Johnson County was in Stott's Company I, but there is no official record of his capture.

14. Almost half of the officers and men of the Twenty-sixth Indiana were captured in an engagement at Camp Sterling, Morganza, Louisiana, on September 29. See Ann Turner, *Guide to Indiana Civil War Manuscripts* (Indianapolis: Indiana Civil War Centennial Commission, 1965), 86.

15. This Latin phrase, as noted in note 48 of the third section of the Diary, may be translated "Marvelous in the saying." Obviously, in this instance Stott uses the phrase sarcastically.

16. Burns's "The Cottar's Saturday Night" surely would have appealed to Stott, given the poignant passages in which the cottar kneels in prayer and Burns reflects that "'An honest man's the noblest work of God;' / And certes, in fair virtue's heavenly road, / The cottage leaves the palace far behind." Stott also refers to Burns's poem, "To a Louse. On Seeing One on a Lady's Bonnet at Church." See Robert Burns, *Poems and Songs, Complete*, 4 vols. (Edinburgh: James Thin, 1896), 1:144–50, 211–13.

17. Private Thomas J. Hall of Lawrence County was in Company B, Eighteenth Indiana. See *AGI*, 4:375.

18. Private Thomas McCracken of Johnson County was in Stott's Company I. See *AGI*, 4:386.

19. Historian David Edmonds indicates that October 25 was "a clear and cold Sunday morning" at Barre's Landing as the regiments prepared "for an open-air religious ceremony." In nearby Opelousas, where Union soldiers "outnumbered the citizens by a ratio of about ten to one," most churches flew the Stars and Stripes and preached "a Union sermon." See David C. Edmonds, *Yankee Autumn in Acadiana: A Narrative of the Great Texas*

Overland Expedition through Southern Louisiana, October–December, 1863 (Lafayette, LA: Acadiana Press, 1979), 241.

20. Burns enclosed "My Nanie's Away" in a December 1749 letter to George Thompson, indicating that it should be sung to "There'll Never Be Peace." Burns's "To a Mouse" of 1785 includes the famous lines: "The best-laid schemes o' mice and men / Gang aft agley." See *The Works of Robert Burns: With an Account of His Life and a Criticism of His Writings*, 6th ed., 4 vols. (London: T. Cadell and W. Davies, 1809), 4:213–14; Burns, *Poems and Songs*, 4:124–25.

21. The verses paraphrased by Stott are from Sir Walter Scott's epic poem *The Lady of the Lake*, part 1, stanza 31, which reads: "Soldier rest, they warfare's o'er / Sleep the sleep that knows not breaking." See Scott, *The Lady of the Lake* (New York and London: International Art Pub. Company, [ca. 1898?]). Corporal James O. Boggs of Vermillion County, Indiana, was in Company C of the Eighteenth Indiana. See *AGI*, 4:376.

22. George S. Hankins of Sardinia, near Vernon, was a sergeant in Company I of the Sixty-eighth Indiana. He was killed in action at Chickamauga on September 20, 1863. See ACWRD.

23. The reference here is to the Battle of Bayou Bourbeau on November 2–3 in which Brigadier General George F. McGinnis's Third Division and Brigadier General Stephen G. Burbridge's Fourth Division of the XIII Corps bore the brunt of a Confederate cavalry assault but valiantly held their ground. See note 28 of the introduction to this section of the diary for bibliographic information on the battle.

24. Hirelings "whose own the sheep are not" is quoted from John 10:12. In standard Civil War language, nine-month men were those "soldiers who enlisted for no less and no more than nine months." Stott is using it here to indicate that in nine months he and his colleagues would be completing their terms of enlistment. See Webb Garrison, *The Encyclopedia of Civil War Usage* (Nashville, TN: Cumberland House, 2001), 172. Stott recalls that General Zachary Taylor arrived at Corpus Christi at the beginning of the Mexican War (in 1845, not 1846). See Holman Hamilton, *Zachary Taylor: Soldier of the Republic* (Hamden, CT: Archon Books, 1966), 162–63; H. Jack Bauer, *Zachary Taylor: Soldier, Planter, Statesman of the Old Southwest* (Baton Rouge: Louisiana State University Press, 1985), 116–19.

25. The ship boarded by Stott's men was the *Clinton*, not Cliffton. There were two Duprees in Company I, Edward and Joseph T., so it is unclear which one was the deserter. Since there is no record of a "muster out" date for Joseph, and Edward is recorded as mustering out on August 28, 1865, it could be that the deserter was Joseph. Both were privates and neither one received promotion. See *AGI*, 4:386. Morgan is Stott's fellow graduate of Franklin College, Thomas Jefferson Morgan, who left the Seventieth Indiana to recruit and lead black troops. He became colonel of the Fourteenth U.S. Colored Infantry in 1864 and was later brevetted brigadier general. See *DAB*, 7:187–88.

26. Henry Bogard, identified earlier, was now a sergeant in Company I. Jeremiah Warren was recruited on September 26, 1862, probably by Stott on his recruiting leave that fall. See *AGI*, 4:386–87.

27. Private William S. Snow of Johnson County and Company I. See *AGI*, 4:386.

28. Patmos was an island in the Aegean Sea to which the Roman Empire banished political dissenters, particularly Christians. It was the location to which Saint John was sent because of his preaching of "the word of God, and for the testimony of Jesus Christ," and where he experienced apocalyptic revelations from God that he shared with the persecuted

churches to which he wrote. See Revelation 1:9.

29. In his official report on the Fort Esperanza campaign, Colonel Henry D. Washburn notes that he lost one man killed and ten wounded, "among the latter Lieutenant George H. Fifer, acting aide-de-camp, a gallant and brave officer." Fifer was in the Thirty-third Illinois Infantry. See OR, 26(1):422; ACWRD.

30. John Carson of Franklin and Company I received promotion to first lieutenant on December 1, 1863. Major General Benjamin F. Butler replaced Major General John G. Foster as commander of the Department of Virginia and North Carolina on November 11, 1863. Stott is mistaken regarding General David Hunter. See Long, *Civil War Day by Day*, 432.

31. Benjamin Fisher of Vermillion County was a private in Company C, Eighteenth. See *AGI*, 4:376.

32. Stott first reflects in this entry on Saint Paul's words in 1 Corinthians 15:54. *Veni, Vidi, Vici* is, of course, most popularly (and loosely) translated "I came, I saw, I conquered."

33. The celebration may have been in response to the Battle of Chattanooga on November 23–25. It is clear that Stott no longer can put full trust in the numerous camp rumors about distant battles, since so many in the past have proven to be incorrect. On Chattanooga, see Long, *Civil War Day by Day*, 436–38.

34. Stott first read Francis Wayland's *Elements of Moral Science* (first published in 1835) as a junior student at Franklin College. Wayland (1796–1865) was a major figure in the reform of higher education during the early nineteenth century. As president of Brown University from 1827 to 1855, he championed "a theory of democracy that led inevitably to a conception of universal education" and regularly taught the senior course in moral philosophy. According to Joseph L. Blau, Wayland's lectures in that course became the basis for the *Elements of Moral Science*, "the first American textbook in Moral Philosophy" and a didactic handbook that challenged the utilitarian ethics of William Paley (1743–1805). Relying heavily on the insights of Stott's beloved Bishop Joseph Butler, Wayland insisted that religion should be the primary focus of philosophy because of its stress on morality, and that "moral science lies at the foundation of all science." Stott was particularly enamored of Wayland's chapter on the "Nature of Virtue," which he mentions in his diary entry of February 15, 1864. See *Catalogue of the Officers and Students of Franklin College for the Academic Year 1860–61* (Indianapolis: Indianapolis Journal Company, 1861), 14; Francis Wayland, *The Elements of Moral Science*, Joseph L. Blau, ed. (Cambridge: Belknap Press of Harvard University Press, 1963), xi, xii–xiii, xxviii, xliv, 76–88; Francis Wayland and Heman Lincoln Wayland, *A Memoir of the Life and Labors of Francis Wayland*, 2 vols. (New York: Sheldon and Company, 1867), 2:379–85. Richard Whately (1787–1863) was the Archbishop of Dublin and a follower of Bishop Butler in his views on ethics. His cardinal tenet was: "the Bible, the Bible alone, is the religion of Protestants." Stott studied Whately's *Logic* as a junior at Franklin College. See Leslie Stephen and Sidney Lee, eds., *Dictionary of National Biography*, 22 vols. (New York: Macmillan, 1908–9), 20:1334–40; *Catalogue of the Officers and Students of Franklin College for the Academic Year 1860–61*, p. 14.

35. The chaplain of the Twenty-third Iowa was Baptist minister Arthur J. Barton. John S. Donaldson was still the chaplain of the Eighteenth Indiana. See Brinsfield et al., *Faith in the Fight*, 132, 149.

36. Luke 2:14 (KJV).

37. John 1:29 (KJV).

38. Luke 16:2 (KJV).

39. Proverbs 29:2 (KJV).

40. The man on trial was Colonel Lemuel Parke, apparently the same "Col. Park" Stott accused of cowardice during the assault at Vicksburg on May 22, 1863. No record of the court-martial has been found. See ACWRD.

41. Stott was apparently reading or recalling James Russell Lowell's satirical protest of the Mexican War published in 1846 as *The Biglow Papers*. Quite possibly he was quoting the poem "What Mr. Robinson Thinks" from memory since he does not employ the exact New England country farmer dialect Lowell employed for his fictional protagonist, Hosea Biglow. See Thomas Wortham, *James Russell Lowell's The Biglow Papers [First Series]: A Critical Edition* (Dekalb: Northern Illinois University Press, 1977), 72; James Russell Lowell, *The Biglow Papers*, second series (Boston: Houghton, Mifflin and Company, 1885), 9, 22; Harry Hayden Clark and Norman Foerster, *James Russell Lowell* (New York: American Book Company, 1947), xxx–xxxii.

42. Stott is reflecting on recent developments for his Franklin College friends. Casabianca Byfield and Simpson Burton were in the class of 1860. Miss Graves may have been Carrie Graves, a Franklin resident and friend of Stott's correspondent Carrie Morrison. William Elgin of the class of 1862 was in the Seventieth Indiana Infantry. Elgin's classmate, Lorenzo W. Billingsley, served in the Fourth Indiana Cavalry. See *Jubilee*, 127, 130, 138. On Elgin and Billingsley, see also ACWRD.

43. Privates Lucian A. Gray and James W. Feagler, both of North Vernon, enlisted in Company C of the Thirteenth Indiana Cavalry on January 13, 1864. Reuben Patterson was captain of Company I, Sixty-eighth Indiana Infantry. See ACWRD,

44. Lorenzo D. McCallister of Anderson was captain of Company K, Eighth Indiana. See *AGI*, 2:55.

45. Basil B. Brashear was surgeon of the Nineteenth Ohio Infantry. The "amateur" statement was apparently directed toward him. See ACWRD. S. Clay Brown was an assistant surgeon with the Eighth Indiana, as was Peter M. Bigney with the Eighteenth. Brown became surgeon of the Eighteenth in June 1864. See *AGI*, 2:159.

46. It is unclear to what "Substitute" Stott was writing. It is possible, however, that it was the nineteenth-century biblical journal *The Substitute*, a "Repository of Scripture Testimony," published in Philadelphia. See *NUC: Pre-1956*, vol. 575:311.

47. Andrew Jackson Hamilton, a native of Alabama, served the state of Texas in Congress from 1859 to 1861. In November 1862 President Abraham Lincoln appointed him a brigadier general and military governor of Texas. See Warner, *Generals in Blue*, 198.

48. Also known as "dog tents," these small, two-man tents replaced the larger, more cumbersome Sibley tents. See Wright, *Language of the Civil War*, 91–92.

49. Private Lewis Williams of Johnson County was in Stott's Company I. The Indiana Adjutant General cites the date of Corporal Timothy Hays's death as March 19. See *AGI*, 4:387.

50. Ira Butler of Johnson County served in Stott's Company I. In October 1864 he was taken prisoner at the Battle of Cedar Creek, Virginia. See *AGI*, 4:386.

51. Eliza (age thirteen) and Harry (twelve) were the children of Franklin College Professor of Chemistry John S. Hougham and his wife, Mary. Julia Johnson (age sixteen) was the daughter of Charles F. and Elizabeth Johnson. See 1860 U.S. Census—Indiana, micro-

film, Roll 271, pp. 690, 770, ISL. The records of First Baptist Church in Franklin indicate that a Maria Mixsell was baptized in February 1864. She could be the Mary Meixwell mentioned by Stott. Mary Alice Medlicott graciously conducted a thorough search of the First Baptist Church records, but did not find the Houghams or Julia Johnson among the list of persons baptized. John T. and Emily Forsythe had five daughters—Mary, Alice, Elizabeth, Frances, and Emma. In March 1864 Alice—to use Stott's spelling—would have been age eighteen or nineteen. No Dora is listed in the census, though that could have been the nickname of one of Alice's sisters. See 1860 Census—Indiana, microfilm, Roll 271, p. 706. David McCaslin of Johnson County was a private in Stott's Company I. See *AGI*, 4:386.

52. Captain James A. Bell of Company C, Eighteenth Indiana, resigned his commission on March 24, 1864. See *AGI*, 2:161.

53. John McCrea of Bloomington was chaplain of the Thirty-third Indiana Infantry. See ACWRD.

54. Stott may have been confused in this biblical reference. It was Isaac who "went out to meditate in the field at the eventide." See Genesis 24:63. Then again, Stott may have been thinking of Psalm 63, attributed to David, in which he says, "When I remember thee upon my bed, and meditate on thee in the night watches." See Psalm 63:6. The article from *Atlantic Monthly* asserts that, historically, "Northern invasions, when successful, advance the civilization of the world." The unknown author cites the Tartar invasion of China and the fact that Greece "died out" because of its lack of "Gothic blood" as proofs of his thesis. He also commends Lincoln's Reconstruction plan, especially its proclamation of amnesty, and urges Northerners to settle in the South after Union victory and "to establish there free institutions." See "Northern Invasions," *Atlantic Monthly* 13 (February 1864): 245–47, 249.

55. The struggle for equal pay for black troops had been ongoing ever since they were first enlisted in the fall of 1862. The issue boiled over, however, in June 1863 when a review of the Militia Act of July 1862 led to a War Department decision to "pay black soldiers at the same rate as black government employees." This resulted in a reduction of pay for black troops from thirteen dollars per month to ten dollars, with the additional three dollars being used as a clothing allowance. Protests broke out in the black ranks. In March 1864 twenty-four members of the black Fourteenth Rhode Island Heavy Artillery, then stationed at Fort Jefferson, Florida, were arrested and sentenced to hard labor for "refusing to accept their pay." See Keith P. Wilson, *Campfires of Freedom: The Camp Life of Black Soldiers during the Civil War* (Kent, OH and London: Kent State University Press, 2002), 44, 45, 47; James M. McPherson, *The Negro's Civil War* (New York: Pantheon Books, 1965), 198–203.

56. Harvey D. Crane, first lieutenant of Company C, Eighteenth Indiana, resigned his commission on March 29, 1865. See *AGI*, 2:161. See also diary entry of April 3, 1864.

57. Jane Vawter Storey (1809–1864) was the daughter of the founder of Vernon, Indiana, John Vawter, and his first wife, Polly Smith Vawter. Jane married Thomas J. Storey in 1825 and was the mother of Stott's good friend Riley Storey. She died on March 8, 1864, at the age of fifty-three. See Grace Vawter Bicknell, *The Vawter Family in America* (Indianapolis: Hollenbeck Press, 1905; reprint, Atlanta: Thorpe and Associates, 1969), 59–60.

58. James V. Bridges of Johnson County was a private in Company I. See *AGI*, 4:386.

59. Nathaniel P. Banks launched his ill-fated Red River campaign of March to May 1864 in an attempt to capture Shreveport, Louisiana, the headquarters of the Confederate

Trans-Mississippi Department, a major supply depot, and "gateway to Texas." It essentially ended with Banks's overwhelming defeat in the battle of Mansfield on April 8. See Patricia L. Faust, ed., *Historical Times Illustrated Encyclopedia of the Civil War* (New York: Harper and Row, 1971), 619–20.

60. Stott is referring to Victor Hugo's graphic account of Waterloo and reflections upon that battle. Hugo wrote of the "indescribable terror" of war and its "frightful beauties"— the dead stripped naked after a battle, the multitude of soldiers filling the roads "wild with terror," interloping sutlers who "steal things which they sell again," and the horror of living "to see the sun" after all the carnage. See Victor Hugo, *Works of Victor Hugo*, vol. 2, *Les Miserables* (London and New York: Chesterfield Society, n.d.), 43, 60, 63.

61. Methodist Nelson L. Brakeman of the First Indiana Heavy Artillery also served as a hospital chaplain. His message was based on Psalm 122:1. See Brinsfield et al., *Faith in the Fight*, 136.

62. Charles Elliott Lippincott served valiantly in the Thirty-third Illinois at Pea Ridge and through the entire Vicksburg Campaign, becoming a brigadier general by brevet in February 1865. See ACWRD.

63. Brigadier General Philip Saint George Cooke (1809–1895), a native Virginian, was an 1827 graduate of West Point and veteran of McClellan's Peninsular campaign, but he saw limited field service after that operation. His son, John Rogers Cooke, remained loyal to his Southern upbringing and became one of Robert E. Lee's leading brigadiers. See Warner, *Generals in Blue*, 89–90.

64. Isaac Ferris, a Dutch Reformed minister, was chancellor of the University of the City of New York from 1852 to 1870. See *DAB*, 3:340. The text for his sermon came from either Matthew 22:21, Mark 12:17, or Luke 20:25.

65. Lionel Allen Sheldon of Columbus, Ohio, became a brigadier general by brevet in March of 1865. See ACWRD.

66. Lieutenant Colonel Frederick A. Boardman of LaCrosse, Wisconsin, was the officer killed in the Battle of Olive Branch Bayou near Comite River two days earlier. See ACWRD.

67. Paraphrase of Isaiah 66:24.

68. A thorough search uncovered no book with this title. It is quite possible, however, that Stott was reading Charles Wesley Alexander's novel, *Maud of the Mississippi*, published in Philadelphia in 1863. The *NUC:Pre-1956*, vol. 8:225, describes this book as "A thrilling narrative of the adventures of Miss Pauline d'Estrage, a young and beautiful French lady . . . during the Vicksburg Campaign under Major-General U.S. Grant."

69. In early May, Grant and Lee had "come together" in Virginia in the battle of the Wilderness (May 5–7) and, at the time of Stott's writing, were engaged at Spotsylvania (May 8–19). In regard to the sermons Stott heard, it is not clear which chaplain made the comments on courage and bravery. Brigadier General Henry Warner Birge led a division of the XIX Corps in the campaign against Port Hudson and during the abortive Red River operation. See Warner, *Generals in Blue*, 33–34.

70. David V. Burns of Sharpsville was in Company C and Richard Stott in Company H of the Twenty-sixth Indiana. See ACWRD. Grant crossed the Rapidan River with his Army of the Potomac shortly after midnight on May 3, thus beginning the Union push toward Petersburg. General Benjamin Butler was moving his Army of the James up the river of that name toward Richmond. See Long, *Civil War Day by Day*, 492.

71. Confederate General James Longstreet received wounds in the throat and shoulder,

severing several nerves, as a result of "friendly fire" during the battle of the Wilderness. He did not return to duty until November. See Jeffry D. Wert, *General James Longstreet: The Confederacy's Most Controversial Soldier* (New York and London: Simon and Schuster, 1993), 387.

72. Alvan Jones Bates was a Congregational minister with the Fourteenth Maine Infantry. His sermon was on John 16:33. See ACWRD.

73. Sherman arrived in the Kingston, Georgia, area on Saturday, May 21. Franz Sigel met defeat in the battle of New Market, Virginia, on the previous Sunday, May 15. See Long, *Civil War Day by Day*, 502–4, 506.

74. Joseph Bailey of Kilbourn City, Wisconsin, enlisted in the Fourth Wisconsin Cavalry in April 1861. He was commissioned into the U.S. volunteers general staff as a brigadier general on November 10, 1864. See ACWRD. Stott's uncle, Philemon C. Vawter, was correct in his judgment of Franklin College's situation. The resignation of Bailey in December 1862 due to a physical breakdown, competition from other educational institutions, and lack of support from the insufficiently organized Baptist Convention led to a board decision on June 27, 1864, to temporarily suspend all operations at the college. See John F. Cady, *The Centennial History of Franklin College* (Franklin, IN: Franklin College, 1934), 85–91.

75. First published in 1863, *Peculiar: A Hero of the Southern Rebellion* by Epes Sargent (1813–1880) is a melodramatic tale of the advent of the war and the war itself. Its setting is primarily in New Orleans, though some scenes occur in New York. Clearly an antislavery novel, its main character is Peculiar Institution, a slave separated from his wife, who works to undermine the slave system in attempts to find her. The book is rabidly anti-Southern. All of its Southern characters are depicted as evil and vicious until they "convert" to antislavery views. See Epes Sargent, *Peculiar: A Hero of the Southern Rebellion* (Boston: Lee and Shepard Publishers, 1892).

76. Joseph M. Thompson of Marion was at that time captain of Company I, Eighth Indiana. He became a lieutenant colonel on May 1, 1865. See *AGI*, 2:48, 54.

77. Doctor Henry Day, pastor of First Baptist Church, now had a new parsonage. William C. Smock was in the Franklin College class of 1859. Wallace is, of course, Stott's friend Barnett Wallace. Riesa Adams could not be identified. See *Jubilee*, 168, 174.

78. Colonel James Blake was the chief marshal for all the receptions of returning Indiana troops. See W. H. H. Terrell, *Indiana in the War of the Rebellion: Report of the Adjutant General* (Indianapolis: Indiana Historical Society, 1960), 43. John Caven was the Republican mayor of Indianapolis from 1863 to 1867 and from 1875 to 1881. See David J. Bodenhamer and Robert G. Barrows, eds., *The Encyclopedia of Indianapolis* (Bloomington and Indianapolis: Indiana University Press, 1994), 391–92. Founded in 1854 in Indianapolis, the *Indiana State Journal* was a Republican newspaper edited by Berry Sulgrove. See John W. Miller, *Indiana Newspaper Bibliography* (Indianapolis: Indiana Historical Society, 1982), 274.

79. The Spencer House, M. Harth proprietor, was located at the corner of South Illinois and Louisiana streets in Indianapolis. See *Indianapolis City Directory and Business Mirror* (Indianapolis: H. H. Dodd and Company, 1863), 77.

80. Mrs. Forsythe was probably Emily Forsythe, the mother of the late Alice. Miss Morrison is, of course, Stott's good friend and correspondent Carrie Morrison. See 1860 Census—Indiana, microfilm, Roll 271, pp. 706, 751.

81. John Charles Frémont was the nominee of a group of dissenting Radical Republicans who, disgruntled by Lincoln's handling of emancipation, chose the general as an alternative candidate at a meeting in Cleveland on May 31, 1864. See Long, *Civil War Day by Day*, 511–12. The proposed military professorship never materialized. Williamson D. Vawter was the third child of Stott's grandparents, William and Frances Vawter, and the brother of his mother, Elizabeth Vawter Stott. Williamson, who was married twice, had eight children. See Bicknell, *Vawter Family in America*, 92.

82. Josiah G. Holland (1819–1881), using the pseudonym Timothy Titcomb, wrote *Letters to the Joneses* in 1863. All of the Joneses were fictional characters whom Titcomb claimed to have taught in "the district schools in Jonesville" while "'boarding around according to the primitive New England fashion." Having maintained acquaintance with their "lives and fortunes," Titcomb seeks to "furnish motives and means for their improvement and reform." Pure satire, the letters go to such recipients of his advice as F. Mendelssohn Jones, Singing Master, who needs to improve his personal character; Reverend Jeremiah Jones, D.D., who is failing in the pulpit; Benjamin Franklin Jones, mechanic, who is habitually absent from church; and Jefferson Davis Jones, politician, whose pursuits are immoral. See J. G. Holland [Timothy Titcomb, pseud.], *Letters to the Joneses* (New York: Scribners, 1863).

83. Andrew Wallace, the paternal grandfather of General Lew Wallace, ran an inn known as the Brookville Hotel at the heart of the town. In 1852, on the site of Wallace's hotel, the Valley House was erected and, beginning in 1856, its proprietor was John W. King, a general merchant and real estate agent. The building still stands. See Franklin County Historical Society Web site, franklinchs.com.

84. Ira Stout was the father of Martha, the "Mattie" to whom both Stott and Eddelman wrote during the war. Fannie could be the thirty-six-year-old Anna Stout who lived at the same residence in 1860, possibly Ira's younger sister. Mattie's husband was Harvey S. Jacques, a schoolteacher in Franklin County. See 1860 U.S. Census—Indiana, microfilm, roll 259, p. 116; unidentified newspaper clipping of the obituary of Harvey S. Jacques, Martha Stout Papers of the Stout-Jacques Families, 1834–1936, IHS. Elizabeth Shirk, in her mid-sixties in 1864, lived in nearby Whitcomb, Indiana, as did Albert Shirk, age eighteen. Elizabeth McNutt, age twenty-one, lived in Metamora and had two younger sisters, Margaret and Ellenora, either of whom could have been Lida. See 1860 Census—Indiana, microfilm, Roll 259, pp. 114, 376.

85. The farming family of Michael Owen in nearby Springfield included daughter Rachel Ann, age twenty-five in 1864, and her older brother James W., who, in the 1860 census, was identified as a "student." "Rate" often was a nickname for Rachel. Given the brief mention Stott makes of her, this would not be the "Rate" with whom he corresponded. See 1860 Census—Indiana, microfilm, Roll 259, p. 117.

86. William Holsclaw, approximately twenty-eight in 1864, was a common laborer in Vernon, Indiana. He married Stott's cousin, Almira Vawter. See 1860 Census—Indiana, microfilm, Roll 271, p. 149; Bicknell, *Vawter Family in America*, 95.

87. May and Elizabeth (Lib) were the daughters of Stott's uncle, Williamson D. Vawter. See Bicknell, *Vawter Family in America*, 92–93.

88. Doctor Philander W. Payne was a leading physician and surgeon in Franklin. Interestingly, he had also lived in Vernon and attended the Jennings County Seminary during the years Stott was growing up, so their acquaintance was perhaps a long one. Stott's

friend, Barnett Wallace, studied under Payne and was about to become a new partner in his practice. On Payne, see David Demaree Banta, *History of Johnson County, Indiana* (Chicago: Brant and Fuller, 1888), 648–49; Elba L. Branigin, *History of Johnson County, Indiana* (Indianapolis: B. F. Bowen and Company, 1913), 580–82. Arta was Wallace's first wife, the former Artemisia Williams of Franklin. Franklin College President Silas Bailey conducted their marriage service on December 20, 1860. Arta died less than four years later, on January 15, 1864. Stott and Wallace were visiting her burial place at Greenlawn Cemetery in Franklin. See obituaries of Doctor Barnett Wallace in the *Franklin Evening Star*, May 24, 1932, and the *Franklin Democrat*, May 26, 1932; also "Old Melodeon Given to County Museum by Doctor Wallace," unidentified newspaper clipping, all in Barnett Wallace Scrapbook #2, SCFC. See also Certificate of Marriage, Marriage Book C, 391, Johnson County Museum, Franklin, IN.

89. Confederate Major General Jubal A. Early moved into Maryland on July 5, took Hagerstown the next day, and advanced to Chambersburg, Pennsylvania, by the end of the month, torching the latter place on July 30. His raid was the event that prompted General Philip Sheridan's Shenandoah Valley campaign in early fall 1864, in which Stott and the Eighteenth Indiana fought. See Long, *Civil War Day by Day*, 531–32, 548.

90. Joseph E. McDonald of Crawfordsville was a moderate Democrat who had served in Congress and as state attorney general. He was overwhelmingly selected for the nomination over the "peace" candidate, Lambdin P. Milligan. David Turpie (not Turpin) was U.S. Senator from Indiana, having been chosen to complete Jesse D. Bright's term after the latter's expulsion from the Senate. He declined the nomination for lieutenant governor. See Emma Lou Thornbrough, *Indiana in the Civil War Era, 1850–1880* (Indianapolis: Indiana Historical Bureau and Indiana Historical Society, 1965), 185, 211–12; John T. Hubbell and James W. Geary, eds., *Biographical Dictionary of the Union: Northern Leaders of the Civil War* (Westport, CT: Greenwood Press, 1995), 542.

CHAPTER 8

1. Eugene Houghton to mother, July 21, 1864, Civil War Letters and Diary of Major William Houghton, 14th Regiment, and Letters of Walter Houghton, 137th Regiment, and Eugene Houghton, 18th Regiment, IHS (hereafter cited as Houghton Collection); *Brookville National Defender*, August 5, 1864.

2. Another brief account of the march through Washington, D.C., appears in *Brookville National Defender*, August 5, 1864. Not all soldiers responded to the capital city positively. Rookie Private Eugene Houghton wrote his mother that he "was Deceived in Washington. I thought I would see a nice place But it was the Blackest place that I saw on my travels." He did find the White House to be "the finest Building that ever I saw." Eugene to mother, July 21, 1864. Stott experienced one embarrassment on the trip. In a report of August 31 "near Harpers Ferry, Va.," he admitted losing "One Ax & Helve, Two Spades, Two Camp Kettles, Three Mess Pans" on the train from Indianapolis. He explained that, since they did not arrive with all the other supplies at their destination, the loss was "beyond my control." See William T. Stott Civil War Papers, 1863–64, SCFC.

3. *Brookville National Defender*, August 5, September 23, 1864; Eugene to mother, July 21, 1864; Frank J. Welcher, *The Union Army, 1861–1865: Organization and Operations*, 2 vols. (Bloomington: Indiana University Press, 1989), 1:489; Catharine Merrill, *The Soldier of Indiana in the War for the Union*, 2 vols. (Indianapolis: Merrill and Company, 1866),

2:684. See also Richard J. Sommers, *Richmond Redeemed: The Siege of Petersburg* (Garden City, NY: Doubleday, 1981), 7, 74–75.

4. Eugene to mother, July 21, 1864; Taylor Pierce to Catharine, July 26, 1864, Richard L. Kiper, ed., *Dear Catharine, Dear Taylor: The Civil War Letters of a Union Soldier and His Wife* (Lawrence: University Press of Kansas, 2002), 243–44.

5. Sommers, *Richmond Redeemed*, 7, 24–25; Merrill, *Soldier of Indiana in the War for the Union*, 2:684; *Brookville National Defender*, September 23, 1864; Welcher, *Union Army*, 1:490. On General Foster, who was only two years older than Stott, see Ezra J. Warner, *Generals in Blue: Lives of the Union Commanders* (Baton Rouge: Louisiana State University Press, 1964), 158–59.

6. David Coffey, *Sheridan's Lieutenants: Phil Sheridan, His Generals, and the Final Year of the Civil War* (New York and Oxford: Rowman and Littlefield, 2005), 45; Merrill, *Soldier of Indiana in the War for the Union*, 2:684; *Brookville National Defender*, September 23, 1864. The camp chair Stott purchased in Washington is probably the one now in the archives at Franklin College.

7. Richard O'Connor, *Sheridan, the Inevitable* (Indianapolis: Bobbs-Merrill, 1953), 193; Coffey, *Sheridan's Lieutenants*, 38–39; Jeffry D. Wert, *From Winchester to Cedar Creek: The Shenandoah Campaign of 1864* (New York: Simon and Schuster, 1987), 6–8, 27–28. For excellent assessments of the value of the Shenandoah Valley for both sides in the war, see Gary W. Gallagher, "The Shenandoah Valley in 1864," in *Struggle for the Shenandoah: Essays on the 1864 Valley Campaign*, Gary W. Gallagher, ed. (Kent, OH and London: Kent State University Press, 1991), 1–18; Benjamin W. Crowninshield, *The Battle of Cedar Creek: A Paper Read before the Massachusetts Military Historical Society, December 8, 1879* (Cambridge, MA: Riverside Press, 1879), 4–7. Readers should note that the branches of the Shenandoah River flow southwest to northeast, so to travel northward in the Valley is to go "down" it and to move in a southerly direction is to go "up" the Valley.

8. Jeffry D. Wert, *Custer: The Controversial Life of George Armstrong Custer* (New York: Simon and Schuster, 1996), 168; Wert, *From Winchester to Cedar Creek*, 9–10. The quotes from Wert and the *New York Times* appear in the Custer biography.

9. Brooks D. Simpson, *Ulysses S. Grant: Triumph over Adversity, 1862–1865* (Boston: Houghton Mifflin, 2000), 367; Philip H. Sheridan, *Personal Memoirs of P. H. Sheridan*, 2 vols. (New York: Charles L. Webster and Company, 1888), 1:462; O'Connor, *Sheridan*, 190; Eric J. Wittenberg, *Little Phil: A Reassessment of the Civil War Leadership of Gen. Philip H. Sheridan* (Washington, D.C.: Brassey's, 2002), 59; Charles C. Osborne, *Jubal: The Life and Times of General Jubal A. Early, CSA, Defender of the Lost Cause* (Baton Rouge and London: Louisiana State University Press, 1992), 313.

10. Wert, *From Winchester to Cedar Creek*, 12–13, 17; Osborne, *Jubal*, 313; Thomas A. Lewis, *The Guns of Cedar Creek* (New York: Harper and Row, 1988), 33; Wittenberg, *Little Phil*, 59.

11. Osborne, *Jubal*, 313–14; Lewis, *Guns of Cedar Creek*, 34.

12. Wittenberg, *Little Phil*, 59; John Y. Simon et al., eds., *Papers of Ulysses S. Grant*, 31 vols. (Carbondale: Southern Illinois University Press, 1967–2009), 12:96–97; Theodore C. Mahr, *Early's Valley Campaign: The Battle of Cedar Creek, Showdown in the Shenandoah, October 1–30, 1864*, 2nd edition (Lynchburg, VA: H. E. Howard, 1992), 25–26; Wesley Merritt, "Sheridan in the Shenandoah Valley," in *Battles and Leaders of the Civil War*, R. U. Johnson and C. C. Clough Buel, eds., 4 vols. (New York: Century Company, 1887), 4:500; A. Wilson

Greene, "Union Generalship in the 1864 Valley Campaign," in Gallagher, ed., *Struggle for the Shenandoah*, 43; George T. Stevens, *Three Years in the Sixth Corps* (Albany, NY: S. R. Gray Publishers, 1866), 392; Wert, *From Winchester to Cedar Creek*, 13, 29, 37; Sheridan, *Personal Memoirs of P. H. Sheridan*, 1:463.

13. Wert, *Custer*, 170; Sheridan, *Personal Memoirs of P. H. Sheridan*, 1:465; Wert, *From Winchester to Cedar Creek*, 12–13; O'Connor, *Sheridan*, 195.

14. Wert, *From Winchester to Cedar Creek*, 16; Osborne, *Jubal*, 316; Greene, "Union Generalship in the 1864 Valley Campaign," 44; *OR*, 43(1):18–19; Sheridan, *Personal Memoirs of P. H. Sheridan*, 1:481, 484.

15. *Vevay Indiana Reveille*, September 8, 1864; *Brookville National Defender*, September 23, 1864; Merrill, *Soldier of Indiana in the War for the Union*, 2:684.

16. Osborne, *Jubal*, 320–24; Sheridan, *Personal Memoirs of P. H. Sheridan*, 1:480–81, 483, 489; Jubal Anderson Early, *War Memoirs*, Frank E. Vandiver, ed. (Bloomington: Indiana University Press, 1960), 407; Welcher, *Union Army*, 1:491, 1024; *Vevay Indiana Reveille*, September 8, 1864; *Brookville National Defender*, September 23, 1864; Merrill, *Soldier of Indiana in the War for the Union*, 2:684.

17. Sheridan to Grant, August 18–19, 1864, Simon, ed., *Papers of Ulysses S. Grant*, 12:23–24; Osborne, *Jubal*, 313; Merrill, *Soldier of Indiana in the War for the Union*, 2:684; Stevens, *Three Years in the Sixth Corps*, 388.

18. Swain Marshall to friends at home, August 27, 1864, Thomas Marshall Papers, 1821–1920, IHS; James Harrison Wilson, *Under the Old Flag: Recollections of Military Operations in the War for the Union, the Spanish War, the Boxer Rebellion, etc.*, 2 vols. (New York and London: D. Appleton and Company, 1912), 1:545; Stevens, *Three Years in the Sixth Corps*, 389–90; Merrill, *Soldier of Indiana in the War for the Union*, 2:684.

19. *Vevay Indiana Reveille*, September 8, 1864; August 23, 29, September 3, 1864, Henry Keiser Diary, Harrisburg Civil War Round Table Collection, USAMHI (hereafter cited as Keiser Diary); Taylor to Catharine, September 7, 1864, Kiper, ed., *Dear Catharine*, 268; John William DeForest, *A Volunteer's Adventures: A Union Captain's Record of the Civil War*, James H. Croushore, ed. (New Haven, CT: Yale University Press, 1946), 169; *OR*, 43(1):20.

20. Taylor to sister, September 2, 1864, Kiper, ed., *Dear Catharine*, 260–61, 263; Will Porter to Will [Houghton], September 16, 1864, Civil War Letters and Diary of Major William Houghton, IHS; Wert, *From Winchester to Cedar Creek*, 39.

21. Simon, ed., *Papers of Ulysses S. Grant*, 12:139; Wittenberg, *Little Phil*, 63; Sheridan, *Personal Memoirs of P. H. Sheridan*, 2:10–11; Early, *War Memoirs*, 413; Osborne, *Jubal*, 332–33; Adam Badeau, *Military History of Ulysses S. Grant*, 3 vols. (New York: D. Appleton and Company, 1881), 3:28; Roy Morris Jr., *Sheridan: The Life and Wars of General Phil Sheridan* (New York: Crown, 1992), 195; Wert, *From Winchester to Cedar Creek*, 43–45.

22. Wert, *From Winchester to Cedar Creek*, 20, 47, 49–52; *OR*, 43(1):279, 318; September 19, 1864, Francis A. Dawes Diary, *Civil War Times Illustrated* Collection, USAMHI (hereafter cited as Dawes Diary); Sheridan, *Personal Memoirs*, 2:18; Morris, *Sheridan*, 195–96; DeForest, *Volunteer's Adventures*, 172–73, 175; Merritt, "Sheridan in the Shenandoah Valley," 4:507; John Ely Briggs, "In the Battle of Winchester," *The Palimpsest* 6 (November 1925): 297; George E. Pond, *The Shenandoah Valley in 1864* (New York: Charles Scribner's Sons, 1883), 155–58; Osborne, *Jubal*, 335; Coffey, *Sheridan's Lieutenants*, 52. Historian Jeffry Wert correctly blames Sheridan for what the general called these "unavoidable delays," claiming the fiasco on Berryville Pike "resulted from Sheridan's serious mismanage-

ment to funnel over 20,000 soldiers through a confining gorge," a virtually impossible feat to accomplish with any speed. See Wert, *From Winchester to Cedar Creek*, 50–51. Similar criticism came from officers in Sheridan's ranks. See DeForest, *Volunteer's Adventures*, 173; Stevens, *Three Years in the Sixth Corps*, 396.

23. OR, 43(1):279, 318; DeForest, *Volunteer's Adventures*, 175; Richard B. Irwin, *History of the Nineteenth Army Corps* (New York and London: G. P. Putnam and Sons, 1892), 380; Wert, *From Winchester to Cedar Creek*, 52–55; Stevens, *Three Years in the Sixth Corps*, 398; O'Connor, *Sheridan*, 202 (Sheridan quote); Monday, September 19, 1864, Israel M. Ritter Diary, USAMHI. (Below the entry are the words, "copied by his wife Julia Barnes Ritter from the diary sent her after the battle of Winchester.")

24. Wert, *From Winchester to Cedar Creek*, 56; *Brookville National Defender*, October 28, 1864; Stevens, *Three Years in the Sixth Corps*, 398–99.

25. Merrill, *Soldier of Indiana in the War for the Union*, 2:686; Pond, *Shenandoah Valley in 1864*, p. 160; Merritt, "Sheridan in the Shenandoah Valley," 4:507–9; Briggs, "In the Battle of Winchester," 399–400; Coffey, *Sheridan's Lieutenants*, 55; Sheridan, *Personal Memoirs of P. H. Sheridan*, 2:21–22; OR, 43(1):279, 318–19, 346; DeForest, *Volunteer's Adventures*, 176–77; Wert, *From Winchester to Cedar Creek*, 57; Irwin, *History of the Nineteenth Army Corps*, 383–86.

26. John B. Gordon, *Reminiscences of the Civil War* (New York: Charles Scribner's So, 1903), 321–22; Ralph Lowell Eckert, *John Brown Gordon: Soldier, Southerner, American* (Baton Rouge and London: Louisiana University Press, 1989), 87–88; Wert, *From Winchester to Cedar Creek*, 59–60; Sheridan, *Personal Memoirs of P. H. Sheridan*, 2:22–23; Pond, *Shenandoah Valley in 1864*, pp. 161–63.

27. Gary W. Gallagher, *Stephen Dodson Ramseur: Lee's Gallant General* (Chapel Hill and London: University of North Carolina Press, 1985), 143; Wert, *From Winchester to Cedar Creek*, 80, 83, 93–94; OR, 43(1):280; Wittenberg, *Little Phil*, 63–64; Sheridan, *Personal Memoirs of P. H. Sheridan*, 2:24–25; Irwin, *History of the Nineteenth Army Corps*, 389–92; Stevens, *Three Years in the Sixth Corps*, 400–401; Osborne, *Jubal*, 339; Merrill, *Soldier of Indiana in the War for the Union*, 2:687.

28. September 23, 1864, Dawes Diary; Wert, *From Winchester to Cedar Creek*, 98, 103; Irwin, *History of the Nineteenth Army Corps*, 393; Briggs, "In the Battle of Winchester," 402; OR, 43(2):118.

29. Sheridan, *Personal Memoirs of P. H. Sheridan*, 2:33–34; Wert, *From Winchester to Cedar Creek*, 107–8; Joseph Hergesheimer, *Sheridan: A Military Narrative* (Boston and New York: Houghton Mifflin, 1931), 201–2; Henry A. DuPont, *The Campaign of 1864 in the Valley of Virginia* (New York: National Americana Society, 1925), 133; September 20, 1864, Dawes Diary; September 20, 1864, Keiser Diary.

30. DeForest, *Volunteer's Adventures*, 191–92; Stevens, *Three Years in the Sixth Corps*, 406–7; Wert, *From Winchester to Cedar Creek*, 109–10.

31. Early, *War Memoirs*, 429; Gallagher, *Stephen Dodson Ramseur*, 147; Badeau, *Military History of Ulysses S. Grant*, 3:31; Hergesheimer, *Sheridan*, 202; Pond, *Shenandoah Valley in 1864*, p. 173; Wert, *Custer*, 184.

32. DeForest, *Volunteer's Adventures*, 192; Osborne, *Jubal*, 342; Wittenberg, *Little Phil*, 67–68; DuPont, *Campaign of 1864 in the Valley of Virginia*, 135; Wert, *From Winchester to Cedar Creek*, 111–12; Sheridan, *Personal Memoirs of P. H. Sheridan*, 2:35.

33. Wert, *From Winchester to Cedar Creek*, 113; Stevens, *Three Years in the Sixth Corps*,

407; Pond, *Shenandoah Valley in 1864*, p. 174; Merritt, "Sheridan in the Shenandoah Valley," 4:510; Sheridan, *Personal Memoirs of P. H. Sheridan*, 2:35–36; Hergesheimer, *Sheridan*, 203; *OR*, 43(1):346; September 21, 1864, Dawes Diary.

34. Wert, *From Winchester to Cedar Creek*, 115, 117; *OR*, 43(1):282; Welcher, *Union Army*, 1:1031; Stevens, *Three Years in the Sixth Corps*, 408; Early, *War Memoirs*, 430.

35. Wittenberg, *Sheridan*, 67–68; Stevens, *Three Years in the Sixth Corps*, 408; Sheridan, *Personal Memoirs of P. H. Sherman*, 2:36, 38; Wert, *From Winchester to Cedar Creek*, 118–23.

36. September 22, 1864, Dawes Diary; *OR*, 43(1):283, 351; DeForest, *Volunteer's Adventures*, 194–95; Merrill, *Soldier of Indiana in the War for the Union*, 2:688; Morris, *Sheridan*, 203.

37. Stevens, *Three Years in the Sixth Corps*, 408; O'Connor, *Sheridan*, 209; *Brookville National Defender*, October 28, 1864; Wert, *From Winchester to Cedar Creek*, 126; *OR*, 43(1):283, 357; Wittenberg, *Little Phil*, 67; Early, *War Memoirs*, 430; September 22, 1864, Keiser Diary.

38. *OR*, 43(1):26–27, 283; Greene, "Union Generalship in the 1864 Valley Campaign," 60.

39. *OR*, 43(1):283; O'Connor, *Sheridan*, 210; Pond, *Shenandoah Valley in 1864*, p. 178n1; Osborne, *Jubal*, 344; Wert, *From Winchester to Cedar Creek*, 130; DeForest, *Volunteer's Adventures*, 196.

40. *Brookville National Defender*, October 28, 1864; September 23, 1864, Keiser Diary; September 24, 1864, Dawes Diary; Early, *War Memoirs*, 432.

41. Merrill, *Soldier of Indiana in the War for the Union*, 2:690; Wert, *From Winchester to Cedar Creek*, 134; Early, *War Memoirs*, 432; Stevens, *Three Years in the Sixth Corps*, 409–10; *OR*, 43(1):28.

42. September 25, 1864, Dawes Diary; Gordon, *Reminiscences of the Civil War*, 326; Sheridan, *Personal Memoirs of P. H. Sheridan*, 1:485–87; Lewis, *Guns of Cedar Creek*, 59; Merritt, "Sheridan in the Shenandoah Valley," 4:512–13; Stevens, *Three Years in the Sixth Corps*, 410–11.

43. DeForest, *Volunteer's Adventures*, 197; *Brookville National Defender*, October 28, 1864; September 29, 1864, Dawes Diary; Mahr, *Early's Valley Campaign*, 28; Wittenberg, *Little Phil*, 70–71.

44. *OR*, 43(1):30; Wert, *From Winchester to Cedar Creek*, 142–43; Mahr, *Early's Valley Campaign*, 27. Historians A. Wilson Greene and Jeffry Wert underscore the importance of the "Burning," contending that it was second only to Sherman's march to the sea in its devastation. Greene, "Union Generalship in the 1864 Valley Campaign," 64; Wert, *From Winchester to Cedar Creek*, 160.

45. Mahr, *Early's Valley Campaign*, 58, 74–75; DeForest, *Volunteer's Adventures*, 198, 201; Early, *War Memoirs*, 436; Eckert, *John Brown Gordon*, 92; Wert, *From Winchester to Cedar Creek*, 168–70; Sheridan, *Personal Memoirs of P. H. Sheridan*, 2:93.

46. Greene, "Union Generalship in the 1864 Valley Campaign," 68; Merritt, "Sheridan in the Shenandoah Valley," 4:514.

47. Irwin, *History of the Nineteenth Army Corps*, 413; Pond, *Shenandoah Valley in 1864*, p. 223; Crowninshield, *Battle of Cedar Creek*, 11–12; Wert, *From Winchester to Cedar Creek*, 170–71; O'Connor, *Sheridan*, 331; Wittenberg, *Little Phil*, 74.

48. A. Bayard Nettleton, "How the Day Was Saved at the Battle of Cedar Creek," (Minnesota) *MOLLUS*, 265; Wert, *Custer*, 193; Wert, *From Winchester to Cedar Creek*, 174;

James Franklin Fitts, "In the Ranks at Cedar Creek," *Galaxy* 1 (July 15, 1866): 534. On the October 13 skirmish, see October 13, 1864, Dawes Diary. There was also a brief scare on October 16, when Union officers, using a captured Confederate code book, intercepted a message from a Confederate signal station that read: "TO LIEUTENANT-GENERAL EARLY: 'Be ready to move as soon as my forces join you, and we will crush Sheridan.' Longstreet, Lieutenant-General." But that was merely a ruse meant to deceive the Union forces into pulling back. Even Sheridan, then away in Washington to confer with Henry Halleck and Secretary Edwin Stanton, recognized it as such. Early himself wrote, "The signal message was altogether fictitious," intended "to induce Sheridan to move back." See Sheridan, *Personal Memoirs of P. H. Sheridan*, 2:63; Crowninshield, *Battle of Cedar Creek*, 9; Irwin, *History of the Nineteenth Army Corps*, 407n2.

49. Stevens, *Three Years in the Sixth Corps*, 414; Mahr, *Early's Valley Campaign*, 98; Nettleton, "How the Day Was Saved at the Battle of Cedar Creek," 265–66; Fitts, "In the Ranks at Cedar Creek," 536.

50. Mahr, *Early's Valley Campaign*, 81–89; Gordon, *Reminiscences*, 333–36; Eckert, *John Brown Gordon*, 93; Lewis, *Guns of Cedar Creek*, 121–22; Early, *War Memoirs*, 438–39; Crowninshield, *Battle of Cedar Creek*, 13–14.

51. Gordon, *Reminiscences*, 335; Eckert, *John Brown Gordon*, 94–95; Fitts, "In the Ranks at Cedar Creek," 235–36; Coffey, *Sheridan's Lieutenants*, 76; Irwin, *History of the Nineteenth Army Corps*, 411–12; Early, *War Memoirs*, 440–41.

52. Osborne, *Jubal*, 359; DeForest, *Volunteer's Adventures*, 202–3; Mahr, *Early's Valley Campaign*, 96–97; Pond, *Shenandoah Valley in 1864*, 220n1; *OR*, 43(1):248, 347, 352; William Elliott to cousin, October 22, 1864, William Elliott Papers, 1864, IHS.

53. Eckert, *John Brown Gordon*, 95; Gordon, *Reminiscences*, 337–38; Gallagher, *Stephen Dodson Ramseur*, 158; Stevens, *Three Years in the Sixth Corps*, 417; Lewis, *Guns of Cedar Creek*, 183; Coffey, *Sheridan's Lieutenants*, 80. Eyewitnesses and historians differ greatly in their assessment of the exact time of the Confederate assault, with estimates of anywhere between 4:30 and 5:30, although 5:00 was the appointed time.

54. Merritt, "Sheridan in the Shenandoah Valley," 4:517; Osborne, *Jubal*, 361; Wert, *Custer*, 193; Gallagher, *Stephen Dodson Ramseur*, 158; Wert, *From Winchester to Cedar Creek*, 178–87; Gordon, *Reminiscences*, 339–40; Stevens, *Three Years in the Sixth Corps*, 417. James F. Fitts, adjutant of the 114th New York, XIX Corps, credited the strategic genius of the Confederate attack. "[T]here was not, during the whole course of the rebellion," he claimed, "a movement so original in its conception, so audacious in its execution, or so threatening in its results, as that by which the Rebel army crept tiger-like upon our left flanks on the early morning of October 19." Fitts, "In the Ranks at Cedar Creek," 534.

55. DeForest, *Volunteer's Adventures*, 208–9; *OR*, 43(1):284; Irwin, *History of the Nineteenth Army Corps*, 418; Pond, *Shenandoah Valley*, 225.

56. *OR*, 43(1):347; Fitts, "In the Ranks at Cedar Creek," 211; Taylor to Catharine and Friends, October 23, 1864, Kiper, ed., *Dear Catharine*, 288; Wert, *From Winchester to Cedar Creek*, 191–92.

57. *OR*, 43(1):347–48, 353; Mahr, *Early's Valley Campaign*, 150, 152, 156; Fitts, "In the Ranks at Cedar Creek," 537–38.

58. Marshall to friends at home, October 23, 1864, Marshall Papers; *OR*, 43(1):348–53; Wert, *From Winchester to Cedar Creek*, 192–93; Mahr, *Early's Valley Campaign*, 140, 160–61, 164; Taylor to Catharine, October 23, 1864, Kiper, ed., *Dear Catharine*, 288; Stevens, *Three*

Years in the Sixth Corps, 418; O'Connor, *Sheridan*, 225.

59. For scenes on the battlefield, see Merrill, *Soldier of Indiana in the War for the Union*, 2:694; Lewis, *Guns of Cedar Creek*, 217; Mahr, *Early's Valley Campaign*, 165–66; Fitts, "In the Ranks at Cedar Creek," 538; Wert, *From Winchester to Cedar Creek*, 193.

60. Elliott to cousin, October 22, 1864, Elliott Papers; Marshall to brothers, October 24, 1864, Marshall Papers.

61. Crowninshield, *Battle of Cedar Creek*, 19; Merrill, *Soldier of Indiana in the War for the Union*, 2:695; DeForest, *Volunteer's Adventures*, 216.

62. Wert, *From Winchester to Cedar Creek*, 194–95, 198–200; Fitts, "In the Ranks at Cedar Creek," 539; Pond, *Shenandoah Valley in 1864*, p. 227n1; *OR*, 43(1):353. Accounts by Union soldiers of the fighting on the "positions beyond Meadow Brook," Jeffry Wert correctly notes, "increase in vagueness," a factor that makes a reconstruction of that period in the battle difficult for the historian. Wert, *From Winchester to Cedar Creek*, 203.

63. Gordon, *Reminiscences*, 341–42; Early, *War Memoirs*, 447–48; Eckert, *John Brown Gordon*, 97-98; Wert, *From Winchester to Cedar Creek*, 215–19. See the latter source for an excellent negative assessment of Gordon's account of his discussion with Early and of the whole "fatal halt" theory. It should be noted that no love was ever lost between Early and Gordon. On the Confederates' lost momentum and the plundering of the Union camps, see Mahr, *Early's Valley Campaign*, 136, 184–85; Crowninshield, *Battle of Cedar Creek*, 20–21; H. M. Pollard, "Recollections of Cedar Creek," (Missouri) *MOLLUS*, 280–81; Lewis, *Guns of Cedar Creek*, 194–95; DuPont, *Campaign of 1864 in the Valley of Virginia*, 169–70.

64. Elliott to cousin, October 22, 1864, Elliott Papers; DuPont, *Campaign of 1864 in the Valley of Virginia*, 267; Crowninshield, *Battle of Cedar Creek*, 23, 25; Irwin, *History of the Nineteenth Army Corps*, 425; Lewis, *Guns of Cedar Creek*, 259; *OR*, 43(1):285; DeForest, *Volunteer's Adventures*, 218.

65. Sheridan, *Personal Memoirs of P. H. Sheridan*, 2:67–71; O'Connor, *Sheridan*, 223; Wittenberg, *Little Phil*, 75.

66. Sheridan, *Personal Memoirs of P. H. Sheridan*, 212–13; Mahr, *Early's Valley Campaign*, 24–41.

67. Wittenberg, *Little Phil*, 75; Wert, *Custer*, 195; Wert, *From Winchester to Cedar Creek*, 221–23; Sheridan, *Personal Memoirs of P. H. Sheridan*, 2:83; Coffey, *Sheridan's Lieutenants*, 88.

68. Irwin, *History of the Nineteenth Army Corps*, 431–32; Wert, *From Winchester to Cedar Creek*, 224; Osborne, *Jubal*, 372; Mahr, *Early's Valley Campaign*, 243, 264; Wittenberg, *Little Phil*, 75.

69. Eckert, *John Brown Gordon*, 99; Lewis, *Guns of Cedar Creek*, 259–60; *OR*, 43(1):285; Coffey, *Sheridan's Lieutenants*, 89.

70. Sheridan, *Personal Memoirs of P. H. Sheridan*, 2:86–87; Wert, *From Winchester to Cedar Creek*, 230; Lewis, *Guns of Cedar Creek*, 262; Morris, *Sheridan*, 216; Mahr, *Early's Valley Campaign*, 275, 284–85; *OR*, 43(1):348, 353; Irwin, *History of the Nineteenth Army Corps*, 433.

71. Fitts, "In the Ranks at Cedar Creek," 541–42; Pond, *Shenandoah Valley in 1864*, pp. 237–38; Lewis, *Guns of Cedar Creek*, 230–31, 233; Sheridan, *Personal Memoirs of P. H. Sheridan*, 2:89; Morris, *Sheridan*, 217.

72. Mahr, *Early's Valley Campaign*, 272; Fitts, "In the Ranks at Cedar Creek," 542; Osborne, *Jubal*, 374; DeForest, *Volunteer's Adventures*, 227; Gallagher, *Stephen Dodson*

Ramseur, 161–65; Pollard, "Recollections of Cedar Creek," 283–84; Lewis, *Guns of Cedar Creek*, 281; October 19, 1864, Dawes Diary; Nettleton, "How the Day Was Saved," 272; P. B. Boarts to parents, October 21, 1864, Peter B. Boarts Letters, Earl Hess Collection, USAMHI.

73. DeForest, *Volunteer's Adventures*, 228; Marshall to brother, October 24, 1864, Marshall Papers; Merrill, *Soldier of Indiana in the War for the Union*, 2:696–99. See also Elliott to cousin, October 22, 1864, Elliott Papers.

74. *OR*, 43(1):32–33; Early, *War Memoirs*, 451; Lewis, *Guns of Cedar Creek*, 239; Richard E. Beringer, Herman Hattaway, Archer Jones, and William N. Still Jr., *Why the South Lost the Civil War* (Athens and London: University of Georgia Press, 1986), 320, 348, 351; Wert, *From Winchester to Cedar Creek*, vii.

75. William T. Stott to Captain [Finlay, Ass't Commissary of Muster, 2nd Div., 19th AC], December 10, 1864, Military Service File, William Taylor Stott, NARA.

CHAPTER 9

1. Ripraps are ragged rocks thrown into harbors or rivers to create a firm basis for a breakwater. During the war the military would sometimes punish soldiers by sentencing them to a stint at "breaking up the rip-raps," i.e., crushing the rocks used for the breakwater's foundation. See John D. Wright, *The Language of the Civil War* (Westport, CT: Oryx Press, 1001), 253.

2. A possible reference to the Zouave regiments that wore baggy red pants as part of their colorful uniforms. They were also noted for their impressive military drills. See Wright, *Language of the Civil War*, 332–33; Webb Garrison, *The Encyclopedia of Civil War Usage* (Nashville, TN: Cumberland House, 2001), 209, 268.

3. William T. Sherman began his move toward Decatur, Georgia, on July 13, 1864, as part of his Atlanta Campaign. Skirmishes occurred there on July 20, 22, 26, and 28. See E. B. Long, *The Civil War Day by Day: An Almanac, 1861–1865* (New York: DaCapo Press, 1971), 538–47. "Sergt. Johnston" is probably James R. Johnson of Johnson County and Company I. See *AGI*, 4:385.

4. Stott refers to what slaves called "patting juba," the rhythmic clapping of hands on the knees and shoulders, and striking of the hands together while keeping time to the music with the feet. This was a regular part of slave worship experiences down in the hollows. See John W. Blassingame, *The Slave Community: Plantation Life in the Antebellum South* (New York and Oxford: Oxford University Press, 1979), 125.

5. Stott observed the work of the Quartermaster's (Q.M.) and Commissary Service (C.S.) Departments, among others. The U.S.C.C. was the United States Christian Commission, a relief society begun by the YMCA and made up of ministers and laity who assisted the soldiers in camp and on the battlefield, distributed Bibles, and provided newspapers, foodstuffs, bandages, and other necessities for the troops. U.S.S.C. referred to the United States Sanitary Commission, a private relief agency headed by Frederick Law Olmsted that did work similar to today's Red Cross. Its volunteers were mostly women who sent blankets, food, and other personal items to the soldiers, as well as medical supplies. See Wright, *Language of the Civil War*, 61–62, 261–62.

6. Union Major General James Birdseye McPherson received a fatal wound somewhere between Decatur and Atlanta on July 22. Lieutenant General John Bell Hood assumed command of the Confederate Army of Tennessee at Atlanta on July 17, succeeding Joseph

E. Johnston, who was relieved of command by President Jefferson Davis. See Patricia L. Faust, ed., *Historical Times Encyclopedia of the Civil War* (New York: Harper and Row, 1986), 368–69, 400, 466.

7. A British essayist, lecturer, and Baptist minister, John Foster (1770–1843) first published his *Essays in a Series of Letters* in 1805. Highly popular, the volume went through nine editions during his lifetime. The lead essay, "On a Man's Writing Memoirs of Himself," first piqued Stott's interest, and it is from that piece that he quoted Foster's comments on soldiers' memoirs, with which he disagreed. In his diary entry of July 30, he quotes from Foster's last essay in the volume, "On Some of the Causes by which Evangelical Religion has been rendered unacceptable to Persons of Cultivated Taste." It is not clear what edition Stott read. See John Foster, *Essays in a Series of Letters*, 7th ed. (Andover, MA: Flagg and Gould, 1826), 52, 159; Leslie Stephens and Sidney Lee, eds., *Dictionary of National Biography*, 22 vols. (New York: Macmillan, 1908–9), 7:497–99.

8. Stott refers to the experience of the Israelites who rebuilt the walls of Jerusalem in 445–44 BCE while still fighting their enemies. They are depicted in Nehemiah 4:17: "They which builded the wall, and they that bare burdens, with those that laded, every one with one of his hands wrought in the work, and with the other hand held a weapon."

9. An anonymous poem, "The Heart of War," was a plaintive story of a New England man who holds his son, Marty, to his breast as he tries to decide whether to go to war as a soldier. He reflects on "all the boys have done / And suffered in this weary war!" and struggles with "Which way my duty lies / Or where the Lord would have me build / My fire of sacrifice." So he and Marty "pray to Heaven for light." The poem ends with a widow kneeling "among her sleeping babes," weeping and praying alone. See "The Heart of War," *Atlantic Monthly* 14 (August 1864): 240–42.

10. Thomas Crawford (1813?–1857) was the sculptor who created the marble pediment and bronze doors for the Senate wing of the Capitol, as well as the bronze statue of *Armed Liberty* at the top of the Capitol dome. He also supervised the sculpting of the marble figures of *History* and *Justice* that appear over the doors of the old Senate chamber and designed the equestrian statue of George Washington in Richmond. See *DAB*, 2:524–26. The *Course of Empire*, five paintings by American landscape artist Thomas Cole (1801–1848), depicts five scenes of the creation and decline of empires: the savage state, the pastoral state, the consummation of empire, destruction, and desolation. James Fenimore Cooper called the work "a great epic poem," and "the work of the highest genius this country has ever produced." Art historians have seen it as an outstanding example of "the Romantic spirit and imagination." See Earl A. Powell, *Thomas Cole* (New York: Henry N. Abrams, 1990), 64, 70. The portrait Stott identifies as "Thomas Benton" is of the Missouri Senator Thomas Hart Benton. "Robert Taney" is, of course, Supreme Court Chief Justice Roger Taney, who presided over the *Dred Scott* case in 1857.

11. There is no record of a G. E. Trautwine in the Eighteenth Indiana. John H. Troutwine of Johnson County was a private in Company I and could well have been the Company Clerk (C.C.), though it is not clear why Stott would cite his name incorrectly. See *AGI*, 4:387.

12. On August 5, 1864, the Union fleet, under Admiral David Farragut's command, steamed into Mobile Bay and battled a number of Confederate vessels, including the CSS *Tennessee*, considered the "most powerful ironclad afloat." Three of Farragut's four ironclads rammed the *Tennessee*, which then surrendered ending the battle of Mobile Bay. See

Long, *The Civil War Day by Day*, 551–52.

13. Fort Gaines was located on Dauphin Island in Mobile Bay and surrendered to the Union army on August 7, 1864. See ibid., 553.

14. John H. Popp of Richmond was first lieutenant and quartermaster of the Eighteenth Indiana from the beginning of the war. See *AGI*, 2:159. The chaplain affected by the lightning strike was Reverend John S. Donaldson (previously identified).

15. There is much confusion in the early sections of this entry. Stott mistakenly places William and Mary College at Staunton, Virginia; it is at Williamsburg. He also identifies its president as a "Dr. Jenkins," the "father in law of 'Stonewall' Jackson." Jackson's first wife was, in fact, Eleanor Junkin, the oldest daughter of Doctor George Junkin, president of Washington College, Lexington, Virginia (not William and Mary). Junkin, a Presbyterian clergyman and educator, who had an influence on Jackson's religious thought, conducted their wedding in August 1853. Junkin had been president of Miami University, Oxford, Ohio, in the 1840s and was an adamant supporter of the Union. The latter fact led to his departure from Washington College and from the South in 1861. See James I. Robertson Jr., *Stonewall Jackson: The Man, the Soldier, the Legend* (New York: Macmillan, 1997), 144, 147, 213, 233; *DAB*, 5:248–49. Stott's eagerness to have "long talks" with the men of his Company and his desire to make them "interesting" for the soldiers suggest traits that may have been setting the stage for his work in the ministry and education after the war.

16. General Winfield Scott Hancock's corps of the Army of the Potomac severed the Weldon Railroad, a major supply route for Lee's Army of Northern Virginia on August 23, 1864. See Long, *Civil War Day by Day*, 559.

17. Julius J. Van Houten of Patriot in Switzerland County, Indiana, enlisted in 1861 as a sergeant. He became captain of Company D on August 22, 1864. See *AGI*, 2:161, 4:377.

18. Following a major bombardment by Union land batteries, Fort Morgan, the last of the major Confederate installations at Mobile Bay, fell to the Union forces on August 23, 1864—the same day the Union forces destroyed sections of the Weldon Railroad at Petersburg. See Long, *Civil War Day by Day*, 559.

19. The opening quotation of the September 1 entry comes from William Cullen Bryant's poem, "The Death of the Flowers." Stott substituted "Autumn" for Bryant's "Melancholy." See Bryant, *Poems*, 2 vols. (New York: D. Appleton, 1871), 1:206. Colonel Henry D. Washburn, longtime commander of the Eighteenth Indiana, faced Democrat Daniel D. Voorhees of Terre Haute in a bid for a seat in Congress. Voorhees prevailed in the election, but in 1866 Washburn, a Republican, was selected by the House of Representatives to replace Voorhees "on the grounds that there were frauds in the votes cast for Voorhees." See Emma Lou Thornbrough, *Indiana in the Civil War Era, 1850–1880* (Indianapolis: Indiana Historical Bureau and Indiana Historical Society, 1965), 233n13.

20. Before firing, all muskets had to be "capped" by placing a percussion cap, "a small container of explosive charge" on the firing "nipple" of the gun. "Traps" were the soldier's gear. See Wright, *Language of the Civil War*, 227, 302.

21. William H. Mitchell was a student at Franklin College, 1858–59. See *Catalogue of the Officers and Students of the Franklin College for the Academical Year, 1858–59* (Indianapolis: Indiana Journal Company, 1859), 7.

22. Renowned Unitarian clergyman, statesman, and orator Edward Everett (1794–1865), in one of his last major speeches, praised Sherman for his successful campaign against Atlanta and associated his successes with those of Grant and Farragut. Sherman

wrote Everett to thank him for "so high a Compliment." The general felt deeply honored to receive such commendation "from one who looks deep into the Causes of Events, and who foreshadows the judgment of History to which all men must submit." See Sherman to Everett, September 17, 1864, in Brooks D. Simpson and Jean V. Berlin, *Sherman's Civil War: Selected Correspondence of William T. Sherman, 1861–1865* (Chapel Hill and London: University of North Carolina Press, 1999).

23. The chaplain noted here is probably Methodist John T. Simmons. See John W. Brinsfield, et al., eds., *Faith in the Fight: Civil War Chaplains* (Mechanicsburg, PA: Stackpole Books, 2003), 194

24. Thomas B. Woods of Crawfordsville was a student in the classical preparatory program at Franklin College, 1858–59. He went into the Eleventh Indiana Volunteer Infantry in April 1861, rising to the rank of first lieutenant in 1862. See *Catalogue of the Officers and Students of Franklin College for the Academical Year 1858–1859*, 9; *AGI*, 2:81.

25. English translation: "Truly beyond value."

26. The volume Stott read was likely Andrew W. Young, *The Citizen's Manual of Government and Law* (Cleveland: J. B. Cobb and Company, 1853). It may be found on microform in the American Culture Series, no, 6, USF.

27. First Lieutenant John Carson of Franklin and Company I assumed command of Company B. This freed Captain Doil R. Bowden of Bedford and Company B to serve as field officer, in which capacity he was joined by Captain Silas A. Wadsworth of Daviess County and Company E. See *AGI*, 2:160, 163, 165,

28. Corporal William S. Crawford of Johnson County and Company I. See *AGI*, 4:386.

29. The adjutant of the Eighteenth Indiana at this time was William W. Zener of Vermillion County. See *AGI*, 2:159. 4:376.

30. Stott identifies the Massanutten range as Round Mountain.

31. There is confusion in Stott's dating of events at this point. The next paragraph actually describes the Eighteenth Indiana's fighting during the Battle of Fisher's Hill, which occurred on September 22, not on the 21st. The brief entry of September 22 refers to events on the 23rd.

32. George W. Bailey of Aurora was first lieutenant in Company A. At the time of the battle, Peter D. Pelser of Metamora was captain of Company F, and Lemmon Ross of Patriot was musician and wagoner in Company D. See *AGI*, 2:160, 4:377.

33. William Young, an October 1862 recruit, was captured at Cedar Creek; it is not known why he was left behind in Texas. The "Doctors Book" was probably John Cordy Jeafferson's *A Book about Doctors*, first published in London in 1860 by Hurst and Blackett. It was a volume of anecdotes and satires about the medical profession. See *NUC, Pre-1956*, p. 466. James Green and Richard Hall, both October 1862 recruits from Johnson County, deserted on July 8, 1864. Stott's good friend Sergeant Henry Bogard, mustered out on August 18, 1864. See *AGI*, 386–87.

34. Mitchell Seminary, a Baptist school, was founded in 1864 at Mitchell, Indiana. Reverend J. K. Howard was graduated that year from Franklin College and became Mitchell's principal and professor of languages, serving on the faculty with Stott's friend Simpson Burton, who taught mathematics. See William T. Stott, *Indiana Baptist History, 1798–1908* (Franklin, IN: W. T. Stott, 1908), 341–42.

35. John Greenleaf Whittier, born in December 1807, would have been fifty-six years old *aetat* (of age) in 1864. See *DAB*, 10:173–76. English poet John Keats (1795–1821)

wrote *Endymion*, a book-length "metrical romance" when he was eighteen years old. The poem emerged from Keats's deep reflections on "the relation between sleep and poetry" and told the tale of a "dreamy, indolent youth" in love with Phoebe, who "sleeps (or dies) into immortal life." The poem was, some literary critics believe, "an ideal vehicle" for Keats's own "personal allegory." His ambiguous epitaph, biographer Andrew Motion states, suggests that Keats's "poetry had come to him 'as naturally as leaves to a tree'; now it was part of nature—part of the current of history." See Stephen T. Steinhoff, *Keats's* Endymion: *A Critical Edition* (Troy, NY: Whitson Publishing Company, 1987), 1, 39–40; Andrew Motion, *Keats* (New York: Farrar, Strauss and Giroux, 1997), 564–65.

36. A possible reference to Mark 10:37–40, in which the disciples James and John request to be given the seats on the right and left hand of Jesus when he enters his glory. Jesus' response is that such a place is not his to give, "but it shall be given to them for whom it is prepared."

37. Psalm 104:24.

38. A dispute arose after Third Winchester between Generals William Dwight and Cuvier Grover. Dwight accused Grover's division of "flying in so much disorder" when pressed by Gordon's forces during the battle. Grover responded by accusing Dwight of eating his lunch while the XIX Corps fought the Confederates. When Emory tried twice to get Dwight to rewrite his report, in which he leveled the charges against Grover, Dwight refused. At that point, Emory relieved Dwight of command. By the time of the corps's next battle at Cedar Creek, Dwight's arrest was lifted. See Jeffry Wert, *From Winchester to Cedar Creek: The Shenandoah Campaign of 1864* (New York: Simon and Schuster, 1987), 189.

39. General Stephen Burbridge led two raids on salt mines at Saltville, VA. The first, on October 2, resulted in a repulse of his small force; in the second, on December 20, Union forces destroyed the saltworks. See Long, *Civil War Day by Day*, 578, 612.

40. Congregational clergyman and educator Joseph Haven (1816–1874) was one of the founding faculty members of Chicago Theological Seminary in 1858. He held the chair of systematic theology and wrote extensively in the field of philosophy, including renowned works on *Mental Philosophy* (1857) and *Moral Philosophy* (1869). Stott's references are to the former work, in which Haven first stated: "The Will is free unless its appropriate Action is hindered. . . . My will is free, when I can *will to do* just what I *please*." Later, he contends, however, that "Whatever freedom a man has . . . it must be such a freedom as is consistent with God's complete control and government of him"—an assertion that places him in concert with Jonathan Edwards's work on Freedom of the Will. See Joseph Haven, *Mental Philosophy: Including the Intellect, Sensibilities, and Will*, improved edition (New York: Sheldon and Company, 1879), 544–45, 526, 577–81; *DAB*, 4:409–10.

41. Private Henry J. Goodman of Johnson County was in Stott's Company I. See *AGI*, 4:386.

42. John W. Hickman of Shelby County was now a captain in Company K. Captain Benjamin H. Robinson of Salem was in Company G. See *AGI*, 164–65.

43. All of these men were, of course, from Johnson County. See *AGI*,, 4:386–87.

44. There was no sergeant named Hover in the Eighteenth Indiana. Stott probably meant Sergeant Samuel B. Hovey of Yorktown and Company D. See *AGI*, 4:377.

45. See Lincoln to Sheridan. October 22, 1864, in Roy P. Basler et al., eds., *The Collected Works of Abraham Lincoln*, 9 vols. (New Brunswick, NJ: Rutgers University Press, 1953–55), 8: 73–74.

46. At Westport, Missouri, south of Kansas City, Samuel Curtis defeated his old nemesis, Sterling Price, along Brush Creek on October 23. The Battle of Westport ended all Confederate efforts in Missouri. See Long, *Civil War Day by Day*, 587–88.

47. Election Day, 1864—Lincoln reelected.

48. On July 17, Jefferson Davis removed General Joseph Johnston from command of the Army of Tennessee because of his failure to stop Sherman's advance on Atlanta, replacing him with thirty-three-year-old Lieutenant General John Bell Hood, who proceeded to lose Atlanta to Sherman's forces. As Sherman set off on his march through Georgia to the sea, realizing that he had not destroyed Hood's army, which was now seeking to retake Tennessee, he placed Brigadier General George H. Thomas in command at Nashville to prevent its capture by Hood. On December 15–16, 1864, Thomas defeated Hood at Nashville, just days after Sherman reached the coast at Savannah (see Stott Diary entry of December 16). See James M. McPherson, *Battle Cry of Freedom: The Civil War Era* (New York and Oxford: Oxford University Press, 1988), 753, 807–8, 813–15.

49. After his defeat in the presidential election, McClellan resigned from the army. See Long, *Civil War Day by Day*, 594.

50. The Union League of America, first formed in 1862, rallied patriotic feelings, fought disloyalty in the East and Midwest, promoted enlistment, and championed support of the Lincoln administration's war policies. Though bipartisan, it received the moral and financial backing of the Republican Party. See Faust, ed., *Encyclopedia of the Civil War*, 772.

51. Thomas De Witt Talmage (1832–1902) was the pastor of the Second Dutch Reformed Church of Philadelphia in 1864. Known as a "Magnetic and rather sensational" preacher, he attracted large crowds to the church, thus giving it new influence in the city. See *DAB*, 9:287–88. Benjamin Silliman (1779–1864) was one of the most influential and renowned American scientists of the early nineteenth century. A professor of chemistry and natural history at Yale from 1802 to 1863, Silliman wrote the chemistry textbook Stott studied during his sophomore year at Franklin College. A deeply religious man, Silliman appealed to the students at Franklin because of his belief that the study of science was an avenue to understanding how God is manifested in the natural world. See ibid., 8(1):160–63; *Catalogue of Officers and Students of Franklin College for the Academic Year, 1860–61*, p. 13.

52. Mrs. Williams was the widow of Major Jonathan H. Williams.

53. James Thomas Fields (1817–1881) and William Davis Ticknor (1810–1864) had been publishers of the *Atlantic Monthly* since 1859. Fields became the publisher of the *North American Review* beginning with its 1865 volume, retaining Ticknor's name on its masthead. See *DAB*, 3:378–79, 9:528–29; *North American Review* 100 (1865): cover.

54. December 6 was the date of Lincoln's annual message to Congress for 1864. See Basler et al., eds., *Collected Works of Abraham Lincoln*, 8:136–53.

55. In Civil War usage, a "play-out" was a soldier who was worn out or demoralized, possibly even to the point of a breakdown. The term also applied to one who was "suspected of malingering." See Wright, *Language of the Civil War*, 1, 232.

56. Gideon Welles was secretary of the navy throughout the war and was considered one of the most effective members of Lincoln's cabinet. Salmon P. Chase, one of Lincoln's rivals for the Republican presidential nomination in 1860, became his secretary of the treasury. Chase's tensions with fellow cabinet members and his own presidential ambitions and manipulations in 1864 led Lincoln to appoint him as Chief Justice upon the death of Roger

Taney. See Balser et al., eds., *Collected Works of Abraham Lincoln*, 8:154.

57. Second Lieutenant George W. Bailey of Aurora and Company A of the Eighteenth Indiana mustered out of the army on December 13, 1864. See *AGI*, 2:160.

58. William Steele Holman of Aurora attended Franklin College from 1838 to 1840. The son of Judge Jesse Lynch Holman, a founder of the college and author of its first constitution, William served in the U.S. House of Representatives four times (1859–65, 1867–77, 1881–95, and 1897). See *Jubilee*, 50, 146; *DAB*, 5:158–59; I. George Blake, *The Holmans of Veraestau* (Oxford, OH: Mississippi Valley Press, 194), 44.

59. The statue of Washington mentioned here is probably that of the sculptor Hiram Powers (1805–1873), who portrayed the first president as a Freemason in a work of 1858. See *DAB*, 8:158–60.

60. For Stott, reading Henry Wadsworth Longfellow's epic poem *Evangeline: A Tale of Acadie* no doubt brought back memories of his campaign in the Cajun country of Louisiana in 1863. The poem, which author Oliver Wendell Holmes Sr. called Longfellow's "masterpiece," told the story of the young French Canadian woman whose fiancé was seized and shipped off to New England on their wedding day. Evangeline searched for him throughout New England and finally in the Acadian settlements of Louisiana, where she found him on his deathbed. The shock of this discovery caused her death. Holmes called Longfellow "our chief singer" and said of the character Evangeline: "And what a beautiful creation is the Acadian maiden!" See *The Compleat Poetical Works of Henry Wadsworth Longfellow*, Cambridge edition (Boston and New York: Houghton Mifflin, 1893), 70–98.

61. The reference to Davy Crockett is probably to the frontiersman's autobiography, originally published in the 1830s, which Stott may have purchased in Washington. Though the book was "unquestionably related to reality," writes literary critic Joseph Arpad, it was "something of a hoax, an imaginative story told by Crockett to satisfy America's desire for a romantic frontier hero." See David Crockett, *A Narrative of the Life of David Crockett*, edited by Joseph Aprad (New Haven, CT: College and University Press, 1972), 7–8, 10. The Reverend Doctor Phineas D. Gurley was pastor of the New York Avenue Presbyterian Church in Washington where the Lincoln family rented a pew. Gurley served as the president's pastor and counselor, particularly during the time of his son Willie's death. He was also present at the Peterson house when Lincoln died. See David Donald, *Lincoln* (New York and London: Simon and Schuster, 1995), 337, 599.

62. Unitarian theologian Orville Dewey's *The Problem of Human Destiny* had just been published when Stott read it. Dewey delivered the essence of the book as the Lowell Lectures of 1851, the goal of which was to address what Dewey called the "world-problem," i.e., what is the end and the highest purpose of man. Dewey sought, writes historian Stow Persons, "to show the correspondence between Unitarianism and the primitive Christianity of Scriptures." In *Human Destiny*, Dewey concluded that "progress redeems all, pays for all; shows that in all things, however dark and mysterious, there has been a good intent and tendency, a good Providence, ruling all." The "voice of humanity," he contended, comes also "from Heaven," calling the American people to "do our Part" in responding to the "tears and groans of long-suffering and sighing humanity." See Dewey, *The Problem of Human Destiny; or, The End of Providence in the World and Man*, fifth edition (New York: James Miller, 1864), 12–15, 253, 275; Stow Persons, *Free Religion: An American Faith* (New Haven, CT: Yale University Press, 1947), 6.

63. It is unclear which Wisconsin senator was speaking, but the two senators from that

state in 1864 were Timothy Otis Howe and James Rood Doolittle. See *Biographical Directory of the United States Congress, 1774–2005* (Washington, D.C.: U.S. Government Printing Office, 2005), 973, 1287. Hoosier Schuyler Colfax served as Speaker of the House from 1863 to 1869. See Faust, ed., *Encyclopedia of the Civil War*, 150–51.

64. Melancthon Williams Jacobus taught oriental and biblical literature at Western Theological Seminary from 1851 to 1876. He was author of commentaries on Genesis, Matthew, Mark, Luke, and Acts. See *National Encyclopedia of American Biography*, vol. 3 (New York: James T. White, 1893), 344–45. Archibald Alexander Hodge, the son of famed theologian Charles Hodge of Princeton, began his professorship in theology at Western in 1864. His *Outline of Theology* (1860) was widely used as a textbook in seminaries. See *DAB*, 5(1): 97–98.

CHAPTER 10

1. Declaration for Invalid Army Pension, July 3, 1888, Full Pension File, William Taylor Stott, NARA; William Stott to Bel and Wilfred and Grace and Ede and Roy, November 23, 1894, Stott Family Papers, in possession of the editor, courtesy of Frances Killpatrick (hereafter cited as Stott Family Papers).

2. Rochester Theological Seminary, *General Catalogue, 1850–1900* (Rochester, NY: n.p., n.d.), 14–16; Christopher H. Evans, *The Kingdom Is Always but Coming: A Life of Walter Rauschenbusch* (Grand Rapids, MI: and Cambridge: William B. Eerdmans, 2004), 11–12. A zealot of German pietism, August Rauschenbusch was a stern but skillful teacher, able to make complex concepts "understandable to an audience of generalists." He displayed a high-strung temperament, especially at home where his family occasionally had to endure angry tirades. His son, though sometimes rebellious, accepted his father's faith but demonstrated signs of the independence of thought that led to the development of a far more liberal theology. When the boy was born in 1861, August prayed *"Walt' herr, überdiesem kinde"* ("Rule, Lord, over this child"). In this prayer, as biographer Paul Minus notes, August "found the newborn's name": Walther. Young Rauschenbusch's famous work, *Christianity and the Social Crisis*, written in 1907 while he too served as a professor at Rochester, would make him the leading spokesman for the Social Gospel—a far cry from August's pietistic mindset. See Evans, *Kingdom Is Always but Coming*, xviii –xix, 1–2; Paul M. Minus, *Walter Rauschenbusch: American Reformer* (London: Collier Macmillan, 1988), 1–2.

3. *Seventeenth Annual Catalogue of Rochester Theological Seminary, 1867–1868* (Rochester, NY: n.p., n.d.), 13–15; *General Catalogue*, 81–83. After serving as an officer in the Seventieth Indiana, Morgan commanded the Fourteenth U.S. Colored Infantry and attained the rank of brevet brigadier general because of his gallantry at the battle of Nashville. He later taught homiletics and ecclesiastical history at the Baptist theological school in Chicago, wrote books on pedagogy, and severed as President Benjamin Harrison's commissioner of Indian Affairs. Elgin was in the Union army from 1862 to 1865 and was chaplain of U.S. Volunteers in the last year of the war. He later was pastor of churches in Indiana, Ohio, New York, and Michigan and was corresponding secretary of the Indiana Baptist Convention from 1882 to 1884. See *DAB*, 13:187–88; *The Colgate-Rochester Divinity School Bulletin: General Catalogue, 1819–1930* (Rochester, NY: n.p., n.d.), 58–59.

4. Memoir of Eleanor Parker Van Cleave, Stott Family Papers; Aunt Polly to Rosemary Laycock, undated, ibid.; Bureau of Pensions Questionnaire, compiled by William Taylor Stott, March 31, 1915, Full Pension File, NARA.

5. *History of Bartholomew County, Indiana–1888* (Columbus, IN: Bartholomew County Historical Society, 1976), 103; John F. Cady, *The Centennial History of Franklin College* (Franklin, IN: Franklin College, 1934), 92; John F. Cady, *The Baptist Church in Indiana* (Franklin, IN: Franklin College, 1942), 205.

6. FC Minutes, February 27, April 27, May 25, 1869.

7. Entries of March 23 and September 2, 1863, O. M. Merrick Diary, Charles S. Merrick Papers, S941, Manuscript Section, ISL; W. T. Stott, "Sketch of One Hundred Years of Baptist History in Indiana, 66, William T. Stott Presidential Papers, 1874–1965, SCFC; Cady, *Centennial History of Franklin College*, 85–91; Dewitt C. Goodrich and Charles R. Tuttle, *An Illustrated History of the State of Indiana* (Indianapolis: Robert S. Peale and Company, 1875), 526; FC Minutes, June 1, 29, 1964. At its June 29 meeting, the board voted to confer the master of arts degree on the entire class of 1861, including Stott. Some of the opponents to the reopening of the college, viewing it as a "defunct institution," preferred to support schools in other states, such as Shurtleff in Illinois or Kalamazoo in Michigan, Still others wanted to transfer the Franklin institution to Indianapolis. See Cady, *Centennial History of Franklin College*, 96–98; I George Blake, *Finding a Way through the Wilderness: The Indiana Baptist Convention, 1833–1983* (Indianapolis: Central Publishing Company, 1983), 71.

8. B. Wallace to Stott, May 1, 1884, Alumni Letter Book, 1883–1884, SCFC.

9. Cady *Centennial History of Franklin College*, 94–95, 98; *Jubilee*, 42. See also "Advertisement for Franklin Seminary," December 1, 1865, Franklin College History Collection, 1843–1909, box 2, SCFC.

10. Cady, *Centennial History of Franklin College*, 99–101, 98; *Jubilee*, 42–43; William T. Stott, *Indiana Baptist History, 1798–1908* (W. T. Stott, 1908), 352; Cady, *Baptist Church in Indiana*, 163–64; FC Minutes, May 25, 1869.

11. Stott, *Indiana Baptist History*, 353;*Catalogue of Officers and Students of Franklin College for the Year 1869–'70* (Indianapolis: Braden and Burford, 1869), 12–19, 21–22; FC Minutes, May25, June 21, 1869.

12. FC Minutes, June 9, July 14, November 9, 1869, February 2, July 20, 1870; *Jubilee*, 43; Cady, *History of Franklin College*, 101–6.

13. Stott, *Indiana Baptist History*, 353; Cady, *History of Franklin College*, 104–6; I. George Blake, *The Holmans of Veraestau* (Oxford, OH: Mississippi Valley Press, 1943), 43–44, 152–54; Blake, *Finding a Way through the Wilderness*, 90. For Holman's complete address, see W. S. Holman, *Capital and Labor* (Washington, D.C., 1871).

14. Stott, *Indiana Baptist History*, 353–54; Cady, *History of Franklin College*, 106; FC Minutes, February 1, November 15, 1871.

15. FC Minutes, January 31, 1872; Cady, *History of Franklin College*, 106; *Baptist Standard*, February 15, 18, 1872, clippings, Barnett Wallace Scrapbook #2, p. 25, SCFC.

16. W. T. Stott, *History of Franklin College* (Indianapolis: Journal and Messenger, 1874), 10. To examine the journalistic exchange between Wayland and college leaders, see the extensive clippings in Wallace Scrapbook, 22–27.

17. FC Minutes, January 31, June 21, July 25, 1872; Stott, "Sketch of One Hundred Years of Baptist History in Indiana," 66; *Jubilee*, 44–45; *Journal and Messenger*, May 15, June 21, 1872, clippings, Wallace Scrapbook, 25–27. See also Silas Bailey, "College Matters in Indiana," *Journal and Messenger*, May 29, 1872, ibid., 27.

18. Elba Branigin, *History of Johnson County, Indiana* (Indianapolis: B. F. Bowen and

Company, 1913), 598; Cady *History of Franklin College*, 110; Clifton J. Phillips, *Indiana in Transition: The Emergence of an Industrial Commonwealth, 1880–1920* (Indianapolis: Indiana Historical Bureau and Indiana Historical Society, 1968), 427–28.

19. Cady, *History of Franklin college*, 110–11; Stott letter, May 8, 1884, Alumni Letter Book, SCFC; Stott, *Indiana Baptist History*, 355; Franklin College Circular, 1872–73, p. 3, SCFC; Branigin, *History of Johnson County*, 295.

20. Stott, *Indiana Baptist History*, 356; FC Minutes, September 11, 1872; T. R. Palmer, "Franklin College Flyer," 1873, p. 1, Franklin College Miscellaneous Publications, SCFC; Franklin College Circular, 1872–73, p. 6.

21 Cady, *History of Franklin College*, 112–16 (quote on 116).

22. Stott, *Indiana Baptist History*, 356–57; FC Minutes, November 20, 1872, February 15, April 23, June 19, 1873, March 4, July 7, 1874, June 4, September 3, 1877, September 9, 1878; Palmer, "Franklin College Flyer," 2–3; *Jubilee*, 46; Cady, *History of Franklin College*, 112.

23. FC Minutes, March 4, 1874, December 22, 1875; Wallace to Stott, May 1, 1884, Alumni Letter Book.

24. FC Minutes, June 14, 1876, April 1, November 4, 1878, January 4 1881; *Jubilee*, 27 (Wyeth quote); Stott, *Indiana Baptist History*, 151–52.

25. FC Minutes, April 9, 1877, December 16 1881, September 11, 1883; Stott, *Indiana Baptist History*, 338.

26. *Catalogue of Franklin College, 1874–75* (Indianapolis: Journal and Messenger, 1875), 16; FC Minutes, March 21, June 13, 1882; Stott to Rachel Butts, February 29, 1884, Stott Presidential Papers; "Franklin College Women's Professorship," flyer, Franklin College Miscellaneous Publications; Branigin, *History of Johnson County*, 298; *Blue and Gold* (1900), 23–24; Cady, *History of Franklin College*, 115–16, 121–22; Stott, *Indiana Baptist History*, 244. Also in the 1890s, Stott solicited the assistance of the school's alumni. In an address to the 1894 graduation class, sent by Carr to all previous graduates, the president spoke of "The Banyan Tree." It is a strange tree, he said, for "from its branches smaller branches grow downwards to the ground, take root, and in turn become supporters of the life of the tree." The alumni are to the college, Stott asserted, what the smaller branches are to the Banyan Tree. As the college's graduates support it, "its growth and usefulness are assured." Stott, "the Banyan Tree," Stott Presidential Papers.

27. FC Minutes, March 19, June 11, 1889, December 22, 1891, December 17, 1895, June 14, 1898, December 16, 1902; Cady, *History of Franklin College*, 120, 125; Cady *Baptist Church in Indiana*, 224. Tensions developed between Stott and Carr, apparently over the latter's methods and possibly personality clashes that led to Carr's resignation in June 1902. In the rather melodramatic letter Carr read to the board, he asserted his love for the institution and belief the $100,000 "will flow to you on account of the influence of my work." Stott joined the board in praise of Carr as a "enthusiastic, faithful and loving servant of the Lord." FC Minutes, June 10, 1902; Cady, *History of Franklin College*, 126–27; Stott, *Indiana Baptist History*, 367.

28. Cady, *Baptist Church in Indiana*, 224–25; Vawter to Stott, July 4, 1883, Alumni Letter Book; Cady *History of Franklin College*, 112–16; Blake *Finding a Way through the Wilderness*, 71–72. A highlight of Stott's presidency was the Jubilee celebration held on campus from June 5 to 12, 1884. It was not only an observance of the college's fiftieth anniversary but it also provided administrators, faculty, alumni, donors, and the Baptist Convention an

opportunity to rehearse the institution's history and to express their justifiable pride over its survival through five decades.

29. Richard J. Storr, *Harper's University: The Beginnings* (Chicago and London: University of Chicago Press, 1966), 5–6, 11, 14–16.

30. FC Minutes, December 16, 1896, March 16, 1987, March 22, December 20, 1898, June 13, 1899; Phillips, *Indiana in Transition*, 431–32; Cady *History of Franklin College*, 125–26.

31. FC Minutes, December 15, 1897, March 22, December 20, June 13, 1899; Phillips, *Indiana in Transition*, 431–32; Cady, *History of Franklin College*, 125–26.

32 "Old Students Revere Memory of Dr. Stott," *Baptist Observer*, November 14, 1918; *The Franklin Almanack* (1919), 8.

33. "Old Students Revere Memory of Dr. Stott."

34. Letter of Martha Carter, *Baptist Observer*, January 2, 1919; Palmer, "Extolled Life of Dr. Stott," Stott Family Papers; Edgar Fay Daugherty, *A Hoosier Parson: Boosts and Bumps (An Apologia Pro Mea Vita)* (Boston: Meador, 1952), 29.

35. *Blue and Gold* (1898), 27; *Annual Catalogue of Franklin College, 1904–1905*, pp. 36–37.

36. Cady, *History of Franklin College*, 122–23; FC Minutes, December 18, 1881, September 16, 1891, September 25, 1901; Wallace to Stott, May 1, 1884, Alumni Letter Book.

37. FC Minutes, December 17, 1889, December 21, 1892, March 20, June 12, 1894, June 13, 1899, December 16, 1902, February 27, July 14, September 30, December 22, 1903; Cady, *History of Franklin College*, 122.

38. Millard F. Kennedy, *Schoolmaster of Yesterday: A Three-Generation Story* (New York: McGraw-Hill, 1940), 263; Branigin, *History of Johnson County*, 296–97; *Catalogue of the Officers and Students of Franklin College, 1883–84* (Cincinnati: Journal and Messenger, 1884), 39; FC Minutes, March 18, June 10, 1884, June 12,1888. On September 12, 1884, Barnett Wallace informed the contractor who was to lay the foundation for the new structure: "College opened yesterday with full attendance. Every available space in aisle of chapel was filled with chairs and still the people overflowed. . . . It was very suggestive of the need of a new chapel at least." Wallace to W. W. Lowes, September 12, 1884, Wallace Letters.

39. Wallace to Gaddis Elgin, July 28, 1884, Wallace Letters; Wallace to R. P. Daggett, August 9, September 12, 1884, July 4, 11, 1887, ibid.; Wallace to George A. Misch, December 12, 1890, ibid.; FC Minutes, June 11, 1889, June 12, 1894, March 17, 1896, June 9, 1903, June 14, 1904; Branigin, *History of Johnson County*, 297.

40. C. H. Hall, "Christianity and Culture," *Franklin College Quarterly* (September 1897): 86–89; Stott, "Sketch of One Hundred Years of Baptist History in Indiana," 67; "Report to the Indiana Baptist Convention," September 1901, Barnett Wallace, Writing and Papers, 1897–1927, SCFC. In addition to regular chapel worship, Stott maintained the focus of faculty and students on the school's Christian foundation in his Saturday morning lectures on Bible doctrines. Students also held biweekly prayer meetings. See *Franklin College Quarterly* (June 1897): 45; FC Minutes, December 20, 1887; Cady, *History of Franklin College*, 140–41.

41. *Blue and Gold* (1898), 29, (1899), n.p., (1902), 24, (1910), n.p.; Cady *History of Franklin College*, 151–52; FC Minutes, August 11, 1887.

42. Wallace to Daggett, October 14, 1884, Wallace Letters; Calvin DeArmand Davis, *A History of the Albert Carter Moncrief Family* (© 1997), 57; *Blue and Gold* (1898), 33–34, (1902), 23; FC Minutes, December 20, 1881, December 22, 1885, June 10–11, 1890,

March 20 1894; *Catalogue of Franklin, 1874–75* (Indianapolis: Journal and Messenger, 1875), 3: *Annual Catalogue of Franklin College, 1904–1905* (Indianapolis: Journal and Messenger, 1905), 25–30; Cady, *History of Franklin College*, 150–52. Music also became a focal point in the last years of Stott's presidency, as graduate Clarke R. Parker created a much-lauded glee club. Stott's daughter, Grace, became Parker's wife in 1900. See FC Minutes, June 12, 1900.

43. For discussion of faculty development opportunities and faculty roles in student recruitment, see FC Minutes, October 7, 1878, May 5, October 7, 1879, March 20, 1888, June 11, 1895, September 14, 1892, September 30, 1903. The unsavory methods of agent Sumner are briefly mentioned in Cady, *History of Franklin College*, 103

44. *Blue and Gold* (1902), 147.

45. Faculty's Secretary's Book, 3, 21–22, Franklin College History Collection, SCFC.

46. Phillips, *Indiana in Transition*, 430–31; Cady, *History of Franklin College*, 141–42, 146–47; Faculty Secretary's Book, 21; *Annual Catalogue, Franklin College, 1904–05*, pp. 11–17. Despite the faculty's many obligations and heavy teaching loads, salaries "remained exceedingly low until well after the turn of the century," according to John Cady. Strong pleas for increases in salary from some board members were regularly expressed, but the first raises did not occur until 1885. See Cady, *History of Franklin College*, 153; FC Minutes, December 19, 1882, December 12, 1884, December 16, 1890.

47. FC Minutes, June 14, 1887, June 13, 1899; Branigin, *History of Johnson County*, 125, 128, 149; *Annual Catalogue of Franklin College, 1904–05*, pp. 58–70.

48. *Franklin College Circular, 1873–74* (Cincinnati: Journal and Messenger, 1874), n.p.; *Annual Catalogue of Franklin College, 1904–05*, p. 45; FC Minutes, March 28, 1879, December 22, 1885, March 22, 1898, June 12, 1900; Cady, *History of Franklin College*, 150. Millard Kennedy recorded that during his student days in the 1880s, "nearly three quarters" of the students were studying "either for the ministry or education." Some had their "eye on the law" or the "notion of being doctors," but a few, like himself, "didn't know where they were going." See Kennedy, *Schoolmaster of Yesterday*, 263.

49. Emma Lou Thornbrough, *Indiana in the Civil War Era, 1850–1880* (Indianapolis: Indiana Historical Bureau and Indiana Historical Society, 1965), 523; Cady, *Franklin College*, 128–30; Branigin, *History of Johnson County*, 298–99.

50. Cady, *History of Franklin College*, 129–30; *Blue and Gold* (1898), 60, 84; S. P. Smith to W. T. Stott, February 16, 1883, Alumni Letter Book.

51. *The Collegiate* (June 1881): 4; Cady, *History of Franklin College*, 132–34, 147–48, especially 153–57, for a more extensive treatment of the themes of student orations.

52. Daugherty, *Hoosier Parson*, 27, 29; Branigin, *History of Johnson County*, 296.

53. FC Minutes, June 1884, December 19, 1893; Cady, *Franklin College*, 134–36; Branigin, *History of Johnson County*, 296; Kennedy, *Schoolmaster of Yesterday*, 267–70.

54. Branigin, *History of Johnson County*, 296; Faculty Secretary's Book, April 9, June 7, 15, 1883, March 19, 1884, June 13, 1892. Interestingly, in 1902, when the front alcove and stairwell beneath the tower of Stott Hall became a "Lover's Retreat," Stott and the faculty "agreed to keep the main entrance to the chapel closed at all times so that the steps and vestibule might be appropriated by the sentimentally inclined." See *Blue and Gold*, (1902), 145.

55. *The Collegiate* (March 1881): 3–4; Cady, *History of Franklin College*, 138.

56. FC Minutes, March 22, 1886; Phillips, *Indiana in Transition*, 434–35; Faculty Secre-

tary's Book, February 1888; Cady *History of Franklin College*, 138.

57. FC Minutes, June 13, 1893, March 19, 1895, December 21, 1897; Wallace to A. G. Spalding & Bros., February 28, 1890, and Wallace to W. G. Everson, December 18, 1898, Wallace Letters; *Blue and Gold* (1898), 100; Cady, *History of Franklin College*, 138–39.

58. FC Minutes, June 9, September 22, December 1897, June 15, December 20, 1898, December 18, 1900, September 25, 1901; *Blue and Gold* (1898), 7 (1900), 110; Cady, *History of Franklin College*, 139–40. Stott's sword now resides in the Franklin College Archives, a gift from his great-grandchildren.

59. Blake, *Finding a Way through the Wilderness*, 92; Grace Vawter Bicknell, *The Vawter Family in America* (Indianapolis: Hollenbeck Press, 1905; reprint Atlanta, GA: Thorpe and Associates, 1969), 107; FC Minutes, June 12, 1888; George S. Cottman, "Indiana Baptist History," *Indiana Magazine of History* 4 (September 1908): 149–50; *Franklin Jeffersonian*, August 31, 1882; Mary A. Medlicott, *First Baptist Church, Franklin, History, 1832–1982* (Franklin: Schumacher Printing, 1983), 8, 12. Stott dedicated his *Indiana Baptist History* to Franklin College.

60. Branigin, *History of Johnson County*, 536; *Franklin Evening Star*, November 1, 1918; *Commemorative Biographical Record of Prominent and Representative Men of Indianapolis an Vicinity* (Chicago: J. H. Beers, 1908), 99; Margaret Leech, *In the Days of McKinley* (New York: Harper and Brothers, 1959), 85; Stott to Mrs. A. A. Wood, October 19, 1896, and Dorothy W. Lawliss to William Bryan Martin, September 14, 1993, Stott File. One biographer, in commenting on Stott's service on the city council, indicates that he was "very liberal" in local matters and "his aim was not to advance party, but to faithfully serve the city." See *Commemorative Biographical Record of Prominent and Representative Men of Indianapolis and Vicinity*, 99.

61. David Demaree Banta, *History of Johnson County, Indiana* (Chicago: Brant and Fuller, 1888), 525; *The Home, 1865–1965: Centennial Souvenir of the Soldiers' and Sailors' Orphans' Home, Knightstown, Indiana* (microfilm), Manuscript Section, ISL; Indiana–Vicksburg Military Park Commission, *Indiana at Vicksburg* (Indianapolis: Wm. Burford, 1911), 433–34, 466; James H. Madison, "Civil War Memories and 'Pardnership Fogettin'," 1865–1913," *Indiana Magazine of History* 99 (September 2003): 215, 223.

62. Bicknell, *Vawter Family in America*, 104–8; Eleanor Van Cleave, "Personal Memoirs," Stott Family Papers; clipping from the *Indiana Baptist*, September 27, 1883, Stott File.

63. Will to Bel, September 17, 1894, Stott letters from Europe and the Holy Land, Stott Family Papers.

64. Will to Bel September 17, 1894, Papa to Ede, September 28, 1894, and Papa to Grace and Ede, November 2–3, 1894, ibid.; Wilfred to Father, May 24, 1901, Stott Presidential Papers. The last letter is on the letterhead of the *Chicago Tribune*, of which Wilfred was an editor. Wilfred also was captain of Company K, 161st Indiana, during the Spanish-American War. See Military File of Wilfred T. Stott, Stott/Stotts file, Genealogical Records, Johnson County Museum of History, Franklin, IN.

65. FC Minutes, March 12, June 9–10, 1885, December 21, 1897.

66. Stuart McConnell, *Glorious Contentment: The Grand Army of the Republic, 1865–1900* (Chapel Hill and London: University of North Carolina Press, 1992), 143, 146, 149; Declaration of Invalid Army Pension, July 3, 1888, Full Pension File, William Taylor Stott, NARA; Surgeon's Certificates, March 6, 1889, April 16, 1890, November 5, 1902, April 19, 1905, ibid.; General Affidavits of C. H. Hall, John Carson, and Maxa Moncrief, March

2, 1889, Louis W. Knobe, April 24, 1889, ibid.; Physician's General Affidavit of Barnett Wallace, December 5, 1902, ibid.; Invalid pensions–rejections, November 17, 1895, May 8, 1905, ibid.; An Act Granting an Increase of Pension to William T. Stott, June 6, 1906, ibid.

67. FC Minutes, June 15, December 21, 1904, January 6, June 14, July 27, 1905. For tributes to Stott at the time of his retirement by the board of directors and Columbus H. Hall, see ibid., June 15, 1905; *Blue and Gold*, (1905), 5–6.

68. Aunt Polly to Boo [Laycock], n.d., and Frances Killpatrick to Lloyd A. Hunter, April 15, 2002, Stott Family Papers; Van Cleave, "Personal Memoir."

69. Report of Superintendent M. M. Wishard, Indiana Soldiers' Orphans' Home, February 24, 1876, Historical sketches, Goals, Organizational Structures, etc. of Miscellaneous Charitable Institution in the State, S2233, Manuscript Section ISL; *Home*, 8. 12, 14, 64–65, 75 (photograph); Van Cleave "Personal Memoir."

70. Roscoe Gilmore Stott, "Their Golden Wedding Day," May 21, 1918, Stott Family Papers.

71. *Baptist Observer*, November 7, 1918, pp. 1–2; *Franklin Evening Star*, November 1, 2, 4, 5, 1918; *Franklin Democrat*, November 8, 1918. Stott's death certificate gives the time of death as 9:25 a.m. and the cause of death as "arterio sclerosis, with contributory (secondary) Bright's disease" (chronic kidney inflammation). Stott Death Certificate, Full Pension File.

72. *Baptist Observer*, November 7, 14, 21, 1918, January 2, 1919.

Bibliography

Unpublished Primary Sources

Editor's Collection.
    Moncrief Family Papers, courtesy of Calvin Davis.
    Stott Family Papers, courtesy of Rosemary Laycock and Frances Killpatrick.
Franklin College Archives, Special Collections, Franklin, IN.
    Alumni Letter Book, 1883–1884.
    Alumni Register.
    Franklin College Alumni Record to 1910, Franklin College Manuscript
        Collection.
    Franklin College Bulletin, 1834–1928.
    Franklin College History Collection, 1843–1909.
    Franklin College Miscellaneous Publications, 1844–1894.
    Franklin College Publications.
        Blue and Gold.
        Catalogues of Franklin College, 1856–1905.
        The Collegiate, 1881.
        The Franklin Almanack 20 (1919).
        Franklin College Quarterly 1 (1897).
        Minutes of the Board of Trustees of the Indiana Baptist Manual Labor Institute,
            1835–1836.
        Minutes of the Indiana Baptist Education Society, 1834–1858.
        Minutes of the Indiana General Association, 1833–1862.
        Carrie Morrison Correspondence, 1860–1864.
        Stott File, Franklin College Collection.
        William T. Stott Civil War Papers, 1863–1864.
        W.T. Stott Presidential Papers, 1874–1905.
        Barnett Wallace Letters, 1882–1918.
        Barnett Wallace Scrapbook #2.
        Barnett Wallace "Sketches of the Early History of Franklin College (to 1904)."
        Barnett Wallace, Writings and Papers, 1897–1927.
Franklin College Business Office, Franklin, IN.
    Franklin College Board of Directors Minutes, 1869–1905.
Iberia Parish Library, New Iberia, LA.
    Civil War Letters of Dan Camp, 24th Iowa.
Indiana Historical Society, William Henry Smith Memorial Library, Indianapolis, IN.
    Erastus G. Burget Diaries.
    Letters of Gilbert H. Denny.
    William Elliott Papers.
    Stephen S. Harding Papers.
    Civil War Letters and Diary of Major William Houghton, and Letters of Walter
        Houghton and Eugene Houghton.
    James Leeper Papers.

McLaughlin-Jordan Family Papers.

Thomas Marshall Papers.

John William Prentiss Collection.

Bernard F. Schermerhorn Papers.

David S. Scott Papers.

Civil War Files of Edward P. Stanfield.

Martha Stout Papers of the Stout-Jacques Families.

John C. Swift Diaries.

William A. Van Buskirk Papers.

Samuel B. Voyles Civil War Correspondence.

Indiana State Library, Indianapolis, IN.

Census Records, Indiana, 1850 (microfilm).

Census Records, Indiana, 1860 (microfilm).

Indiana Division, Manuscript Section.

George F. Chittenden Papers.

Jefferson Columbus Davis Papers.

Historical Sketches, Goals, Organizational Structure, etc. of Miscellaneous Charitable Institutions, 1876.

Louis W. Knobe Diary.

Charles S. Merrick Papers.

Daniel Roberts Letters.

Asa E. Sample Civil War Diary.

Augustus E. Sinks, "Four Years in Dixie," Journal of the Campaign of the 46th Indiana Regiment.

James R. Slack Papers.

Mrs. F. A. Thomas Civil War Diaries and Letters.

Harry Watts Civil War Reminiscence.

Johnson County Museum and Historical Society, Franklin, IN.

Stott/Stotts File. Genealogical Records.

Rebecca S. Wallace Biographical Data Scrapbook.

National Archives and Records Administration, Washington, D.C.

Full Pension File, William Taylor Stott.

Military Service File, William Taylor Stott.

Pea Ridge National Military Park, Pea Ridge, AR.

Grenville M. Dodge Papers.

Henry W. Dysart Diary.

Samuel A. McKay [pseudonym Jim Hardtack] War Reminiscences.

Asa Payne, "Story of the Battle of Pea Ridge."

Henry Voelkner Papers.

United States Army Military History Institute, Carlisle Barracks, PA.

Peter B. Boarts Letters, Earl Hess Collection.

Eugene A. Carr Papers.

Civil War Times Illustrated Collection.

Henry Curtis, Jr., Papers.

Francis A. Dawes Diary.

George W. Gordon Papers.

Samuel P. Herrington Diary, Rudolph Haerle Collection
Henry Keiser Diary, Harrisburg Civil War Round Table Collection.
George S. Marks Papers and Diary, Civil War Miscellaneous Collection.
Israel M. Ritter Diary.
University of Louisiana, Lafayette, Dupree Library Archives.
Walter Burke Papers.
University of South Florida, Tampa, Library, Florida Documents.
E. E. Johnson, "Notes by the Way," Diary of E. E. Johnson, 1862.
Vicksburg National Military Park Archives, Vicksburg, MS.
Regimental Files.
99th Illinois Infantry.
8th Indiana Infantry.
18th Indiana Infantry.
Indiana Light Artillery, 1st Battery.
21st Iowa Infantry.
23rd Iowa Infantry.
11th Wisconsin Infantry.
Western Historical Manuscript Collection, University of Missouri, Rolla.
Lyman G. Bennett Collection.
Henry Perrin Mann Civil War Diaries.
James S. Rogers Papers.
Aquilla Standifird Civil War Diary.

Indiana Newspapers

Baptist Observer: Official Paper of Indiana Baptists (weekly).
Brookville Franklin Democrat.
Brookville National Defender.
Franklin Democrat.
Franklin Evening Star.
Greensburg Standard.
Indianapolis Daily Sentinel.
Rockville Parke County Republican.
Vevay Indiana Reveille.

Published Primary Sources

Baxter, William. *Pea Ridge and Prairie Grove; or, Scenes and Incidents of the War in Arkansas.*
Fayetteville: University of Arkansas Press, 2000.
Bennett, L. G., and William M. Haigh. *History of the Thirty-Sixth Regiment Illinois*
Volunteers, during the War of the Rebellion. Aurora, IL: Knickerbocker and Hodder, 1876.
Bigelow, James K. *Abridged History of the Eighth Indiana Volunteer Infantry from Its*
Organization, April 21st, 1861, to the Date of Re-enlistment as Veterans, January 1, 1864.
Indianapolis: Ellis Barnes, 1864.
Blodgett, Edward A. "The Army of the Southwest and the Battle of Pea Ridge." In *Military*
Essays and Recollections: Papers Read before the Commandery of the State of Illinois, Mili-
tary Order of the Loyal Legion of the United States. Wilmington, NC: Broadfoot, 1992.
Burns, Harrison. *Personal Recollections of Harrison Burns.* Indianapolis: Indiana

Historical Society, 1975.

Cadwallader, Sylvanus. *Three Years with Grant.* Edited by Benjamin Thomas. New York: Alfred A. Knopf, 1955.

Clarke, Norman, ed. *Warfare along the Mississippi: The Letters of Lieutenant Colonel George E. Currie.* Mount Pleasant: Central Michigan University, 1961.

Colgate-Rochester Divinity School Bulletin: General Catalogue, 1819–1930. Np., np.

Cozzens, Peter, and Robert L. Girardi, eds. *The Military Memoirs of General John Pope.* Chapel Hill and London: University of North Carolina Press, 1998.

Crabtree, John D. "Recollections of the Pea Ridge Campaign and the Army of the Southwest." In *Military Essays and Recollections: Papers Read before the Commandery of the State of Illinois, Military Order of the Loyal Legion of the United States.* Chicago: A. C. McClurg, 1897.

Crowninshield, Benjamin W. *The Battle of Cedar Creek: A Paper Read before the Massachusetts Military Historical Society.* Cambridge, MA: Riverside Press, 1879.

Dana, Charles A. *Recollections of the Civil War.* New York: D. Appleton, 1899.

Daugherty, Edgar Fay. *A Hoosier Parson: Boosts and Bumps (An Apologia Pro Mea Vita).* Boston: Meador, 1951.

DeForest, John William. *A Volunteer's Adventures: A Union Captain's Record of the Civil War.* Edited by James H. Croushore. New Haven, CT: Yale University, 1946.

Deputy, Malcolm. *"The Land of Winding Waters."* Montezuma, IN: Wabash Valley Press, 1963.

DuPont, Henry A. *The Campaign of 1864 in the Valley of Virginia.* New York: National Americana Society, 1925.

Early, Jubal Anderson. *War Memoirs.* Edited by Frank E. Vandiver. Bloomington: Indiana University Press, 1960.

Elliott, Isaac H. *History of the Thirty-Third Illinois Veteran Volunteer Infantry in the Civil War.* Gibson City, IL: Regimental Association, 1902.

First Half Century of Franklin College, 1834–1884: Jubilee Exercises, June 5 to 12, Cincinnati: Journal and Messenger, 1884.

Foster, John W. *War Stories for My Grandchildren.* Cambridge, MA: Riverside Press, 1918.

Gordon, John B. *Reminiscences of the Civil War.* New York: Charles Scribner's Sons, 1903.

Grant, Ulysses S. *Personal Memoirs of U. S. Grant.* 2 vols. New York: Charles L. Webster and Company, 1885.

Harwood, Nathan S. "The Pea Ridge Campaign." In *Civil War Sketches and Incidents: Papers Read before the Nebraska Commandery of the Military Order of the Loyal Legion of the United States.* Omaha, 1887.

George W. Herr. *Episodes of the Civil War: Nine Campaigns in Nine States.* San Francisco: Bancroft Company, 1890.

The Home, 1865–1965: Centennial Souvenir of the Soldiers' and Sailors' Orphans' Home, Knightstown, Indiana. Indianapolis: Mitchell-Fleming, 1965.

"Indiana Troops at Helena," Pts. 3–6. *Phillips County (AR) Historical Quarterly* 17 (March/June 1979): 11–21, 34–42; 18 (June/December 1980), 1–8, 1–7.

Indianapolis Directory and Business Mirror. Indianapolis: H. H. Dodd and Company, 1862

Irwin, Ray W., ed. "Missouri in Crisis: The Journal of Captain Albert Tracy, 1861, Part III." *Missouri Historical Review* 51 (April, 1957): 270–83.

Johnson, R. U., and C. C. Buel, eds. *Battles and Leaders of the Civil War.* 4 vols.

New York: Century Company, 1887.

Kennedy, Millard Fillmore. *Schoolmaster of Yesterday: A Three-Generation Story.* New York: McGraw-Hill, 1940.

Kiper, Richard L., ed. *Dear Catharine, Dear Taylor: The Civil War Letters of a Union Soldier and His Wife.* Lawrence: University of Kansas Press, 2002.

Lathrop, David. *The History of the Fifty-Ninth Regiment Illinois Volunteers; or, A Three Years' Campaign through Missouri, Arkansas, Mississippi, Tennessee, and Kentucky.* Indianapolis: Hall and Hutchinson, 1865.

Marshall, R. V. *An Historical Sketch of the Twenty-Second Regiment Indiana Volunteers.* Madison, IN: Courier Company, 1884.

Memorial Volume of Rev. Silas Bailey, D.D., LL.D. Lafayette, IN: Spring and Robertson, 1876.

Moore, Frank, ed. *The Rebellion Record: A Diary of American Events.* 12 vols. New York: Putnam, 1861–68.

Nettleton, A. Bayard. "How the Day Was Saved at the Battle of Cedar Creek." In *Glimpses of the Nation's Struggle, Minnesota Commandery, Military Order of the Loyal Legion of the United States.* Wilmington, NC: Broadfoot, 1992.

Oldroyd, Osborne H. *A Soldier's Story of the Siege of Vicksburg.* Springfield, IL, 1885.

Perry, Oran. "The Entering Wedge." In *Indiana Commandery, Military Order of the Loyal Legion of the United States.* Wilmington, NC: Broadfoot, 1992.

Pollard, H. M. "Recollections of Cedar Creek." In *War Papers and Personal Reminscences, 1861–1865, Commandery of Missouri, Military Order of the Loyal Legion of the United States.* Wilmington, NC: Broadfoot, 1992.

Rochester Theological Seminary. *General Catalogue, 1850–1900.* N.p., n.d.

———. *Seventeenth Annual Catalogue of Rochester Theological Seminary.* N.p., n.d.

Sheridan, Philip H. *Personal Memoirs of P. H. Sheridan.* 2 vols. New York: Charles L. Webster and Company, 1888.

Simon, John Y., ed. *The Papers of Ulysses S. Grant.* 31 vols. Carbondale: Southern Illinois University Press, 1967–2009.

Simpson, Brooks D., and Jean Berlin. *Sherman's Civil War: Selected Correspondence of William Tecumseh Sherman, 1861–1865.* Chapel Hill and London: University of North Carolina Press, 1999.

Starr, William C. "Cedar Creek." In *War Papers Read before the Indiana Commandery, Military Order of the Loyal Legion of the United States.* Indianapolis: The Commandery, 1898.

Stevens, George T. *Three Years in the Sixth Corps.* Albany: S. R. Gray, 1866.

Stevenson, David. *Indiana's Roll of Honor*, vol. 1. Indianapolis: By Author, 1864.

Stevenson, William G. *Thirteen Months in the Rebel Army.* New York: A. S. Barnes and Company, 1959.

Taylor, Richard. *Destruction and Reconstruction: Personal Experiences of the Late War.* New York: D. Appleton, 1879.

Terrell, W. H. H. *Indiana in the War of the Rebellion: Report of the Adjutant General.* 8 vols. Indianapolis: W. R. Holloway, State Printer, 1865–69.

United States War Department. *The War of the Rebellion: A Compilation of the Official Records of the Union and Confederate Armies.* 128 vols. Washington, D.C.: U.S. Government Printing Office, 1880–1901.

Wilson, James Harrison. *Under the Old Flag: Recollections of Military Operations in the War for the Union, the Spanish War, the Boxer Rebellion, etc.* New York and London: D. Appleton and Company, 1912.

Winters, William. *The Musick of the Mocking Birds, the Roar of the Cannon: The Civil War Diary of William Winters.* Edited by Steven E. Woodworth. Lincoln and London: University of Nebraska Press, 1998.

Works Read or Cited by William Taylor Stott

Allyn, Robert. "A Gossip about Poets and Poetry." *The Ladies' Repository* 21 (May, 1861): 297–300.

Bryan, William Cullen. *Poems.* 2 vols. New York: D. Appleton, 1871.

Buck, William C. *Theology: The Philosophy of Religion.* Nashville, TN: Southwestern Publishing House, 1857.

Burns, Robert. *Poems and Songs, Complete.* 4 vols. Edinburgh: James Thin, 1896.

———. *The Works of Robert Burns: With an Account of His Life and a Criticism of His Writings.* 6th ed. London: T. Cadell and W. Davies, 1809.

Butler, Joseph. *The Analogy of Religion, Natural and Revealed, to the Constitution and Course of Nature.* Cambridge, MA: Hilliard and Brown, 1827.

Byron, George Gordon. *The Complete Poetical Works.* 7 vols. Edited by Jerome J. McGann. Oxford: Oxford University Press, 1980–93.

Cicero. *In Catilinam, I–V. Cicero in Twenty-Eight Volumes.* Cambridge, MA: Harvard University Press, 1977.

Christopherson, H. "Home—Its Enchantments." *The Ladies Repository* 20 (July 1860): 386–87.

Crockett, David. *A Narrative of the Life of David Crockett.* Edited by Joseph J. Arpad. New Haven, CT: College and University Press, 1972.

Dewey, Orville. *The Problem of Human Destiny; or, The End of Providence in the World and Man.* 5th ed. New York: James Miller, 1864.

Dick, John. *An Essay on the Inspiration of the Holy Scriptures, of the Old and New Testaments.* 2nd American ed. Philadelphia: James C. Howe, 1818.

———. *Lectures on Theology.* Philadelphia: W. G. Wardle, 1844.

Festus. *The Brevarium of Festus: A Critical Edition with Historical Commentary.* Edited by J. W. Eadie. London: University of London Athlone Press, 1967.

Fields, William. *The Scrap-Book.* 2d ed. Philadelphia: J. B. Lippincott, 1861.

Foster, John. *Essays in a Series of Letters.* Andover, MA: Flagg and Gould, 1826.

Gray, Thomas. *The Works of Thomas Gray, In Prose and Verse.* 4 vols. Edited by Edward Gosse. London and New York: Macmillan, 1902–6.

Greenwood, Grace. [Jane Clarke Lippincott]. *Greenwood Leaves: Collection of Sketches and Letters.* 2d ed. Boston: Ticknor, Read, and Fields, 1852.

Haven, Joseph. *Mental Philosophy: Including the Intellect, Sensibilities, and Will.* Improved edition. New York: Sheldon and Company, 1879.

"The Heart of War." *Atlantic Monthly* 14 (August 1864): 240–42.

Horace. *Horace: The Odes and Epodes.* Translated by C. E. Bennett. Cambridge, MA: Harvard University Press, 1960.

Hugo, Victor. *Works of Victor Hugo.* Vol. 2, *Les Miserables.* London and New York: Chesterfield Society, n.d.

Leslie, E. "Mr. and Mrs. Woodbridge." *Godey's Lady's Book and Ladies' American*

Magazine 22 (Jan.–June 1841): 2–6, 74–78, 109–13, 168–74.

Lichen, Lily. [Mary A. A. Phinney]. "Sweet Home." *The Ladies' Repository* 21 (May 1861): 304.

Longfellow, Henry W. *The Complete Poetical Works of Henry Wadsworth Longfellow.* Cambridge Edition. Boston and New York: Houghton Mifflin, 1893.

Lowell, James Russell. *The Biglow Papers.* Second series. Boston: Houghton Mifflin and Company, 1885.

———. *James Russell Lowell's The Biglow Papers: A Critical Edition.* Edited by Thomas Wortham. Dekalb: Northern Illinois University, 1977.

[Judge Halliburton]. *Sam Slick: The Clockmaker.* Philadelphia: T. B. Peterson, n.d.

Mill, John Stuart. "The Contest in America." *Harper's New Monthly Magazine* 24 (April 1862): 677–84.

Moore, Thomas. *The Poetical Works of Thomas Moore.* Boston: Phillips, Sampson, and Company, 1855.

Nevins, William. *Practical Thoughts.* In *The Evangelical Family Library*, vol. 13. New York: American Tract Society, 1836.

Newman, Samuel Phillips. *A Practical System of Rhetoric; or, The Principles and Rules of Style.* Andover, MA: Gould and Newman, 1835.

"Northern Invasions." *Atlantic Monthly* 13 (February 1864): 245–50.

Ovid. *The Metamorphoses of Ovid.* Translated by Michael Simpson. Amherst: University of Massachsetts Press, 2001.

Pope, Alexander. *An Essay on Man.* Vol. 3 of *Poems of Alexander Pope.* 10 vols. Edited by Maynard Mack. New Haven: Yale University Press, 1951.

Sargent, Epes. *Peculiar: A Hero of the Southern Rebellion.* New edition. Boston: Lee and Shepard Publishers, 1892.

Scott, Walter. *The Lady of the Lake: A Poem in Six Cantos.* Boston: Thomas O. Walker, n.d.

Sophocles. *Oedipus the King.* San Francisco: Chandler Pub. Co., 1961.

Steinhoff, Stephen T. *Keat's Endymion: A Critical Edition.* Troy, NY: Whitson, 1987.

Titcomb, Timothy. [J. G. Holland]. *Lessons in Life: A Series of Familiar Essays.* New York: Charles Scribner's Sons, 1881.

———. *Letters to the Joneses.* New York: Scribners, 1863.

"Victory." *Harper's New Monthly Magazine* 25 (July 1862): 265–70.

Wayland, Francis. *The Elements of Moral Science.* Edited by Joseph L. Blau. Cambridge, MA: Belknap Press of Harvard University, 1963.

Young, Edward. *Night Thoughts on Life, Death, and Immortality.* New York: A. S. Barnes and Company, 1852.

Writings of William Taylor Stott

"History of Fifty Years of the First Baptist Church of Franklin, Indiana." In *Franklin Jeffersonian,* August 31, 1882.

History of Franklin College: A Brief Sketch. Indianapolis: Journal and Messenger, 1874.

Indiana Baptist History, 1798–1908. By the author, 1908.

Secondary Sources

Ambrose, Stephen E. *Halleck: Lincoln's Chief of Staff.* Baton Rouge: Louisiana State

University Press, 1962.

Ammerman, Lois, April Nicole Compton, and Merideth Ertel. *Reminiscences of Vernon: Stories of the Early Days of Vernon, Indiana*. Vernon: Jennings County Historical Society, 2002.

Arceneaux, William. *Acadian General: Alfred Mouton and the Civil War*. Lafayette: University of Southwestern Louisiana, 1981.

Arnold, James R. *Grant Wins the War: Decision at Vicksburg*. New York: John Wiley and Sons, 1997.

Badeau, Adam. *Military History of Ulysses S. Grant*. 3 vols. New York: D. Appleton and Company, 1881.

Ballard, Michael B. *Pemberton: A Biography*. Jackson and London: University Press of Mississippi , 1991.

———. *Vicksburg: The Campaign That Opened the Mississippi*. Chapel Hill and London: University of North Carolina Press, 2004.

Banta, David Demaree. *History of Johnson County, Indiana*. Chicago: Brant and Fuller, 1888.

Barnes, Kenneth C. "The Williams Clan: Mountain Farmers and Union Fighters in North Central Arkansas" *Arkansas Historical Quarterly* 52 (Autumn 1993): 286–317.

Barr, Alwyn. "Texas Coastal Defenses, 1861–1863." *Southwestern Historical Quarterly* 45 (July 1961): 1–31.

Basler, Roy P., et al., eds. *The Collected Works of Abraham Lincoln*. 9 vols. New Brunswick, NJ: Rutgers University Press, 1953–55.

Bearss, Edwin C. "The Battle of Pea Ridge." *Arkansas Historical Quarterly* 20 (Spring 1961): 74–94.

———. "The First Day at Pea Ridge, March 7, 1862." *Arkansas Historical Quarterly* 17 (Summer 1958): 132–54.

———. "From Rolla to Fayetteville with General Curtis." *Arkansas Historical Quarterly* 19 (Autumn 1960): 225–59.

———. "Grand Gulf's Role in the Civil War." *Civil War History* 5 (March 1959): 5-29.

———. *The Vicksburg Campaign*. 3 vols. Dayton, OH: Morningside, 1985–86.

Bergeron, Arthur W., Jr. *The Civil War in Louisiana, Part A: Military Activity*. In *The Louisiana Purchase Series in Louisiana History*, vol. 5. Lafayette: University of Louisiana, Lafayette, 2002.

Bicknell, Grace Vawter. *The Vawter Family in America*. Indianapolis: Hollenbeck Press, 1905. Reprint, Atlanta, GA: Thorpe and Associates, 1969.

Blake, I. George. *Finding a Way through the Wilderness: The Indiana Baptist Convention, 1833–1983*. Indianapolis: Central Publishing Company, 1983

———. *The Holmans of Veraestau*. Oxford, OH: Mississippi Valley Press, 1943.

Bond, John W. "The History of Elkhorn Tavern." *Arkansas Historical Quarterly* 21 (Spring 1962): 3–15.

Branigin, Elba L. *History of Johsnon County, Indiana*. Indianapolis: B. F. Bowen and Company, 1913.

Brasseaux, Carl A. *Acadian to Cajun: Transformation of a People, 1803–1877*. Jackson and London: University Press of Mississippi, 1992.

Briggs, John Ely. "In the Battle of Winchester." *The Palimpsest* 6 (November 1925): 394–402.

Brinsfield, John W., et al., eds. *Faith in the Fight: Civil War Chaplains.* Mechanicsburg, PA: Stackpole Books, 2003.

Brown, Walter L. "Pea Ridge: Gettysburg of the West." *Arkansas Historical Quarterly* 15 (Spring 1856): 3–16.

Buley, R. Carlyle. *The Old Northwest: Pioneer Period, 1815–1840.* 2 vols. Bloomington: Indiana University Press, 1950.

Bundy, Alice Ann. *A Glimpse of Pioneer Life in Jennings County.* Vernon, IN: Jennings County Preservation Association, 1992.

Cady, John F. *The Baptist Church in Indiana.* Franklin, IN: Franklin College, 1942.

———. *The Centennial History of Franklin College.* Franklin, IN: Franklin College, 1934.

Cain, Marvin R., and John F. Bradbury. "Union Troops and the Civil War in Southwestern Missouri and Northwestern Arkansas." *Missouri Historical Review* 88 (October 1993): 29–47.

Carter, Arthur B. *The Tarnished Cavalier: Major General Earl Van Dorn, C.S.A.* Knoxville: University of Tennessee Press, 1999.

Carter, Samuel, III. *The Final Fortress: The Campaign for Vicksburg, 1862–1863.* New York: St. Martin's Press, 1980.

Castel, Albert. *General Sterling Price and the Civil War in the West.* Baton Rouge: Louisiana State University Press, 1968.

Catton, Bruce. *Grant Moves South.* Boston and Toronto: Little, Brown and Company, 1960.

Christ, Mark K., ed. *Rugged and Sublime: The Civil War in Arkansas.* Fayetteville: University of Arkansas Press, 1994.

Coffey, David. *Sheridan's Lieutenants: Phil Sheridan, His Generals, and the Final Years of the Civil War.* New York and Oxford: Rowman and Littlefield, 2005.

Commemorative Biographical Record of Prominent Men of Indianapolis and Vicinity. Chicago: J. H. Beers, 1908.

Cottman, George S. "Indiana Baptist History." Review of *Indiana Baptist History*, by W. T. Stott. *Indiana Magazine of History* 9 (September 1908): 149–50.

Cozzens, Peter. *General John Pope: A Life for the Nation.* Urbana and Chicago: University of Illinois Press, 2000.

Cutrer, Thomas W. *Ben McCulloch and the Frontier Military Tradition.* Chapel Hill and London: University of North Carolina Press, 1993.

Davis, Barbara Butler, ed. *Affectionately Yours: The Civil War Home-Front Letters of the Ovid Butler Family.* Indianapolis: Indiana Historical Society, 2004.

Davis, Calvin DeArmond. *A History of the Albert Carter Moncrief Family.* By the author, 1997.

Davis, Edwin Adam. *Heroic Years: Louisiana in the War for Southern Independence.* Baton Rouge: Louisiana University Press, 1964.

Donald, David Herbert. *Lincoln.* New York and London: Simon and Schuster, 1995.

Duncan, Bingham. *Whitelaw Reid: Journalist, Politician, Diplomat.* Athens: University of Georgia Press, 1975.

Eckert, Ralph Lowell. *John Brown Gordon: Soldier, Southerner, American.* Baton Rouge and London: Louisiana University Press, 1989.

Edmonds, David C. *Yankee Autumn in Acadiana: A Narrative of the Great Texas Overland Expedition through Southern Louisiana, October–December, 1863.*

Lafayette, LA: Acadiana Press, 1979.

Engle, Stephen D. "Franz Sigel at Pea Ridge." *Arkansas Historical Quarterly* 50 (Autumn 1991): 249–70.

———. *Yankee Dutchman: A Life of Franz Sigel*. Fayetteville: University of Arkansas Press, 1993.

Evans, Christopher H. *The Kingdom Is Always but Coming: A Life of Walter Rauschenbusch*. Grand Rapids, MI and Cambridge: Wm. B. Eerdmans, 2004.

Faust, Patricia L., ed. *Historical Times Illustrated Encyclopedia of the Civil War*. New York: Harper and Row.

Fitts, James Franklin. "In the Ranks at Cedar Creek." *Galaxy* 1 (July 15, 1866): 533–43.

Fitzhugh, Lester N. "Saluria, Fort Esperanza, and Military Operations on the Texas Coast, 1861—1864." *Southwestern Historical Quarterly* 61 (July 1957): 66–100.

Fleischer, Jennifer. *Mrs. Lincoln and Mrs. Keckley*. New York: Broadway Books, 2003.

Fletcher, John Gould. *Arkansas*. Chapel Hill: University of North Carolina Press, 1947.

Gallagher, Gary W. *Stephen Dodson Ramseur: Lee's Gallant General*. Chapel Hill and London: University of North Carolina Press, 1985.

———, ed. *Struggle for the Shenandoah: Essays on the 1864 Valley Campaign*. Kent, OH and London: Kent State University Press, 1991.

Garrison, Webb. *The Encyclopedia of Civil War Usage*. Nashville, TN: Cumberland House, 2001.

Gerteis, Louis. *Civil War St. Louis*. Lawrence: University Press of Kansas, 2001.

Grabau, Warren E. *Ninety-Eight Days: A Geographer's View of the Vicksburg Campaign*. Knoxville: University of Tennessee Press, 2000.

Greene, Francis V. *The Mississippi*. New York: Charles Scribner's Sons, 1882.

Hartje, Robert G. *Van Dorn: The Life and Times of a Confederate General*. Nashville, TN: Vanderbilt University Press, 1967.

Hattaway, Herman. *General Stephen D. Lee*. Jackson: University Press of Mississippi, 1976.

Hergesheimer, Joseph. *Sheridan: A Military Narrative*. Boston and New York: Houghton Mifflin, 1931.

Hess, Earl J. "Battle in the Brush: Davis' Division at Pea Ridge, 7 March 1862." *Indiana Military History Journal* 8 (May 1983): 12–20.

History of Bartholomew County, Indiana—1888. Columbus, IN: Bartholomew County Historical Society, 1976.

History of Jennings County, Indiana. 1956. Reprint, Evansville, IN: Unigraphic, 1979.

History of Jennings County: Jennings County, Indiana, 1816–1999. Vernon, IN: Jennings County Historical Society, 1999.

Hollandsworth, James G., Jr. *Pretense of Glory: The Life of General Nathaniel P. Banks*. Baton Rouge: Louisiana State University Press, 1998.

Hoosier Journal of Ancestry: Jennings County. Little York, IN, n.d.

Hubbell, John T., and James W. Geary, eds. *Biographical Dictionary of the Union: Northern Leaders of the Civil War*. Westport, CT: Greenwood Press, 1995.

Huffstodt, Jim. *Hard Dying Men: The Story of General W. H. L. Wallace, General T. E. G. Ransom and Their "Old Eleventh" Illinois Infantry in the Civil War, 1861–1865*. Bowie, MD: Heritage Books, 1991.

Hughes, Nathaniel Cheairs, Jr., and Gordon D. Whitney. *Jefferson Davis in Blue: The Life of Sherman's Relentless Warrior*. Baton Rouge: Louisiana State University Press, 2002.

Hurley, Phyllis, and Mischell Ferguson. *The Way They Were: Jennings County, Indiana.* N.p: 1995.

Indiana-Vicksburg Military Park Commission. *Indiana at Vicksburg.* Indianapolis: Wm. B. Burford, 1911.

Johnson, Allen, and Dumas Malone, eds. *Dictionary of American Biography.* 20 vols. New York: Scribner's Sons, 1927–37.

Jones, James P. "Jefferson Davis in Blue: The Military Career of Jefferson C. Davis, U.S.A." Master's thesis, University of Florida, 1954.

Kerby, Robert L. *Kirby Smith's Confederacy: The Trans-Mississippi South, 1863–1865.* Tuscaloosa and London: University of Alabama, 1972.

King, James T. *War Eagle: A Life of General Eugene A. Carr.* Lincoln: University of Nebraska Press, 1963.

Kiper, Richard L. *Major General John Alexander McClernand: Politician in Uniform.* Kent, OH and London: Kent State University Press, 1999.

Kohl, Rhonda M. "'This Godforsaken Town': Death and Disease at Helena, Arkansas, 1862–1863." *Civil War History* 50 (June 2004): 109–44.

Lewis, Thomas A. *The Guns of Cedar Creek.* New York: Harper and Row, 1988.

Long, E. B., *The Civil War Day by Day: An Almanac, 1861–1865.* New York: DaCapo Press, 1971.

Lowe, Richard. *The Texas Overland Expedition of 1863.* Fort Worth and Boulder: Ryan Place Publishers, 1996.

McConnell, Stuart. *Glorious Contentment: The Grand Army of the Republic, 1865–1900.* Chapel Hill and London: University of North Carolina Press, 1992.

McPherson, James M. *Battle Cry of Freedom: The Civil War Era.* New York and Oxford: Oxford University Press, 1988.

———. *The Negro's Civil War.* New York: Pantheon Books, 1965.

———. *What They Fought For, 1861–1865.* Baton Rouge: Louisiana State University Press, 1994.

McReynolds, Edwin C. *Missouri: A History of the Crossroads State.* Norman: University of Oklahoma Press, 1962.

Madison, James H. "Civil War Memories and 'Pardnership Forgittin'," 1865–1913." *Indiana Magazine of History* 99 (September 2003): 198–230.

Mahr, Theodore C. *Early's Valley Campaign: The Battle of Cedar Creek, Showdown in the Shenandoah, October 1–30, 1864.* 2d ed. Lynchburg, VA: H. E. Howard, 1992.

Medlicott, Mary Alice. *First Baptist Church, Franklin, Indiana, History, 1832–1982.* Franklin, IN: Schumacher Printing, 1983.

Merrill, Catharine. *The Soldier of Indiana in the War for the Union.* 2 vols. Indianapolis: Merrill and Company, 1866.

Miers, Earl Schenk. *The Web of Victory: Grant at Vicksburg.* New York: Alfred A. Knopf, 1955.

Miller, John W. *Indiana Newspaper Bibliography.* Indianapolis: Indiana Historical Society, 1982.

Minus, Paul M. *Walter Rauschenbusch: American Reformer.* London: Collier Macmillan, 1988.

Monaghan, Jay. *Civil War on the Western Border, 1854–1865.* Boston and Toronto: Little, Brown and Company, 1955.

Morris, Roy, Jr. *Sheridan: The Life and Wars of General Phil Sheridan*. New York: Crown, 1992.

Nevins, Allen. *Fremont in the Civil War*. New York: Frederick Ungar, 1961.

O'Connor, Richard. *Sheridan, The Inevitable*. Indianapolis: Bobbs-Merrill, 1953.

Osborne, Charles C. *Jubal: The Life and Times of General Jubal A. Early, CSA, Defender of the Lost Cause*. Baton Rouge and London: Louisiana State University Press, 1992.

Parrish, William E. *A History of Missouri*. Vol. 3, *1860–1875*. Columbia: University of Missouri Press, 1973.

———. *Turbulent Partnership: Missouri and the Union, 1861–1865*. Columbia: University of Missouri Press, 1963.

Parsons, Joseph A., Jr. "Indiana and the Call for Volunteers, April 1861." *Indiana Magazine of History* 54 (March 1958): 1–23.

Phillips, Clifton J. *Indiana in Transition: The Emergence of an Industrial Commonwealth, 1880–1920*. Indianapolis: Indiana Historical Bureau and Indiana Historical Society, 1968.

Piston, William Garrett, and Richard W. Hatcher III. *Wilson's Creek: The Second Battle of the Civil War and the Men Who Fought It*. Chapel Hill and London: University of North Carolina Press, 2000.

Pond, George E. *The Shenandoah Valley in 1864*. Campaigns of the Civil War, vol. 11. New York: Charles Scribner's Sons, 1883.

Powell, Earl A. *Thomas Cole*. New York: Harry N. Abrams, 1990.

Raphael, Morris. *The Battle in the Bayou Country*. Detroit: Harlo Press, 1975.

Rolle, Andrew. *John Charles Fremont: Character as Destiny*. Norman and London: University of Oklahoma Press, 1991.

Seidel, Michael. *Robinson Crusoe: Island Myths and the Novel*. Boston: Twayne, 1991.

Shalhope, Robert. *Sterling Price: Portrait of a Southerner*. Columbia: University of Missouri Press, 1971.

Shea, William L. "The Confederate Defeat at Cache River." *Arkansas Historical Quarterly* 52 (Summer 1993): 129–55.

———, and Earl J. Hess. *Pea Ridge: Civil War Campaign in the West*. Chapel Hill and London: University of North Carolina Press, 1992.

Shea, William L. "The Road to Pea Ridge." *Arkansas Historical Quarterly* 52 (Autumn 1993): 205–22.

———, and Terrence J. Winschel. *Vicksburg Is the Key: The Struggle for the Mississippi River*. Lincoln and London: University of Nebraska Press, 2003.

Simpson, Brooks D. *Ulysses S. Grant: Triumph over Adversity, 1822–1865*. Boston and New York: Houghton Mifflin, 2000.

Smith, Timothy B. *Champion Hill: Decisive Battle for Vicksburg*. New York: Savas Beattie, 2004.

Sommers, Richard. *Richmond Redeemed: The Siege at Petersburg*. Garden City, NY: Doubleday and Company, 1981.

Stephens, Leslie, and Sidney Lee, eds. *Dictionary of National Biography*. 22 vols. New York: Macmillan, 1908–9.

Storr, Richard J. *Harper's University: The Beginnings*. Chicago and London: University of Chicago Press, 1966.

Thornbrough, Emma Lou. *Indiana in the Civil War Era, 1850–1880*. Indianapolis: Indiana

Historical Bureau and Indiana Historical Society, 1965.

Turkoly-Joczik, Robert L. "Fremont and the Western Department." *Missouri Historical Review* 82 (July 1988): 363–85.

Warner, Ezra. *Generals in Blue: Lives of the Union Commanders*. Baton Rouge: Louisiana State University Press, 1964.

Welcher, Frank J. *The Union Army, 1861–1865: Organization and Operations*. 2 vols. Bloomington: Indiana University Press, 1989.

Wert, Jeffry D. *Custer: The Controversial Life of George Armstrong Custer*. New York: Simon and Schuster. 1996.

———. *From Winchester to Cedar Creek: The Shenandoah Campaign of 1864*. New York: Simon and Schuster, 1987.

Williams, Kenneth P. *Lincoln Finds a General: A Military Study of the Civil War*. 5 vols. New York: Macmillan, 1949–59.

Williams, Richard Brady. *Chicago's Battery Boys: The Chicago Mercantile Battery in the Civil War Western Theater*. New York: Savas Beattie, 2005.

Wilson, James Grant, and John Fiske, eds. *Appleton's Cyclopedia of American Biography*. 7 vols. New York: D. Appleton and Company, 1888.

Wilson, Keith P. *Campfires of Freedom: The Camp Life of Black Soldiers during the Civil War*. Kent, OH and London: Kent State University Press, 2002.

Winschel, Terrence J. *Triumph and Defeat: The Vicksburg Campaign*. 2 vols. El Dorado Hills, CA: Savas Beattie, 2006.

Winslow, Hattie Lou, and Joseph R. H. Moore. *Camp Morton, 1861–1865: Indianapolis Prison Camp*. Indianapolis: Indiana Historical Society, 1940.

Winsor, Bill. *Texas in the Confederacy: Military Installations, Economy and People*. Hillsboro, TX: Hill Junior College Press, 1978.

Winters, John D. *The Civil War in Louisiana*. Baton Rouge: Louisiana State University Press, 1963.

Wittenberg, Eric J. *Little Phil: A Reassessment of the Civil War Leadership of Gen. Philip H. Sheridan*. Washington, D.C.: Brassey's, 2002.

Woodworth, Stephen E., ed. *Grant's Lieutenants: From Cairo to Vicksburg*. Lawrence: University of Kansas Press, 2001.

———. *Nothing but Victory: The Army of the Tennessee, 1861–1865*. New York: Alfred A. Knopf, 2005.

Wooster, Ralph A. *Civil War Texas: A History and a Guide*. Austin: Texas State Historical Association, 1999.

Wright, John D. *The Language of the Civil War*. Westport, CT: Oryx Press, 2001.

Index